Customer Satisfaction and Sustainability Initiatives in the Fourth Industrial Revolution

Cecilia Silvestri
University of Tuscia, Viterbo, Italy

Michela Piccarozzi
University of Tuscia, Viterbo, Italy

Barbara Aquilani
University of Tuscia, Viterbo, Italy

A volume in the Advances in Marketing, Customer Relationship Management, and E-Services (AMCRMES) Book Series

IGI Global
DISSEMINATOR OF KNOWLEDGE

Published in the United States of America by
IGI Global
Business Science Reference (an imprint of IGI Global)
701 E. Chocolate Avenue
Hershey PA, USA 17033
Tel: 717-533-8845
Fax: 717-533-8661
E-mail: cust@igi-global.com
Web site: http://www.igi-global.com

Library of Congress Cataloging-in-Publication Data

Names: Silvestri, Cecilia, 1982- editor. | Piccarozzi, Michela, 1982- editor. | Aquilani, Barbara, 1969- editor.
Title: Customer satisfaction and sustainability initiatives in the fourth industrial revolution / Cecilia Silvestri, Michela Piccarozzi, and Barbara Aquilani, editors.
Description: Hershey, PA : Business Science Reference, [2020] | Includes bibliographical references and index. | Summary: “”This book links together three highly relevant topics in the business of modern economy-innovation, customer satisfaction, and sustainability-and analyzes their synergies”--Provided by publisher”-- Provided by publisher.
Identifiers: LCCN 2019029256 (print) | LCCN 2019029257 (ebook) | ISBN 9781799814191 (hardcover) | ISBN 9781799814207 (paperback) | ISBN 9781799814214 (ebook)
Subjects: LCSH: Consumer satisfaction. | Consumption (Economics)--Environmental aspects. | Sustainable development.
Classification: LCC HF5415.335 .C869 2020 (print) | LCC HF5415.335 (ebook) | DDC 658.8/343--dc23
LC record available at https://lccn.loc.gov/2019029256
LC ebook record available at https://lccn.loc.gov/2019029257

This book is published in the IGI Global book series Advances in Marketing, Customer Relationship Management, and E-Services (AMCRMES) (ISSN: 2327-5502; eISSN: 2327-5529)

British Cataloguing in Publication Data
A Cataloguing in Publication record for this book is available from the British Library.

Advances in Marketing, Customer Relationship Management, and E-Services (AMCRMES) Book Series

Eldon Y. Li
National Chengchi University, Taiwan & California Polytechnic State University, USA

ISSN:2327-5502
EISSN:2327-5529

Mission

Business processes, services, and communications are important factors in the management of good customer relationship, which is the foundation of any well organized business. Technology continues to play a vital role in the organization and automation of business processes for marketing, sales, and customer service. These features aid in the attraction of new clients and maintaining existing relationships. **The Advances in Marketing, Customer Relationship Management, and E-Services (AMCRMES) Book Series** addresses success factors for customer relationship management, marketing, and electronic services and its performance outcomes. This collection of reference source covers aspects of consumer behavior and marketing business strategies aiming towards researchers, scholars, and practitioners in the fields of marketing management.

Coverage

- Telemarketing
- Database marketing
- Ethical Considerations in E-Marketing
- Cases on Electronic Services
- CRM strategies
- Data mining and marketing
- Online Community Management and Behavior
- Cases on CRM Implementation
- B2B marketing
- Social Networking and Marketing

IGI Global is currently accepting manuscripts for publication within this series. To submit a proposal for a volume in this series, please contact our Acquisition Editors at Acquisitions@igi-global.com or visit: http://www.igi-global.com/publish/.

The Advances in Marketing, Customer Relationship Management, and E-Services (AMCRMES) Book Series (ISSN 2327-5502) is published by IGI Global, 701 E. Chocolate Avenue, Hershey, PA 17033-1240, USA, www.igi-global.com. This series is composed of titles available for purchase individually; each title is edited to be contextually exclusive from any other title within the series. For pricing and ordering information please visit http://www.igi-global.com/book-series/advances-marketing-customer-relationship-management/37150. Postmaster: Send all address changes to above address.

Titles in this Series

For a list of additional titles in this series, please visit:
https://www.igi-global.com/book-series/advances-marketing-customer-relationship-management/37150

Digital Marketing Strategies for Tourism, Hospitality, and Airline Industries
José Duarte Santos (Instituto Superior Politécnico Gaya, Portugal) and Óscar Lima Silva (Instituto Superior Politécnico Gaya, Portugal)
Business Science Reference • copyright 2020 • 267pp • H/C (ISBN: 9781522597834) • US $225.00 (our price)

Exploring the Power of Electronic Word-of-Mouth in the Services Industry
Sandra Maria Correia Loureiro (Instituto Universitário de Lisboa, Portugal) and Hans Ruediger Kaufmann (University of Applied Management Studies, Germany)
Business Science Reference • copyright 2020 • 463pp • H/C (ISBN: 9781522585756) • US $265.00 (our price)

Green Marketing as a Positive Driver Toward Business Sustainability
Vannie Naidoo (University of KwaZulu-Natal, South Africa) and Rahul Verma (Department of Training and Technical Education, India)
Business Science Reference • copyright 2020 • 356pp • H/C (ISBN: 9781522595588) • US $225.00 (our price)

Strategies and Tools for Managing Connected Consumers
Ree C. Ho (Taylor's University, Malaysia)
Business Science Reference • copyright 2020 • 365pp • H/C (ISBN: 9781522596974) • US $275.00 (our price)

Handbook of Research on Narrative Advertising
Recep Yilmaz (Ondokuz Mayıs University, Turkey)
Business Science Reference • copyright 2019 • 400pp • H/C (ISBN: 9781522597902) • US $285.00 (our price)

Breaking Down Language and Cultural Barriers Through Contemporary Global Marketing Strategies
Mehdi Khosrow-Pour, D.B.A. (Information Resources Management Association, USA)
Business Science Reference • copyright 2019 • 339pp • H/C (ISBN: 9781522569800) • US $235.00 (our price)

Myth in Modern Media Management and Marketing
Jan Kreft (Jagiellonian University, Poland) Sylwia Kuczamer-Kłopotowska (University of Gdańsk, Poland) and Anna Kalinowska-Żeleźnik (University of Gdańsk, Poland)
Business Science Reference • copyright 2019 • 317pp • H/C (ISBN: 9781522591009) • US $215.00 (our price)

Predicting Trends and Building Strategies for Consumer Engagement in Retail Environments

IGI Global
DISSEMINATOR OF KNOWLEDGE

701 East Chocolate Avenue, Hershey, PA 17033, USA
Tel: 717-533-8845 x100 • Fax: 717-533-8661
E-Mail: cust@igi-global.com • www.igi-global.com

Editorial Advisory Board

Table of Contents

Detailed Table of Contents

Almost all firms are involved in challenges linked to Industry 4.0 that represent a new logic for business models focused on innovation, technology, and sustainability. In this domain, the support and integration of digital innovations is assuming ever greater importance and a key role is played by the so-called "industrial symbiosis." Looking more in depth at industrial symbiosis literature, which practically developed within the engineering domain, it is clear that most of its particular traits can also be found in management literature when referring to value co-creation, especially in the business to business domain. Given the above, the aim of this work is twofold: to analyze the role of Industry 4.0 digital platforms as a tool for the development of environmental sustainability and to understand how Industry 4.0 as a whole can support the achievement of environmental sustainability goals. The only Italian case will be used to validate the proposed theoretical framework.

The global commitment to drastically curb greenhouse gas emissions towards a sustainable development is strongly connected to the development and usage of renewable energy (RE), such as solar and wind. Between 2006 and 2016, world's total RE consumption, excluding hydro-electricity, increased by almost 350%, and RE investment grew from US $47 billion in 2004 to 279.8 billion in 2017. The importance of RE has attracted a lot of attention from the economic literature as well, since a growing body of empirical research is investigating the relationships between RE and economic growth. The general outcome is the existence of a positive bi-directional (direct and reverse) link between RE consumption and real GDP, though it also emerges evidence showing no statistically significant relationship. This Chapter provides i) an overview of the recent world's trends of RE production and investment, ii) an extensive and detailed review of the recent advances in the RE-growth empirical literature, highlighting the main methodologies adopted and the main findings emerged.

The 17 Sustainable Development Goals (SDGs) of the United Nations 2030 Agenda for Sustainable Development intends to improve efforts of governments, societies, and companies to deal with major social and environmental problems affecting contemporary societies. From a business perspective, companies can find a propulsive boost of innovation looking at different models of production and use of services/products. This new perspective is radically changing the ways companies and consumers interact, and the role of companies in supporting the achievement of SDGs through service innovation is becoming pervasive. In addition, the emerging digital economy represents a great opportunity opening up to sustainability-oriented service innovation and firms are developing their competitive advantage based on the introduction of new digital business models. This chapter explores this issue through an explorative case study based on the MyTaxi business model. Implications for managers and researchers and opportunities for future research are highlighted.

The interest of scientists and companies in understanding the business implications of environmental commitments is timely; however, a dilemma remains at the firm level: is environmental sustainability a strategic factor for business competitiveness? The author contributes to this international end interdisciplinary debate through a double analysis, theoretical and empirical. Starting from a systematic literature review, the main correlations between environmental commitments and business performance are identified in a scholar's perspective. Based on the results from an Italian survey, the main added values associated with certified environmental management system are verified with a manager's perspective. Finally, the findings obtained from theoretical and empirical points of view are compared, to discuss confirmations or contradictions and underline questions still open.

The chapter deepens the theme of sustainability in fashion products, exploring the importance of sustainable innovation as a competitive driver. The fashion industry is not exempt from issues related to sustainability, in its economic, environmental, and social sense, since it is one of the most polluting industries in the world, in addition to being often shaken by scandals related to the poor working conditions for many fashion factory workers around the world. Given the relevance of the issue of sustainability in the fashion supply chains, the chapter will provide food for thought on the question of managerial behaviors based on sustainability and deepen the knowledge on the need of a collaborative approach among firms and within the supply chains of the fashion system.

Preface

The dramatic increase in competition, the progressive and widespread globalization of markets and the technological, often radical, innovations which occur with increasing frequency, make it very difficult for firms to know what the consumer really wants.

Globalization has created a rise in competition on a worldwide scale, causing a drop in traditional methods of achieving competitive advantage and making factors, like tacit knowledge and other intangible assets, crucial for firm success.

In this scenario, firms must be increasingly consumer-oriented and design their product offering in order to even better meet customer expectations.

Not only are customer-focused firms' expert in supplying products, but also in building long lasting relationships with customers; in other words, they are skilled not exclusively in the product concept and launch, but also in marketplace creation and development.

In an extremely dynamic context, anticipating customer needs is the key to marketing decisions. This stand point, defined as the customer-based view, does not just deal with marketing policies and market analysis procedures, but implies alignment of all business activities to target customer needs.

Therefore, cultivating long term relationships with consumers is a winning strategy to face challenges from a highly competitive market, even if it is necessary to go beyond traditional quality and satisfaction issues in order to achieve a good customer retention strategy and to be successful both from a market share and a profit point of view.

Indeed, quality, satisfaction and loyalty are all factors of a cause-effect chain; in fact, increased customer satisfaction and retention increases profits. However, in designing a quality-oriented strategy nowadays it is even more important to pay attention to innovation in that combining quality and innovation can pave the way to success for firms.

In this winning combination both customer attention towards sustainability issues, in particular environmental ones, and innovations put forward by Industry 4.0 can play an important role, especially if taken together.

Indeed, if it is true that today's customers are always more informed and aware of their choices and pay particular attention to sustainability issues, especially environmental ones (i.e. recycled plastics, Circular Economy initiatives, etc.), Industry 4.0 can also greatly support firms in satisfying these consumer needs through its innovations and tools.

In fact, Industry 4.0, the so-called Fourth Industrial Revolution, has radically changed the traditional concept of innovation in business; it encompasses new highly mechanized and automatized ways to produce goods even if it also includes numerous areas like: smart factory, Cyber-physical Systems, Internet of Things (IoT), new distribution systems, and so on.

All these innovations represent further possibilities for firms to achieve high quality standards in products and services offered, but also new sustainable ways of production and operation in order to meet all consumer needs, also those pertaining to environmental protection, without forgetting market share, higher revenues, lower costs and, as a consequence, better firm performance also from an economic point of view.

In this scenario, this book seeks to provide new insights and investigate issues relating to the main topics already mentioned, combining three highly relevant topics for businesses in the modern economy: innovation, customer satisfaction and sustainability (declined in its three dimensions, economic, social and environmental).

The impact is undoubtedly relevant, stimulating scientific debate on the issues, increasing and adding value to the current knowledge base in this particular area of research, still quite neglected by literature, which is not so focused on the multi-facet relationships between sustainability, customer satisfaction and Industry 4.0 issues as a whole.

The book "Customer Satisfaction and Sustainability Initiatives in the Fourth Industrial Revolution" is ideally designed for researchers, post-graduate students, managers, consultants and entrepreneurs who want to understand the impact of innovation, in particular Industry 4.0, on their businesses. Indeed, Industry 4.0 can greatly help firms enhance their customer relationships, satisfaction etc. also focusing on sustainability both from a customer point of view (i.e. attention to issues by customers) and from a firm standpoint which are, inevitably, linked together in an inseparable way.

The book is structured in fifteen chapters, divided into three major sections, considering their main focus, while chapters in each section are ordered putting first theoretical contributions and/or literature reviews and then case studies and/or empirical studies on specific topics and/or industries and/or firms:

- Industry 4.0;
- Sustainability and environmental sustainability;
- Customer satisfaction/behaviour.

Section 1, Industry 4.0, aims to explain the characteristics of the Fourth Industrial Revolution, laying the foundations for understanding subsequent sustainability and consumer behavior analysis, assuming an innovative and technology-oriented perspective.

This section is made up of three chapters.

Chapter 1, "Industry 4.0 in the context of the Triple Bottom Line of Sustainability: A Systematic Literature Review" by Julian M. Müller, presents a comprehensive overview of Industry 4.0 in the context of the Triple Bottom Line.

Chapter 2 entitled "How Industry 4.0 Changes the Value Co-Creation Process" by Rebecca Castagnoli, Giacomo Büchi and Monica Cugno analyzes the literature on Industry 4.0 in order to understand the effect that Industry 4.0 can have on customer co-creation processes.

Chapter 3, "Achieving Environmental Sustainability Through Industry 4.0 Tools: The Case of the 'Symbiosis' Digital Platform" by Barbara Aquilani, Michela Piccarozzi, Cecilia Silvestri and Corrado Gatti, analyzes the role of Industry 4.0 digital platforms as a tool for the development of environmental sustainability and seeks to understand how Industry 4.0, as a whole, can help in achieving environmental sustainability goals.

Section 2, Sustainability and Environmental Sustainability, focuses on how Industry 4.0 innovations and/or tools can help protect the environment or foster sustainability, understood in its triple perspective (economic, environmental and social).

This section encompasses six chapters.

Chapter 4, "Renewable Energy and Economic Growth: An Overview of the Literature" by Patrizio Morganti and Giuseppe Garofalo, provides an overview of recent world trends of renewable energy (RE) production and investment as well as an extensive and detailed review of recent advances in RE-growth empirical literature, highlighting the main methodologies adopted and the main findings.

Chapter 5, "Innovative Business Models in Digital Firms: The Challenge of Sustainability" by Patrizia Accordino, Tindara Abbate, Daniela Rupo, Raffaella Coppolino and Elvira Tiziana La Rocca, aims at exploring the introduction of new digital business models, through an explorative case study: MyTaxi.

Chapter 6, "Environmental Sustainability to Support Competitiveness" by Anna Mazzi, first performs a systematic literature review aimed at identifying the main correlations between environmental commitments and business performance. A survey carried out in Italy then validates the main added values associated with certified environmental management systems, already present in literature.

Chapter 7, "Sustainable Innovation in Fashion Products: An Opportunity for Italian SMEs" by Alessandra De Chiara and Floriana Iannone, puts forward the question of managerial behaviors based on sustainability and deepens the need for a collaborative approach between firms within the supply chains, choosing the fashion industry to carry out this study.

Chapter 8, "Life Cycle Management and Sharing Economy: Methodological Framework and Application in Sustainable Mobility" by Roberta Guglielmetti Mugion, Gabriella Arcese, Martina Toni and Luca Silvestri, proposes some indicators for the assessment of sustainability in urban shared mobility based on the Life Cycle Management (LCM) general framework. The LCA analysis was then tested following the ISO Standard 14040 and 14044. The authors through the proposed research framework aim to realize a new general approach to the management of materials, products and services, called "strategic lifecycle management".

Chapter 9, "B Corp Certification for a Circular Economy Approach and a Sustainable Pathway" by Enrico Maria Mosconi, Stefano Poponi, Simona Fortunati and Michelangelo Arezzo di Trifiletti, identifies and discusses the potential of B Corp certification in applying Circular Economy. In particular, compared multiple case study analysis is used to evaluate how the requirements of the B Corp certification are able to influence the circularity of the enterprises analyzed.

Section 3, Customer Satisfaction/Behaviour, aims at analyzing and describing new trends in consumer behavior in the light of Industry 4.0 technologies, also considering sustainability issues.

Chapter 10, "Ecodesign Strategies and Customer Value: A Conjoint Approach" by Anna Codini, Giuseppe Bertoli and Riccardo Frassine revises the literature on ecodesign, adopting a customer-based perspective focusing on the controversial results regarding eco-products and customer value. After that, with the aim of identifying techniques suitable to support ecodesign strategies in a customer-based perspective, and considering the challenges affecting customer perception of eco-products, the chapter shows—through an empirical analysis conducted on washing machines—how conjoint analysis can be successful in this domain.

Chapter 11, "Consumer Perceptions of CSR and Sustainable Consumption: What Relationships? Insights From the Sportswear Sector" by Giovanna Pegan, Gabriella Schoier and Patrizia de Luca, presents a theoretical overview of the importance of investigating the perceptions of CSR - to be understood as a three-dimensional construct - from a consumer perspective and explores the crucial theme of sustainable consumption, completing the chapter with a quantitative empirical research carried out on Italian consumers.

Chapter 12, "The Effect of Packaging Material on Consumers' Evaluation and Choice: A Comparison Between Glass and Tetra-pak in the Olive Oil Sector" by Beatrice Luceri, Donata Tania Vergura and Cristina Zerbini, aims at contributing to the knowledge of the role of packaging material in influencing product evaluation processes. Specifically, a between-subjects experimental design was adopted in order to investigate whether the product quality judgment and the purchase intention towards extra virgin olive oil differ between tetra-pak and glass bottle.

Chapter 13, "The Evolution of Fast Food in a Customer-Driven Era: Innovation and Sustainability for Customers' Needs" by Alessandro Bonadonna, Chiara Giachino, Francesca Pucciarelli and Bernardo Bertoldi analyzed how both International Hamburger Foodservices (IHF), such as McDonalds and Burger King, and Local Hamburgher Foodservice (LHF), such as M**Bun and Burgheria, are changing their strategies to meet customer needs.

Chapter 14, "Consumer Behavior: Motivational Factors for the Decision to Purchase Organic Products in the Municipality of Guadalajara" by Jalisco José G Vargas-Hernández and Jovanna Nathalie Cervantes Guzmán, develops a model for ecological consumer behavior in order to identify the motivations that influence decisions to purchase organic products in citizens from 25 to 45 years old in the municipality of Guadalajara.

Finally, Chapter 15, "The Millennial's Involvement in Corporate Social Responsibility" by Eleonora Rapiti and Cecilia Silvestri, focuses on the behavior of Millennials to whom CRS is an integral part of their lives. The study first identifies, through a factor analysis, the dimensions of CSR and then analyzes, through a cluster analysis, the relationships between CSR, Customer Satisfaction (CS) and Customer Loyalty (CL) of different Millennials groups.

Acknowledgment

The editors would like to acknowledge the help of all the people involved in this project and, more specifically, the Editorial Advisory Board, the Authors for their contributions and all the Reviewers that took part in the double blind review process. Without their support, this book would not have become a reality.

Moreover, we would like to greatly thank IGI Global Editorial/Production Team for its continuous and helpful support.

Chapter 1
Industry 4.0 in the Context of the Triple Bottom Line of Sustainability:
A Systematic Literature Review

Julian M. Müller
https://orcid.org/0000-0002-7372-2405
Salzburg University of Applied Sciences, Austria

ABSTRACT

Industry 4.0 and sustainability are trending topics in the industry and scientific research. However, there is currently no comparable study, which summarizes the impacts of Industry 4.0 on all three dimensions of the Triple Bottom Line at the same time. This chapter aims to present a comprehensive overview of Industry 4.0 in the context of the Triple Bottom Line of sustainability. For this reason, a systematic literature review is conducted to find out the current state of literature about this topic. The chapter presents a systematic literature review on 64 peer-reviewed journal articles, which have been published between 2014 and 2019. An in-depth analysis of the content as well as an analysis of the empirical methodologies are conducted. To structure the existing knowledge, a framework is developed, and the findings are categorized into ecological and social aspects. On this basis the content is evaluated to discuss key findings and relating interdependencies.

INTRODUCTION

So far, Industry 4.0-related literature has mainly concerned technical aspects of the phenomenon (Kiel et al., 2017). Whereas further research disciplines, such as business management have begun to examine Industry 4.0 (Piccarozzi et al., 2018), ecological and social aspects of Industry 4.0 have been even less regarded. In particular, integrative investigations of economic, ecological, and social aspects remain rare (Birkel et al., 2019; Kiel et al., 2017). Several authors find that improving ecological and social aspects of industrial value creation whilst maintaining economic profitability is a challenging task. Several po-

DOI: 10.4018/978-1-7998-1419-1.ch001

tentials and challenges of Industry 4.0 seem contradictory in each of the three dimensions of the Triple Bottom Line. For instance, working conditions shall be improved, whilst job losses are expected through Industry 4.0. Therefore, an interdisciplinary and integrative investigation of Industry 4.0 is necessary, not only balancing, but combining ecological and social potentials with market success (Müller et al., 2018a; Müller & Däschle, 2018; Stock et al., 2018). Further, several authors find that sustainability aspects of Industry 4.0 differ across countries and need to be incorporated in managerial practice and policy, for instance been the German initiative "Industry 4.0" and the "Internet Plus" initiative within the concept "Made in China 2025" (Müller and Voigt, 2018).

Still, sustainability in the context of Industry 4.0 has been addressed by some authors in recent time. According to Scopus, out of 137 articles that have "Industry 4.0" and "Sustainability" in abstract, title or keywords, 103 were published since 2018. This relates to articles in English language in journals or conference proceedings.

In order to provide a comprehensive overview of the current state of research regarding Industry 4.0 in the context of the Triple Bottom Line of sustainability, the article performs a systematic literature review. Thereupon, the article discusses and evaluates recent research findings, presenting managerial and theoretical implications, and promising avenues for future research.

Background

The term "Industry 4.0" is derived from the German "Industrie 4.0" initiative launched by the German government in 2011. It aims at ensuring future competitiveness of the German manufacturing industry (Kagermann et al., 2013; Lasi et al., 2014; Müller et al., 2017). In this context, Industry 4.0 indicates a predicted fourth industrial revolution. Industry 4.0 builds on several technological developments, including the Internet of Things and Cyber-Physical Systems, that shall enable real-time interconnection of products, production facilities, humans, and smart devices in a vertical and horizontal manner. Vertical interconnection means across several departments within an enterprise, horizontal interconnection expresses digital information sharing across several partners within a supply chain, including the customer. Further, the entire product lifecycle shall be encompassed, from production, to product usage, to recycling (Kagermann et al., 2013; Lasi et al., 2014; Liao et al., 2017; Müller et al., 2018b).

After 2011, when the German initiative "Industrie 4.0" was launched in the "High tech strategy" of the German federal government, several comparable programs and initiatives have been launched worldwide. For instance, the European Union initiated a program called "Factories of the Future". It intends to ensure a digital and sustainable production in order to maintain global competitiveness. In the United States of America, The "Industrial Internet Consortium" represents a comparable initiative, whereas China launched the program "Internet Plus" within the program "Made in China 2025" (Liao et al., 2017; Müller & Voigt, 2018).

As the first industrial revolution (mechanization), the second industrial revolution (electrification), and the third industrial revolution, Industry 4.0 is expected to inflict changes in an economic, ecological, and social context (Birkel et al., 2019; Maynard, 2015; Kiel et al., 2017; Müller & Voigt, 2018).

Economic, ecological and social aspects subsume the Triple Bottom Line of sustainability (Elkington, 1987; Elkington, 1998; Norman et al., 2004). Since the World Commission on Environment and Development's "Brundtland report" in 1987 (World Commission on Environment and Development, 1987), an increasing expectation of society to achieve ecological and social welfare whilst maintaining economic success can be observed. This is also and especially true for industrial value creation, which is built on global supply chains, requiring, among many further aspects, large amounts of energy and fuels, whilst social conditions might not always be acceptable in many manufacturing locations. The United Nations' Sustainable Development Goal 12 - "Ensure sustainable consumption and production patterns" expresses this increased attention on sustainable industrial value creation (Glavič & Lukman, 2007; McWilliams et al., 2016; Müller & Voigt, 2018). While many authors regard sustainability mainly from an ecological or social perspective, mostly without combining both, the Triple Bottom Line of sustainability must also consider economic aspects and their interplay with ecological and social considerations in order to achieve the maximum possible benefits (Littig & Griessler, 2005). In recent time, the term "circular economy" can be found increasingly, subsuming the sustainability initiatives towards industrial value creation.

For Industry 4.0, most authors have focused on technological aspects, whilst economic, ecological and social aspects are comparably less understood. Especially their interplay has hardly been investigated so far, as most authors focus on one of the three dimensions within the Triple Bottom Line of sustainability (Birkel et al., 2019; Kiel et al., 2017; Müller & Voigt, 2018). In order to further develop the understanding of benefits and challenges in each of the three dimensions, the present article systematically reviews extant literature, as explained in the following.

Methodology

This chapter is based on a systematic literature review of extant literature. The Scopus database was used to find relevant articles. The keywords "Industry 4.0 AND sustainability" and "Industry 4.0 AND circular economy" were used for the systematic literature search. Only journals and proceedings in English were selected. The specified keywords were used to search the title, the abstract and the keywords. This resulted in a list of 100 articles from journals and proceedings. After a thorough selection of results for relevance to this topic, taking into account any duplications, the researchers obtained a total number of 64 relevant and qualitative articles. In particular, articles that solely focus on technical solutions or economic considerations without ecological and social aspects were excluded from the further research process. As articles on economic aspects are found considerably more in literature than those on the ecological and social dimensions, only such articles that investigate economical aspects together with ecological and social aspects were analyzed in order to avoid an imbalance towards the economic dimension.

FINDINGS

For the search term "Industry 4.0 AND sustainability", 42 journal papers and 17 proceedings were included in the literature review, and the search term "Industry 4.0 AND circular economy" included 5 journal papers. From the final sample of 64 research articles found in journals or conference proceedings, 14 articles were published in 2019, 39 articles in 2018, 8 in 2017 and one was published in 2016, 2015 and 2014 each. The most used empirical methods are literature review (15 times), case studies (14 times). Also interviews (9 times) and surveys (6 times) were used in a quarter of the articles. Further used empirical methodologies are mathematical modelling or programming (4 times), application cases (2 times) and experiments (2 times). Further, 14 articles are not based on an empirical methodology.

Relating to the journal or conference proceedings the articles were published in, the following picture can be obtained, as shown in Table 1 below.

Most frequently, publications from the journal Sustainability were found, namely 13 articles. Furthermore, 8 articles of Procedia Manufacturing and 6 articles of Procedia CIRP were added to the list. Four articles were published in Process Safety and Environmental Protection, whereas in Computers and Industrial Enginering, IFAC-PapersOnLine, and Journal of Manufacturing Technology Management, three articles were published each. Further, two articles were published in Entrepreneurship and Sustainability Issues and Ressources, Conservation and Recycling. Further journals and conference proceedings only list one article so far, as can be obtained from Table 1.

Table 1. Journals and conference proceedings in which articles were published (n = 64)

Journal	2019	2018	2017	2016	2015	2014	Total
Sustainability	5	7	1				13
Procedia Manufacturing		7	1				8
Procedia CIRP		2	2	1		1	6
Process Safety and Environmental Protection		4					4
Computers and Industrial Engineering	1	2					3
IFAC-PapersOnLine		3					3
Journal of Manufacturing Technology Management	1	2					3
Entrepreneurship and Sustainability Issues	1		1				2
Resources, Conservation and Recycling	1	1					2
Advances in Manufacturing			1				1
Annals of Operations Research		1					1
Annual Reviews in Control	1						1
Applied Sciences		1					1
Benchmarking		1					1
Economies		1					1
Energies		1					1
IEEE Access		1					1
International Journal of Agile Systems and Management			1				1
International Journal of Energy Research	1						1
International Journal of Environmental Research and Public Health	1						1
International Journal of Information Management	1						1
International Journal of Innovation Management			1				1
International Journal of Precision Engineering and Manufacturing		1					1
International Journal of Production Research	1						1
Journal of Cleaner Production		1					1
Journal of Management Analytics					1		1
Research Technology Management		1					1
Social Sciences		1					1
Technological Forecasting and Social Change		1					1
Total	**14**	**39**	**8**	**1**	**1**	**1**	**64**

When examining the methodology used within the research articles, Table 2 presents an overview.

Additionally to Tables 1 and 2, Table 3 in the appendix gives an overview to all 64 articles reviewed and their respective titles, authors, methods used, and further publication details.

Regarding the aspects covered in the 64 articles reviewed, the following picture can be obtained:

Articles covering ecological and social aspects: 28 articles
Articles covering only ecological aspects: 19 articles
Articles covering only social aspects: 17 articles

However, the aspects covered in the 64 research articles sometimes cannot be clearly assigned to one dimension of the Triple Bottom Line, since there are certain dependencies that relate to two or more dimensions simultaneously.

One of the most important effects results from the effects of energy efficiency on the potential of cost efficiency. Since electrical energy accounts for a large part of the costs in industrial value creation, Industry 4.0 offers several potentials. With smart energy distribution, improved process efficiency and improved design efficiency, the eco-effective production of the future can also make a significant contribution to the economic dimension (Kiel et al., 2017). For example, intelligent energy systems are capable of predicting a company's energy consumption and adjusting it to energy production (Birkel et al., 2019). Through the intelligent planning and scheduling of energy peaks, times with cheaper energy costs can be used with the possibility of adapting production speed to the energy supply (Stock et al., 2018). On the other hand, Birkel et al. (2019) and Stock et al. (2018) argue that Industry 4.0 leads to higher energy consumption, for instance through required data centers. Furthermore, new technologies and machines related to Industry 4.0 must be produced first, which requires a great deal of additional resources (Birkel et al., 2019).

Another issue that needs to be critically assessed is the creation of new jobs and job losses inflicted by Industry 4.0 (Birkel et al., 2017; Kiel et al., 2017). While there is no doubt in academic research that industry 4.0 will influence the labor market, it is still unclear which kind of jobs will develop in which direction.

Table 2. Methods used within articles published (n = 64)

Methodology	Number
Systematic literature review	15
Case study	14
Theoretical (not empirical-based)	14
Interviews (semi- structured interviews, expert interviews, …)	9
Surveys (questionnaire-based surveys, online surveys)	7
Mathematical programming or modelling	4
Application case	2
Experiments	2

FUTURE RESEARCH DIRECTIONS

In the following, six recommendations for future research are presented, that were identified in the literature analysis.

First, small and medium-sized enterprises (SMEs) have been shown to play a decisive role for the unfolding of Industry 4.0 across the supply chain, relating to their importance within industrial value creation, but have lacking resources and lacking understanding of the concept Industry 4.0, among further (Müller, 2019a; Müller et al., 2018b; Müller & Voigt, 2016). However, for sustainability aspects within the Triple Bottom Line, only one article within the sample of 64 articles is directly related to SMEs (Müller & Voigt, 2018). Therefore, it is recommended to further regard SMEs, focusing on sustainability aspects within the Triple Bottom Line in future research.

Second, only two articles within the total sample of 64 articles are related directly to supply chain management and logistics, referring to for sustainability aspects within the Triple Bottom Line (Kayikci, 2018; Strandhagen et al., 2017). However, the benefits of Industry 4.0 relating to horizontal interconnection of the supply chain for sustainability aspects necessarily require the integration and adaption of supply chain management (Birkel et al., 2019). Therefore, it is recommended to regard supply chains, logistics, and supply chain management more closely in the context of Industry 4.0 and the Triple Bottom Line of sustainability.

Third, new technologies such as digital platforms and ecosystems (Müller, 2019b; Schmidt et al., 2019; Veile et al., 2019) are comparably less understood from a sustainability perspective. The same applies for technologies such as blockchain, 3D-printing, or artificial intelligence, which have been investigated from a mainly technological perspective so far, but neglecting aspects within the Triple Bottom Line (Birkel et al., 2019).

Fourth, only few articles compare sustainability and Industry 4.0 in an international comparison, where perceptions, necessities and expectations towards sustainability might be different, showing a fourth possible research avenue for the future (Müller & Voigt, 2018).

Fifth, the majority of articles rather describes the opinions of experts or technological showcases descriptively. A critical assessment of their implementation, especially across the supply chain, is still missing and should be achieved, combining expert opinions and, for instance, process data, that shows benefits towards sustainability.

Sixth, the interdependencies among several dimensions of the Triple Bottom Line of sustainability must still be understood better, as the majority of articles does not cover all three dimensions of the Triple Bottom Line simultaneously. This is especially true for research across the supply chain and linking research areas like business model innovation to sustainability (Birkel et al., 2019; Müller et al., 2018b).

Conclusion

The chapter is able to present a comprehensive overview of research articles dedicated to the Triple Bottom Line of sustainability in the context of Industry 4.0. A final sample of 64 research articles was examined, highlighting methods used, publication focuses, compound effects of several aspects within the Triple Bottom Line, aspects less regarded in current literature, and possible future research directions.

Regarding the limitations of this chapter, it has to be noted that the majority of journals and conference proceedings are listed in Scopus. However, a few of them might not appear in Scopus and are therefore also not regarded in this chapter. The same is true for the term "Industry 4.0": Articles related to terms like "Smart Manufacturing", "Smart Factory" or comparable terms might not all be covered in this literature review. Several articles, but not presenting an extensive list, are presented in the section dedicated to Further Reading of this chapter.

APPENDIX

Table 3. List of articles reviewed in this chapter (n = 64)

Authors	Title	Year	Journal	Volume/Issue/ Pages	Methodology	Sample	Aspect
Bányai, T., Tamás, P., Illés, B., Stankevičiūtė, Ž., Bányai, Á.	Optimization of municipal waste collection routing: Impact of industry 4.0 technologies on environmental awareness and sustainability	2019	International Journal of Environmental Research and Public Health	16 (4), art. No. 634	Systemic literature review	227 journal articles	Ecological/ Social
Birkel, H.S., Veile, J.W., Müller, J.M., Hartmann, E., Voigt, K.-I.	Development of a risk framework for Industry 4.0 in the context of sustainability for established manufacturers	2019	Sustainability	11 (2), art. No. 384	Semi-structured expert interviews	14 interviews	Ecological/ Social
Gu, F., Guo, J., Hall, P., Gu, X.	An integrated architecture for implementing extended producer responsibility in the context of Industry 4.0	2019	International Journal of Production Research	57 (5), pp. 1458-1477	Case study	1 refrigerator plant	Ecological
Kusiak, A.	Fundamentals of smart manufacturing: A multi-thread perspective	2019	Annual Reviews in Control		Theoretical (not empirical-based)		Ecological
Limba, T., Stankevičius, A., Andrulevičius, A.	Industry 4.0 and national security: The phenomenon of disruptive technology	2019	Entrepreneur-ship and Sustainability Issues	6 (3), pp. 1528-1535	Theoretical insights obtained by document analysis, classification, critical analysis, abstraction methods		Social
Manavalan, E., Jayakrishna, K	A review of Internet of Things (IoT) embedded sustainable supply chain for industry 4.0 requirements	2019	Computers and Industrial Engineering	127, pp. 925-953	Literature review (analysing number of publications on IoT, SSCM and Industry 4.0) for identifying the research gap, building on it, a conceptual framework model has been formulated	Publications from the past ten years	Social/ Eco-logical
Nascimento, D.L.M., Alencastro, V., Quelhas, O.L.G., Caiado, R.G.G., Garza-Reyes, J.A., Lona, L.R., Tortorella, G.	Exploring Industry 4.0 technologies to enable circular economy practices in a manufacturing context: A business model proposal	2019	Journal of Manufacturing Technology Management	30 (3), pp. 607-627	Semi-structured interviews with managers, researchers and professors and literature review		Ecological
Rajput, S., Singh, S.P.	Connecting circular economy and industry 4.0	2019	International Journal of Information Management	49, pp. 98-113	Online survey	161 question-naires	Social/ Eco-logical

continued on following page

Table 3. Continued

Authors	Title	Year	Journal	Volume/Issue/ Pages	Methodology	Sample	Aspect
Salah, B., Abidi, M.H., Mian, S.H., Krid, M., Alkhalefah, H., Abdo, A.	Virtual reality-based engineering education to enhance manufacturing sustainability in industry 4.0	2019	Sustainability	11 (5), art. No. 1477	VR-based experiments with students	50 participants	Social
Savastano, M., Amendola, C., Bellini, B., D'Ascenzo, F.	Contextual impacts on industrial processes brought by the digital transformation of manufacturing: A systematic review	2019	Sustainability	11 (3), art. No. 891	Literature review	156 primary publications	Social
Scharl, S., Praktiknjo, A.	The Role of a Digital Industry 4.0 in a Renewable Energy System	2019	International Journal of Energy Research		Semi- structured interviews with industry managers and energy researchers		Ecological/ Social
Stachová, K., Papula, J., Stacho, Z., Kohnová, L.	External partnerships in employee education and development as the key to facing industry 4.0 challenges	2019	Sustainability	11 (2), art. No. 345	Quantitative survey	1482 organi-sations	Social
Tseng, M.-L., Chiu, A.S.F., Chien, C.-F., Tan, R.R.	Pathways and barriers to circularity in food systems	2019	Resources, Conservation and Recycling,	pp. 236-237	Theoretical (not empirical-based)		Ecological/ Social
Varela, L., Araújo, A., Ávila, P., Castro, H., Putnik, G.	Evaluation of the relation between lean manufacturing, industry 4.0, and sustainability	2019	Sustainability	11 (5), art. No. 1439	Questionnaire based survey	252 question-naires	Ecological/ Social
Bag, S., Telukdarie, A., Pretorius, J.H.C., Gupta, S	Industry 4.0 and supply chain sustainability: framework and future research directions	2018	Benchmarking	Article in Press	Systemic literature review	53 papers	Social
Bonilla, S.H., Silva, H.R.O., da Silva, M.T., Gonçalves, R.F., Sacomano, J.B.	Industry 4.0 and sustainability implications: A scenario-based analysis of the impacts and challenges	2018	Sustainability	10 (10), art. No 3740	Literature Review and theoretical analysis of scenarios	4 scenarios	Ecological
Braccini, A.M., Margherita, E.G.	Exploring organizational sustainability of Industry 4.0 under the triple bottom line: The case of a manufacturing company	2018	Sustainability	11 (1), art. No. 36	Case Study	1 company	Social/ Eco-logical
Bressanelli, G., Adrodegari, F., Perona, M., Saccani, N.	Exploring how usage-focused business models enable circular economy through digital technologies	2018	Sustainability	10 (3), art. No. 639	Case Study	1 company (ALPHA)	Ecological
Carvalho, N., Chaim, O., Cazarini, E., Gerolamo, M.	Manufacturing in the fourth industrial revolution: A positive prospect in Sustainable Manufacturing	2018	Procedia Manufacturing	21, pp. 671-678	Theoretical (not empirical-based)		Ecological

continued on following page

Table 3. Continued

Authors	Title	Year	Journal	Volume/Issue/ Pages	Methodology	Sample	Aspect
Chaim, O., Muschard, B., Cazarini, E., Rozenfeld, H.	Insertion of sustainability performance indicators in an industry 4.0 virtual learning environment	2018	Procedia Manufacturing	21, pp. 446-453	Case study	1 company	Social/ Eco-logical
Dassisti, M., Siragusa, N., Semeraro, C.	Exergetic Model as a Guideline for Implementing the Smart-factory Paradigm in Small Medium Enterprises: The Brovedani Case	2018	Procedia CIRP	67, pp. 534-539	Systemic literature review	339 papers	Ecological
de Sousa Jabbour, A.B.L., Jabbour, C.J.C., Foropon, C., Filho, M.G.	When titans meet – Can industry 4.0 revolutionise the environmentally-sustainable manufacturing wave? The role of critical success factors	2018	Technological Forecasting and Social Change	132, pp. 18-25	Theoretical (not empirical-based)		Ecological
Ding, B.	Pharma Industry 4.0: Literature review and research opportunities in sustainable pharmaceutical supply chains	2018	Process Safety and Environmental Protection	119, pp. 115-130	Literature review	33 articles	Social
Dossou, P.-E.	Impact of Sustainability on the supply chain 4.0 performance	2018	Procedia Manufacturing	17, pp. 452-459	Case study	1 company	Social
Franciosi, C., Iung, B., Miranda, S., Riemma, S.	Maintenance for Sustainability in the Industry 4.0 context: a Scoping Literature Review	2018	IFAC- PapersOnLine	51 (11), pp. 903-908	Literature review	68 papers	Ecological
Garcia-Muiña, F.E., González-Sánchez, R., Ferrari, A.M., Settembre-Blundo, D.	The paradigms of Industry 4.0 and circular economy as enabling drivers for the competitiveness of businesses and territories: The case of an Italian ceramic tiles manufacturing company	2018	Social Sciences	7 (12), art. No. 255	Case study	1 ceramic tiles manu-facturing company in Italy	Social
Garrido-Hidalgo, C., Hortelano, D., Roda-Sanchez, L., Olivares, T., Ruiz, M.C., Lopez, V.	IoT Heterogeneous Mesh Network Deployment for Human-in-the-Loop Challenges Towards a Social and Sustainable Industry 4.0	2018	IEEE Access	6, pp. 28417-28437	Experiments		Social
Gregori, F., Papetti, A., Pandolfi, M., Peruzzini, M., Germani, M.	Improving a production site from a social point of view: An IoT infrastructure to monitor workers condition	2018	Procedia CIRP	72, pp. 886-891	Case study	1 company	Social
Kamble, S.S., Gunasekaran, A., Gawankar, S.A.	Sustainable Industry 4.0 framework: A systematic literature review identifying the current trends and future perspectives	2018	Process Safety and Environmental Protection	117, pp. 408-425	Systemic literature review	85 papers	Social/ Eco-logical

continued on following page

Table 3. Continued

Authors	Title	Year	Journal	Volume/Issue/ Pages	Methodology	Sample	Aspect
Kayikci, Y.	Sustainability impact of digitization in logistics	2018	Procedia Manufacturing	21, pp. 782-789	Case study, Qualitative expert interviews and secondary data		Ecological/ Social
Kenett, R.S., Zonnenshain, A., Fortuna, G.	A road map for applied data sciences supporting sustainability in advanced manufacturing: The information quality dimensions	2018	Procedia Manufacturing	21, pp. 141-148	Theoretical (not empirical-based)		Social/ Eco-logical
Kumar, R., Singh, S.P., Lamba, K.	Sustainable robust layout using Big Data approach: A key towards industry 4.0	2018	Journal of Cleaner Production	204, pp. 643-659	(Mathe-matical) model development		Social/ Eco-logical
Latorre-Biel, J.-I., Faulín, J., Juan, A.A., Jiménez-Macías, E.	Petri Net Model of a Smart Factory in the Frame of Industry 4.0	2018	IFAC-PapersOnLine	51 (2), pp. 266-271	Application case		Social
Lin, K.-Y.	User experience-based product design for smart production to empower industry 4.0 in the glass recycling circular economy	2018	Computers and Industrial Engineering	125, pp. 729-738	Literature review + empirical study with a glass recycling company in Taiwan	11 papers (circular economy), 35 studies (product design), 9 resources to compare the level of literature)	Social
Lopes de Sousa Jabbour, A.B., Jabbour, C.J.C., Godinho Filho, M., Roubaud, D.	Industry 4.0 and the circular economy: a proposed research agenda and original roadmap for sustainable operations	2018	Annals of Operations Research	270 (1-2), pp. 273-286	Theoretical (not empirical-based)		Ecological
Lugert, A., Batz, A., Winkler, H.	Empirical assessment of the future adequacy of value stream mapping in manufacturing industries	2018	Journal of Manufacturing Technology Management	29 (5), pp. 886-906	Empirical survey	170 participants	Ecological
Luthra, S., Mangla, S.K.	Evaluating challenges to Industry 4.0 initiatives for supply chain sustainability in emerging economies	2018	Process Safety and Environmental Protection	117, pp. 168-179	Questionnaire based survey	96 responses	Social/ Eco-logical
Maresova, P., Soukal, I., Svobodova, L., Hedvicakova, M., Javanmardi, E., Selamat, A., Krejcar, O.	Consequences of industry 4.0 in business and economics	2018	Economies	6 (3), art. No. 46	Literature Review	67 papers	Social
Mattsson, S., Fast-Berglund, Å., Li, D., Thorvald, P.	Forming a cognitive automation strategy for Operator 4.0 in complex assembly	2018	Computers and Industrial Engineering	Article in Press	Theoretical (not empirical-based)		Social
Müller, J.M., Kiel, D., Voigt, K.-I.	What drives the implementation of Indusrry 4.0? The role of opportunities and challenges in the context of sustainability	2018	Sustainability	10 (1) art. No. 247	Quantitative study (partial least square structural equation modelling)	746 manu-facturing companies	Ecological/ Social

continued on following page

Table 3. Continued

Authors	Title	Year	Journal	Volume/Issue/ Pages	Methodology	Sample	Aspect
Müller, J.M., Voigt, K.-I.	Sustainable Industrial Value Creation in SMEs: A Comparison between Industry 4.0 and Made in China 2025	2018	International Journal of Precision Engineering and Manufacturing-Green Technology	5 (5), pp. 659-670	Questionnaire based survey (for SMEs in China and Germany)	329 SMEs (222 Germany, 107 China)	Ecological/ Social
Murmura, F., Bravi, L.	Additive manufacturing in the wood-furniture sector: Sustainability of the technology, benefits and limitations of adoption	2018	Journal of Manufacturing Technology Management	29 (2), pp. 350-371	Questionnaire based survey	234 Italian companies	Ecological
Nagy, J., Oláh, J., Erdei, E., Máté, D., Popp, J.	The role and impact of industry 4.0 and the internet of things on the business strategy of the value chain-the case of hungary	2018	Sustainability	10 (10), art. No. 3491	Questionnaire based survey/ expert interviews	43 question-naires/ 4 expert interviews	Ecological
Okorie, O., Salonitis, K., Charnley, F., Moreno, M., Turner, C., Tiwari, A.	Digitisation and the circular economy: A review of current research and future trends	2018	Energies	11 (11), art. No. 3009	Systematic literature review	174 articles	Social
Paravizo, E., Chaim, O.C., Braatz, D., Muschard, B., Rozenfeld, H.	Exploring gamification to support manufacturing education on industry 4.0 as an enabler for innovation and sustainability	2018	Procedia Manufacturing	21, pp. 438-445	Systematic literature review	51 articles	Ecological/ Social
Sénéchal, O.	Performance indicators nomenclatures for decision making in sustainable conditions based maintenance	2018	IFAC-PapersOnLine	51 (11), pp. 1137-1142	Application case		Ecological/ Social
Sjödin, D.R., Parida, V., Leksell, M., Petrovic, A.	Smart Factory Implementation and Process Innovation: A Preliminary Maturity Model for Leveraging Digitalization in Manufacturing Moving to smart factories presents specific challenges that can be addressed through a structured approach focused on people, processes, and technologies.	2018	Research Technology Management	61 (5), pp.22-31	Case Study	5 companies	Social/ Eco-logical
Stock, T., Obenaus, M., Kunz, S., Kohl, H.	Industry 4.0 as enabler for a sustainable development: A qualitative assessment of its ecological and social potential	2018	Process Safety and Environmental Protection	118, pp 254-267	Literature review and case study with expert interviews		Ecological/ Social
Tsai, W.-H., Lu, Y.-H.	A framework of production planning and control with carbon tax under industry 4.0	2018	Sustainability	10 (9), art. No. 3221	Mathematical programming model		Ecological/ Social
Tseng, M.-L., Tan, R.R., Chiu, A.S.F., Chien, C.-F., Kuo, T.C.	Circular economy meets industry 4.0: Can big data drive industrial symbiosis?	2018	Resources, Conservation and Recycling	131, pp 146-147	Literature review (analysing the number of publications on different keywords)		Ecological/ Social

continued on following page

Table 3. Continued

Authors	Title	Year	Journal	Volume/Issue/ Pages	Methodology	Sample	Aspect
Waibel, M.W., Oosthuizen, G.A., Du Toit, D.W.	Investigating current smart production innovations in the machine building industry on sustainability aspects	2018	Procedia Manufacturing	21, pp. 774-781	Interviews	12 companies	Ecological/ Social
Yang, S., Raghavendra, M.R.A., Kaminski, J., Pepin, H.	Opportunities for industry 4.0 to support remanufacturing	2018	Applied Sciences	8 (7), art. No. 1177	Case Study	2 cases	Ecological
Yazdi, P.G., Azizi, A., Hashemipour, M.	An empirical investigation of the relationship between overall equipment efficiency (OEE) and manufacturing sustainability in industry 4.0 with time study approach	2018	Sustainability	10 (9), art. No. 3031	Time study-based methodology		Ecological
Gregori, F., Papetti, A., Pandolfi, M., Peruzzini, M., Germani, M.	Digital Manufacturing Systems: A Framework to Improve Social Sustainability of a Production Site	2017	Procedia CIRP	63, pp. 436-442	Case study	1 production line	Social
Kiel, D., Müller, J.M., Arnold, C., Voigt, K.-I.	Sustainable industrial value creation: Benefits and challenges of industry 4.0	2017	International Journal of Innovation Management	21 (8) art. no. 1740015	Multiple case study with expert interviews	46 manu-facturing companies	Social/ Eco-logical
Lin, K.C., Shyu, J.Z., Ding, K.	A cross-strait comparison of innovation policy under industry 4.0 and sustainability development transition	2017	Sustainability	9 (5), art. No. 786	Literature review of policies	107 policy tools from China, 103 policy tools from Taiwan	Social
Man, J.C.D., Strandhagen, J.O.	An Industry 4.0 Research Agenda for Sustainable Business Models	2017	Procedia CIRP	63, pp. 721-726	Theoretical (not empirical-based)		Ecological
Prause, G., Atari, S.	On sustainable production networks for industry 4.0	2017	Entrepreneurship and Sustainability Issues	4 (4), pp 421-431	Case study+ semi- structured expert interviews+ quantitative analysis of internal business process data	1 company	Social/Eco-logical
Rauch, E., Dallasega, P., Matt, D.T.	Distributed manufacturing network models of smart and agile mini-factories	2017	International Journal of Agile Systems and Management	10 (3-4), pp 185-205	Case Study	2 companies	Social/ Eco-logical
Strandhagen, J.O., Vallandingham, L.R., Fragapane, G., Strandhagen, J.W., Stangeland, A.B.H., Sharma, N.	Logistics 4.0 and emerging sustainable business models	2017	Advances in Manufacturing	5 (4), pp. 359-369	Theoretical (not empirical-based)		Ecological
Waibel, M.W., Steenkamp, L.P., Moloko, N., Oosthuizen, G.A.	Investigating the Effects of Smart Production Systems on Sustainability Elements	2017	Procedia Manufacturing	8, pp. 731-737	Theoretical (not empirical-based)		Ecological/ Social
Stock, T., Seliger, G.	Opportunities of Sustainable Manufacturing in Industry 4.0	2016	Procedia CIRP	40, pp. 536-541	Theoretical (not empirical-based)		Social/ Ecological

continued on following page

Table 3. Continued

Authors	Title	Year	Journal	Volume/Issue/ Pages	Methodology	Sample	Aspect
Branger, J., Pang, Z.	From automated home to sustainable, healthy and manufacturing home: a new story enabled by the Internet-of-Things and Industry 4.0	2015	Journal of Management Analytics	2 (4), pp 314-332	Theoretical (not empirical-based)		Social/ Eco-logical
Stark, R., Grosser, H., Beckmann-Dobrev, B., Kind, S.	Advanced technologies in life cycle engineering	2014	Procedia CIRP	22 (1), pp. 3-14	Theoretical (not empirical-based)		Ecological

REFERENCES

Bag, S., Telukdarie, A., Pretorius, J. H. C., & Gupta, S. (in press). Industry 4.0 and supply chain sustainability: Framework and future research directions. *Benchmarking: An International Journal.*

Bányai, T., Tamás, P., Illés, B., Stankevičiūtė, Ž., & Bányai, Á. (2019). Optimization of Municipal Waste Collection Routing: Impact of Industry 4.0 Technologies on Environmental Awareness and Sustainability. *International Journal of Environmental Research and Public Health, 16*(4), 634. doi:10.3390/ijerph16040634

Birkel, H. S., Veile, J. W., Müller, J. M., Hartmann, E., & Voigt, K. I. (2019). Development of a risk framework for Industry 4.0 in the context of sustainability for established manufacturers. *Sustainability, 11*(2), 384. doi:10.3390u11020384

Bonilla, S., Silva, H., Terra da Silva, M., Franco Gonçalves, R., & Sacomano, J. (2018). Industry 4.0 and sustainability implications: A scenario-based analysis of the impacts and challenges. *Sustainability, 10*(10), 3740. doi:10.3390u10103740

Braccini, A. M., & Margherita, E. G. (2018). Exploring Organizational Sustainability of Industry 4.0 under the Triple Bottom Line: The Case of a Manufacturing Company. *Sustainability, 11*(1), 1–17. doi:10.3390u11010036

Branger, J., & Pang, Z. (2015). From automated home to sustainable, healthy and manufacturing home: A new story enabled by the Internet-of-Things and Industry 4.0. *Journal of Management Analytics, 2*(4), 314–332. doi:10.1080/23270012.2015.1115379

Bressanelli, G., Adrodegari, F., Perona, M., & Saccani, N. (2018). Exploring how usage-focused business models enable circular economy through digital technologies. *Sustainability, 10*(3), 639. doi:10.3390u10030639

Carvalho, N., Chaim, O., Cazarini, E., & Gerolamo, M. (2018). Manufacturing in the fourth industrial revolution: A positive prospect in sustainable manufacturing. *Procedia Manufacturing, 21*, 671–678. doi:10.1016/j.promfg.2018.02.170

Chaim, O., Muschard, B., Cazarini, E., & Rozenfeld, H. (2018). Insertion of sustainability performance indicators in an industry 4.0 virtual learning environment. *Procedia Manufacturing, 21*, 446–453. doi:10.1016/j.promfg.2018.02.143

Dassisti, M., Siragusa, N., & Semeraro, C. (2018). *Exergetic Model as a Guideline for Implementing the Smart-factory Paradigm in Small Medium Enterprises: The Brovedani Case. In Procedia CIRP* (Vol. 67, pp. 534–539). Amsterdam, Netherlands: Elsevier.

de Man, J. C., & Strandhagen, J. O. (2017). *An Industry 4.0 research agenda for sustainable business models. In Procedia CIRP* (Vol. 63, pp. 721–726). Amsterdam, Netherlands: Elsevier.

de Sousa Jabbour, A. B. L., Jabbour, C. J. C., Foropon, C., & Godinho Filho, M. (2018). When titans meet–Can industry 4.0 revolutionise the environmentally-sustainable manufacturing wave? The role of critical success factors. *Technological Forecasting and Social Change, 132*, 18–25. doi:10.1016/j.techfore.2018.01.017

de Sousa Jabbour, A. B. L., Jabbour, C. J. C., Godinho Filho, M., & Roubaud, D. (2018). Industry 4.0 and the circular economy: A proposed research agenda and original roadmap for sustainable operations. *Annals of Operations Research, 270*(1-2), 273–286. doi:10.100710479-018-2772-8

Ding, B. (2018). Pharma industry 4.0: Literature review and research opportunities in sustainable pharmaceutical supply chains. *Process Safety and Environmental Protection, 119*, 115–130. doi:10.1016/j.psep.2018.06.031

Dossou, P. E. (2018). *Impact of Sustainability on the supply chain 4.0 performance. In Procedia Manufacturing* (Vol. 17, pp. 452–459). Amsterdam, Netherlands: Elsevier.

Elkington, J. (1987). Towards the Sustainable Corporation. Win-Win-Win Business Strategies for Sustainable Development. *California Management Review, 36*(2), 90–100. doi:10.2307/41165746

Elkington, J. (1998). Partnerships from cannibals with forks: The triple bottom line of 21st-century business. *Environmental Quality Management, 8*(1), 37–51. doi:10.1002/tqem.3310080106

Franciosi, C., Iung, B., Miranda, S., & Riemma, S. (2018). Maintenance for Sustainability in the Industry 4.0 context: a Scoping Literature Review. In *IFAC-PapersOnLine* (vol. 51(11), pp. 903-908). Laxenburg, Austria: IFAC (International Federation of Automatic Control).

Garcia-Muiña, F., González-Sánchez, R., Ferrari, A., & Settembre-Blundo, D. (2018). The Paradigms of Industry 4.0 and Circular Economy as Enabling Drivers for the Competitiveness of Businesses and Territories: The Case of an Italian Ceramic Tiles Manufacturing Company. *Social Sciences, 7*(12), 255. doi:10.3390ocsci7120255

Garrido-Hidalgo, C., Hortelano, D., Roda-Sanchez, L., Olivares, T., Ruiz, M. C., & Lopez, V. (2018). IoT Heterogeneous Mesh Network Deployment for Human-in-the-Loop Challenges Towards a Social and Sustainable Industry 4.0. *IEEE Access: Practical Innovations, Open Solutions, 6*, 28417–28437. doi:10.1109/ACCESS.2018.2836677

Glavič, P., & Lukman, R. (2007). Review of sustainability terms and their definitions. *Journal of Cleaner Production, 15*(18), 1875–1885. doi:10.1016/j.jclepro.2006.12.006

Gregori, F., Papetti, A., Pandolfi, M., Peruzzini, M., & Germani, M. (2017). *Digital manufacturing systems: a framework to improve social sustainability of a production site. In Procedia CIRP* (Vol. 63, pp. 436–442). Amsterdam, Netherlands: Elsevier.

Gregori, F., Papetti, A., Pandolfi, M., Peruzzini, M., & Germani, M. (2018). *Improving a production site from a social point of view: an IoT infrastructure to monitor workers condition. In Procedia CIRP* (Vol. 72, pp. 886–891). Amsterdam, Netherlands: Elsevier.

Gu, F., Guo, J., Hall, P., & Gu, X. (2018). An integrated architecture for implementing extended producer responsibility in the context of Industry 4.0. *International Journal of Production Research*, 1–20.

Kagermann, H., Wahlster, W., & Helbig, J. (2013). *Recommendations for implementing the strategic initiative Industrie 4.0.* Final report of the Industrie 4.0 Working Group. Frankfurt am Main, Germany: acatech.

Kamble, S. S., Gunasekaran, A., & Gawankar, S. A. (2018). Sustainable Industry 4.0 framework: A systematic literature review identifying the current trends and future perspectives. *Process Safety and Environmental Protection*, *117*, 408–425. doi:10.1016/j.psep.2018.05.009

Kayikci, Y. (2018). *Sustainability impact of digitization in logistics. In Procedia Manufacturing* (Vol. 21, pp. 782–789). Amsterdam, Netherlands: Elsevier.

Kenett, R. S., Zonnenshain, A., & Fortuna, G. (2018). *A road map for applied data sciences supporting sustainability in advanced manufacturing: the information quality dimensions. In Procedia Manufacturing* (Vol. 21, pp. 141–148). Amsterdam, Netherlands: Elsevier.

Kiel, D., Müller, J. M., Arnold, C., & Voigt, K. I. (2017). Sustainable industrial value creation: Benefits and challenges of industry 4.0. *International Journal of Innovation Management*, *21*(08), 1740015. doi:10.1142/S1363919617400151

Kumar, R., Singh, S. P., & Lamba, K. (2018). Sustainable robust layout using Big Data approach: A key towards industry 4.0. *Journal of Cleaner Production*, *204*, 643–659. doi:10.1016/j.jclepro.2018.08.327

Kusiak, A. (2019). Fundamentals of smart manufacturing: A multi-thread perspective. *Annual Reviews in Control*, *47*, 214–220. doi:10.1016/j.arcontrol.2019.02.001

Lasi, H., Fettke, P., Kemper, H.-G., Feld, T., & Hoffmann, M. (2014). Industry 4.0. *Business & Information Systems Engineering*, *6*(8), 239–242. doi:10.100712599-014-0334-4

Latorre-Biel, J. I., Faulín, J., Juan, A. A., & Jiménez-Macías, E. (2018). Petri net model of a smart factory in the frame of Industry 4.0. *IFAC-PapersOnLine*, *51*(2), 266–271. doi:10.1016/j.ifacol.2018.03.046

Liao, Y., Deschamps, F., Loures, E., & Ramos, L. F. P. (2017). Past, present and future of Industry 4.0 - a systematic literature review and research agenda proposal. *International Journal of Production Research*, *55*(12), 3609–3629. doi:10.1080/00207543.2017.1308576

Limba, T., Stankevičius, A., & Andrulevičius, A. (2019). Industry 4.0 and national security: The phenomenon of disruptive technology. *Entrepreneurship and Sustainability Issues*, *6*(3), 1528–1535. doi:10.9770/jesi.2019.6.3(33)

Lin, K., Shyu, J., & Ding, K. (2017). A cross-strait comparison of innovation policy under industry 4.0 and sustainability development transition. *Sustainability*, *9*(5), 786. doi:10.3390u9050786

Lin, K. Y. (2018). User experience-based product design for smart production to empower industry 4.0 in the glass recycling circular economy. *Computers & Industrial Engineering*, *125*, 729–738. doi:10.1016/j.cie.2018.06.023

Littig, B., & Griessler, E. (2005). Social sustainability. A catchword between political pragmatism and social theory. *International Journal of Sustainable Development*, *8*(1-2), 65–78. doi:10.1504/IJSD.2005.007375

Lugert, A., Batz, A., & Winkler, H. (2018). Empirical assessment of the future adequacy of value stream mapping in manufacturing industries. *Journal of Manufacturing Technology Management*, *29*(5), 886–906. doi:10.1108/JMTM-11-2017-0236

Luthra, S., & Mangla, S. K. (2018). Evaluating challenges to Industry 4.0 initiatives for supply chain sustainability in emerging economies. *Process Safety and Environmental Protection*, *117*, 168–179. doi:10.1016/j.psep.2018.04.018

Manavalan, E., & Jayakrishna, K. (2019). A review of Internet of Things (IoT) embedded sustainable supply chain for industry 4.0 requirements. *Computers & Industrial Engineering*, *127*, 925–953. doi:10.1016/j.cie.2018.11.030

Maresova, P., Soukal, I., Svobodova, L., Hedvicakova, M., Javanmardi, E., Selamat, A., & Krejcar, O. (2018). Consequences of Industry 4.0 in business and economics. *Economies*, *6*(3), 46. doi:10.3390/economies6030046

Mattsson, S., Fast-Berglund, Å., Li, D., & Thorvald, P. (in press). Forming a cognitive automation strategy for Operator 4.0 in complex assembly. *Computers & Industrial Engineering*.

Maynard, A. D. (2015). Navigating the fourth industrial revolution. *Nature Nanotechnology*, *10*(1), 1005–1006. doi:10.1038/nnano.2015.286

McWilliams, A., Parhankangas, A., Coupet, J., Welch, E., & Barnum, D. T. (2016). Strategic Decision Making for the Triple Bottom Line. *Business Strategy and the Environment*, *25*(3), 193–204. doi:10.1002/bse.1867

Müller, J., Dotzauer, V., & Voigt, K. I. (2017). Industry 4.0 and its impact on reshoring decisions of German manufacturing enterprises. In Supply Management Research (pp. 165-179). Springer Gabler.

Müller, J., & Voigt, K. I. (2016). Industrie 4.0 für kleine und mittlere Unternehmen. *Productivity Management*, *3*, 28–30.

Müller, J. M. (2019a). Business model innovation in small-and medium-sized enterprises: Strategies for industry 4.0 providers and users. *Journal of Manufacturing Technology Management*. doi:10.1108/JMTM-01-2018-0008

Müller, J. M. (2019b). Antecedents to Digital Platform Usage in Industry 4.0 by Established Manufacturers. *Sustainability*, *11*(4), 1121. doi:10.3390u11041121

Müller, J. M., Buliga, O., & Voigt, K.-I. (2018b). Fortune favors the prepared. How SMEs approach business model innovation in Industry 4.0. *Technological Forecasting and Social Change*, *132*, 2–17. doi:10.1016/j.techfore.2017.12.019

Müller, J. M., & Däschle, S. (2018). Business Model Innovation of Industry 4.0 Solution Providers Towards Customer Process Innovation. *Processes*, *6*(12), 260. doi:10.3390/pr6120260

Müller, J. M., Kiel, D., & Voigt, K. I. (2018a). What drives the implementation of industry 4.0? The role of opportunities and challenges in the context of sustainability. *Sustainability*, *10*(1), 247. doi:10.3390u10010247

Müller, J. M., & Voigt, K. I. (2018). Sustainable industrial value creation in SMEs: A comparison between industry 4.0 and Made in China 2025. *International Journal of Precision Engineering and Manufacturing-Green Technology*, *5*(5), 659–670. doi:10.100740684-018-0056-z

Murmura, F., & Bravi, L. (2018). Additive manufacturing in the wood-furniture sector: Sustainability of the technology, benefits and limitations of adoption. *Journal of Manufacturing Technology Management*, *29*(2), 350–371.

Nagy, J., Oláh, J., Erdei, E., Máté, D., & Popp, J. (2018). The Role and Impact of Industry 4.0 and the Internet of Things on the Business Strategy of the Value Chain—The Case of Hungary. *Sustainability*, *10*(10), 3491. doi:10.3390u10103491

Nascimento, D. L. M., Alencastro, V., Quelhas, O. L. G., Caiado, R. G. G., Garza-Reyes, J. A., Lona, L. R., & Tortorella, G. (2018). Exploring Industry 4.0 technologies to enable circular economy practices in a manufacturing context: A business model proposal. *Journal of Manufacturing Technology Management*, *30*(3), 607–627. doi:10.1108/JMTM-03-2018-0071

Norman, W., MacDonald, C., & Arnold, D. G. (2004). Getting to the Bottom of "Triple Bottom Line". *Business Ethics Quarterly*, *14*(2), 243–262. doi:10.5840/beq200414211

Okorie, O., Salonitis, K., Charnley, F., Moreno, M., Turner, C., & Tiwari, A. (2018). Digitisation and the circular economy: A review of current research and future trends. *Energies*, *11*(11), 3009. doi:10.3390/en11113009

Paravizo, E., Chaim, O. C., Braatz, D., Muschard, B., & Rozenfeld, H. (2018). *Exploring gamification to support manufacturing education on industry 4.0 as an enabler for innovation and sustainability. In Procedia Manufacturing* (Vol. 21, pp. 438–445). Amsterdam, Netherlands: Elsevier.

Piccarozzi, M., Aquilani, B., & Gatti, C. (2018). Industry 4.0 in management studies: A systematic literature review. *Sustainability*, *10*(10), 3821. doi:10.3390u10103821

Prause, G., & Atari, S. (2017). On sustainable production networks for Industry 4.0. *Entrepreneurship and Sustainability Issues*, *4*(4), 421–431. doi:10.9770/jesi.2017.4.4(2)

Rajput, S., & Singh, S. P. (2019). Connecting circular economy and industry 4.0. *International Journal of Information Management*, *49*, 98–113. doi:10.1016/j.ijinfomgt.2019.03.002

Rauch, E., Dallasega, P., & Matt, D. T. (2017). Distributed manufacturing network models of smart and agile mini-factories. *International Journal of Agile Systems and Management*, *10*(3-4), 185–205. doi:10.1504/IJASM.2017.088534

Salah, B., Abidi, M. H., Mian, S. H., Krid, M., Alkhalefah, H., & Abdo, A. (2019). Virtual Reality-Based Engineering Education to Enhance Manufacturing Sustainability in Industry 4.0. *Sustainability, 11*(5), 1477. doi:10.3390u11051477

Savastano, M., Amendola, C., Bellini, F., & D'Ascenzo, F. (2019). Contextual Impacts on Industrial Processes Brought by the Digital Transformation of Manufacturing: A Systematic Review. *Sustainability, 11*(3), 891. doi:10.3390u11030891

Scharl, S., & Praktiknjo, A. (2019). The Role of a Digital Industry 4.0 in a Renewable Energy System. *International Journal of Energy Research, 43*(8), 3891–3904. doi:10.1002/er.4462

Schmidt, M.-C., Veile, J. W., Müller, J. M., & Voigt, K.-I. (2019). *Kick-start for connectivity – How to implement digital platforms successfully.* Paper presented at the International Society for Professional Innovation Management (ISPIM) Innovation Conference, Florence, Italy.

Sénéchal, O. (2018). Performance indicators nomenclatures for decision making in sustainable conditions based maintenance. *IFAC-PapersOnLine, 51*(11), 1137–1142. doi:10.1016/j.ifacol.2018.08.438

Sjödin, D. R., Parida, V., Leksell, M., & Petrovic, A. (2018). Smart Factory Implementation and Process Innovation: A Preliminary Maturity Model for Leveraging Digitalization in Manufacturing Moving to smart factories presents specific challenges that can be addressed through a structured approach focused on people, processes, and technologies. *Research Technology Management, 61*(5), 22–31. doi:10.1080/08956308.2018.1471277

Stachová, K., Papula, J., Stacho, Z., & Kohnová, L. (2019). External partnerships in employee education and development as the key to facing industry 4.0 challengesn. *Sustainability, 11*(2), 345. doi:10.3390u11020345

Stark, R., Grosser, H., Beckmann-Dobrev, B., & Kind, S. (2014). Advanced technologies in life cycle engineering. *Procedia CIRP, 22*, 3–14. doi:10.1016/j.procir.2014.07.118

Stock, T., Obenaus, M., Kunz, S., & Kohl, H. (2018). Industry 4.0 as enabler for a sustainable development: A qualitative assessment of its ecological and social potential. *Process Safety and Environmental Protection, 118*, 254–267. doi:10.1016/j.psep.2018.06.026

Stock, T., & Seliger, G. (2016). *Opportunities of sustainable manufacturing in industry 4.0. In Procedia CIRP* (Vol. 40, pp. 536–541). Amsterdam, Netherlands: Elsevier.

Strandhagen, J. O., Vallandingham, L. R., Fragapane, G., Strandhagen, J. W., Stangeland, A. B. H., & Sharma, N. (2017). Logistics 4.0 and emerging sustainable business models. *Advances in Manufacturing, 5*(4), 359–369. doi:10.100740436-017-0198-1

Tsai, W. H., & Lu, Y. H. (2018). A framework of production planning and control with carbon tax under industry 4.0. *Sustainability, 10*(9), 3221. doi:10.3390u10093221

Tseng, M. L., Chiu, A. S., Chien, C. F., & Tan, R. R. (2019). Pathways and barriers to circularity in food systems. *Resources, Conservation and Recycling, 143*, 236–237. doi:10.1016/j.resconrec.2019.01.015

Tseng, M. L., Tan, R. R., Chiu, A. S., Chien, C. F., & Kuo, T. C. (2018). Circular economy meets industry 4.0: Can big data drive industrial symbiosis? *Resources, Conservation and Recycling, 131*, 146–147. doi:10.1016/j.resconrec.2017.12.028

Varela, L., Araújo, A., Ávila, P., Castro, H., & Putnik, G. (2019). Evaluation of the Relation between Lean Manufacturing, Industry 4.0, and Sustainability. *Sustainability, 11*(5), 1439. doi:10.3390u11051439

Veile, J. W., Kiel, D., Müller, J. M., & Voigt, K.-I. (2019). *Ecosystem 4.0: A Supply Chain Perspective on Business Model Innovation.* Paper presented at the International Society for Professional Innovation Management (ISPIM) Innovation Conference, Florence, Italy.

Waibel, M. W., Oosthuizen, G. A., & du Toit, D. W. (2018). *Investigating current smart production innovations in the machine building industry on sustainability aspects. In Procedia Manufacturing* (Vol. 21, pp. 774–781). Amsterdam, Netherlands: Elsevier.

Waibel, M. W., Steenkamp, L. P., Moloko, N., & Oosthuizen, G. A. (2017). *Investigating the effects of smart production systems on sustainability elements. In Procedia Manufacturing* (Vol. 8, pp. 731–737). Amsterdam, Netherlands: Elsevier.

World Commission on Environment and Development. (1987). *Our Common Future.* Oxford University Press.

Yang, S., MR, A., Kaminski, J., & Pepin, H. (2018). Opportunities for industry 4.0 to support remanufacturing. *Applied Sciences, 8*(7), 1177. doi:10.3390/app8071177

Yazdi, G. P., Azizi, A., & Hashemipour, M. (2018). An empirical investigation of the relationship between overall equipment efficiency (OEE) and manufacturing sustainability in Industry 4.0 with time study approach. *Sustainability, 10*(9), 3031. doi:10.3390u10093031

ADDITIONAL READING

Beier, G., Niehoff, S., Ziems, T., & Xue, B. (2017). Sustainability aspects of a digitalized industry–A comparative study from China and Germany. *International Journal of Precision Engineering and Manufacturing-Green Technology, 4*(2), 227–234. doi:10.100740684-017-0028-8

Bonekamp, L., & Sure, M. (2015). Consequences of Industry 4.0 on Human Labour and Work Organisation. *Journal of Business and Media Psychology, 6*(1), 33–40.

Herrmann, C., Schmidt, C., Kurle, D., Blume, S., & Thiede, S. (2016). Sustainability in manufacturing and factories of the future. *International Journal of Precision Engineering in Manufacturing-Green Technology, 1*(4), 283–292. doi:10.100740684-014-0034-z

Müller, J. M., Maier, L., Veile, J., & Voigt, K. I. (2017). Cooperation strategies among SMEs for implementing industry 4.0. In *Proceedings of the Hamburg International Conference of Logistics (HICL)* (pp. 301-318). Berlin, Germany: epubli.

Müller, J. M., Veile, J., & Voigt, K. I. (2018). Supplier Integration in Industry 4.0–Requirements and Strategies. In *Proceedings of the Hamburg International Conference of Logistics (HICL)* (pp. 23-36). Berlin, Germany: epubli.

Müller, J. M., & Voigt, K. I. (2018). The Impact of Industry 4.0 on Supply Chains in Engineer-to-Order Industries-An Exploratory Case Study. *IFAC-PapersOnLine*, *51*(11), 122–127. doi:10.1016/j.ifacol.2018.08.245

Peukert, B., Benecke, S., Clavell, J., Neugebauer, S., Nissen, N. F., & Uhlmann, E. (2015). *Addressing Sustainability and Flexibility in Manufacturing Via Smart Modular Machine Tool Frames to Support Sustainable Value Creation. Procedia CIRP* (Vol. 29, pp. 514–519). Amsterdam, Netherlands: Elsevier.

Shrouf, F., & Miragliotta, G. (2015). Energy Management Based on Internet of Things: Practices and Framework for Adoption in Production Management. *Journal of Cleaner Production*, *100*, 235–246. doi:10.1016/j.jclepro.2015.03.055

Veile, J. V., Kiel, D., Müller, J. M., & Voigt, K.-I. (2019). (in press). Lessons learned from Industry 4.0 implementation in the German manufacturing industry. [available online.]. *Journal of Manufacturing Technology Management*, *ahead-of-print*(ahead-of-print). doi:10.1108/JMTM-08-2018-0270

Veile, J. W., Schmidt, M.-C., Müller, J. M., & Voigt, K.-I. (2019). *Buyer-supplier relationships in Industry 4.0 – A comparison across industries.* Paper presented at the European Operations Management Association (EurOMA) conference, Helsinki, Finland.

KEY TERMS AND DEFINITIONS

Circular Economy: Reduction of resource consumption, wastage, and energy consumption through more efficient end-to-end processes along the entire product lifecycle.

Cyber-Physical Systems: Allow a fusion of the real and virtual worlds through sensor, data transmission, and data evaluation technologies.

Industry 4.0: The term relates to a predicted fourth industrial revolution through horizontal and vertical interconnection in real-time based on digital technologies.

Internet of Things: Extending the internet through internet-ready products and production facilities ("things") with their own IP-addresses.

Small and Medium-Sized Enterprises: Within the European Union, enterprises with up to 250 employees and 50 million Euros of annual turnover.

Sustainability: Ensuring economic viability while achieving ecological and social welfare.

Triple Bottom Line: The combination of economic, ecological, and social aspects and their interdependency.

Chapter 2
How Industry 4.0 Changes the Value Co-Creation Process

Rebecca Castagnoli
University of Turin, Italy

Giacomo Büchi
University of Turin, Italy

Monica Cugno
https://orcid.org/0000-0001-8305-8248
University of Turin, Italy

ABSTRACT

The chapter analyses the literature on Industry 4.0 to understand the effect that Industry 4.0 has on customer co-creation process. The chapter is conceptual and is based on a literature analysis—conducted through ISI-Thompson Web of Science—that answers two research question: (RQ1) if and (RQ2) how the Industry 4.0 changes the customer value co-creation process. The results are summarized into a conceptual framework that shows how Industry 4.0 transforms the creation of value for customers, of customers, and with customers. The implications encourage managers and policymakers to implement a wider range of enabling technologies along the various phases of the supply chain and to adopt a new way to manage the company itself and the relations with customers involving them in the co-creation of products.

INTRODUCTION

The Fourth Industrial Revolution or Industry 4.0 (Kagerman, Helbig & Wahlster, 2013), has profoundly modified the factory by transforming it into a smart factory. The new scenario comes from the convergence of different emerging technologies that allow the transition to a digitalized era that introduces in the factories a smart environment in which machines, devices and products are interconnected to adapt, be flexible and respond quickly to market changes (Wei et al, 2017). Industry 4.0 has received increas-

DOI: 10.4018/978-1-7998-1419-1.ch002

ing attention from policy makers, managers and academics. Current researches are mainly focused on technological development (more than 50% of existing studies are of engineering), while are still limited studies on how the changes in technical and production developments transform the factory, the management, the relations with stakeholders and the way value is created. Management research explores the phenomenon almost exclusively through conceptual studies or case studies that verify the effects of Industry 4.0 on individual and isolated aspects of the value creation such as the customer relationship management (Dukić, Dugandžić & Dukić, 2017), the business model innovation (Müller et al., 2018) and the service dominant logic (Bullinger et al., 2017). Industry 4.0 modifies genetic heritage and strategic design of the factory creating new opportunities and threats that need to be managed. Early studies show that these changes have a significant impact on relationships with several stakeholders. For instance, Industry 4.0 introduces controversial changes in the relationships with internal stakeholders reducing low skill occupations and introducing new high skill occupations. However, since the 90-95% of the value of a company is made by customers (Gupta & Lehmann, 2006), the paper aims to fill the gap investigating the potential changes that Industry 4.0 brings to the customer value co-creation process.

The paper has two research questions:

Research Question One: Does the Industry 4.0 changes the customer value co-creation process?
Research Question Two: How does the Industry 4.0 changes the customer value co-creation process?

The paper is conceptual and is based on a literature analysis conducted through ISI-Thompson Web of Science database to identify two research objects: (1) to analyze opportunities and threats of the single enabling technologies; (2) to identify if and how the Industry 4.0 modifies the customer value co-creation process.

The research is based on a critical review because there are only few studies that analyze the topic and the most of them are based on specific case studies. In addition, the studies identified analyze how Industry 4.0 changes individual aspects of the value creation, of the business model innovation, or of the supply chain. However, there are no studies that analyze, with a holistic approach, the specific implications of the Industry 4.0 in the customer value co-creation process.

The contribution to scholarship of the paper is to create an abstracting description of the Industry 4.0 phenomenon (finding its definitions and its main characteristics and mapping its opportunities and threats) and to re-conceptualize the existing theory on customer value co-creation process in the light of the Industry 4.0.

The originality of the paper is that it has reconstruct a conceptual framework, with a holistic approach, on opportunities and threats that Industry 4.0 has on customer value co-creation process.

The paper is divided into five paragraphs. The second paragraph summarizes the theoretical background on Industry 4.0. The third paragraph responds to research object 1 by describing the opportunities and threats of Industry 4.0. The fourth responds to research object 2 by outlining the theoretical framework. The fifth paragraph reports discussions and conclusions enriched by practical implications, limits and future research developments.

THEORETICAL BACKGROUND ON INDUSTRY 4.0

Industry 4.0 is a controversial process by nature, definition, enabling technologies, opportunities and threats.

The expression the 'Fourth Industrial Revolution' took on the current name of Industry 4.0 after Germany's industrial plan (Industrie 4.0, Kagermann, Helbig & Wahlster, 2013). Actually, Industry 4.0 also has other names used in different countries, such as Industrial Internet or Advanced Manufacturing (US), Factories of the Future (European Commission), Future of Manufacturing (UK) or more used terms such as Digital Factory, Digital Manufacturing, Smart Factory, Interconnected Factory, Integrated Industry, Production 4.0, Internet Plus.

No conceptual or operative definition of Industry 4.0 has yet been identified so far that is universally accepted (Piccarozzi et al., 2018). This is because of: the many enabling technologies that it is made up of, in fact more than 1200 enabling technologies are estimated (Chiarello et al., 2018); the rapid obsolescence of its innovations; the variety of domains where it can be applied such as smart products and services (Schmidt et al., 2015; Porter & Heppelmann; 2014), smart objects (Atzori et al., 2014), smart machines and factories (Kagermann et al., 2013), smart manufacturing and industry (Davis et al., 2012), smart spaces (Leminen et al., 2012) or smart cities (Letaifa, 2015); the different disciplines that analyze the subject such as engineering, ICT, economics, management, etc.; the different points of view of the various stakeholders such as policy makers, managers, entrepreneurs and academics. However, it is possible to determine certain common elements such as automation systems, Internet, connections between the physical and virtual worlds, recognition of a set of enabling technologies, digitalization, changes in the relationships with stakeholders and in the governance and some common principles such as smartness, interoperability, virtualization, decentralization, real-time capability, service orientation and modularity (Hermann et al., 2015) and controlling complex systems (Müller, Kiel & Voigt, 2018; Liao et al., 2017).

In particular, the introduction of the internet of things realizes an environment 4.0 establishing global networks that incorporate machinery, warehousing systems and production facilities in the shape of Cyber-Physical Systems (CPS) and Cyber Physical Production System (CPPS). In the environment 4.0, the Cyber-Physical Systems are based on smart machines, storage systems and production facilities capable of autonomously exchanging information, triggering actions and controlling each other independently. This allows improvements of the industrial processes involved, optimizing value chain and supply chain (Kagermann, 2013).

A more embracing definition of the phenomenon Industry 4.0 is the adoption of industrial automation systems over the entire value chain and throughout the product's life cycle (Liao et al., 2017; Reischauer, 2018; Yin et al., 2017).

The two key factors for Industry 4.0's success are: integration and interoperability (Lu, 2017; Lasi et al., 2014; Wei et al., 2017).

Integrating industrial automation systems results in greater and more innovative features via networking with stakeholders (both horizontally and vertically). It also helps to create connections between the cyber and physical worlds.

CPS and CPPS are based on the creation of a virtual image of all physical non-human components involved in the production process, such as machinery, plant, products and devices. These physical components do not only exist as we perceive them with the five senses, but they also exist within a virtual image found in the world of information technology that represents all the possibilities and capabilities of the physical components as well as their current states. On the basis of the information provided by the virtual image, the single decentralized physical component is able to make decisions autonomously and to communicate them directly to nearby physical components (Lasi et al., 2014).

Interoperability in fact facilitates production processes, even without continuity, within and beyond the bounds of a business interconnecting systems and exchanging know-how and skills.

Industry 4.0 uses a series of enabling technologies which can be categorized into ten macro-categories: advanced manufacturing solution, augmented reality, internet of things, big data analytics, cloud computing, cyber-security, additive manufacturing, simulation, horizontal and vertical integration, other enabling technologies. The first nine categories come from a study by the Boston Consulting Group (Rußmann et al., 2015) and some Authors (Wan et al., 2015; Kinsy et al., 2011) add the last one 'Others enabling technologies' that include a series of no-less significant innovations, but with limited application domains: agri-food, bio-based economy, technologies supporting the optimization of energy consumption (Maksimchuk & Pershina, 2017; Birkel et al., 2019).

METHODOLOGY

The paper is conceptual and aims at answering two research questions.

Research Question One: Does Industry 4.0 change the customer value co-creation process?
Research Question Two: How does Industry 4.0 change the customer value co-creation process?

Starting from these RQs the study is divided into two main parts answering two research objectives.

Research Objective One: To analyze opportunities and threats of the single enabling technologies.
Research Objective Two: To identify which elements of the customer value co-creation process are modified by Industry 4.0.

The first part creates an abstracting description of the Industry 4.0 phenomenon (mapping its opportunities and threats). The second part re-read the existing theory on customer value co-creation process in the light of the Industry 4.0. Both the research parts are based on a critical review that aims to reconstruct a conceptual framework on the possible influence that Industry 4.0 has on the customer value co-creation process.

The research is based on a critical review because there are only few studies that analyze the topic and the most of them are based on specific case studies. In addition, the studies identified analyze how Industry 4.0 changes individual aspects of the value creation, of the business model innovation, or of the supply chain. However, there are no studies analyzing with a holistic approach the specific implications of the Industry 4.0 in the customer value co-creation process.

RESEARCH OBJECT 1: OPPORTUNITIES AND THREATS OF ENABLING TECHNOLOGIES

With lab tests results, managerial literature on Industry 4.0 shows how openness to enabling technologies in one or more phases of the value chain allows a business to obtain some opportunities. These opportunities can be classified into six main macro-typologies (Davies, 2015; Mejtoft, 2011): production flexibility (manufacturing small lots); speed of serial prototypes; greater output capacity; reduced set-up costs and fewer errors and machine stoppages; higher product quality and less production rejects; clients' better opinion of products. However, the current literature on Industry 4.0 does not report in a holistic way the opportunities and threats of the individual enabling technologies. The paper reconstructs them in Table 1 thanks to a precise examination of the literature on the individual enabling technologies.

RESEARCH OBJECT 2: TO IDENTIFY WHICH ELEMENTS OF THE CUSTOMER VALUE CO-CREATION PROCESS ARE MODIFIED BY INDUSTRY 4.0

Traditionally, the value of companies has always been created within the company itself with minimal customer interaction. However, the process has evolved as a result of three technological developments: first the Internet, then Web 2.0 and finally Industry 4.0. This is how co-creation develops, based on the collaboration between the actors (producers and consumers) facilitated by technology. The third phase of development of co-creation, Industry 4.0, adds a new dimension to the ordinary "anytime, anyplace connectivity for anyone", to include this type of connectivity for everything. (Mejtoft, 2011).

The customer value co-creation process approach sees the participation of customers in the value creation processes as receiving, generating and co-producing subjects of value. The three elements feed into each other creating a result that is superior to the sum of the parts. On the other hand, if left to chance or if improperly managed, they can cause conflicting effects that risk amplifying negative effects by creating an impoverishment of value more than proportional. The perspective is based on the observation that a loyal and collaborative customer base is one of the main forms of wealth of the company not only for the contribution it makes in terms of current cash flows but also for the potential and further increase in value that the stability of relations with customers can generate over time (Gupta & Lehmann, 2006).

Depending on the role played by the customer, it is possible to distinguish between three value configurations: value for customer; value of customer (or customer equity), co-creation of value with customer.

The plurality of opportunities and threats derived from the enabling technologies of Industry 4.0 and the smart environment in which people, objects, machines, products and plants are interconnected even without solutions of continuity impact on the customer value co-creation process and this requires the need to realize a conceptual framework.

Value for Customer

The value for customer is based on the company's ability to deliver a system of supply to which customers assign, at the level of perception, a value in use greater than or less than the expected value. A company that wishes to manage relations with its customers will have to make available to the customer a value proposal (value offer) that allows to create a satisfaction for the customer and that the offer over time can be able to create a degree of trust and loyalty.

Table 1. Macro-categories of enabling technologies: definition, opportunities, threats and authors

Macro-categories of enabling technologies	Definition	Opportunities	Threats	Authors
Advanced manufacturing solution	The term advanced manufacturing solution refers to the creation of interconnected and modular systems that guarantee automated industrial plans. These technologies include automatic material-moving systems and advanced robotics that are now on the market as cobots (collaborative robots) or automated guided vehicles and unmanned aerial vehicle.	-Reduction of set-up cost, errors and machine downtime, given by the capacity to learn the tasks from the operator; -Flexibility, given by direct participation of men in the most complex work and control phases and by the elimination of structural and technological constraints of automatic and fixed systems; - Higher production capacity, given by the possibility to modify the criteria for the attribution of work activities between operator and machine and to allow greater efficiency and effectiveness of work.	-problems linked to a reduction of low-skilled employees.	Durakbasa et al., 2013; Szalavetz, 2018
Augmented reality	The concept of augmented reality indicates a series of devices that enriches (or lessens) human sensory perception via access to virtual environments and accompanied by elements of sound, smell, touch, etc. These elements can be added to mobile devices (smartphones, tablets, pcs) or other sensors for vision (augmented-reality glasses) or sound (earphones) or touch (gloves) that provide multimedia information.	-Higher speed in prototyping, given by the possibility to design products and process with augmented-virtual reality; - Reduction of set-up cost, errors and machine downtime + Better product quality and less production waste, due to the possibility to receive information in real time and to provide virtual training and consequently improving work procedures and decision-making processes.	The literature analysis didn't found any threats related to this technology. However, the threats could be linked to the general problems of Industry 4.0 such as privacy implications etc.	Gorecky et al., 2014
Internet of things	The term internet of things (IoT) corresponds to a set of devices and intelligent sensors that facilitate communication between people, products and machines.	-Higher product evaluation by the customer, given by: the greater knowledge of customer needs and preferences with the aim of personalizing products; the inclusion of the customers in the production (co-creation of value); the greater guarantee regarding origin, use and destination of products, guaranteeing effective traceability of the product from the factory to the customer; -Reduction of set-up cost, errors and machine downtime + Better product quality and less production waste, due to the greater interconnection along the supply and distribution chain and due to the ability to reveal machinery wear, tear and breakdown in real time allowing for preventive/ predictive maintenance.	-greater risk of hacking; -privacy issues: need to protect the bigger exchange of data throughout the supply and distribution chains.	Gershenfeld & Euchner, 2015; Euchner, 2018; Rong et al., 2015; Lu, Papagiannidis & Alamanos, 2018
Big data analytics	The concept of big data analytics (BDA) is related to the technologies that capture, archive, analyze and disseminate large quantities of data that derive from products, processes, machines and people interconnected and the environment around a company.	-Higher product evaluation by the customer due to a faster communication and customized products and to the capacity to profile customers and relative needs; - Flexibility due to the possibility of demand estimation; - Better product quality and less production waste optimizing supply chain thanks to improved efficiency of the warehouse, distribution and sales and thanks to the contained production costs.	-privacy issues; -possible threats to democracy in the absence of transnational regulations; -lack of skills because big data present the need for companies to have the in-house skills to analyse the information.	Lee, 2015; McAffee & Brijolfsson, 2012a; McAffee & Brijolfsson, 2012b; Wamba et al., 2015; Yadegaridehkordi et al., 2018

continued on following page

Table 1. Continued

Macro-categories of enabling technologies	Definition	Opportunities	Threats	Authors
Cloud computing	Cloud computing technologies facilitate the archiving and processing of large quantities of data with high performance in terms of speed, flexibility and efficiency. Cloud computing also results in developing a greater number of services based on data for the productive system including monitoring and control functions in order to ensure quality and improve operative and productive excellence.	The opportunities and threats of these technologies can be added to those big data analytics and the internet of things technologies.	The opportunities and threats of these technologies can be added to those big data analytics and the internet of things technologies.	Mitra et al., 2018; Nieuwenhuis et al., 2018
Cyber-security	The concept of cyber-security includes security measures designed to protect the flow of information over interconnected corporate systems.	These technologies are designed to support others by limiting the threats linked to the ever increasing spread of information.	These technologies are designed to support others by limiting the threats linked to the ever increasing spread of information.	Tuptuk & Hailes, 2018
Additive manufacturing	Additive manufacturing is a process of additive production allowing for complex products through depositing layers of material including different types of material (plastic, ceramic, metals, resins, …) onto each other thus eliminating the need to assemble the material. A significant example is 3D printing.	-Higher speed in prototyping due to faster times in complex design and prototyping phases; -Reduction of set-up cost, errors and machine downtime + Better product quality and less production waste creating small customized production lots with possible advantages in terms of lower production costs and waste and eliminating the separation between manufacturing and assembly phases allows a significant reduction in lead time between order and delivery.	-possible inefficiencies due to the lack of economies of scale. Their use is generally limited to prototypes, high-value products or spare parts for products no longer available and for customised production.	Lasi et al., 2014; Weller et al., 2015; Janssen et al., 2014; Sasson & Johnson, 2016; Laplume et al., 2016; Borger et al., 2016; Baumers et al., 2016; Jiang, Kleer & Piller, 2017
Simulation	The term simulation means reproducing the physical world into virtual models and allowing operators to test and optimize the settings in order to obtain materials, productive processes (discrete elements) and products (finished or distinct elements).	-Higher speed in prototyping that increase production times; - Reduction of set-up cost, errors and machine downtime.	The literature analysis didn't found any threats related to this technology. However, the threats could be linked to the general problems of Industry 4.0 such as privacy implications etc.	Rodič, 2017
Horizontal e vertical integration	The integration offered by Industry 4.0 is characterized by two dimensions: one internal, the other external. The first, called horizontal integration, concerns the integration and exchange of information between the different areas of the company. The second, called vertical integration, concerns the relationships with suppliers and customers.	- Reduction of set-up cost, errors and machine downtime + Better product quality and less production waste due to: lower cost; ability to self-learn in order to identify, diagnose and solve problems; better connections in the in-coming and out-going supply chains; -Higher production capacity and increased productivity.	The literature analysis didn't found any threats related to this technology. However, the threats could be linked to the general problems of Industry 4.0 such as privacy implications etc.	Anderl et al., 2018; Lu, 2017
Other enabling technologies	Other enabling technologies are several technologies used for specific fields (see agrifood, bio-based economy, …) and tools determining where, when and how energy resources are used with the aim of eliminating or reducing waste.	- Better product quality and less production waste, to optimize productions and to decrease waste costs.	The literature analysis didn't found any threats related to this technology. However, the threats could be linked to the general problems of Industry 4.0 such as privacy implications etc.	Maksimchuk & Pershina, 2017

Source: own elaboration

Industry 4.0 impacts on the value of the offer in four areas.

1. Increased knowledge of the customer's needs: A set of technologies, among which big data and the Internet of Things play a predominant role, allow for better profilation of customers and of their needs.
2. Impact on product regards three areas.
   a Product development. Enabling technologies of Industry 4.0 (such as augmented reality) allow customers to actively participate in the prototyping and testing phase of products.
   b Product realization. Industry 4.0 allows the realization of production, even without spatial continuity, within and beyond the company's borders, thanks to the combination of three production scenarios (Büchi, Cugno & Castagnoli, 2018): the traditional mass production (scenario i) can be joined with mass customization (scenario ii) and mass personalization (scenario iii). Mass customization, is where products are made to satisfy the need of individual customers whose efficiency of production is near the mass (production) but with limited volumes (Fogliatto, da Silvera, & Borenstein, 2012; Tseng, Jiao & Wang, 2010). Mass personalization is where products and purchase experiences are created for individual customer tastes based on their preferences and in contained volumes (Tseng, Jiao & Wang, 2010; Chellappa & Sin, 2005). Mass customization and mass personalization help implement a varied product range – from many of a kind to one of a kind – which can then be adapted as demand changes over time, leading to further reductions of average unit costs.
   c Product differentiation. Enabling technologies of Industry 4.0 also increase the number and quality of pre and post sales services that are added to the core product through CPS-based platforms. These services provide greater benefits to the customer and a greater differentiation of its offer compared to that of competitors. This implementation of services is strictly linked to the service dominant logic in two ways. Firstly, the co-creation itself is considered as a service offered to the client in a broad sense. Secondly although product personalization and customization can concerne physical and technological features of a product, it is evident that in many cases the personalization can consist of one or more service linked to the product.

Value of Customer

The value of the customer or customer equity refers to the ability to define and monitor the economic value of the customer base during the life cycle of the relationship, through the configuration of specific measures.

The customer's life cycle in relation to the time and value created for the company generates a cost of customer acquisition for the company. Subsequently, the break even point is reached, after which the customer becomes profitable.

To increase profitability, it is necessary to reduce acquisition costs - acquisition strategy -; bring the break-even point of the customer's profitability closer; increase customer loyalty, generating more sales through up-selling, cross-selling and trading-up. These three objectives can be pursued individually or through a combination of these - loyalty strategy - to increase the company's profits.

The creation of customer value, however, should not be limited to considering only the historical and prospective value of the cash flows that each customer generates for the company. The evaluation of these should also highlight the intangible values that they are able to exercise, in terms of reputation and contributions to strengthening the image, the ability to generate input to innovation and learning (Niray et al., 2001).

Enabling technologies of Industry 4.0 enable the company to improve customer loyalty strategies through the use of big data, cloud computing and the Internet of things.

On the other hand, the same technologies also allow customers to obtain more information in real time on the offer of the various manufacturers on the market.

This means that the life cycle of the customer changes significantly, as customers can choose to change supplier at any time. Customer loyalty tends to be more variable with the risk for companies to lose their customer base more quickly.

Value with Customer

The creation of value with the customer is based on the ability of the company to build and manage a space around the customer's experiences, through interactions with the company. The customer becomes a co-creator and co-producer of the system of offering of the company of which he is a user (Prahalad et al. 2000, 2003 and 2004; Bendapudi et al., 2003).

In the context of Industry 4.0 the creation of value with the customer becomes more relevant because some technologies, such as additive manufacturing or augmented reality, allow the decentralization of production and the direct involvement of the consumer in the conception and design of the final product.

DISCUSSION AND CONCLUSION

In the conclusions, the results are summarized with particular attention to the comparison with the existing literature on the topic. As a preliminary observation, it must be underlined that the paper discusses as a main goal the relationships between Industry 4.0 and co-creation process analyzing if and how Industry 4.0 changes the value creation for customer, of customer and with customer.

Since this literature is still limited with reference to the purposes of the paper, it is also analyzed the general literature related to co-creation, servitization and business model innovation.

Answering to the RQ1 (Does the Industry 4.0 changes the customer value co-creation process?) it is possible to state that as the previous Industrial Revolutions, Industry 4.0 transforms workplaces and society implying social, environmental and economic changes (Kiel et al., 2017) and modifies the value creation for customer, of customer and with customer. The paper answers the RQ2 (How does the Industry 4.0 changes the customer value co-creation process?) in the following section to better understand how Industry 4.0 changes the value co-creation process (Figure 1).

As the previous Industrial Revolutions, Industry 4.0 aims to transform workplaces and society implying social, environmental and economic changes (Kiel et al., 2017).

The productive flexibility allows to improve the creation of value with the customer and for the customer. The increased amount of customer data owned by companies has two consequences: companies can reach new customers who are either or not satisfied with current solutions (Jhonson et al., 2008) or cannot access them (Yunus et al., 2010); companies can increase customer loyalty through more comprehensive value offer (Enkel & Mezger, 2013) or to reduce costs faced by customers (Mitchell & Coles, 2004).

Figure 1. Results: Changes of Industry 4.0 on value co-creation process
Source: own elaboration

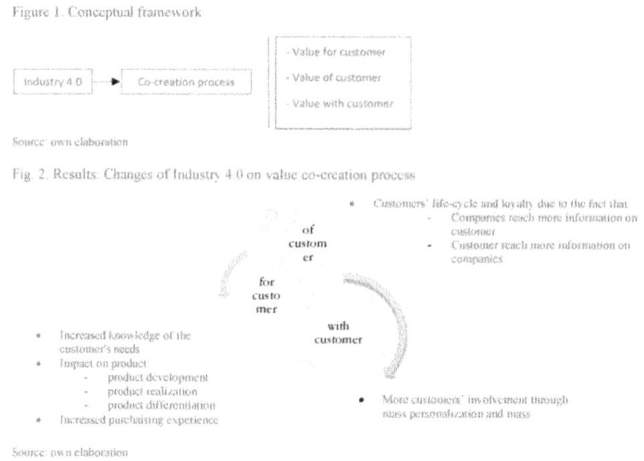

In addition, Industry 4.0 allows the supply of customized and personalized products at lower and lower prices in the long run, but these remain strongly influenced by the huge initial investments. For this reason, a strong increase in pre-sales and after-sales services is necessary to justify the price increase due to investments in new technologies (Schlechtendahl et al., 2015; Xu et al., 2014). Adding services to the original products allows companies to create value added or barriers to customer exit (Dukić, Dugandžić & Dukić, 2017; Rennung, 2016). The increasing servitization of production results in a further change in the value creation for the customer.

The need of additional services results that is no more enough to create value by identifying customer needs and producing state of the art products. Through a product customers access to a web-based services (Ferber, 2013) and are these services, and not only the product itself, that generate income (Carruthers, 2014).

As previously explained, the company modifies the customer value co-creation process through the availability of large amounts of information on customer preferences. On the other hand, customers change suppliers by obtaining real-time information on product characteristics and prices of competitors with lower information costs. This changes some prerequisites of the customer co-creation process with shorter customer's life cycle and less loyalty in the long run.

However, there are also some dark side of the Industry 4.0. These dark sides are mainly related to economic, social, legal/political, ecological, technical risks (Birkel et al., 2019) such as privacy concerns, initial costs and standardization. In addition, there is the network effect occurring when value depend on the number of other users. For Industry 4.0 a driving force but also one of the initial problems for the obstacles above. Finally, the information on customers and on their needs that Industry 4.0 provides must be managed and analyzed with the necessary skills in order to respond to the emerging needs by identifying ad hoc solutions.

Industry 4.0 promotes the emergence of new business models mainly related to digital platforms. These have the potential to cannibalize existing business models, making implementation difficult. At present, many companies are (still) focused on marketing their products. In the future, the focus will rather be on providing solutions and addressing customer problems. Therefore, companies face the risk that their business models will not be able to adapt quickly enough to these future requirements. At the same time, radical changes are necessary in order to implement new models, which inherently creates severe challenges for companies with a variety of potential issues. Since these developments are difficult to predict, there are particularly considerable risks for the existence of a company (Birkel et al., 2019).

The main contribution of the study is the integration of the theoretical framework of the customer co-creation process (Vargo & Lusch, 2008; Grönroos & Voima, 2013) in the context of the transformations of the Industry 4.0.

Despite the still limited application of Industry 4.0, the results obtained encourage managers and policy makers to implement a wider range of enabling technologies along the various phases of the supply chain and to adopt a new way to manage the company itself and the relations with customers involving them in the co-creation of products.

The limited number of studies currently available on the subject highlights the need for further investigation.

In addition, it is interesting to develop empirical research that verifies the validity of the theoretical framework on a sample of companies and customers.

REFERENCES

Anderl, R., Haag, S., Schützer, K., & Zancul, E. (2018). Digital twin technology – An approach for Industrie 4.0 vertical and horizontal lifecycle integration. *Información Tecnológica, 60*(3), 125–132.

Atzori, L., Iera, A., & Morabito, G. (2014). From "Smart Objects" to "Social Objects": The Next Evolutionary Step of the Internet of Things. *Communication Magazine, IEEE, 52*(1), 97–105. doi:10.1109/MCOM.2014.6710070

Baumers, M., Dickens, P., Tuck, C., & Hague, R. (2016). The cost of additive manufacturing: Machine productivity, economies of scale and technology-push. *Technological Forecasting and Social Change, 102*, 193–201. doi:10.1016/j.techfore.2015.02.015

Bendapudi, N., & Leone, R. P. (2003). Psycologic Implications of Customer Participation in Co-Production. *Journal of Marketing, 67*(1), 14–28. doi:10.1509/jmkg.67.1.14.18592

Birkel, H. S., Veile, J. W., Muller, J. M., Hartmann, E., & Voigt, K. I. (2019). Development of a Risk Framework for Industry 4.0 in the context of sustainability for established manufacturers. *Sustainability, 11*(2), 384. doi:10.3390u11020384

Bogers, M., Hadar, R., & Bilberg, A. (2016). Additive manufacturing for consumer-centric business models: Implications for supply chains in consumer goods manufacturing. *Technological Forecasting and Social Change, 102*, 225–239. doi:10.1016/j.techfore.2015.07.024

Büchi, Cugno, & Castagnoli. (2018). Economies of Scale and Network Economies in Industry 4.0. *Symphonya, 2*, 1–11.

Bullinger, H.-J., Neuhüttler, J., Nägele, R., & Woyke, I. (2017). Collaborative Development of Business Models in Smart Service Ecosystems. PICMET 2017: Technology Management for Interconnected Word, 1-9.

Carruthers, K. (2014). How the Internet of Things Changes Everything: the Next Stage of the Digital Revolution. *Australian Journal of Telecommunications and the Digital Economy, 2*(4), 69.1-69.13.

Chellappa, R. K., & Sin, R. G. (2005). Personalization versus privacy: An empirical examination of the online consumer's dilemma. *Information Technology Management, 6*(2-3), 181–202. doi:10.100710799-005-5879-y

Chiarello, F., Trivelli, L., Bonaccorsi, A., & Fantoni, G. (2018). Extracting and mapping industry 4.0 technologies using Wikipedia. *Computers in Industry, 100*, 244–257. doi:10.1016/j.compind.2018.04.006

Davies, R. (2015). *2015, Industry 4.0 Digitalisation for productivity and growth, EPRS, European Parliamentary*. Research Service.

Davis, J., Edgar, T., Porter, J., Bernaden, J., & Sarli, M. (2012). Smart manufacturing, manufacturing intelligence and demand-dynamic performance. *Computers & Chemical Engineering, 47*, 145–156. doi:10.1016/j.compchemeng.2012.06.037

Dukić, B., Dugandžić, S., & Dukić, S. (2017). Conceptual CRM Application database Model in the Function of Physical products distribution for Known Customer. *17th International Scientific Conference Business Logistics in Modern Management*, 369-383.

Durakbasa, N. M., Bas, G., & Krauter, L. G. (2013). The Assessment of Industrial Manufacturing Systems Towards Advanced Operations by Means of Integrated Modeling Approach. *Vision 2020: Innovation, Development Sustainability, and Economic Growth, 21st International-Business-Information-Management-Association Conference on Vision 2020: Innovation, Development Sustainability, and Economic Growth*, 1418-1426.

Enkel, E., & Mezger, F. (2013). Imitation Processes and their Application for Business Model Innovation: An Explorative Study. *International Journal of Innovation Management, 17*(1), 1340005. doi:10.1142/S1363919613400057

Euchner, J. (2018). The Internet of Things. *Research Technology Management, 61*(5), 10–11. doi:10.1080/08956308.2018.1495971

Ferber, S. (2013). *How the Internet of Things Changes Everything*. HBR Blog Network.

Fogliatto, F. S., da Silvera, G. J., & Borestein, D. (2012). The mass customization decade: An updated review of the literature. *International Journal of Production Economics, 138*(1), 14–25. doi:10.1016/j.ijpe.2012.03.002

Gerbert, P., Lorenz, M., Rüßmann, M., Waldner, M., Justus, J., Engel, P., & Harnisch, M. (2015). *Industry 4.0: The future of Productivity and growth in Manufacturing Industries*. BCG Perspectives.

Gershenfeld, N. G., & Euchner, J. (2015). Atoms and bits: Rethinking manufacturing. Conversations. *Research Technology Management, 58*(5), 16–21. doi:10.5437/08956308X5805003

Gorecky, D., Schmitt, M., Loskyll, M., & Zühlke, D. (2014). Human-machine-interaction in the industry 4.0 era. *2014 12th IEEE International Conference on Industrial Informatics (INDIN).*

Grönroos, C., & Voima, P. (2013). Critical Service Logic: Making Sense of Value Creation and Co-creation. *Journal of the Academy of Management Science, 41*(2), 133–150. doi:10.100711747-012-0308-3

Gupta, S., & Lehmann, D. R. (2006). *Customers as Assets*. Milano: Pearson.

Hermann, M., Pentek, T., & Otto, B. (2015). *Design Principles for Industrie 4.0 Scenarios: A Literature Review*. Dortmund: Technische UniversitäT Dortmund.

Janssen, Blankers, Moolenburgh, & Posthumus. (2014). *The Impact of 3-D Printing on Supply-Chain Management*. TNO Transport and Mobility.

Jhonson, M. W., Christensen, C. M., & Kagermann, H. (2008). Reinventing your Business Model. *Harvard Business Review, 86*(12), 51–59.

Jiang, R., Kleer, R., & Piller, F. T. (2017). Predicting the future of additive manufacturing: A Delphi study on economic and societal implications of 3D printing for 2030. *Technological Forecasting and Social Change, 117*, 84–97. doi:10.1016/j.techfore.2017.01.006

Kagermann, W. W. H., Helbig, J., & Wahlster, W. (2013). Recommendations for implementing the strategic initiative Industrie 4.0. Final report of the Industrie 4.0 working group.

Kiel, Müller, Arnold, & Voigt. (2017). Sustainable Industrial Value Creation: Benefits And Challenges Of Industry 4.0. *International Journal of Innovation Management, 21*(8).

Kinsy, M., Khan, O., Ivan, C., Majstorovic, D., Celanovic, N., & Devadas, S. (2011). Time-predictable computer architecture for cyber-physical systems: digital emulation of power electronics systems. *Proceedings of 2011 IEEE 32nd Real-Time Systems Symposium (RTSS)*, 305-316. 10.1109/RTSS.2011.35

Laplume, A. O., Petersen, B., & Pearce, J. M. (2016). Global value chains from a 3D printing perspective. *Journal of International Business Studies, 47*(5), 595–609. doi:10.1057/jibs.2015.47

Lasi, H., Fettke, P., Kemper, H. G., Feld, T., & Hoffmann, M. (2014). Industry 4.0. *Business & Information Systems Engineering, 6*(4), 239–242. doi:10.100712599-014-0334-4

Lee, J., Bagheri, B., & Kao, H. A. (2015). A Cyber-Physical Systems architecture for Industry 4.0-based manufacturing systems. *Manufacturing Letters, 3*, 18–23. doi:10.1016/j.mfglet.2014.12.001

Leminen, S., Westerlund, M., Rajahonka, M., & Siuruanien, R. (2012). Towards IOT Ecosystems and Business Models. In S. Andreev, S. Balandin, & Y. Koucheryavy (Eds.), *Internet of Things, Smart Spaces, and Next Generation Networking* (pp. 15–26). Berlin: Springer. doi:10.1007/978-3-642-32686-8_2

Letaifa, S. B. (2015). How to Strategise Smart Cities: Revealing the SMART model. *Journal of Business Research, 68*(7), 1414–1419. doi:10.1016/j.jbusres.2015.01.024

Liao, Y., Deschamps, F., Loures, E. D. F. R., & Ramos, L. F. P. (2017). Past, present and future of Industry 4.0-a systematic literature review and research agenda proposal. *International Journal of Production Research, 55*(12), 3609–3629. doi:10.1080/00207543.2017.1308576

Lu, Y. (2017). Industry 4.0: A survey on technologies, applications and open research issues. *Journal of Industrial Information Integration, 6*, 1–10. doi:10.1016/j.jii.2017.04.005

Lu, Y., Papagiannidis, S., & Alamanos, E. (2018). Internet of Things: A systematic review of the business literature from the user and organisational perspectives. *Technological Forecasting and Social Change, 136*, 285–297. doi:10.1016/j.techfore.2018.01.022

Maksimchuk, O., & Pershina, T. (2017). A new paradigm of industrial system optimization based on the conception "Industry 4.0". *MATEC Web of Conferences*, 1-5.

McAfee, A., & Brynjolfsson, E. (2012a). Big data: The management revolution. *Harvard Business Review, 90*(10), 61–67.

McAffee, A., & Brynjolfsson, E. (2012b). Big Data: The Management Revolution Exploiting vast new flows of information can radically improve your company's performance. But first you'll have to change your decision-making culture. *Harvard Business Review*, 3–9.

Mejtoft, T. (2011). Internet of Things and Co-Creation of Value. *2011 International Conference on Internet of things & 4th International Conference on Cyber, Physical and Social Computing*, 672-677.

Mitchell, D. W., & Coles, C. B. (2004). Business Model Innovation breakthrough moves. *The Journal of Business Strategy, 25*(1), 16–26. doi:10.1108/02756660410515976

Mitra, A., O'Regan, N., & Sarpong, D. (2018). Cloud resource adaptation: A resource based perspective on value creation for corporate growth. *Technological Forecasting and Social Change, 130*, 28–38. doi:10.1016/j.techfore.2017.08.012

Müller, J. M., Buliga, O., & Voigt, K. (2018). How SMEs approach business model innovations in Industry 4.0. *Technological Forecasting and Social Change, 132*, 2–17. doi:10.1016/j.techfore.2017.12.019

Müller, J. M., Kiel, D., & Voigt, K. I. (2018). What Drives the Implementation of Industry 4.0? The Role of Opportunities and Challenges in the Context of Sustainability. *Sustainability, 10*(1), 247. doi:10.3390u10010247

Nieuwenhuis, L. J. M., Ehrenhard, M. L., & Prause, L. (2018). The shift to Cloud Computing: The impact of disruptive technology on the enterprise software business ecosystem. *Technological Forecasting and Social Change, 129*, 308–313. doi:10.1016/j.techfore.2017.09.037

Niray, R., Gupta, M., & Narasimhan, C. (2001). Customer profitability in a Supply Chain. *Journal of Marketing, 65*(3), 1–16. doi:10.1509/jmkg.65.3.1.18332

Piccarozzi, M., Aquilani, B., & Gatti, C. (2018). Industry 4.0 in management studies: A systematic literature review. *Sustainability, 10*(10), 3821. doi:10.3390u10103821

Porter, M. E., & Heppelmann, J. E. (2014). How smart, connected products are transforming competition. *Harvard Business Review, 92*(11), 64–88.

Prahalad, C. K., & Ramaswamy, V. (2000). Co-Opting Customer Competence. *Harvard Business Review*, 79–87.

Prahalad, C. K., & Ramaswamy, V.The Experience Economy. (2004). *Work is Theatre & Every Business a Stage*. Boston: Harvard Business School Press.

Prahalad & Ramaswamy. (2003). Experience Innovation. *MIT Sloan Business Review, 44*(4), 12-18.

Reischauer, G. (2018). Industry 4.0 as policy-driven discourse to institutionalize innovation systems in manufacturing. *Technological Forecasting and Social Change, 132*, 26–33. doi:10.1016/j.techfore.2018.02.012

Rennung, F., Luminosu, C. T., & Draghici, A. (2016). Service Provision in the framework of Industry 4.0. *Procedia: Social and Behavioral Sciences, 221*, 372–377. doi:10.1016/j.sbspro.2016.05.127

Rodič, B. (2017). Industry 4.0 and the New Simulation Modelling Paradigm. *Organizacija, 50*(3), 193–207. doi:10.1515/orga-2017-0017

Rong, K., Hu, G., Lin, Y., Shi, Y., & Guo, L. (2015). Understanding business ecosystem using a 6C framework in Internet-of-Things-based sectors. *International Journal of Production Economics, 159*, 41–55. doi:10.1016/j.ijpe.2014.09.003

Sasson, A., & Johnson, J. C. (2016). The 3D printing order: Variability, supercenters and supply chain configurations. *International Journal of Physical Distribution & Logistics Management, 46*(1), 82–94. doi:10.1108/IJPDLM-10-2015-0257

Schlechtendahl, J., Keinert, M., Kretschmer, F., Lechler, A., & Verl, A. (2015). Making Existing Production Systems Indutry 4.0-ready, production. *Engineering, 9*(1), 143–148.

Schmidt, R., Möhring, M., Härting, R. C., Reichstein, C., Neumaier, P., & Jozinović, P. (2015). Industry 4.0 - Potentials for Creating Smart Products: Empirical Research Results. In W. Abramowicz (Ed.), *Business Information Systems, 18th International Conference, BIS*. Poznan, Poland: Springer International Publishing.

Szalavetz. (2018). Industry 4.0 and capability development in manufacturing subsidiaries. *Technological Forecasting and Social Change.*

Tseng, Jiao, & Wang. (2010). Design for mass personalization. *CIRP Annals Manufacturing Technology, 59*(1), 175-178.

Tuptuk, N., & Hailes, S. (2018). Security of smart manufacturing systems. *Journal of Manufacturing Systems, 47*, 93–106. doi:10.1016/j.jmsy.2018.04.007

Vargo, S. L., & Lush, R. F. (2008). Service-dominant logic: Continuing the evolution. *Journal of the Academy of Marketing Science, 36*(1), 1–10. doi:10.100711747-007-0069-6

Wamba, S. F., Akter, S., Edwards, A., Chopin, G., & Gnanzou, D. (2015). How 'big data' can make big impact: Findings from a systematic review and a longitudinal case study. *International Journal of Production Economics, 165*, 234–246. doi:10.1016/j.ijpe.2014.12.031

Wan, J., Cai, H., & Zhou, K. (2015). Industrie 4.0: Enabling Technologies. *International Conference on Intelligent Computing and Internet of Things (ICIST)*, 135-140.

Wei, Z., Song, W., & Wang, D. (2017). Manufacturing flexibility, business model design, and firm performance. *International Journal of Production Economics, 193*, 87–97. doi:10.1016/j.ijpe.2017.07.004

Weller, C., Kleer, R., & Piller, F. T. (2015). Economic implications of 3D printing: Market structure models in light of additive manufacturing revisited. *International Journal of Production Economics, 164*, 43–56. doi:10.1016/j.ijpe.2015.02.020

Woodall. (2003). Conceptualizing Value for the Customer. An Attributional Structural and Dispositional Analysis. *Academy of Marketing Science Review, 12*, 1-44.

Xu, L. D., He, W., & Li, S. (2014). Internet of Things in industries: A survey. *IEEE Transactions on Industrial Informatics, 10*(4), 2233–2243. doi:10.1109/TII.2014.2300753

Yin, Y., Stecke, K. E., & Li, D. (2017). The evolution of production systems from Industry 2.0 through Industry 4.0. *International Journal of Production Research, 7543*, 1–14.

Yunus, M., Moingeon, B., & Lehmann-Ortega, L. (2010). Building Social Business Models: Lessons from the Grameen Experience. *Long Range Planning, 43*(2), 308–325. doi:10.1016/j.lrp.2009.12.005

Chapter 3
Achieving Environmental Sustainability Through Industry 4.0 Tools:
The Case of the "Symbiosis" Digital Platform

Barbara Aquilani
University of Tuscia, Italy

Michela Piccarozzi
https://orcid.org/0000-0001-9717-9462
University of Tuscia, Italy

Cecilia Silvestri
https://orcid.org/0000-0003-2528-601X
University of Tuscia, Italy

Corrado Gatti
Sapienza University of Rome, Italy

ABSTRACT

Almost all firms are involved in challenges linked to Industry 4.0 that represent a new logic for business models focused on innovation, technology, and sustainability. In this domain, the support and integration of digital innovations is assuming ever greater importance and a key role is played by the so-called "industrial symbiosis." Looking more in depth at industrial symbiosis literature, which practically developed within the engineering domain, it is clear that most of its particular traits can also be found in management literature when referring to value co-creation, especially in the business to business domain. Given the above, the aim of this work is twofold: to analyze the role of Industry 4.0 digital platforms as a tool for the development of environmental sustainability and to understand how Industry 4.0 as a whole can support the achievement of environmental sustainability goals. The only Italian case will be used to validate the proposed theoretical framework.

DOI: 10.4018/978-1-7998-1419-1.ch003

INTRODUCTION

The Fourth Industrial Revolution – i.e., Industry 4.0-, today involves the majority of firms and institutions and emerges as a new logic for business models focused on innovation, technology and sustainability (Pan et al., 2015; Burritt, 2016; Piccarozzi et al., 2018). In this domain, integration of digital innovations in industrial production is assuming ever greater importance and a very important role is played by the so-called "industrial symbiosis" (IS). IS, a term introduced in 1992 by Robert Ayres (i.e., Ayres 1989, 1994) and then adopted by other scholars (i.e., Hawken, 1993; Chertow, 2000), involves "traditionally separate industries adopting an integrated approach aimed at generating competitive advantages through the exchange of materials, energy, water and/or by-products" (Chertow, 2000, pp. 314).

Looking more in depth at the literature on IS, which practically belongs to the engineering domain, it is clear that most of its particular traits can be found in management literature when referring to value co-creation, especially in business to business (B2B) environments. Indeed, "*the co-creation view starts with interactions as the locus of value and platforms of engagements with individuals are the locus of value creation, and co-creative enterprises follow a single principle: they focus their entire organization on the engagements with individuals*" (Leavy, 2014, p. 11). In this context, digital platforms can be understood as engagement platforms (i.e., Ramaswamy & Ozcan, 2014), therefore tools which can provide valuable support for both the development of value co-creation processes among firms and IS (please see section Background). Indeed, through digital platforms it is possible to coordinate, manage, promote and create synergies between firms (de Reuver et al., 2018) which are essential for realizing both value co-creation processes and IS. Defined as above, digital platforms can be framed in the so-called external (industrial) platforms which can be understood as "manegeable objects" that organizations purposely manage to bring multiple parties within the industry together" (Gawer & Cusumano, 2014, p. 8). Inside these digital platforms firms collaborate generating various network effects and, as consequence, building an ecosystem able to support various firm activities, especially innovative ones, on behalf participants in the platform ecosystem (Gawer & Cusumano, 2014).

Moreover, these same platforms can be a valuable tool for orienting firms further towards sustainability (i.e., Garg & Buyya, 2012), in particular environmental sustainability, without neglecting the economic perspective (saving costs of management services, infrastructures and natural resources, increasing productivity, reducing firm dependence on non-renewable resources; Brousseau & Penard, 2007).

However, online platforms can also be understood as tools pertaining to Industry 4.0 in that they are the *locus* of interactions needed to implement the smart factory, for example (i.e. Erro-Garcés, 2019) or to collect, store and manage data (i.e. Klingenberg et al., 2019), etc. In this domain it can be easily said that Industry 4.0 technologies can contribute significantly to solve demographic, climate and productive resource changes, all issues which today are among the priorities in the environmental sustainability domain (Pan, 2015; Prause, 2015, 2017; Frolov, 2017; de Sousa Jabbour, 2018). Indeed, from the connection between objects, systems, people and value co-creation processes, online platforms enable and support useful information exchange in real time leading to both optimizing the use of resources and supporting the development of new strategies and actions towards environmental sustainability, where information and data are of paramount importance (i.e. Klingenberg et al., 2019).

Given the above, the aim of this work is twofold: to analyze the role of Industry 4.0 digital platforms as a tool for the development of environmental sustainability and to understand how Industry 4.0 as a whole can support the achievement of firm environmental sustainability goals. The role of industrial platforms, in this domain, has been completely neglected by literature, while some more studies are needed to understand the link between Industry 4.0 and sustainability as also recently claimed by Erro-Garés (2019).

The study will be based on a qualitative approach with the analysis of the only Italian case, the digital "Symbiosis" platform created by the Italian ENEA (National Agency for New Technologies, Energy and Sustainable Economic Development) that will give a first validation of what has emerged from the literature.

From a theoretical point of view this chapter will contribute to deepen the theme of Industry 4.0, still new but growing, and will also examine the unexplored role of digital platforms for environmentally sustainable firm goals, also helping in enhancing our understanding of industrial platforms following the invitation for "cross-fertilize several disciplines" thanks to their study (Gawer & Cusumano, 2014, p. 25). Indeed, this study will help in bridging the concepts of IS and value co-creation, whose foundations can be found in two different streams of literature, into the broad domain of Industry 4.0. From a managerial point of view, this work will support firms in better understanding the contribution of technology and Industry 4.0 features and tools - especially digital platforms - in the ongoing challenge to environmental sustainability.

Basing its original traits on these contributions the chapter starts with a literature review on the relevant ties to build the proposed framework: Industry 4.0 and IS contributing to environmental sustainability and IS as a value co-creation process developing in digital platforms. It then presents the proposed framework followed by the case study and its discussion. Limitations and future avenues of research will be presented, followed by the conclusion which highlights the main contributions of the chapter.

BACKGROUND

Industry 4.0 and IS: An Underexplored Link Towards Environmental Sustainability

Industry 4.0 is based on the development of a completely automated and intelligent production, capable of communicating autonomously with the main corporate players (Piccarozzi et al., 2018). The term was coined in Germany and was first used in 2011 to identify the new proposal for the German economic policy to come; it was based on high-tech strategies (Mosconi, 2015).

Industry 4.0 focused on horizontal and vertical integration of production systems driven by real-time data interchange and flexible manufacturing to enable customized production (Li et al., 2017; Thoben et al, 2017). These innovations will lead to full automation and digitalization processes, and the use of electronics and information technologies (IT) in manufacturing and services in a private environment (Sommer et al., 2015).

The topic is quite new, but in the last four years' theoretical studies have multiplied considering various management issues (i.e., Production Method, Business Model, Strategy, Impacts and Consequences of Industry 4.0, Human Resources in SMEs - Small Medium Enterprise-, Supply Chain, Sustainability, Information System and Social Innovation) (Piccarozzi et al., 2018).

However, a shared definition of Industry 4.0 does not yet exist; the need for a shared language represents the first point of the research agenda in the Industry 4.0 domain (Erro-Garcés, 2019).

In this respect, in fact, the existence of similar terms such as the "Internet of Things", "Industrial Internet", or related issues called "Smart Factory" or "Human-Machine-Cooperation" have not facilitated finding a common understanding of what really constitutes Industry 4.0 (Wang, 2016).

The McKinsey Global Institute, for example, identifies the Fourth Industrial Revolution as the age of "cyber–physical systems"—systems that integrate at least computation, networking and physical processes, including a myriad of technologies that span mobile devices, the Internet of Things (IoT), artificial intelligence (AI), robotics, cyber security and 3D printing (Buguin et al., 2013).

Through a systematic review of the literature a recent paper combined the peculiarities of various definitions that have already emerged in literature embracing a management perspective and defined Industry 4.0 as "*the integration of Internet of Things technologies into industrial value creation enabling manufacturers to harness entirely digitized, connected, smart, and decentralized value chains" (Prause, p. 423) able to "deliver greater flexibility and robustness to firm competitiveness and enable them to build flexible and adaptable business structures, [acquiring] the permanent ability for internal evolutionary developments in order to cope with a changing business environment" (Koether, p. 583), as the result of a purposely formulated strategy implemented over time*"(Piccarozzi et al., 2018, p. 16).

Indeed, Industry 4.0 and its innovations have led to a profound digitalization of operating methods in everyday life and above all in firms, radically modifying their business models; this development provides great opportunities to achieve sustainable manufacturing (Stock et al., 2016). In particular, the emergence of Industry 4.0 has profoundly changed, and will continue to do so, the world economy affecting various variables like "*investment, consumption, growth, employment, trade and so on*" (Piccarozzi et al., 2018, p. 2).

Therefore, it's not surprising that Industry 4.0 has strong ties with many other literature streams like IS, through for example Big Data (Tseng et al., 2018).

IS "*engages traditionally separate industries in a collective approach to competitive advantage involving physical exchange of materials, energy, water, and/or by-products. The keys to industrial symbiosis are collaboration and the synergistic possibilities offered by geographic proximity*" (Chertow, 2000, p. 314).

In fact, IS describes the "*mutualistic interaction of different industries for beneficial reuse of waste flows or energy cascading that results in a more resource-efficient production system and fewer adverse environmental impacts*" (Grant et al., 2010, p. 750).

IS provides various advantages, both from a cost saving point of view and in terms of the reuse of materials and resources, contributing to respect of the environment while enabling operations towards its conservation (Goodland et al., 1996; Leigh, 2005; Mirata et al., 2005; Chertow, 2007).

IS falls in the new field of interdisciplinary studies dedicated to industrial ecology (Chertow, 2004) to be understood as a science of sustainability (Allenby et al., 1999; Ehrenfeld, 2004; Gibbs, 2008).

IS is mainly realized by firms following three different methods (Chertow et al., 2008):

- The use of materials traditionally understood as waste or by-products to replace commercial products or raw materials;
- The sharing of utilities and infrastructures for the use and management of resources, such as steam, energy, water and wastewater;
- The joint supply of services to meet accessory needs common to businesses related to safety, hygiene, transport and waste management.

From the aforementioned issues it clearly emerges that the link between Industry 4.0 and IS is really tight and twofold even if this topic is still understudied in literature, above all in the management domain.

On the one hand Industry 4.0 shares attention to sustainability issues with IS, especially environmental ones concerning the reuse of materials, pollution, water saving, etc.

Today sustainability is a central topic in social science studies as a whole (Piccarozzi, 2017). In particular, the major turning point was made with the Brundtland Report, which introduced the concept of sustainable development as a "*development that meets the needs of the present without compromising the ability of future generations to meet their own needs*" (WCED, p. 41).

Since the Brundtland Report, the concept of sustainability has evolved dramatically and three essential and interrelated dimensions of it have emerged: social, economic, and environmental (Piccarozzi, 2017). These three dimensions have been defined as the pillars of sustainability which show that responsible development requires the simultaneous consideration of natural, human, and economic capital or, in other words, a direct exchange between planet, people and profits (Elkington et al., 1997; Kajikawa, 2008; Schoolman et al., 2012).

In this domain, environmental sustainability can be defined as "*a condition of balance, resilience, and interconnectedness that allows human society to satisfy its needs while neither exceeding the capacity of its supporting ecosystems to continue to regenerate the services necessary to meet those needs nor by our actions diminishing biological diversity*" (Mehta, 2019, p. 156).

Over the years, environmental sustainability has assumed a fundamental role in terms of sustainable development. The pinpoint is on a more rational and conscious use of resources (The Natural Step, 2018) for example:

- To reduce the extraction of natural substances;
- To reduce the production of chemical substances and compounds (plastic, dioxins, etc.);
- To reduce the physical degradation of nature and natural processes;
- To reduce the barriers to meet human needs.

In this domain, it is quite clear that innovations of Industry 4.0 could provide an important step forward in IS processes and, in this way, could allow better achievement of environmental sustainability goals.

Indeed, Ferrera et al. (2017), for example, affirm that in order to achieve levels of environmental sustainability, firms must exploit technological innovations (such as IoT and Big Data, both tools of Industry 4.0) also in the services needed in order to achieve IS processes.

Stock (2016), on the other hand, states that "*the cross-linking of value creation networks in Industry 4.0 offers new opportunities for realizing closed-loop product life cycles and industrial symbiosis. It allows the efficient coordination of the product, material, energy, and water flows throughout the product life cycles as well as between different factories*" (Stock et al., 2016, p. 540).

From the above it is clear that both Industry 4.0 and IS are based on the respect and achievement of environmental sustainability and can contribute to achieve its goals.

On the other hand, Industry 4.0 can offer its tools to IS processes and among them especially digital platforms, also because Big Data is generated and available from them, where data can also be extracted and elaborated.

Indeed, Industry 4.0 with its innovations and tools can enable and promote IS processes.

In particular, it can be said that (Piccarozzi et al., forthcoming): (a) Industry 4.0 tools, such as mathematical and computer models, can support decision-making processes enabling and enhancing IS paths

Figure 1. Enhancing environmental sustainability through Industry 4.0 and its tools: a conceptual framework
Source: (authors' elaboration)

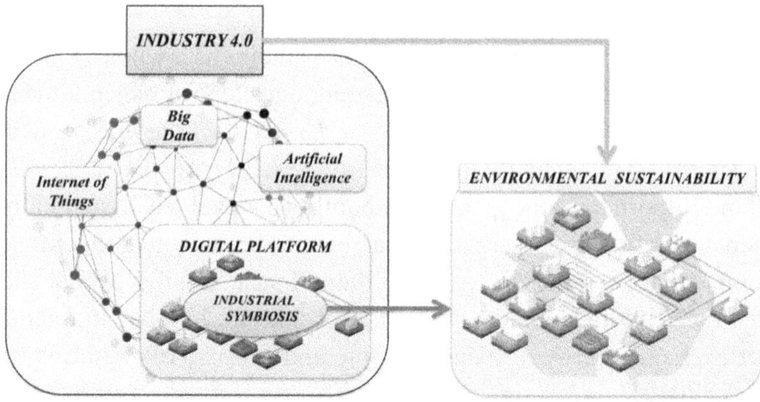

(Ferrera, 2017); (b) Big Data and analyses of them could help in optimizing the use of scarce resources (Tseng, 2018); (c) Industry 4.0 technologies can help in assessing models and metrics for resource usage optimization to be used in IS (Chalkias, 2019).

Figure 1 shows both the aforementioned links, even if further details are necessary to understand the role of digital platforms to carry out IS processes and why the latter can be considered a value co-creation process; the following section is dedicated to these issues.

Digital Platforms as Milieu in Which IS Develops; A Type of Value Co-Creation Process

Most of the particular traits of IS can be found in management literature when referring to value co-creation processes developed in B2B environments, the same domain in which IS emerges.

Value co-creation can be defined as a "*view start[ing] with interactions as the locus of value*" being "*platforms of engagements with individuals [...] the locus of value creation, and co-creative enterprises follow[ing] a single principle: they focus their entire organization on the engagements with individuals*" (Leavy, 2014, p. 11). In this context interactions are the *locus* of value (Leavy, 2014, p. 11) and each individual co-creates value related to all other individuals collaborating in co-creation processes (Ind et al., 2013).

Even if the value co-creation approach embraces an individual perspective (i.e. Ramaswamy, 2011), it is important to point out that in its domain value can no longer be identified exclusively with profit to be captured by firms, it must be understood as a set of different values able to be appropriated by all individuals participating in value co-creation pertaining to firms (Denning, 2014).

These values which can be interpreted as a value able to change in form during co-creation processes is made by intrinsic and extrinsic benefits (Antikainen et al., 2010) that individuals capture for themselves in light of their participation in co-creation. Partners should therefore participate in firm innovation processes, not only concerning product and/or services, but also collaborating on organizational changes or even setting new firm goals and/or strategies if desired and/or required (Ramaswamy & Ozcan, 2014).

Indeed, value co-creation doesn't only concern innovation in products and/or processes, but goes beyond to the strategic firm goals which can be shared with partners (Ramaswamy & Ozcan, 2014) of the same industry or outside it. This implies that through co-creation processes individuals pertaining to different firms, but also industries, are able to collaborate enabling IS.

However, value co-creation processes need engagement platforms to develop (i.e. Ramaswamy & Ozcan, 2014); the latter can be divided in offline, such as call centers (i.e. Leavy, 2013; Ramaswamy & Ozcan, 2014), temporary shops (Russo Spena et al., 2012), etc. and online. Among online engagement platforms digital ones (Aquilani et al., 2013, 2014, 2016) can be considered tools that can provide support for the development of value co-creation processes among firms. Indeed, through digital platforms "it is possible to coordinate, manage, promote and create synergies between firms" (Piccarozzi et al., 2019, forthcoming). Digital platforms can be defined as purely technical elements where the platform is an extensible codebase, and the ecosystem comprises third-party modules complementing this codebase (Tiwana et al., 2010; Boudreau, 2012; de Reuver, 2018); in this case digital platforms can easily be encompassed in Industry 4.0 tools.

However, digital platforms can also be characterized as a socio-technical assemblage encompassing technical elements (hardware and software) and associated organizational processes and standards (Tilson et al., 2012). Following this different definition, apart from the technical elements which virtually refer back to Industry 4.0 features, it is easy to encompass engagement platforms in which co-creation processes develop. Indeed, processes and standards can be understood as the rules to co-create value through interactions – the social side of the platform - which are, *per se*, co-created by the participants of the platform (Ramaswamy & Ozcan, 2014). From another standpoint, engagement platforms can also be understood as external (industrial) platforms (Gawer & Cusumano, 2014) in which interactions among both internal and external partners happen on behalf of all participants.

In this *milieu* IS processes can develop. Indeed, digital platforms allow information exchanges like those relevant to developing the economic viability of participating in IS; one of the main threats in implementing IS (Raabe, 2017). Moreover, digital platforms such as globally accessible engagement platforms allow both value co-creation processes and IS at a world level, making possible, especially for the latter, the expansion of symbiotic exchanges beyond the industrial district boundaries and, in this way, contributing to their success but also even to new outcomes (Taddeo et al., 2017). In this domain, it is worth remembering that engagement platforms can converge and individuals can pertain to more than a single engagement platform at the same time, making the ecosystem of capabilities emerge (i.e. Ramaswamy & Ozcan, 2014). Indeed, an ecosystem of capabilities can be understood as the ability of a group of individuals pertaining to the same ecosystem to design and implement coordinated processes of value co-creation, thanks to the exchange of information very often made possible through the new technological functions available today (Aquilani, 2016).

In this domain it is clear that "*ecosystem capacities are critical in constituting ecosystems of enterprise capabilities, since all agents in the system possess an indefinite number of affects that can be converted into capabilities in co-dependencies with other agencies in an enterprise's strategic architecture of multiple engagement platforms*" (Ramaswamy & Ozcan, 2014, p. 84). Given the above, it is clear that IS shares some particular traits with value co-creation processes; this leads to the affirmation that IS can be considered a value co-creation process. Indeed, if it is true that IS supports a group of firms to jointly achieve profit maximization through the internalization of their externalities (Desrochers & Leppala, 2010), it can also be said that benefits are shared among partners who have collaborated towards a common goal. Moreover, with reference to DART - Dialogue, Access, Risk (Ramaswamy 2009a, 2009b)

-Reward assessment or Reflexivity, Transparency (Ramaswamy & Ozcan, 2014) – it can also be said that it is of paramount importance for IS to start and nurture interactions. Considering "access", it is clear that access to knowledge, resources, tools, experiences, capabilities, etc. is essential both for value co-creation and IS and just in this domain the role of technology, especially digital platform features and enabled operations, is strategic (Ramaswamy, 2009b; Ramaswamy & Ozcan, 2014). The risk-reward assessment involves partners collaborating to co-create value who need to jointly consider the risks of collaborating and the benefits of doing so (Ramaswamy 2009a, 2009b). To assess this issue, partners need more and more information but also new tools and supports in order to reduce risks, making more and more informed choices (Aquilani, 2016); in this domain Big Data and related metrics and analytics can play a very important role. The risk issue in IS is also of paramount importance in that each firm collaborating must disclose some resources and/or information and/or knowledge, making it more vulnerable under various profiles; selective revealing in innovation activities can become a successful strategic choice (Harhoff et al., 2003; Henkel, 2006; Alexy et al., 2013), although it is not without risks. Reflexivity deals once again with information, suggestions, recommendations, tools made available to individuals to co-create, but highlights that they are all essential to enhance the value to be co-created in the engagement platform (Ramaswamy & Ozcan, 2014). In this context, the value co-creation view underlines that the risk must be constantly considered, in that it is embedded in value co-creation processes and therefore is a fundamental element of the co-creative enterprise (i.e., Frigo & Ramaswamy, 2009; Frigo, CMA, CPA, Læssøe, 2012; Læssøe et al., 2013). Transparency is about the complete availability of information and interactions, information being the essential element of transparency and interactions entailing trust among individuals who participate. Indeed, trust can only develop when information is freely available and transferred in a totally open domain at each stage and moment in which the co-creation processes develop (Prahalad & Ramaswamy, 2014) and this applies to value co-creation as well as to IS.

Based on the shared traits of value co-creation and IS, it is clear that even if they start in two different streams of literature, engineering and management respectively, the processes they suggest to firms and industries to innovate and be successful are really similar, even if not equal due, at least, to the distribution of value among individuals; this is more precisely defined by the value co-creation approach than by IS.

Indeed, in the value co-creation approach individuals must play an active role (i.e., Prahalad & Ramaswamy, 2003, 2004) and obtain some kind of benefit – psychological or economic (Ramaswamy & Gouillart, 2010b) - for their activity in value co-creation processes (Saarijärvi, Kannan & Kuusela, 2013). Even if IS only considers that some firms jointly achieve profit maximization (Desrochers & Leppala, 2010), it can be said that each partner must implicitly play an active role and that profit must be shared. Surely this issue deserves more attention in future research, given that this is not in the aim of this chapter and that, apart from the profit – the outcome of the collaboration - also in terms of knowledge, resources, etc. to be understood as benefits, must be exchanged in order to adopt an integrated approach in separate industries as IS suggests (i.e. Hawken, 1993; Chertow, 2000).

The outlined parallel between value co-creation and IS appears really interesting. It seems that the two approaches have initiated from two different stand points, the first at a management and general level though based on human experiences and the second focusing on the operational level of firms and industries searching for an integrated approach in manufacturing activities. However, IS can be read almost through the lens of the value co-creation approach while co-creation processes can also develop in digital platforms, one of the tools of Industry 4.0.

Methodology

The methodology used in this chapter to initially validate the proposed framework is the single case study.

The case-based method is preferable in situations in which "*the main research questions are "how" or "why" questions [and] a researcher has little or no control over behavioral events and the focus of the study is a contemporary phenomenon in depth and within its real-world context, especially when the boundaries between phenomenon and context may not be clearly evident*" (Yin 2014, p. 216).

Indeed, in accordance with the methodology of Yin (2002, 2014), the case study was structured in different steps of analysis using a variety of qualitative data collection both primary (interview with platform manager) and secondary (i.e. published papers, internet resources and reports).

The first step was the choice of the case study to analyze. For the purposes of this research, a case study (*Symbiosis*) that presented theoretical and practical reflections useful for validating the proposed theoretical model was selected (Siggelkow, 2007) (see below).

The second step was the collection of secondary data like information material on the case study, drawing on information available both online and offline.

The analysis of secondary data highlighted the information gaps that determine the basis for the interview with the platform manager.

In particular, the information needed for the second step of analysis was effectively found online through the official website of the platform (http://www.industrialsymbiosis.it/) and subsequently deepened through a series of publications and presentations available online.

Finally, the last step was a direct interview (conducted in May-June 2019) with the platform manager Ing. Laura Cutaia from ENEA in order to complete the information set. The semi-structured interview provided an understanding of the technical and operational side of the platform as well as an appreciation of the results already achieved. It also provided further future prospects for the platform. Questions formulated for the semi-structured interview, including these aspects of the case study, were sent to the platform manager on the 15th of May and were returned on the 4th of June by e-mail. This information was then integrated into the results section of the chapter. In doing this the latter was triangulated with information derived from secondary data (Eisenhardt, 1989), also in order to increase construct validity, mitigating the risk of bias in information and as a control for the individual judgments of authors (Gibbert et al., 2008). Finally, the chapter draft was written and sent to the platform manager to gather some lacking information and to be sure that all details about the case study were correctly assessed into the prepared chapter. Some more adjustments were made by authors after the platform manager check to match some requests coming from her, who, after a second check round, approved the whole resulting chapter.

The research design just outlined guarantees the validity of the analysis through the interweaving of information and news from different sources, internal and external, direct and indirect (Yin, 2002).

Figure 2 shows the design of the methodology.

Figure 2. Research design
Source: (authors' elaboration)

The selected case study was the digital platform "*Symbiosis*", created by the Italian ENEA.

This case was selected because it represents the first IS platform launched in Italy, more precisely in Sicily which, as it will emerge, has given rise to a national synergistic process and to the birth of the first IS network in Italy called SUN - Symbiosis User Network (Cutaia et al., 2015a).

THE ITALIAN ENEA SYMBIOSIS PLATFORM

The Project and the Origin of the Platform

As has already emerged from the analysis of the literature, IS has become a topic of considerable interest at a global level (Ayres 1989, 1994; Hawken, 1993; Chertow, 2000).

In Europe it has taken on prominence in the EU Cohesion Policy and European growth strategies. In Italy, for example, a lot of activities have been implemented by the Department for Development Policies and Economic Cohesion (DPS) of the Italian Ministry of Economic Development (MISE), with the support of local Governments, to improve and support the diffusion of IS, in the lens of a circular economy (Cutaia, 2014d).

In particular, two Italian regions, Emilia Romagna and Lazio have included IS in their strategic plans, to reduce the quantity of waste, to increase regional sustainability, to reuse materials and save raw materials (Cutaia et al., 2016 p. 12).

In Emilia-Romagna, for example, five technological specializations were considered strategic and relevant for a growth strategy of the territory and for each specialization some key-subjects were identified for implementation (Iacondini et al., 2014):

- Agri-food (biomasses management, smart water management, sustainable production systems, smart packaging);
- Building (waste valorization, energy efficiency, renewable resources);
- Mechatronics and motor design, and manufacture (eco-design, energy efficiency, critical and substitutive materials);
- Health and wellbeing industries;
- Creative and cultural industries.

An application of IS was developed in this region in 9 months, from the end of June 2013 to the beginning of March 2014, contributing to paving the way for the above-mentioned initiatives.

In fact, this first application has created great interest in IS and was the starting point for the project which then developed in Sicily.

In this Region, the Italian agency for new technologies, energy and sustainable economic development (ENEA), promoted the development and the implementation of the first Italian Platform for IS (2011-2015).

The goals of the interesting new project were to provide a methodology and a tool for IS implementation at a regional level and at the same time promote the creation of an IS platform to support small and medium-sized enterprises (SMEs) in search of IS opportunities (Cutaia et al., 2019).

In particular, the platform aims at creating IS networks and mechanisms in a functional way in order to support SMEs in:

1. Geo-referencing the organization;
2. Entering and updating information regarding the production;
3. Inserting, updating and managing resources through a system of input/output record cards;
4. Sharing resources;
5. Searching for possible symbiosis projects (http://www.industrialsymbiosis.it/a-cosa-serve).

In this context the search for symbiosis opportunities takes place through the direct connection between a firm's input and/or output (firm seeking IS) and inputs and/or outputs coming from another or more firms through a search algorithm. The latter enables the connection between similar resources; therefore a process of resource transformation and/or valorization takes place, making them perfectly compatible (http://www.industrialsymbiosis.it/a-cosa-serve).

Indeed, this platform enables the transfer of resources (materials, energy products, water, services and expertise) offering, at the same time, other operational instruments (like for example: legal database, tools for Life Cycle Assessment (LCA) and Eco-design, best practices database, etc.) in order to support firms in achieving IS.

The path to create the platform and its launch was structured in a series of steps from the beginning of the project (2011) till its programmed end in 2015.

First of all, the platform was designed and implemented from an architectural point of view, it was then equipped with all deemed ICT and tools (Cutaia et al., 2015a). Then, a promotion campaign was launched for the involvement of both local enterprises and national/international ones, in order to create a starting database of firms and carry out the subsequent steps to identify possible synergies (Cutaia et al., 2015c).

The first operative meeting with firms was held in Syracuse in March 2014 with the aim of involving firms in the platform. Forty out of the 1,500 firms in the area of Syracuse took part in the event and were allowed to create the first synergic links among them.

Data provided during the workshop was elaborated and individual firm reports were generated and sent out to other enterprises with information about potential matches. Thus, Cutaia et al. (2014c) affirm that "*potential matches found during the workshop are part of the whole potential matches that are potentially possible, since information provided by firms before the meeting, filling in input-output table are much more detailed and large than those provided during the workshop. For this reason, ongoing activity foresee the completion of elaboration of input-output data provided, as a whole, by the firms*" (Cutaia et al., 2014c, p. 7).

Looking more in-depth at the phases of the project, it can be said that the platform in Sicily was implemented following three main steps (Brunori et al., 2016).

The first organizational phase included (Cutaia et al., 2019):

1. The creation of a geo-referenced database of firms;
2. Networking with selected firms;
3. Sending and receiving input/output data collection forms to identify resources;
4. The organization of workshops aimed at identifying potential symbiotic synergies.

At this point these meetings can be considered a first moment of "data processing" (Cutaia, interview) useful for sharing input and output resources of one's production process.

The second executive phase included the following main activities (Cutaia et al., 2019):

1. The development of workshops with involved firms;
2. The analysis of all data collected in the first phase and the identification of potential synergies;
3. The upload of all data collected on the IS platform;
4. The selection of IS paths to be proposed to firms;
5. The in-depth study of all possible problems linked to the proposed project of IS;
6. The first draft of operative handbooks of the paths of IS identified during the project.

An interesting aspect is precisely the definition and draft of operative handbooks.

These documents assume a basic cognitive function which is essential for the effective realization of IS between interested partners (Cutaia et al., 2019).

In fact, the operative handbooks allow assessment of feasibility of the synergies identified by the platform from a technical, economic and regulatory point of view.

The operative handbooks also identify factors to be investigated and/or overcome in order to achieve successful synergies, such as the characterization and qualification of materials or administrative requirements (Cutaia et al., 2019).

In Figure 3 it is possible to see both the layout and the summary table of an operative handbook.

The third phase of the project is the organization of consultation tables in which firms, stakeholders and ENEA, discussed the feasibility and the different particularities of the identified IS paths.

Furthermore, still in this last operational phase, the revision of the operative handbooks in the light of observations that emerged from the consultation phase lead to the final drafts of the operative handbook.

The success of this first project was crucial to start a series of related activities that developed in sequence through numerous Italian cities and regions and also with an international focus (see Lubiana project below).

Figure 3. Example of layout and summary table included in the initial part of the operative handbook
Source: (Cutaia et al., 2019, available online at http://astrolabio.amicidellaterra.it/node/1324 © [2019] [ENEA]. Used with permission).

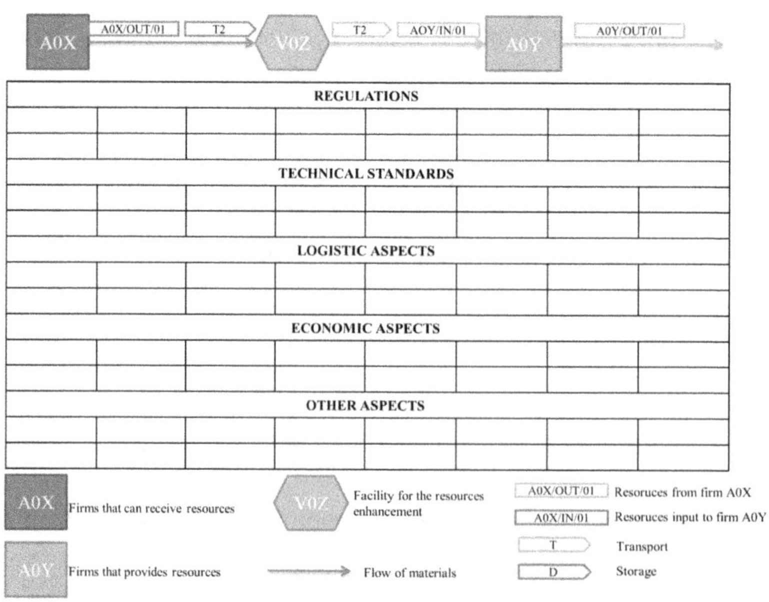

Figure 4. Resources and potential synergies in ENEA projects
Source: (ENEA presentation available online at https://www.minambiente.it/sites/default/files/archivio/allegati/CReIAMO_PA/L3/WP3/Silvia_Sbaffoni_roma_12102018.pdf © [2018] [ENEA]. Used with permission).

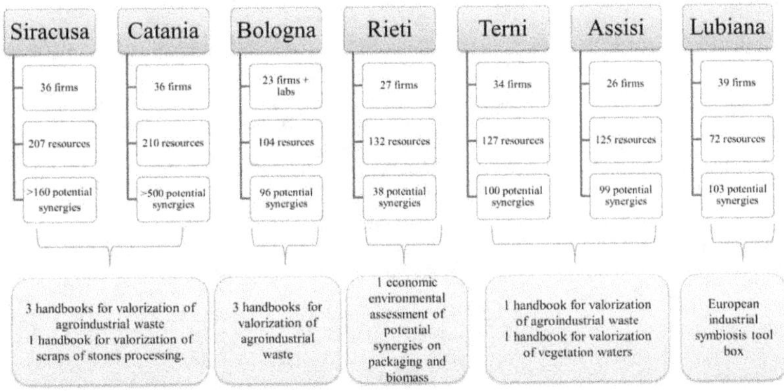

As is clear from Figure 4, the seven projects that started in sequence have involved a large number of resources generating various potential synergies for IS.

Individual projects, or in some cases considerations emerging from the above-mentioned projects all together led to the draft of joint operative handbooks.

These first drafts of operative handbooks are then presented to Consultation tables in which local authorities, category associations, etc. participate in order to review and eventually enrich them with insights suggested by stakeholders; critical issues are also identified and overcome.

These operative handbooks analytically describe the layouts of the synergies and detail, step by step, the legal-administrative requirements, the technical standards, the economic aspects as well as any further information necessary to allow firms to effectively achieve synergies.

Finally, the operative handbooks are completed by ENEA and sent to involved firms.

For the above-mentioned projects, Figure 4 illustrates six operative handbooks and a handbook as well as a set of European tools, which have been formulated for this precise purpose.

Following the numerous projects, the platform has obviously evolved over the years.

Today, 168 firms are participating (please see Figure 5) with a total of 2,604 resources made available and shared and 1,923 IS processes activated (http://www.industrialsymbiosis.it/network, accessed on June 12, 2019).

Figure 5 also shows how firms participating in the platform can be located on a map using a search engine operating through three different filters:

- Name of firm, if known;
- Code relating to the activity performed by the firm;
- Geographical location.

Symbiosis platforms must also be analyzed from a technical/operational point of view to understand methods and steps that can achieve IS.

Figure 5. Distribution of firms registered on the platform: access page
Source: (http://www.industrialsymbiosis.it/network © [2019] [ENEA]. Used with permission).

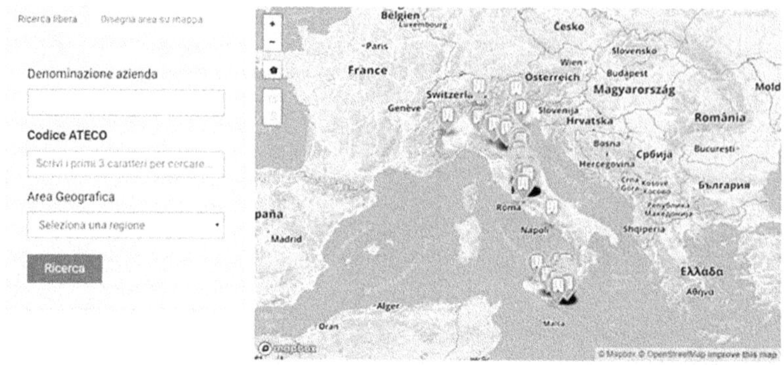

Characteristics and Operational Mechanisms of *Symbiosis*

The *Symbiosis* platform is managed by ENEA and is based on an integrated system of Information and Communication Technology (ICT) and Database (DBs) tools in order to support firm interactions and stakeholder networks (Cutaia et al., 2015c).

The basic idea (please see Figure 6) was to create a tool facilitating the match of resources (understood as waste materials, waste, energy waste, capacity, services, etc.) between firms traditionally non-cooperating at an industrial level.

At the same time, the platform can offer a series of additional services and operational tools (Best Available Technology (BA), regulations, databases, rapid LCA and eco-design tools among others) to firms involved in IS (Cutaia et al., 2014a, 2015c).

To access the platform, firms insert their general information (name, address, activity sector and so on) directly on the www.industrialsymbiosis.it portal, creating their profile.

Figure 6. Functional hierarchy of the industrial Symbiosis platform
Source: (Cutaia et al., 2014a © [2014] [ENEA]. Used with permission).

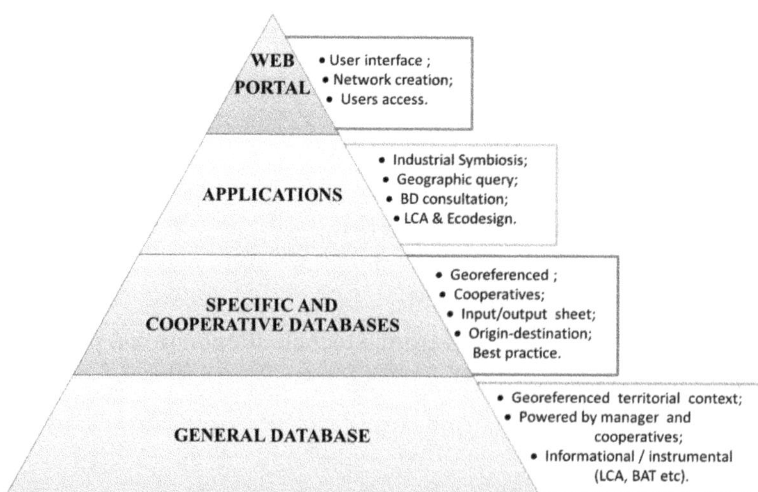

Figure 7. How the platform works: an example
Source: (Cutaia et al., 2014c, p. 3© [2014] [ENEA]. Used with permission).

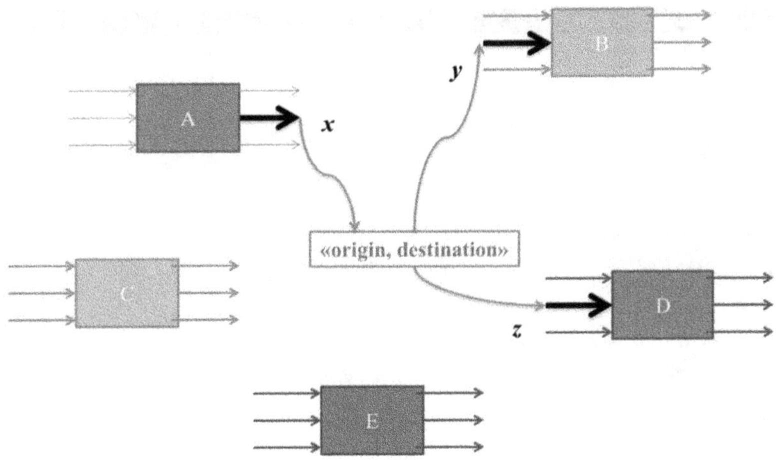

Then firms, through projects each accessible to an *ad hoc* fee, both to ensure better functioning and effectiveness of the platform and profit from all the functions provided by the platform, are encouraged to go from the "registered company" level to the "associated" one (queries, DBs, results in terms IS matching) (Cutaia et al., 2014c). Indeed, to facilitate the match, "*registered firms can become "associated", providing their own information about inputs and outputs they want to share within the industrial symbiosis network*" (Cutaia et al., 2015a, p. 1523).

Figure 7 shows both the relationships and synergic combinations that can be realized between firms "associated" on the platform.

The boxes (A, B, C, etc.) represent the "associated" firms, and the bolt their own input-output (going in and out from the respective boxes) and the possible synergies. "*This connection goes through a string origin-destination which allows to find relation between one waste/by product with its potential of productive use*" (Cutaia et al, 2014c, p. 3).

All registered firms therefore insert information on the platform regarding: availability, quantity and units of measurement for resources together with the coding for their management (e.g. Nace code, or CER code – EWC code).

At this point, IS platform software connects inputs and outputs through the "bridge" represented by the <origin, destination> string.

As shown in Figure 7, for example, the platform searches possible matches for output x (resources made available by firm A) and the string identifies two possible destinations as inputs for firm B and/or D as inputs y or z.

The <origin, destination> strings when originated are fed, either directly during the workshops or through the analysis of good practices, literature, industrial practices, patents, applied research, etc., by the platform manager and, as a consequence, new possible synergies are identified and/or realized.

As emerged from the platform manager interview, through the <origin, destination> string, using an already existing coding, two "worlds" which normally "speak different languages", are put in communication, i.e., inputs and outputs. Firms involved receive an *ad hoc* report that lists possible identified

Figure 8. Example of structure of an <origin, destination> string
Source: (Cutaia et al.,2014c, p. 4 © [2014] [ENEA]. Used with permission).

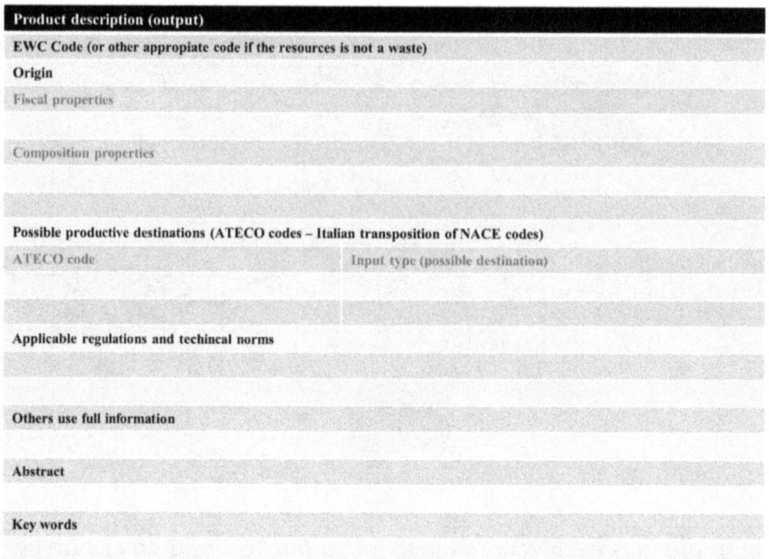

Product description (output)
EWC Code (or other appropiate code if the resources is not a waste)
Origin
Fiscal properties
Composition properties
Possible productive destinations (ATECO codes – Italian transposition of NACE codes)
ATECO code | Input type (possible destination)
Applicable regulations and techincal norms
Others use full information
Abstract
Key words

matches in detail, no matter whether they can be directly realized by firms participating in the workshops or just hypothesized by the string among partners not participating in the workshops.

The structure showing the information appearing to firms in the <origin, destination> string is shown in Figure 8.

After the match made by the string, firms involved are asked by ENEA if they are willing to proceed with IS and in this case the procedure is activated through an active participation by firms until release of the resulting operative handbooks (please see above).

Table 1. Relevant data of the most important projects realized

Project	Partners	No. of Firms	No. Workshops	Shared Resources	No. of Potential Synergies	No. Operative Handbooks
Sicily Eco-Innovation Project	Confindustria Catania, Syracuse Chamber of Commerce, Sicily Region, University of Catania	100	3	400	690	4
Green Industrial symbiosis in Emilia Romagna	Chamber of Commerce of Bologna, ASTER	13	1	104	96	3
Eco-industrial park in the Rieti-Cittaducale Industrial Development Area	University of Tuscia (co-founder)	27	2	146	110	1 (Economic-environmental assessment of potential synergies)
Industrial symbiosis in Umbria	"Sviluppumbria" (Regional Agency for Economic Development of Umbria)	60	2	250	259	2

Source: (authors' elaboration from Cutaia interview)

This represents the last step of IS in which ENEA participates; any commercial agreements between partners is handled directly by them.

Data about the most important projects realized until now are shown in Table 1.

Benefits, Threats and Future Prospects of *Symbiosis*

Results generated by *Symbiosis* can be identified as follows:

- Business awareness of opportunities deriving from IS;
- Improved resource efficiency;
- Value co-creation outcomes;
- Positive environmental fallouts.

First of all, the platform has enabled firms to understand that it is possible to share all types of resources, not only materials (by-products or waste), but also energy waste, services, expertise. Therefore, they become aware that IS can be a driver for an increasingly strong dialogue between various firms also pertaining to different industries.

Indeed, IS achieved through *Symbiosis* allows firms to make more efficient use of resources; it can be understood as a "diagnostic tool" in order to optimize the use and/or reuse of resources.

Moreover, the platform, through the transfer of waste resources, either in excess or underutilized, from one firm to another, provides economic and environmental benefits deriving from both non-disposal of waste and avoids the consumption of primary resources.

In this way, *Symbiosis* processes lead to "win more-win more solutions", in which all actors involved can take advantage of interactions in terms of value created at least at an economic, relational and business strategy level. IS is also useful as a territorial planning tool for local valorization of resources, which can be considered an important factor in order to achieve eco-innovation and to enrich the territory in which it is developed. Embracing a holistic view for the management of industrial areas, it can also become an essential tool to guarantee more efficient use of resources and to trigger the conditions behind better territorial and economic competitiveness.

The environmental impact has risen in importance for *Symbiosis* in that in the most recent IS projects already closed specific indicators have been included to measure the relative environmental impact where the comparative environmental assessment part has been included with and without symbiosis using life cycle assessment (LCA) according to ISO 14000 standards; this issue is considered even more crucial in order to fully exploit IS opportunities.

In this domain, even if the sample of industrial symbiosis projects is very small, it is possible to state that environmental performances when IS is achieved are more sustainable than those for which it has not been realized. For example, looking at the Rieti-Cittaducale project, Cutaia affirms that it has been estimated, in the best-case scenario, that an important improvement in waste management could be achieved through *Symbiosis*, precisely following the principles and objectives of the circular economy.

This is due to:

- A decrease of 32 t of biodegradable and construction waste, not disposed in landfills because recycled;
- An extension of the life cycle of approximately 50 industrial wooden crates, equal to 3.5 t, reused and not disposed.

Notwithstanding the above-mentioned benefits, some threats emerge during both the planning and the implementation phases of IS.

The main threat is obviously the firms' lack of trust when coming to share certain information, especially that relating to more sensitive data, such as waste, in any form, and production residues.

According to the platform manager, this lack of trust is essentially referable to a structural defect concerning the economic system as a whole, which has emerged over the years managing *Symbiosis.*

Cutaia (interview) states that "*In Italy as well as in other Countries, above all in the Mediterranean ones, there is not a "culture of waste"; the latter to be understood as the ability to see how waste can be reused and/or transformed in order to add value to resources resultant from a given production process. Such a cultural bias against the resource discarded inhibits any revaluations of the same*".

Against this bias only awareness among firms of opportunities to be grasped from IS can lead to the valorization of waste, in any form, initiating both the recovery and the optimization processes on which circular economy models are based.

Given these threats some improvements have been considered for *Symbiosis.*

For example, the STORM project - Industrial Symbiosis for the Sustainable Management of Raw Materials - was recently launched at an international level.

STORM, carried out within EIT Raw Materials, is a "Network of Infrastructures" project based on IS, aimed at creating a network of excellence in order to provide services and tools to external customers to support them in the implementation of innovative and sustainable business and cooperation models.

The project which began in 2016 involved 11 European partners coordinated by ENEA.

Among the various activities, two IS workshops were held with the involvement of Slovene firms in Ljubljana (39 firms involved) and Italian ones in Assisi (26 firms involved) organized respectively with the Slovenian Chamber of Commerce and Industry and "Sviluppumbria".

Both in Italy and in Slovenia 125 resources were shared and 99 and 100 potential synergies respectively were identified.

Moreover, as IS allows a better and more efficient use of resources, an important step forward could be the realization of a voluntary discipline by firms in order to achieve a resource diagnosis through a system of accounting. The latter will provide the exact state of management in the domain of such resources and also carry out a monitoring schedule in order to develop an efficiency plan. This will also allow easier access to IS opportunities. For this reason, ENEA, in collaboration with "Sviluppumbria", started a pilot project in an Umbrian firm based on this type of methodology for the diagnosis of resources.

FUTURE RESEARCH DIRECTIONS AND LIMITATIONS

The main limitation of the present research work is the analysis of a single case study in the domain of IS, although this is the only case at a National level. Therefore, further work is needed, above all, at an

International level, to validate the proposed model through a cross-Country analysis. The results of this analysis will "measure" the differences in the way and measure IS contributes to environmental sustainability in different Countries, also from a value co-creation point of view. This same analysis can then be carried out at a global level and, in this context, it would also be interesting to understand whether there are differences among the various industries in which firms embracing IS pertain.

Furthermore, by comparing operating platforms also at an international level, it will be possible to evaluate the contribution of policies and/or tools made available by single Countries for IS, to understand their impact on performance and therefore on the level of achieved environmental sustainability. Another future avenue of research could also be found in directly investigating firm reasons to collaborate in digital platforms to achieve environmental sustainability, for example, also through a questionnaire.

CONCLUSION

The *Symbiosis* case study shows how, as suggested by the framework, Industry 4.0 platforms devoted to IS contribute to environmental sustainability, in that the latter is one of its main benefits. Indeed, this contribution can grow if firms become more aware of the opportunities and benefits of IS.

Moreover, it emerges that both Industry 4.0 and IS pay great attention to sustainability issues and among them to those pertaining to environmental sustainability, i.e., waste.

Industry 4.0 also provides new innovations and tools which can be really useful to start and achieve IS, fostering environmental sustainability, as the case study suggests. The latter also highlights how firms can exploit technological innovations through IS, i.e. platforms, pertaining to Industry 4.0 and in this way can support firms in fulfilling their environmental sustainability goals (Ferrera et al., 2017).

Moreover, the case study also shows how IS permits various and valuable relationships among firms also pertaining to different industries, thus recalling the contribution of Stock (2016) which links value creation and LCA to IS.

Apart from the development of the *Symbiosis* platform, the IS experience achieved by ENEA allows its platform manager to state that, unfortunately, there is not yet a shared methodology or standard for the development of a resource efficiency plan at both a National or European Community level; a plan is already in use for example for energy efficiency (European directive 2012/27/EU).

The case study, therefore, helps in firstly validating the proposed framework and, in this way contributes, from a theoretical point of view, to deepen the theme of Industry 4.0, still new but growing, through the use of digital platforms to achieve environmental sustainability. It attempts to bridge the literature on IS with the one on value co-creation in the broad domain of Industry 4.0. It also adds some insights on industrial platforms functioning, considering an industrial platform in which the innovator's dilemma as well as other trade-offs couldn't emerge (Gawer and Cusumano, 2014); it is a third-party owned platform. However, standards and common rules are needed anyway and as for all other industrial platforms "platform leaders [ENEA] first have to evolve their own internal capabilities and approaches to technological innovation and business strategy" and then, "equally important, they must bring along with them an entire ecosystem of users and partners, and coordinate at least incremental innovation on a broad scale" (Gawer & Cusumano, 2014, p. 19).

From a managerial point of view, the study can be of help in creating awareness in firms about IS opportunities, from both an economic and environmental point of view, a more informed use and reuse of waste, in whichever form, and can help in paving the way for an energy efficiency plan first at a firm level and then at an industrial level and beyond; all this as a whole representing a potential great enhancement towards shared environmental sustainability goals. Moreover, this chapter reinforce the awareness of the valuable contribution industrial platforms can generate for both implementing Industry 4.0 and support firms activities with partners which today represents a profiting avenue for growing rapidly and successfully. From a more operational point of view, this paper sheds light on a special kind of Industry 4.0 platform, suggesting a way to easily access and profit from IS processes. Finally, to have linked *Symbiosis* to Industry 4.0, industrial platform literature and environmental sustainability can suggest to their leaders new ways to develop it profiting at the best from all its opportunity or even enhance them trying to better support participating firms.

ACKNOWLEDGMENT

This research received no specific grant from any funding agency in the public, commercial, or not-for-profit sectors.

The research was supported by ENEA, in particular we greatly acknowledge Dr. Erika Mancuso, Dr. Marco La Monica and Ing. Laura Cutaia, the *Symbiosis* platform manager, who has been really helpful both with information and the interview provided for the case study release.

REFERENCES

Alexy, O., George, G., & Salter, A. J. (2013). Cui bono? The selective revealing of knowledge and its implications for innovative activity. *Academy of Management Review*, *38*(2), 270–291. doi:10.5465/amr.2011.0193

Allenby, B. R., & Braden, R. (1999). Industrial ecology: policy framework and implementation. Prentice Hall.

Antikainen, M., Makipaa, M., & Ahonen, M. (2010). Motivating and supporting collaboration in open innovation. *European Journal of Innovation Management*, *13*(1), 100–119. doi:10.1108/14601061011013258

Aquilani, B. (2016). *La co-creazione di valore nei processi di innovazione aperta: verso un modello di analisi*. Padova: Cedam.

Aquilani, B., & Abbate, T. (2013). Le piattaforme di innovazione online: la prospettiva delle imprese. *Proceedings of XXV Convegno annuale di Sinergie*.

Aquilani, B., & Abbate, T. (2014). Open Innovation through Customers: Collaborative Web-Based Platforms for Ethically and Socially Responsible New Products Part 1. In Handbook of Research on Consumerism in Business and Marketing: Concepts and Practices (pp. 335-374). IGI Global.

Aquilani, B., Abbate, T., & Dominici, G. (2016). Choosing Open Innovation Intermediaries through their web-based platforms. *The International Journal of Digital Accounting Research*, *16*, 35–60. doi:10.4192/1577-8517-v16_2

Aquilani, B., Silvestri, C., Ioppolo, G., & Ruggieri, A. (2018). The challenging transition to bio-economies: Towards a new framework integrating corporate sustainability and value co-creation. *Journal of Cleaner Production, 172*, 4001–4009. doi:10.1016/j.jclepro.2017.03.153

Ayres, R. U. (1989). Industrial Metabolism. In *Technology and Environment*. Washington, DC: National Academy Press.

Ayres, R. U. (1994). Industrial metabolism: Theory and policy. In R. U. Ayres & U. K. Simonis (Eds.), *Industrial Metabolism: Restructuring for Sustainable Development* (pp. 3–20). Tokyo: United Nations University Press.

Boudreau, K. J. (2012). Let a Thousand Flowers Bloom? An Early Look at Large Numbers of Software App Developers and Patterns of Innovation. *Organization Science, 23*(5), 1409–1427. doi:10.1287/orsc.1110.0678

Brousseau, E., & Penard, T. (2007). The economics of digital business models: A framework for analyzing the economics of platforms. *Review of Network Economics, 6*(2). doi:10.2202/1446-9022.1112

Brunori, C., Mancuso, E., Luciano, A., Sbaffoni, S., Barberio, G., La Monica, M., ... Cutaia, L. (2016). L'economia circolare per il contenimento delle emissioni di gas serra. *Energia Ambiente e Innovazione, 1*, 46–49.

Buguin, J., Dobbs, R., Bisson, P., & Marrs, A. (2013). *Disruptive Technologies: Advances That Will Transform Life, Business, and the Global Economy*. San Francisco, CA: McKinsey Global Institute.

Burritt, R., & Christ, K. (2016). Industry 4.0 and environmental accounting: A new revolution? *Asian Journal of Sustainable Society Responsibility, 1*(1), 23–38. doi:10.118641180-016-0007-y

Chalkias, G. (2019). *Industrial Symbiosis: A Circular Manufacturing Strategy for Industry 4.0*. Retrieved from https://www.crit-research.it/wp-content/uploads/2018/04/20180419CRIT_Circular-manufacturing-strategies-for-I40-Chalkias-IRIS.pdf

Chertow, M. R. (2000). Industrial Symbiosis: Literature and Taxonomy. *Annual Review of Energy and the Environment, 25*(1), 313–337. doi:10.1146/annurev.energy.25.1.313

Chertow, M. R. (2007). "Uncovering" industrial symbiosis. *Journal of Industrial Ecology, 11*(1), 11–30. doi:10.1162/jiec.2007.1110

Chertow, M. R., Ashton, S. A., & Espinosa, J. C. (2008). Industrial symbiosis in Puerto Rico: Environmentally related agglomeration economies. *Regional Studies, 42*(10), 1299–1312. doi:10.1080/00343400701874123

Cutaia, L., Barberio, B., Luciano, A., Mancuso, E., Sbaffoni, S., La Monica, M., & Scagliarino, C. (2015a). The experience of the first industrial symbiosis platform in Italy. *Environmental Engineering and Management Journal, 14*(7), 1521–1533. doi:10.30638/eemj.2015.164

Cutaia, L., Barberio, G., La Monica, M., Luciano, A., Mancuso, E., Sbaffoni, S., & Scagliarino, C. (2019). *La Prima Piattaforma Italiana per la Simbiosi Industriale*. Retrieved from http://astrolabio.amicidellaterra.it/node/1324

Cutaia, L., Boncio, E., Barberio, G., Beltrani, T., La Monica, M., Mancuso, E., ... Paoni, S. (2017). Industrial symbiosis network in Umbria, Italy, in methods and tools for the implementation of industrial symbiosis best practices and business cases in Italy. *Proceedings of the first SUN Conference Rome.*

Cutaia, L., La Monica, M., Scagliarino, S., Barberio, G., Sbaffoni, S., Luciano, A., & Mancuso, M. (2015b). Recovery of waste streams from agroindustry through industrial symbiosis in Sicilia. In *LCA for feeding the planet and energy for life, International conference on Life Cycle Assessment as reference methodology for assessing supply chains and supporting global sustainability challenges.* ENEA.

Cutaia, L., Mancuso, E., Barberio, G., Sbaffoni, S., Luciano, A., La Monica, M., & Scagliarino, C. (2015c). The Experience of the First Industrial Symbiosis Platform in Italy. In *Experiences of Industrial Symbiosis in Italy. Proceedings of conferences promoted by ENEA at Ecomondo in 2012, 2013 and 2014.* ENEA.

Cutaia, L., Mancuso, E., Sbaffoni, S., Luciano, A., & Barberio, G. (2014c). First results of the implementation of the Industrial Symbiosis Platform in Italy. *Proceedings Symbiosis Conference.*

Cutaia, L., Morabito, R., Barberio, G., Mancuso, E., Brunori, C., Spezzano, P., ... Cappello, F. (2014a). The Project for the Implementation of the Industrial Symbiosis Platform in Sicily: The Progress After the First Year of Operation. In R. Salomone & G. Saija (Eds.), *Pathways to Environmental Sustainability.* Springer International Publishing. doi:10.1007/978-3-319-03826-1_20

Cutaia, L., Sbaffoni, S., Mancuso, E., Barberio, G., Luciano, A., Scagliarino, C., & La Monica, M. (2014b). Un esempio di eco-innovazione di sistema attraverso la valorizzazione territoriale di risorse: Nuovo approccio cooperativo tra mondo industriale, scientifico e istituzionale. *EAI Energia, Ambiente e Innovazione. Energia Ambiente e Innovazione, 60*(5), 76–88.

Cutaia, L., Scagliarino, C., Mencherini, U., & Iacondini, A. (2014d). Industrial symbiosis in Emilia-Romagna region: Results from a first application in the agroindustry sector. *Procedia Environmental Science. Engineering and Management, 2*, 11–36.

Cutaia, L., Scagliarino, C., Mencherini, U., & La Monica, M. (2016). Project green symbiosis 2014 - II phase: Results from an industrial symbiosis pilot project in Emilia Romagna region (Italy). *Environmental Engineering and Management Journal, 15*(9), 1949–1961. doi:10.30638/eemj.2016.210

de Reuver, M., Sørensen, C., & Basole, R. C. (2018). The digital platform: A research agenda. *Journal of Information Technology, 33*(2), 124–135. doi:10.105741265-016-0033-3

de Sousa Jabbour, A. B. L., Jabbour, C. J. C., Foropon, C., & Godinho Filho, M. (2018). When titans meet–Can industry 4.0 revolutionise the environmentally-sustainable manufacturing wave? The role of critical success factors. *Technological Forecasting and Social Change, 132*, 18–25. doi:10.1016/j.techfore.2018.01.017

Denning, S. (2014). Navigating the phase change to the creative economy. *Strategy and Leadership, 42*, 3–11.

Desrochers, P., & Leppälä, S. (2010). Industrial symbiosis: Old wine in recycled bottles? Some perspective from the history of economic and geographical thought. *International Regional Science Review, 3*(3), 338–361. doi:10.1177/0160017610375441

Ehrenfeld, J., & Gertler, N. (1997). Industrial ecology in practice: The evolution of interdependence at Kalundborg. *Journal of Industrial Ecology*, *1*(1), 67–79. doi:10.1162/jiec.1997.1.1.67

Elkington, J. (1997). *Cannibals with Forks: The Triple Bottom Line of 21st Century Business*. Oxford, UK: Capstone Publishing.

Erro-Garcés, A. (2019). Industry 4. 0: Defining the research agenda. *Benchmarking: An International Journal*, (ahead-of-print). doi:10.1108/BIJ-12-2018-0444

Ferrera, E., Rossini, R., Baptista, A. J., Evans, S., Hovest, G. G., Holgado, M., & Silva, E. J. (2017). Toward Industry 4.0: efficient and sustainable manufacturing leveraging MAESTRI total efficiency framework. In *International Conference on Sustainable Design and Manufacturing* (pp. 624-633). Springer. 10.1007/978-3-319-57078-5_59

Frolov, V. G., Kaminchenko, D. I., Kovylkin, D. Y., Alex, J., & Alex, A. (2017). The Main Economic Factors of Sustainable Manufacturing within the Industrial Policy Concept of Industry 4.0. *Academy Strategic Management Journal*, *16*, 1–11.

Frosch, R. A. (1992). Industrial ecology: A philosophical introduction. *Proceedings of the National Academy of Sciences of the United States of America*, *89*(3), 800–803. doi:10.1073/pnas.89.3.800

Garg, S. K., & Buyya, R. (2012). Green cloud computing and environmental sustainability. *Harnessing Green IT: Principles and Practices*, 315-340.

Gawer, A., & Cusumano, M. A. (2014). Industry platforms and ecosystem innovation. *Journal of Product Innovation Management*, *31*(3), 417–433. doi:10.1111/jpim.12105

Gibbs, D. (2008). Industrial Symbiosis and Eco-Industrial Development: An Introduction. *Geography Compass*, *2*(4), 1138–1154. doi:10.1111/j.1749-8198.2008.00123.x

Grant, G. B., Seager, T. P., Massard, G., & Nies, L. (2010). Information and communication technology for industrial symbiosis. *Journal of Industrial Ecology*, *14*(5), 740–753. doi:10.1111/j.1530-9290.2010.00273.x

Harhoff, D., Henkel, J., & Von Hippel, E. (2003). Profiting from voluntary information spillovers: How users benefit by freely revealing their innovations. *Research Policy*, *32*(10), 1753–1769. doi:10.1016/S0048-7333(03)00061-1

Hawken, P. (1993). *The Ecology of Commerce*. New York: Harper Business.

Henkel, J. (2006). Selective revealing in open innovation processes: The case of embedded Linux. *Research Policy*, *35*(7), 953–969. doi:10.1016/j.respol.2006.04.010

Iacondini, A., Mencherini, U., Morselli, L., Passarini, F., & Vassura, I. (2014). Industrial symbiosis in Italy as a tool for sustainability: Case study analysis and replicability, *Procedia Environmental Science. Engineering and Management*, *1*, 19–24.

Ind, N., Iglesias, O., & Schultz, M. (2013). Building brands together. *California Management Review*, *55*(3), 5–26. doi:10.1525/cmr.2013.55.3.5

Kajikawa, Y. (2008). Research core and framework of sustainability science. *Sustainability Science, 3*(2), 215–239. doi:10.100711625-008-0053-1

Klingenberg, C. O., Viana Borges, M. A., & Valle Antunes Jr, J. A. (2019). Industry 4.0 as a data-driven paradigm: A systematic literature review on technologies. *Journal of Manufacturing Technology Management*, JMTM-09-2018-0325. doi:10.1108/JMTM-09-2018-0325

La Monica, M., Cutaia, L., & Franco, S. (2014). La simbiosi industriale come modello per lo sviluppo sostenibile dei sistemi economici territoriali. *Proceedings XXVI Convegno annuale di Sinergie —Manifattura: quale futuro?,* 151-164.

Leavy, B. (2014). Venkat Ramaswamy–how value co-creation with stakeholders is transformative for producers, consumers and society. *Strategy and Leadership, 42*(1), 9–16. doi:10.1108/SL-09-2013-0072

Leigh, M., & Li, X. (2015). Industrial ecology, industrial symbiosis and supply chain environmental sustainability: A case study of a large UK distributor. *Journal of Cleaner Production, 106*, 632–643. doi:10.1016/j.jclepro.2014.09.022

Li, G., Hou, Y., & Wu, A. (2017). Fourth Industrial Revolution: Technological drivers, impacts and coping methods. *Chinese Geographical Science, 27*(4), 626–637. doi:10.100711769-017-0890-x

Mehta, P. (2019). E-Waste, Chemical Toxicity, and Legislation in India. In Advanced Methodologies and Technologies in Engineering and Environmental Science. IGI Global.

Mirata, M., & Emtairah, T. (2005). Industrial symbiosis networks and the contribution to environmental innovation: The case of the Landskrona industrial symbiosis programme. *Journal of Cleaner Production, 13*(10-11), 993–1002. doi:10.1016/j.jclepro.2004.12.010

Moore, J. F. (2006). Business ecosystems and the view from the firm. *The Antitrust Bulletin, 51*(1), 31-75.

Mosconi, M. (2015). *The New European Industrial Policy*. London, UK: Routledge. doi:10.4324/9781315761756

Pan, M., Sikorski, J., Kastner, C. A., Akroyd, J., Mosbach, S., Lau, R., & Kraft, M. (2015). Applying Industry 4.0 to the Jurong Island Eco-Industrial Park. *Energy Procedia, 75*, 1536–1541. doi:10.1016/j.egypro.2015.07.313

Piccarozzi, M. (2017). Does Social Innovation Contribute to Sustainability? The Case of Italian Innovative Start-Ups. *Sustainability, 9*(12), 2376. doi:10.3390u9122376

Piccarozzi, M., Aquilani, B., & Gatti, C. (2018). Industry 4.0 in Management Studies: A Systematic Literature Review. *Sustainability, 10*(10), 3821. doi:10.3390u10103821

Piccarozzi, M., Silvestri, C., & Aquilani, B. (forthcoming). Achieving environmental sustainability: the role of Industry 4.0 in industrial symbiosis processes (work-in-progress). *Conference Proceedings Sinergie-Sima 2019.*

Prahalad, C. K., & Ramaswamy, V. (2003). The new frontier of experience innovation. *MIT Sloan Management Review, 44*, 4, 12–18.

Prahalad, C. K., & Ramaswamy, V. (2004). *The future of competition: Co-creating unique value with customers*. Boston, MA: Harvard Business School Publishing.

Prause, G. (2015). Sustainable Business Models and Structures for Industry 4.0. *Journal of Secure Sustainability*, *5*(2), 159–169. doi:10.9770/jssi.2015.5.2(3)

Prause, G., & Atari, S. (2017). On sustainable production networks for Industry 4.0. *Entreprise Sustainability*, *4*(4), 421–431. doi:10.9770/jesi.2017.4.4(2)

Raabe, B., Low, J. S. C., Juraschek, M., Herrmann, C., Tjandra, T. B., Ng, Y. T., & Tan, Y. S. (2017). Collaboration platform for enabling industrial symbiosis: Application of the by-product exchange network model. *Procedia CIRP*, *61*, 263–268. doi:10.1016/j.procir.2016.11.225

Ramaswamy, V., & Gouillart, F. (2010). Building the co-creative enterprise. *Harvard Business Review*, (October): 100–109.

Ramaswamy, V., & Ozcan, K. (2014). *The Co-creation Paradigm*. Stanford, CA: Stanford University Press.

Saarijärvi, H., Kannan, P. K., & Kuusela, H. (2013). Value co-creation: Theoretical approaches and practical implications. *European Business Review*, *25*(1), 1, 6–19. doi:10.1108/09555341311287718

Schoolman, E. D., Bush, J. S., & Bell, K. F. (2012). How interdisciplinary is sustainability research? Analyzing the structure of an emerging scientific field. *Sustainability Science*, *7*(1), 67–80. doi:10.100711625-011-0139-z

Siggelkow, N. (2007). Persuasion with case studies. *Academy of Management Journal*, *50*(1), 20–24. doi:10.5465/amj.2007.24160882

Sommer, L. (2015). Industrial revolution-industry 4.0: Are German manufacturing SMEs the first victims of this revolution? *Journal of Industrial Engineering and Management*, *8*(5), 1512–1532. doi:10.3926/jiem.1470

Stock, T., & Seliger, G. (2016). Opportunities of sustainable manufacturing in Industry 4.0. *Procedia Cirp*, *40*, 536–541. doi:10.1016/j.procir.2016.01.129

Taddeo, R., Simboli, A., Ioppolo, G., & Morgante, A. (2017). Industrial symbiosis, networking and innovation: The potential role of innovation poles. *Sustainability*, *9*(2), 169. doi:10.3390u9020169

The Natural Step. (2018). *Strategic Life Cycle Assessment (SLCA)*. Available at https://thenaturalstep.org/wp-content/uploads/2018/01/SLCA-matrix-structure.pdf

Thoben, K. D., Wiesner, S., & Wuest, T. (2017). "Industrie 4.0" and smart manufacturing-a review of research issues and application examples. *International Journal of Automotive Technology*, *11*(1), 4–16.

Tilson, D., Sørensen, C., & Lyytinen, K. (2012). Change and Control Paradoxes in Mobile Infrastructure Innovation: The Android and iOS Mobile Operating Systems Cases. *45th Hawaii International Conference on System Science (HICSS 45)*. 10.1109/HICSS.2012.149

Tiwana, A., Konsynsky, B., & Bush, A. A. (2010). Platform Evolution: Coevolution of Platform Architecture, Governance, and Environmental Dynamics. *Information Systems Research*, *21*(4), 675–687. doi:10.1287/isre.1100.0323

Tseng, M. L., Tan, R. R., Chiu, A. S., Chien, C. F., & Kuo, T. C. (2018). Circular economy meets industry 4.0: Can big data drive industrial symbiosis? *Resources, Conservation and Recycling, 131*, 146–147. doi:10.1016/j.resconrec.2017.12.028

Venkatraman, N. V., El Sawy, O. A., Pavlou, P. A., & Bharadwaj, A. (2014). Theorizing digital business innovation: platforms and capabilities in ecosystems. *Fox School of Business Research Paper,* (15-080).

Wang, S., Wan, J., Li, D., & Zhang, C. (2016). Implementing smart factory of industrie 4.0: An outlook. *International Journal of Distributed Sensor Networks, 12*(1), 3159805. doi:10.1155/2016/3159805

World Commission on Environment and Development (WCED). (1987). *Our Common Future.* New York, NY: Oxford University Press.

Yin, R. K. (2002). *Case study research: Design and methods.* Thousand Oaks, CA: SAGE Publications.

Yin, R. K. (2014). *Case study research: Design and methods.* SAGE Publication.

KEY TERMS AND DEFINITIONS

Big Data: Extremely large data sets that may be analyzed computationally to reveal patterns, trends, and associations, especially relating to human behavior and interactions.

Digital Platforms: They can be understood as technical elements based on a codebase, but also as an assemblage of hardware and software elements from one hand and *ad hoc* organizational routines and standards, from the other hand.

Engagement Platform: Is an offline (i.e., temporary shops) or online platform (i.e., open innovation platform) in which interactions among individuals happen. This is one of the pillars of the value co-creation approach.

Environmental Sustainability: Is the conscientious development of a society through the responsible use and hopefully reuse of natural resources, reducing any form of waste.

Industrial Symbiosis: Is a match among resources coming from different firms not necessarily pertaining to the same industry allowing to improve business processes.

Industry 4.0: Industry 4.0 aims at realizing an entirely digitized, connected, smart, and decentralized production system guided by a purposely formulated strategy.

Sustainability: Sustainability is the art of combining economic, environmental and social aspects meeting the needs of the present generation without compromising the future ones.

Value Co-Creation: Views the active role of individuals in creating benefits, economic and not, which are shared among them and by them appropriated simultaneously.

Chapter 4
Renewable Energy and Economic Growth:
An Overview of the Literature

Patrizio Morganti
University of Tuscia, Viterbo, Italy

Giuseppe Garofalo
University of Tuscia, Viterbo, Italy

ABSTRACT

The global commitment to drastically curb greenhouse gas emissions towards a sustainable development is strongly connected to the development and usage of renewable energy (RE), such as solar and wind. Between 2006 and 2016, world's total RE consumption, excluding hydro-electricity, increased by almost 350%, and RE investment grew from US $47 billion in 2004 to 279.8 billion in 2017. The importance of RE has attracted a lot of attention from the economic literature as well, since a growing body of empirical research is investigating the relationships between RE and economic growth. The general outcome is the existence of a positive bi-directional (direct and reverse) link between RE consumption and real GDP, though it also emerges evidence showing no statistically significant relationship. This Chapter provides i) an overview of the recent world's trends of RE production and investment, ii) an extensive and detailed review of the recent advances in the RE-growth empirical literature, highlighting the main methodologies adopted and the main findings emerged.

INTRODUCTION

The global commitment to drastically curb greenhouse gas emissions towards a sustainable development is strongly connected to the development and usage of renewable energy (RE). RE is sourced from natural processes and is either inexhaustible or can be replenished. Examples of renewable energy are solar photovoltaic (PV), wind, geothermal, hydropower, bio-energy, and ocean power. The share of renewables has increased significantly in the recent years. Between 2006 and 2016, world's total renewable energy

DOI: 10.4018/978-1-7998-1419-1.ch004

consumption, excluding hydro-electricity, increased by almost 350% (from 93 to 420 million tonnes of oil equivalent), and renewable energy investment grew from 47 US$ billion in 2004 to 279.8 billion in 2017 (BP 2017, FS 2018). The growth of renewables has been faster in the developing non-OECD countries compared with the OECD countries (REN21 2019 and FS 2018). Also, emerging countries are largely investing in renewables (IEA 2013). In 2018, global investment in RE was USD 288.9 billion, mostly in PV and wind. Developing and emerging economies accounted for 53% of total RE investment, with China alone accounting for 32% of the total. In 2018, China led in global investment in RE, followed by the U.S., Japan, India, and Australia (REN21 2019). In particular, China led in hydropower, solar PV, wind, and solar water heating, in terms of total capacity or generation.

The growing role of renewables has attracted a lot of attention from both academics and energy policy analysts. In particular, there exists a growing body of empirical research which examines the relationship between renewables and economic growth, with important implications for policy makers.

The aim of this Chapter is to is to provide an overview of i) the world's trends of RE production and investment since 2000, ii) the recent advances in the RE-growth literature by highlighting methodologies, main findings, and policy implications. The questions addressed by this paper are: i) Which is the current state of art of the literature in renewables and economic growth?, ii) Does exist a statistically significant relationship between RE and real GDP growth?, iii) What is the sign of this relationship?, iv) What are the effects across-countries and over-time?, v) What policy lessons can we learn?

It emerges that different outcomes can be obtained depending on i) the energy variables involved, ii) the existing causal relationship, iii) the econometric technique adopted, and iv) the countries included in the sample of the analysis. The causal relationship between RE and growth is indeed investigated according to different hypotheses, such as 1) the "growth" hypothesis, assuming the existence of a uni-directional link between RE consumption and economic growth (for instance, Fang 2011, Tiwari 2011, Bilgili and Ozturk 2015), 2) the "feedback" hypothesis, implying a bi-directional link between renewables and economic growth (Apergis and Payne 2010a, Apergis and Payne 2010b, Apergis and Payne 2011, Salim and Rafiq 2012, Bhattacharya et al 2016), 3) the "conservative" hypothesis, meaning that there exists a uni-directional link from economic growth to energy consumption (Sadorsky 2009, Tugcu et al. 2012, Al-Mulali et al. 2013, Cho et al. 2015, Inglesi-Lotz 2016), 4) the "neutrality" hypothesis, implying no effect among each other (Menegaki 2011, Al-Mulali et al 2013). From the perspective of policy makers, this literature overview offers important lessons for the implementation of future policies on promoting renewable energy in combination with macroeconomic policies aimed to a sustainable growth and development. Governments, energy planners, international cooperation agencies, utilities, and associated bodies must act together in implementing strategies for renewable deployment across countries. Therefore, it is crucial to have as much as reliable information regarding the direction of the potential link between RE and growth

The Chapter is organized as follows. Section 2 provides an overview of the recent global trends in renewable production and investment, while Section 3 reviews the main contributions which investigates the empirical link between renewable and economic growth. Section 4 concludes. A comprehensive description of variables and data sources is available at the end of the paper in Appendix A.

GLOBAL TRENDS

The rising importance of renewable energy at a global level is shown in Figure 1. World's total energy production from renewables slightly rose from 1130 million of toe in 1990 to 1306 million of toe in 2000 (15.6%), while it is during the 2000s that it emerges a remarkable upward tendency (see Panel A, Figure 1). Renewable production increased by 24.4% between 2000 and 2010 (from 1306 to 1626 million of toe) and by 18% between 2016 and 2010 (from 1626 to 1919 Mtoe). Electricity output from renewable sources of energy follows a kind of exponential trend (see Panel B, Figure 1). During the period 1990-2000 electricity output increased by 23.3% (from 2299312 GWh in 1990 to 2835801), while the most remarkable increase occurred during the 2000s as also emerged for renewable production: electricity output from renewables rose from 2835801 GWh in 2000 to 4199621 GWh in 2010 (48% increase), and to 5938892 GWh in 2016 (41.4% increase with respect to 2010).

Figure 2 shows the importance of renewable energy in the global electricity generation mix. The upper line shows The percentage of yearly net new generating capacity from renewable technologies (upper line - excluding hydro) has drastically increased over the years, from just under 20% in 2007, to 39% in 2013, to 57% 2016 and 61% in 2017. The middle line on Figure 1 shows the percentage of cumulative world generating capacity that is accounted for by renewables excluding large hydro. This has increased in almost a straight line, from 7.5% in 2007 to 13% in 2013 and 19% in 2017, as the gigawatts of new wind and solar plants added have grown and the net additions of fossil fuel power stations have decreased. The lower line on the chart shows that, in 2017, their share of total electricity produced grew to 12.1%, a record, up from 5.2% in 2007, 8.6% in 2013 and 11% in 2016.[1]

FS (2018) reports that renewables capacity, excluding large hydro, added 157GW last year, made up of 98GW of solar (almost all PV but with a few hundred MW of solar thermal), wind 52GW (mostly onshore but with about 5GW of offshore), biomass and waste-to-energy just over 3GW, small hydro just under 3GW and geothermal about 700MW (FS 2018). For fossil-fuel technologies, in 2017 a net 35GW of coal-fired generation were added, while the net addition of gas-fired plants was 38GW. The net addition of oil-fired capacity was minus 3GW (more capacity was switched to gas or closed, than opened). It is estimated that a net 19GW of large hydro dams were added, plus a net 11GW of nuclear. In terms of renewable power capacity per capita, the five top countries are Iceland, followed by Denmark, Germany and Sweden, and Finland. Rankings for different sources based on capacity per capita were: i) solar PV - Germany, Australia, Japan, Belgium, and Italy, ii) wind power - Denmark, Ireland, Germany, Sweden, and Portugal, iii) solar water heating - Barbados, Austria, Cyprus, Israel, and Greece. Several developing countries are investing equivalent or higher amounts in RE than developed countries on a

Figure 1. Renewables production and electricity output from renewables (1990-2016)

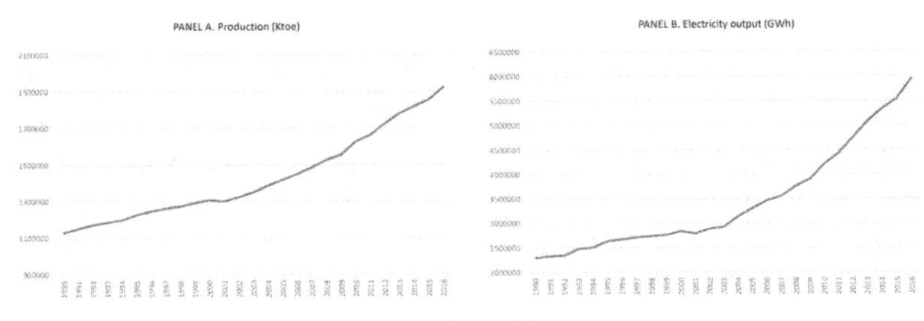

Figure 2. Renewable power generation and capacity as a share of global power (percentages, 2007-2017)

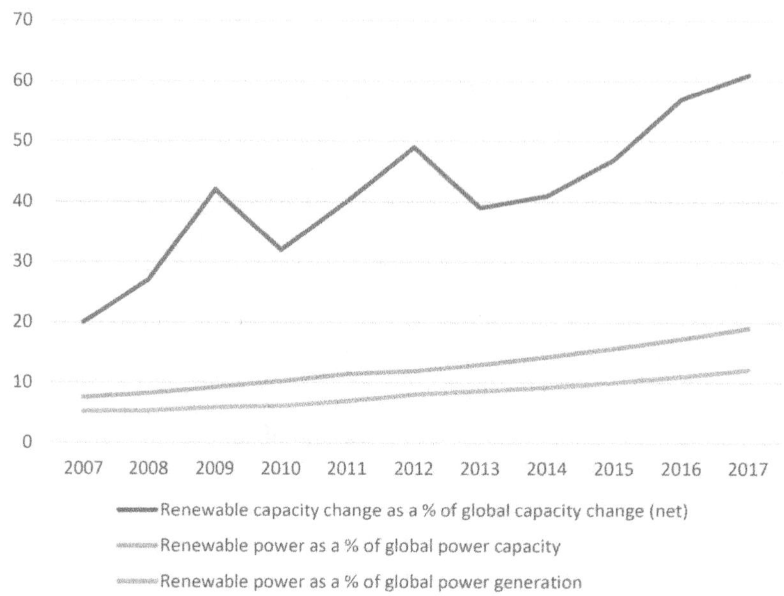

Source: our elaboration on data from FS (2018).

per gross domestic product (GDP) basis, particularly as energy demand continues to increase at a faster rate in developing markets, such as in Djibouti, Morocco and Palau (REN21 2019).

Figure 3 shows the estimated net addition of generating capacity in 2017 according to technology. It emerges the domination of solar energy, not just in the context of renewables but in terms of all generating sources. Solar's 98GW of installations outnumbered by far wind's 52GW and the net 70GW of all fossil fuel technologies. Solar was equivalent to 38% of all the net new power capacity added worldwide in 2017.[2]

FS (2018) provides a very detailed report on renewable energy investment. According to FS (2018), developing economies have confirmed their leadership over developed economies in 2017 in terms of investment in RE: excluding large hydro-electric projects (more than 50MW), emerging economies attracted $177.1 billion of new investment. Meanwhile, developed economies saw investment to $102.8 billion, their lowest level since 2006 (FS 2018). Figure 4 plots renewable investment by three categories of economies: developed, the "big three" developing countries, i.e. China, India and Brazil (those developing countries which recently showed the best performances in terms of renewable production, investment, and consumption), and other developing economies. RE investment in China, India and Brazil together hit $143.6 billion in 2017, their highest total ever and with an increase of 24% with respect to the level of 2016.

In 2017, investment of developed economies dropped by 19% (reached $102.8 billion). Much of this decline reflected the trend in Europe, where there were fewer big offshore wind financings in 2017 than in the previous two years, and both lower capital costs per MW and policy changes also had an impact.[3]

Figure 5 highlights the dominance of China in last year: $126.6 billion of renewable investment out of the global total of $279.8 billion (equivalent to a 45% share), followed by Europe (40.9%), and the U.S. (40.5%).[4]

Figure 3. Net power generating capacity added by type of technology (2017, gigawatts)

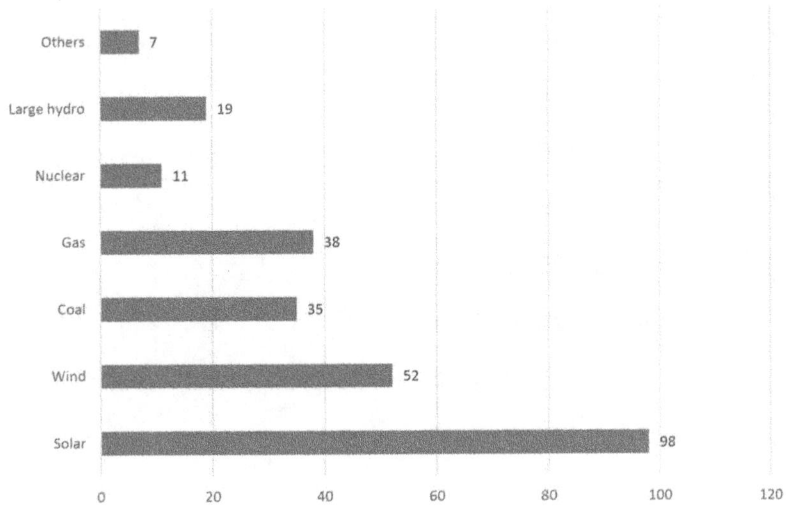

Source: our elaboration on data from FS (2018).

THE NEXUS BETWEEN RENEWABLE ENERGY AND ECONOMIC GROWTH

The energy and growth nexus can be analyzed from different perspectives according to i) the energy variables involved, ii) the existing causal relationship, iii) the econometric technique adopted, and iv) the countries included in the sample of the analysis (e.g. emerging or non-emerging economies). Following Tugcu et al. (2012), Al-Mulali et al. (2013), Battarchaya et al. (2016), and Inglesi-Lotz (2016) which provide a literature review of the renewables and economic growth nexus, Table 1 summarizes

Figure 4. Global new investment in renewable energy by type of economy (2004-2017, US$ billions)

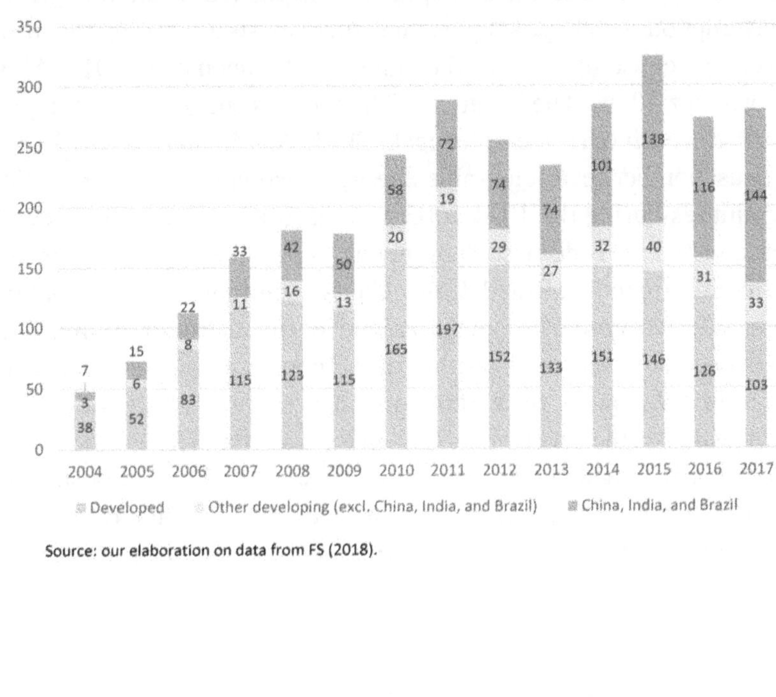

Source: our elaboration on data from FS (2018).

Figure 5. Global new investment in renewable energy by region (2017, US$ billions)

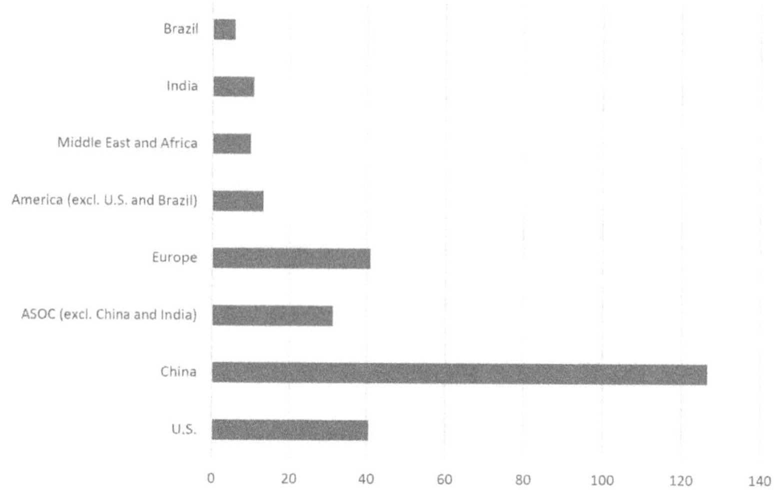

Source: our elaboration on data from FS (2018).

the methodology, time span, sample of countries included, and main findings, of the most relevant recent contributions in this strand of the literature.

Over the past decades, research has produced different findings but no unanimous consensus has emerged. According to Bhattacharya et al (2016), the nexus between energy consumption and economic growth can be investigated under four hypotheses. The "growth" hypothesis, which considers energy as an input of the growth process, shows the existence of a uni-directional link between energy consumption and economic growth (for instance, Fang 2011, Tiwari 2011, Bilgili and Ozturk 2015). The "feedback" hypothesis implies a bi-directional relationship between energy consumption and economic growth, suggesting that any change in energy consumption affects economic growth with a reverse effect (Apergis and Payne 2010a, Apergis and Payne 2010b, Apergis and Payne 2011, Salim and Rafiq 2012, Bhattacharya et al 2016). The "conservative" hypothesis means that economic growth is the dynamic which causes the consumption of energy sources, thus there exists a uni-directional causality link from economic growth to energy consumption (see Sadorsky 2009, Tugcu et al. 2012, Al-Mulali et al. 2013, Cho et al. 2015, Inglesi-Lotz 2016). The "neutrality" hypothesis suggests that energy consumption and growth are not related with each other (see Menegaki 2011, Al-Mulali et al 2013).

A bi-directional causation between renewable energy consumption and economic growth emerges, for a sample of 18 countries during the 1994-2003 period, from the study by Sadorsky (2009), which reports that an increase in real gross domestic product has a positive impact on per capita RE consumption. Included countries are Argentina, Brazil, Chile, China, Colombia, Czech Republic, Hungary, India, Indonesia, South Korea, Mexico, Peru, Philippines, Poland, Portugal, Russia, Thailand, Turkey. Supposing a linear relationship between the natural logarithm of RE consumption per capita and the logarithm of real gross domestic product per capita, the author computes long-run elasticities using panel cointegration techniques and investigates the short-run effects using a vector error correction (VEC) model. The author considers two empirical models. The first one investigates the relationship between renewable energy consumption and income for the full sample of 18 countries, while the second one investigates the relationship between renewable energy consumption, income and electricity prices for a subsample

Table 1. A summary of the recent empirical contributions in the renewable-growth nexus

Study	Methodology	Period	Country	Findings
Sadorsky (2009)	Panel, FMOLS	1994-2003	18 emerging countries	GDP > RE
Apergis and Payne (2010a)	Panel	1985-2005	20 OECD countries	GDP < > RE
Apergis and Payne (2010b)	Panel	1992-2007	13 Eurasian countries	GDP < > RE
Apergis and Payne (2011)	Panel	1980-2006	6 Central American countries	GDP < > RE
Menegaki (2011)	Panel, random effect	1997-2007	27 European countries	GDP and RE are neutral to each other
Fang (2011)	OLS	1978-2008	China	RE > GDP
Tiwari (2011)	Structural VAR	1960-2009	India	RE > GDP
Apergis and Payne (2012)	Panel	1990-2007	80 countries	GDP < > EC (RE, NRE)
Salim and Rafiq (2012)	Panel	1980-2006	6 major emerging countries	GDP < > RE in the short-run
Tugcu et al. (2012)	ARDL approach for cointegration; Hatemi J (2012) for causality test	1980-2009	G7 countries	The relationship is different for countries and varies with specification
Ai-mulali et al. (2013)	FMOLS	1980-2009	108 countries	79% feedback; 2% conservation; 19% neutrality
Ozturk and Bilgili (2015)	Dynamic panel analysis	1980-2009	51 Sub-Sahara African countries	Biomass has positive effect on GDP
Cho et al. (2015)	Panel vector error correction model	1990-2010	31 OECD and 49 non-OECD countries	GDP > RE for developed and GDP < > RE for less developed countries
Bilgili and Ozturk (2015)	Panel, DOLS	1980-2009	G7 countries	Biomass has positive effect on GDP
Battarchaya et al. (2016)	OLS, DOLS, FMOLS	1991-2012	38 countries	GDP < > RE, and also a neutral relationship for some countries
Inglesi-Lotz (2016)	Panel	1990-2010	OECD countries	GDP > RE

of 10 countries (Czech Republic, Hungary, India, Indonesia, Korea (South), Mexico, Poland, Portugal, Thailand, and Turkey), where the author includes an electricity price variable and the vector error correction model. Panel estimates show that an increase in per capita gross domestic product has a positive impact on per capita renewable energy consumption: in particular, a 1% increase in real GDP per capita increases the consumption of renewable energy per capita in emerging economies by nearly 3.4% in the long run. The long-run income elasticities found from this model are similar in sign, significance and magnitude to the ones found for the full sample. The fully modified ordinary least square (FMOLS) shows that the long-run price elasticity of demand is approximately -0.70. By comparison, the own price elasticity of electricity demand is low with long-term price elasticities ranging from -0.01 to -0.04 and electricity demand in emerging economies being the most sensitive to price changes. This suggests that renewable energy consumption is more responsive to price changes than electricity demand. This is good news in the case of falling electricity prices since a drop in electricity prices spurs renewable energy consumption more than electricity consumption. The results of this paper are important in showing that renewable energy income elasticities are much larger than electricity income elasticities. A 1% change in income has a much bigger effect on increasing renewable energy consumption than it does on increasing electricity consumption.

Apergis and Payne have provided several important contributions to the literature: the authors have basically analyzed the link between renewable energy consumption and economic growth for different macro-areas, in particular OECD countries, Eurasia, and Central America. Apergis and Payne (2010a) examine the relationship between renewable energy consumption and economic growth for a panel of 20 OECD countries between 1985 and 2005. The authors use a panel error correction (PEC) model in order to overcome the drawback related to the short time span. The countries included are Australia, Austria, Belgium, Canada, Denmark, France, Germany, Iceland, Italy, Japan, Luxembourg, Netherlands, New Zealand, Norway, Portugal, Spain, Sweden, Switzerland, United Kingdom, and the United States. Control variables are real gross domestic product in constant 2005 US dollars, real gross fixed capital formation in constant 2005 US dollars, and labor force. After performing panel unit root and cointegration tests, the authors compute panel fully modified ordinary least square long-run estimates and find that the short-run and long-run Granger-causality tests reveal positive bi-directional causality between renewable energy consumption and economic growth. Furthermore, renewable energy consumption indirectly affects economic growth through its positive impact on real gross fixed capital formation. This result highlights the importance of renewable energy in OECD countries. Likewise, economic growth shows a crucial role in providing the resources for the development and usage of renewable energy.

A similar study is carried out by the same authors for the Eurasia macro-area (Apergis and Payne 2010b). The authours investigate the causal relationship between renewable energy consumption and economic growth for 13 countries within Eurasia (Armenia, Azerbaijan, Belarus, Estonia, Georgia, Kazakhstan, Kyrgyzstan, Latvia, Moldova, Russia, Tajikistan, Ukraine, and Uzbekistan) over the period 1992-2007 using a multivariate panel data framework with fully modified ordinary least square long-run estimates.[5] Given the inclusion of Russia, the authors employs two panel data sets: with and without Russia. The results show the existence of a long-run equilibrium relationship between real GDP, RE consumption, real gross fixed capital formation, and the labor force. The long-run elasticity estimates for renewable energy consumption with respect to real gross domestic product are larger for the panel data set which includes Russia than the panel set data set that does not (the majority of energy consumption from renewable energy sources in Eurasia comes from Russia). The results from the PEC models support the feedback hypothesis given that both short-run and long-run bi-directional causality exists between RE consumption and economic growth.

Apergis and Payne (2011) study the relationship between RE consumption and economic growth for a panel of six Central American countries (Costa Rica, El Salvador, Guatemala, Honduras, Nicaragua, and Panama) over the period 1980-2006, using a multivariate framework, similar to the authors' previous works, which includes real GDP in constant 2000 US dollars, real gross fixed capital formation in constant 2000 US dollars, labor force in millions, and RE consumption defined as total renewable electricity net consumption in millions of kilowatt hours. The authors' interest to Central America is motivated by the recent gradual transition from agricultural exports towards the manufacturing and tourism sectors of many countries belonging to this macro-area which, in turn, has arisen several concerns related i) the high volatility of oil prices, ii) the high dependency on foreign energy sources, iii) the severe environmental consequences of carbon emissions. renewable energy sources are thus needed to diversify the region's energy consumption. The results show the presence of both short-run and long-run bi-directional causality links between renewable energy consumption and economic growth; in particular a 1% increase in renewable energy consumption increases real gross domestic product by 0.244% in the long run.

Menegaki (2011) conducts an empirical study on the causal relationship between economic growth and RE for 27 European countries in a multivariate panel framework using a random effect model. The author uses annual data ranging from 1997 to 2007 obtained from Eurostat. The multivariate framework encompasses real GDP per capita in purchasing power parity (PPP) terms, the percentage of RE sources in gross inland energy consumption, final energy consumption in 1000 toe, greenhouse emissions in CO2 equivalents with base year 1990, and employment rate calculated as number of people with ages between 15 and 64 years divided by the corresponding population size. While in fixed models the interest lays in the individual means across the levels of the fixed factor, in random effect models the interest lays in the variance of means across the levels of a random factor. The random effect model employed reveals the long-run relationship between gross domestic product, RE consumption, CO2 emissions and employment: in particular, a 1% increase of greenhouse gas emissions has a larger positive effect on GDP as compared to an increase in RE sources and this can be motivated by the high cost faced in RE investments which makes them a less competitive GDP growth driver than the greenhouse gas emissions. According to the panel error correction model, it emerges neither short- nor long-run Granger causality from RE consumption to economic growth, thus providing some evidence for the "neutrality" hypothesis. This implies that RE consumption has a minor role in affecting gross domestic product (in PPP terms) in Europe. Such a neutral relationship between gross domestic product and renewable energy consumption may be due to the early stages of development and market penetration of renewable energy.

A specific focus on the Chinese experience is provided by Fang (2011), who analyzes the impact of both the amount and the share of RE consumption on economic welfare, using a Coob-Douglas production function in multivariate ordinary least square (OLS) from 1978 to 2008. The author uses gross domestic product and other indicators which reflect economic welfare, such as gross domestic product per capita, per capita annual income of rural households, and per capita annual income of urban households, as dependent variables, while the amount and share of RE consumption are treated as independent variables. Other control variables are gross capital formation, total number of employees, and research and development expenditure. According to the author's findings, China shows high correlation between economic variables and RE consumption, though increases in per capita annual income of rural and urban households are not closely related with the share of RE consumption increases due to policies and institutional factors. In particular, a 1% increase in RE consumption increases, respectively, real GDP by 0.120%, GDP per capita by 0.162%, per capita annual income of rural households by 0.444%, and per capita annual income of urban households by 0.368% respectively.

Another case-study analysis is provided by Tiwari (2011) who investigates the dynamics of RE consumption, economic growth, and CO2 emissions for India, using a structural VAR (SVAR) approach. It emerges that a positive shock on renewable energy consumption increases gross domestic product and decreases CO2 emissions, and that a positive shock on gross domestic product have a very high positive impact on the CO2 emissions.

Apergis and Payne (2012) perform another econometric exercise this time aimed to examine the relationship between renewable and non-RE consumption and economic growth for 80 countries within the same multivariate panel framework as that used in their previous contributions. The time span ranges between 1990 and 2007 and the included countries are (Algeria, Argentina, Australia, Austria,

Bangladesh, Belgium, Bolivia, Brazil, Bulgaria, Canada, Cameron, Chile, China, Comoros, Costa Rica, Denmark, Dominican Republic, Ecuador, Egypt, El Salvador, Ethiopia, Finland, France, Gabon, Germany, Ghana, Greece, Guatemala, Guinea, Honduras, Hungary, Iceland, India, Indonesia, Iran, Ireland, Italy, Japan, Jordan, Kenya, Korea, Luxembourg, Madagascar, Malawi, Malaysia, Mali, Mauritius, Mexico, Morocco, Mozambique, Netherlands, New Zealand, Nicaragua, Norway, Pakistan, Panama, Paraguay, Peru, Philippines, Poland, Portugal, Romania, Senegal, South Africa, Spain, Sri Lanka, Sudan, Swaziland, Sweden, Switzerland, Syria, Thailand, Tunisia, Turkey, Uganda, United Kingdom, United States, Uruguay, Venezuela, Zambia). The authors regress real GDP in billions of constant 2000 U.S. dollars on renewable electricity consumption (defined in million of kilowatt hours), total non-renewable electricity consumption (defined in million of kilowatt hours), real gross fixed capital formation in billions of constant 2000 U.S. dollars, and total labor force in millions. The authors this time control for the simultaneous use of renewable and non-renewable energy (NRE) consumption in order to distinguish their relative impact to economic growth. The estimates of the panel error correction model show the existence of a bi-directional causality between renewable and NRE energy consumption and economic growth in both the short- and long-run. Also, there is bi-directional short-run causality between renewable and NRE consumption which may suggest a kind of substitutability between the two sources of energy.

Salim and Rafiq (2012) analyzes the determinants of renewable energy consumption in a panel of six major emerging economies whose adoption of RE is increasing at a very fast pace, i.e. Brazil, China, India, Indonesia, Philippines and Turkey. The authors compute estimates through fully modified ordinary least square, dynamic ordinary least square (DOLS), and Granger causality methods. The RE variable used in this study is a composite variable reflecting RE from several different sources (i.e. biomass, solar, wind and hydroelectricity) for which no reliable price measure is available. In the long run, it emerges that renewable energy consumption is significantly determined by income and pollutant emission in Brazil, China, India and Indonesia, while mainly by income in Philippines and Turkey. Causal link between i) renewable energy and income, and ii) renewable energy and pollutant emission, emerge to be bi-directional in the short-run, showing the appropriateness of the efforts by emerging countries in reducing carbon emissions through the adoption of energy efficiency policies aimed to drastically increase the share of renewable in the overall energy mix.

G7 countries are object of study from Tugcu et al. (2012). Their goal is to investigate the long-run relationships between RE and NRE consumption on the one side, and economic growth on the other side, using classical and augmented production functions, during 1980-2009. G7 economies are among the major i) energy consumers of World's total energy production, and ii) pollutant in terms of World's total CO2 emissions (Tugcu et al. 2012). The multivariate framework adopted by the authors includes real GDP in constant 2005 US dollars, real gross fixed capital formation in constant 2005 US dollars, labor force in millions, total number of the full and part time students enrolled in public and private tertiary education, the number of patent applications, RE consumption in millions of kilowatt hours as net geothermal, solar, wind and biomass energy, and non-renewable energy consumption is the total of energy consumption related to coal, natural gas, and petroleum. The analysis leads to different outcomes depending on the type of causal relationship investigated: i) between non-renewable energy consumption and economic growth (estimated from augmented production function), it emerges a short-run significant evidence for the "growth" hypothesis only for Japan, while for other countries, findings provide the absence of causality, ii) there is no causal relationship between RE consumption and economic growth (estimated from augmented production function) in France, Italy, Canada and the United States, while the "feedback" hypothesis is present for England and Japan, iii) between RE and NRE consumption and economic growth (estimated from classical production function), the "feedback" hypothesis is supported for all countries.

Al-Mulali et al. (2013) focus their study on the analysis of the bi-directional long-run relationship between renewable energy consumption and the growth rate of gross domestic product during the period 1980-2009, by grouping the full sample of countries (108) into different income categories, i.e. upper-middle income, lower-middle income, and high-income countries. The authors adopt the fully modified ordinary least square approach, and use electricity consumption from renewable sources (measured in kilowatt-hour) to approximate renewable energy consumption. The results support the "feedback" hypothesis for the 79% of the countries, the "neutrality" hypothesis for the 19% of the countries, the "conservative" hypothesis for the 2% of the countries. It also emerges that the higher the income of countries the more persistent and significant is the bi-directional long-run link.

Ozturk and Bilgili (2015) investigate the long-run impact of biomass consumption on the growth rate of real gross domestic product for 51 Sub-Sahara African countries during the 1980-2009 period. Panel cointegration, conventional ordinary least square, and dynamic ordinary least square analyses are conducted considering both homogeneous and heterogeneous variance structures. The authors regress real GDP on population, openness and biomass energy consumption. The results show a significant and substantive influence of biomass energy consumption on economic growth. According to homogeneous variance structure, a 1% increase in biomass consumption increases GDP by 1.818%. However, when considering heterogeneous variance structure, a 1% increase in biomass produces a smaller increase in gross domestic product (0.820%). Thus, energy conservation policies aimed at reducing energy consumption seem to produce negative effects on the economic growth of Sub-Sahara African countries.

The analysis of the renewable-growth nexus according to different country's classification by income has been also investigated by Cho et al. (2015) which compare the long-run causal relationship between renewable energy consumption and economic growth of developed countries with that of less-developed countries. Their analysis is carried out over the 1990-2010 period for 31 OECD countries (developed countries) and 49 non-OECD countries (less-developed countries) in the multivariate panel vector error correction model. The results support the conservation hypothesis for OECD countries, and the "feedback" hypothesis for non-OECD countries, implying that RE is not as much important for the economic growth of developed countries as it is for less-developed countries.

Bilgili and Ozturk (2015) provide another study related to the investigation of the long run link between biomass energy consumption and the growth rate of real gross domestic product growth, again considering homogeneous and heterogeneous variance structures, but this time for G7 countries. The time coverage is 1980-2009. Their econometric methodology is basically the same as in Ozturk and Bilgili (2015), i.e. panel cointegration, conventional OLS, and dynamic OLS analyses. The findings show that the long run elasticities of panel real GDP data are significant and positive, thus confirming the "growth" hypothesis in which biomass energy consumption positively affects the economic growth of G7 countries.

Bhattacharya et al (2016) analyzes the long-run link between economic growth on the one side, and traditional and energy-related inputs on the other side, for a sample of 38 top RE consuming countries from 1991 to 2012.[6] The authors consider a simple production function with renewable and non-renewable sources of energy included in the production process along with traditional inputs. Two energy sources are used in the production function, being renewable energy consumption, and non-renewable energy consumption. They use energy consumption as electricity consumption generated from various RE sources and measured in billion kilowatt hours. On the other hand, non-renewable energy sources include coal and coal products, oil, and natural gas. In their study, the non-renewable energy consumption is used as the aggregate of these four energy sources. The authors normalize the data series and transform the data for all these four fuel sources into a common unit, and they use a balanced panel of 38 countries. They regress real GDP in constant 2005 US dollar on renewable energy consumption, NRE consumption, real gross fixed capital formation in constant 2005 US dollar, and total labor force. The countries included in the analysis are Australia, Austria, Belgium, Brazil, Bulgaria, Canada, Chile, China, the Czech Republic, Denmark, Finland, France, Germany, Greece, India, Ireland, Israel, Italy, Japan, Kenya, Republic of Korea, Mexico, Morocco, the Netherlands, Norway, Peru, Poland, Portugal, Romania, Slovenia, South Africa, Spain, Sweden, Thailand, Turkey, Ukraine, the United Kingdom, and the United States. The authors estimate ordinary least square, dynamic ordinary least square, and fully modified ordinary least square models. The three approaches produce very similar results for each variable in terms of sign and significance, however in terms of magnitude they vary slightly. In general, RE consumption has a long-run significant positive impact on economic growth. For the empirical interpretation, the authors only consider dynamic ordinary least square and fully modified ordinary least square, since these two approaches account for serial correlation and endogeneity that may exist in the model. According to DOLS estimates, a 1% increase in RE consumption increases output by 0.101%, while a 1% increase in NRE consumption increases growth by 0.280%. According to FMOLS estimates, a 1% increase in renewable energy consumption produces a positive impact on growth by 0.109%, while a 1% increase in NRE consumption produces a positive impact on growth by 0.277%. According to these findings, the authors argue that non-renewable energy consumption plays a bigger role in economic output, therefore policy advisers need to promote the generation and use of renewable energy to ensure sustainable economic development in future. The authors also examined the time-series analysis of long-run output elasticities for each individual country, allowing to understand the impact of renewable energy consumption on output across the sample countries. The authors established that i) RE is an important driver for the economic growth of Austria, Bulgaria, Canada, Chile, China, the Czech Republic, Denmark, Finland, France, Germany, Greece, Italy, Kenya, Republic of Korea, Morocco, the Netherlands, Norway, Peru, Poland, Portugal, Romania, Spain and the United Kingdom (in most of these countries, significant shift towards renewables has occurred during the time span of the analysis[7]), ii) RE has a negative effect on economic growth for five countries, i.e.India, Ukraine, the United States, and Israel, iii) there is no significant relationship between RE and economic growth for the remaining countries, i.e. Australia, Belgium, Brazil, Ireland, Japan, Mexico, Slovenia, South Africa, Sweden, Thailand and Turkey, suggesting as a possible explanation for this result that these countries had not been able to make use of RE sources effectively in the production process, and it therefore has almost no impact on the economic output. Therefore, policy advisers of these countries should focus on investing renewable energy effectively so the increase in demand for energy consumption from various economic activities can make use of RE sources. The authors conclude that the effects of renewable deployment are different across countries due to many factors, and their findings support the heterogeneity across countries in their stages of deployment process and the role of RE in influencing the economic growth process.

Inglesi-Lotz (2016) considers a panel dataset including all the OECD countries for the period from 1990 to 2010. The author shows that renewable energy consumption, or its share to the total energy mix, is positively, and statistically significant, related to economic growth. The theoretical basis of the work is a general Cobb-Douglas production function a salso used by Fang (2011) in his effort to evaluate the influence of renewable energy consumption to the Chinese economy. The energy variables employed are total renewable energy consumption and the share of RE consumption to the energy mix. The author regresses GDP and GDP per capita on RE variables and on a set of control variables such as gross fixed capital formation, number of employees, and amount of R&D expenditure. The authors estimate four different models in order to ensure the robustness of the results (see Inglesi-Lotz (2016) for more details). It emerges that a long-run equilibrium relationship between real GDP or real GDP per capita, total RE consumption or share of total RE consumption, real gross fixed capital formation, employment and the R&D expenditures of the countries. The estimations show that a 1% increase in renewable energy consumption increases GDP by 0.105% and GDP per capita by 0.100%, while a 1% increase of the share of RE to the energy mix of the countries increases gross domestic product by 0.089% and GDP per capita by 0.090%. These findings support the advantages of government policies of OECD countries promoting the use of RE by establishing RE markets, RE portfolio standards not only to improve the environmental conditions but also from a macroeconomic point of view. The study promotes the idea that policies in favor of renewable energies will at least not harm the economic welfare of the countries. The results also suggest that policy makers should not only focus on the rise of RE consumption but also on its position and contribution to the overall energy mix.

CONCLUSION

In recent years, dependence on the non-renewable energy sources has declined due to increasing awareness about environmental concern and focus of energy generation through renewable energy sources. This has increased renewable generation of energy in both developed and developing countries in recent years, either due to national and international regulatory measures imposed by governments and environmental body, or to the growing awareness of the consequences of environmental degradation on humankind.

The literature overview provided by this Chapter shows that the investigation of the relationship between RE and economic growth leads to different outcomes, such as 1) a uni-directional link exists from energy consumption to economic growth (the "growth" hypothesis, Fang 2011, Tiwari 2011, Bilgili and Ozturk 2015), 2) a bi-directional link between energy and economic growth (the "feedback" hypothesis, Apergis and Payne 2010a, Apergis and Payne 2010b, Apergis and Payne 2011, Salim and Rafiq 2012, Bhattacharya et al 2016), 3) a uni-directional link from economic growth to energy consumption (the "conservative" hypothesis, Sadorsky 2009, Tugcu et al. 2012, Al-Mulali et al. 2013, Cho et al. 2015, Inglesi-Lotz 2016), 4) no effect among each other (the "neutrality" hypothesis, Menegaki 2011, Al-Mulali et al 2013). In addition, the current state of art of the literature can offer important lessons for the implementation of future policies aimed to promote renewable energy in combination with sustainable growth and development. Governments, energy planners, international cooperation agencies, utilities, and associated bodies must act together in implementing strategies for renewable deployment across countries. Designing effective energy policies requires a good understanding of the relationship between income and renewable energy consumption. In particular, it is very important to have as much as reliable information regarding the direction of the potential link between renewable and growth (the so-called "growth", "feedback", "conservative", and "neutral" hypotheses): for instance, small changes in real per capital income may have an higher impact on per capita renewable energy consumption or vice versa. It also emerges that across countries and over time, renewable energy consumption per capita in emerging economies is expected to grow faster than real per capita income as economic development takes place. Renewable energy infrastructures should be improved since they emerge to be the appropriate options for developed countries since renewable consumption increases economic growth. In other words, advanced economies should invest more on renewable energy sources to reduce greenhouse gas emissions, promote sustainable growth, improve energy security, and reducing energy dependency. Policy makers should encourage a multilateral effort to promote renewable energy and energy efficiency across countries, and should introduce appropriate incentive mechanisms for the development and market accessibility of renewable energy, such as green or white certificates, renewable production tax credits, rebates for the installation of renewable energy systems, renewable energy portfolio standards. Improving energy efficiency can contribute to meet several goals such as energy security, economic efficiency, technological development, business competitiveness, job creation and consumers' welfare. The expansion of renewable energy could also curb the dependence on foreign energy sources for many countries, leading to a decrease in the volatility of oil and natural gas prices on international markets, and reducing the degree of long-run environmental degradation related to carbon emissions. In addition, the cooperation among stakeholders, both in the public and the private sector, is needed, paying particular attention to spread and share information across countries with respect to on-going projects, technologies, financing and investment strategies.

The trade-off between regulation and discretion is, therefore, very crucial. When formulating policy interventions, regulators should provide more transparent information about industrial processes and technologies adopted, internalize externalities associated with energy use (thus address market failures such as information asymmetries, credit constraints, or organizational inefficiencies), and foster economic growth and social welfare towards a sustainable development.

REFERENCES

Al-Mulali, U., Fereidouni, H. G., Lee, J. Y., & Sab, C. N. B. C. (2013). Examining the bi-directional long run relationship between renewable energy consumption and GDP growth. *Renewable & Sustainable Energy Reviews*, *22*, 209–222. doi:10.1016/j.rser.2013.02.005

Apergis, N., & Payne, J. E. (2010a). Renewable energy consumption and economic growth: Evidence from a panel of OECD countries. *Energy Policy*, *38*(1), 656–660. doi:10.1016/j.enpol.2009.09.002

Apergis, N., & Payne, J. E. (2010b). Renewable energy consumption and growth in Eurasia. *Energy Economics*, *32*(6), 1392–1397. doi:10.1016/j.eneco.2010.06.001

Apergis, N., & Payne, J. E. (2011). The renewable energy consumption-growth nexus in Central America. *Applied Energy*, *88*(1), 343–347. doi:10.1016/j.apenergy.2010.07.013

Apergis, N., & Payne, J. E. (2012). Renewable and non-renewable energy consumption-growth nexus: Evidence from a panel error correction model. *Energy Economics*, *34*(3), 733–738. doi:10.1016/j.eneco.2011.04.007

Bilgili, F., & Ozturk, I. (2015). Biomass energy and economic growth nexus in G7 countries: Evidence from dynamic panel data. *Renewable & Sustainable Energy Reviews*, *49*, 132–138. doi:10.1016/j.rser.2015.04.098

British Petroleum (BP). (2017). Statistical Review of World Energy, June.

Cho, S., Heo, E., & Kim, J. (2015). Causal relationship between renewable energy consumption and economic growth: Comparison between developed and less-developed countries. *Geosystem Engineering, 18*(6), 284–291. doi:10.1080/12269328.2015.1053540

Fang, Y. (2011). Economic welfare impacts from renewable energy consumption: The China experience. *Renewable & Sustainable Energy Reviews, 15*(9), 5120–5128. doi:10.1016/j.rser.2011.07.044

Frankfurt School of Finance and Management (FS). (2018). *Global trends in renewable energy investment 2018*. Frankfurt School-UNEP Centre/BNEF.

International Energy Agency (IEA). (2013). Renewable energy: Medium-term market report, OECD/IEA, Paris.

Menegaki, A. N. (2011). Growth and renewable energy in Europe: A random effect model with evidence for neutrality hypothesis. *Energy Economics, 33*(2), 257–263. doi:10.1016/j.eneco.2010.10.004

Ozturk, I., & Bilgili, F. (2015). Economic growth and biomass consumption nexus: Dynamic panel analysis for Sub-Sahara African countries. *Applied Energy, 137*, 110–116. doi:10.1016/j.apenergy.2014.10.017

Renewable Energy Policy Network for the 21st Century (REN21). (2019). Renewables 2019 Global Status Report. Paris, REN21 Secretariat.

Sadorsky, P. (2009). Renewable energy consumption and income in emerging economies. *Energy Policy, 37*(10), 4021–4028. doi:10.1016/j.enpol.2009.05.003

Salim, R. A., & Rafiq, S. (2012). Why do some emerging economies proactively accelerate the adoption of renewable energy? *Energy Economics, 34*(4), 1051–1057. doi:10.1016/j.eneco.2011.08.015

Tiwari, A. K. (2011). A structural VAR analysis of renewable energy consumption, real GDP and CO2 emissions: Evidence from India. *Economic Bulletin, 31*(2), 1793–1806.

Tugcu, C. T., Ozturk, I., & Aslan, A. (2012). Renewable and non-renewable energy consumption and economic growth relationship revisited: Evidence from G7 countries. *Energy Economics, 34*(6), 1942–1950. doi:10.1016/j.eneco.2012.08.021

KEY TERMS AND DEFINITIONS

Economic Growth: Real GDP per capita growth rates, usually measured at constant prices with respect to a base year.

Kilowatt-Hour: The kilowatt hour (kWh) is a unit of energy commonly used as a billing unit for energy delivered to consumers by electric utilities. If energy is transmitted or used at a constant rate (power) over a period of time, the total energy in kilowatt hours is equal to the power in kilowatts multiplied by the time in hours.

Ktoe: 1000 toe.

Renewable Energy: Energy that is collected from renewable resources, which are naturally replenished on a human timescale, such as hydro, geothermal, solar, wind and tide/wave/ocean energy, as well as from biofuels and renewable waste. Renewable energy often provides energy in four important areas: electricity generation, air and water heating/cooling, transportation, and rural (off-grid) energy services.

Renewable Energy Consumption: The sum of the energy consumption from renewable sources in the end-use sectors. Energy used for transformation processes and for own use of the energy producing industries is excluded. Final consumption reflects for the most part deliveries to consumers.

Renewable Energy Production: Production of primary energy from renewable sources, i.e. hydro, geothermal, solar, wind and tide/wave/ocean energy, as well as from biofuels and renewable waste.

Renewable Investment: Investment in technologies aimed to generate primary energy from renewable sources.

Tonne of Oil Equivalent (TOE): A unit of energy defined as the amount of energy released by burning one tonne of crude oil. It is approximately 42 gigajoules or 11,630 kilowatt hours, although as different crude oils have different calorific values, the exact value is defined by convention; several slightly different definitions exist. The toe is sometimes used for large amounts of energy. Multiples of the toe are used, in particular the megatoe (Mtoe, one million toe) and the gigatoe (Gtoe, one billion toe).

ENDNOTES

1 FS (2018).

2 Ibidem.

3 Ibidem.

4 Ibidem.

5 Eurasia's countries have an high dependency on fossil fuel.

6 The 38 countries have been selected by the authors according to the 'Renewable Energy Country Attractiveness Index' (RECAI) prepared by the Ernst & Young (Bhattacharya et al (2016).

7 See Battarchaya et al. (2016).

Chapter 5
Innovative Business Models in Digital Firms:
The Challenge of Sustainability

Patrizia Accordino
University of Messina, Italy

Tindara Abbate
University of Messina, Italy

Daniela Rupo
University of Messina, Italy

Raffaella Coppolino
https://orcid.org/0000-0002-7312-0922
Department of Economics, University of Messina, Italy

Elvira Tiziana La Rocca
University of Messina, Italy

ABSTRACT

The 17 Sustainable Development Goals (SDGs) of the United Nations 2030 Agenda for Sustainable Development intends to improve efforts of governments, societies, and companies to deal with major social and environmental problems affecting contemporary societies. From a business perspective, companies can find a propulsive boost of innovation looking at different models of production and use of services/products. This new perspective is radically changing the ways companies and consumers interact, and the role of companies in supporting the achievement of SDGs through service innovation is becoming pervasive. In addition, the emerging digital economy represents a great opportunity opening up to sustainability-oriented service innovation and firms are developing their competitive advantage based on the introduction of new digital business models. This chapter explores this issue through an explorative case study based on the MyTaxi business model. Implications for managers and researchers and opportunities for future research are highlighted.

DOI: 10.4018/978-1-7998-1419-1.ch005

INTRODUCTION

Over recent decades, the expansion of Internet and related digital technologies has strongly revolutionized the directions for the value creation of organizations and, in general, of the whole ecosystem (Moore, 1993), determining various business opportunities (Amit and Zott, 2001) and inevitable threats related to the volatility and unpredictable nature of technology (Trimi and Berbegal-Mirabent, 2012). Indeed, digital technologies have the potential of generating incredible new wealth, commonly through entrepreneurial start-ups and corporate ventures (Amit and Zott, 2001). However, the digital revolution has mainly imposed the definition of new business models to create, deliver and capture value (Zott et al., 2011) by addressing customer needs, providing new products and solutions to innovation problems and transforming the rules of competition for established businesses and new ventures in unusual ways (Osterwalder et al., 2005; Teece, 2010; Zott et al., 2011; Massa et al., 2016; Foss and Saebi, 2018). This vortex has involved a large set of industries and contexts in its continuous movement toward a "digital center" in which business models are strongly digitized (Bradley et al., 2015). On the other hand, the development of ways dedicated to value creation, delivery and appropriation has provided potential spaces for the definition and implementation of unconventional exchange mechanisms and transaction architectures (Amit and Zott, 2001) and, consequently, increased the opportunities of designing new boundary-spanning organizational forms (Zott et al., 2011). Specifically, these developments have revealed different horizons for the design and experimentation of e-business models (Osterwalder and Pigneur, 2003) by fostering firms to fundamentally change the way they organize and participate in economic exchanges, both within and across firm and industry boundaries in the context of highly interconnected electronic markets (de Reuver et al., 2007).

Although management literature is increasingly focused on e-business models, it is necessary to underline that contributions show various approaches to the business logic of firms characterized by ICT-driven innovations but less importance is dedicated to how innovations in the business models may contribute to create economic, environmental and social value (Evans et al., 2017). Notably, business model innovation is increasingly considered as "a potential mechanism to integrate sustainability into the business" (Evans et al., 2017, p. 597), suggesting that business models must be transformed, incorporating social and environmental priorities for sustainability (Carayannis et al., 2014, pp. 122-123). Indeed, new business models may help to develop integrative and competitive solutions by either radically reducing negative and/or creating positive external effects for the environment and society as a whole (Presenza et al., 2019).

With this in mind, the chapter intends to analyze the e-business model of a digital firm operating in the travel industry, where facing the challenge of sustainability is fundamental. The aim is to identify distinctive elements related to sustainability of the application of innovative digital technologies without neglecting recent developments linked to legal factors like the rules on fair competition and taxation.

The research question is: to *what extent do e-business models support sustainable innovations in a real context*?

To achieve the research objective, the study performs an explorative qualitative analysis based on a single case study, represented by MyTaxi, an innovative digital firm operating in the Italian travel industry.

There are several reasons for this choice. Firstly, the travel and tourism industry is facing the pressure of digital transformation. According to UNTWO, in 2018 it campaigned for tourism and digital transformation and propelled the industry into realizing the potential of digitization in destination management and marketing. Additionally, a growing number of companies is embracing sustainability and integrating sustainable innovation into their entire business model, by observing it as a future business opportunity for innovating and building a competitive advantage. On the other hand, travel industry data can be considered among the first product/service categories sold online, thus making most online customers feel at ease when purchasing tickets online (Shankar et al., 2003).

Secondly, the experience of MyTaxi is emblematic in terms of the definition and implementation of a new business model focused on innovation, by using digital platforms that strongly change the relationship between firms and customers and firms and the environment. On the other hand, the way in which MyTaxi is evolving shows incremental attention to sustainability issues in the logic of creating, delivery and capturing value.

This research provides various contributions to the literature focused on the innovation of business models stimulated by the use of digital technologies and platforms that enhance the interactions among different actors for efficacious pathways to value co-creation (Aquilani, 2016). It increases the comprehension of how businesses operating in the travel and tourism industry can innovate their business models to promote sustainable goals. Moreover, there are further insights into the literature on digital firms, by presenting the main characteristics of their business model configurations.

The chapter is organized as follows. Section 2 includes a concise overview of e-business model literature with particular attention to the sustainability of these models, followed by the analysis of the principal components used in this study. Section 3 describes some methodological aspects concerning research setting, selected case study, research design and data collection. Section 4 contains the results and discussions of this study. Theoretical and managerial implications, limitations and further research options are developed in Section 5.

LITERATURE BACKGROUND

Business Model

A business model shows how firms earn money by addressing two fundamental issues: how they identify and create value for customers and how they capture some of this value as their profit in the process (Casadesus-Masanell and Ricart, 2010; Teece, 2010; George and Bock, 2011; Zott et al., 2011; Foss and Saebi, 2017). It describes the logic of firms, the way they operate and how they create value for their stakeholders (MacMillan et al., 2008). Creating and capturing value reflect two relevant functions that all organizations must perform to survive over an extended period of time. Firstly, successful organizations "create substantial value by doing things in ways that differentiate them from the competition" (Shafer et al., 2005) and develop core competencies, capabilities, and positional advantages that are different from their competitors. Secondly, organizations must earn money to survive; therefore, "their viability is tied both to the value they create and to the way they capture the value and resultantly generate profit" (Shafer et al., 2005). However, value creation and capture occur within a value network, which can consider partners, distribution channels, suppliers and coalitions that extend the company's resources (Hamel, 2002). The role a firm plays within its value network is an important element of its business model.

In the context of Information Technology (IT), the term e-business model means "doing business electronically" (Zott et al., 2011), by encompassing e-markets, e-commerce and Internet-based business (Afuah and Tucci, 2001) and referring to firms that conduct transactions with their business partners and buyers through the Internet. In this respect, Shapiro and Varian (1999) propose that e-business value creation can result from combinations of information, physical products and services, innovative configurations of transactions, and the reconfiguration and integration of resources, capabilities, roles, and relationships among suppliers, partners, and customers. Nevertheless, research on e-business models can be structured within two complementary streams: the former is oriented to describe generic e-business models and provide typologies; the latter examines the components of e-business models (Zott et al., 2011). Several studies suggest the decomposition of the "atomic elements" of the business models which describe a different way of conducting business electronically; in particular, e-business initiatives can be exemplified by pure atomic business models or by combining them (Hamel 2000; Afuah and Tucci 2001; Petrovic et al. 2001; Rayport and Jaworski 2001; Weill and Vitale 2001). Applegate (2001) presents six e-business models focused on distributors, portals, infrastructure distributors, infrastructure producers, and infrastructure portals. Dubosson-Torbay et al. (2002) recognize the principal dimensions for classifying business models: user role, interaction pattern, nature of the offering, pricing system, level of customization, and economic control.

Additionally, scholars have deepened the principal components of e-business models by providing different representations (i.e., a mixture of informal textual, verbal, and ad hoc graphical representations) or schemas for the analysis of (new) ways of doing business and the (new) roles that firms play in their respective ecosystems. In particular, they mainly focus to the notion of value (e.g., value stream, customer value, value proposition), financial aspects (e.g., revenue streams, cost structures), and aspects related to the architecture of the network between the firm and its exchange partners (e.g., delivery channels, network relationships, logistical streams, infrastructure). Each of these components can constitute part of a generic business model, and "it could be a source of differentiation among business model types" (Zott et al. 2011).

In this respect, this study considers the contribution of Osterwalder and Pigneur (2003) who provide a business model "ontology", which is a conceptualization of the elements and their relationships, vocabulary, and semantics of a business model, through the expression of the business logic of a specific firm. In particular, this ontology is broken down into four pillars that describe what a firm offers, who it targets with this, how this can be realized and how much can be earned (Osterwalder and Pigneur, 2003). These pillars can be translated into four business model blocks: 1) product innovation block, which considers the value proposition and capabilities of firms; 2) customer relationship block, which describes how firms get in touch with their customers and what kind of relationships they intend to establish with them; 3) infrastructure management block, which considers what activities/processes, resources/assets and partners are necessary to provide the first two blocks, and finally 4) financial aspects concerning the revenue flows and the pricing mechanisms of firms.

Sustainability

The concept of sustainable development was launched in 1972 during the UN Conference on the Human Environment held in Stockholm, initiating the academic and institutional debate on the subject. Then, in 1983, the United Nations World Commission on Environment and Development was established and in 1987, the organization, actualizing its conclusions in the Brundtland Report, underlined that sustainable development ensures the needs of the present, while not compromising the ability to meet those of the future (WCED, 1987).

In 1992, the United Nations Conference on Environment and Development was held in Rio de Janeiro and a document called the Rio Declaration - consisting of 27 principles developed in Agenda 21 - was adopted defining the first concept of sustainable development based on three relevant factors acting in a synergic way: economic growth, social equity, and environmental protection. They represent the traditional 'triangle' formed by People, Planet and Profit (Barbier,1987), which are considered the three fundamental pillars of sustainable development (Mitcham, 1995; Mebratu, 1998). The economic side of sustainability is linked to the firm ability to make profits, ensuring long-term survival and favoring poverty alleviation, equity, and income redistribution. The social factors are influenced by the human capital involved and, specifically, by related skills and experience as well as cultural implications. The environmental factors are the biological elements and processes - relevant in their interconnection - that must be preserved in order to ensure human survival.

Over the following decades, this became a priority for Countries and a fundamental goal in their policies, and the United Nations Commission on Sustainable Development was specifically set up to monitor the implementation of the outcomes of the Rio Conference. Since then, the aim of sustainable development has remained a core issue at different levels and is being pursued through a broad variety of initiatives all over the world.

The current period represents a crucial moment in the path towards sustainability, given the landmark achievement set out by the adoption of the 2030 Agenda for Sustainable Development. The Agenda provides "a shared blueprint for peace and prosperity for people and the planet, now and into the future", and establishes some sustainable development goals (SDGs) built on decades of work by various Countries and the UN. Accomplishment is some way off but the challenges posed by this issue are rapidly and deeply changing the roadmap of innovation both in production methods and in consumption habits.

As a result of the broad debate on sustainability, it soon became clear that, although the 'three pillars' were commonly accepted throughout the literature, they could not be considered universal: environmental, social and economic aspects must be placed side by side with other enabling factors which have become additional pillars. One of the most relevant is the institutional dimension of sustainability (Pfahl, 2005; Turcu, 2013) which deepens the interaction between institutions and members of the society, specifically considering how the former perceives citizen expectations and manages the mutual relationship in a sustainable way.

All these different aspects of sustainability must be concurrently enhanced in order to maintain a whole sustainable system (Daly, 1996). In view of the most recent implications, it is a fact that sustainability is strongly connected to innovation, intended as the search for new ways and new methods or as the implementation of new or significantly improved procedures (Etzkowitz and Zhou, 2006): indeed, the UN Sustainable Development summit of 2015 establishing the new 2030 sustainable development Agenda, has clarified the importance of e-business and digitalization in the product lifecycle and underlined that they can save resources, offering better services, ensuring their continuous improvement.

The concept of sustainability must be identified from a wide perspective, as today's challenge is to define operational and consistent terms of sustainability from an integrated social, ecological, and economic system point of view. In this vein, among the emerging paradigms, the perspective of "value cocreation" can be considered useful to handle sustainable issues (Rupo et al., 2018). Value cocreation "is the process of creating something together in a process of direct interactions between two or more actors, where the actors' processes merge into one collaborative, dialogical process" (Grönroos and Gummerus 2014, p. 209). The value co-creation paradigm provides a clear framework that is useful for understanding how to add value to "existing value" or for using this latter concept to facilitate the growth process through interactions between the firm and actors (Ramaswamy and Ozcan, 2014). It describes how actors can be involved as active partners in service innovation through multiple interactive channels.

The value co-created with the contribution of different actors shows how it is possible for each one to obtain benefits from collaboration, rendering the relationship active, effective, durable (Aquilani and Abbate, 2016) and profitable for participants.

Business Model for Sustainability

As just highlighted, for companies operating in the travel industry it is essential to have an innovative business model that allows them to be flexible and competitive in a world where being proactive makes the difference between winning or perishing. At the same time, it is crucial that this business model should be sustainable or better be built for supporting organizations to pursue the vital goal of sustainability.

Scholars' contributions to the topic have progressively increased over the last ten years focusing, *inter alia*, on the importance of the sustainable business model (Carayannis, 2014; Evans et al., 2017; Geissdoerfer et al., 2018) and on evolving innovations (Joyce and Paquin, 2016), also dealing with the circular economy (Evans et al., 2017; Rosa et al., 2019). This chapter focuses on the way through which the business model can enhance sustainable innovation (Boons and Lüdeke-Freund, 2013; Schaltegger et al., 2016).

The difference is not merely terminological. In fact, the aim is not to analyze how business models support innovation to be or become sustainable but concerns how sustainability is embedded in the business model. Specifically, the goal is to investigate how an innovative business model, i.e. the e-business model adopted by the firm selected here, can be analyzed as a driving force for sustainable strategic choices "creating economic success through (and not just along with) a certain environmental or social activity" (Schaltegger et al., 2012, p.98).

The basic idea that suggests this choice is that digital companies do not need to transform their business model, but are already born with an intrinsically sustainable business model. In fact, as well as allowing quick answers and effective, the key technologies involved reduce paper consumption, minimize costs and provide services to everyone, without distinction, because of the ability to customize services and make them usable, even in particular situations. Moreover, the direct relationship with customers and/or partners with the possibility of networking naturally favors the co-creation of value and also the possibility of establishing value constellations (Normann and Ramirez, 1993; Vanhaverbeke and Cloodt, 2006).

DESIGN AND METHODOLOGY

In this section, the study describes the following elements: research setting, case study research design as well as data collection and analysis.

Research Setting

Recently, disruptive business model innovations are increasingly emerging in the travel and tourism industry (Nosratabadi et al., 2019) seeking to satisfy economic, environmental, and social goals simultaneously (Evans et al., 2017). Different solutions are continually emerging with the idea of inverting the current tendency "that sustainability issues with their major societal and environmental effects influencing human beings and nature had not been the priorities of most business model types" (Nosratabadi et al., 2019,

p. 2). This underlines that business models, designed to realize the sustainability goals of organizations, under the inevitable pressure, have in fact been transformed into a more sustainable economic system.

Significant examples can be identified in the development of app-based smart-sharing systems, electric vehicle use, bike-sharing, intelligent mobility, and eco-safe driving such as: Musement, Guide Me Right, Sharewood and Sailsquare. In particular, Musement, the multi-platform booking service has innovated travel experiences around the world through *digitization* and *personalization*. In 2018, the company became part of TUI Group, leader in the global travel market. This acquisition represents the most important exit in the Italian tech travel sector in the last decade and gives Musement new opportunities and synergies to a sustainability approach.

However, these digital firms must face different pressure challenges linked to the fact that the modern global economy often cannot capture business models achieving profit from digital services while a company can generally avoid the physical presence in a Country and, consequently, the right taxation. Therefore, the definition of "Permanent Establishment" marking the concept of significant economic presence could be relevant (Hongle andPistone, 2015; Blum, 2015).

One must note that article 101 of the Treaty on the Functioning of the European Union (TFEU) imposes fair competition in the internal market, prohibiting anti-competitive actions and ensuring that markets remain open.

Various proposals have been put forward to find a common solution appropriate to the taxation of firms operating within the digital economy. At the OECD level (OECD, 2015), Action 1 of the OECD BEPS Project15 addresses three options: defining the aforementioned concept of a "significant economic presence", introducing withholding taxes on digital transactions or, equalization levies.

The European Commission (EU COM, 2018) has released long and short-term solutions regarding taxing multinational corporations that provide digital services. According to the long-term proposal, the Institution suggests the Member States adopting a uniform definition of a "Digital Permanent Establishment" with at least one of the following criteria: a) €7 million ($8.1 million) in annual revenues; b) more than 100,000 users; and c) more than 3,000 contracts for digital services with businesses in the EU.

The short-term digital tax proposal is the Digital Service Taxation, a turnover tax levied by individual countries at a rate of 3 percent on revenues derived from the sale of advertising space, digital intermediary activities like online marketplaces, and sales of user-collected data. It would apply to companies with both: a) total annual worldwide revenues of €750 million ($868 million); and b) total EU revenues of €50 million ($58 million).

Although these are only proposals, the new taxation approaches to the digital economy are in the tax agenda of several Member States. The 2019 Italian budget law (30/12/2018, no. 145) introduces a 3 percent digital service tax on revenues from digital services if the company has both more than €750 million ($835 million) in worldwide revenue and revenues in Italy of €5.5 million ($6.1 million). Nevertheless, the web tax needs an implementing decree of the Ministry of Economy that has not yet been issued.

Case Study: MyTaxi

A qualitative methodological approach was used in this study to achieve the research aims of gaining deeper insights into e-business models for sustainability through personal interviews, company documents, institutional sites and published data sources (Eisenhardt and Graebner, 2007; Eisenhardt, 1989).

The method used to carry out the research is a single case study (Yin, 1984), which seems the correct research strategy for the analysis of the contemporary phenomenon within its real-life context (Yin, 1984) and the development of a holistic understanding of a phenomena under investigation. Furthermore, the single case study method is considered the most suitable methodology to in-depth examination (Miles and Huberman, 1994) and to answer the following research question: *to what extent does the e-business model support sustainable innovations in the real context?* To carry out the research, the study focused on MyTaxi in order to provide empirical insights concerning the phenomenon of innovation of a business model oriented to achieve sustainability objectives.

Mytaxi, the largest taxi app in Europe, was founded in June 2009 in Germany by the startup Intelligent Apps GmbH, initially under the name of 1TouchTaxi. The idea of creating a direct connection between a licensed taxi driver and passenger, offering both a digital reservation management system and high-quality service, has been innovating within the industry.

This direct connection "passenger - taxi driver" has been the main strength, in addition to another key component, that Mytaxi has been operating exclusively through licensed taxi drivers, thus ensuring consumers reliability, safety and high quality.

Traveling with Mytaxi is easier, faster, more convenient and efficient than traditional lines. Via the app, the customer can request or book a taxi, see it live on the digital map, contact the driver, rate the journey, pay for it by smartphone and receive the receipt as a PDF in his email inbox.

The following table 1 shows the main stages of the evolution of the Mytaxi company.

Mytaxi's goal is to provide innovative and up-to-date services, able to continuously integrate new features, helping to create modern, safe and affordable urban mobility, using existing resources without adding other vehicles to the road. A recent study (CERTeT 2018)[1] of Mytaxi app, provides important input on strategic issues in which Mytaxi invests. According to this study, real benefits brought by e-hailing to mobility are the improvement in safety, reliability, and transparency of the transport service. CERTeT 2018 survey shows that the introduction of e-hailing is able to generate a reduction in average waiting times between one run and another. The e-hailing platform use is very high compared to other call and booking methods, it also generates a change in the payment methods and increases the number of trips, as it allows taxi drivers to intercept the demand more effectively. In addition, the CERTeT 2018 survey investigated the issue of changing the relationship between the taxi driver and passenger, highlighting the perception of greater relaxation of customers with respect to the route and the price of the ride. Information and transparency regarding costs and the path provided through the e-hailing platform appear to have a fundamental role in the relationship of trust between user and service provider.

Regarding firm performance, in 2018, Mytaxi in Italy recorded a 110% sales growth and over 2 million rides, with relevant growth also at a European level with over 40 million rides. The waiting time has dropped to 3.5 minutes thanks to a wide fleet of licensed taxi drivers. With a record-breaking 2018, Mytaxi aims to improve further thanks to new investments.

The process of acquisitions and alliances for building a synergic network of companies in order to combine and integrate complementary services is a crucial key factor. It is possible to consider the merger with Hailo. Mytaxi became Europe's largest cab hailing operator when its parent company Daimler[2] absorbed the UK platform Hailo, the leading UK and Ireland app for taxi bookings, active also in Spain, as well as in the United States. Mytaxi name and technique and Hailo offerings to be migrated to Mytaxi have been maintained. It has avoided many of Uber's pitfalls by matching customers with registered drivers. When Hailo decided to join with Mytaxi, the goal was to become the dominant force in Europe through solid relationships with its drivers - something Uber cannot always boast of.

Table 1. Mytaxi: main data and facts

Foundation	June 2009
Headquarter	Hamburg
Employees	over 500
Major shareholder	Daimler AG
App Mytaxi	Available for Apple iOS, Android, BlackBerry 10 and Windows Phone 7.x and 8.x, as well as a web app. User interface with the languages German, English, French and Spanish. Languages available for the web app: German and English.
Peculiarity	Internationality of Mytaxi, or the possibility of using the same app, with the same account, in most cities in European countries where the service is provided.
Main phases	
By July 2012	15,000 taxis connected in Germany download about 1.7 million times
In mid-2012	Integration of pre-order and mobile payment options
At CeBIT 2012	Award as "The most innovative business idea" among 50 international participants
At the beginning of 2012	Daimler joined as an investor
From September 2014	Mytaxi is a subsidiary of Daimler Mobility Services GmbH (part of the Daimler Group).
October 2014	Available in over 40 cities in Germany, as well as internationally in Austria (Vienna, Graz, Salzburg), Switzerland (Zurich), Spain (Barcelona, Madrid), Poland (Warsaw) and the United States (Washington).
2015	Offer progressively extended to Australia (license), Italy, Portugal and Sweden by 2015.
May 2015	Innovation service: trips with Mytaxi drivers can be paid for with the app even if the taxi wasn't ordered through the app
July 2016	Mytaxi and Hailo, leading UK and Ireland app for taxi bookings, announced their merger
2017	Acquisition of CleverTaxi, leading taxi call app in Romania, and the acquisition of Taxibeat, leading market taxi app in Greece.
From December 2017	*Match service*, a new taxi sharing service that offers customers a more advantageous and efficient travel experience in pooling. Initially in Hamburg followed by other major cities such as Berlin or Munich.
2018	Mytaxi has been downloaded over 10 million times and provides its customers with a fleet of 120,000 licensed taxi drivers available in over 70 European cities in 11 European countries: Germany, Austria, Poland, Spain, Portugal, Italy, United Kingdom, Ireland, Sweden, Greece and Romania.
February 2019	Alliance Daimler AG (Mytaxi's majority shareholder) and BMW Group for combining their "existing offers in the areas of car-sharing, ride, parking, *recharge* and multimodality".
May 2019	*Hive* project in Lisbon, a shared transport version

Source: Our elaboration.

The Mytaxi merging process with other European hailers continues (recent acquisitions include Romanian market leader Clever Taxi and Taxibeat the leading market taxi app in Greece) by relying on its trustworthy and cab-friendly reputation.

In February 2019, it was announced that the majority shareholder of Mytaxi, Daimler AG, would be allied with the BMW Group and that the two would combine their "existing offers in the areas of car-sharing, ride, parking, recharge and multimodality" under a common family of brands. Mytaxi will be renamed "Free Now"[3] this year to join the network of five new brands: Reach Now (Multimodal),

Charge Now (Charging), Free Now (Ride-Hailing), Park Now (Parking) and Share Now (CarSharing). The app's logo and appearance will also change. Therefore, the trips' services will be expanded. For example, customers should also be offered rental cars with drivers (radio rental cars) through the app.

Data Collection and Analysis

The study collected data concerning MyTaxi in order to explore the innovative activity in a context that faces particular challenges such as sustainability, diversity of laws and rules between nations as well as increased customer expertise fostering ever-changing needs.

Information was collected through direct interview, triangulated with other secondary data sources (Gibbert et al., 2008), such as the analysis of archival data, published reports, official documents, and scientific articles. In detail, the study performed three main steps. In the first step, it examined the company's official website in order to obtain general information concerning the aspects related to history, main characteristics, and components of its business model (i.e., services, customers, commercial partners and so on). Additionally, the analysis was oriented to the MyTaxi app developed to provide an alternative method of booking a taxi by connecting both driver and customer directly.

In the second step, the study proceeded to examine diverse materials available online, such as official documents, articles and interviews in newspapers and magazines, reports and scientific contributions (Kozinets, 2002). Not neglecting new "scenarios" derived from issuing rules concerning relevant factors like the taxation of web digital platform transactions and problems connected with fair competition.

In the third step, the study collected primary data through a semi-structured interview with several key informants. The importance of these actors as most relevant sources of data and information is given by their centrality to decision-making processes.

The interview was conducted during the period May to June 2019, and transcribed and focused on the firm's e-business model components, including the analysis of the development of practices to accomplish the sustainable goals of its business model.

Thanks to these different sources, a rich collection of data was gathered. The analysis of data followed an iterative process, in accordance with suggestions by Strauss and Corbin (1998). Initially, the authors individually read the various archival data in an attempt to analyse the main components of the business model. Then, they collectively discussed and developed a first framework of analysis. Then they analysed data derived from the interview, hence refining the framework and organizing the various data into the dimensions underpinning the theorizing of the study.

The integrity of data was guaranteed in different ways. Firstly, the multiple sources were triangulated to improve the robustness of the findings, thus company documentation, secondary data together with primary data enhance the credibility of the case study (Patton 2001; Yin 2009). Secondly, each researcher independently read all the data and information collected. Then, researchers intensively discussed their interpretations, the main purpose being to reach a common agreement about their inferences by activating a necessary process of interaction between theoretical concepts and collected data.

FINDINGS AND DISCUSSIONS

In the context just outlined, the digital firm under investigation is exponentially growing, riding (and maybe driving) the wave of the phenomenon of e-hailing, or the call to the taxi through the app, gaining ground even in the tourist sector and potentially becoming a driver of change in travel approach, due to the reduction of waiting times, the new ways of booking and paying.

Starting from the idea of speeding up and, at the same time, customizing the driver/customer relationship, MyTaxi has expanded its range of action becoming highly competitive in a sector characterized by the presence of stringent constraints and increasingly sustainable priorities.

According to Elkington, the challenge of integration of new priorities in business will increasingly play out in four key areas: boards, balance sheets, brands, and business models. The last realm of integration moves "beyond the corporate hearts and minds to the very DNA of business" (Elkington, 2013, p.36). For this reason, we sought to look at the four pillars of MyTaxi's business model with the lens of the triple bottom line (Elkington, 1998). In this context, value proposition provides measurable economic value in the structure of costs and revenue, ecological value in its smart way to travel; social value in the way to take care of customers and own resources and when interacting on the network with other organizations. Moreover, customer interface motivates customers to take responsibility for creating value by their active participation in the evaluation of the service (Boons et al., 2013)

MyTaxi and the Challenge of Economic Sustainability

MyTaxi brings together selected individual drivers and connects them to customers, facilitating and speeding up access to the service and payment through a user-friendly app and personalizes booking and payment formula both in B2C and in B2B versions. In B2C customers book-check-pay, using the App, saving time and increasing security (only licensed drivers); while in B2B drivers (considered by the firm as *partners*) can create/expand their customer portfolio and firms getting the service (even for hospitality), saving time, reducing costs and accounting times, simply accessing Europe's largest taxi network. Moreover, there is administrative support for firms in travel accounting, i.e. the opportunity for companies to connect MyTaxi with their SAP account (but administrative support is also provided for those without SAP), streamlining accounting procedures. Furthermore, the "Hospitality" service gives firms the opportunity to book for guests by pressing a single button of the MyTaxi modem or with the app.

Within such activities, it is interesting to highlight that both passengers and, especially, firms should manage their costs in an easier and faster way.

Therefore, the Mytaxi business model contributes to economic sustainability in the following ways. The first is purely *economic*. For drivers Mytaxi is a partner that helps to expand their customer portfolio at paltry costs compared with gained advantages (taxi drivers are given the opportunity to sign up without registration or withdrawal fees and the commissions on rides are applied based on local rates); for passengers, payment by direct debit (Gpay credit card and similar pay tools) facilitates the travel experience, for firms, the administrative support for travel accounting facilitates the monitoring of travel expenses. The second is *strategic*. This app implies designing a customer-centered sustainable value, where the feedback from the customer (tips and/or positive evaluation) contribute to co-creating value. In fact, customers become multi-role stakeholders who are directly involved in the co-creation of value moving from mere feedback of their entire experience to active participation in the definition of innovative services/solutions. The last is *reputational*, such as the opportunity to have qualified and licensed drivers that assure greater attention to results and to the professionalism of their behaviour and in return increase the quality of the service and, consequently, the potential of customer attraction and *fidelization*.

MyTaxi and the Challenge of Social Sustainability

Social sustainability can be defined as the equitable distribution of social classes of the main conditions of wellbeing and improvement of the quality of life. MyTaxi is a service facilitating, personalized and faster travel experiences for individuals and business purposes, doing so it makes travel for business, leisure and for everyday needs much simpler. In this context, the e-business model supported the direct customer/taxi driver relationship through the app: customers can book their service, traveling without having to think about "pulling out the wallet" and being able to check the itinerary of the taxi arriving by geolocation.

Moreover, with Mytaxi *Match*, the App allows customers to share a taxi ride with one or more unknown passengers who wish to join along the route and proceed in the same direction. Travel expenses are cheaper for passengers, thus attracting new groups of financially weak customers, who previously barely used taxis. In October 2018, the company launched a new version of the app that allows customers to choose different types of vehicles (for example Eco or those equipped with a wheelchair).

Consequently, MyTaxi appears to support the social sustainability of innovation in three main ways. The first is the "*globalization*" of access either in terms of customer diversity, or as concerns the international diffusion of the app. International distribution of the app, in fact, is facilitated by the way it functions: MyTaxi operates in the same way everywhere, even if services seem to change on the basis of the pervasiveness of the app as well as the legal constraints and culture of travelers. In this way, even in different nations with different rules for transportation, travelers perform the same routines to have the same service. The social sustainability of MyTaxi also includes the realm of *security*: the choice of enrolling only licensed drivers to improve the security of passenger experiences and the relative perception of the quality of the service. Last but not least, the study can underline the social sustainability of this business model analyzing *HRM policies*. Attention to the competitive arena but also to specific local areas where MyTaxi operates is underlined by two peculiarities: its attention to enroll VRIO resources (Barney,1991) (for example the developers of solutions, programs and owners responsible for the service are embedded in the organizational system) and its polycentric staffing approach (for example, law experts and other key-positions for local growth -i.e. taxi drivers- seem to be enrolled only from the local country since the calls-for-job on the platform are in the local language while other calls are also in English). Moreover, the HRM policies include thematic workshops and courses at the headquarters in Hamburg, where teams from various countries exchange best practices. Furthermore, every country in which Mytaxi is active periodically conducts off-site meetings in which the working group meets for a brainstorming to define plans, strategies, activities and future goals without neglecting participation in recreational activities, allowing the team to collaborate and strengthen relationships.

From the local point of view, as just underlined, MyTaxi has a proactive approach and continuously interacts with the local institutions to improve competitiveness. In Italy, an interesting example is the AGCM resolution. In fact, the Antitrust Italian authority has established that the restrictive clauses of the exclusiveness of the big companies of Rome and Milan are "restrictive of competition in violation of Article 101 of the TFEU", so even taxi drivers already engaged with other companies can register with MyTaxi and have their own customers. Consequently, MyTaxi will be able to enrich its offer by acquiring taxi drivers already engaged in other companies as partners, thus becoming more competitive in the Italian context. But this case is also an example of how important the firm's continuous monitoring of the external environment is: new rules concerning web tax transactions could, in fact, distort the positive outcomes and the AGCM solutions could follow a different and less liberal path.

MyTaxi and the Challenge of Environmental Sustainability

In the challenge of environmental sustainability, disruptive business model innovation has emerged, among these: car-pooling, expanded electric vehicle use, bike-sharing, intelligent mobility, eco-safe driving, app-based car sharing and so on. This has happened because one of the most significant challenges facing global sustainable development is mobility, which has great potential in reducing carbon emissions.

MyTaxi faces the challenge of environmental sustainability in two ways: the first concerns the reduction of paper use, both in the application of direct debit and in the management of online administrative support; the second concerns the integration of the transport network available to passengers. This firm seems to concentrate on building collaborative networking both for the integration of services, for example Trenitalia, and for the diversification of outcomes, or for the facilitation of travel accounting for firms. At the same time, it seems to move towards integration within groups of homogeneous thinking, i.e. FreeNow that seems to be in search of a smart and sustainable way to travel. A significant example is what is happening in Lisbon, where thanks to the pilot project Hive users can easily use the App to find, unlock and pay for the use of scooters, enjoy their experience and block them once they reach their destination. This type of transport provides a service also called "last mile" because drivers can park their cars where possible and travel the last stretch to their destination without having to walk or wait for public transport.

Hive confirms and enhances the "green" image of the company because its debut takes place in a Country whose national electricity production comes from green renewable sources, satisfying 100% of the national electricity demand as well as providing a considerable surplus.

CONCLUSION

The purpose of this research was to deepen the understanding of the e-business model defined and implemented by digital firms operating in the travel and tourism industry, seeking to face the increasing challenge of sustainability. In order to achieve this goal, it firstly identified and described a specific theoretical framework, highlighting the main peculiarities of the business model concept in digital contexts, thus emphasizing that the essential value elements of organizations are concerned with proposition, creation, delivering, and capturing value. Additionally, it focused on sustainability underlining that the theoretical lenses adopted to develop the study, were drawn from the conceptualization that business models are increasingly considered as potential mechanisms for achieving the sustainability goals of companies (Nosratabadi et al., 2019).

To explore such theoretical aspects, the study selected MyTaxi, as a fruitful case study to investigate how a firm incorporated the principles of sustainability and integrated sustainability into its value proposition, value creation, and value capture activities of business.

Regarding the economic perspective, the study shows that MyTaxi is oriented to the adoption of sustainability in its business model because it increases the opportunities to activate and maintain value networks, by reducing the related investment and improving benefits for all participants in the network. In this way, MyTaxi seeks to integrate economic purposes with sustainability ambitions in such a way that the benefits of all the stakeholders (i.e., customers, taxi drivers, local institutions, etc.) are achieved simultaneously.

From the environmental perspective, Mytaxi is strongly committed to identifying innovative and adequate mechanisms to offer travel experiences that provide value not only to its customers, but also generate benefits for society and the environment. In this sense, the effort to reduce the use of paper and the activity of environmental monitoring is emblematic, by reinforcing the idea that a firm's value creation logic should consider the integration of environmental goals into a more holistic meaning of value (Schaltegger et al., 2012).

From the social perspective, MyTaxi addresses its efforts and energies to different activities oriented to create social impacts. In this respect, this firm uses advanced digital technologies and platforms that improve the globalization of access and the security of the service. This means that value propositions can be efficaciously designed on customer values to provide social benefits.

The research provides several contributions to the literature focused on the innovation of the business models stimulated by the use of digital technologies and platforms and by the intent for integration of sustainability principles in business practices. Specifically, it increases the comprehension of how businesses operating in the travel and tourism industry can concretely create customer and social value by integrating social, environmental, and business activities. Moreover, new insights are added to the literature on digital firms, by presenting the main peculiarities of their business model configurations.

This study offers insights from a managerial point of view, since firms may be inspired by the definition and implementation of e-business models based on sustainability concerns to explore innovative business opportunities and to achieve a better competitive advantage.

In particular, from a managerial perspective, it is important to understand how firms can design, combine and adopt their business models by integrating sustainability principles in their logic of generating and capturing value, being more responsive to the dynamics of the industry, environment, etc. Although, this path is not easy, sustainability "is a mother lode of organizational and technological innovations that yield both bottom-line and top-line returns." (Nidumolu et al., 2009, p. 2).

Additionally, managers should understand the new opportunities offered by advanced Internet technologies and, consequently, use them for the development of their business models. Then, by moving from the various underlined components, they should be able to differentiate their e-business model from the competition and take advantage of their core competences.

Moreover, with a view on the new European strategies to achieve income from web-platform transactions, it is clear that firms must consider recently issued new rules of Member States in order to avoid their limitations but also to respect tax obligations and the rules on fair competition. The previous assumption should also influence the legislator in order to suggest avoiding restrictions imposed on innovative enterprises without considering their positive outcomes and the growth of the business ecosystem.

This research is not without limitations, which may present interesting opportunities for future research. Firstly, the study is based on a single case study, therefore, it is impossible to make generalizations regarding the findings. In this respect, an explorative qualitative analysis, based on different cases of innovative startups, could be useful to compare their e-business models and to obtain various insights for the step of quantitative analysis. Additionally, large quantitative data could be collected to empirically test the results of this study.

ACKNOWLEDGMENT

The authors are grateful to Mytaxi Italia for the kind cooperation.

REFERENCES

Afuah, A., & Tucci, C. L. (2001). *Internet business models and strategies*. Boston, MA: McGraw-Hill, Irwin.

Amit, R., & Zott, C. (2001). Value creation in e-Business. *Strategic Management Journal, 22*(6/7), 493–520. doi:10.1002mj.187

Applegate, L. M. (2001). E-business models: Making sense of the Internet business landscape. In G. W. Dickson & G. DeSanctis (Eds.), Information technology and the future enterprise: New models for managers. Upper Saddle River, NJ: Prentice Hall. 49-94.

Aquilani, B. (2016). *La co-creazione di valore nei processi di innovazione aperta: verso un modello di analisi*. Milano, Italy: CEDAM.

Aquilani, B. & Abbate, T. (2016). Co-creation and open innovation: Bridging the two paradigms. In *Proceedings of the R&D Management Conference Titled from Science to Society: Innovation and Value Creation*, Cambridge, UK, July 3–6, 2016.

Barbier, E. B. (1987). The concept of sustainable economic development. *Environmental Conservation, 14*(2), 101–110. doi:10.1017/S0376892900011449

Barney, J. (1991). Firm resources and sustained competitive advantage. *Journal of Management, 17*(1), 99–120. doi:10.1177/014920639101700108

Blum, D. W. (2015). Permanent establishments and action 1 on the digital economy of the OECD base erosion and profit shifting initiative – the Nexus criterion redefined? *69 Bulletin of International Taxation*, 6/7, 3.2., *Journals IBFD*. Retrieved from http://www.ibfd.org/sites/ibfd.org/files/

Boons, F., & Lüdeke-Freund, F. (2013). Business models for sustainable innovation: State-of-the-art and steps towards a research agenda. *Journal of Cleaner Production, 45*, 9–19. doi:10.1016/j.jclepro.2012.07.007

Bradley, J., Loucks, J., Macaulay, J., Noronha, A., & Wade, M. (2015). *Digital vortex how digital disruption is redefining industries. Global Center for Digital Business Transformation*. Retrieved from https://www.cisco.com/c/dam/en/us/solutions/collateral/industry-solutions/digital-vortex-report.pdf

Carayannis, E. G., Sindakis, S., & Walter, C. (2015). Business model innovation as lever of organizational sustainability. *The Journal of Technology Transfer, 40*(1), 85–104. doi:10.100710961-013-9330-y

Casadesus-Masanell, R., & Ricart, J. E. (2010). From strategy to business models and onto tactics. *Long Range Planning, 43*(2–3), 195–215. doi:10.1016/j.lrp.2010.01.004

Daly, H. E. (1996). *Beyond growth: the economics of sustainable development*. Boston, MA: Beacon Press.

de Reuver, M., Bouwman, H., & MacInnes, I. (2007, July). What drives business model dynamics? A case survey. In *Eighth World Congress on the Management of eBusiness* (WCMeB 2007). IEEE.

Dubosson-Torbay, M., Osterwalder, A., & Pigneur, Y. (2002). E-business model design, classification, and measurements. *Thunderbird International Business Review, 44*(1), 5–23. doi:10.1002/tie.1036

Eisenhardt, K. M. (1989). Building theories from case study research. *Academy of Management Review*, *14*(4), 532–550. doi:10.5465/amr.1989.4308385

Eisenhardt, K. M., & Graebner, M. E. (2007). Theory building from cases: Opportunities and challenges. *Academy of Management Journal*, *50*(1), 25–32. doi:10.5465/amj.2007.24160888

Elkington, J. (1998). Partnerships from cannibals with forks: The triple bottom line of 21st century business. *Environmental Quality Management*, *8*(1), 37–51. doi:10.1002/tqem.3310080106

Elkington, J. (2013). Enter the triple bottom line. In *The triple bottom line* (pp. 23–38). Routledge.

Etzkowitz, H., & Zhou, C. (2006). Triple helix twins: Innovation and sustainability. *Science & Public Policy*, *33*(1), 77–83. doi:10.3152/147154306781779154

EU COM. (2018) *Proposal for a COUNCIL DIRECTIVE laying down rules relating to the corporate taxation of a significant digital presence*. Brussels, Belgium. 21.3.2018, 147 final 2018/0072 (CNS). Retrieved from https://ec.europa.eu/taxation_customs/business/company-tax/fair-taxation-digital-economy_en

Evans, S., Vladimirova, D., Holgado, M., Van Fossen, K., Yang, M., Silva, E., & Barlow, C. (2017). Business model innovation for sustainability: Towards a unified perspective for creation of sustainable business models. *Business Strategy and the Environment*, *26*(5), 597–608. doi:10.1002/bse.1939

Foss, N. J., & Saebi, T. (2017). Fifteen years of research on business model innovation: How far have we come, and where should we go? *Journal of Management*, *43*(1), 200–227. doi:10.1177/0149206316675927

Foss, N. J., & Saebi, T. (2018). Business models and business model innovation: Between wicked and paradigmatic problems. *Long Range Planning*, *51*(1), 9–21. doi:10.1016/j.lrp.2017.07.006

García-Gutiérrez, I., & Martínez-Borreguero, F. J. (2016). The innovation pivot framework. Fostering business model innovation in startups. *Research Technology Management*, (September-October): 48–56.

Geissdoerfer, M., Vladimirova, D., & Evans, S. (2018). Sustainable business model innovation: A review. *Journal of Cleaner Production*, *198*, 401–416. doi:10.1016/j.jclepro.2018.06.240

George, G., & Bock, A. J. (2011). The business model in practice and its implications for entrepreneurship research. *Entrepreneurship Theory and Practice*, *35*(1), 83–111. doi:10.1111/j.1540-6520.2010.00424.x

Gibbert, M., Ruigrok, W., & Wicki, B. (2008). What passes as a rigorous case study? *Strategic Management Journal*, *29*(13), 1465–1474. doi:10.1002mj.722

Grönroos, C., & Gummerus, J. (2014). The service revolution and its marketing implications: Service logic vs service-dominant logic. *Managing Service Quality*, *24*(3), 206–229. doi:10.1108/MSQ-03-2014-0042

Hamel, G. (2000). *Leading the revolution*. Boston, MA: Harvard Business School Press.

Hamel, G. (2002). *Leading the revolution: How to thrive in turbulent times by making innovation a way of life*. Boston, MA: Harvard Business School Press.

Hongle, P. & Pistone, P. (2015). *Blueprints for a new PE Nexus to tax business income in the era of the digital economy*. White Papers IBFD. Retrieved from http://www.ibfd.org/sites/ibfd.org/files/

Joyce, A., & Paquin, R. L. (2016). The triple layered business model canvas: A tool to design more sustainable business models. *Journal of Cleaner Production*, *135*, 1474–1486. doi:10.1016/j.jclepro.2016.06.067

Joyce, A., & Paquin, R. L. (2016). The triple layered business model canvas: A tool to design more sustainable business models. *Journal of Cleaner Production*, *135*, 1474–1486. doi:10.1016/j.jclepro.2016.06.067

Kozinets, R. V. (2002). The field behind the screen: Using netnography for marketing research in online communities. *JMR, Journal of Marketing Research*, *39*(1), 61–72. doi:10.1509/jmkr.39.1.61.18935

MacMillan, I., Roberts, E., Livada, V., & Wang, A. (2008). *Corporate venture capital (CVC): Seeking innovation and strategic growth.* National Institute of Standards and Technology-US Department of Commerce 08-916.

Massa, L., Tucci, C., & Afuah, A. (2017). A critical assessment of business model research. *The Academy of Management Annals*, *11*(1), 73–104. doi:10.5465/annals.2014.0072

Mebratu, D. (1998). Sustainability and sustainable development: Historical and conceptual review. *Environmental Impact Assessment Review*, *18*(6), 493–520. doi:10.1016/S0195-9255(98)00019-5

Miles, M. B., & Huberman, A. M. (1994). *Qualitative data analysis: An expanded sourcebook.* Thousand Oaks, CA: Sage.

Mitcham, C. (1995). The concept of sustainable development: Its origins and ambivalence. *Technology in Society*, *17*(3), 311–326. doi:10.1016/0160-791X(95)00008-F

Moore, J. F. (1993). Predators and prey: A new ecology of competition. *Harvard Business Review*, *71*(3), 75–86. PMID:10126156

Nidumolu, R., Prahalad, C. K., & Rangaswami, M. R. (2009). Why sustainability is now the key driver of innovation. *Harvard Business Review*, *87*(9), 56–64.

Normann, R., & Ramirez, R. (1993). From value chain to value constellation: Designing interactive strategy. *Harvard Business Review*, *71*(4), 65–77. PMID:10127040

Nosratabadi, S., Mosavi, A., Shamshirband, S., Kazimieras Zavadskas, E., Rakotonirainy, A., & Chau, K. W. (2019). Sustainable business models: A review. *Sustainability*, *11*(6), 1663. doi:10.3390u11061663

OECD. (2015). *Addressing the tax challenges of the digital economy, action 1 - 2015 Final Report, OECD/G20 base erosion and profit shifting project.* Paris, France: OECD Publishing. doi:10.1787/9789264241046-

Osterwalder, A., & Pigneur, Y. (2003). Modeling value propositions in e-Business. In *Proceedings of the 5th International Conference on Electronic Commerce*, 429-436.

Osterwalder, A., Pigneur, Y., & Tucci, C. L. (2005). Clarifying business models: origins, present, and future of the concept. *Communications of the Association for Information Systems*, *16*(1), 1–25.

Patton, M. Q. (2001). *Qualitative evaluation and research methods.* Thousand Oaks, CA: Sage.

Petrovic, O., Kittl, C., & Teksten, R. D. (2001). Developing business models for eBusiness. *International Conference on Electronic Commerce* 2001, Vienna, Austria.

Pfahl, S. (2005). Institutional sustainability. *International Journal of Sustainable Development*, *8*(1/2), 80–96. doi:10.1504/IJSD.2005.007376

Presenza, A., Messeni Petruzzelli, A., & Natalicchio, A. (2019). Business model innovation for sustainability. Highlights from the tourism and hospitality industry. *Sustainability*, *11*(1), 212–216. doi:10.3390u11010212

Ramaswamy, V., & Ozcan, K. (2014). *The co-creation paradigm*. Stanford University Press.

Rayport, J. F., & Jaworski, B. J. (2001). *Cases in e-Commerce*. Boston, MA: McGraw-Hill/Irwin.

Rosa, P., Sassanelli, C., & Terzi, S. (2019). Towards circular business models: A systematic literature review on classification frameworks and archetypes. *Journal of Cleaner Production*, *236*, 117696. doi:10.1016/j.jclepro.2019.117696

Rupo, D., Perano, M. & Vargas-Sanchez, A. (2018). A framework based on sustainability, open innovation, and value cocreation paradigms—a case in an Italian maritime cluster. *Sustainability, 10*(3), 729. 1-28. doi:10.3390u10030729

Schaltegger, S., Hansen, E. G., & Lüdeke-Freund, F. (2016). Business models for sustainability: Origins, present research, and future avenues. *Organization & Environment*, *29*(1), 3–10. doi:10.1177/1086026615599806

Schaltegger, S., Lüdeke-Freund, F., & Hansen, E. G. (2012). Business cases for sustainability: the role of business model innovation for corporate sustainability. *International Journal of Innovation and Sustainable Development, 6*(2), 95-119.

Shafer, S. M., Smitha, H. J., & Linder, J. C. (2005). The power of business models. *Business Horizons*, *48*(3), 199–207. doi:10.1016/j.bushor.2004.10.014

Shankar, V., Smith, A. K., & Rangaswamy, A. (2003). Customer satisfaction and loyalty in online and offline environments. *International Journal of Research in Marketing*, *20*(2), 153–175. doi:10.1016/S0167-8116(03)00016-8

Shapiro, C., & Varian, H. R. (1999). *Information rules: A strategic guide to the network economy*. Boston, MA: Harvard Business School Press.

Strauss, A., & Corbin, J. (1998). *Basics of qualitative research techniques*. Thousand Oaks, CA: Sage.

Teece, D. J. (2010). Business models, business strategy and innovation. *Long Range Planning*, *43*(2–3), 172–194. doi:10.1016/j.lrp.2009.07.003

Trimi, S., & Berbegal-Mirabent, J. (2012). Business model innovation in entrepreneurship. *The International Entrepreneurship and Management Journal*, *8*(4), 449–465. doi:10.100711365-012-0234-3

Turcu, C. (2013). Re-thinking sustainability indicators: Local perspectives of urban sustainability. *Journal of Environmental Planning and Management*, *56*(5), 1–25. doi:10.1080/09640568.2012.698984

Vanhaverbeke, W. & Cloodt, M. (2006). Open innovation in value networks. *Open innovation: Researching a new paradigm*, 258-281.

WCED. (1987, December). Report of the World Commission on Environment and Development. *General Assembly Resolution, 42/187*, 11.

Weill, P., & Vitale, M. R. (2001). *Place to space. Migrating to eBusiness models*. Boston, MA: Harvard Business School Press.

Yin, R. K. (1984). *Case study research: design and methods*. Beverly Hills, CA: Sage.

Yin, R. K. (2009). *Case study research: design and methods*. London, UK: Sage.

Zott, C., Amit, R., & Massa, L. (2011). The business model: Recent developments and future research. *Journal of Management*, *37*(4), 1019–1042. doi:10.1177/0149206311406265

KEY TERMS AND DEFINITIONS

Business Model Innovation: The complex architecture of connected components/elements underlying value creation, delivery and capture and assuming that innovation is a necessary part of business model concept.

Digital Platforms: Electronic ecosystems where technology enables interactions and transactions among multiple players, generating value and knowledge.

E-Business Model: A different way of conducting business electronically by encompassing e-markets, e-commerce and Internet-based business and referring to firms that conduct transactions with their partners and buyers through the Internet.

Fair Competition: An open and equitable competition between business players operating in a free market.

Sustainable Development: Development that meets the needs of the present, without compromising the ability of future generations to meet their own needs (from Brundtland Report).

Tax Rules: Sets of constitutional, common-*law*, statutory and regulatory rules concerned with the legal aspects of taxation.

Value Cocreation: The process of creating something together through direct interactions between two or more actors (such as the company and consumers), in which the joint collaboration of each party is aimed at creating value for all parties.

ENDNOTES

1 In September 2018 Mytaxi presented the results of the study "Urban Mobility and Technology: the impact of e-hauling", carried out by a research team of the Bocconi University CERTeT. The aim is to understand the influences and implications of e-hailing, that is the taxi call through application, in urban mobility, today increasingly complex and characterized by a growing demand for flexibility and services on demand. The study considered the numbers of mytaxi app in Milan and Rome, over a 12-month period, between October 2016 and September 2017, highlighting the differences between the two contexts with regard to seasonality, level of activity on weekdays and holidays and in different time slots

2 Daimler is one of the biggest producers of premium cars and the world's biggest manufacturer of commercial vehicles with a global reach. Daimler provides financing, leasing, fleet management, insurance and innovative mobility services.

3 However, in UK this rebranding has caused some criticism because this will be the second rebranding in two years for the popular taxi app. Just when customers start to get used to referring to Hailo as MyTaxi, they have decided to change the name and rebrand yet again (Kelly 2019).

Chapter 6
Environmental Sustainability to Support Competitiveness:
From Theory to Practice

Anna Mazzi
https://orcid.org/0000-0001-7870-5535
University of Padova, Italy

ABSTRACT

The interest of scientists and companies in understanding the business implications of environmental commitments is timely; however, a dilemma remains at the firm level: is environmental sustainability a strategic factor for business competitiveness? The author contributes to this international end interdisciplinary debate through a double analysis, theoretical and empirical. Starting from a systematic literature review, the main correlations between environmental commitments and business performance are identified in a scholar's perspective. Based on the results from an Italian survey, the main added values associated with certified environmental management system are verified with a manager's perspective. Finally, the findings obtained from theoretical and empirical points of view are compared, to discuss confirmations or contradictions and underline questions still open.

INTRODUCTION

Since the 1980s the concerns of the international community linked to the consequences of an irresponsible development have determined the progressive affirmation of the concept of sustainability and the issue of environment is of great interest for companies today. Among scientists a lively debate concerning corporate sustainability has determined multiple epistemological and theoretical paradigms (Vildåsen et al., 2017). On the other hand, over the years the attention to environmental problems has grown in consumers, pushing companies to introduce the sustainability as strategic variable in their business (Roulet and Touboni, 2015; Xu et al., 2018). In order to answer the increasing pressure of legislation and market of environmental issues, many organizations are committed to reducing environmental impacts

DOI: 10.4018/978-1-7998-1419-1.ch006

(Ren et al., 2019). To support the growing needs of sustainable management in many sectors around the world, the standards and guidelines have gradually multiplied in recent years (Toniolo et al., 2019/b).

To gain increase of market credibility and legitimacy, many organizations around the world have chosen to achieve voluntary environmental certifications, beyond the legal requirements (Chen et al, 2012; Neuteleers and Engelen, 2015; Wijethilake, 2017). The environmental management system is certainly the most widespread tool to improve the environmental performances of an organization; moreover, thanks to its applicability in all economic sectors, it represents the best-known environmental label on the market (Ni, 2018). However, in several cases the organizations not always are able to quantify costs and benefits related their environmental procedures and performances (Mazzi et al., 2016/b; Lee et al., 2017).

The focus of this chapter is the discussion about the relevance of the environmental sustainability (ES) in supporting the business competitiveness (BC). In the international debate this topic has already been widely discussed by many authors. The so-called "neoclassical" approach that considers the environment as a negative externality and focuses on the environment in terms of compliance with regulatory requirements is considered to be outdated (Bhat, 1998; Bithas, 2011). However, a dilemma thus arises: is it convenient for a company to invest in the environment? (Porter, 1991; Boons, 2002). The international debate concerning this question starts from the awareness of the complexity related to measure the relationship between environmental commitment and business success factors; in the last thirty years through empirical and theoretical studies the scientists come to conflicting conclusions. In other words, looking for an answer to this dilemma is "like finding the Holy Grail" (Boons and Wagner, 2009).

The chapter contributes to this long-standing question starting from a double perspective, theoretical and practical, and looking for a meeting point. From a systematic literature review, the theoretical evidences related the relationship on ES and BC are underlined and the scholars' perspective is clarified. Through the investigation of the opinion of companies with ES commitments, the practical experiences related the relationship on ES and BC are verified. Finally, comparing the results derived by the literature review and the opinion of companies, the similarities and differences between theoretical and practical outcomes are underlined.

The novelty of this research concerns in the adoption of this double approach. Indeed, even if the papers discussing the existence of a relationship between ES and BC are very numerous in a theoretical or experiential perspective, very few studies have explored this topic in both perspectives (Raut et al., 2019). At the same time, in this topic the need to compare theories and practices is known, in order to overcome the redundancy of assessing and bring theoretical reflections closer to real experiences (Büyüközkan & Karabulut, 2018; Genovese et al., 2017).

The chapter is structured as follows. Section 2 explains the research design, through the formulation of research questions and the phases with which the research is structured. Section 3 is dedicated to the presentation of the first part of the research: the exploration of the topic with the perspective of scholars, through the analysis of the literature published in the last twenty years. The goal is to identify the main findings obtained by the scientists regarding the ES-BC relationship. In section 4 the second part of the research is presented: its aim is to investigate the point of view of managers, obtained by a survey among firms. The purpose is to investigate the opinion of companies regarding how ES contributes to BC, through a national survey. Section 5 presents the third part of the research, dedicated to comparing the two different points of view, scholars, from literature review, and practitioners, from survey among companies. The purpose is to identify similarities and differences between theoretical and practical analysis in investigating the question of ES-BC relationship. Final propositions and future perspectives conclude the chapter, underlying the relevance of environmental sustainability in competitiveness of firms and suggesting further directions of the research in this topic.

BACKGROUND AND RESEARCH DESIGN

From Knowledge Gaps to Research Goals

Already in the 1930s economists begin discussing the unsustainability of welfare in an economy that uses non-renewable resources (Hotelling, 1931). In the 1960s the attention toward adverse environmental effects caused by environmental pollution increases and transparent and science-based information begin to be demanded by environmental scientists (Carsol, 1962). From 1970s the concerns of international community regarding environmental problems created by some industrial activities are growing (Meadows et al., 1972). From 1980s resource consumption and waste production are recognized as the main causes of environmental problems and the principles to guide countries in future sustainable development are defined (UN, 1992).

The concept of sustainability should ideally improve the quality of life for every individual without expending the earth's resources beyond its capacity. Researchers have attempted to quantify carrying capacities of ecosystem that must not be exceeded to maintain functions, as well as other ecosystem aspects of interest, named as planetary boundaries (Rockström et al., 2009; Steffen et al., 2015).

Acting to reduce the impact on the ecosystem is therefore necessary and urgent, needing a collective effort: both businesses, governments and individuals must take actions, changing consumption and production behaviors, setting policies and changing practices, including the "people, planet and prosperity" in sustainable development agenda (UN, 2002).

In designing, manufacturing, delivering, using, recovering and disposing products various requirements have to be integrated with environmental aspects: feasibility, convenience, security, acceptability; often conflicting requirements have to be fulfilled in a life cycle perspective (Bonan and Doney, 2018; Acquaye et al., 2018). Therefore, to support complex decisions, multidimensional approaches are necessary (Taghikhah et al., 2019). In this direction moves the model of triple bottom line, coined by Elkington (1994): it explains the three dimensions of sustainability assessment, considering them in an integrative model, correlating economic prosperity, social justice and environmental protection with long-term objectives (Mattioda et al., 2015).

The market seems to reward environmentally responsible organizations, and many companies around the world are increasingly becoming interested in environmental issues (O'Rourke, 2014; Álvarez-García & Del RíoRama, 2016). Environmental labelling standards are fundamental tools to guide and support sustainable business strategies of companies (Toniolo et al., 2019/a). The choice of many organizations around the world is to achieve environmental certifications, as official recognitions by accredited third bodies, beyond the legal requirements. An independent certification allows organizations to gain increase of market credibility, stakeholders transparency and community legitimacy (Kogg and Mont, 2012; Xu et al., 2018).

Undoubtedly, the scientists and practitioners are interested to study the issues underpinning the adoption of sustainable practices by organizations, especially considering the benefits related the environmental certification (Kollmann and Prakash, 2001; Ren et al., 2019). With the aim to upgrade the knowledge in this context, the author focuses the research on the added values of environmental certification, comparing two perspectives: the vision of scientific community and the opinion of firms.

The **research goal** is to verify if ES favors BC, considering both scholars' theories and practitioners' opinions and comparing them, if possible.

The **research questions** are formulated as follow:

RQ1: What is the relationship between ES and BC in a scholar perspective?
RQ2: What is the relationship between ES and BC in a manager perspective?
RQ3: Is there a coherence between scholars and managers points of view concerning relationship between ES and BC?

Structure and Scope of the Research

In order to pursue the research goal and to answer to the research questions, the **structure of the research** includes three main parts:

1. **First part: Literature review**, with the aim of summarizing the main relationships between ES and BC deriving by the opinion of scholars;
2. **Second part: Survey on companies**, with the aim of knowing the opinion of practitioners related existing relationships between ES and BC;
3. **Third part: Comparison of results**, to underline coherences or inhomogeneities between theories of scholars and opinions of practitioners.

The research will be rigorous and lead to solid results, if it adopts valid criteria to identify firm's commitment in ES and BC.

Concerning the concept of ES, ISO 14001 certification is the universally recognized tool to distinguish in the market the companies engaged in environmental improvement (ISO, 2018). Approved by International Organization for Standardization in 1996 and revised in 2004 and again in 2015, ISO 14001 is the most widespread international standard that supports organizations in the implementation and maintenance of an environmental management system, defining a list of requirements through which any organization, of any size and any sector, can develop a systematic approach to improve environmental performance, coherently and consistently with its specific context (ISO, 2015). The key concept of this standard is the voluntary decision of companies to implement a systematic approach in order to reduce environmental impacts and control significant environmental aspects, with an ongoing commitment to improving the overall environmental performance, through a virtuous circle with a preventive and proactive approach.

Concerning the concept of BC, triple bottom line represents the key strategy to improve compatibility between the increasing resource needs and the dwindling natural resource stocks. Triple bottom line means that decision making on product and process development, investment and policy must address the three dimensions of sustainability: economy, environment and society (Valdivia et al., 2012).

From previous reasonings the **research scope** is defined by the following items:

- The concept of firm's ES corresponds to the environmental management system consistent with ISO 14001 standard;

- The concept of firm's BC corresponds to the parameters adopted in scientific debate concerning the triple bottom line;
- The scholars' point of view is represented by papers recently published in scientific journals that discuss the relationship between ES and BC;
- The practitioners' point of view is represented by the opinion of ISO 14001 certified companies related the ES-BC relationship.

Through a block diagram figure 1 shows the research structure. In the third, fourth and fifth sections the methodology adopted for each phase is explained and the results are described.

THE OPINION OF SCHOLARS: LITERATURE REVIEW

Design of the Literature Review

To obtain significant results from literature review, the methodological recommendations suggested by notable papers were considered (Luederitz et al., 2016; Mazzi et al., 2016/a; Büyüközkan and Karabulut, 2018; Koberg and Longoni, 2019).

Consequently, the framework adopted to support the literature review is described follows and graphically represented in figure 2.

Step 1: Material collection. To identify international papers related implications of ES and BC, a bibliographical survey was conducted through the international database ISI Web of Knowledge, integrated by the libraries of the main editors in sustainable topics. The research keywords adopted to screening the papers from the libraries are: "environmental sustainability", "sustainability commitment", "environmental management", "ISO 14001 certification", "business performance", "business competitiveness", "triple bottom line", and their synonymous. Only papers published in international journals in English language from 2000 and 2018 are included in the material collection. In order to include in the following steps only the papers really concerned the research goal, a cleaning step of the selected papers was been made through the detailed analysis of the abstracts, with the aim to verify the coherence of each paper in the topic "ES-BC relationship at firm level".

Figure 1. Block diagram of the research phases

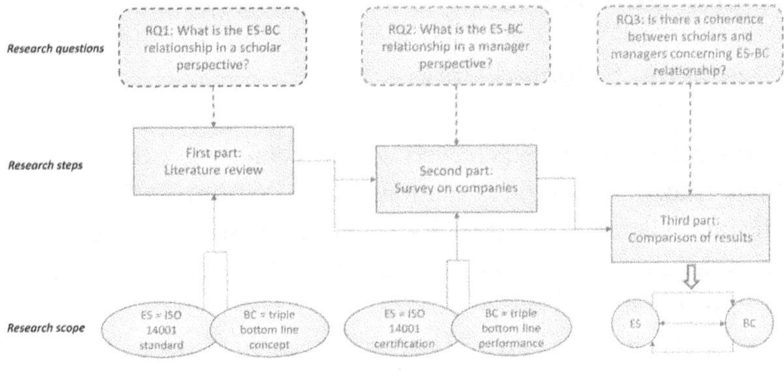

Figure 2. Research steps related the literature review

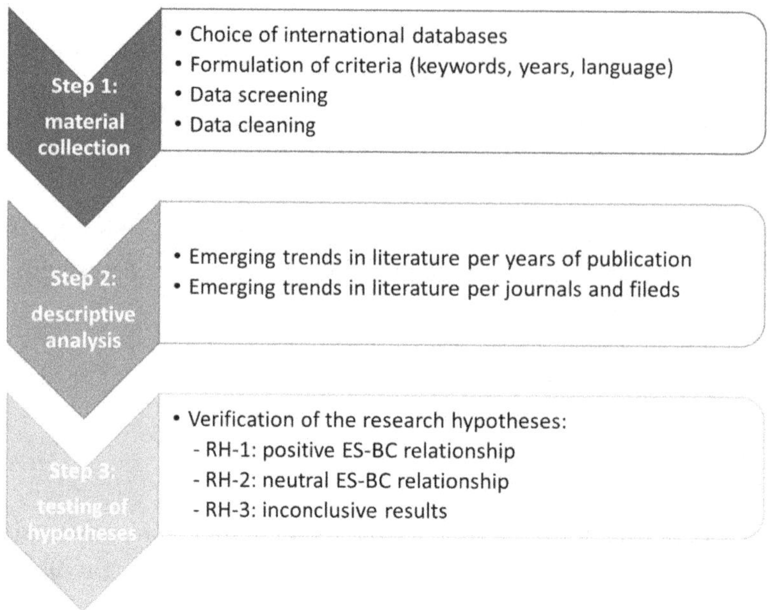

Step 2: Descriptive analysis. A descriptive analysis of the papers selected in the first step was been made, with the aim of underline the emerging trends in the literature review in terms of temporal evolution of the research topic, considering the number of papers published during the years and the research fields interested in this topic.

Step 3: Testing of hypotheses. Each paper selected in the first step was analyzed in depth through a detailed content analysis, with the aim of knowing the main contents and of understanding the results in terms of relationship between ES and BC. The results of the selected papers were synthesized with the aim to verify the following research hypotheses:

- **Research hypothesis RH-1:** There is a positive relationship between ES and BC;
- **Research hypothesis RH-2:** The relationship between ES and BC is neutral;
- **Research hypothesis RH-3:** Results concerning ES-BC relationship are inconclusive.

Results from the Literature Review

Descriptive Analysis of the Selected Papers

At the end of the material collection, 95 papers were selected concerning the role of ES in BC. This huge amount of literature published in indexed international journals from 2000 and 2018 demonstrates that the questions about the interrelationships between ES and BC are still interested in a scholar perspective.

Figure 3 synthesizes the growing number of papers published during the years. About half of these papers were published in the last five years.

Other characteristics emerged by the analysis of the selected papers are the following.

Figure 3. Number of papers published from 2000 and 2018 discussing the ES-BC relationship

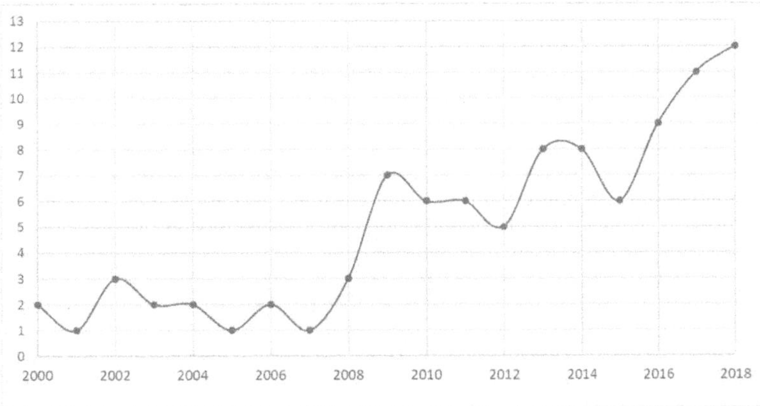

- The debate regarding the ES-BC relationship currently takes place in various disciplines, as environment, management, business and ethics;
- The relationship between ES and BC has been studied both in large companies and in small-medium enterprises; the studies cover several industries, especially those with high environmental concerns;
- To verify the relationship between ES and BC, more frequently the scientists have adopted official statistics and publicly available data to investigate the ES and BC of firms; on the other hand, several studies have utilized a survey to learn about companies on this topic.

Testing of the Research Hypotheses RH-1, RH-2, and RH-3

A detailed content analysis was conducted related the 95 selected papers, focused on the results, discussion and conclusions sections, in order to test the research hypotheses previously formulated, and then confirm or deny them.

The emerging trends from literature review concerning the validity of each research hypothesis are shown in figure 4.

Literature review revealed that the first hypothesis investigated, "there is a positive relationship between ES and BC", is confirmed.

Almost all of the authors agree that there is a relationship between sustainability and competitiveness in a business perspective. This agreement is notable because it includes different case studies in different countries and from different industrial sectors.

Investigating in more depth the papers, there are different ways to confirm RH-1 hypothesis:

- Several papers confirm a positive and bidirectional relationship between environment and competitiveness in firm's performance; this seems that a positive two-way relationship between ES and BC exists, in a "win-win" perspective (see also: Porter and Kramer, 2011;-Gallego-Álvarez et al., 2014; Ni, 2018).

Figure 4. Number of papers that confirm the research hypotheses

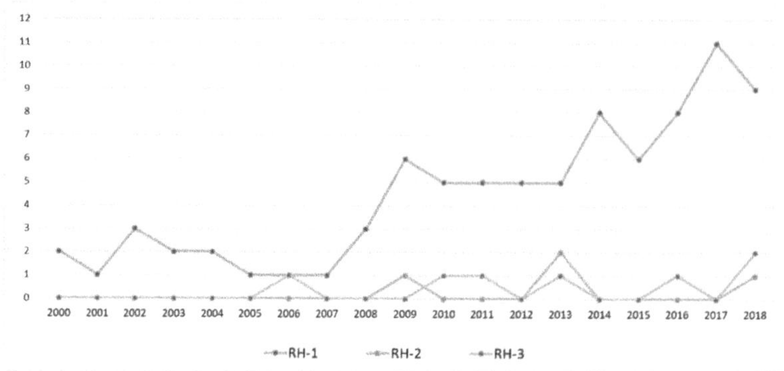

- Some authors demonstrate the existence of a "cyclic hypothesis", in which better BC determines better ES that in turn determines better BC (more recently, see also: Morioka et al., 2017; Katiyar et al., 2018).
- Several papers discuss various "conditional relationships" between ES and BC: some variables are identified by several authors conditioning the ES-BC relationship through potential moderator roles. The more frequently identified variable strictly correlated to complexity of firms, measured by the size, the internal processes and technologies, and the geographical location (more recently, see also: Wijethilake, 2017; Antonioli and Mazzanti, 2018).
- Some authors recently have demonstrated the existence of other "mediating factors" to support the positive relationship between ES and BC. The more frequently cited factors are related the maturity of ES practices adopted by firms, the relevance of sustainability in the firm's strategies, the external pressures and the corporate reputation (more recently, see also: Morioka et al., 2017; Guimarães et al., 2018; Rivas-Asanza et al., 2018).

To test the research hypothesis RH-2, few studies conclude with a "neutral hypothesis", in which different sustainable practices determine the same business results or similar sustainable practices determine different business results (see also: Dragomir, 2013; Qorri et al., 2018).

To test the research hypothesis RH-3, some notable reviews substantially demonstrate that there is no univocal consensus about the convenience of ES in order to support economic or business performance (see also: Horváthová, 2010; Albertini, 2013).

From the analysis of the papers more recently published, is it possible to identify new emerging drivers associated to the ES-BC relationship. In the last years the interests of scholars are related to the following fields associated to the ES-BC relationship:

- Management operations and practices, as the human resource management (Morioka et al., 2017; Matinaro et al., 2019) or the innovation processes (Garcés-Ayerbe and Cañón-de-Francia, 2017; Antonioli and Mazzanti, 2017; Pesce et al, 2018);
- Internal and external pressures, as the supply chain management (Acquaye et al., 2018; Katiyar et al. 2016) or the risk management (Giannakis and Papadopoulos, 2016; Lintukangas et al., 2016);
- Circular economy perspectives, as the life cycle management approach and the reuse/recycle opportunities (Acquaye et al., 2018; Kalmikova et al., 2018).

Emerging Trends from a Scholar Perspective

Summarizing the literature review results, it is possible to conclude with the following outcomes:

- There is a consensus among scholars to recognize a positive relationship between ES and BC;
- ES and BC support each other positively and mutually;
- ES and BC determine positive effects both in internal and external performances of firms, through the management of resources, the control of processes, the credibility in the market and the collaboration with the supply chain;
- The strength of the ES-BC relationship is conditioned by some "moderator factors" related the characteristics, practices and policies of firms;
- The main notable "moderator factors" for a positive ES-BC relationship are: the complexity of firms, the maturity of sustainable commitment, and the strategic interest in sustainability practices.

A critical aspect emerging from the literature review is the extreme heterogeneity of the variables used to measure the sustainability and competitiveness of firms (see also: Horváthová, 2012; Schneider and Meins, 2013; Raut et al., 2019). This lack of homogeneity, certainly linked to the complexity of the topic, however leads to incomparable results because of the adoption of different indicators (see also: Mazzi et al, 2016/a; Genovese et al., 2017).

Finally, many authors complain about the difficulty of understanding the critical factors for a successful implementation of environmental commitments and practices (see also: Boiral and Henri, 2012; Merli et al., 2016), which is considered a relevant gap within the scientific knowledge. In other words, the methodological approaches to study the relationship between EP and BC are evolving during the last twenty years, but the scientific knowledge still appears to be that described by Ullmann in 1985: as "empirical data in search of a theory".

To synthesize these outcomes, figure 5 represents the emerging trends in literature review concerning the role of ES in BC.

THE OPINION OF PRACTITIONERS: SURVEY AMONG COMPANIES

Design of the Survey

In this section, the research investigates the opinion of companies regarding how ES contributes to BC.

Figure 5. Emerging trends on ES-BC relationship in a scholar's perspective from the literature review

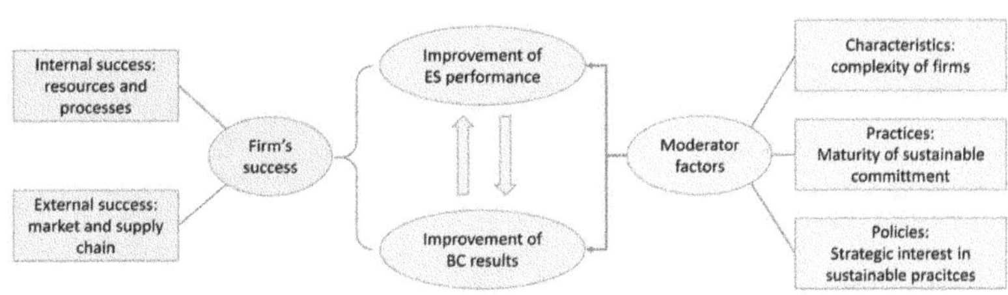

To design the survey, first of all it is necessary to define the variables that characterize ES and BC. Then, the methodology adopted to conduct the survey must be explained using the variables defined as representative for ES and BC concepts. The research hypotheses verified through the survey are explained, coherently with the results from the literature review. Finally, the questionnaire utilized to collect the opinion of practitioner and the conducting of survey are presented.

Variables Assumed to Characterize ES and BC

As previously demonstrated in section 2, at firm's level the more significant element to demonstrate a strategic commitment in ES policy and obtain a continuous improvement in ES operations is the adoption of the environmental management system consistent with ISO 14001 standard.

In the world, Italy is one of the countries with the largest number of companies with this environmental certification. With reference of the survey periodically conducted by ISO concerning the diffusion of international standards in the world, figure 6 shows the top ten countries with the largest number of ISO 14001 certifications: Italy is the second country in Europe and the fourth in the world (ISO, 2018).

Undoubtedly, Italy is a relevant player in the context of ISO 14001: to do this, Italian context was chosen to realize the second research phase. The survey was conducted, involving the managers of Italian companies with a certified environmental management system.

The elements characterizing the concept of BC are derived by scientific literature concerning the main benefits correlated with ISO 14001 certification:

- Environmental performance improvement, including environmental impacts reduction and environmental prevention (Nguyen and Hens, 2015; Singh et al., 2015; Pesce et al., 2018);
- Internal organization improvement, related organizational management, operations performance, human resource management, and strategic business goals (Ismail et al., 2014; Paillé et al., 2014; Álvarez-García and Del Riorama, 2016);

Figure 6. The top ten countries in the world as number of ISO 14001 certifications (data source: ISO, 2018)

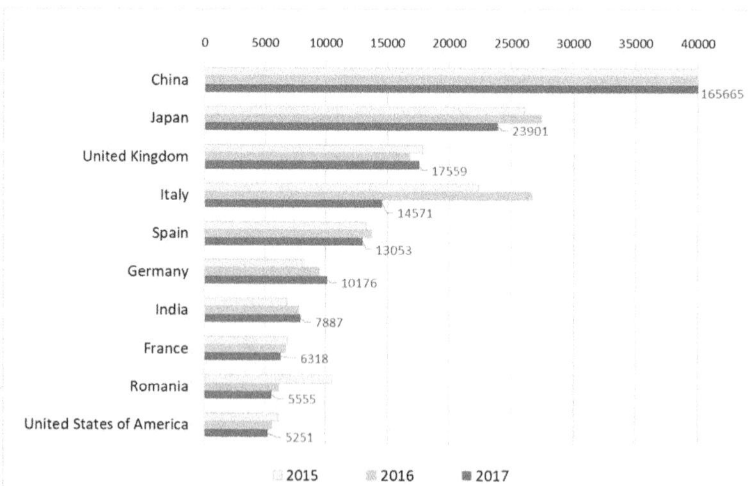

- Economic performance improvement, that include increase profitability and market share and external image and reputation (Jørgensen and Jensen, 2012; Ferenhof et al., 2014; Lee et al., 2017);
- Legal compliance improvement, as assurance of regulatory compliance in practices and documents (Heras-Saizarbitoria et al., 2015; Mazzi et al., 2016/b).

Consequently, the research assumptions adopted to design and conduct the survey are the following:

- ES is represented by the adoption of ISO 14001 certification of Italian companies;
- BC is explained by economic performance improvement, internal organization improvement, environmental performance improvement, legal compliance improvement, and other benefits.

Methodology to Conduct the Survey

To consider the opinion of Italian practitioners, related implications of ES and BC, primary data derived by the Italian firms with ISO 14001 certification have been considered, using the survey methodology.

To obtain significant results from the Italian survey, in line with the methodological recommendations by Corbetta (1999), Dillman (2000) and Raut et al. (2019), the following framework was adopted, graphically represented in figure 7.

Step 1: Survey preparing. To know the opinion of Italian firms regarding the ES-BC relationship, the following question was asked: "How many benefits derive from the ISO 14001 certification?". In line with the previous literature analysis, the variables considered as benefits are: "economic performance improvement", "internal organization improvement", "environmental performance improvement" and "legal compliance improvement". The possible answers are defined in a 3-point Likert scale, with the following alternatives: "Relevant benefits", "Few benefits", "No benefit", "I don't know". In order to facilitate the participation in the survey, the questionnaire was developed in an electronic form.

Step 2: Data collection. Italian firms with ISO 14001 certification were selected, by reference to the national database of certified firms, managed by the national accreditation body, ACCREDIA. To effectively investigate the opinion of practitioners in ES, the questionnaire was addressed to the employees that are environmental managers or that have specific responsibilities in the environmental management system of company. The survey was conducted during the 2018. In order to collect as many answers as possible, the questionnaire was sent to managers by email, and online completed by managers.

Step 3: Data analysis. Answers collected by the managers of Italian firms with certified environmental management system were analyzed through descriptive statistics. In accordance with the results derived by the previous literature analysis, the moderator factors assumed to analyze the opinion of practitioners concerning the BC benefits associated to the ES are the following:

- "Complexity of firm", represented by the dimension of respondent firms, as small-medium enterprise or large company;
- "Environmental management experience", translated in maturity or youth of the system and measured by the year of ISO 14001 certification attendance;
- "Strategic interest in sustainability", measured in terms of other environmental sustainability certifications obtained by the company.

Step 4: Data synthesis. The answers collected and analyzed were synthesized on the base of the following research hypotheses, derived by the previous literature analysis and data analysis:

- **Research hypothesis RH-1.1:** The adoption of ISO 14001 certification determines benefits in economic performance improvement, internal organization improvement, environmental performance improvement, legal compliance improvement, and other benefits;
- **Research hypothesis RH-1.2:** The complexity of firm represents a moderator factor in the positive relationship between ISO 14001 certification and economic performance improvement, internal organization improvement, environmental performance improvement, legal compliance improvement, and other benefits;
- **Research hypothesis RH-1.3:** The environmental management experience represents a moderator factor in the positive relationship between ISO 14001 certification and economic performance improvement, internal organization improvement, environmental performance improvement, legal compliance improvement, and other benefits;
- **Research hypothesis RH-1.4:** The strategic interest in sustainability represents a moderator factor in the relationship between ISO 14001 certification and economic performance improvement, internal organization improvement, environmental performance improvement, legal compliance improvement, and other benefits.

Results From the Survey

Descriptive Analysis of Respondent Firms

Italian organizations invited in the survey were approximatively 5000; respondent firms were 452, with an approximatively 9% response rate. Tables 1, 2 and 3 show the type of responding organizations distinguished through the moderator factors assumed in the research hypotheses RH-1.2, RH-1.3 and RH-1.4:

- To consider the complexity of firm, the respondent firms are distinguished in small-medium and large enterprises;
- To consider the environmental management experience, the respondent firms are distinguished on the base of the year of certification:
- To consider the strategic interest in sustainability the respondent firms are distinguished on the base of other environmental sustainability certifications obtained.

Coherently with the industrial characteristics of the Italian economic context, the percentage of small-medium enterprises in the survey's results is relevant.

Half of the responding companies have been certified for less than 10 years; the pioneer companies of ISO 14001 certification are only 3%, while companies with a more recent certification are more than 10%.

Almost all the responding companies declare to have already obtained other certifications, first of all the quality management system; the second certification obtained by respondent firms is health and safety management system, followed by social management system and energy management system. A small group of firms has adopted other product environmental labels, as life cycle assessment, product environmental declaration, carbon footprint or other ecolabels. More than 30% of respondent firms own

Figure 7. Framework for the research steps related the Italian survey

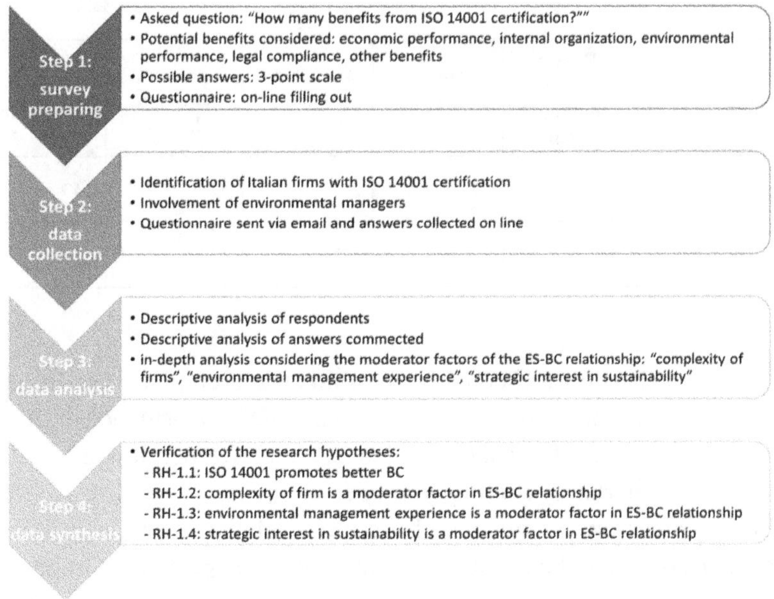

other certificates not directly correlated the environmental sustainability, as food safety, information security, testing, or other technical standards. Few firms (3%) have not adopted any other standards.

Verification of Research Hypothesis RH-1.1

Analyzing the answers collected by respondent companies at the question "How many benefits derive from the ISO 14001 certification?", the author obtains the graph in figure 8, that represents the percentage of firms considering relevant, few or null the BC benefits derived by the adoption of ISO 14001. As

Table 1. Number and percentage of respondent firms distinguished by the moderator factor "complexity of firm"

	Large companies	Small-medium enterprises
N° of firms	86	366
% of firms	19%	81%

Table 2. Number and percentage of respondent firms distinguished by the moderator factor "environmental management experience"

	Certified from 1996 to 2000	Certified from 2001 to 2005	Certified from 2006 to 2010	Certified from 2010 to 2015	Certified from 2016 to 2018
N° of firms	14	106	115	159	58
% of firms	3%	24%	25%	35%	13%

Table 3. Number and percentage of respondent firms distinguished by the moderator factor "strategic interest in sustainability"

	Quality manag. systems	Health & Safety manag. systems	Social manag. systems	Energy manag. systems	Product environ. labels	Other standards	No other standards
N° of firms	401	219	37	24	22	143	15
% of firms	89%	48%	8%	5%	5%	32%	3%

described previously, the benefits for BC considered in this research phase are: economic performance improvement, internal organization improvement, environmental performance improvement, legal compliance improvement, and other benefits (not included in the abovementioned).

From the figure 8 some remarkable findings emerge.

Legal compliance improvement is considered the more relevant benefit by Italian certified firms. Almost no managers have answered the question stating that this aspect is not important. Environmental performance and internal organization are also very significant for Italian firms: approximately 60% of managers states that environmental certification has allowed company to achieve important improvements in these two aspects. On the contrary, economic performances seem the least important benefit derived by an environmental certification: less than 16% of companies believe they have achieved significant improvements in economic performance, instead more than 55% has achieved little economic improvement and more than 20% declares any benefit from ISO 14001 certification in terms of economic performance.

It is possible to confirm the research hypothesis RH-1.1. The relationship between ES and BC is proven by the opinion of Italian managers in the following terms:

- The main added value derived by ISO 14001 certification is the legal compliance;
- Internal organization and environmental performance are strictly correlated to ISO 14001 certification;

Figure 8. Answers by Italian firms of the question "How many benefits derive from the ISO 14001 certification?"

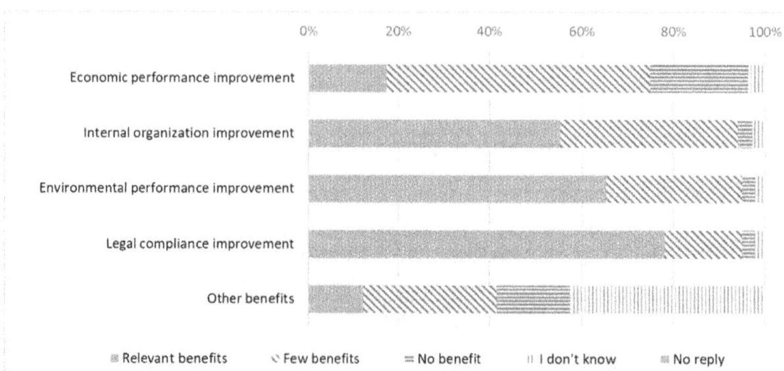

- The relationship between environmental certification and economic benefits is weakly confirmed.

Verification of Research Hypotheses RH-1.2, RH-1.3, and RH-1.4

The answers obtained by the Italian survey are now analyzed by subdividing the respondent companies according to three parameters, assumed as potential moderator factors: complexity of firm, environmental management experience and strategic interest in sustainability. To better highlight the differences between the groups of responses, the author focus the attention, in each group, on the percentage of companies that responded "Relevant benefits" for each item.

To verify the hypothesis RH-1.2, the answers collected by large and small-medium Italian companies are compared, in line with table 1. Figure 9 shows the percentage of large companies and small-medium enterprises that consider relevant benefits correlated to environmental certification.

Looking at the radar graph in figure 9, the two lines related large and small-medium companies essentially have an overlapping trend. Only the parameter "economic environmental performance" demonstrates a difference: more than 20% of large companies considers it as a relevant added value of environmental certification. Instead, in the group of small-medium enterprises, this percentage drops to 15%.

The author can affirm that the size of firm is a conditioning factor in ES-BC relationship only for the economic performance. Instead, related the other dimensions of competitiveness, as environmental performance, legal compliance and internal organization, the size of company does not affect the relationship between ES and BC.

To verify the hypothesis RH-1.3, the author considers the answers collected by Italian companies grouped on the base of seniority or youth of environmental management system: this corresponds to consider the year of obtaining ISO 14001 certification. Figure 10 compares the percentage of companies that consider relevant benefits related BC, grouped on the base of year of certification, in line with the classification in table 2.

Figure 9. Percentage of large and small-medium companies that consider relevant the benefits of ISO 14001 certification

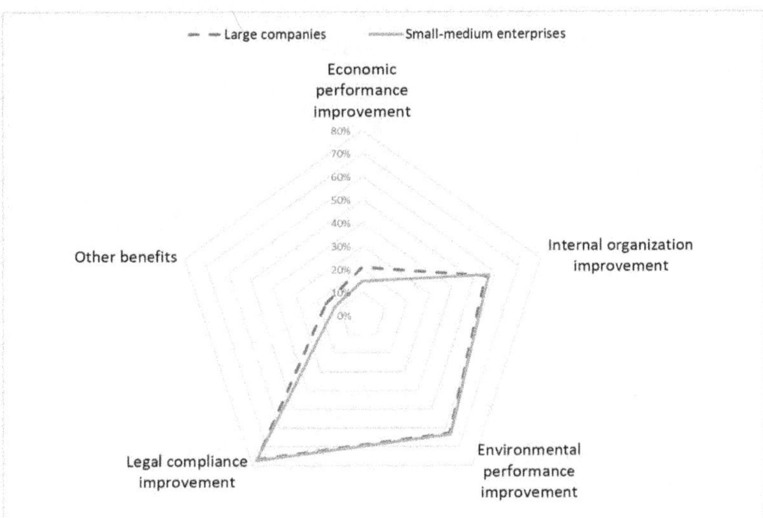

All the groups confirm legal compliance, environmental performance and internal organization as the main benefits obtained by ISO 14001 certification.

Basically, the lines in the graph in figure 10 overlap: this means that responding companies got the same benefits from ISO 14001, regardless of the year in which they have obtained the certification.

However, there are slight differences in the trends:

- Among companies certified for the longest time (group 1996-2000), very few firms claim to have obtained economic benefits from the environmental certification;
- Among recently certified companies (group 2016-2018), the percentage of firms that feel relevant economic benefits increases, reaching 20%; on the other hand, in this group environmental performance, internal organization and legislative compliance are important for a smaller number of companies.
- The companies included in the other groups (2001-2005, 2006-2010, and 2011-2015) have similar trends, with overlapped lines.

It is possible to state that the maturity of environmental management system can influence the awareness of organizations in appreciating the benefits of environmental certification in company competitiveness. At the same time, the seniority of ISO 14001 certification is a moderator factor for the ES-BC relationship in terms of economic performance improvement.

To verify the hypothesis RH-1.4, the answers must be grouped on the base of other certifications obtained by firms, in line with the classification adopted in table 3.

Figure 11 compares the percentage of Italian companies that have obtained relevant benefits from ISO 14001 certification, grouped on the base of other certifications achieved.

The radar graph in figure 11 shows some relevant information:

Figure 10. Percentage of companies that consider relevant the benefits of ISO 14001 certification, grouped on the base of year of certification

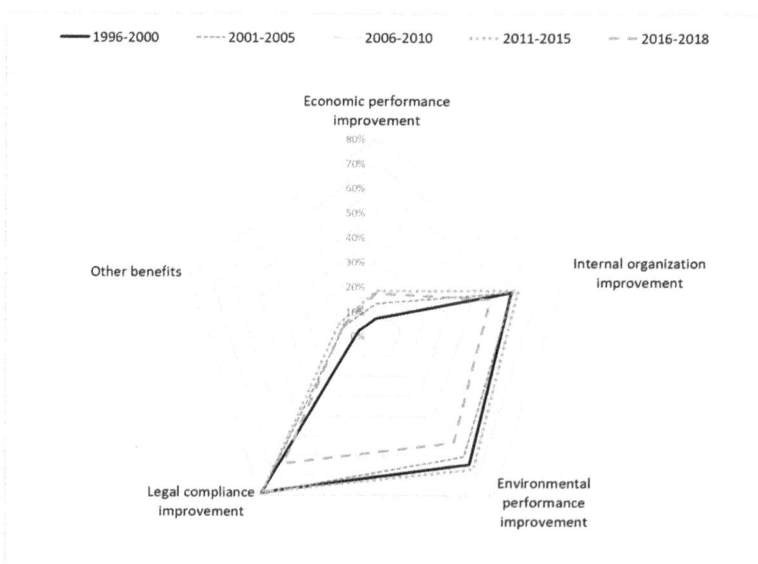

Figure 11. Percentage of companies that consider relevant the benefits of ISO 14001 certification, grouped on the base of other certifications obtained

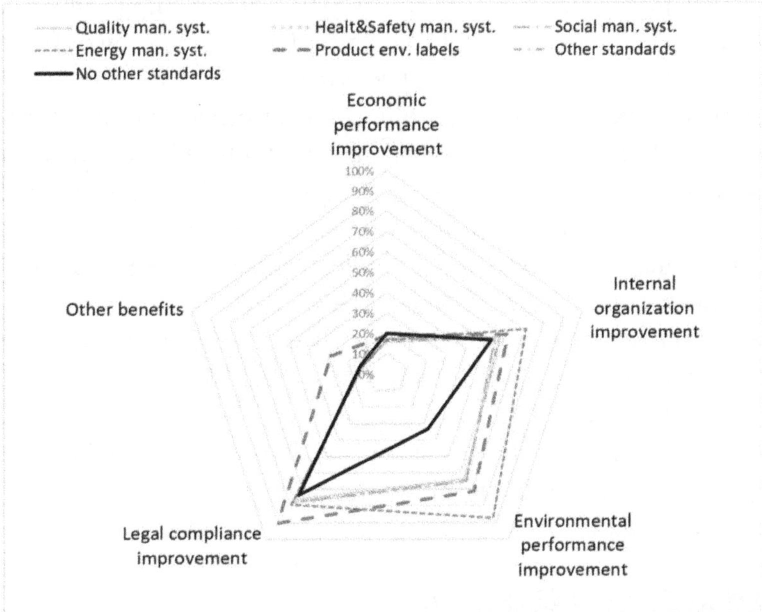

- in the group of companies that have other environmental certifications (as energy management system and product environmental labels), the percentage of them recognizing important benefits from ISO 14001 increases;
- among Italian firms with energy management system, almost 90% have achieved high environmental improvements and over 70% have achieved important results as internal organization;
- if companies have obtained other environmental product labels, the benefits of ISO 14001 in BC are even more evident;
- if companies have obtained other certifications not strictly related to environment, the answers are not affected by changes: lines related quality management system, health and safety management system, social management system and other standards appear to overlap;
- not having any other certification makes the trend worse: in this group, a lower percentage of companies declares to obtain organizational and environmental benefits from ISO 14001.

From these results, the author states that the presence of other environmental certifications is a multiplicator factor for the relationship between ES and BC. On the other hand, the presence of other certifications not strictly correlated to environmental commitments is a neutral factor in the ES-BC relationship. Finally, the absence of other certifications is a moderator factor in the relationship.

Emerging Trends from the Empirical Perspective

Summarizing the previous results, several findings emerge from the opinion of Italian managers concerning the relationship between ES and BC.

The research hypothesis RH-1.1 is partially confirmed. The positive relationship between ES and BC is strongly confirmed in terms of legal compliance, internal organization and environmental performance. Considering the economic performance, the positive ES-BC relationship is only weakly confirmed.

The research hypothesis RH-1.2 is partially confirmed. Large dimension of firms slightly favors the ES-BC positive relationship in terms of economic performance. Positive ES-BC relationship concerning legal compliance, internal organization and environmental performance is not affected by size of firms.

The research hypothesis RH-1.3 is not confirmed and partially refused. The maturity of ISO 14001 certification is a moderator in ES-BC relationship, because Italian companies certified for the longest time do not recognize economic benefits related to environmental certification. On the other hand, the youth of environmental management system is a moderator factor in ES-BC relationship in terms of environmental performance, internal organization and legal compliance.

The research hypothesis RH-1.4 is confirmed. The positive ES-BC relationship appears to be strengthened in companies that have achieved other environmental certifications, while the absence of other certifications weakens this relationship.

To synthesize these results, figure 12 represents the trends emerging from Italian companies involved in the national survey, concerning the relationship between environmental management system certification and business competitiveness.

Lessons Learned and Open Questions

This chapter has addressed the long-standing question concerning "does it pay to be green?", comparing two analytical perspectives: the vision of scientific community and the opinion of firms. A double-level survey, among scholars through a literature review and among managers through a national survey, has given very interesting results, through the confirmation or not of a series of research hypotheses.

The author resumes the research questions and tries to give the answers.

RQ1: What is the relationship between ES and BC in a scholar perspective?

As demonstrated in the third section if this chapter, from a scholar perspective there is a positive relationship between ES and BC. Furthermore, there are factors that can strengthen or weaken this relationship, such as the complexity of firms, the experience in environmental commitments, and the strategic interest in sustainability practices.

RQ2: What is the relationship between ES and BC in a manager perspective?

As illustrated in the fourth section, from the opinion of managers, in Italian companies the positive relationship between ES and BC is strongly confirmed with reference of better performance in legal compliance, internal organization and environmental impacts. On the other hand, the positive relationship between ES and economic performance is weekly confirmed.

RQ3: Is there a coherence between scholars' and managers' points of view concerning relationship between ES and BC?

Figure 12. Emerging trends on ES-BC relationship in a managers' perspective from the Italian survey

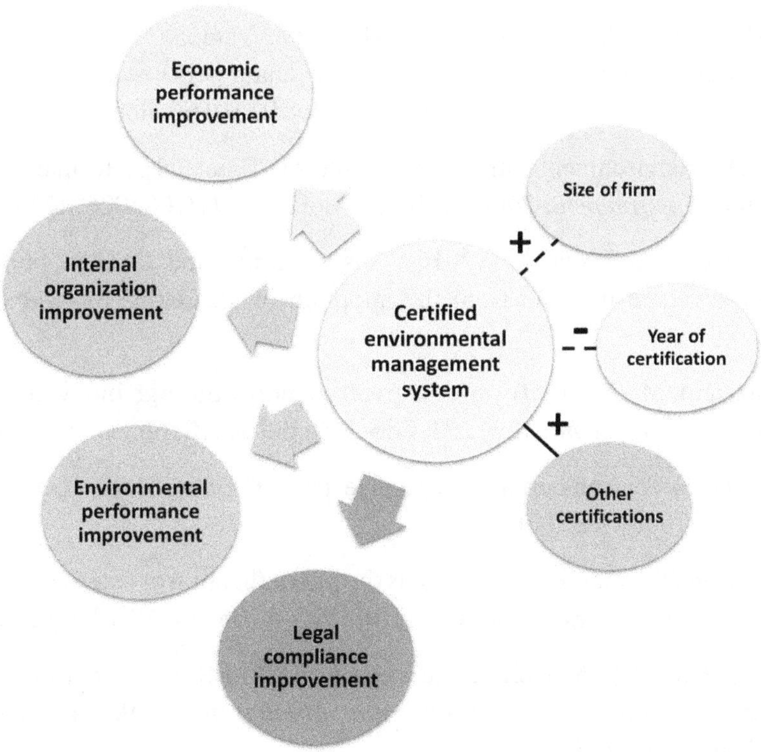

As explained in the fifth section, the moderator factors identified from the literature review are only partially confirmed by the managers' opinion. The size of firm positively affects the economic benefits associated with ES. The maturity of environmental commitments does not confirm seems to be a weakening factor in the relationship between ES and BC. Other environmental certifications strengthen the relationship between ES and environmental performance, legal compliance and internal organization.

The author concludes taking up the research goal: verify if ES favors BC, considering both scholars' theories and practitioners' opinions and comparing them, if possible.

The positive relationship between ES and BC is confirmed both by the international scientific papers published in the last 20 years and by the Italian companies certified with ISO 14001 standard. This positive relationship is coherently recognized by scholars and managers. Some firms' characteristics reinforce this relationship, both in a scholar and in a manager perspective: size of firms and presence of other environmental certifications contribute to increasing the benefits linked to ES.

In some cases, scholars' and managers' opinions reach different conclusions. Italian companies struggle to associate significant economic benefits with ES, probably because of the known difficulty of companies in quantifying the economic aspects associated with BC.

Based on this sentence, the author underlines the responsibility of scholars in this topic: they must develop effective tools easily usable by managers to quantify the economic benefits linked to environmental sustainability. This is a necessary task, to guide companies and market towards economically and environmentally sustainable choices.

REFERENCES

Acquaye, A., Ibn-Mohammed, T., Genovese, A., Afrifa, G., Yamoah, F. A., & Oppon, E. (2018). A quantitative model for environmentally sustainable supply chain performance measurement. *European Journal of Operational Research, 269*(1), 16, 188–205. doi:10.1016/j.ejor.2017.10.057

Albertini, E. (2013). Does environmental management improve financial performance? A meta-analytical review. *Organization & Environment, 26*(4), 431–457. doi:10.1177/1086026613510301

Álvarez-García, J., & del RíoRama, M. (2016). Sustainability and EMAS: Impact of motivations and barriers on the perceived benefits from the adoption of standards. *Sustainability, 8*(10), 1057. doi:10.3390u8101057

Antonioli, D., & Mazzanti, M. (2017). Towards a green economy through innovations: The role of trade union involvement. *Ecological Economics, 131*, 286–299. doi:10.1016/j.ecolecon.2016.09.003

Bhat, V. N. (1998). Does environmental compliance pay? *Ecotoxicology (London, England), 7*(4), 221–225. doi:10.1023/A:1008938811813

Bithas, K. (2011). Sustainability and externalities: Is the internalization of externalities a sufficient condition for sustainability? *Ecological Economics, 70*(10), 1703–1706. doi:10.1016/j.ecolecon.2011.05.014

Boiral, O., & Henri, J. F. (2012). Modelling the impact of ISO 14001 on environmental performance: A comparative approach. *Journal of Environmental Management, 99*, 84–97. doi:10.1016/j.jenvman.2012.01.007 PMID:22326757

Bonan, G. B. & Doney, S. C. (2018). Climate, ecosystems, and planetary futures: The challenge to predict life in Earth system models. *Science*, 359(6375), eaam8328.

Boons, F. (2002). Greening products: A framework for product chain management. *Journal of Cleaner Production, 10*(5), 495–505. doi:10.1016/S0959-6526(02)00017-3

Boons, F., & Wagner, M. (2009). Assessing the relationship between economic and ecological performance: Distinguishing system levels and the role of innovation. *Ecological Economics, 68*(7), 1908–1914. doi:10.1016/j.ecolecon.2009.02.012

Büyüközkan, G., & Karabulut, Y. (2018). Sustainability performance evaluation: Literature review and future directions. *Journal of Environmental Management, 217*, 253–267. doi:10.1016/j.jenvman.2018.03.064 PMID:29605780

Carsol, R. (1962). *Silent spring*. Boston, MA: Houghton Mifflin Harcourt.

Chen, Y. S., Chang, C. H., & Wu, F. S. (2012). Origins of green innovations: The differences between proactive and reactive green innovations. *Management Decision, 50*(3), 369–398. doi:10.1108/00251741211216197

Corbetta, P. G. (1999). *Metodologia e tecniche della ricerca sociale (Methodology and methods of the social research)*. Bologna, Italy: Il Mulino.

Dillman, D. A. (2000). *Mail and internet surveys: the Taylored design method* (2nd ed.). New York, NY: John Wiley & Sons.

Dragomir, V.D. (2013). Environmental performance and responsible corporate governance: An empirical note. *Ekonomika a management*, 16, 33-51.

Elkington, J. (1994). Towards the sustainable corporation: Win-win business strategies for sustainable development. *California Management Review, 36*(2), 90–100. doi:10.2307/41165746

Ferenhof, H. A., Vignochi, L., Selig, P. M., Lezana, A. G. R., & Campos, L. M. S. (2014). Environmental management systems in small and medium-sized enterprises: An analysis and systematic review. *Journal of Cleaner Production, 74*, 44–53. doi:10.1016/j.jclepro.2014.03.027

Gallego-Álvarez, I., García-Sánchez, I. M., & Vieira, C. D. (2014). Climate change and financial performance in times of crisis. *Business Strategy and the Environment, 23*(6), 361–374. doi:10.1002/bse.1786

Garcés-Ayerbe, C., & Cañón-de-Francia, J. (2017). The relevance of complementarities in the study of the economic consequences of environmental proactivity: Analysis of the moderating effect of innovation efforts. *Ecological Economics, 142*, 21–30. doi:10.1016/j.ecolecon.2017.06.022

Genovese, A., Morris, J. L., Piccolo, C., & Koh, S. C. L. (2017). Assessing redundancies in environmental performance measures for supply chains. *Journal of Cleaner Production, 167*, 1290–1302. doi:10.1016/j.jclepro.2017.05.186

Giannakis, G., & Papadopoulos, T. (2016). Supply chain sustainability: A risk management approach. *International Journal of Production Economics, 171*(4), 455–470. doi:10.1016/j.ijpe.2015.06.032

Guimarães, J. C. F., Severo, E. A., & Vasconcelos, C. R. M. (2018). The influence of entrepreneurial, market, knowledge management orientations on cleaner production and the sustainable competitive advantage. *Journal of Cleaner Production, 174*, 1653–1663. doi:10.1016/j.jclepro.2017.11.074

Heras-Saizarbitoria, I., Arana, G., & Boiral, O. (2015). Exploring the dissemination of environmental certifications in high and low polluting industries. *Journal of Cleaner Production, 89*, 50–58. doi:10.1016/j.jclepro.2014.10.088

Horváthová, E. (2010). Does environmental performance affect financial performance? A meta-analysis. *Ecological Economics, 70*(1), 52–59. doi:10.1016/j.ecolecon.2010.04.004

Horváthová, E. (2012). The impact of environmental performance on firm performance: Short-term costs and long-time benefits. *Ecological Indicators, 84*, 91–97.

Hotelling, H. (1931). The economics of exhaustible resources. *Journal of Political Economy, 39*(2), 137–175. doi:10.1086/254195

Ismail, M. S., Ramli, A., & Darus, F. (2014). Environmental management accounting practices ad Islamic corporate social responsibility compliance: Evidence from ISO14001 companies. *Procedia: Social and Behavioral Sciences, 145*, 343–351. doi:10.1016/j.sbspro.2014.06.043

ISO. (2015). *ISO 14001:2015 Environmental management systems – Requirements with guidance of use*. Geneva, Switzerland: International Organization for Standardization.

ISO. (2018). T*he ISO survey of management system standard certifications – 2017*. International Organization for Standardization. Available at https://isotc.iso.org/livelink/livelink?func=ll&objId=18808772&objAction=browse&viewType=1

Jørgensen, M. S., & Jensen, C. L. (2012). The shaping of environmental impacts from Danish production and consumption of clothing. *Ecological Economics*, *83*, 164–173. doi:10.1016/j.ecolecon.2012.04.002

Kalmykova, Y., Sadagopan, M., & Rosado, L. (2018). Circular economy – From review of theories and practices to development of implementation tools. *Resources, Conservation and Recycling*, *135*, 190–201. doi:10.1016/j.resconrec.2017.10.034

Katiyar, R., Meena, P. L., Barua, M. K., Tibrewala, R., & Kumar, G. (2018). Impact of sustainability and manufacturing practices on supply chain performance: Findings from an emerging economy. *International Journal of Production Economics*, *197*, 303–316. doi:10.1016/j.ijpe.2017.12.007

Koberg, E., & Longoni, A. (2019). A systematic review of sustainable supply chain management in global supply chains. *Journal of Cleaner Production*, *207*, 1084–1098. doi:10.1016/j.jclepro.2018.10.033

Kogg, B., & Mont, O. (2012). Environmental and social responsibility in supply chains: The practice of choice and inter-organisational management. *Ecological Economics*, *83*, 154–163. doi:10.1016/j.ecolecon.2011.08.023

Kollmann, K., & Prakash, A. (2001). Green by choice? Cross-national variation in firms' responses to EMS-based environmental regimes. *World Politics*, *53*(3), 399–430. doi:10.1353/wp.2001.0010

Lee, S. M., Noh, Y., Choi, D., & Rha, J. S. (2017). Environmental policy performances for sustainable development: From the perspective of ISO 14001 certification. *Corporate Social Responsibility and Environmental Management*, *24*(2), 108–120. doi:10.1002/csr.1395

Lintukangas, K., Kähkönen, A. K., & Ritala, P. (2016). Supply risks as drivers of green supply management adoption. *Journal of Cleaner Production*, *112*(3), 1901–1909. doi:10.1016/j.jclepro.2014.10.089

Luederitz, C., Meyer, M., Abson, D. J., Gralla, F., Lang, D. J., Rau, A. L., & von Wehrden, H. (2016). Systematic student-driven literature review in sustainability science—An effective way to merge research and teaching. *Journal of Cleaner Production*, *119*, 229–235. doi:10.1016/j.jclepro.2016.02.005

Matinaro, V., Liu, Y., Le, T. R. J. S., & Poesche, J. (2019). Extracting key factors for sustainable development of enterprises: Case study of SMEs in Taiwan. *Journal of Cleaner Production*, *209*, 1152–1169. doi:10.1016/j.jclepro.2018.10.280

Mattioda, R. A., Mazzi, A., Canciglieri, O., & Scipioni, A. (2015). Determining the principal references of the social life cycle assessment of products. *The International Journal of Life Cycle Assessment*, *8*(8), 1155–1165. doi:10.100711367-015-0873-z

Mazzi, A., Toniolo, S., Manzardo, A., Ren, J., & Scipioni, A. (2016, Nov. 19). (2016/a). Exploring the direction on the environmental and business performance relationship at the firm level. Lessons from a literature review. *Sustainability*, *8*(11), 1200. doi:10.3390u8111200

Mazzi, A., Toniolo, S., Mason, M., Aguiari, F., & Scipioni, A. (2016, December). (2016/b). What are the benefits and difficulties in adopting an environmental management system? The opinion of Italian organizations. *Journal of Cleaner Production, 139*, 873–885. doi:10.1016/j.jclepro.2016.08.053

Meadows, D. H., Meadows, D. L., Randers, J., & Behrens, W. W. (1972). The limits to growth. New York, NY: Potomac Associates - Universe Books.

Merli, R., Preziosi, M., & Ippolito, C. (2016). Promoting sustainability through EMS application: A survey examining the critical factors about EMAS registration in Italian organizations. *Sustainability, 8*(3), 197. doi:10.3390u8030197

Morioka, S. N., Bolis, I., Evans, S., & Carvalho, M. M. (2017). Transforming sustainability challenges into competitive advantage: Multiple case studies kaleidoscope converging into sustainable business models. *Journal of Cleaner Production, 167*, 723–738. doi:10.1016/j.jclepro.2017.08.118

Neuteleers, S., & Engelen, B. (2015). Talking money: How market-based valuation can determine environmental protection. *Ecological Economics, 117*, 253–260. doi:10.1016/j.ecolecon.2014.06.022

Ni, B. (2018). Productivity, capital intensity, and ISO 14001 adoption: Theory and evidence. *Review of Development Economics, 23*(1), 395–414. doi:10.1111/rode.12547

O'Rourke, D. (2014). The science of sustainable supply chains. *Science, 344*(6188), 1124–1127. doi:10.1126cience.1248526 PMID:24904157

Paillé, P., Chen, Y., Boirla, O., & Jin, J. (2014). The impact of human resource management on environmental performance: An employee-level study. *Journal of Business Ethics, 121*(3), 451–466. doi:10.100710551-013-1732-0

Pérez-Calderón, E., Milanés-Montero, P., & Ortega-Rossel, F. J. (2012). Environmental performance and firm value: Evidence from Dow Jones Sustainability Index Europe. *International Journal of Environmental of Research, 6*, 1007–1014.

Pesce, M., Shi, C., Critto, A., Wang, X., & Marcomini, A. (2018). SWOT analysis of the application of International Standard ISO 14001 in the Chinese context. A case study of Guangdong Province. *Sustainability, 10*(9), 3196. doi:10.3390u10093196

Porter, M. E. (1991). America's green strategy. *Scientific American, 264*(4), 168. doi:10.1038cientific american0491-168

Porter, M. E., & Kramer, M. (2011). Creating shared value. How to reinvent capitalism and unleash the wave of innovation and growth. *Harvard Business Review, 89*, 62–77.

Qorri, A., Mujkić, A., & Kraslawski, A. (2018). A conceptual framework for measuring sustainability performance of supply chains. *Journal of Cleaner Production, 189*, 570–584. doi:10.1016/j.jclepro.2018.04.073

Raut, R. D., Mangla, S. K., Narwane, V. S., Gardas, B. B., Priyadarshinee, P., & Narkhede, B. E. (2019). Linking big data analytics and operational sustainability practices for sustainable business management. *Journal of Cleaner Production, 224*, 10–24. doi:10.1016/j.jclepro.2019.03.181

Ren, S., He, D., Zhang, T., & Chen, X. (2019). Symbolic reactions or substantive pro-environmental behavior? An empirical study of corporate environmental performance under the government's environmental subsidy scheme. *Business Strategy and the Environment*, in press. doi:10.1002/bse.2308

Rivas-Asanza, W., Celleri-Pacheco, J., Andrade-Garda, J., García-Vázquez, R., Mato-Abad, V., Rodríguez-Yáñez, S., & Suárez-Garaboa, S. (2018). Environmental sustainability in information technologies governance. *Sustainability*, *10*(12), 4792. doi:10.3390u10124792

Rockström, J., Steffen, W., Noone, K., Persson, Å., Chapin, F. S., Lambin, E., ... Foley, J. (2009). Planetary boundaries: exploring the safe operating space for humanity. *Ecology and Society*, *14*(2), 32. doi:10.5751/ES-03180-140232

Roulet, T., & Touboul, S. (2015). The intentions with which the road is paved: Attitudes to liberalism as determinants of greenwashing. *Journal of Business Ethics*, *128*(2), 305–320. doi:10.100710551-014-2097-8

Schneider, A., & Meins, E. (2013). Two dimensions of corporate sustainability assessment: Towards a comprehensive framework. *Business Strategy and the Environment*, *21*(4), 211–222. doi:10.1002/bse.726

Singh, N., Jain, S., & Sharma, P. (2015). Motivations for implementing environmental management practices in Indian industries. *Ecological Economics*, *109*, 1–8. doi:10.1016/j.ecolecon.2014.11.003

Steffen, W., Richardson, K., Rockström, J., Cornell, S. E., Fetzer, I., Bennett, E. M., ... Sörlin, S. (2015). Planetary boundaries: Guiding human development on a changing planet. *Science*, *347*(6223). doi:10.1126cience.1259855 PMID:25592418

Taghikhah, F., Voinov, A., & Shukla, N. (2019). Extending the supply chain to address sustainability. *Journal of Cleaner Production*, *229*, 652–666. doi:10.1016/j.jclepro.2019.05.051

Toniolo, S., Mazzi, A., Mazzarotto, G., & Scipioni A. (2019/a). International standards with a life cycle perspective: which dimension of sustainability is addressed? *International Journal of Life Cycle Assessment*, (in press). doi:10.100711367-019-01606-w

Toniolo, S., Mazzi, A., Simonetto, M., Zuliani, F., & Scipioni, A. (2019/b). Mapping diffusion of environmental product declarations released by European program operators. *Sustainable Production and Consumption*, 17, 85-94.

Ullmann, A. (1985). Data in search of a theory: A critical examination of the relationship among social performance, social disclosure and economic performance of U.S. firms. *Academy of Management Review*, *10*, 540–557.

UN. (1992). *Report of the United Nations Conference on Environment and Development. Annex I - Rio Declaration on Environment and Development*. United Nations, Rio de Janeiro. Retrieved from https://www.un.org/documents/ga/conf151/aconf15126-1annex1.htm

UN. (2002). *Plan of implementation of the world summit on sustainable development. United Nations, UN Documents*, A/CONF.199/20. United Nations, Johannesburg. Retrieved from http://www.un-documents.net/jburgpln.htm

Valdivia, S., Ugaya, C. M. L., Hildenbrand, J., Traverso, M., Mazijn, B., & Sonnemann, G. (2013). A UNEP/SETAC approach towards a life cycle sustainability assessment—Our contribution to Rio+20. *The International Journal of Life Cycle Assessment*, *18*(9), 1673–1685. doi:10.100711367-012-0529-1

Vildåsen, S. S., Keitsch, M., & Fet, A. M. (2017). Clarifying the epistemology of corporate sustainability. *Ecological Economics*, *138*, 40–46. doi:10.1016/j.ecolecon.2017.03.029

Wijethilake, C. (2017). Proactive sustainability strategy and corporate sustainability performance: The mediating effect of sustainability control systems. *Journal of Environmental Management*, *196*, 569–582. doi:10.1016/j.jenvman.2017.03.057 PMID:28351823

Xu, X., Zeng, S., & Chen, H. (2018). Signaling good by doing good: How does environmental corporate social responsibility affect international expansion? *Business Strategy and the Environment*, *27*(7), 946–959. doi:10.1002/bse.2044

KEY TERMS AND DEFINITIONS

Certification: The confirmation of certain characteristics of an object, person, or organization, provided by some form of external review, education, assessment, or audit.

Circular Economy: An economic system aimed at minimizing resource input and waste, emission, and energy by slowing, closing, and narrowing energy and material loops; this can be achieved through long-lasting design, maintenance, repair, reuse, remanufacturing, refurbishing, and recycling.

Competitiveness: The set of strategies, policies and factors that determine the level of productivity of a company; competitive economies are most likely to be able to grow more sustainably and inclusively, meaning more likelihood that everyone in society will benefit from the fruits of economic growth.

Environment: All of the natural materials and living things, which include air, water, sunlight and their relationships.

Environmental Management System: The framework that helps an organization achieve its environmental goals, reduce its environmental impacts and improve its environmental performance through systematic plans, effective processes and practices, consistent monitoring and evaluation, in a continuous improvement perspective.

International Standards: Technical or organizational rules developed by international standards organizations, with a large user base worldwide, to overcome technical barriers in international commerce caused by differences among technical regulations and standards developed independently and separately by each nation or industry.

Literature Review: A critical analysis of published sources, or literature, on a particular topic, through collection, classification, comparison and evaluation of contents.

Survey Methodology: A research methodology that studies a sampling of individual units from a population through associated techniques of survey data collection, such as questionnaire construction and methods to ask one or more questions that may or may not be answered.

Sustainability: The process of people maintaining change in a balanced environment, in which the exploitation of resources, the direction of investments, the orientation of technological development and institutional change are all in harmony and enhance both current and future potential to meet human needs and aspirations.

Triple Bottom Line: An accounting framework with three parts, social, environmental (or ecological) and financial, adopted by organizations to evaluate their performance in a broader perspective to create greater business value coherently in the concept of sustainability.

Chapter 7
Sustainable Innovation in Fashion Products:
An Opportunity for Italian SMEs

Alessandra De Chiara
University of Naples "L'Orientale", Italy

Floriana Iannone
University of Naples "L'Orientale", Italy

ABSTRACT

The chapter deepens the theme of sustainability in fashion products, exploring the importance of sustainable innovation as a competitive driver. The fashion industry is not exempt from issues related to sustainability, in its economic, environmental, and social sense, since it is one of the most polluting industries in the world, in addition to being often shaken by scandals related to the poor working conditions for many fashion factory workers around the world. Given the relevance of the issue of sustainability in the fashion supply chains, the chapter will provide food for thought on the question of managerial behaviors based on sustainability and deepen the knowledge on the need of a collaborative approach among firms and within the supply chains of the fashion system.

INTRODUCTION

The fashion industry is not exempt from the issues related to sustainability. Within its economic, environmental, and social meaning, it is one of the most polluting industries in the world. In fact, 20% of the global waste of water is attributed to the industry's production, and 10% of carbon dioxide emissions, a strong incidence in the production of greenhouse gases that is expected, in the next 12 years, to increase by 60%, contributing massively to global warming (United Nations, 2018). The release of highly harmful substances in so many rivers is alarming (Greenpeace, 2011), as well as the data on unbridled consumerism against very low percentages of recycling; 85% of the clothes produced end up in landfills and only 1% are recycled. The fashion industry has important repercussions on social well-being, too,

DOI: 10.4018/978-1-7998-1419-1.ch007

considering its massive outsourcing practices to countries that pay less attention to workers' rights, and also without underestimating its implications on ethical issues related to animal abuse.

The Italian fashion industry is a fundamentally important sector for the economy of the country. Its competitiveness is based on a mix of tradition, style, and innovation, which has also led Italy to register positive trends in the last year (+ 2.5% growth in turnover in 2017, + 4.3% exports), with an estimated positive trend for 2018, which confirms fashion as the second largest industry in the country (Confindustria Moda, 2017). However, many opportunities are still available, especially by smaller companies and, in this perspective, sustainability can be a key factor to strengthen the competitiveness of the sector. Although the theme of sustainability is a very topical issue, and there are many examples that evoke the commitment of large companies and big brands, the theoretical debate does not go deep into the opportunities existing for small and medium-sized fashion companies. Sustainability could act as a distinctive feature, further defending these Italian companies' offers against competition from firms of developing countries that often embrace a model of low quality/price.

The present work intends to contribute to debate to identify the characteristics of a sustainable innovation strategy as a driver of SMEs' competitiveness, and to answer the question: what are the resources needed to implement this strategy?

Above all, this paper presents some elements of originality that can be traced in an effort to deepen the theme of sustainability in the fashion system with reference to SMEs. The discussion about which resources are required to face the challenge of sustainability and which ones are most relevant to pursue this type of strategy is an element of absolute importance, too; this is the aspect to stress in order to stimulate a concrete commitment of fashion companies towards sustainability and to implement policies to support them.

The work is structured as follows: the first part deals with the issue of the sustainable innovation strategy and the resources needed to develop this strategy, with particular reference to textile apparel companies; in the second part the work reports the results of the empirical survey carried out on a sample of opinion leaders (institutional representatives of the sector in Italy), the managerial implications and conclusions, as well as the limits of the research and the future trajectories of research.

SUSTAINABLE INNOVATION STRATEGY: A FOCUS ON FASHION PRODUCTS

Corporation as citizen is a concept which emphasizes a corporations' social function, underlining companies' abilities to bring benefits to society and the environment while improving its competitiveness (Porter & Kramer, 2002; Husted & Allen 2007). Starting the analysis from Caroll's thought which provides, at the end of the 1970s, a pyramidal structure for illustrating the priorities that all businesses should consider while defining their conduct and pursuing their objectives; literature has proposed corporate social responsibility as an essential element for doing business, as institutional guidelines pointed out that companies must find the most viable solutions to create a shared value for owners, stakeholders, and society (European Commission on CSR strategy 2011-2014), until they recognize in the concept of corporate social responsibility a competitive strategy when there is a clear statement of social/environmental objectives in the business mission and strategies (Porter & Kramer, 2006). Other essential elements are the formalization of organizational processes and structures, the implementation of policy and effective measures (to reduce the impact of business practices on the environment or ensure a higher social cohesion), and the communication of social and environmental performances (De

Chiara, 2016). Based on the presence of these elements, the sustainable strategy can be considered a competitive strategy formed on "the creation of the business offer through its ethical connotations, namely adding an "ecological value" or "social value" to the product/service it intends to provide" (De Chiara, 2016, p.12). The response to environmental and social instances has been described as one of the best market opportunities that allows businesses to differentiate market position, improving the competitive advantage (Porter & Kramer, 2011).

Literature and institutions have also stressed the important role of SMEs in diffusion of the sustainable business behaviors (Battaglia et al., 2010; Testa et al., 2012; UNIDO, 2007; EC, 2013), underlining the strategic asset of social capital while engaging in responsible conducts by virtue of their strong ties to the local system (Harvey et al., 1991; Perrini & Tencati, 2008). Collaborations and networks seem to be special pre-conditions for the identification of sustainable paths and for developing all the necessary competences to raise awareness of sustainability issues in defining business strategies (Molteni et al., 2006). In SMEs, the ability to maintain relationships and build confidence among stakeholders is considered a strategic resource. "If social capital is a strategic asset, its management is strategic too (De Chiara, 2012). For the purposes of responsible social capital management, SMEs will be able to strengthen the relationship nature of these actors, in other words, the corporate social responsibility will help increase SMEs' social capital" (De Chiara, 2016, p.26).

If literature agrees that for SMEs sustainability principles to be applied through a network-based approach, equally shared is the thesis that, in this highly globalized scenario, sustainable-driven strategies become a safe differentiation factor and a generator of competitive advantage, ensuring each enterprise enhanced visibility and increased profit margin (Molteni & Todisco, 2008). Unfortunately, as pointed out by several international organizations (UNIDO, 2007, EC, 2011), SMEs hardly engage in responsible conduct, probably due to cultural or financial barriers. Several studies underline that this kind of firms have relatively minor importance individually, while collectively they can generate a great impact. According to Lawrence et al. (2006) while individually small and medium sized enterprises (SMEs) may have small social, environmental and financial impacts, cumulatively their impact is significant. The question is how a single economic entity, especially a small-scale enterprise, can be engaged in the uptake of sustainability practices. Between the barriers to SMEs adoption of environmental practices, the first limit can be traced back to self-perception about the impact they have on the environment (Ammenberg & Hjelm, 2003; Hillary, 1995; Simpson et al., 2004). Some authors focus the problem underlining the lack of expertise and understanding of strategies to address environmental issues (Ammenberg & Hjelm, 2003; Simpson et al., 2004; Tilley, 1999; Welford, 1994); others identify the 'cost' as the major barrier to more proactive environmental behavior in SMEs, with mangers perceiving little financial benefit from environmental investments (Petts et al., 1998; Revell & Rutherfoord, 2003; Simpson et al., 2004).

Then the institutions have to propose practical approaches for SMEs based on dialogue with stakeholders or the creation of business clusters (i.e. business networks and business clusters) to boost growth and increase competitiveness (De Chiara, 2016). The role of associations is important in generating growth, depending on their ability «to improve the performance of individual firms through offering selective benefits (such as information and advice); through collective supports it is important for society to also build-up structures where SMEs will be enabled to enhance their contribution to the common good» (Bennett, 1999, p.593).

In the Italian economic-productive tissue, characterized almost exclusively by SMEs, it becomes important to adopt a collaborative approach in order to foster corporate social responsibility practices in SMEs.

The planning of this strategy «must primarily focus on the 'hierarchical' level of all potential decisions for planning sustainable projects that would comply with the business resources/abilities and be credible for all stakeholders» (De Chiara, 2016, p.13), not to be appreciated as an additional element in business strategies implementation, but as an integral part of management (Molteni & Todisco, 2008). This consideration could imply radical change of strategic and management perspective (Perrini & Pivato, 2007), including the implementation of innovations in terms of how business practices and processes are sustainably driven.

Innovation is the key that allows change to the production processes and its output towards sustainability levels. Companies with sustainability integrated in their orientation and innovation processes show value creation: the development of products new to the market (radical innovations) and cooperation with stakeholders (Bos-Brouwers, 2010). In recent years, many scholars have dealt with the combination of sustainability and innovation as a new and further challenge for businesses. Blowfield, Visser & Livesey (2007) describe innovation as a key to responding to sustainability; in fact, scholars have taken up previous scientific works (Andersson & Bateman, 2000) in which the transformation of the problems deriving from a low level of sustainability into business growth opportunities was proposed. In this way, the company can succeed in developing ideas and customized solutions around sustainable prospects. Several studies have examined the positive results (Bhattacharya, 2001; Porter & Kramer, 2002, Knox & Maklan, 2004; Swaen & Vanhamme, 2005) so it is no surprise that CSR has increasingly been referred to as a major asset in the core business, rather than a peripheral decision with philanthropic connotations (Bhattacharya et al., 2004). However, some studies denounce that companies often opt for spot initiatives (as proposed, among others, by Becker-Olsen in 2006) with effects that can be reached quickly and in the short term, but without the possibility of continuation in the medium-long term.

With regard to SMEs, a qualitative research on a sample of 68 German SMEs from three industries (automotive suppliers, mechanical and plant engineering, as well as electrical engineering and ICT), demonstrated that Industry 4.0 affects the three business model elements of manufacturing SMEs – value creation, value capture, and value offer – by giving specific examples for business model innovation in each of the three elements (Müller et al., 2018). A company internally motivated and/or externally pressured towards implementation has an impact on which business model elements are innovated. In addition, many sustainable innovations are directed at the improvement of technological processes (eco-efficiency) and to lower costs of production (Müller et al., 2018).

Innovation is identified as the keystone towards achieving better environmental and social performance conditions in the fashion supply chain both in the theoretical debate and in business studies. Niinimäki's studies (2015) tackle the question by showing that innovation should not be understood solely as technological development for the achievement of tools to support the fashion supply chain, but also as the stimulus towards the structuring of new interactions and partnerships between the various stakeholders that revolve around the supply chain, without excluding a direct involvement of the consumer. The latter is not only the mere recipient of a piece of clothing, but is the one who can guide the behavior of companies through responsible choices in terms of sustainability. Consumers are aware of the fact that the location of the production plant, the configuration of the manufacturing process, the useful life of the product, as well as the distance in geographical terms from the places of production to those of distribution and, then, to the places of final purchase, have a significant impact on the environment and on the social contexts in which production processes materialize (Niinimäki and Hassi, 2011).

In the study of Armstrong et al. (2015), it has been shown that consumers are able to discern the effects of their actions with respect to the consequences in terms of sustainability. In particular, the choices of repair and re-design of the item of clothing, restitution of used garments, personalization, design in autonomy, advice on fashion styles to use neglected garments, borrowing clothing, and product exchange were considered. The primary result that emerges in this study concerns the role of consumers in increasing the useful life of the product: the repair choices prolong the period of use; customization makes the product unique and, therefore, perceived as more durable; the choice to borrow allows the use of the item of clothing by multiple users, and the stylistic consultancy service makes it possible to identify new opportunities for the use of a garment. The second consequence is the reduction of waste deriving from abandoned garments as a result of repairs and re-design, or due to the return to the sales points. Furthermore, the research also gives an indication of which age groups seem most favorably affected by the possibilities offered by these actions: consumers under 40 express a preference on the exchange of clothing and the possibility of returning clothes used, followed by the granting of vouchers to be used within the same point of sale where the item was purchased; consumers over 40 prefer stylistic consultancy in a store.

Sustainability criteria are considered important in the choice of a garment (indicated in third place after form, style, and price) and the trend of sustainable fashion seems to grow, especially due to millennials that are revolutionizing consumer models and pay more attention to the eco-ethical component of what they buy (Albouy & Adesida, 2018).

The thesis of sustainable innovation as a driver of competitiveness has been adopted and also testified by some recent surveys. In particular, in the textile sector, recent research identifies among the reasons for the development of green products:

1. The need to differentiate the production from that of competitors;
2. The need to adapt to customer requests;
3. The need to adapt to standards imposed by the countries in which products are exported;
4. The production of articles consistent with their ethical values (Blumine - Acimit, 2016).

Sourcing fashion products from abroad is one of the factors against which the finger is pointed by those who are interested in sustainability. In fact, the favorable economic aspects sought by manufacturing companies do not match beneficial effects for the environment, for workers, for the use of natural resources, and for transparency towards consumers (Farrer, 2018).

This theoretical debate supports the thesis that the participation and integration of the supply chain and the sharing of objectives and practices is not only desirable to have a greater impact in terms of sustainable processes and products, but is also necessary where it is not possible to pursue a high level of monitoring and control, or even these practices could be harmful in supply chain relations (Wiemere & Plugge, 2007; Russo Spena & De Chiara, 2012). The engagement approach represents, therefore, a model of management of the activities necessary to collect the experiences related to the specificities of each activity of the supply chain, to obtain the support of resources and capacity of the actors, as well as to collect the necessary support and guarantee understanding and the sharing of sustainable innovation strategies (De Chiara, 2016).

Logistics social responsibility, purchasing social responsibility (Carter & Jennings 2002, 2004), as well as sustainable supply chain management (Teuscher et al., 2006) are some of the first approaches that have emphasized the effectiveness of the adoption of social responsibility practices in a collaborative logic, underlining the strategic role played by the supplier (Maignan et al., 2002; Vurro et al., 2009; Andersen & Skjoett-Larsen, 2009). These studies tend to converge on a definition of sustainable supply

Figure 1. Strategic assets for sustainable innovation strategy
Source: (our elaboration)

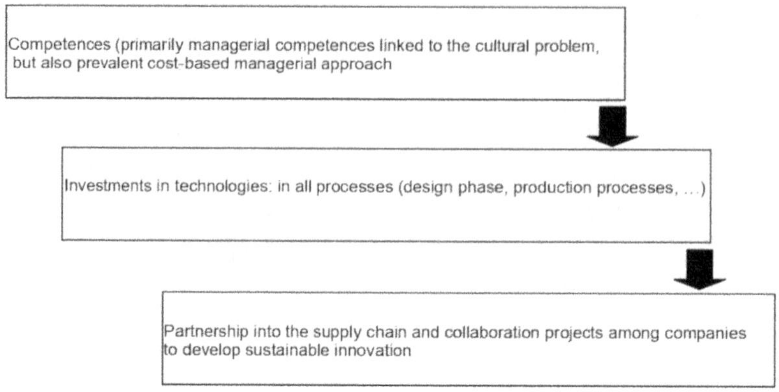

chain that places emphasis on the voluntary integration of policies and tools aimed at involving and empowering suppliers and distributors on social, environmental, and safety issues.

WHAT RESOURCES EXIST FOR SUSTAINABLE INNOVATION STRATEGY IN FASHION INDUSTRY?

The sustainable approach to the production of fashion products involves every phase of the production process, from design to product development, up to the sale. Most critical issues in adopting a sustainable approach in the fashion industry are individuated:

1. Lack of awareness, which leads managers and designers not to deal with sustainability right from the start;
2. The lack of specific tools to assess the impact of materials, colors, and printing techniques;
3. The tendency of many brands to the so-called "design to cost", i.e. to design taking into consideration the immediate costs of production without paying attention to the costs, economic or not, during the entire life cycle of the garment.

However, there is a significant increase in the commitment of companies regarding the attention paid to the socio-environmental impact of productions, through greater investments in technology and training; from Adidas to Nike, and Asos to Levi's, many important brands are investing in sustainable design.

Summarizing essential assets can be identified in: competences, investments in technologies, and engagement into the supply chain (Figure 1).

The development of sustainable business models calls into question specific sensitivity and skills starting from the manager now asked to implement new approaches. The lack of awareness of the need for a planned process becomes an obstacle, just as the lack of awareness of the binomial sustainability-competitiveness is an important cultural problem. Many brands tend to consider the immediate costs of production without paying attention to the costs in economic, social, and environmental dimensions over a long period.

In Italy, despite the growing attention to sustainability issues (see also the annual Green Carpet Award 2018), fashion has not started a profound reflection on its behaviors and the change in the competitive model. It must be said that fashion sustainability cannot be treated as a fashionable topic, but requires a radical change in the management model of one of the largest global industries, a change that involves chemistry, textiles, the world of technology and logistics, the accessories industry, distribution, the tertiary sector, and agriculture.

At the international level, some studies show that an improvement in the sustainable performance of the companies in the sector is underway: the report "Seven Years of Detoxing the Clothing Industry of Greenpeace" reports the important results regarding the complete elimination of perfluorinates (Pfc), difficult chemical substances to dispose of and are very harmful to the environment, yet widely used for the production of sportswear; as well as the important effects in terms of greater consumer awareness that has stimulated greater traceability of the supply chains in companies and a growing attention to the sustainability of all the major luxury brands.

Investment in technology seems to be the crucial driver for sustainable innovation. Already in the first phase of design and development, some decisions were taken that could significantly influence the environmental impact that a fashion product will have: the materials to be used and the colors with which the products and printing methods of the fabrics are dyed. Therefore, it is important to plan how the fashion product can be designed to reduce environmental impact during the design phase.

Many companies have chosen to invest in technology; Nike, in collaboration with the London College of Fashion, has developed 'MAKING,' an app that makes it easy for designers to design taking into account the cost of various materials in terms of water, chemicals, energy, and waste; Adidas has opted, instead, for an improvement in the research and development area from which Parley Ocean Plastic was born, a range of innovative and ecological materials created starting from the recycling of plastic waste, intercepted before they are dispersed in the sea. From this waste, Ultraboost, the record sneakers, were produced, selling one million pieces in a year. Besides, in the search for sustainable materials, we must mention the creators of Orange Fiber, a fiber obtained from the waste of oranges, and New Life, obtained instead from the recycling of plastic bottles, both winners of the Technology and Innovation Award.

Even in the phase of industrial development it is important to invest in technology: eco-friendly production technologies, but also management applications that can ensure product traceability (e.g. sourcemap)- as well as allowing those who buy to verify the production process and buy consciously- are vital.

In the Italian textile segment, data shows that companies have already started investing in the use of technologies to reduce environmental impact. In particular, investments are recorded to limit the consumption of water and energy in the dyeing and finishing phases; investments in industrial processes based on biochemistry and biotechnology to limit the use of chemicals; and investments to optimize the production chain, from design to distribution, rationalizing processes and reducing waste (TextileEvolution, Made in Italy 4.0). Investments in technologies are considered a valid tool to support the necessary synergy between textile producers and textile machinery (Bluesign - Acimit, 2016), as they produce the following main improvements: energy saving, versatility, reduction of process chemicals, increase in safety at work, reduction of water consumption, increasing the speed of data management, and reducing emissions.

Supply chain management is certainly a critical phase, but even in this case some technological applications can be implemented in order to monitor the processes carried out elsewhere (for example the software sourcemap). Beyond the use of technological solutions to manage information flows, in the strongly de-verticalized fashion system chains, which involve numerous actors to pass from the raw material to the finished product, it is necessary to share knowledge and experience to better align the processes towards sustainability. Collaborating not only implies the continuous exchange of information, but requires the definition of a collaborative model and operational tools to make the collaboration work. The engagement can be considered the main approach to define and implement sustainability strategies, as it represents a necessary condition to guarantee the inclusion of the various requests and ensure the choice of shared sustainable initiatives and policies that satisfy all the parties involved; as well as an indispensable approach to implement strategies, to put sustainability initiatives into practice and to have an effective impact in terms of sustainable development (De Chiara, 2017).

Barratt's work (2004) identifies the elements necessary to support collaboration:

1. A collaborative culture, which is composed of additional elements such as trust, reciprocity, exchange of information, openness and communication;
2. The strategic elements, which include resources, intra-organizational support, the point of view of the company (corporate focus), and technology.

Companies must develop the ability to select the supplier with whom to collaborate (Espino-Rodriguetz & Rodriguez-Diaz, 2008), and the ability to identify the most appropriate engagement model (Greenwood, 2007), as well as identify the governance mechanisms for coordination and communication (Huang et al., 2014; Tachizawa & Wong, 2015; United Nation Global Compact, 2015).

Some Italian studies shows that fashion companies, attentive to the impact of the supply chain in terms of sustainability, pay particular attention to the supply of raw materials, favoring short supply chains (Caniato, 2012). This is evident both upstream of the supply chain, favoring nearby suppliers, in some cases all processing is carried out in Italy, precisely to ensure the ethicality of the products, with particular reference to working conditions and the selection of raw materials. Differently, in the case of supply from abroad, there is a prevalence of the choice to rely on a first level of suppliers, appropriately selected and with whom they maintain long-lasting relationships.

The adoption of shorter supply chains is also found in reference to the disintermediation of commercial relations (Caniato, 2012), with choices for the distribution of products directly to end consumers. Numerous forms make it possible to activate these operating modes of distribution, focusing above all on proximity relationships (in particular geographical) between consumers, with one of them playing the role of pivot of the final distribution phase and which is the only counterpart of the distribution with respect to company. These operations were first proposed to other goods, especially those of a food nature, but were subsequently expanded also to different sectors, including the fashion sector. These practices bring out a discrepancy in the relationship between the sustainability of purchasing behavior and the cost-effectiveness of the purchase; in fact, in the short distribution systems to the purchase cheapness there are also positive consequences for the environment, given the reduced use of resources for transport. On the contrary, it is argued that purchasing choices aimed at reducing the economic impact on the consumer (Hawley, 2018) tend to aggravate the balance of resources used, if the products are the result of supply chains originated by some operators of countries with little attention to the sustainability of their productions.

The improvement of the interaction skills among the firms of the supply chain helps to extract the innovative potential inherent in the cooperation (Dyer & Singh, 1998; Tencati & Zsolnai, 2008), increasing the value and quality of operations and process outputs (Dallocchio et al., 2010) and, consequently, allowing the support of competitive models linked to differentiation advantages (Burgess et al., 2006; Robinson & Malhotr, 2005). Literature and institutions (Unido, 2007) have repeatedly underlined the functionality of creating the network for the development of the necessary skills that can help the interpenetration of sustainability issues in the definition of corporate strategies, becoming an integral part of it (Molteni, Pedrini & Bertolini, 2006).

In the field of innovation, stakeholder collaborations seem to be a key perspective. As Vezzoli (2007) argued, the discussion of radical innovations, new interactions, and partnerships between different stakeholders, as well as new sustainable relationships between consumers and products, might be fundamental for technological development and innovations. This seems to be particularly appropriate to stimulate the fashion industry towards a new kind of balance, new kinds of radical design, and business thinking. Talking about sustainable innovation means considering products, services, or processes that offer value not only for both the business and customer but also to the environment through a significant decrease in environmental impact. Sustainable innovation is a larger systemic approach where sustainability thinking is integrated in all levels of the business (products, technologies, services, new business models, organization model and relationship with stakeholders) (Niinimäki, 2013).

In the same way, alliances among companies are considered strategic and there are numerous examples in the fashion sector to implement product and process innovation: from the partnership between the company Vibrama (which specialized in rubber soles) and Eurojersey (which specialized in technical materials) was born Vibrama Furoshiki the Wrapping Sole, a shoe that can adapt to different morphologies of the foot and reduce industrial molds.

From a more operational point of view, the presence of standards can be considered a strategic marketing tool to direct the consumer to make informed purchase choices, but at the same time it represents a stimulus for companies to renew products and processes. Both environmental and social standards are considered, and obtaining certifications entails a review of the processes in the technical and organizational aspects.

Considering the nature (public/private), the object (product/process), the method, the extension, or even the possibility of affixing a trademark, a classification of the major standards related to the fashion, textile and clothing industry, is presented in Figure 2.

METHODOLOGICAL CHOICES

The methodological choices of empirical research refer to different tools related to the qualitative research method and collected data from a range of sources (Yin, 1994).

Although the primary source of data for this study was interviews with opinion leaders, which provided an understanding of sustainability in the fashion industry, several other sources have been used: contextual data gathered through the participation in various events organized by operators in the sector, such as conventions, exhibitions, workshops and fashion shows; consultation of documents (business and association reports, policy documents, magazine articles); and focus groups held during the period of survey, with some meetings organized with representatives of trade associations, in particular at the Fashion Academy (Milan-Naples) in March and April 2019, at the Italian Leather Research Institute (Naples) in May 2019, at the Union of Industrialists - Fashion Section (Naples) May 2019.

In order to clarify the set of opinion leaders to investigate, a preliminary desk analysis was conducted on documentations relating to the fashion industry. Then 16 semi-structured interviews were conducted (see Table 1 for details) with selected stakeholders who were part of the fashion industry, as well as part of the broader field of the industry (faculty at fashion design institutes). The interviews took place

Figure 2. The complex universe of certifications in the textile and clothing sector
Source: (our elaboration)

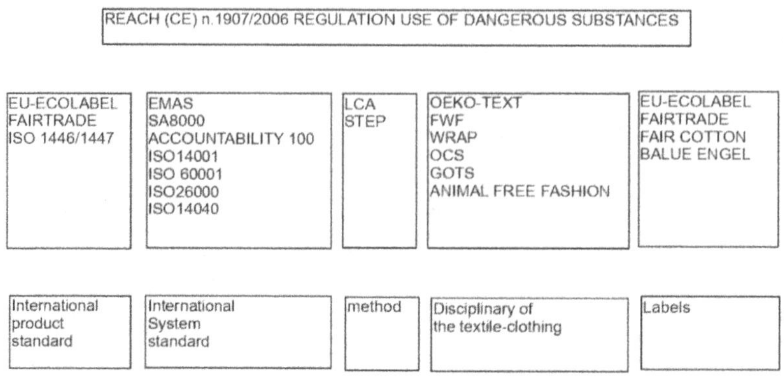

between October 2018 and May 2019, usually lasted between 45 minutes and 1 hour, and were recorded and later transcribed. Initially, the interview process followed a purposeful sampling, logically interviewing the major representatives of the various trade associations at national and local level. The interviews were central to delineating the cognitive processes underlying the sustainability strategies and practices in fashion industry.

The semi-structured questionnaire consisted of 5 parts:

1. Introduction and presentation of the study;
2. Initiation and start recording and presentation of the initial topic;
3. Main narration by the interviewees, with no questioning;
4. Questioning phase;
5. Concluding talk.

Due to concerns over the analysis of data, the interviews were analyzed in accordance with accepted methods (Glaser & Strauss, 1967; Locke, 2001): key concepts, actions, and events were identified and were grouped into categories and, during this stage, a triangulation of data sources (literature review, interviews, and event observation) helped to refine and strengthen the categories (Glaser & Strauss, 1967).

Table 1. The interviewed opinion leader

Affiliation	Key Informant Number
Accademia della Moda Milano-Napoli	2
Sistema Moda Italia	2
Camera della Moda	1
Confindustria Napoli	6
Confindustria Caserta	1
Italian Leather Research Institute Naples	1
Isprambiente	1

Source: (our elaboration)

RESULTS

The survey allows to affirm that opinion leaders reserve a great attention to the issue of sustainability and corporate social responsibility in the fashion system. The textile and clothing industry are considered sectors with the greatest environmental problems: massive production involves the emission of polluting substances in the atmosphere and in the waste water, together with the waste of processing residues. As presented in Table 2, the different themes that emerged during the interview activities have been considered and have been object of successive in-depth analysis based on their degree of frequency.

First of all, sustainability represents a strategic issue. On this point the President of Accademia della Moda affirmed that sustainability is an important issue both for the future and for the current scenarios of fashion business. In his opinion one of the first consequences for companies not oriented towards sustainability might be, in the medium term, the final exit from the market.

Looking at the SMEs, sustainability practices are often associated to an additional cost for these firms that should not be able to support it. The results of survey photograph a picture in which the social and environmental responsibility is associated with additional investments and costs for these companies. On this point, for example, the President of the Confindustria Campania - Fashion Section - noted that sustainability in general involves investments in various areas that, at this phase of the national and international economy crisis, SMEs – and in particular those operated in the fashion industry - cannot afford. Another important aspect – as noted by the President of Accademia della Moda – is related to the costs and the difficulty of verifying the productions and the relationships with the suppliers, especially abroad. He referred to the case of the brand Diesel that makes 36 million garments per season to be produced in 2 months. The organization is structured to operate in proximity to its suppliers and foreign producers. This strategy, adopted to carry out and guarantee procedural checks, generate costs unsustainable for SMEs declaring their ethical choice to be attentive to sustainability but operating in the supply chain with inadequate control tools.

Table 2. The different themes emerged during the interview activities

Main Issue	Number of Agreement to the Issue
Relevance of the theme of sustainability for the industry	13
Association between sustainability practices and additions costs for SMEs	9
Sustainability innovation as a key driver for SMEs	13
Need for different governance tools of a sustainable supply chain	13
Need for managerial competences	8
Need for technical competences	10
Raise awareness of the demand for sustainable fashion products	6
Implementation of partnership, especially between SMEs	1
More re-use and recycling policies in the textile and clothing sector	10
Network for driving sustainable innovation strategies, especially for SMEs	13
Raising awareness of the demand and exploring sustainable luxury-oriented segments	5
Politics and practice to sustain firm especially SMEs	11

Source: (our elaboration)

The respondents recognize that while generating costs in the short term, investing in sustainability might produce economic advantages both to management efficiency and to product innovation, as well as process, but only in the medium term.

Reasoning about the role of sustainability innovation as a possible key driver for strengthening the Italian fashion SME's competitiveness, the President of Sistema Moda Italia provided an important perspective. In fact, he pointed out that, today, sustainability is felt as an additional cost and an imposition by the brands in turn pressed by NGOs, but in the medium term it would have had a positive impact on the future of the company and therefore it has now become a fundamental asset. Besides, the President of Confindustria Campania - Fashion Section, in this regard argued that companies that aim at long-term strategies must transform their ethical intuition into tangible elements for the market. Therefore, for the opinion leaders, creating sustainable fashion products could be a key factor to strengthen a firm's competitiveness, also acting as a further distinctive feature for Italian companies that are increasingly committed to meet the challenges of companies that base their competitiveness on price policies.

Concerning the commitment in sustainable activities, empirical research shows a clear focus on internal aspects of sustainability regarding the responsible management of human resources aimed at improving the conditions of workers and their families. The application of sustainability standards is limited and not clear to opinion leaders; the level of adoption of formal tools, such as the ethical code or the sustainability report, is very low and used mainly by big companies in the luxury segments.

The interviews recognized the importance of a greater commitment to all strategic assets, competences, investments in technologies, and engagement into the supply chain. They recognized the importance of having to invest in all: from a greater awareness of the company's top management, with the necessary inclusion within the staff of specialized managerial figures, to the need for innovation in product and process allowing to meet better market opportunities and allowing to differentiate the business from competitors and gain sustainable competitive advantages.

The President of Accademia della Moda recalled the complexity of these processes linked to the responsibility of the supply chain; SMEs, engaged in the respect of a sustainable operating, have to act consequently investing in technologies, enhancing competences, and in the engagement into the supply chain. As there is no control but only a set of standards/certifications and self-declarations, these companies have to be capable to address sustainability issues individually with their suppliers. Besides, it would also be desirable to make more demands for sustainability issues, such as banishing obsolete materials (f.e. acrylic) and promoting material recycling systems in those countries more involved in the delocalization of supply chains process. At the same time, the President of Sistema Moda Italia highlighted that central problems for SMEs are the traceability both of the products and of the process in relation to sustainability, as well as problems related to the cost of energy, water and sludge disposal, and - in addition – the introduction of pre-retirement measures that can negatively affect the availability of professional resources. These issues are difficult to deal with for small and poorly structured companies. Besides, with regard to sustainability standards, the President of Sistema Moda Italia declared that these tools can be appropriate and useful for the selection of suppliers (especially those having a greater international recognition), but the strongest tools are often training, collaboration, and dialogue with suppliers, which lead to a consolidation of the supplier/customer relationship.

The opinion leaders recognize a need for innovation while complaining about the lack of preparation of the managers regarding sustainability themes. Underlining the lack of specialized technical competence regarding the development of new products and processes, opinion leaders stress the need of greater technical expertise in the design phase or in the process traceability pointing up the need for economic-financial resources, as well as appropriate partnerships, to implement shared innovative projects, especially for SMEs. The President of Sistema Moda Italia, talking about the most critical issues in the production and sale of sustainable products (for Italian companies and SMEs in particular), highlighted a lack of technicians able to interpret and manage specifications and ecotoxicological requirements/standards; and the underestimation of design as a function already oriented to sustainability, together with a lack of familiarity with marketing strategies for semi-finished manufacturers all of which combined with the difficulties in balancing production flexibility with environmental impact reduction.

Furthermore, some opinion leaders have expressed the need for expansion of re-use and recycling policies in the textile and clothing sector, recognizing the need to move in the direction of expanding politics of recycling and reusing products, together with the research for technical solutions and materials that prolong textile lifecycle. They admit the need to convert the destinations of use of many fashion products at the end of their life cycle, for example by transforming "waste" products into new raw materials or into new products. This orientation appears to be fundamental for the President of the Italian Leather Research Institute but it is a perspective shared by all the interviewed, especially for the purpose of reducing the environmental impact of the production chain and the supply chain. However, opinion leaders believe it is also necessary to consider the "upstream" impacts of the process, the production of the raw material, as well as those related to the use of the product and its disposal.

Not all the respondents agreed on the point of the importance of the network for driving sustainable innovation strategies, especially for SMEs, often penalized by lack of knowledge and skills. For example, the President of Confindustria Campania - Fashion Section, considers it very important as a driving element for companies that do not have the skills and resources to invest in sustainability projects. President of Accademia della Moda is skeptical on usefulness of networks as a driver of sustainability that remain, in his opinion, an entrepreneurial vision linked to the demand dynamics. For the President of Confindustra Caserta – Fashion Section the networking for companies is always important, however, companies have faced the issue of sustainability individually with our suppliers and especially when requested by the customers.

The importance of the network at all levels of the supply chain, but above all among producers, distributors and consumers, is shared by the opinion leaders for implementing sustainable practices. Consumers, in most cases, rely on the brands and distributors they trust to monitor sustainability along the entire production chain. The need was acknowledged by the major distribution chains (as well as some of the most important fashion brands) that, in this case, also relied on technology with the consequent introduction of digital platforms and up in support of a more performing government of these processes.

Another emerging theme, derived from the survey, is the necessity to raise the awareness of the demand for sustainable fashion products. As the President of Sistema Moda Italia underlined, a good number of Italian SMEs are already operating in this way, not only supporting new product lines but also bringing traditional productions towards ever greater sustainability. Many opinion leaders declare it necessary to have a reversal in the mentality of consumers. In fact, while paying attention to the price of products in relation to their aesthetic and functional characteristics, consumers should be sensitized to the criteria of sustainability, to the recognition of the labels certifying the sustainability of the products and perhaps, and encouraged to purchase those products. Additionally, when concerning the so-called luxury goods, they declare that it is possible to find new segments of demand "sustainability oriented", much work needs to be done in relation to the demand for fast fashion products. Carlo Casillo, President of Confindustria Campania - Fashion Section, stated that sustainability is a fundamental factor for companies that want to act more and more competitively and want to position themselves on a high segment, but, in his opinion, contemporary consumers are increasingly attentive to the problem of pollution and respect for ethical and social values.

Looking at the need for policies and practice to sustain firms, especially SMEs, in the ambitious and complex challenge of sustainability, all the respondents recognize the need for policies and practices addressed to the development of new opportunities in the field of sustainability in the fashion industry and agree in stating that there is a lack of material and immaterial resources to be addressed to the development of appropriate tools to support the dissemination of sustainability practices of firms. As the President Lettieri noted, the most famous Italian brands have decided to bring the productions back to Italy and the Milan fashion shows are all about sustainability. The traditional high-end productions, for example, are already in line with the theme of sustainability. Under this line in April 2019 Naples hosted the footwear industry conference that is all about sustainability. The problem is that the topic should be transferred to everyone: from the big corporations to the SMEs, from the entrepreneurs to the consumers. And in addition to policies and practices, more controls must be made on the products placed in the shops.

DISCUSSION

Results allow to identify two main trajectories: sustainability as a driver for competitiveness and innovation; a starting phase in the implementation of managerial approach for sustainable innovation in Italian fashion industry.

The Italian fashion system is aware of the possible benefits connected to the adoption of sustainable behavior and it considers environmental and social sustainability a 'non-reversible commitment,' as a part of the activities of political orientation, of associative engagement. But the survey shows that the commitment to sustainability is essentially linked to the impact on reputation, to the improvement of the relations with the stakeholders, in particular with the territory where the company resides and with the firm's employees. It would seem possible to affirm that in the fashion industry there is a real national delay (and even more of a local delay) in the adoption of the new paradigms of sustainability, especially in comparison to other industries more directly involved in the application of innovation in production processes (energy production, cars, design, construction). In the fashion industry, in fact, market dynamics are historically and substantially based almost exclusively on evocation, image, and communication, rather than on the production processes. The fashion industry engine is represented by creativity and originality rather than by the development of sustainable assets.

Innovation is mainly conceived as an activity aimed at improving product quality by implementing its sustainable characteristics with a significant increase in production costs. Facing a sustainable path requires making non-recoverable investments (especially in research and innovation) and transforming the organizational structure of the company together with the relationship dynamics with customers and suppliers.

The environmental and social challenges that affect the global clothing supply chain also influence the entire industry and no company can deal with them alone. If the prevailing orientation is to entrust the productions to a first level of contracting, losing sight of the dynamics of further subcontracting, it should be underlined that the proactive and the multi-stakeholder collaboration could accelerate the improvement of the environmental and social performances for the industry as a whole. One of the direct consequences might be the costs reduction for the companies and shared product and process innovation.

At a more operational level, the system of sustainable standards imposes adjustments that can act as a driving force for product and process innovations, but it appears to be very expensive for the companies, especially SMEs, and - although "the costs of non-quality" are clearly perceived by the interviewees, sustainable development strategies are not yet clear and shared in the supply chain. Opinion leaders affirm that companies recognize that a fundamental aspect of corporate social responsibility is linked to the environmental impact of production along the entire production chain. However, though declaring that they operate in order to reduce the consumption of natural resources, polluting emissions and waste, adopting environmental management systems, so many firms are not yet certified and present a certain difficulty of orientation in the complex world of standards and certifications. The set of tools used in governing relations, such as, audits, for example, are often limited to the first and second level of suppliers. So, if the survey shows a clear focus of the opinion leaders on the aspects of sustainability with declarations of commitment regarding the responsible management of human resources and investments, aimed at improving the conditions of workers and their families, this orientation does not correspond to the real knowledge of the related certifications, standards, and codes of conduct necessary and sufficient to trigger basic sustainable management mechanisms.

Despite that the survey confirms a great attention from the opinion leaders to the issue of corporate social responsibility in the fashion system, and despite the resonance that this topic, it seems impossible to identify a unified and clear corpus of CSR and sustainable development within this economic sector, especially with regard to managerial prospects. The survey highlights the need for resources and skills, managerial at first; it finds a certain lack in the structuring of sustainable development models capable of overcoming the crisis of the current production model, where the textile and clothing sector can be considered one of those with the greatest environmental criticality, with a production that involves the emission of polluting substances in the atmosphere and in the waste water and the waste of processing residues. A lack of knowledge related to the most famous sustainability standards (generic, of product, of process, or of sector) is a further result. These data testify the implementation of managerial approach to sustainable innovation is still at starting phase. A real need for sustainable innovation has to be articulated both in terms of product and process; whether sustainable behavior is an ethical or marketing issue, the result of a "push" or "pull" process, the empirical research describes that it involves investments in various areas that at this time may be not within the reach of companies, those of smaller size, in particular.

CONCLUSION

The research clearly highlights the belief in the sector's trade associations of the need to concretely start implementing sustainable innovations, not only in view of the high impact this industry has on the environment, and the implications of social problems, but because implementation of sustainable business models helps improve business performance. This is even more true in view of the characteristics of the Italian fashion system, which presents, alongside the big names of luxury, a multiplicity of small and medium-sized enterprises that compete on medium/low quality proposals that are seen daily attacked by the offer coming from those countries with low costs of production factors, which realize the so-called fast fashion.

However, the lack of full awareness in companies of the importance of sustainability as a driver of competitiveness represents an important obstacle, alongside the need to provide specific resources and skills to implement these processes. Still, often in the sector there is an idea of sustainability associated with an improvement of the image rather than of sustainable behaviors activated to improve the performance of the company. Cultural skills, even before being managerial, are therefore indispensable for starting this change of perspective. The adoption of sustainable practices has repercussions on social and cultural changes (for example, the effect that the extension of the life cycle of a fashion collection could have), so it appears important to start from the assumption that sustainability only looks at the material production of goods, but also at the cultural dimension of the products, their symbolic production and their immaterial content.

From this derives the first managerial implications on the importance of training and of management company "sustainability oriented" and policy implications for trade associations on the need to inform and train managerial skills on sustainability issues as a competitive strategy.

The implementation of a sustainable strategy requires the development of process and product innovations, which require specific human skills and investments in technologies that could probably be onerous for a SME. Hence, again, the important role that trade associations have in stimulating partnerships to support innovation and also of local institutions in providing financial support programs as well as specific training.

Finally, the research underlines an important role that the consumer has in orienting the offer of companies when they make their purchase choices. If, on the one hand, consumers as a special kind of stakeholder have a crucial role in stimulating sustainable innovation of companies focused on the fashion system; on the other, as highlighted in the research, often consumers have no specific knowledge for orienting their choices and would also need them to be informed. To reach consumers' trust it seems important to have an open communication and information to sustainability commitment at all levels of the company's practices. Consumers in the fashion industry requires and needs a lot of information gathering about the different stages in manufacturing and communicating because of the intrinsic characteristics of the industry itself: the attribute 'Made in' is today less relevant than the attribute 'Made by' and these aspects are relevant not only to consumers but also to all stakeholders. In this direction, in supporting consumers, even an intervention on the sustainability standards system would be necessary.

At the moment the whole system appears little known by firms, difficult to recognize and hard to apply by managers, and tricky to interpret even by the opinion leaders. A set of valid standards and certifications, with a strong level of credibility, practicability, and universality should be recognized and adopted in the entire industry as basic tools able to support the interests of all stakeholders and to allow better governance of relations between business and supply chain.

In short, sustainability represents a source of competitive advantage that implies serious reflections and reinterpretations of internal processes and a greater socio-environmental sensitivity on the part of the company. The roads wind along the following trajectories: a better management of the risks related to the less responsible behaviors (just think of waste disposal, working conditions, supply chain management); improve the attractiveness of the human capital enterprise (management, in particular) 'sustainability oriented' with obvious possible repercussions on the corporate climate, processes, and performance; implement innovations in products and aimed at maximizing efficiency and optimizing sustainability costs; increase the capacity to attract financial resources in support of sustainable innovation, with repercussions on trust in relations with the market and institutions; increase relationships with sustainability stakeholders with repercussions on brand value.

This work tries to bring out these issues, with known limitations due to having conducted a survey on trade associations but not on companies, too. However, all these issues are research themes that could be deepened, since the latest market data (Lyst 2019)[1] shows that the development of the sustainable market in many northern European countries, in North America, and Singapore is even three-digit growth and that sustainable fashion is now an established reality, representing a great business opportunity.

REFERENCES

Abhijit, M. & Sanjib, K. S. (2019). Analyzing the barriers of green textile supply chain management in Southeast Asia using interpretive structural modeling. *Sustainable Production and Consumption, 17.*

Albouy, D., & Adesida, O. (2018). *Sustainable fashion blueprint report.* Cambridge University Judge Business School.

Alvarez, G., Colin Pilbeam, C., & Wilding, R. (2010). Nestlé Nespresso AAA sustainable quality program: An investigation into the governance dynamics in a multi-stakeholder supply chain network. *Supply Chain Management, 15*(2), 165–182. doi:10.1108/13598541011028769

Andersen, M., & Skjoett-Larsen, T. (2009). Corporate social responsibility in global supply chains. *Supply Chain Management, 14*(2), 75–86. doi:10.1108/13598540910941948

Anderson, E., & Weitz, B. (1992). The use of pledges to build and sustain commitment in distribution channels. *JMR, Journal of Marketing Research, 29*(1), 18–34. doi:10.1177/002224379202900103

Anderson, L. M., & Bateman, T. S. (2000). Individual environmental initiative: Championing natural environmental issues in US business organizations. *Academy of Management Journal, 43*, 548–570.

Armstrong, C. M., Niinimaki, K., Kujala, S., Karell, E., & Lang, C. (2015). Sustainable product-service systems for clothing: Exploring consumer perceptions of consumption alternatives in Finland. *Journal of Cleaner Production, 97*, 30–39. doi:10.1016/j.jclepro.2014.01.046

Barnett, C., Cloke, P., Clarke, N., & Malpass, A. (2005). Consuming ethics: Articulating the subjects and spaces of ethical consumption. *Antipode, 37*(1), 23–45. doi:10.1111/j.0066-4812.2005.00472.x

Barratt, M. (2004). Understanding the meaning of collaboration in the supply chain. *Supply Chain Management, 9*(1), 30–42. doi:10.1108/13598540410517566

Battaglia, M., Bianchim, L., Frey, M., & Iraldo, F. (2010). An innovative model to promote CSR among SMEs operating in industrial clusters: evidence from an EU project. *Corporate Social Responsibility and Environmental Management, 17*(3), 133–141. doi:10.1002/csr.224

Becker-Olsen, K. L., Cudmore, B. A., & Hill, R. P. (2006). The impact of perceived corporate social responsibility on consumer behavior. *Journal of Business Research, 59*(1), 46–53. doi:10.1016/j.jbusres.2005.01.001

Belz, F. M., & Peattie, K. (2010). *Sustainability marketing. A global perspective.* Chichester, UK: John Wiley & Sons.

Bennett, R. (1999). Business associations: Their potential contribution to government policy and the growth of small and medium-sized enterprises. *Environment and Planning. C, Government & Policy, 17*(5), 593–608. doi:10.1068/c170593

Bhattacharya, C. B., & Sen, S. (2004). Doing better at doing good: When, why, and how consumers respond to corporate social initiatives. *California Management Review*, *47*(1), 9–24. doi:10.2307/41166284

Birtwistle, G., & Moore, C. M. (2007). Fashion clothing–where does it all end up? *International Journal of Retail & Distribution Management*, *35*(3), 210–216. doi:10.1108/09590550710735068

Blome, C., Schoenherr, T., & Kaesser, M. (2013). Ambidextrous governance in supply chains: the impact on innovation and cost performance. *The Journal of Supply Chain Management*, *49*(4), 59–80. doi:10.1111/jscm.12033

Blowfield, M., Visser, W., & Livesey, F. (2007). Sustainability innovation - mapping the territory, Cambridge Programme for Sustainability Leadership Paper Series, 2.

BLUMINE-ACIMIT. (2016). *Le tecnologie green nella filiera tessile: un valore aggiunto nei processi di innovazione sostenibile.* Report presented during the Plenary Meeting of ACIMIT, 21 giugno 2016.

IEFE Bocconi & Ricardo-AEA (2015). *Evaluation of the Implementation of the EU Ecolabel Regulation.*

Bos-Brouwers, H. E. J. (2010). Corporate sustainability and innovation in SMEs: Evidence of themes and activities in practice. *Business Strategy and the Environment*, *19*(7), 417–435.

Bouzon, M. & Govindan, K. (2015). Reverse logistics as a sustainable supply chain practice for the fashion industry: an analysis of drivers and the Brazilian Case. In T. C. E. Cheng & T.-M. Choi (Eds.), Sustainable fashion supply chain management (pp. 85-104). Cham, Switzerland: Springer.

Bowie, N. E. (2000). *Ethical theory and business* (6th ed.). New York, NY: Prentice Hall.

Burgess, K., Singh, P. J., & Koroglu, R. (2006). Supply chain management: A structured literature review and implications for future research. *International Journal of Operations & Production Management*, *26*(7), 703–729. doi:10.1108/01443570610672202

Caniato, F., Caridi, M., Crippa, L., & Moretto, A. (2012). Environmental sustainability in fashion supply chains: An exploratory case-based research. *International Journal of Production Economics*, *135*(2), 659–670. doi:10.1016/j.ijpe.2011.06.001

Carroll, A. B. (1979). A three-dimensional conceptual model of corporate performance. *Academy of Management Review*, *4*(4), 497–505. doi:10.5465/amr.1979.4498296

Carter, C. R., & Jennings, M. M. (2002). Logistics social responsibility: An integrative framework. *Journal of Business Logistics*, *23*(1), 145–180. doi:10.1002/j.2158-1592.2002.tb00020.x

Carter, C. R., & Jennings, M. M. (2004). The role of purchasing in the socially responsible management of the supply chain: A structural equation analysis. *Journal of Business Logistics*, *25*(1), 145–186. doi:10.1002/j.2158-1592.2004.tb00173.x

Clark, H. (2008). SLOW+ FASHION—an oxymoron—or a promise for the future...? *Fashion Theory*, *12*(4), 427–446. doi:10.2752/175174108X346922

CNTAC (2015-2017). *Annual report on social responsibility of Chinese textile and apparel industry.*

CNTAC (2016-2017). *Annual report on social responsibility of Chinese textile and apparel industry.*

Cullen, J. G. (2017). Educating business students about sustainability: A bibliometric review of current trends and research needs. *Journal of Business Ethics, 145*(2), 424–439. doi:10.100710551-015-2838-3

Daddi, T., Gusmerotti, N. M., Iraldo, F., & Frey, M. (2014). EMAS and ISO 14001: The differences in effectively improving environmental performance. *Journal of Cleaner Production, 68*(1), 165–173.

Daddi, T., Magistrelli, M., Frey, M., & Iraldo, F. (2011). Do environmental management systems improve environmental performance? Empirical evidence from Italian companies. *Environment, Development and Sustainability, 13*(5), 845–862. doi:10.100710668-011-9294-8

Daddi, T., Testa, F., Iraldo, F., & Frey, M. (2014). Removing and simplifying administrative costs and burdens for EMAS and ISO 14001 certified organizations: Evidence from Italy. *Environmental Engineering and Management Journal, 13*(3), 689–698. doi:10.30638/eemj.2014.073

Dallocchio, M., Perrini, F., Russo, A., & Vurro, C. (2010). *Creare valore nella supply chain: Modelli di gestione a confronto*. Milano, Italy: Egea.

De Chiara, A. (2015). *Stakeholder engagement per strategie di sostenibilità*. Torino, Italy: Giappichelli Editore.

De Chiara, A. (2016). *Implementing sustainability strategies in networks and clusters - principles, tools and new research outcomes, Series: CSR, Sustainability, Ethics & Governance*. Berlin, Germany: Springer.

De Chiara, A. (2017). *Distretti industriali e sostenibilità. Analisi nei distretti e nei poli industriali della Campania,* University Press, Università degli Studi di Napoli "L'Orientale".

De Chiara, A. (2018). Strategie sostenibili nei distretti industriali: opportunità per piccole imprese e sistemi locali. In V. Maggioni & P. Stampacchia (Eds.), *L'impresa del XXI secolo. Scritti di economia e gestione delle imprese in onore del prof. Sergio Sciarelli*. Cedam.

Drucker, P. F. (1992). The new society of organizations. *Harvard Business Review*, (September–August), 95–104.

Dyer, J., & Singh, H. (1998). The relational view: Cooperative strategy and sources of interorganizational competitive advantage. *Academy of Management Review, 23*(4), 660–679. doi:10.5465/amr.1998.1255632

Egels-Zandén, N., & Wahlqvist, E. (2007). Post-partnership strategies for defining corporate responsibility: The business social compliance initiative. *Journal of Business Ethics, 70*(2), 75–189. doi:10.100710551-006-9104-7

Elkington, J. (1994). Towards the sustainable corporation: Win-win-win business strategies for sustainable development. *California Management Review, 36*(2), 90–100. doi:10.2307/41165746

Elkington, J. (2004). Enter the triple bottom line. In *The triple bottom line: Does it all add up, 11*(12), 1-16. Retrieved from http://www. johnelkington.com

Ellis, J. L., McCracken, V. A., & Skuza, N. (2012). Insights into willingness to pay for organic cotton apparel. *Journal of Fashion Marketing and Management, 16*(3), 290–305. doi:10.1108/13612021211246053

EMAS. (2013). *EMAS implementation in the EU: level of adoption, benefits, barriers and regulatory relief, BRAVE Project – Survey on European EMAS organizations*. Scuola Superiore Sant'Anna, November.

Espino-Rodrìguez, T., & Rodrìguez-Diaz, F. M. (2008). A model of strategic evaluation of a tourism destination based on internal and relational capabilities. *Journal of Travel Research, 45*(4), 368–380. doi:10.1177/0047287507308324

European Commission. (2011). Communication from the Commission to the European Parliament, the Council, the European Economic and Social Committee and the Committee of the Regions. A renewed EU strategy 2011–14 for Corporate Social Responsibility. COM (2011) 681, Brussels, Belgium.

European Commission. (2013). *La responsabilità sociale d'impresa per le piccole e medie imprese. Consigli e Strategie per i consulenti.*

Farrer, J. (2018). Remediation: discussing fashion textiles sustainability. In A. Gwilt & T. Rissanen (Eds.), *Shaping sustainable fashion.* Washington, DC: Earthscan.

Fletcher, K. (2007). Slow fashion. *The Ecologist, 37*(5), 61.

Fletcher, K. (2008). *Sustainable fashion & textiles: design journeys.* Oxford, UK: Earthscan.

Fondazione Symbola. (2015). *Certificare per Competere. Dalle certificazioni ambientali nuova forza al made in Italy.*

Galaskiewicz, J. (2011). Studying supply chains from a social network perspective. *The Journal of Supply Chain Management, 47*(1), 4–8. doi:10.1111/j.1745-493X.2010.03209.x

Glaser, B. G., & Strauss, A. (1967). *The discovery of grounded theory.* New York, NY: Aldine.

Greenwood, M. (2007). Stakeholder engagement: Beyond the myth of corporate responsibility. *Journal of Business Ethics, 34*(4), 315–327. doi:10.100710551-007-9509-y

Harvey, B., Van Luijk, K., & Corbetta, G. (1991). *Market morality and company size.* London, UK: Kluver. doi:10.1007/978-94-011-3556-6

Hawley, J. M. (2018). Textile recycling options: Exploring what could be. In A. Gwilt & T. Rissanen (Eds.), *Shaping sustainable fashion.* Washington, DC: Earthscan.

Horne, R. E. (2009). Limits to labels: The role of eco-labels in the assessment of product sustainability and routes to sustainable consumption. *International Journal of Consumer Studies, 33*(2), 175–182. doi:10.1111/j.1470-6431.2009.00752.x

Huang, M. C., Cheng, H. L., & Tseng, C. Y. (2014). Re-examining the direct and interactive effects of governance mechanisms upon buyer–supplier cooperative performance. *Industrial Marketing Management, 43*(4), 704–716. doi:10.1016/j.indmarman.2014.02.001

Husted, B., & Allen, D. (2007). Corporate social strategy in multinational enterprises: antecedents and value creation. *Journal of Business Ethics, 74*(4), 345–361. doi:10.100710551-007-9511-4

Husted, B. W., & de Jesus Salazar, J. (2006). Taking Friedman seriously: Maximizing profits and social performance. *Journal of Management Studies, 43*(1), 75–91. doi:10.1111/j.1467-6486.2006.00583.x

Iraldo, F., Lanzini, P., Melis, M., Kahlenborn, W., Freier, I., Rubik, F., ... Petersen, A. (2006). *EVER: Evaluation of EMAS and Eco-Label for their revision.* Research Findings.

Ireland, R. & Bruce, R. (2000). CPFR: only the beginning of collaboration, *Supply Chain Management Review*, September/October, 80-88.

Jacoby, J., Berning, C. K., & Dietvorst, T. F. (1977). What about disposition. *Journal of Marketing*, *41*(2), 22–28. doi:10.1177/002224297704100212

Jin Gam, H., Cao, H., Farr, C., & Heine, L. (2009). C2CAD: A sustainable apparel design and production model. *International Journal of Clothing Science and Technology*, *21*(4), 166–179. doi:10.1108/09556220910959954

Joergens, C. (2006). Ethical fashion: Myth or future trend?, *Journal of Fashion Marketing and Management*: An *International Journal (Toronto, Ont.)*, *10*(3), 360–371.

Kleine, A., & Von Hauff, M. (2009). Sustainability-driven implementation of corporate social responsibility: Application of the integrative sustainability triangle. *Journal of Business Ethics*, *85*(3), 517–533. doi:10.100710551-009-0212-z

Knox, S., & Maklan, S. (2004). Corporate social responsibility: Moving beyond investment towards measuring outcome. *European Management Journal*, *22*(5), 508–516. doi:10.1016/j.emj.2004.09.009

Lawrence, S. R., Collins, E., Pavlovich, K., & Arunachalam, M. (2006). Sustainability practices of SMEs: The case of NZ. *Business Strategy and the Environment*, *15*(4), 242–257. doi:10.1002/bse.533

Lawrence, T., Dyck, B., Maitlis, S., & Mauws, K. M. (2006). The underlying structure of continuous change. *MIT Sloan Management Review*, *47*, 59–66.

Li, Y., Zhao, X., Shi, D., & Li, X. (2014). Governance of sustainable supply chains in the fast fashion industry. *European Management Journal*, *32*(5), 823–836. doi:10.1016/j.emj.2014.03.001

Lii, Y. S., & Lee, M. (2012). Doing right leads to doing well: When the type of CSR and reputation interact to affect consumer evaluations of the firm. *Journal of Business Ethics*, *105*(1), 69–81. doi:10.100710551-011-0948-0

Lillywhite, S. (2007). Corporate social responsibility home and away. *Age*, *14*(June).

Lim, S. J., & Phillips, J. (2008). Embedding CSR values: The global footwear industry's evolving governance, structure. *Journal of Business Ethics*, *81*(1), 143–156. doi:10.100710551-007-9485-2

Locke, K. (2001). *Grounded theory in management research*. London, UK: Sage.

Maignan, I., Hillebrand, B., & McAlister, D. (2002). Managing socially-responsible buying. *European Management Journal*, *20*(6), 641–648. doi:10.1016/S0263-2373(02)00115-9

McCarthy, S., & Golocic, S. (2002). Implementing collaborative planning to improve supply chain performance. *International Journal of Physical Distribution & Logistics Management*, *32*(6), 431–454. doi:10.1108/09600030210437960

McEvily, B., Perrone, V., & Zaheer, A. (2003). Trust as an organizing principle. *Organization Science*, *14*(1), 91–103. doi:10.1287/orsc.14.1.91.12814

Miemczyk, J., Johnsen, T. E., & Macquet, M. (2012). Sustainable purchasing and supply management: A structured literature review of definitions and measures at the dyad, chain and network levels. *Supply Chain Management, 17*(5), 478–496. doi:10.1108/13598541211258564

Molteni, M. (2004). *Responsabilità sociale e performance d'impresa*. Milano, Italy.

Molteni, M., Antoldi, F., & Todisco, A. (2016). SMEs and CSR: An empirical survey in Italian industrial district. In *EABIS/CBS International Conference on The Social Responsibility of Small and Medium Sized Enterprises. Integration of CSR into SMEs Business Practice*, Copenhagen, Vol. 26.

Molteni, M., Pedrini, M., & Bertolini, S. (Eds.). (2006). *La responsabilità sociale d'impresa nelle aziende familiari italiane*. Milano, Italy: Franco Angeli.

Molteni, M. & Todisco, A. (2008). *Piccole e medie imprese e CSR. La CSR come leva di differenziazione*. Retrieved from http://www.isvi.org

Müller, J. M., Buliga, O., & Voigt, K. I. (2018). Fortune favors the prepared: How SMEs approach business model innovations in Industry 4.0. *Technological Forecasting and Social Change, 132*, 2–17. doi:10.1016/j.techfore.2017.12.019

Müller, J. M., & Voigt, K. I. (2018). Sustainable industrial value creation in SMEs: A comparison between industry 4.0 and made in China 2025. *International Journal of Precision Engineering and Manufacturing-Green Technology, 5*(5), 659–670. doi:10.100740684-018-0056-z

Nadvi, K. (2008). Global standards, global governance and the organization of global value chains. *Journal of Economic Geography, 8*(3), 323–343. doi:10.1093/jeg/lbn003

New, S. (2010). The transparent supply chain. *Harvard Business Review, 88*(10), 1–11.

Niinimaki, K. (2010). Eco-clothing, consumer identity and ideology. *Sustainable Development, 18*(3), 150–162. doi:10.1002d.455

Niinimaki, K. (2015). Ethical foundations in sustainable fashion. *Textiles and Clothing Sustainability, 1*(1), 3. doi:10.118640689-015-0002-1

Niinimaki, K., & Hassi, L. (2011). Emerging design strategies in sustainable production and consumption of textiles and clothing. *Journal of Cleaner Production, 19*(16), 1876–1883.

Nishitani, K., Kaneko, S., Fujii, H., & Komatsu, S. (2012). Are firms' voluntary environmental management activities beneficial for the environment and business? An empirical study focusing on Japanese manufacturing firms. *Journal of Environmental Management, 105*, 121–130. doi:10.1016/j.jenvman.2012.03.054

Oehmen, J., De Nardo, M., Schonsleben, P., & Boutellier, R. (2010). Supplier code of conduct - state of the art and customisation in the electronics industry. *Production Planning and Control, 21*(7), 664–679. doi:10.1080/09537280903547785

Parboteeah, K., Addae, H., & Cullen, J. B. (2012). Propensity to support sustainability initiatives: A cross- national model. *Journal of Business Ethics, 105*(3), 403–413. doi:10.100710551-011-0979-6

Perrini, F. & Pivato, S. (2007). Responsabilità sociale e competitività delle piccole-medie imprese. In R. Benini (Ed.), L'impresa responsabile e la comunità intraprendente (73–94). Halley Editrice, MC.

Perrini, F., & Tencati, A. (2008). *Corporate social responsibility*. Milano, Italy: Egea.

Petersen, A. (2006). *EVER: Evaluation of EMAS and Eco-Label for their Revision*. Research Findings.

Phu-Hop, M. (2017). The corporate social responsibility in Vietnam today. *Journal of Business and Economic Development*, *2*(3), 170–175.

Plambeck, E. L., Lee, H. L., & Yatsko, P. (2012). Improving environmental performance in your Chinese supply chain. *MIT Sloan Management Review*, *53*(2), 43–52.

Pookulangara, S., & Shephard, A. (2013). Slow fashion movement: Understanding consumer perceptions— An exploratory study. *Journal of Retailing and Consumer Services*, *20*(2), 200–206. doi:10.1016/j.jretconser.2012.12.002

Pookulangara, S., Shephard, A., & Mestres, J. (2011). University community's perception of sweatshops: A mixed method data collection. *International Journal of Consumer Studies*, *35*(4), 476–483. doi:10.1111/j.1470-6431.2010.00950.x

Porter, M., & Kramer, M. (2006). Strategy and society: the link between competitive advantage and corporate social responsibility. *Harvard Business Review*, (December): 78–93.

Porter, M. & Kramer, M. (2011). Creating shared value, *Harvard Business Review*, Jan-Feb, 1-17.

Porter, M. E., & Kramer, M. R. (2002). The competitive advantage of corporate philanthropy. *Harvard Business Review*, *80*(12), 56–68.

Powell, W. W. (1990). Neither market nor hierarchy. *Research in Organizational Behavior*, *12*, 295–336.

Prahalad, C. K. (2005). *The fortune at the bottom of the pyramid, Pearson Education, Inc.* Upper Saddle River, NJ: Publishing as Warthon School Publishing.

Pui-Yan Ho, H., & Choi, T.-M. (2012). A five-R analysis for sustainable fashion supply chain management in Hong Kong: A case analysis. *Journal of Fashion Marketing and Management: An International Journal*, *16*(2), 161–175. doi:10.1108/13612021211222815

Rennings, K., Ziegler, A., Ankeleb, K., & Hoffmann, E. (2006). The influence of different characteristics of the EU environmental management and auditing scheme on technical environmental innovations and economic performance. *Ecological Economics*, *57*(1), 45–59. doi:10.1016/j.ecolecon.2005.03.013

Repubblica, D. (2019). Moda sostenibile: da trend a realtà. La richiesta di abiti etici cresce in tutto il mondo, 9 aprile. Retrieved from https://d.repubblica.it/moda/2019/04/09

Robinson, C. J., & Malhotra, M. K. (2005). Defining the concept of supply chain quality management and its relevance to academic and industrial practice. *International Journal of Production Economics*, *96*(3), 315–337. doi:10.1016/j.ijpe.2004.06.055

Rodriguez-Melo, A., & Mansouri, S. A. (2011). Stakeholder engagement: Defining strategic advantage for sustainable construction. *Business Strategy and the Environment*, *20*(8), 539–552. doi:10.1002/bse.715

Russo Spena, T., & De Chiara, A. (2012). CSR, innovation strategy and supply chain management: Toward an integrated perspective. *International Journal of Technology Management*, *58*(1/2), 83–108. doi:10.1504/IJTM.2012.045790

Sabath, R., & Fontanella, J. (2002). The unfulfilled promise of supply chain collaboration. *Supply Chain Management Review*, *6*(4), 24–29.

Sarkis, J., Zhu, Q., & Lai, K. H. (2011). An organizational theoretic review of green supply chain management literature. *International Journal of Production Economics*, *130*(1), 1–15. doi:10.1016/j.ijpe.2010.11.010

Sciarelli, S. (1999). Responsabilità sociale ed etica d'impresa: una relazione finalizzata allo sviluppo aziendale, *Finanza, Marketing e Produzione, 17(1).*

Sciarelli, S. (2007). *Etica e responsabilità sociale nell'impresa.* Milano, Italy: Giuffrè Editore.

Shaw, D. S., & Connolly, J. (2006). Identifying fair trade in consumption choice. *Journal of Strategic Marketing*, *14*(4), 353–368. doi:10.1080/09652540600960675

She, B. (2014). Sustainable fashion supply chain: Lessons from H&M. *Sustainability*, *6*(9), 6236–6249. doi:10.3390u6096236

Shen, B., Wang, Y., Lo, C., & Shum, M. (2012). The impact of ethical fashion on consumer purchase behaviour. *Journal of Fashion Marketing and Management*, *16*(2), 234–245. doi:10.1108/13612021211222842

Shen, B., Zheng, J. H., Chow, P. S., & Chow, K. Y. (2014). Perception of fashion sustainability in online community. *Journal of the Textile Institute*, *105*(9), 971–979. doi:10.1080/00405000.2013.866334

Swaen, V., & Vanhamme, J. (2005). The use of corporate social responsibility arguments in communication campaigns: does source credibility matter. *Advances in Consumer Research. Association for Consumer Research (U. S.)*, *32*, 590–591.

Tachizawa, E. M., & Wong Chee, Y. (2015). Towards a theory of multi-tier sustainable supply chains: A systematic literature review. *Supply Chain Management*, *19*(5/6), 643–663. doi:10.1108/SCM-02-2014-0070

Tencati, A., & Zsolnai, L. (2008). The collaborative enterprise. *Journal of Business Ethics*, *85*(3), 367–376. doi:10.100710551-008-9775-3

Testa, F., Battaglia, M., & Bianchi, L. (2012). The diffusion of CSR initiatives among SMEs in industrial clusters: Some findings from Italian experiences. *International Journal of Technology Management*, *58*(1-2), 152–170. doi:10.1504/IJTM.2012.045793

Testa, F., Rizzi, F., Daddi, T., Gusmerotti, N. M., Iraldo, F., & Frey, M. (2014). EMAS and ISO 14001: The differences in effectively improving environmental performance. *Journal of Cleaner Production*, *68*(1), 165–173. doi:10.1016/j.jclepro.2013.12.061

Teuscher, P., Grüninger, B., & Ferdinand, N. (2006). Risk management in sustainable supply chain management (SSCM) lessons learnt from the case of GMO-free soybeans. *Corporate Social Responsibility and Environmental Management*, *13*(1), 1–10. doi:10.1002/csr.81

Tischner, U., Schmincke, E., Rubik, F., & Prosler, M. (2000). *How to do ecodesign? - A guide for environmentally and economically sound design*. Berlin, Germany: German Federal Environmental Agency.

UNIDO. (2007). *The UN global compact operational guide for medium-scale enterprise*. July.

United Nations Global Compact. (2010). *Supply chain sustainability. A practical guide for continuous improvement.*

United Nations Global Compact. (2015). Supply chain sustainability. A practical guide for continuous improvement, Second Edition.

Vezzoli, C. (2007). *System design for sustainability. Theory, methods and tools for a sustainable "satisfaction-system" design*. Milan, Italy: Maggioli Editore.

Vurro, C., Russo, A., & Perrini, F. (2009). Shaping sustainable value chains: Network determinants of supply chain governance models. *Journal of Business Ethics*, *90*(4), 607–621. doi:10.100710551-010-0595-x

Wang, Y. & Fesenmaie, D. R. (2007). Collaborative destination marketing: A case study of Elkhart County, Indiana, *Tourism Management, 28*, 863-875.

Werbach, A. (2009). *Strategy for sustainability: A business manifesto*. London, UK: McGraw-Hill.

Wiemer, J. & Plugge, L. (2007). Transparency in the supply chain GRI, *Briefing Paper*, July 23, 2007.

Williamson, O. E. (1981). The economics of organization: The transaction cost approach. *American Journal of Sociology*, *87*(3), 548–577. doi:10.1086/227496

Wognum, P. M., Bremmers, H., Trienekens, J. H., van der Vorst, J. G. A. L., & Bloemhof, J. M. (2011). Systems for sustainability and transparency of food supply chains-current status and challenges. *Advanced Engineering Informatics*, *25*, 65–76. doi:10.1016/j.aei.2010.06.001

Wrana, J., & Revilla Diez, J. (2018). Multinational enterprises or the quality of regional institutions – What drives the diffusion of global CSR certificates in a transition economy? Evidence from Vietnam. *Journal of Cleaner Production*, *186*, 168–179. doi:10.1016/j.jclepro.2018.03.113

Yin, R. K. (1994). *Case study research, design and methods*. Londres, UK: Sage.

ADDITIONAL READING

Battaglia, M., Testa, F., Bianchi, L., Iraldo, F., & Frey, M. (2014). Corporate Social Responsibility and Competitiveness within SMEs of the Fashion Industry: Evidence from Italy and France. *Sustainability*, *6*(2), 872–893. doi:10.3390u6020872

Diddi, S., & Niehm, L.S. (2017). Exploring the role of values and norms towards consumers' intentions to patronize retail apparel brands engaged in corporate social responsibility (CSR), *Fashion and Textiles*, 4 (5).

Gaskill-Fox, J., Hyllegard, K. H., & Paff Ogle, J. (2014). CSR reporting on apparel companies' websites: Framing good deeds and clarifying missteps. *Fashion and Textiles*, *1*(1), 11. doi:10.118640691-014-0011-8

Graafland, J. J. (2002). Sourcing ethics in the textile sector:Thecase of C&A. *Business Ethics European Review*, *11*(3), 282–294. doi:10.1111/1467-8608.00286

Koszewska, M. (2010). CSR standards as a significant factor differentiating textile and clothing goods. *Fibres & Textiles in Eastern Europe*, *18*(6), 14–19.

Morgan, L. R., & Birtwistle, G. (2009). An investigation of young fashion consumers' disposal habits. *International Journal of Consumer Studies*, *33*(2), 190–198. doi:10.1111/j.1470-6431.2009.00756.x

Navaretti, B., Falzoni, G., & Turrini, A. (2001). The decision to invest in a low-wage country: Evidence from Italian textiles and clothing multinationals. *The Journal of International Trade & Economic Development*, *10*(4), 451–470. doi:10.1080/09638190110074588

Nicholls, A. J. (2002). Strategic options in fair trade retailing. *International Journal of Retail & Distribution Management*, *30*(1), 6–17. doi:10.1108/09590550210415220

Parker, E. (2011) Steps towards Sustainability in Fashion: Snapshot Bangladesh, Hammond, L., Higginson, H. & Williams, D (EDS), London College of Fashion and Fashioning an Ethical Industry.

Testa, F., Battaglia, M., & Bianchi, L. (2012). The diffusion of CSR initiatives among SMEs in industrial clusters: Some findings from Italian experience. *International Journal of Technology Management*, *58*(1/2), 152–170. doi:10.1504/IJTM.2012.045793

Ul Haque, H., & Md, M. (2018). Corporate Social Responsibility (CSR) Driven Innovation & Opportunities for Sustainable International Business. *International Journal of Business and Social Research*, *8*(3), 19–28.

KEY TERMS AND DEFINITIONS

Corporate Social Responsibility: CSR represents one of the theoretical frameworks aimed at clarifying the role of business in society. "The new concept of social responsibility recognizes the intimacy of the relationship between the corporation and society and realizes that such relationships must be kept in mind by top managers as the corporation and the related groups pursue their respective goals" (Walton 1967, p. 18).

Fashion Industry: Fashion industry consists of enterprises from textile, clothing and accessories, and tanning sectors.

Small and Medium-Sized Enterprises (SMEs): Defined in the EU recommendation 2003/361. The main factors determining whether an enterprise is an SME are: 1. staff headcount; 2. either turnover or balance sheet total.

Stakeholder Engagement: Stakeholder engagement is the process by which an organization involves people who may be affected by the decisions it makes or can influence the implementation of its decisions. The stakeholders' engagement has increasingly become the most viable approach for the implementation of sustainability plans.

Supply Chain Sustainability: Supply chain sustainability is the management of environmental, social and economic impacts and the encouragement of good governance practices, throughout the lifecycles of goods and services. The objective of supply chain sustainability is to create, protect and grow long-term environmental, social and economic value for all stakeholders involved in bringing products and services to market (UN Global Compact, 2010).

Sustainability: Originated with the Brundtland Report in 1987, this concept describes sustainable development as one that satisfies the needs of the present without adversely affecting the conditions for future generations.

Sustainability Strategy: A competitive strategy based on the creation of the business offer through its ethical connotations, namely adding an "ecological value" or "social value" to the product/service it intends to provide.

Sustainable Innovation: The application of a new technologies or production methods as well as the development of new products - or the use of new materials and components in the manufacture of products - that aim to design a profitable product or service in an innovative and user-oriented way that benefits the environment and society.

ENDNOTE

1 According to the latest data from Lyst, a leading search engine in the fashion world, which we publish as a preview, the demand for sustainable fashion is growing worldwide. For more details: https://d.repubblica.it/moda/2019/04/09/news/moda_sostenibile_sostenibilita_dati_lyst_italia_prodotti_piu_cercati_stella_mccartney_stansmith_adidas_parley_ultraboost-4363600/

Chapter 8
Life Cycle Management and Sharing Economy:
Methodological Framework and Application in Sustainable Mobility

Roberta Guglielmetti Mugion
University of Roma Tre, Italy

Gabriella Arcese
Niccolò Cusano University, Italy

Martina Toni
University of Roma Tre, Italy

Luca Silvestri
Niccolò Cusano University, Italy

ABSTRACT

The life cycle sustainability assessment based on Life Cycle Thinking is currently considered the most crucial paradigm that includes three kinds of sustainability variables. Life cycle management (LCM) is the most holistic approach in promoting sustainable value creation, embedding the social, economic, and environmental dimensions as a management tool. LCM is mainly applied in the manufacturing and products chain, whereas it is understudied in the service industry. This chapter proposes the development of the LCM general framework and the definition of indicators for the assessment of sustainability in the urban shared mobility. The research framework has been tested in the transportation sector focusing on car sharing context.

DOI: 10.4018/978-1-7998-1419-1.ch008

INTRODUCTION

The globalization process, the growth of urbanization, and the excess of automobile usage impacts on the environmental, economic and social facets of urban life (Haghshenas and Vaziri, 2012; Florida, 2010), highlighting that is necessary adopting behaviour and practices that are socially and environmentally robust (Birkin and Polesie, 2012).

Disruptive technologies inspires the emergence of new business models and they need to embed social and environmental issues, besides the economic goals (Hart, 2007). Currently, innovative business models based on shared service are widespread especially in the mobility sector.

In particular, car sharing is a growing phenomenon that proposes to merge the three facets of sustainability (environmental, social and economic) and it represents a continuously rising trend, confirmed by the high number of overall registered users. Indeed, over 4.8 million members share more than 100 thousand vehicles worldwide (Shaheen, 2015; Lane et al., 2015).

According to Schiller et al., (2017) these business models are characterized by four features:

- Usage area of shared vehicles: city center broader city area or regional;
- Vehicles type: small/city cars, compact cars, SUVs and MPVs;
- Pricing: by time, by distance, fixed prices;
- Parking co-operations: parking permits, commercial, private.

It represents a flexible solution for fulfilling needs of transportation of an urban area, striving to solve issues related to car ownership.

Mobility concepts can be classified by the flexibility offered to customers as well the distance travelled which take into account the variation in usage areas (Schiller et al., 2017). Particularly, social and environmental effects are recognized by several authors (Shaheen and Cohen, 2012; Nijland and Van Meerkerk, 2017). . However, potential impacts of car sharing on the society are widely discussed, although they lack of directions and empirical contributions.

Hence, shared mobility can contribute as a tool for improving sustainability at environmental and social levels; on this strength, a 'green image' is usually associated to car sharing (Nijland and Van Meerkerk, 2017).

In addition, in the last decade, the European Commission has strived to identify useful means for reducing the environmental impacts caused by the interaction of humans with the environment (EU, 2006).

Life Cycle Sustainability Assessment (hereafter LCSA) framework provides specific tools to evaluate each sustainability area (Kloeppfer 2007, Finkbeiner et al. 2010). Moreover, Life Cycle Management (LCM) is a strategic framework for industrial application and evaluation of the sustainability concept.

Using the LCM tools, the authors define the indicators for quantifying the real and potential impacts in term of economic environmental and social sustainability using the cradle to grave approach.

This chapter proposes a theoretical framework that is applied to the sharing mobility, focusing on car sharing, based on principles for global sustainability.

The aim is to realize a new general approach to the management of materials products and services, here termed "strategic lifecycle management".

More specifically, it deals with the analysis of the actual state of car sharing services, adopting the LCM approach and comparative analysis, and defining a set of indicators for evaluating the environmental and social impacts.

The lifecycle stages considered in the study include production activities, use phase and end of life and the indicator considering environmental, economic and social aspects.

This chapter is organized as follows. First, the Background section presents a review on LCM, sharing economy and car sharing. Then, the methodology is introduced and consequently the main Results of this study are proposed. Afterward, Discussions and Conclusions are illustrated.

BACKGROUND

In this section, sharing economy and car sharing (i), a review on LCM approach (ii) and on automotive (iii) are briefly presented. Finally, the main literature gaps are highlighted (iv).

Sharing Economy and car sharing

Urban transport habits have been redefined in order to address sustainable mobility, considering the necessity to face overconsumption of natural resources, global warming, ozone depletion and water and air pollution that seriously threaten quality of life (Tanner and Wölfing Kast, 2003).

Sustainable mobility is a mobility which is in accordance with the demands for sustainable development, considering the core characteristics of ecological sustainability, human sustainability (basic needs satisfaction), future responsibility and global responsibility (Lafferty & Langhelle, 1995; Høyer, 1997). It provides an alternative paradigm within which to investigate the complexity of cities, and to strengthen the links between land use and transport (Banister, 2008).

As delineated by Banister (2008) in attempting to understand how to implement effectively sustainable cities, sustainable mobility has a central role, especially concerning the need to raise awareness and change consumer behaviour, values, and motivations. First, in order to face environmental issues, the dependence on one's own private car needs to be overcome (Marshall and Banister, 2000; Banister, 2007). Currently, the actual challenge is to break the norm of using cars and one solution is represented by switching from private cars to alternative sustainable means of transportation (Gärling et al., 2013; Hajer *et al.*, 2012; Guglielmetti Mugion et al., 2018). It implies a preference for accessing rather than buying, contributing to an improvement in wellbeing and quality of life (Jackson, 2005). Human behavior covers a critical role in this changing, and the cost of car ownership (i.e. purchasing and maintenance costs, fuel prices) and the restricted available parking space in urban areas, both contribute on this purpose (Efthymiou et al., 2013). Car sharing is a falls within the access based consumption form of transaction in which no transfer of ownership takes place during the usage. Hence, users can access a vehicle, attaining benefits through the usage (Lovelock and Gummesson 2004) and, in this way, the businesses sell the utilization instead of the ownership.

Car sharing - that is defined by The Carsharing Association (2011) as '*access to shared vehicles 24 hours, seven days a week at unattended self-service locations, among other social and environmental criteria*'- is contributing on this purpose. Conventional car-sharing may not require additional infrastructure, and it leads to time and money savings, lower emissions and car-sharing participants report increased environmental awareness after joining the program and, the more environmentally conscious the respondents declares to be, the more possible it is that they will join one of the two schemes (Efthymiou et al., 2013). Indeed, car sharing change the mobility patterns, provides various benefits from the environmental and social perspectives. First, it induces people to decrease car ownership, by substituting the purchase of the first or additional cars; moreover, the number of kilometers travelled became fewer (Nijland and Van Meerkerk, 2017). Shaheen and Cohen (2013) demonstrate also that there could be also long-term impacts due to the environmental awareness after the adoption of car sharing. This trend is due also to the cost of purchasing and maintaining a car, the increasing fuel prices and the restricted available parking space in urban areas (Millard-Ball et al., 2005; Shaheen and Cohen, 2007). All of these costs linked to owning a car, make car ownership a luxury that not many people can afford. From one side car ownership becomes a luxury and from the other side public transport restricts the freedom and quality of travel, thus car-sharing seem to be the solution. Moreover, the global pressure to reduce greenhouse gases (GHG) (Walsh, 1990; EEA, 2010) in order to fulfill obligation toward the environmental protocols, in turn forces them to encourage the investment on alternative, sustainable, urban transport schemes, such as conventional or electrified carsharing (Millard-Ball et al., 2005; Shaheen and Cohen, 2007; Barth and Shaheen, 2002; Shaheen et al., 2010a, 2010b, 2010c). Car sharing can be a solution because, as Millard-Ball et al. (2006) illustrate it reduces the vehicle ownership; indeed each car-sharing vehicle replaces between 4 and 23 vehicles depending on the characteristics of the city, since after joining a car-sharing program, people tend to sold their car. Further study (Martin et al., 2010) shows that car-sharing has removed between 75,000 and 94,000 vehicles, with a reduction in air pollution and traffic congestion and increases the available parking slots. Hence, both short and long-term effects need to be considered in analyzing the effects of sustainable mobility. Mattia et al. (2019) showed that economic, environmental, and social benefits indicate the attitude toward the free-floating car sharing and that attitude, perceived behavioral control, and subjective norm have a significant influence on the future intention to re-use the service.

Review on LCM

Sustainable aspects cover a strategic function for business strategy for both companies and policy makers. The sustainable evaluations of materials, products and services require constant monitoring and estimations of environmental, economic and social factors. The most comprehensive tools and indicators for supporting these evaluations is the life-cycle assessment (LCA).

Life Cycle Management (LCM) is, at the same time, a management concept and an opportunity for applying in the industrial and service sectors overall sustainability performance in business and along its value chains (Sonnemann et Margni, 2015). Sustainability performance contributes to differentiating the products and survives in the market, and the LCM pattern aims at long-term achievements minimizing environmental and socioeconomic burden while maximizing economic and social value.

In the literature, it is possible to found different LCM definitions that start in 1995 by Linneman and the three vision on LCM:

(1) A managerial perspective for the integration of environmental issues into the companies' decision-making processes
(2) An engineering perspective for the optimization of the environmental impact considering all the product life cycle
(3) The leadership point of view for the creation of a different organizational and culture model to approach the business strategy

Since 2000, LCM considers only the environmental impacts and it is linked at Life Cycle Assessment applications. In 2002, Heiskanen considers LCA as an accounting model and a "social planner's view on environmental issues, rather than the minimization of a company's direct environmental liabilities".

The theoretical evolution derives from different authors contributions, such as Hunkeler et al. (2004); Baumann and Tillman (2004) and Remmen et al. (2007). The first contribution considers the LCM is an "integrated framework of concepts and techniques to address environmental, economic, technological and social aspects of products, services and organizations". The second one introduces "the managerial practices and organizational arrangements that apply life cycle thinking", and the last contribute underline the importance of socio-economic burdens associated with the system during its entire life cycle and value chain.

In 2009, the breakthrough came from the UNEP/Setac document entitled "Life cycle management: how business uses it to decrease footprint, to create opportunities and make value chains more sustainable" where it is possible to read "… a business management approach that can be used by all types of businesses (and other organizations) to improve their products and thus the sustainability performance of the companies and associated value chains" "It can be used to target, organize, analyze and manage product-related information and activities towards continuous improvement along the life cycle".

The LCM framework represents the triple bottom line (3BL), that is a model that integrates the "three dimensions of sustainability: economic, environmental and social" and cover the three Ps: people, planet and profit (Remmen et al., 2007) (Figure 1).

In this context, environmental life cycle assessment (LCA), social life cycle assessment (SLCA) and life cycle costing (LCC) are essential techniques for realizing, implement and measure LCM model.

LCA follow the ISO Standards procedures (ISO 14040, 14044) and it is a methodological framework for estimating and assessing the environmental impacts attributable to the life cycle of a product, such as climate change and toxicological stress on human health and ecosystems, the depletion of resources, water use, land use, energy and others (Rebitzer et al., 2004).

S-LCA is defined as "a social impact (and potential impact) assessment technique that aims to assess the social and socio-economic aspects of products and their potential positive and negative impacts along their life cycle encompassing extraction and processing of raw materials, manufacturing, distribution, use, re-use, maintenance, recycling, and final disposal" (Unep/Setac, 2009).

Figure 1. The triple bottom line

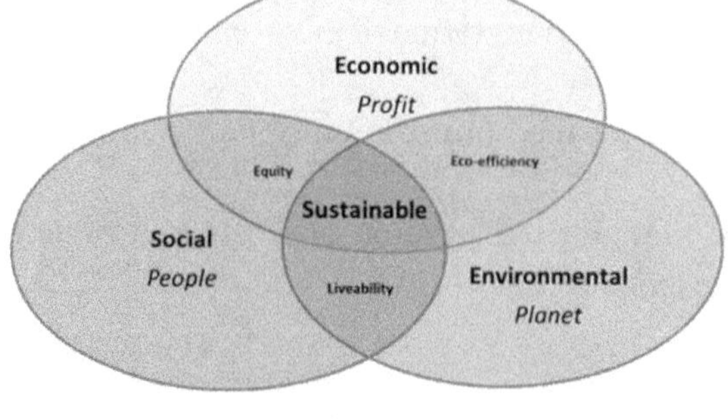

Life cycle costing, which is used in parallel with an LCA, covers all the costs incurred by the extended waste management system, as though the LCA system was a single economic actor, including the environmental costs for environmental LCC.

However, LCA analysis often has a lack in the sustainability perspective. This lack is probably due to the difficulties in obtaining trade-offs between specificity and depth, comprehension and applicability.

LCM in Automotive Industry

The mobility sector is a key field for the development of technologies that help to minimize environmental impacts. Many automotive companies apply LC tools for sustainability evaluations of impact (Toyota, Volkswagen, BMW, and other). A crucial role is covered by energy consumption for transportation, prevented food losses, differences in thermal insulation properties, and fuel savings due to the lower mass of plastic automotive components.

The mobility sector companies are continuously working for developing technologies able to minimize environmental impacts. Volkswagen Group, i.e. includes in the performance evaluation, its responsibility for the sustainable development of the economy, the environment and the society and set itself the goal to become its automobile manufacturer more sustainable and respect the international emissions limits plan for 2020.

A set of essential sustainable targets has been elaborated for each business units (R&D, Production phase and sales) and involve the external actor along the value chain. The Volkswagen LCAs contribute the LCIA composition like data on vehicle, component, technology, raw materials information and energy consumptions. Mainly data source for this information is the internal Material Information System (MISS), technical data sheets and drawings. For the use phase modelling, instead, fuel consumption and the resultant emissions are worked out based on the New European Driving Cycle (NEDC). The end of life (EoL) consider the amount of energy consumed during the dismantling and/or recycling of the vehicle parts. The WorldAutoSteel is a useful data source for LCT in the sector (World Steel Association, www.worldsteel.org).

Concerning the development of LCM framework for automotive, it is possible to summarize the LC stages into three categories:

i. Production stage: with an average contribution in the GHG emissions of 19% in term of CO2-eq, and include raw material extraction to semi-finished products or components and finally the car's production and assembly
ii. Use stage: the average valued data for GHG emissions amount is 72% and
iii. EoL stage characterized by a good contribution of recovery materials, in fact the attribute level does not exceed the 2% for GHG emission.

From the BMW's experiences instead, it is possible to include in the analysis the use of new and green technologies. They could contribute to better environmental performance and green product design, in particular, referring to the GHG reduction.

A valid example of these technologies is the electric car, more efficient combustion engines, hybrid engines and emission control systems, aerodynamic drag (Boureima, 2009.). The usage of energy-intensive technologies, like lithium-ion accumulators or lightweight materials, can lead to a higher burden in the production and recovery phase, combined with a lower burden in the use phase (Sonneman & Margni, 2015).

Through the analysis of the comparative analysis between LPG, hybrid and Battery Electric Vehicle (BEV), it is possible to verify that the use phase still constitutes the significant portion because the role of energy consumption and it has a direct economic impact on the users. In detail, it is possible to quantify the average consumption for the electricity for the production phase (23.6 kWh) and Fuel (0.44 MJ) and to consider the specifications of the Lithium-ion battery (2 for car) by Tesla data (Lifetime 160934 km for 2 battery per F.U.),

The LCI data of the electrolyte of the lithium-ion battery which is the lithium hexafluorophosphate (LiPF6) was not available in the Ecoinvent database but it is possible to complete LCI through CONCAWE Report (www.concawe.eu) and MIRAI Toyota Lifecycle Environmental Action (https://www.toyota-global.com/sustainability/environment/challenge2/lca-and-eco-actions/).

With the past increase of crude oil prices and the introduction of emission limits for the vehicles, the interest for less consuming and more efficient cars has led most automotive companies to reduce the cars' weight by choosing lighter materials and improving their efficiency in the use phase. The use phase is the hotspot related the GWP and air quality value (the EU lists the limit values pay attention to (PM2.5: 25 µg/m3, PM10: 50 µg/m3 and NO2: 40 µg/m3 refer to the annual mean). For those pollutants with more than one metric.

Several analysis includes different solutions for improving the aerodynamics, choosing lighter materials and materials substitution for reducing tailpipe emissions and fuel consumption, and introducing technologies (i.e. start & stop), energy regeneration.

In the solutions consideration, we have also to consider the other aspect of sustainability. GHG could be reduced by using renewable raw materials, but at the same time, this practice could cause negative impacts like biodiversity alterations, social risks for developing countries (working conditions, wages, and human rights and externalities across productivity sector (agro-food sector).

Regarding LCC, the monetization of the environmental externalities and economic costs are crucial (first of all carbon tax, carbon compensation and carbon neutrality). The hotspots related to the paid expenses and obtained revenues by the manufacturing company or when they are connected to the consumer.

SLCA for vehicle considers the social hotspots at the company level, but this approach is not useful for this work. It is necessary to collect data for every single product and assess social performance and considering all stakeholders' categories: workers, customers, local community, society, and value chain actors not including consumers (UNEP/SETAC 2009).

Literature Gaps

The literature review mainly investigate the application of LCM in the automotive industry, whereas there a scarcity of contributions on sharing services. Thus, LCM remains an understudied topic in the sharing mobility industry, mainly in the car sharing services. On this strength, this chapter represents the first attempt to propose a theoretical framework for adopting LCM in the car sharing.

METHODOLOGY

Based on the LCM approach, a comparative analysis of the LCM for a car is developed. Then, an evaluation of the main types of car sharing was identified. Second, the life cycle stages of the car sharing service are described and the main involved stakeholders, subcategories and their activities are identified. Then, the service blueprint map is depicted, showing the customer journey on backstage and on-stage activities. It allowed highlighting the crucial role of customer and technology in the car sharing system, which should be included in the assessment of economic, social and environmental impacts.

It was clear from the beginning that a full sustainability assessment would require at least two further dimensions, the economic and the social ones. The authors LCM model adapted for sharing mobility was based on Life cycle sustainability assessment (LCSA) and include global sustainability indicators.

It was based on the following assumption:

$$LCSA = LCA + LCC + SLCA$$

This formal equation underlines how the sustainability assessment of the product must to consider jointly the environmental performance evaluation, the economic aspects and the social performance definition along the product's life cycle.

LCA should also eventually take into account the economic consequences of alternative products or product designs. Neither the internal nor the external economic aspects of the decisions are within the scope of developed LCA methodology.

LCC was considered based on Norris' approach (cost-effective and environmental-related consequences of alternative decisions. The process scope of the LCC includes only those processes imposing direct economic costs (or benefits) upon the decision maker, and there are accounted selling prices of inputs to the investment's economic life.

S-LCA is a social impact assessment technique that aims to assess the social and socio-economic aspects of products and the related potential positive and negative impacts along their life cycle based on UNEP/SETAC Guideline with a consequential S-LCA, which aims to evaluate the social implications caused by choosing among several alternatives.

RESULTS

In this section, the results of the LCM application are presented focusing on the car sharing services, namely free-floating and stationary types. Then, a comparative analysis of cars is described.

Car Sharing Services: Actual State And Future Trends

The growth of car sharing phenomenon is continuous and it has high potential trigger expansion especially in Southern and Easter Europe. It competes with car ownership and other transportation services even though it is still a niche market, since the car ownership seems to be dominant analyzing the number of cars per inhabitants still rising in most European Countries. Its major diffusion is registered in dense urban context where it is possible to see also bike and scooter sharing as well as ride sharing/hailing, through the strong entry of Uber especially in US market. Anyway, car-hailing platforms are more restricted in Europe, in which there is a strict market regulation.

Car sharing is very different from car rental that implies to pay a car for a number of days and from car lease and ownership that means pay a car to own. However, it is worth to emphasize that there is not a unique definition of car sharing, that can be defined as the "membership-based, self-service, short term car access system with a network of vehicles for which members pay by time and/or distance". Thus, it provides short term, pay per use car access. With a payment per minute and /or hour based on the distance driven. The service providers can own the car itself, function as an intermediary and connect private individuals (peer-to-peer). Cars are distributed in different city locations and cars have to be picked up and drive directly by end users. Different forms of car sharing are identified: free floating (pick up/drop off anywhere), point to point (pick up/drop off in fixed location) and peer to peer (pick up/drop off private car owner).

Currently, the majority of the car sharing operators provide traditional fuel vehicles, even if some companies offer electrical vehicles to end-customers. The car sharing usage is strongly affected by the use of Mobile Apps, that represent the unique way to have access to the service from the starting registration to the vehicles check out. This implies the fact that car sharing is more diffused among young and young adults, that still perceive the cost of car sharing as a barrier.

Anyway, the car sharing can represent a good transitional option toward the sustainable mobility even if environmental and social impact should be further analyzed. Car manufacturers should take into consideration into their strategic plans this new tendency, investing in technology and platforms for sharing cars.

Car Sharing Service Analysis: Life Cycle, Stakeholders, Activities

The life cycle analysis allowed to identify the following 3 main stages, that compose the car sharing services focusing on free floating and stationary car sharing: i) "Processing and Planning Shared mobility"; ii) "Usage"; and iii) "End of life".

Firstly, the "Processing and Planning shared mobility" phase is identified, which involves the selection and utilization of resources (raw materials, energy, components and semi-finished goods etc.) for the production and assembly of vehicles. Then, the car sharing service is planned and implemented by the operators and intermediaries. Indeed, they handle the vehicles by renting or buying them from car manufacturers.

Second, the "Usage" phase is strongly related to the customer engagement in adopting car sharing services. The customer behavior is vital for defining economic (internal perspective), environmental and social impacts (external perspective). In this stage, the technology represents enablers that allow to match customer and shared vehicles. The technology is mainly represented by digital platforms and Apps, which guarantee the efficiency and effectiveness of the service.

Finally, the "End of life" stage concerns the treatment, collection, recycling and disposal of finished goods and components involved in the service namely cars, battery, digital and electrical devices, etc.

Here following the 3 phases are shown below (Figure 2).

It is worth to specify that the assessment of the economic, environmental and social impacts is transversal to the three main phases.

Afterward, the identification of the main stakeholders involved in the car sharing service and their main activities is presented.

Figure 2. The three phases of Life cycle analysis

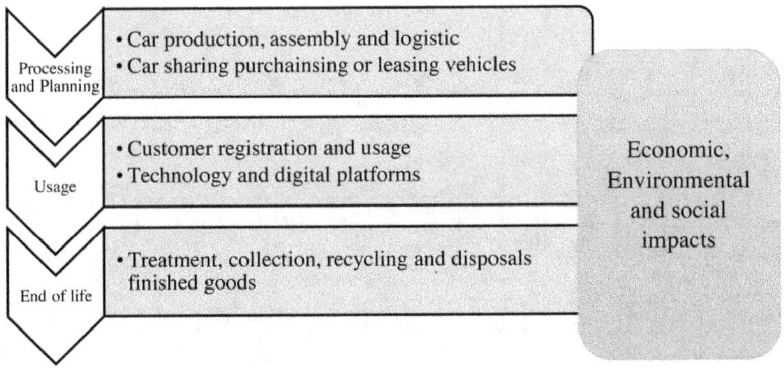

Concerning the free floating and point-to-point car sharing, several stakeholders are involved in the value chain and the technological operators and customers cover a crucial role.

Following a table of the main stakeholders is described. According to SLCA approach, the subcategories are identified.

The service blueprint map below (Figure 3) shows the steps that a customer has to follow in order to use a car sharing service, explaining the contact points between customer and technology, and evidencing the interaction line (on stage and back stage). In the process, the registration and booking system are vital for ensuring the service provision and allowing matching demand and offer.

Table 1. Stakeholders involved according to SLCA approach

Stakeholders categories	Detail	Activities
Value chain actors	Car manufactures	They produced cars (fuels, electrics, hybrid etc.) that can be used for car sharing
	Car sharing operators/ Intermediaries	Provide cars, amenities and their access; manage maintenance and fuel costs; offer the availability of website and Mobile Apps.
	Technological handlers	Provide vehicles shared technological platforms
	Suppliers of car sharing operators/ intermediaries	Provide maintenance and fuel services; Provide accessories to cars such as child seat, electric infrastructure for cars battery charge etc.
	Supplier of car manufacturer	Provide raw materials and semi-finished goods
	Technological handlers	Provide software platforms and Apps
Employees	Car manufacturer, car sharing operators Technological handlers	Manage back office processes
Consumers	Car sharing users	Pick up, drive and drop-off vehicles
Local communities	Municipality	Provides free parking and permission for forbidden area in the center of the city
	Citizens and tourists	Environmental and social awareness and behavior
Society	Public commitment	Sustainability, economic development, market regulation
	Transportation institutions	Agreement and urban city mobility plan

Figure 3. The service blueprint map

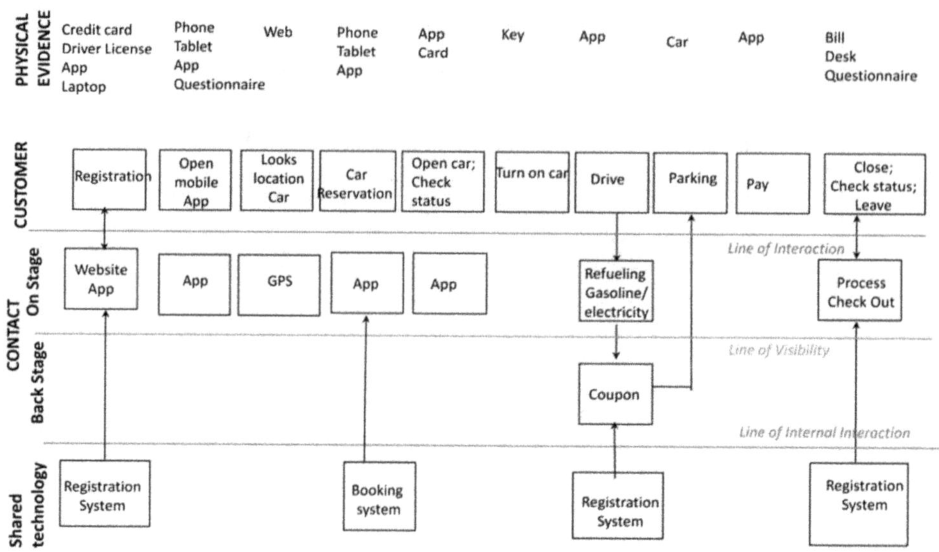

The LCSA analysis followed the ISO Standard 14040 and 14044, including the same system boundary. It refers to the equivalent functional unit and includes the corresponding component of the supply chain. The LCA steps definition as represented in Table 2.

Table 2. LCM framework for sharing mobility (authors' elaboration)

LCM phases	LCA	LCC	SLCA
1. Goal and Scope definition	F.U. has been defined as the shared cars usage of a passenger during the years of lifetime driven distance		
2. Life cycle Inventory (LCI)	Eco invent and Gabi Database; CONCAWE; MIRAI; Environmental Certifications	Accounting internal data sources; Input-Output database for each Country	SHDB Primary data (in-depth interview etc.)
3. Life cycle impact assessment (LCIA)	Focus on the GWP, Human Health and Air Acidification (Urban pollution)	Economic and environmental costs; Externalities (positive and negative)	Stakeholder categories and focus on consumers and society and local communities (Use phase)
4. Interpretation of results	Better solutions in the urban areas consider the Percentage of population living close to major roads and the Percentage of population exposed to background concentrations	Focus on economic barriers; Relation between (economic and environmental) costs and market price	Focus on stakeholder sub-categories: Community Engagement, Safe and Healthy Living Conditions, Supplier Relationship, Promoting Social Responsibility, Health and Safety, Social Benefit/Social Security

DISCUSSIONS

In the course of the years, technological evolution and green technologies introduction contribute to the natural turnover of the vehicle fleet. Indeed, significant reductions in term of NOx and PMx emissions has been obtained with Euro 6 and hybrid vehicles.

The purpose of zero emissions in the passenger cars will be as effective as zero emission vehicles in helping cities become compliant with air quality standards.

Despite technological advances, NO2 compliance issues in traffic "hot-spots" persist until 2030 in some European cities. Although the conditions concerning GWP improve, it is unlikely that the measures that the European Union reserves for diesel cars will definitively resolve the problem because, in the use phase, the chemical is produced by mechanical abrasion (tire wear, roads and tires). The percentage of population living close to major roads: 4.9 and the percentage of population exposed to background concentrations: 95.1 (EEA, 2014 data for IT) represent significant indicators for traffic management and transport modes.

CONCLUSIONS

Due to a literature gap, this chapter represented the first attempt to apply the LCM framework in the sustainable mobility field namely in the car sharing. The study evidences that three main phases are needed that are: i) Processing and Planning shared mobility; ii) Usage; iii) End of Life. The main findings that it is possible to detect is that the role of the consumer and his/her engagement is vital for defining the economic, environmental and social impacts and that the linkage between resources and customers is created by technology. The originality of this chapter is to be identified in the integration of the usage of the Service Blueprint map in the LCM framework in order to analyse the conjointly analyse the internal and perspectives. Moreover, a sustainability vision of car sharing is proposed that enables the usage of LCM as a strategic tools for supporting the decision making process. Finally, some useful indicators for the assessment of sustainability in the shared mobility are defined.

REFERENCES

Banister, D. (2007). Is paradigm shift too difficult in UK transport? *Journal of Urban Technology, 14*(2), 71–86. doi:10.1080/10630730701531732

Banister, D. (2008). The sustainable mobility paradigm. *Transport Policy, 15*(2), 73–80. doi:10.1016/j.tranpol.2007.10.005

Baumann H. & Tillman A-M. (2004). *The hitchhiker's guide to LCA: an orientation in life cycle*

Birkin, F., & Polesie, T. (2012). *Intrinsic sustainable development epistemes, science, business and sustainability*. Singapore: World Scientific Publishing.

Boureima, F. S., Messagie, M., Matheys, J., Wynen, V., Sergeant, N., Van Mierlo, J., & De Caevel, B. (2009). Comparative LCA of electric, hybrid, LPG and gasoline cars in Belgian context. *World Electric Vehicle Journal, 3*(3), 469–476. doi:10.3390/wevj3030469

Deloitte, M. (2017). Car sharing in Europe: Business models. National variations and upcoming disruptions.

Efthymiou, D., Antoniou, C., & Waddell, P. (2013). Factors affecting the adoption of vehicle sharing systems by young drivers. *Transport Policy*, *29*, 64–73. doi:10.1016/j.tranpol.2013.04.009

Finkbeiner, M., Schau, E. M., Lehmann, A., & Traverso, M. (2010). Towards life cycle sustainability assessment. *Sustainability*, *2*(10), 3309–3322. doi:10.3390u2103309

Florida, R. (2010). *The Great Reset: how new ways of living and working drive post- crash prosperity*. New York, NY: HarperCollins.

Gärling, T., Ettema, D., & Friman, M. (2013). *Handbook of sustainable travel*. Heidelberg, Germany: Springer.

Gärling, T., Ettema, D., & Friman, M. (2013). *Handbook of sustainable travel*. Heidelberg, Germany: Springer.

Guglielmetti Mugion, R., Toni, M., Raharjo, H., Di Pietro, L., & Sebathu, S. P. (2018). Does the service quality of urban public transport enhance sustainable mobility? *Journal of Cleaner Production*, *174*, 1566–1587. doi:10.1016/j.jclepro.2017.11.052

Haghshenas, H., & Vaziri, M. (2012). Urban sustainable transportation indicators for global comparison. *Ecological Indicators*, *15*(1), 115–121. doi:10.1016/j.ecolind.2011.09.010

Hajer, M., Hoen, A., & Huitzing, H. (2012). Shifting gear: beyond classical mobility policies and urban planning. In B. van Wee (Ed.), Keep Moving. The Hague, The Netherlands: Eleven International Publishing.

Hart, S. L. (2007). *Capitalism at the crossroads aligning business, Earth, and humanity*. Upper Saddle River, NJ: Wharton School Publishing.

Hawkins, T. R., Singh, B., Majeau-Bettez, G., & Strømman, A. H. (2013). Comparative environmental life cycle assessment of conventional and electric vehicles. *Journal of Industrial Ecology*, *17*(1), 53–64. doi:10.1111/j.1530-9290.2012.00532.x

Heiskanen, E. (2002). The institutional logic of life cycle thinking. *Journal of Cleaner Production*, *10*(5), 427–437. doi:10.1016/S0959-6526(02)00014-8

Høyer, K. G. (1997). Sustainable development. In D. Brune, D. Chapman, M. Gwynne, & J. Pacyna (Eds.), *The Global Environment. Science, Technology and Management*. Weinheim, Germany: VCH. doi:10.1002/9783527619658.ch74

Hunkeler, D., Saur, K., Rebitzer, G., Schmidt, W., Jensen, A., Stranddorf, H., & Christiansen, K. (2004). *Life cycle management*. Pensacola, FL: SETAC.

ISO 14040 and ISO 14044, Environmental Management – Life Cycle Assessment – Principles and Framework

Kloepffer, W. (2008). Life cycle sustainability assessment of products. *The International Journal of Life Cycle Assessment*, *13*(2), 89–95. doi:10.1065/lca2008.02.376

Lafferty, W., & Langhelle, O. (1995). *Bærekraftig Utvikling*. Oslo, Norway: Ad Notam.

Lane, C., Zeng, H., Dhingra, C., & Carrigan, A. (2015). Car sharing, A vehicle for sustainable mobility in emerging markets. *World Resources Institute Centre for Sustainable Cities.*

Linneman, R. E., & Stanton, J. L. (1995). *Marketing planning in a total quality environment.* Psychology Press.

Lovelock, C., & Gummesson, E. (2004). Whither services marketing?: In search of a new paradigm and fresh perspectives. *Journal of Service Research, 7*(1), 20–41. doi:10.1177/1094670504266131

Marshall, S., & Banister, D. (2000). Travel reduction strategies: Intentions and outcomes. *Transportation Research Part A, Policy and Practice, 34*(5), 321–338. doi:10.1016/S0965-8564(99)00034-8

Mattia, G., Mugion, R. G., & Principato, L. (2019). Shared mobility as a driver for sustainable consumptions: The intention to re-use free-floating car sharing. *Journal of Cleaner Production,* 237.

Mildenberger, U., & Khare, A. (2000). Planning for an environment-friendly car. *Technovation, 20*(4), 205–214. doi:10.1016/S0166-4972(99)00111-X

Millard-Ball, A., Murray G., ter Schure J., Fox, C., & Burkhardt, J., (2005). Car sharing: *Where and how it succeeds.* Transit Cooperative Research Program (TCRP) Report, 108.

Nijland, H., & van Meerkerk, J. (2017). Mobility and environmental impacts of car sharing in the Netherlands. *Environmental Innovation and Societal Transitions, 23,* 84–91. doi:10.1016/j.eist.2017.02.001

Norris, G. A. (2001). Integrating life cycle cost analysis and LCA. *The International Journal of Life Cycle Assessment, 6*(2), 118–120.

Rebitzer, G., Ekvall, T., Frischknecht, R., Hunkeler, D., Norris, G., Rydberg, T., & Pennington, D. W. (2004). Life cycle assessment: Part 1: Framework, goal and scope definition, inventory analysis, and applications. *Environment International, 30*(5), 701–720. doi:10.1016/j.envint.2003.11.005 PMID:15051246

Remmen, A., Jensen, A. A., & Frydendal, J. (2007). *Life cycle management. A business guide to sustainability.* UNEP DTIE.

Shaheen, S. (2015). Mobility + sharing economy: past, present and future. (2015). *International Sharing Economy Symposium. Utrecht,* The Netherlands.

Shaheen, S., Meyn, M., & Wipyewski, K. (2003). US shared-use vehicle survey findings on carsharing and station car growth: Obstacles and opportunities. *Transportation Research Record: Journal of the Transportation Research Board,* (1841), 90-98.

Shaheen, S. A., & Cohen, A. P. (2007). Growth in worldwide carsharing: An international comparison. *Transportation Research Record: Journal of the Transportation Research Board, 1992*(1), 81–89. doi:10.3141/1992-10

Shaheen, S. A., & Cohen, A. P. (2013). Carsharing and personal vehicle services: Worldwide market developments and emerging trends. *International Journal of Sustainable Transportation*, *7*(1), 5–34. doi:10.1080/15568318.2012.660103

Sonnemann, G., & Margni, M. (Eds.). (n.d.). *Life cycle management, LCA compendium*. The Complete World of Life Cycle Assessment.

Tanner, C., & Wölfing Kast, S. (2003). Promoting sustainable consumption: Determinants of green purchases by Swiss consumers. *Psychology and Marketing*, *20*(10), 883–902. doi:10.1002/mar.10101

UNEP. (2009). *SETAC. Guidelines for social life cycle assessment of products. United Nations Environment Programme (UNEP) and Society of Environmental Toxicology and Chemistry*. Belgium: SETAC.

Chapter 9
B Corp Certification for a Circular Economy Approach and a Sustainable Pathway

Enrico Maria Mosconi
https://orcid.org/0000-0001-7065-7313
University of Tuscia, Italy

Stefano Poponi
https://orcid.org/0000-0001-7574-5320
Niccolò Cusano University, Italy

Simona Fortunati
University of Tuscia, Italy

Michelangelo Arezzo di Trifiletti
Embassy of the United States of America, Rome, Italy

ABSTRACT

The "loop" approach of the circular model, which aims to live in the business or market environment, requires a radical evolution of the production techniques, management, and skills in a new concept or idea for the market. Circular Economy results from a long awareness-raising process connected with problems concerning environmental protection. The dissemination of circular economy supposes the adoption of business models which will eventually enable environmental sustainability oriented behaviors, an efficient use of resources, and the respect of ethical, social, and environmental values. Benefit Corporations are companies pursuing these objectives. This chapter identifies and discusses the potential of B Corp certification to apply the principle of Circular economy. In particular, a compared multiple analysis of case studies is used to evaluate how the requirements of the scheme of certification influence the potential circularity of the enterprises analyzed.

DOI: 10.4018/978-1-7998-1419-1.ch009

INTRODUCTION

The new paradigm of circular economy was developed in response to production of the current linear model and to address critical issues due to scarcity and inadequacy in the management of virgin resources by organizations and to the volatility of their prices (Michelini, Moraes, Cunha, Costa, & Ometto, 2017). With proposals that address the full lifecycle of products, new business models aim to increase resource efficiency while respecting the environment so that material from bio-waste is reintegrated, technical waste is refurbished and unused material is re-entered within the industrial cycle, as key resources to close the loop (Ellen-MacArthur Foundation, 2013). Therefore, the transition to circular economics arises as a challenge to slow climate change and to address resource scarcity. Circular economy is applied not only to sustainable development issues, such as environmental or industrial ecology policies (Ghisellini, Cialani, & Ulgiati, 2016) but it extends towards concepts or solutions inspired by "biomimetics", "bioeconomy", sustainability and the green economy (Pomponi & Moncaster, 2017). The new business model goes beyond the economic concept of profit, encouraging the attainment of improving the social-cultural context. In particular, it advocates for minimizing the generation of waste and having as a main objective that of reaching a greater awareness in consumers' perceptions. Therefore, it can be defined as "an economic system that represents a change of paradigm in the world in which the society is correlated with nature and aims to prevent the exhaustion of resources, the circuits of energy and materials" (Prieto-Sandoval, Jaca, & Ormazabal, 2018). There are quite a lot of problems associated to a non-rational use of resources thus technological innovation can represent a valid help for attaining a more favorable transition, by promoting modularity and versatility (Nižetić, Djilali, Papadopoulos, & Rodrigues, 2019). In this context, the stakeholders become an integral part for radically improving this achievement (Højberg, Troldborg, Stisen, Christensen, & Henriksen, 2013). The change must then adopt top-down policies, expressed in policy terms, but even more bottom-up policies for the implementation of production and consumption models increasingly efficient and at the same time environmentally sustainable. The take-make-consume and dispose model (Urbinati, Chiaroni, & Chiesa, 2017) leaves room for circular systems. Products retain their value for as long as possible for subsequent reuse, there by generating value throughout the entire circular lifecycle and reactivating its functionality or use by symbiotic cascade processes, leading towards new production cycles (Holgado, Benedetti, Evans, Baptista, & Lourenço, 2018). Therefore, a characteristic of the circular economy model is given by the interdependency of phases and cascade cycles. This makes it is possible to avoid or at least partly prevent resources from escaping the circle by reducing waste as much as possible. La Ellen MacArthur Foundation has long been committed to strengthening and communicating principles related to circular economy (CE), as well as promoting ideas and opportunities of a new social and environmental business (Ellen-MacArthur Foundation, 2013). The Foundation's contribution was fundamental in the launching of this initiative and to facilitate a transition at the European level of the process change. Among the essential elements that it proposes, there are a series of indicators, including: design (design-of-waste), "the extension of the lifecycle of the product", "renewable energies", the "eco-system" approach, the "recovery of material", the "sharing", the "product as service". The "design-of-waste" contributes to the reduction of waste, promoting a more efficient production, cable of restoring a supply chain through a virtuous process of environmental management. The extension of the lifecycle of the product, together with the repair, resale, regeneration, and reconditioning, allows to affect the profitability of companies, thanks to offer of a new range of services. The use of "renewable energy" contributes to reduce the environmental impact and the use of non-renewable sources, while the eco-system approach operates as a new "Thinking System". That is a way of rethinking the economy, by taking into consideration all the factors that intervene between the action and the consequences that they have on society and on the environment. The recovery of materials through recycling and their subsequent reuse, preserve the quality characteristics, by decreasing their use and at the same time, through sharing models, which act through on-demand platforms, by promoting a facilitation of trade, where the product takes the form of the service.

The concepts expressed by Ellen Mac Arthur (Ellen-MacArthur Foundation, 2013) lead to reconsider and regenerate systems already existing in nature, to build resilience through flexibility. This means equipping organizations with a ductility to cope with / absorb an unexpected or unpredictable event that negatively affects its sustainability. This implies a constructive change based on "resource awareness", "interior strength ", on the set of principles needed to address the challenges of global sustainability through the creation of shared value" (Genovese, Acquaye, Figueroa, & Koh, 2017).

The reduction in consumption is the additional factor for the application of CE. Circular Economy aims to reduce the consumption of raw materials and energy by applying the cascade system to the linear economy model. Unal and Shao define the concept of Circular Economy as "a sustainable development initiative with the objective of reducing the societal production-consumption systems linear material and energy throughout flows by applying materials cycles renewable and cascade - type energy flows to the linear system" (Ünal & Shao, 2019). Circular economy can manufacture resilience-friendly products, using natural systems and likewise contemplate a "vision" that knows how to go beyond the immediate benefit. In Circular Economy systems the re-use of products and regeneration use less resources and energy than traditional recycling methods of raw materials. Ngan et al. emphasize how "the system is designed to be restorative and regenerative" (Ngan et al., 2019), where the "reduction", "reuse", and "re-cycle" represent the three milestones to assess the impact on production and consumption: "The Circular Economy (CE) has gained traction as a pathway towards more sustainable economic growth (Ruggieri, Braccini, Poponi, & Mosconi, 2016). The main actions leading towards a CE have been identified as the 3R principles of "reduce", "reuse", and "recycle". However, understanding is lacking regarding how the adoption of CE using the 3R principles generates value and revenue in a business context" (Ranta, Aarikka-Stenroos, & Mäkinen, 2018).

Taking into consideration the evolution of principles related to the EC's appraisal in the international context, the research will focus on the analysis of the B Corp Certification, on the method of assigning the rankings by the standard and finally a multiple analysis is carried out to compare the impact areas of the certified enterprises. The aim of the paper is to identify and discuss the potential of B Corp certification to apply the principle of Circular economy. In particular, a compared multiple analysis of case studies is used to evaluate how the requirements of the scheme of certification influence the potential circularity of the enterprises analyzed, evaluating the ability/potential of the companies to activate the Circular Business Models. The analysis was based on the value of the ranking obtained, the impact areas covered by enterprises and the requirements defined by the standard.

Background

"The Circular Economy (CE) can be a driver for sustainability and CE can be promoted and supported by the creation of new and innovative business models, which embed CE principles into their value propositions throughout the value chain" (Manninen et al., 2018). The models can assume the characteristic of cascade cycles that describe a flow, narrow or long, that integrates concepts of economic sustainability of resources and operational sustainability in order to determine the efficiency and appropriateness of the exploitation of resources in a given context. In general, narrow cycles preserve the integrity and complexity of a product. In longer cycles instead, there are a series of consecutive steps where the use of new material, energy and manpower needed to create a new product and increase its quality and efficiency contribute to reducing the dispersion of material out of the cycle itself, with pricing benefits and customer satisfaction. The application of the new circular models is based on a number of principles, the list of which is not yet exhaustive due to the lack of uniformity and coding. In order to obtain a continuous improvement within an organization and to improve its efficiency and Implement CE practices, principles that can guide the organization itself to become more sustainable should be applied. In the vast literature on the subject, several authors use a well-established terminology related to the use of 3R to describe concepts of recycle, reuse and reduce (Reike, Vermeulen, & Witjes, 2018; Ranta et al., 2018). "Recycling" implies a "downcycling", that is it reduces the difference between quality of recycled materials and the primary material over time, trying to implement recovery, thereby reducing the potential wastes of renewable materials (Braungart, McDonough, & Bollinger, 2007). The principle of "reduce" is based on the concept of reducing the consumption of raw materials through the design of products that last longer through maintenance and repair techniques which can also have a positive impact on the reduction of costs, impacts (CO_2), raw materials (Moraga et al., 2019).

Ghisellini proposes a classification not only on the bases of 3R, but also of an "appropriate design", a "renewability, and a "reclassification of materials" (Ghisellini et al., 2016). The "appropriate design" implies a search for solutions to avoid excess waste in dumps, thanks to an ease in disassembly and reuse cycle (Ceschin & Gaziulusoy, 2016). When the use of resources is needed, the system must select those to be used and to be preferred from the performance point of view. This new way of working requires a reclassification of materials (raw materials or second raw materials). "Renewability" represents the additional principle. Renewable energy becomes a prerequisite in this context in order to reduce dependence on fossil energy and improve the adaptability (resilience) of the economic system to the negative effects of non-renewable energy (Ghisellini et al., 2016). The "reclassification of materials" is proposed in technical terms. The development of technical materials, such as metals, minerals, plastics, polymers and other artificial materials, introduces the possibility of upgrading, right from the development stage, with a reduction in the loss of resources along the entire value chain, while biological materials can be used to replace those made of non-natural origin, promoting their degradation as a result of usage, without causing damage to the environment.

Further authors extend these concepts by introducing principles evoking the use of "R", generating a sequence of definitions: "4R" for the application of "Recovery"; (Khmara & Kronenberg, 2018) the "5R" for "Reclamation" (Pan et al., 2014); the "6R" for "Repurpose"(Jawahir & Bradley, 2016) until also considering "Recycle Materials" "7R", Recovery energy "8R" and "Re-Mine" "9R" (Reike et al., 2018).

These conditions are necessary to facilitate the transition and to bring about a change also in the use of a product, activating a cultural loop (Geissdoerfer, Morioka, de Carvalho, & Evans, 2018).

Design is one of the principles of the CE. (Bovea & Pérez-Belis, 2018) emphasize "[…] the analysis of how an existing product design meets the design guidelines required from the circular economy perspective, and which are the design guidelines that would need to be incorporated into its design to become a better circular design product" (Bovea & Pérez-Belis, 2018). Design intervenes in regenerative development (Ceschin & Gaziulusoy, 2016) by defining new consumption models such as strategic design or environmental design. The first understood as a sustainable production model that applies to the design to implement innovations within companies and organizations (Baldassarre et al., 2019).

The second "[…] involves overlap of information used and created by the diversity of product design expertises" (Rio, Riel, & Brissaud, 2017). This denotes a difficulty of interrelating design skills with environmental needs, introducing new concepts related to eco-design, design for assembly or disassembly, necessary to ensure full sustainability from "Recovery" (Akanbi et al., 2019).

The circular concept is further linked to the Product Service System (PSS) principle that changes the mode of use of products or access to services (Tukker, 2015). Companies that use the PSS model, integrate products and services to satisfy the consumer and allow the product to be kept in use for as long as possible by changing the relationship between supplier and user. "Industrial symbiosis" is an additional element in promoting the competitiveness of new circular business models. The creation of a network of exchanges in order to be able optimally manage waste and resource depletion is defined by Brian Baldassarre as "[…] a collective approach to competitive advantage in which separate industries created a cooperative network to exchange materials, energy, water and/or by-products" (Baldassarre et al., 2019) and can be mentioned as one of the founding principles of circular economy.

"System thinking" is among the principles of CE, an element of interconnection among all the factors that conditions the complex system of relating to stakeholders. "Systemic thinking" acts in the flows and correlations between space and time, allowing to perceive change in advance, identify future scenarios, in a mid-term approach (Arnold & Wade, 2015). The BSI also focuses on this principle in the 8001 standard.

(British Standards Institution, 2017). It also identifies the capacity of organizations to completely rethink management of resources and energy, in order to improve the financial, environmental and social benefits (British Standards Institution, 2017). Niero and Riviera identify "System thinking" as the core of the lifecycle of the product and present a study on the importance of the integration of the BS 8001 principles. Pauliuk instead focuses on "System Thinking" to understand how management and monitoring policies of services and products affect the use of large-scale materials (Pauliuk, 2018) while Arnold and Wade focus on the role of communication (Arnold & Wade, 2015). Value optimization is identified as a principle by standard BS 8001 (British Standards Institution, 2017). Organizations maintain all components and materials of products to maximum value and utility at all times. Niero and Rivera consider it as an iterative life cycle characteristic that can lead to an improvement in efficiency and performance with a consequent increase and optimization of resources (Niero & Rivera, 2018), other authors (Jiang, Wang, Zhang, Mendis, & Sutherland, 2019) consider it as a way to achieve the recovery of the optimal value of used components and improve the economic benefits resulting from the regeneration of the end-of-life product. Badurdeen and Jawahir focus on the creation and optimisation of value through sustainable production, also supported by academic experts and/or industry professionals and government representatives (Badurdeen & Jawahir, 2017). "Stewardship" is the essence of relationship management (British Standards Institution, 2017). The leaders of organizations pursuing this principle assume an awareness of decisions, responsibility for actions and results. It also used for the quantification of economic social and environmental impacts, for the evaluation and recognition of trade-offs (Niero & Rivera, 2018). Pauliuk defines it as the aspect able to address the review of decisions with respect to the lifecycle of materials (Pauliuk, 2018) while for Kalmykova et al. the conservation of resources should be pursued through methods of recycling or regeneration through a strategy of "product stewardship" or "end-of-life" (Kalmykova, Sadagopan, & Rosado, 2018) which can support circular economy for future challenges and benefits to come (Jensen & Remmen, 2017). In fact, in the form of "shared responsibility", "*product stewardship*" takes on value especially in relation to the packaging supply chain (Lewis, 2005) or as a means to promote significant changes between society and the productive world in a perspective of ecological modernization (Lane & Watson, 2012). "*The Innovation*", although it represents a generic concept that finds within the literature numerous fields of research, it is inserted within CE as a principle to reaffirm the role taken by organizations in the generation of new knowledge focused on the realization or redistribution of value (British Standards Institution, 2017). Niero and Rivera consider "Innovation" as a tool for implementing a social and environmental economy through the opportunities it offers in achieving sustainable goals (Niero & Rivera, 2018). In this context, eco-innovation is the basis for transition (de Jesus, Antunes, Santos, & Mendonça, 2018) of increasing circulation and competitiveness of companies (Pieroni, McAloone, & Pigosso, 2019). The "*Transparency*" assumes an openness for organizations to favor the possibility of promoting transition to a circular model using clear, transparent and timely communication (British Standards Institution, 2017). Certification standards succeed in transfering this degree of transparency, especially in the use of environmental declarations (Kirchherr, Reike, & Hekkert, 2017; Niero & Rivera, 2018) and the progressive improvement of performance sustainability, enhancing the role of the consumer and the community (Mol, 2015).

The "*Collaboration*" allows to create a mutual business value (British Standards Institution, 2017) in a period of sustainable development among stakeholders (Niero & Rivera, 2018) capable of stimulating the search for agreements to put entrepreneurial models and CE principles into practice for promoting new ideas. In this regard Veleva and Bodkin have demonstrated how collaboration between contractors and suppliers throughout the supply chain can lead to reductions in the use of raw materials and waste (Veleva & Bodkin, 2018) by promoting new and more sustainable business models (Witjes & Lozano, 2016).

From the analysis of the literature, however, a gap emerges with respect to the relationship between the new international standard B Corp and the Circular Economy, although they share many principles and aims. The need to bridge this gap starts with the selection of a specific reference area, in order to make comparable the data obtained within the same sector, in which the certified B Corps operate. However, the literature still lacks in these aspects, preventing us from defining a picture a priori about the role that these companies are taking in the transition to the new model. This study, in its preliminary phase, tries to overcome this gap to investigate how these certifications can contribute to the pursuit of the transition to the new model.

B-Corp Perspective and Tool

The concept of "benefit business" is becoming nowadays more and more widely spread thanks to a new mode of conceiving a business. Such term is associated, directly or indirectly, to the modality of managing an organization with respect to objectives that assume a social nature, oriented towards the increase of the benefits of the community and to the protection of the environment[1] (Castellani, Rossi, & Rampa, 2016).

This new business concept aims at consolidating in the medium and long term, principles that can succeed in generating added value to all stakeholders, and to those closely associated to them. The characteristic of this type of society is linked to the ability to generate innovation in different areas, including innovation in the cultural field, environmental, tourism, training, in a collaborative approach, capable of networking for the management of complex projects.

Although benefit companies and B Corporations are used as synonyms, the two corporations have a profound distinction in terms of form and substance. A distinction which, from an economic point of view leads to a hybrid company, one between a profit and non-profit status, which leads to the creation of businesses "for benefit". This changing and moving process leads to a certification process, B Corporation, that promotes the creation of real business communities, thanks to the use of a common brand, certified B Corp, that also promote associations leading to the formal recognition of "for benefit" and to the adoption of an evaluation system (voluntary) capable of expressing the degree of impact and the creation of value.

This certification makes it possible to measure the company's social and environmental performance using new factors to regenerate the production system, offering new opportunities for companies that become vehicles of innovation and sustainable progress. In this way it achieves a dual purpose for the company, that of continuing to make profits and that of achieving benefits, from the point of view of responsibility, sustainability and transparency.

The certification takes into account all the activities of the company in its complexity, including products, services, organizations, environmental performance, the involvement of workers in the collective economy, social, cultural life of the community and the structure of governance. In the world there are currently over 2788 B Corps certified in over 64 countries in 150 different sectors of activity, of which 85 in Italy alone, which identifies itself as the first European country in terms of B-Corps created. Within the certification scheme the first step for a company concerns the measurement of its performance of its social and environmental economic impact. Through a self-assessment of the management system, companies are called upon to define their own B impact assessment and continue through a validation path for the obtainment of the certification.

The B-Corp certification is obtained by scoring between 80 and 200 points. The protocol for certifying a company is based on approximately 150 different models, built according to company size, sector and geographical area. The evaluation is based on the relationship between the benefits generated and the negative impact produced on the environment and society. If these two figures are equivalent, the company does not receive the certification. In the event that the score achieved is greater than 80 points, then the company is returning to society more than what it is subtracting, thus obtaining the certification.

This type of certification, in addition to being voluntary, is also applicable to each sector, regardless of the activity carried out. The system is managed by B-Lab, that is an independent organization which issues the certification attesting to the environmental and social commitment, as well as to the requirements of the norm. "The B-Corps internalize their social and natural contexts and attempt to engage in institutional work to provide a thinking leadership around sustainability and to drive change on a wider scale"(Stubbs, 2017). To support communication among all stakeholders involved, every year B-Lab publishes a list of all the companies that have obtained the best worldwide results in several categories, such as: best for the environment, best for the world, best for the long term, best for community, best for works, best for word.

The GIIRS (Global Impact investing rating system) is a corporate assessment tool, created in 2011 by the Foundation Clinton Global Initiative and developed by B-Lab, with the aim of assessing the degree of corporate impact with respect to 5 areas identified by the certification system and the relative creation of value.

The GIIRS was created to change the way entrepreneurs invest with a rating and analysis approach similar to the tools used by large financial analysis companies. In order for impact investments to gain credibility for each specific sector of activity, investors must have at their disposal a tool capable of verifying investment opportunities and their performance over time. For this reason, the GIIRS has defined a strict evaluation process for companies. The data is provided by the companies themselves to a third-party certification body, before the company can receive an evaluation. Ratings are structured taking into account both a weighted average of the investing company and a valuation of the funds. This allows you to achieve an overall rating that includes an impact assessment, an assessment of the SEM social or environmental business or the KPI performance indicators that are specific to each sector in which the company operates (figure 1).

For impact investments to gain credibility for each specific business sector, investors must have at their disposal a tool capable of verifying investment opportunities and their performance over time. This is why with GIIRS a strict business evaluation process has been defined. The data is provided by the same company to a third-party certification body before the company can receive an assessment. Ratings are structured taking into account both a weighted average of the investing company and a valuation of the funds. This leads to an overall rating that includes an impact assessment, an assessment of the social or environmental business SEM or the KPI performance indicators that are specific to each sector in which the company operates. Through the GIIRS, it is therefore possible to create a benchmark on impact and performance measurements between the various operators and at the same time ensure a reliable tool to monitor performance over time. In particular, the rating of a GIIRS evaluates 5 areas of impact: governance, workers, community, environment, customers.

Through the "Governance" impact area, the system of indicators aims to clearly identify the mission and traceability (monitoring) of environmental and social performance, responsibility, control and stakeholder involvement. A code of conduct associated with internal financial controls, aimed at preventing and managing complaints or corruption and transparent financing, as well as communication with customers and workers.

The "Workers" impact area considers the fairness of performance, in particular it takes into account the adequacy of wages and career progressions/possibilities in the structure. The preparation of the worker and the ability of the organization to maintain the level of training of the staff, guaranteeing a level of transferability of the competences/knowledge and identifying the degree of involvement of the workers takes on a basic role.

Figure 1. Evaluation process
Source: (Our elaboration on Giirs index, 2019)

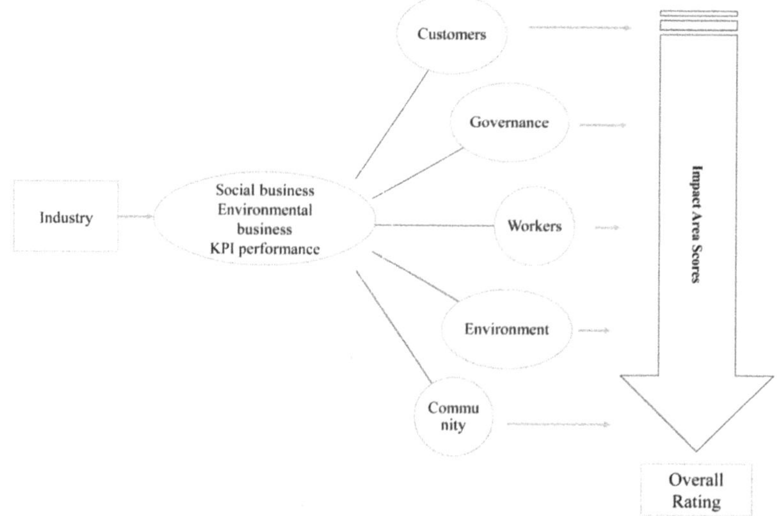

The "Community" impact area focuses on the need to integrate supplier stakeholders (the basis of the total quality approach) and the constant monitoring of the satisfaction of expectations and involvement in the local community. The presence of codes of conduct aimed at ensuring the safety of workers and the working environment, as well as respect for and support for the development of local economies qualify this area. In addition, the promotion of social welfare is added to the impact area by assessing how the organizations succeed, through policies of inclusion and participation in the commitments of society, are transferred and promoted outside, including community services and charitable donations.

The "Environment" area supports the extension of corporate policies with respect to environmental sustainability, in particular towards two types of factors: input and output. Inputs include, for example, energy, water and raw materials, which require a constant and continuous temporal assessment of the reduction of impacts and consumption. Outputs take into account the effects produced by the emissions generated and the different types of waste produced, as well as the impact of transport and distribution. Also in this case, these factors require constant monitoring oriented towards policies to improve environmental performance. In addition, in this Area, the design method is considered as a solution to encourage renewability, preservability, reduction of waste, promotion or conservation of the state of nature. The cultural aspect is also taken into account, i.e. the organization ability to be sensitive or to solve environmental problems.

Through the "Customers" area certification aims to measure the impact that the policies/actions adopted by companies have on customers. In particular, this section goes into the evaluation of the relationships that the company has with its community, measuring relationships with suppliers, diversity and involvement in the local community. The ability to promote public benefits through the sale of its products or through the provision of its services must, for the purposes of evaluation, be able to influence the resolution of a social problem.

This area has the function of verifying how the company products are designed to solve a social problem. The standard in this case goes to consider also aspects related to access to basic services, such as health or training of people or equal opportunities, from the arts and increasing capital to business oriented towards these prospects.

Another type of measurement is the IRIS (Impact reporting and investment standards) which is a collection of shared metrics that measure social, environmental and financial performance with the aim of pursuing criteria of transparency, credibility and accountability in operations that measure impacts. The tool contains all the data of the organizations that adhere to it anonymously.

It is updated periodically on the basis of feedback from experienced users. PULSE is another tool used to collect financial, social and environmental metrics that integrate quantitative data on impact and qualitative performance to demonstrate where and how investments can be most effective according to geographical area, sector and period. IRIS standards are included in PULSE.

MAIN FOCUS OF THE CHAPTER

This work aims to contribute to the debate on the potential applications of B Corp certification to facilitate the transition to the circular economy. The document adopts a methodological approach of qualitative research based on the descriptive protocol of the case study defined by Yin [15], through which a comparative multiple analysis was conducted. The analysis is based on the documentary approach of Silverman, (Silverman, 2008, 2011) and is proposed as an exploratory work for the particularity of the field of reference and the proposed themes. The extraction of the certified companies took place from the official website of B Corp, the sector considered is "food & beverage", while the location chosen for the analysis is that of the Italian territory. The search has produced n.8 results of certified companies B Corp that are: Island Bio, Damiano, Fratelli Carli, Local To You, Filippi, Perlage, Valli del Bitto Trading spa, Wami.

The cases were analysed to identify factors influencing the development of circular economy approaches in the impact areas of the BCorp certification. The analysis was based on secondary data documenting the cases, documents issued by the certifying body (annual reports), on the documentation available to companies.

The next step concerned the analysis of the ranking obtained during certification and of the impact areas identified by the standard. At this point, the authors have provided, through a process of interactive analysis of individual case studies, to define in a shared way a paper-concept table, excluding non-pertinent information, to be used in the discussion of the results. In this way it was possible to reconstruct the picture of the critical factors of the circular economy activated by each company B Corp. A final evaluation was expressed on the ability/potential of the companies to activate circular business models, according to the value of the ranking obtained, the impact areas covered, and the requirements defined by the standard. Within table 1 a description of the companies considered is given.

The ranking analysis (see Table 2) shows a fair result in terms of total score of the companies considered. Although two companies are at the minimum certification threshold, it is possible to identify excellence both in terms of the final evaluation of the entire system and of the individual areas of impact. Of the eight companies considered, in fact, four are able to achieve recognition in terms of global excellence in the areas of the environment (F.lli Carli and Damiano) and in that of Governance (Wami). The companies marked with an asterisk are those that have distinguished themselves with the recognition granted by the B Corp "Best for the Word Honorees for the impact area "Governance", est for Environment for the impact area "Environment" (each asterisk equals more years for the same award. The distribution of scores for each impact area is rather heterogeneous and does not reflect the total score achieved, but where each company seems to excel in a field of certification and not have a good level for all areas. This means that companies are still in a phase of growth in the process of adoption and implementation of B Corp certification to all proposed areas of impact. This is demonstrated by the recent acquisition of the certificate, also by the exception of the company F.lli Carli. In fact, even though this company obtained the certificate in 2014, it was not able to raise the level of all the impact areas, but it showed its strong point in the Environment area, obtaining the Best for the Word Honorees award for three years in a row. A further aspect characterised by all types of company is the absence of an evaluation of the Customer aspect. This measures the positive impact of the company on customers through products and services. The intention is to create benefits for the users, and in general for the stakeholders. This aspect is crucial for the Benefit policies, but it doesn't appear in the cases analyzed.

The scenario that emerges from the concept table highlights the areas of B Corp certification and the way in which the standard manages to activate the principles of CE.

The role of the community, the transfer of values, the participation of staff in the activities of the local community is undoubtedly one of the critical elements of this discussion. Certifying B Corp certainly brings advantages in terms of image for companies, but the real visibility and added value is perceivable from the analysis of cases, in actions to support the community. It becomes a protagonist, in a process of co-participation of social initiatives.

Table 1. Enterprises object of the analysis

Island Bio	The company has an industrial production of organic products such as vegetable beverages, breakfast cereals, cooking creams, fruit juices. It operates under its own brand Isola Bio or through Abafoods. It has an integrated supply chain that goes from the possession of agricultural land in different Italian regions to a network of agricultural producers for the production of high quality cereals, and a storage center for cereals. The biological aspect concerns the production of soya, oats, millet spelt, sorghum and sunflower oil. The marketing is done by Isola Bio, owned by a Dutch food multinational. It obtained B-Corp certification in 2018.
Damiano Srl	The company is a worldwide producer of organic almonds and hazelnuts that it grows in Sicily. The company also manages the production chain (cultivation, control, processing, packaging and distribution) of organic dried fruit, creams, flours, cereals and grains. It has a heterogeneous system of product and process certifications to guarantee the quality, transparency of the supply chain and safety of products sold internationally. Certified B Corp since 2016.
F.lli Carli	The company Fratelli Carli stands out for its ability to sell online its own production products of high quality, such as extra virgin olive oil, vinegar, olives, in oil, sauces, condiments, gastronomic products, wines, cakes, soaps and cosmetics olive oil. The company adopts an innovative production system for the production of oil, which is the company's main product. It obtained B-Corp certification in 2014.
Local To You	The Company operates as an e-commerce platform. It promotes organic farming at competitive prices at local level with wholesale and retail sale of food products with attention to the quality of crops and products. It brings together social cooperatives and farms, managing to make deliveries even at home The company was awarded as "Start up innovative 2017" by the Emilia Romagna Region for the 'high intensity of knowledge. It obtained B-Corp certification in 2017.
Filippi S.r.l	It is a family-run artisan pastry shop of leavened cakes that operates on an international context. He introduced the logic of CRS into his business. It obtained B-Corp certification in 2016.
Perlage	The company deals with biodynamic agriculture for the production of organic prosecco. Strongly internationalized, it selects a variety of grapes for the production of Glera, Merlot, Cabernet, Pinot Grigio, Chardonnay, Verdiso, Rabosa, Incrocio Manzoni types. It has been certified B-Corp since 2016.
Wami S.r.l. S.B.	A brand of highly digestible, oligomineral water with one of the lowest sodium contents in Italy that springs from the Maritime Alps and the Rainbow Spring. It has a national distribution in the form of PET and glass formats. The attention to the environment and to the role of the community is preponderant for the company that contributes to preserving the environmental characteristics of a locality, being its product formtemente linked to a virtuous management of the territory. The B-Corp certification with a score of 96.8.
Valli del Bitto Trading spa	The company promotes and markets the cheese of the Valli del Bitto, which is protected by a product trademark: Storico Ribelle. The traditional production process makes it possible to safeguard quality and territorial identity. The company operates through a Consortium that brings together several producers who continue to produce this cheese with a series of traditional practices in the mountain pasture. Obtains B-Corp certification in 2016.

Source: (Our Elaboration, 2019)

Table 2. Ranking for B Corp enterprises

Enterprises	Governance	Workers	Customers	Community	Environment	Total point
Island Bio	11.1	24.6	/	12.2	32.4	80.4
Damiano	6	17.5	/	22.6	60**	106.1
F.lli Carli	7.2	22.6	/	25.1	42.4***	97.3
Local to you	9.9	15.0	/	45.1	34.6	104.6
Filippi srl	12.1	19.8	/	43.5	13	88.4
Perlage	8.0	17.1	/	20.2	35.5	80.8
Wami	17.6*	/	/	72.1	7.1	96.8
Valli del Bitto Trading spa	9.9	24.2	/	35.8	12.5	82.4

Source: (Our Elaboration on ranking data, 2018)

Table 3. Impact Areas Concept Matrix

Company name	Governance	Workers	Customers	Community	Environment
Organic island	Strengthening of the brand in the communication of values and practices adopted by the company: • biological aspects, • sustainability, vegetable, • certification • innovation, • green culture, • development of new organic markets	Training of workers Worker benefits on achievement of objectives, such as: • life insurance • salary for trainees • virtual meetings to avoid travel	N.A.	Donations in cash and with your own products Collaboration and involvement of charitable organizations and against social distress: • fundraising for charity for earthquake victims (organization of football tournaments) • and disabled people. Purchases from local suppliers who are assessed through social and environmental standards for microfranchising certification-microdistribution Flo Cert certification. Provides support to low-income markets to improve the income of small producers in developing countries Educational projects with schools for Food, Sustainable Development and Respect for Biodiversity	Energy from renewable sources • water zero waste • water treated with more controlled reverse osmosis • plastic-glass recycling -metal-paper and composting • certifications: brc/ifs-fairtrade-iso 22005-kosher-biological certification- IBD organic Brasil-SA8000- CSQA greenhouse gas emissions- • Since 2011 he has been Corporate Golden Donor for the Italian Environmental Fund for the protection of the environment and culture. • It has built a plant for the self-production of clean energy and a zero emission thermal carrier that can reach efficiency over 85%.
Damiano	Acquisition of small processing companies to make production viable in terms of exports. Participates in the "Elite" program of the Italian Stock Exchange Financial operations and aimed at acquiring innovations for packaging Transparency and assurance actions through the use of integrated certifications	Through the Damiano Foundation, the company bears the unforeseen costs of the worker for the purchase of a house (e.g. taking out a loan) or bears the university costs of the children of its employees. employee honor loans	N.A.	Purchase of land and farm in continuity with the old property (involving the old owners) in accordance with the traditional techniques of the company Damiano. Project COCHO, design competition, for the launch of a new product. The company is a Flo-cert operator in Italy for both cocoa and chocolate.	Certification kosher- Fairtrade-Eu BIO/Biosuisse/ NOP/ IBD Vegan gluteen free IFS certification Equipped with an innovative packaging system that allows you to make packaging from 100 grams up to one ton The Damiano Foundation is committed to supporting research into organic farming and new environmentally friendly technologies in the countries of the South of the world. The company Damiano is one of the founding partners of the Bio district of Nebrodi for the sustainable development of the Nebrodi area. Winner of the Best for environment Award
F.lli Carli	Definition of a Welfare Plan and projects in favour of workers. Assumes as its mission a value model of transparency, correctness and competence	Respect for gender equality (Over 42% of shares are pink), of employees with permanent contracts. Project "Free of.... Welfare", the company helps to define a work-life balance and converts part of the production premium or the entire premium between employees by awarding vouchers for shopping, gym, travel or for the babysitter or for health or insurance costs. Promotion of staff training courses. A programme to assess the individual skills and aspirations of employees.	N.A.	She collaborates with AIFO and with the Cambodian missionary sisters in a worldwide voluntary association to which she devolves a part of the proceeds for projects of childcare and development in the countries of the South of the world.	E-Commerce Quality Mark - ISO27001:2013 Management and Safety System Certification SGS food- the choice of materials and products with 100% recyclable packaging with 75% glass recycling rate, 100% vegetable-based printing inks and 100% PEFC pallets certification. Energy produced by photovoltaic systems, CO2 reduction through door-to-door deliveries. The percentage of waste delivered to disposal consortia is also about 100%. Use the Net-Comm seal to demonstrate your commitment to transparency and quality of the consumer you buy online. Recycling Project: this is an educational project funded by the European Community and created in 2011 for the recovery of used vegetable oil of domestic origin, to be used to obtain biofuel with low environmental impact. It has set up a sustainability committee. The "CO.SO. "which is composed of representatives of all business realities that collaborate with the company.

continued on following page

Table 3. Continued

Company name	Governance	Workers	Customers	Community	Environment
Local to you	Definition of a mission to support quality, sustainability and social value creation. Facilitation of corporate walfare policies.	It promotes the training and education of workers. It hires workers who have disadvantaged situations, promotes the reintegration of disadvantaged people (ex-toxicodipents or disabled). Local To You employs 23 low-contract people, 8 of whom are migrants seeking asylum. With a view to corporate welfare, they propose the creation of purchasing groups to receive office expenses and facilitate the working life of employees	N.A.	E-commerce commercialization founded a NEWCO to facilitate the entry of industrial partners to safeguard the social purpose of business decisions for new job opportunities. It develops projects with local agricultural companies and rehabilitation activities (orthotherapy), with the involvement of the "La Nuvoletta Bianca" Centre. It collaborates with social cooperatives for the development of the "SEMINO" project for social agriculture. He collaborates on projects of rural social innovation. It collaborates with schools on the "Vitamin C" school project on the themes of food, environmental protection and sustainable mobility.	Promotes biodynamic and organic farming. It favours the use of methods that respect the environment and health, with respect for seasonal cycles, and favours local production. Cultivate sustainably.
Filippi s.r.l.	Develops corporate welfare programs for economic benefits, improvement of the quality of life and health of employees. Institutes Prevention Day. Transforms its legal status into a Benefit Company (SB). Purchasing policies with fair trade chains. Use of extra virgin olive oil in the production. Buy only free-range eggs of Italian origin.	Organizes professional qualification courses Involvement of staff participates in the social life of the company. Creation of special staff areas (canteen, leisure activities) Organization of a corporate trip with all the staff. Birth bonus (one thousand euros for each employee who becomes a parent).	N.A.	It gives priority in the recruitment of staff with economic disadvantage by favouring women and without discrimination to non-Italian staff. It collaborates with a cooperative of disabled children, non-profit donations to Engim Onlus that promotes the inclusion at work of disabled people, Donation to the women's basketball team of the country for the purchase of sports equipment. Sponsorship of local community sports activities. It supports an association for the promotion and diffusion of theatre and culture in the community. Creation of a local district for interaction with local suppliers.	Product life cycle verification and traceability Maximizing energy efficiency and use of renewable sources, reducing Co2, 72% of waste is recycled. Using FSC Certified Paper Re-use of production waste in beekeeping.
Perlage	Orientation of the company's mission to the guarantee of products through dàm certification, organic certification, responsibility towards social relations. Establishes services of collaboration with suppliers and schools. Reinvestment of 60% of profits in technology and innovation. Publication of objectives and progress in terms of social and environmental performance. The company is established as a BRC - British Retail Consortium.	Promotes internships and flexibility of employees' working hours Join the Social Inclusion Challenge program for the theme of social inclusion in the company with corporate bonuses, health care, internships for disabled children. Promotes internal training (haccp, and on the standard ISO 9001: 2015, team building). It favours the stipulation of permanent employment contracts,. Employee benefits, e.g. fuel bonuses and FASA (Alimentary Health Care) fund access	N.A.	Organization of cultural events Support to companies on the production of organic wine. Attention to social issues through collaboration with associations for the disabled. Develops network projects with competitors. He's got projects in place with high schools. On the reduction of water waste in the cellars. He has collaborations with the school of enelogy of Conegliano and with C.E.O.D. and C.E.C.A.T. It implements social promotion initiatives, such as campaigns to fight breast cancer "Corri in Rosa" of San Vendemiano, screenings of documentaries "Cinema in cantina", art exhibitions and participation in conferences on sustainability issues, cooking classes and dance classes, sensory dinners in the cellar, projects and agreements with research institutions, internships for disabled children and post-graduate internships.	Organic wine production with respect for the soil and biodiversity Certifications: DEMETER BRC/IFS, certified NOP U.S.A., A.V.I. Label Veg in the vegan and organic sector. Equipped with an Eco-point that provides information about the company's commitment to the environment. Use of ecopallet, PerlAPP bottles, recyclable packaging cartons. Investment in a Corporate Purifier. Calculation of the carbon footprint, Differentiation of waste insertion of solar photovoltaic panels and the purchase of green certificates. Joins Rafcycle's wastepaper recovery program. Experimentation for the reduction of copper in agriculture. It promotes biodynamic farming methods to reactivate the microorganisms present in the soil...

continued on following page

Table 3. Continued

Company name	Governance	Workers	Customers	Community	Environment
Wami	A vision oriented towards transparency and engagement on water projects. Transparency towards the community of the benefits achieved, through periodic publication of data. Allocation of part of the profits for water resources. Traceability with unique code bottles. He won the world honoree best for governance award in 2018.	Growth of its employees up to 70% of current hires High working standards and benefits with flexible working hours for employees. Involvement of employees in water projects carried out in the territory. Employee access to financial information.	N.A.	Create an online community with a report of all the liters of water donated and the villages created. Participation in the project conceived by WaniRide With A Mission to reach donations for the construction of a water network in the district of Tenghory in Senegal. It favours the creation, in Africa, of local associations of aqueducts that maintain the efficiency of the structures, through dedicated personnel. He collaborates with Life water international, Acra foundation, Amref and SRI Lanka and with Oxfam. It contributes to the creation and development of disadvantaged communities through the construction of aqueducts and creates new jobs. It encourages education and improves the health of the population. It sensitizes and educates the community to a correct consumption of water, in all its forms, and makes the user responsible for the disposal of de-packaging.	Creation of a shared work environment. Use of 80% recycled, fully recyclable display materials Promotes CO2 savings by encouraging the use of public transport. The packaging used is 100% recyclable. He planted 60 trees at the Parco Nord in Milan for the C02 reduction.
Valli del Bitto Trading spa	The mission of the company oriented towards the pursuit of objectives of social innovation. It favours the association between producers, improving organization and bargaining power. Encourages the creation of rural networks.	Hiring of 3 employees for the point of sale, museum and online promotions Administrators and employees participate as voluntary workers in local associations.	N.A.	Engaged in activities of dissemination of innovative experiences in the field of creativity. commercial, agri-food, economic sustainability, protection of native species. Supports initiatives aimed at creating value for the community also through participation in rural networks at national and international level	It offers sustainable economic solutions to reduce environmental impacts by improving its integration with economic and social networks- energy savings in agriculture, livestock, food. It defines a production specification for the respect of milk processing methods, natural feeding on pastures, rotational grazing, preservation of native breeds, and provides for the exclusion of ferments and feed on pastures.

Source: (Our elaboration on enterprises data, 2019)

The Governance area outlines the management's commitment to promoting sustainable, environmental, social and transparency values. This area also highlights the various initiatives undertaken, such as the use of certifications and the activation of secondary markets for the purchase or sale of products. This is where the "high" principles of the EC concerning "System Thinking", "Stewardship", "Transparency" and "Collaboration" are gathered.

In the cases analysed, it clearly emerges how the Governance area manages to activate them, stimulating organizations to rethink the management of their own resources, in order to assume greater responsibility for the proposed actions, guaranteeing openness and transparency in the adoption of guarantee instruments, such as certifications, or activating behaviour inspired by mutual business value.

The other areas have the capacity to activate mechanisms of circularity, especially from the point of view of behaviour, oriented towards the responsible use of raw materials, the recycling of products, and the involvement of primary and secondary stakeholders. The involvement of the Community offers the possibility of intervening on the capacity to generate new employment, promoting environmental sustainability and solidarity (Poponi, Colantoni, Cividino, & Mosconi, 2019)

The Worker area emphasizes the principle of "Stewardship". Employees are involved in the choices of business policies and social initiatives of the company (see for e.g. Wami and Filippi), with a consequent empowerment of workers that leads to the establishment of a positive corporate climate, also favored by the possibility of access to corporate benefits.

Being a B Corp also means strengthening your brand, generating confidence in your stakeholders and ensuring a return on profit and credibility. The role of the community becomes therefore fundamental, where the principle "Collaboration" finds its maximum expression for its application. The involvement of local suppliers and the activation of secondary markets, as well as the stimuli arising from collaborations with various associations for the inclusion of disadvantaged people in the work, projects with schools aimed at education oriented to sustainability, the environment and food, undoubtedly make this area of strategic impact to activate a virtuous behavior of the consumer. A not insignificant element that the certified company B wants to communicate is the responsible aspect through which it acts in a perspective increasingly focused on the figure of a consumer, attentive to the methods of implementation of the production activities of a 'company and the policies of environmental sustainability of the same. The analysis shows an important gap. The B Corp certification, especially in the 2019 news, includes a section dedicated to Customers stewardship to better understand how companies manage value and impact towards customers, with measurement metrics that refer to inclusion performance, fairness and diversity. All the companies considered did not obtain an adequate score in the Customer area. In fact, although the role of the consumer is indirectly called for in the various areas of impact, especially in the community area, there is no real commitment on the part of organizations in this area. This has two important implications, one on the system of enterprises in the food area, and the other on the B Corp certification system. In the first case, it is necessary to reconsider the strategies of Benefit-Business, considering a direct involvement of the consumer in corporate policies so that the impact of social policies can be measured. Only through this phase it will be possible to undertake a path oriented to the continuous improvement of the presentation (Crosby, 1997; Deming & De Vio, 1991). On the other hand, companies will have to equip themselves with adequate tools, in terms of highly specialized human resources, to facilitate the effective application of the requirements of the area. In the second case, it denotes the need to intervene by the management system of B Corp with systems to assist companies so that this point, so strategic for the set of values Benefit, cannot be omitted from the calculation of the ranking for obtaining certification.

The Environment area, due to the characteristic of the sector identified, is not able to generate a paradigm shift towards the EC. It undoubtedly contributes to an improvement in the environmental performance of companies, thanks to investments in technology to reduce emissions, to include innovative packaging systems, to encourage the internal recycling of waste. The product and system certification tool acts as a bottom-up stimulus, in a bottom-up logic, in line with the literature (see for example (Llorach-Massana, Farreny, & Oliver-Sol, 2016; Merli & Preziosi, 2018; Poponi et al., 2019; Ruggieri et al., 2016; Sousa-Zomer, Magalhães, Zancul, Campos, & Cauchick-Miguel, 2018; Zeller, Towa, Degrez, & Achten, 2018) products more sustainable and in line with EC principles. Companies emphasize the biological aspect of their products, the processing techniques that preserve biodiversity and the environment.

In general, in the cases analysed, there is no real switch to the EC paradigm. Without a doubt, in this particular sector, B Corp acts as a stimulus to the highest principles of the EC, such as System Thinking, Stewardship, Transparency and the Collaboration. This system undoubtedly favours a cultural transition, representing a stimulus from below, which leads to the activation of the principles in a collaborative perspective, where the role of the community and more markedly having adhered to a global movement allows to activate virtuous behaviors of all stakeholders for the pursuit of economic and social growth.

FUTURE RESEARCH DIRECTIONS

A common strategy for implementing the circular economy concerns the application of the principles within the certification standards. Consequently, an implication concerns the need to periodically review the certification framework with potential related to the application of new innovations (e.g industry 4.0) to integrate the principles of the circular economy into business development models, and to improve the environmental sustainability of a production process or product.

Furthermore, the implications concern the identification of standards increasingly coherent with the evolution of consumer behavioral choices, during the purchase and disposal phase of the product.

The exploratory nature of the work and the documentary analysis carried out can represent the main limitations of this work, the uncertainties and discretion were reduced using a replicable approach to conduct studies on the subject of analytical models that consider our scenarios. Among the main limitations of this analysis we find a reduced case of analysis, focused on a defined industry and a lack of clear references in the literature such as to identify a specific set of indicators on which to base a generalized model.

The future research steps concern the study of the stimuli offered by the application of B Corp certifications on wider contexts, which can compare the composition of companies in international contexts.

Further works are needed to collect data on B Corp valuation models and the application of CE principles. This could be done through a systematic analysis of the sector identified on heterogeneous framework. These further analyses will contribute to reveal the role of certification as a bottom up lever for sustainability, and to associate the ranking assigned by the certification to the circularity degree reached by each enterprise.

CONCLUSION

The chapter proposes a critical review of the B Corp certification and its potential application as a tool to facilitate the transition to the Circular Economy.

Circular Economy is the result of the application of the paradigms based on new levers of growth, such as green economy or sustainable development, which include a more efficient use of resources, the respect of ethical, social and environmental values. Benefit Corporations are companies pursuing these objectives with the twofold aim to reconcile business performances (economic and financial) with the ethic and the sustainability principles. In these new business models the idea of social responsibility as a form of self-regulation is strengthened (B-Corporations, 2017; Wilburn & Wilburn, 2014). Through a voluntary certification scheme, these companies aim, in fact, to rebalance their mission and business activities-affirming principles of social responsibility, so simultaneously getting both their profit and non-profit objectives. This approach finds its full application in the management system within a new B-Corp certification frame, to support the creation of a community of companies interested in promoting social and environmental concerns, encourage the development of an adequate legal framework of benefit business, and conceive an innovative evaluation standard.

In the proposed analysis, the ability of companies to activate mechanisms of circularity within the areas of impact of the certification clearly appears. The aspects most stimulated by the certification concern the involvement of governance, the orientation towards the responsible use of raw materials, a higher awareness of product recycling, and a greater involvement of primary and secondary stakeholders. within the context of Circular. The Community impact area offers the possibility to intervene on the ability to stimulate and involve local actors, fostering new employment and an environmental-solidarity sustainability. The characteristics of the selected companies do not allow to have a radical switch toward CE, compare with other industry where B Corp certifications work (Poponi, Colantoni, Cividino, & Mosconi, 2019; Ruggieri, Mosconi, & Poponi, 2018; Ruggieri, Mosconi, & Poponi, 2018). Moreover, the B Corp stimulate the change, pushing on high principles of the CE, such as System Thinking, Stewardship, Transparency and the Collaboration.

REFERENCES

Akanbi, L. A., Oyedele, L. O., Omoteso, K., Bilal, M., Akinade, O. O., Ajayi, A. O., ... Owolabi, H. A. (2019). Disassembly and deconstruction analytics system (D-DAS) for construction in a circular economy. *Journal of Cleaner Production, 223*, 386–396. doi:10.1016/j.jclepro.2019.03.172

Arnold, R. D., & Wade, J. P. (2015). A definition of systems thinking: A systems approach. *Procedia Computer Science, 44*(C), 669–678. doi:10.1016/j.procs.2015.03.050

B-Corporations. (2017). Why B Corps Matter I B Corporation.

Badurdeen, F. & Jawahir, I. S. (2017). Strategies for value creation through sustainable manufacturing. *Procedia Manufacturing, 8*(October 2016), 20–27. doi:10.1016/j.promfg.2017.02.002

Baldassarre, B., Schepers, M., Bocken, N., Cuppen, E., Korevaar, G., & Calabretta, G. (2019). Industrial symbiosis: Towards a design process for eco-industrial clusters by integrating circular economy and industrial ecology perspectives. *Journal of Cleaner Production, 216*, 446–460. doi:10.1016/j.jclepro.2019.01.091

Bovea, M. D., & Pérez-Belis, V. (2018). Identifying design guidelines to meet the circular economy principles: A case study on electric and electronic equipment. *Journal of Environmental Management, 228*(August), 483–494. doi:10.1016/j.jenvman.2018.08.014 PMID:30248643

Braungart, M., McDonough, W., & Bollinger, A. (2007). Cradle-to-cradle design: Creating healthy emissions - a strategy for eco-effective product and system design. *Journal of Cleaner Production, 15*(13–14), 1337–1348. doi:10.1016/j.jclepro.2006.08.003

British Standards Institution. (2017). *Framework for implementing the principles of the circular economy in organizations : guide*. BSI Standards Limited. Retrieved from https://shop.bsigroup.com/ProductDetail?pid=000000000030334443&_ga=2.150628976.710916583.1559852485-363687714.1559679644

Castellani, G., De Rossi, D., & Rampa, A. (2016). *L E S OCIETÀ B ENEFIT La nuova prospettiva di una Corporate Social Responsibility con Commitment*. Fondazione Comerciale Dei Comercialisti.

Ceschin, F., & Gaziulusoy, I. (2016). Evolution of design for sustainability: From product design to design for system innovations and transitions. *Design Studies*, *47*, 118–163. doi:10.1016/j.destud.2016.09.002

Crosby Philip, B. (1997). *Obiettivo qualità*. McGraw-Hil.

de Jesus, A., Antunes, P., Santos, R., & Mendonça, S. (2018). Eco-innovation in the transition to a circular economy: An analytical literature review. *Journal of Cleaner Production*, *172*, 2999–3018. doi:10.1016/j.jclepro.2017.11.111

Deming, W. E., & De Vio, S. (1991). *L'impresa di qualità*. Petrini.

Ellen-MacArthur Foundation. (2013). Toward the circular economy.

Geissdoerfer, M., Morioka, S. N., de Carvalho, M. M., & Evans, S. (2018). Business models and supply chains for the circular economy. *Journal of Cleaner Production*, *190*, 712–721. doi:10.1016/j.jclepro.2018.04.159

Genovese, A., Acquaye, A. A., Figueroa, A., & Koh, S. C. L. (2017). Sustainable supply chain management and the transition towards a circular economy: Evidence and some applications. *Omega (United Kingdom)*, *66*. doi:10.1016/j.omega.2015.05.015

Ghisellini, P., Cialani, C., & Ulgiati, S. (2016). A review on circular economy: The expected transition to a balanced interplay of environmental and economic systems. *Journal of Cleaner Production*, *114*, 11–32. doi:10.1016/j.jclepro.2015.09.007

Højberg, A. L., Troldborg, L., Stisen, S., Christensen, B. B. S., & Henriksen, H. J. (2013). Stakeholder driven update and improvement of a national water resources model. *Environmental Modelling & Software*, *40*, 202–213. doi:10.1016/j.envsoft.2012.09.010

Holgado, M., Benedetti, M., Evans, S., Baptista, A. J., & Lourenço, E. J. (2018). Industrial symbiosis implementation by leveraging on process efficiency methodologies. *Procedia CIRP*, *69*(May), 872–877. doi:10.1016/j.procir.2017.11.078

Jawahir, I. S., & Bradley, R. (2016). Technological elements of circular economy and the principles of 6R-based closed-loop material flow in sustainable manufacturing. *Procedia CIRP*, *40*, 103–108. doi:10.1016/j.procir.2016.01.067

Jensen, J. P. & Remmen, A. (2017). Enabling circular economy through product stewardship. *Procedia Manufacturing*, *8*(October 2016), 377–384. doi:10.1016/j.promfg.2017.02.048

Jiang, Z., Wang, H., Zhang, H., Mendis, G., & Sutherland, J. W. (2019). Value recovery options portfolio optimization for remanufacturing end of life product. *Journal of Cleaner Production*, *210*, 419–431. doi:10.1016/j.jclepro.2018.10.316

Kalmykova, Y., Sadagopan, M., & Rosado, L. (2018). Circular economy - From review of theories and practices to development of implementation tools. *Resources, Conservation and Recycling*, *135*(February 2017), 190–201. doi:10.1016/j.resconrec.2017.10.034

Khmara, Y., & Kronenberg, J. (2018). Degrowth in business: An oxymoron or a viable business model for sustainability? *Journal of Cleaner Production*, *177*, 721–731. doi:10.1016/j.jclepro.2017.12.182

Kirchherr, J., Reike, D., & Hekkert, M. (2017). Conceptualizing the circular economy: An analysis of 114 definitions. *Resources, Conservation and Recycling*, *127*(September), 221–232. doi:10.1016/j.resconrec.2017.09.005

Lane, R., & Watson, M. (2012). Stewardship of things: The radical potential of product stewardship for re-framing responsibilities and relationships to products and materials. *Geoforum*, *43*(6), 1254–1265. doi:10.1016/j.geoforum.2012.03.012

Lewis, H. (2005). Defining product stewardship and sustainability in the Australian packaging industry. *Environmental Science & Policy*, *8*(1), 45–55. doi:10.1016/j.envsci.2004.09.002

Llorach-Massana, P., Farreny, R., & Oliver-Sol, J. (2016). Are cradle to cradle certified products environmentally preferable? Analysis from an LCA approach'. *Journal of Cleaner Production*, *113*, 715–716. doi:10.1016/j.jclepro.2015.11.008

Manninen, K., Koskela, S., Antikainen, R., Bocken, N., Dahlbo, H., & Aminoff, A. (2018). Do circular economy business models capture intended environmental value propositions? *Journal of Cleaner Production*, *171*, 413–422. doi:10.1016/j.jclepro.2017.10.003

Merli, R., & Preziosi, M. (2018). The EMAS impasse : Factors influencing Italian organizations to withdraw or renew the registration. *Journal of Cleaner Production*, *172*, 4532–4543. doi:10.1016/j.jclepro.2017.11.031

Michelini, G., Moraes, R. N., Cunha, R. N., Costa, J. M. H., & Ometto, A. R. (2017). From linear to circular economy: PSS conducting the transition. *Procedia CIRP*, *64*, 2–6. doi:10.1016/j.procir.2017.03.012

Mol, A. P. J. (2015). Transparency and value chain sustainability. *Journal of Cleaner Production*, *107*, 154–161. doi:10.1016/j.jclepro.2013.11.012

Moraga, G., Huysveld, S., Mathieux, F., Blengini, G. A., Alaerts, L., Van Acker, K., & ... Dewulf, J. (2019). Circular economy indicators: What do they measure? *Resources, Conservation and Recycling*, *146*, 452–461. doi:10.1016/j.resconrec.2019.03.045

Ngan, S. L., How, B. S., Teng, S. Y., Promentilla, M. A. B., Yatim, P., Er, A. C., & Lam, H. L. (2019). Prioritization of sustainability indicators for promoting the circular economy: The case of developing countries. *Renewable & Sustainable Energy Reviews*, *111*(May), 314–331. doi:10.1016/j.rser.2019.05.001

Niero, M., & Rivera, X. C. S. (2018). The role of life cycle sustainability assessment in the implementation of circular economy principles in organizations. *Procedia CIRP*, *69*(May), 793–798. doi:10.1016/j.procir.2017.11.022

Nižetić, S., Djilali, N., Papadopoulos, A., & Rodrigues, J. J. P. C. (2019). Smart technologies for promotion of energy efficiency, utilization of sustainable resources and waste management. *Journal of Cleaner Production*, *231*, 565–591. doi:10.1016/j.jclepro.2019.04.397

Pan, S. Y., Du, M. A., Te Huang, I., Liu, I. H., Chang, E. E., & Chiang, P. C. (2014). Strategies on implementation of waste-to-energy (WTE) supply chain for circular economy system: A review. *Journal of Cleaner Production*, *108*, 409–421. doi:10.1016/j.jclepro.2015.06.124

Pauliuk, S. (2018). Critical appraisal of the circular economy standard BS 8001:2017 and a dashboard of quantitative system indicators for its implementation in organizations. *Resources, Conservation and Recycling*, *129*, 81–92. doi:10.1016/j.resconrec.2017.10.019

Pieroni, M. P. P., McAloone, T. C., & Pigosso, D. C. A. (2019). Business model innovation for circular economy and sustainability: A review of approaches. *Journal of Cleaner Production*, *215*, 198–216. doi:10.1016/j.jclepro.2019.01.036

Pomponi, F., & Moncaster, A. (2017). Circular economy for the built environment: A research framework. *Journal of Cleaner Production*, *143*, 710–718. doi:10.1016/j.jclepro.2016.12.055

Poponi, S., Colantoni, A., Cividino, S., & Mosconi, E. (2019). The stakeholders' perspective within the B corp certification for a circular approach. *Sustainability*, *11*(6), 1584. doi:10.3390u11061584

Poponi, S., Colantoni, A., Cividino, S. R., & Mosconi, E. M. (2019). The stakeholders' perspective within the B corp certification for a circular approach. *Sustainability*, *11*(6), 1584. doi:10.3390u11061584

Prieto-Sandoval, V., Jaca, C., & Ormazabal, M. (2018). Towards a consensus on the circular economy. *Journal of Cleaner Production*, *179*, 605–615. doi:10.1016/j.jclepro.2017.12.224

Ranta, V., Aarikka-Stenroos, L., & Mäkinen, S. J. (2018). Creating value in the circular economy: A structured multiple-case analysis of business models. *Journal of Cleaner Production*, *201*, 988–1000. doi:10.1016/j.jclepro.2018.08.072

Reike, D., Vermeulen, W. J. V., & Witjes, S. (2018). The circular economy: New or Refurbished as CE 3.0? — Exploring controversies in the conceptualization of the circular economy through a focus on history and resource value retention options. *Resources, Conservation and Recycling*, *135*(August 2017), 246–264. doi:10.1016/j.resconrec.2017.08.027

Rio, M., Riel, A., & Brissaud, D. (2017). Design to environment: information model characteristics. *Procedia CIRP*, *60*, 494–499. doi:10.1016/j.procir.2017.02.006

Ruggieri, A., Braccini, A. M., Poponi, S., & Mosconi, E. M. (2016). A meta-model of inter-organisational cooperation for the transition to a circular economy. *Sustainability (Switzerland)*, *8*(11). doi:10.3390u8111153

Ruggieri, A., Mosconi, E. M., & Poponi, S. (2018). Can the B corp certification activate the circular economy pathway in a multiple stakeholder perspective? In *ISDRS - The 24th Annual Conference, Actions for a Sustainable World: from theory to practice.*

Ruggieri, A., Mosconi, E. M., & Poponi, S. (2018). The B corp certification as a standard of the entrepreneurial pathway towards the circular economy perspective. In *XXVIII National Congress of Commodity Sciences, Firenze, Italy, Feb. 21-23, 2018.*

Silverman, D. (2008). *Qualitative Research: Theory, Method and Practice*. Sage.

Silverman, D. (2011). *Qualitative Research*. London, UK: Sage.

Sousa-Zomer, T. T., Magalhães, L., Zancul, E., Campos, L. M. S., & Cauchick-Miguel, P. A. (2018). Cleaner production as an antecedent for circular economy paradigm shift at the micro-level: Evidence from a home appliance manufacturer. *Journal of Cleaner Production*, *185*, 740–748. doi:10.1016/j.jclepro.2018.03.006

Stubbs, W. (2017). Characterising B corps as a sustainable business model: An exploratory study of B corps in Australia. *Journal of Cleaner Production*, *144*, 299–312. doi:10.1016/j.jclepro.2016.12.093

Tukker, A. (2015). Product services for a resource-efficient and circular economy - A review. *Journal of Cleaner Production*, *97*, 76–91. doi:10.1016/j.jclepro.2013.11.049

Ünal, E., & Shao, J. (2019). A taxonomy of circular economy implementation strategies for manufacturing firms: Analysis of 391 cradle-to-cradle products. *Journal of Cleaner Production*, *212*, 754–765. doi:10.1016/j.jclepro.2018.11.291

Urbinati, A., Chiaroni, D., & Chiesa, V. (2017). Towards a new taxonomy of circular economy business models. *Journal of Cleaner Production*, *168*, 487–498. doi:10.1016/j.jclepro.2017.09.047

Veleva, V., & Bodkin, G. (2018). Corporate-entrepreneur collaborations to advance a circular economy. *Journal of Cleaner Production*, *188*, 20–37. doi:10.1016/j.jclepro.2018.03.196

Wilburn, K., & Wilburn, R. (2014). The double bottom line: Profit and social benefit. *Business Horizons*, *57*(1), 11–20. doi:10.1016/j.bushor.2013.10.001

Witjes, S., & Lozano, R. (2016). Towards a more circular economy: Proposing a framework linking sustainable public procurement and sustainable business models. *Resources, Conservation and Recycling*, *112*, 37–44. doi:10.1016/j.resconrec.2016.04.015

Zeller, V., Towa, E., Degrez, M., & Achten, W. M. J. (2018). Integration of waste supply and use data into regional footprints: case study on the generation and use of waste from consumption and production activities in Brussels. *Procedia CIRP*, *69*(May), 100–105. doi:10.1016/j.procir.2017.11.116

KEY TERMS AND DEFINITIONS

B-Corp: A new way of doing business through a transparent, sustainable and social business.

Benefits Corporation: Evolution of the corporate concept with social objectives as well as profit objectives.

Business Model: Model through which an organization adopts strategic and organizational solutions to create a competitive advantage.

Circular Economy: A business model for managing sustainable value creation.

Ecodesign: Design of a sustainable product with the consequent reduction of environmental impact.

Sustainability: Process in which economic growth is oriented towards environmental and social respect.

Sustainable Production: Creation of consumer goods with raw materials whose value can be maintained or recovered.

ENDNOTE

1 G.Castellani, A.Rampa, D.De Rossi, Benefit Companies. The new perspective of a Corporate Social Responsibility with Commitment, National Foundation of Accountants FNC document 15 May 2016

Chapter 10
Ecodesign Strategies and Customer Value: A Conjoint Approach

Anna Paola Codini
Università degli Studi di Brescia, Italy

Giuseppe Bertoli
Università degli Studi di Brescia, Italy

Riccardo Frassine
Poste Italiane, Italy

ABSTRACT

Despite increasing attention to environmental issues, studies of ecodesign reveal that the market and the customer are two of the main external barriers to the effective implementation of ecodesign in industrial companies. Moreover, studies adopting this perspective mostly evidence the difficulties in interpreting customer perception as a source of customer value. Contributions exploring specific techniques that may be useful to support ecodesign strategies in a customer-based perspective are scarce. To fill this gap in the literature, this chapter revises the literature on ecodesign, adopting a customer-based perspective focusing on the controversial results regarding eco-products and customer value. To identify techniques suitable to support ecodesign strategies in a customer-based perspective, and considering the challenges affecting customer perception of eco-products, the chapter shows—through an empirical analysis conducted on ecological washing machines—how conjoint analysis can be successful in this aim.

DOI: 10.4018/978-1-7998-1419-1.ch010

INTRODUCTION

Ecodesign is an approach considering environmental aspects and integrating them in the product development process (ISO, 2011) through the application of strategies aimed at reducing the negative environmental impact along the phases of the product lifecycle.

Now that sustainability has been acknowledged as a key driver of innovation (Nidumolu et al., 2009; Hopkins, 2010), research on green product innovation in general (Baumann et al., 2002; Adams et al., 2012; Pereira and Vence, 2012; De Medeiros et al., 2014) and on ecodesign in particular has flourished in recent years (Rossi et al., 2016; Chun et al., 2018). Within this body of literature, many contributions seek to revise the various studies conducted over the years on green product development, focusing on antecedents, on outcomes of the strategies under consideration, and on success factors (Dangelico, 2016). However, the implementation of ecodesign practices in industry is not advancing as rapidly as expected or as would be required to create a more sustainable society (Dekoninck et al., 2016).

Furthermore, looking at the external barriers that prevent the implementation of ecodesign approaches in industrial companies, some authors (e.g., Rossi et al., 2016) have identified "market and customer" as relevant external barriers. The obstacles they present might stem from difficulties in identifying the advantages and disadvantages connected with the application of ecodesign strategies, lack of awareness of benefits, or difficulties in interpreting customer perception (Bey et al., 2013; Boks, 2006; Johansson, 2002; Handfield et al., 2001).

Despite this consciousness, so far studies of ecodesign that adopt a customer-based perspective are scarce (Chun et al., 2018). The literature on green product innovation focuses largely on market outcomes, mostly as evidenced by the impact on sales and market share (Driessen et al., 2013), reputation (Chen, 2008; Driessen et al., 2013; Lin et al., 2013), acquisition of new customers (Liu et al., 2011; Triebswetter and Wackerbauer, 2008a, 2008b), customer loyalty (Aoe, 2007; Plouffe et al., 2011), customer satisfaction (Leonidou et al., 2013), and willingness to pay (Langerak et al., 1998), sometimes using controversial evidence. Few studies have investigated the impact of ecodesign strategies on customer value, using specific techniques aimed at developing eco-design strategies according to the customer value.

Furthermore, the adoption of a customer-based perspective is particularly needed in the context of the Fourth Industrial Revolution, in which companies cannot disregard consumers who nowadays reveal to pay particular attention to the environment and to the ethical aspects (Galbreth and Ghosh, 2013; Ülkü and Hsuan, 2017). As the Fourth Industrial Revolution has radically changed the traditional concept of innovation—requiring and increasing customer orientation—eco-design strategies cannot ignore this claim to the imperative of customer satisfaction, and need for specific tools supporting this transition.

In order to fill this gap in the literature, and consistently with the aim of the book, the current chapter revises the literature on ecodesign, adopting a customer-based perspective focusing on the relationship between ecodesign strategies and customer value. With the aim of identifying useful techniques for supporting ecodesign strategies from a customer-based perspective, the chapter shows—using an empirical analysis of ecological washing machines—how conjoint analysis can be successful in this aim.

Background

Recent studies conducted on ecodesign have evidenced how, in addition to other internal factors, market benefits (such as potential market opportunities, opening of new markets, and increase of market share) influence green product innovation (Dangelico and Pujari, 2010; Green et al., 1994; Keskin et al., 2013;

Pujari and Wright, 1999; Rennings et al., 2006; Triebswetter and Wackerbauer, 2008a; van Hemel and Cramer, 2002) and can be considered as internal antecedents of this phenomenon (Dangelico, 2016). Furthermore, with regard to the antecedents of green product innovation external to the firm, among the most often mentioned are market demand and market stakeholder pressures (Chen et al., 2012; Conway and Stewart, 1998; Foster and Green, 2000; Green et al., 1994; Horbach et al., 2012; Huang et al., 2009; Kivimaa, 2007; Langerak et al., 1998; Lin et al., 2013; Liu et al., 2011; Pujari and Wright, 1999; Triebswetter and Wackerbauer, 2008a; Tsai et al., 2012; van Hemel and Cramer, 2002; Visser et al., 2008). Finally, customer pressures (Guoyou et al., 2013; Pujari and Wright, 1999) and the potential for customer benefit (Kammerer, 2009) also stimulate green product innovation.

The literature focusing on the outcomes of green product innovation has likewise paid attention to market dimensions. Indeed, market outcomes are among the most often mentioned outcomes of green product innovation (Dangelico, 2016). Particularly, these include increased market share (Leonidou et al., 2013; Lin et al., 2013; Liu et al., 2011; Triebswetter and Wackerbauer, 2008a, 2008b), increased sales (Leenders and Chandra, 2013; Leonidou et al., 2013; Lin et al., 2013; Liu et al., 2011), increased turnover (Horbach et al., 2012; Langerak et al., 1998; Triebswetter and Wackerbauer, 2008a, 2008b), and improved reputation (Chen, 2008; Driessen et al., 2013; Lin et al., 2013). Furthermore, customer outcomes of green product innovation are highlighted in the literature as relevant. This dimension of performance includes the acquisition of new customers (Liu et al., 2011; Triebswetter and Wackerbauer, 2008a, 2008b), better customer satisfaction (Leonidou et al., 2013), and increased willingness to pay a premium price (Langerak et al., 1998).

However, even though, theoretically, ecodesign should in general lead to better market performance, the market and the customer are still considered to be among the main external barriers to an effective implementation of ecodesign in industrial companies (Rossi et al., 2016). Indeed, considering that the implementation of ecodesign is not advancing at the rate necessary to achieve a more sustainable society (Dekoninck et al., 2016), members of the ecodesign research community have investigated the reasons behind the slow rate of development of ecodesign in industry, with the aim of identifying, in addition to the drivers of ecodesign implementation, challenges and barriers (Bey et al., 2013; Johansson, 2006; O'Hare, 2010). More precisely, in the review of ecodesign methods and tools conducted by Rossi et al. (2016), the Authors identify the market and the customer as among the external barriers mostly strongly influencing ecodesign implementation. In addition to the high competitiveness of the business, the lack of marketing studies, and the lack of involvement of sales and marketing departments, the authors also stressed the difficulties in identifying the advantages and disadvantages connected with the application of ecodesign strategies for products, the lack of awareness of benefits, the difficulties in interpreting customer perception, and the perception that there is no demand from the market. It is no coincidence that all these market- and customer-related external barriers correspond to the key dimensions of customer value as the driver of an effective implementation of ecodesign strategies. Thus, more market research is needed to better understand customers' needs. In consonance with this perspective, Dangelico (2016), in her resource-based model of success factors in the development of green product innovation, identifies marketing capabilities as a driver. In the specific case of green product innovation, this category of capabilities includes, in addition to the capabilities of developing and managing a good, green corporate image and of scanning for opportunities and threats presented by the green market, the capability of establishing a specific target market for green products and assessing market needs.

Consumers are paying more attention to all aspects of the supply chain; from production, delivery, through to disposal. They're actively learning, becoming more aware of environmental issues, and aren't afraid to question a brand's sustainability claims. According to a recent survey Global Web Index (2018), 61% of consumers are likely to switch to a brand that is more environmentally friendly than their current brand. So, when sustainability enters the equation, brand loyalty gets under immense strain. This should be a wake-up call for manufacturers and brands, as sustainability isn't just another buzzword. Consumers genuinely care, and they're expecting more from brands than ever before (Global Web Index, 2018).

Furthermore, it's not only a demand for sustainability that has grown, but also a willingness among consumers to put their money where their mouth is. At a global level, the number of consumers who say they would be willing to pay more for sustainable/eco-friendly products grew from 49% in 2011 to 57% in 2018 (Global Web Index, 2018).

The growing concern of citizens about environmental issues confirms the presence of a growing commitment to the protection of the ecosystem. Such a sensitivity, however, does not necessarily translate into coherent attitudes and choices reflecting those intentions.

The surveys conducted by Flash Eurobarometer (2013) show, in fact, that only in some cases do the strong emotions of green consumers and their sensitivity to environmental issues actually materialize in a motivational drive that leads to the purchase and consumption of particular goods and services. The same surveys show that only about 30% of consumers are really interested in environmental problems, but only half of that 30% would actually be oriented and inclined to buy eco-designed goods, while the rest would be totally indifferent to or skeptical about these issues.

Sensitivity can therefore be considered a pre-condition for the manifestation of eco-sustainable consumption behavior. However, although environmental awareness often corresponds to a high frequency of green purchasing decisions, sometimes there is no such relation. There has always been, therefore, a great difference between environmental sensitivity and eco-sustainable consumption, as demonstrated by the fact that there is no simple relationship between concern for the state of the environment and consumer choices. Although sensitivity is an essential prerequisite for the development of ecological consumption, it is not sufficient to direct an individual's purchasing behaviors. Eco-sustainable consumption, on the other hand, requires that the individual who wants to show his or her interest in the environment takes direct action to translate his or her interests and intentions into real behavior through the purchase of green goods and to be willing to make a significant commitment of economic resources.

Despite this increasing sensitivity towards sustainable issues, indeed price and brand trust are the most important considerations for consumers above all else, and there's an obvious conflict when it comes to consumers' desire to use sustainable materials versus what they're willing to spend or what they're able to afford. Consumers are price-conscious primarily, and this presents a significant challenge for manufacturers and brands to overcome. Environmentally-friendly alternatives tend to have a higher cost attached to them, so unless there's a way to avoid passing these extra costs on to the consumer, brands may face an uphill battle getting consumers on board, at least in the short term. Even if consumers have the best intentions, price remains an issue (Global Web Index, 2018).

In order to adopt a customer-based approach to the development of ecodesign strategies, it is therefore interesting and necessary to identify the factors that influence the choice of green products. In this regard, the rich literature that has sought, over the years, to identify the factors that constitute a real obstacle to the purchase of SR (social responsibility) products (Kumar and Anand, 2014) has identified the following: *i)* the significantly higher price compared to traditional goods (Pelsmacker, 2006); *ii)* the lower quality level and the lesser ability to meet needs compared to traditional products (Bird and Hughes, 1997, Pelsmacker, 2006; Gielissen and Graafland, 2009); *iii)* the too-often limited amount of information available to consumers (Pelsmacker, 2006); *iv)* the difficulty of finding such products in the distribution network (Vermeir and Verbeke, 2006; Pelsmacker, 2006); and *v)* packaging made with non-eco-friendly materials or that does not communicate the necessary information to the consumer (Immaculate, 2013).

The variables identified as critical reveal how the customer value is a central element in influencing purchase choices, even of eco-products. For this reason, many studies over the years have focused on the issue of the price of ecological products and the related issue of willingness to pay.

In this regard, two interesting works are those of Auger et al. (2003) and Guagnano (2001), in which a growing interest on the part of consumers in the green component is once again highlighted, but above all an interesting contrast is reported. This compares selfishness, by which people seek to satisfy their personal interests without worrying about what happens around them, and altruism, which instead pushes consumers to take into account the needs of the community and to strive to fulfill them even if doing so requires sacrifices, such as forsaking their own interests and incurring a higher purchase price.

Tsen et al. (2006) come to similar conclusions and, through a survey of a sample of 300 subjects, demonstrate the existence of a positive relationship between willingness to pay a *premium price* and the habits, behaviors, and values of consumers. In particular, consumers are willing to pay a higher price for SR products when the ethical, social, and environmental causes in question reflect their values and when consumers "see themselves" in these causes in a way that inspires them to take direct action toward the resolution of *corporate social responsibility* (CSR) issues.

Freestone and McGoldrick (2007) later conducted a study on 1,000 students to investigate their willingness to buy ethical goods at a *premium price;* the results do not clearly demonstrate a willingness to pay a higher price for SR products, but they do identify ethical and environmental characteristics to have a major impact on the purchasing choices of consumers.

Gielissen's (2011) qualitative study investigates SR products under multiple dimensions and extends the analysis to more categories of goods, obtaining interesting results and drawing new conclusions on the subject. First of all, the study shows that the demand for SR products is influenced by a number of factors: *i)* the perception of buying green goods as a moral duty; *ii)* the importance and impact of such goods in solving social problems; *iii)* the influence and opinion of other consumers; *iv)* the significantly higher *premium price* attached to such products; *v)* their quality and functional performance; and *vi)* the proximity and availability of goods. In particular, the study shows that the charging of a *premium price* has a negative impact on actual purchase and represents the biggest obstacle to be overcome.

Other interesting ideas are found in the work of Petricevic and Bell (2010), which analyzes the factors that can affect the propensity of consumers to buy *green products* while also taking into account the fact that people usually look for a *trade-off* between the functional component and the green component. An interesting element that emerges from this survey is that if the price of SR and traditional products is almost identical, people are oriented toward the first category of product, while the situation changes significantly when SR products carry a higher price. Moreover, despite the willingness of a significant proportion of respondents to purchase SR products to support the preservation of the ecosystem and send an important signal of change, they do not want to sacrifice quality or efficiency at a functional level.

This confirms the findings of the study conducted by Auger et al. (2008), namely that individuals are willing to pay a premium price to feel active and environmentally responsible but at the same time do not want to give up the functional component at the expense of the green one.

METHODOLOGY

The Conjoint Analysis: General Insights

Conjoint analysis is a multivariate statistical technique widely used in marketing research (Green and Srinivasan, 1978 and 1990; Green et al., 2001, and Green and Krieger, 2002). It is among the most popular techniques for measuring customer value and it is considered to guarantee valid and affordable results (Green and Srinivasan, 1978, 1990; Gustaffson et al., 2007). According to Green and Srinivasan (1978), the term "conjoint analysis" refers broadly to "any decompositional method that estimates the structure of a consumer preference given his/her overall evaluations of a set of alternatives that are pre-specified in terms of levels of different attributes (Green and Srinivasan, 1978, p. 104)".

The objective of the conjoint analysis is, first of all, to obtain a quantitative measure of the value to the customer of the different levels of the various attributes with which the offer has been articulated, as well as of the overall value attributed to different profiles (Carrol and Green, 1995). The term "offer profile" is used to refer to a combination of different attributes, each of which consists of several levels, into which the product under investigation is broken down. Once the different profiles have been defined, they are submitted, usually by means of a questionnaire, to a sample of potential buyers, who indicate their purchasing preferences. By analyzing the judgments of preference regarding the various offer profiles, it is possible to identify and measure the relative importance of the attributes included in the analysis.

Unlike the "composition approach" (Fishbein, 1963, 1967), the conjoint analysis is defined as a "decomposition approach" (Green and Srinivasan, 1978), as the objective is not achieved on the basis of the evaluations (of importance and performance) expressed by the interviewees with reference to single attributes, but by "breaking down" the overall judgments given by respondents with regard to a set of alternative product profiles. This makes it possible to overcome one of the main obstacles to measuring customer value, which consists of the difficulty of assessing the importance of individual attributes to which the product is de-composed, without excessively simplifying the process of choice. Preferences are formed, in fact, by taking into account all the relevant attributes of the product, and it is therefore unrealistic to totally abstract particular attributes from their reciprocal interrelationships.

The logical process underlying the decomposition approach based on conjoint analysis requires:

1. *Definition of attributes and levels and configuration of virtual profiles*: this selection phase is crucial for the success of the exploratory analysis, since as the number of attributes and levels increases, the number of offer profiles grow exponentially, making it more difficult for respondents to express preferences and for the researcher to elaborate and manage the analysis. In order to better manage the study and to obtain reliable final results, it is therefore necessary to define a limited number of attributes and levels[1] (Green and Srinivasan, 1990);
2. *Estimation of utility values associated with the levels of attributes*: once the necessary data has been collected, thanks to statistical programs it is possible to estimate the utility values assigned to each level of each attribute as well as to calculate the relative importance of each attribute. After the statistical elaboration of expressed references, the program returns the estimates of the utilities associated with the various levels of each attribute. These values must be considered and interpreted in the sense of greater or lesser; therefore a negative value does not mean "disutility," but simply a lower utility than the level corresponding to a positive utility value;

3. *Calculation of relative importance of each attribute included in the analysis*: after obtaining the utilities of each attribute level, one can determine the relative importance of each attribute; the program returns these values by default, applying the formula below:

$$IR_j = \frac{Max[U_j W_{ji}] - Min[U_j W_{jt}]}{\sum_{i-1}^{k} (Max[U_j W_{jt}] - Min[U_j W_{jt}])}$$

where:

IRj corresponds to the relative importance of the jth attribute;
Max[UjWji] indicates the maximum utility value associated with the Wji level of the *j-th* attribute of the *i-th* bidding profile;
Min [UjWji] represents the minimum utility value associated with the Wji level of the *j-th* attribute of the *i-th* bidding profile; and
k is the total number of attributes of the tender;

4. *Conversion of utility into monetary terms*: when price is included among the attributes, it becomes possible to convert the values of the utility values into monetary values, thus determining the economic value of a utility gap.

This conversion can be made using the following formula (Busacca et al., 2019):

Vmut = ΔP / ΔUP

where:

Vmut is the monetary value of a utility unit;
ΔP is the difference between the maximum and minimum price levels;
ΔUP is the difference between the maximum and minimum value of the price level utility.

In this way it is possible to define the price differential to be applied in the event that one wants to make changes to a product already on the market, estimating the impact of the change in terms of value for the customer.

An interesting application of conjoint analysis is that it involves *segmenting the market according to the utility values* obtained through the first processing (Green and Krieger, 1991). Indeed, the processing of aggregated data returns values for the relative importance assigned to the various attributes, with little differentiation between them, all in all. In case of real differences in preferences within the sample of respondents, it is possible to use them to segment the market.

The segmentation can be conducted by trial and error, launching hypothetical segmentations with different cluster numbers, in order to select the optimal number of clusters, corresponding to maximum variance between clusters and minimum variance in clusters.

Finally, after elaborating data to estimate the utility values related to attribute levels, as an expression of their importance, taken in aggregate and by segments, the conjoint analysis output allows to *estimate the customer value assigned to a real or virtual product profile*. The most frequently used method for estimating these values is that of minimum squares. More precisely, multiple regression analysis is applied to a linear system composed of a number of equations equal to that of the selected offer profiles. The assessments expressed for each profile are the dependent variables, while the explanatory variables are represented by the levels (coded by *dummy* variables in the case of qualitative factors) of the product attributes. In analytical terms:

$$Gi = b0 + \sum Uj\,Wji$$

where:

Gi corresponds to the consumer's assessment of the i-offer profile.
b0 is the constant;
Wji indicates the level of the *j-th* attribute of the *i-th* profile;
Uj Wji expresses the value-utility associated with *Wji*.

This application allows to compare the customer value of two or more alternative product profiles, measure the customer value assigned to the overall products and define the value gap emerging in the different options.

The Study Conducted on Ecological Washing Machines

After this brief description of the main steps of conjoint analysis technique, the following empirical study uses conjoint analysis to measure the customer value of certain green attributes of white goods. In particular, the survey refers specifically to the ecological version of the product "washing machine".

Conjoint analysis has been applied to a number of environmental issues since the mid-1990s, and recently an increasing number of conjoint studies have focused on consumer preferences in relation to sustainability characteristics (Sammer and Wustenhagen, 2005; Rokka and Uusitalo, 2008; Achabou and Dekhili, 2013; Osburg et al., 2016; Van Heek et al., 2017; Lieder et al., 2018). Considering that conjoint analysis "is concerned with determining the joint effect of levels of two or more attributes of stimuli on the total evaluative judgment of a set of stimuli [...]" (Rao, 2014, p. 3), it is particularly suitable for supporting ecodesign, since ecodesign adopts an integrated approach, developing products as a system in which all components can be jointly addressed to protect the environment.

The decision to apply the conjoint analysis technique to a durable product such as a washing machine was not a random one. Durable goods require a significant economic outlay at the time of purchase, which, given the length of their lifecycle, takes place with a rather limited frequency. Hence the importance of accurately measuring the value of the product as perceived by the customer (Codini et al., 2012). Durable goods, and washing machines in particular, are also characterized by a significant number of attributes and levels, an essential requirement for the correct application of the technique of conjoint analysis (Green and Srinivasan, 1978).

Moreover, in recent years, sales in this industry have been slowing down, partially due to the changes in consumer preferences, which have moved toward energy-saving appliances and appliances with lower environmental impact (see Growth for Knowledge reports). This trend, along with new, restrictive environmental regulations in the European market in particular, have forced producers of household appliances to invest in ecodesign. Indeed, as pointed out by recent studies, developing sustainable products is not only an important source of differentiation-based competitive advantage (Reinhardt, 1998; Orsato, 2006), but it is also a contributing factor in rejuvenating mature manufacturing industries in developed countries (Dangelico et al., 2013). However, considering that this strategy leads to new products with higher prices, companies operating in this industry need to be conscious of the customer value when buying eco-appliances (Ward et al., 2011; Mills and Schleich, 2010).

In the empirical study reported in this section, the interviewed consumers were asked to evaluate different product profiles consisting of multiple combinations of green attributes; this allowed to obtain the utility values and to assign the consequent relative importance to each of the green attributes included in the analysis. Based on the aim of the chapter—to show how conjoint analysis can support ecodesign strategies from a customer-based perspective—various elaborations of the conjoint analysis output were explored. Indeed, data collected were elaborated, in order to segment the market of ecological washing machines and to measure the customer value of different option of ecological washing machines.

The study was conducted using a sample of 347 Italian consumers. Table 1 reports the main socio-demographic feature of the respondents.

After an analysis of the eco–washing machines in the Italian market, four eco-attributes were identified and used, in addition to the price, in product profiles configurations. These attributes were energy class and the presence or lack of eco-tech, eco-timer, and energy-saver devices. Then, using a factorial design, 13 product profiles were selected and submitted to consumers, who were asked to assign a rating to each profile.

In an attempt to appropriately *define the attributes and levels to be used in the analysis*, the preliminary phase of the work involved the creation of a database cataloging a sample of washing machines

Table 1. Socio-demographic characteristics of respondents

Variables		**Number of respondents**	**Percentage of respondents**
Gender	Male	142	41%
	Female	205	59%
Total		**347**	**100%**
Profession	Students	82	24%
	Employees	83	24%
	Workers	48	14%
	Housewives	36	10%
	Pensioners	26	7%
	Teachers	18	5%
	Executives	11	3%
	Other professions	43	12%
Total		**347**	**100%**

offered by the main brands on the market, with the intention of identifying the most common functional characteristics and green attributes. In order to collect the essential data, the product sections of the websites of the main washing machine manufacturers were analyzed along with the catalogs of the main retail chains of household appliances. In particular, the following were taken into account in the classification phase: energy efficiency class, load capacity, centrifuge, presence or absence of eco-tech and eco-washing programs, and list price. This phase was instrumental in obtaining an overview of the products on the market, as well as in collecting the information necessary to carefully select the attributes and corresponding levels useful for the survey.

Once the tabulation of the washing machines has been completed, the database was segmented into four sales price ranges (€150–€300, €301–€550, €551–€800, and over €800) in order to make a first grouping and identify the attributes most frequently presented as their distribution within each of the price ranges. This made it possible to identify an initial database consisting of the attributes taken into account in the product classification phase and their levels. This first phase allowed to narrow the field of investigation considerably, having identified, from among the theoretical attributes, those prevailing in the actual market. However, the number of attributes and levels was still too high for an effective conjoint analysis. It was therefore necessary to further reduce their number by taking into account only those considered most relevant to consumer choice. Since the real objective of this analysis is to investigate the "green" component of washing machines and the influence that this has on consumers, the next phase of "skimming" focused only on "eco" attributes, omitting traditional ones.

To this end, offer profiles included in the analysis had the same technical characteristics, but differed from each other exclusively in terms of "eco" attributes. In order to identify the "basic" profile, the load capacity expressed in kilograms and the centrifuge in rpm were taken into consideration; analyses were carried out using the wider database of products to identify the levels of the attributes most frequently present. The "basic" product identified has a load capacity of 7 kg and a centrifuge of 1200 rpm. As regards the price, however, a single range between €199 and €699 was used, given that this range contains the largest number of washing machines with the attributes relevant to the survey.

The green attributes identified in the selection phase and the levels of each included in the analysis are as follows:

- Energy efficiency class, divided into levels A+, A++, A+++, classifications corresponding to the levels of energy savings, introduced by the new European energy labeling legislation;
- Eco-tech attributes, divided into two levels: YES (present) and NO (absent), to indicate the presence or absence of recycled materials in the washing machine with consequent high or low environmental impact at the time of disposal;
- Eco-time function, divided into two levels: YES (present) and NO (absent), to indicate the presence or absence of an eco-wash option, that is related to the length of cycle;
- Energy-saver function, divided into two levels: YES (present) and NO (absent), to indicate the presence or absence of an energy-saving program;
- Price, divided into three levels: €289.00, €459.00, and €619.00. These values represent the central points of the three bands (€199.00–€366.00, €367.00–€533.00, and €534.00–€699.00) into which a fair distribution of the products on the market included in the initial database fall (with about 30% of the products on the market falling within each class).

Table 2. Definitive composition of the attributes to be analyzed

Attributes	Levels
Energy efficiency class	A+; A++; A+++
Eco-tech	YES (present); NO (absent)
Eco-time	YES (present); NO (absent)
Energy saver	YES (present); NO (absent)
Price of	€289.00, €459.00, or €619.00

This first phase made it possible to define the set of attributes of washing machines and the corresponding levels that would be used for the configuration of the offer profiles in the survey.

Once the attributes and their levels were identified, they were combined through the use of "R-project" software (R version 2.15.0 conjoint package 1.33) [2] to obtain virtual product profile configurations.

In particular, for the configuration and subsequent selection of the profiles, it was decided to use a full profile mode with a fractioned factorial drawing with 13 profiles. By means of the fractioned factorial selection, the software R automatically returns the 13 profiles it considers statistically most significant.

The questionnaire used in data collection not only contains the product profiles but also had several sections designed to collect specific data relevant to the subject of reference. After a brief introduction in which the objectives of the study were presented, the selected profiles, which detail variations in the ecological characteristics of a single model of washing machine with a load capacity of 7 kilograms and a maximum centrifuge of 1200 rpm, were presented to the interviewee. The respondents were asked to express satisfaction on a scale ranging from 1 (very bad) to 9 (excellent) for each individual "card" of the product presented.

The next section of the questionnaire posed questions about the buying habits of the respondents, especially in relation to the purchase of white goods. Finally, the last part solicited personal information useful for defining the socio-demographic profile of the sample. The administration was partly direct and partly online.

The elaboration of data collected allowed to *estimate the utility values associated with the levels of attributes* (Table 3), to *calculate the relative importance of each attribute included in the analysis* (Table 4), and finally, to *convert utility into monetary terms.*

In order to *segment the market according to utility values,* we started with a number of clusters c = 3 and worked our way up to c = 15. Then, the optimal number of clusters was according to: the "variance between," the "variance in," the total variance, and Pearson's correlation index[3]. In this case, it was decided to group the sample into 13 segments; this may not make much sense according to a marketing logic, but among the different simulations this was the best option from a statistical point of view. When c = 13 we obtain a correlation ratio equal to 71.1%, which is fairly good, statistically, with values within clusters (i.e. "variance in") rather contained than highlighting a good homogeneity within the groups.

After identifying the number of segments on which to conduct the research and analyzing their composition, the next step was to see how the clusters identified relate to the 13 virtual product profiles, in order to identify their essential characteristics, especially in terms of the relative importance each cluster of respondents assigned to the different eco-attributes.

Table 3. Utility Values of Attribute Levels

Attribute	Level	Utility values
Energy class	A+	-0.5722
	A++	0.0724
	A+++	0.4998
Eco-tech	Yes.	0.8024
	No.	-0.8024
Eco-timer	Yes	0.5718
	No.	-0.5718
Energy saver	Yes	0.7601
	No.	-0.7601
Price of	€289.00	0.4769
	€459.00	0.0263
	€619.00	-0.5032
Intercept		5.5324

Table 4. Relative Importance Of The Various Attributes

Attribute	Level	Utility gap	Relative importance
Energy class	A+ A++ A+++	1.072	16.96%
Eco-tech	Yes. No.	1.6048	25.39%
Eco-timer	Yes No.	1.1436	18.09%
Energy saver	Yes No.	1.5202	24.05%
Price of	€289.00 €459.00 €619.00	0.9801	15.51%
Total		6.3207	100%

Table 5. Conversion of Utility into Monetary Terms

Attribute	Level	Utility values	Price gap (ΔP)	Utility gap (ΔUP)	Monetary value of the unitary utility (ΔP / ΔUP)
Price of	€289.00 €459.00 €619.00	0.4769 0.0263 -0.5032	€330.00	0.9801	€336.70

Table 6. R Syntax of Cluster Analysis

Within cluster sum of squares by cluster:
[Cluster 1] 235.63467; [Cluster 2] 433.40843; [Cluster 3] 435.49875; [Cluster 4] 404.29968; [Cluster 5] 472.00926; [Cluster 6] 279.20041; [Cluster 7] 350.11482; [Cluster 8] 252.32279; [Cluster 9] 16.69671; [Cluster 10] 37.65345; [Cluster 11] 206.66622; [Cluster 12] 454.14251; [Cluster 13] 101.11321
(between_SS / total_SS = 71.1%)

Cluster 1, which represents 6.91% of all respondents, was labeled "Economic Eco-friendly" as people belonging to this group are looking for products with high energy efficiency while considering a very low price to be a basic criterion in their purchasing choices.

The second Cluster comprises 10.37% of the total and was called "The Early Economy", because these are consumers who are always attentive to technological innovations, whether functional or eco-sustainable, and are willing to try them out before others, sometimes even running risks to do so. Nevertheless, price has a considerable influence on their final decisions, sometimes representing a real obstacle.

Cluster 3 comprises 15.85% of the sample; these consumers were referred to as "Pragrmatics" because they attach greater importance to the practicality of washing than to green characteristics.

Cluster 4 includes 12.39% of the total; these consumers were called "Energy Efficients," as they pay great attention to features that can minimize energy consumption and waste, even if they have to pay a higher price for a particular product model.

In Cluster 5 10.37% of the sample is included, and these individuals were recognized as "Opportunists"; they are looking for offers that contain some green attributes, but their final decision depends on price.

Cluster 6 is made up of 8.64% of respondents and was called "Super Greens", as these consumers are looking for products with all the eco-sustainable features that the market offers. Here the price does not represent an insurmountable obstacle to the purchase of the goods.

Cluster 7 also includes 8.64% of respondents and was called "Savers" because it is made up of those people for whom the only factor that affects the final purchase is price.

Group 8 is made up of 7.49% of the sample, including consumers who were recognized as "The Avant-Garde", willing to pay even very high prices for the latest, greenest model.

Cluster 9 is composed of just under 1% of the subjects involved in the survey, who were labeled "Environmentalists" because they are looking for products with functional performance that have a very low impact on the environment.

Cluster 10 contains only 1.4% of the sample and was made up of "Eco Calculators": people who will buy a product at a high price, knowing that the energy efficiency of that product will offset the initial investment and allow them to save over time thanks to reduced energy consumption and waste.

Cluster 11 contains 4.89% of the sample. These subjects were described as "The Efficient Thrifty," as they seek green and energy-saving product characteristics, while always also focusing on the price.

Cluster 12 contains 10.66% of the people surveyed, and were labeled as "Rich Greens": individuals for whom price has little influence on their final purchasing decision in comparison to their interest in issues such as respect for the environment, pollution, and energy savings.

The last cluster (13) includes 1.3% of respondents, termed "The Indifferent," since these consumers do not care about features related to eco-sustainability, but give primary importance to functional features and performance. In the last elaboration of conjoint analysis output, two virtual profiles deriving from different combination of levels of attributes were created. After that to each product profile a customer

Table 7. Consumer's Assessment of the "a" and "b" Eco-product Profiles.

Attribute	Level	Eco-product profile "a"
Energy class	A+	-0.5722
Eco-tech	Yes	0.8024
Eco-timer	Yes	0.5718
Energy saver	No	-0.7601
Intercept		5.5324
Global consumer assessment for "a"		**5.5743**
Attribute	**Level**	**Eco-product profile "b"**
Energy class	A++	0.0724
Eco-tech	No	-0.8024
Eco-timer	No	-0.5718
Energy saver	Yes	0.7601
Intercept		5.5324
Global consumer assessment for "b"		**4.9907**

assessment was assigned, basing on the utility values of the single levels of the attributes emerging from the conjoint analysis. This step allowed to *measure the customer value of virtual product profiles.*

DISCUSSION

The empirical analysis reported in this chapter shows how the technique of conjoint analysis can support the development of ecodesign strategies aimed at increasing value for the customer. As can be seen from the results of the analysis, the technique makes it possible, first and foremost, to *measure the relative importance attributed by the consumer to the "eco" components* of a product, to *segment the market according to consumers' different perceptions regarding these "eco" attributes*, and, finally, to *quantify the customer value of different virtual or real eco-product profiles.*

The intention of the empirical study was not so much to focus attention on the results of the survey conducted in relation to the case of washing machines, but rather to highlight—starting from this concrete application—the general potential that this technique may have in defining strategies for ecodesign.

However, discussing the results of the conjoint analysis conducted in the case of ecological washing machines, general insights on the potential of this technique in eco-design strategies can emerge.

As the analysis shows, the first objective of the conjoint analysis technique when applied to products that incorporate "eco" components is to evaluate the reaction of the market to the introduction of these green features, thus assessing in advance the possible response from the market; this information can be used to direct the design of the product itself. In addition, the analysis can accurately quantify the relative importance that customers will attribute to the "eco" characteristics of the product, thus offering indications about their willingness to pay for these characteristics. This information is indispensable when launching new "eco" products and when there is a need to estimate the possible return on investment in these products.

Specifically, in the case of eco-washing machines, the eco-attributes considered as most important by consumers were "eco-tech" (relative importance 25.39%) and "energy-saver" (relative importance 24.05%). Surprisingly, price was the attribute with the lowest relative importance (15.51%), while medium importance was assigned to eco-timer (18.09%), and energy class (16.96%). Furthermore, utility gaps give interesting insights for managers developing new eco-products or revising existing ones, quantifying the potential increase in customer value deriving from a change in the levels of the attributes (i.e. how much does utility value increase moving from an A++ energy class to an A+++ class?).

Another important contribution of the analysis is the so-called "monetary value of unitary utility", which allows the identification of the attributes and levels that generate the greatest increase in perceived utility by quantifying the associated monetary value to the customer. This application of conjoint analysis could certainly have a considerable impact on ecodesign strategies aimed not only at developing radically new offers but also at improving existing products from a green point of view (for example, thanks to the introduction of a green attribute, such as packaging, in an existing product).

In this case, the ΔP is given by the difference between the maximum price level (€619.00) and the minimum price level (€289.00) and is therefore equal to €330.00, while the relative utility gap (ΔUP) results from the difference between 0.4769 (maximum utility value associated with the minimum price) and 0.5032 (minimum utility vaðue associated with the maximum price) and is equal to 0.9801. Therefore, the monetary value of the unitary utility is given by the ratio 330.00/0.9801 and is equal to €336.70. This means that offering a new product version ensuring an increase of 1 utility unit allows to increase the price of the eco-product up to €336.70. Similarly, including "eco-tech" in a washing machine that does not include this attribute, increases perceived utility by 1.6048; this means that consumers are willing to pay for this attribute up to €540.34 (1.6048*336.70) more than what they actually pay for a washing machine that is not "eco-tech".

Furthermore, the use of the results of conjoint analysis to segment the market certainly offers excellent opportunities when defining ecodesign strategies, allowing the identification of different segments according to their sensitivity to the "eco" characteristics of the product, and the consequent differentiation of the marketing policies addressed to them. Indeed, while the discussion reported above considered just the results of the conjoint analysis referred to the overall sample, the most interesting application of the conjoint analysis are those considering the partial results–as to say the different segments emerging from the analysis.

Although the names given to each of the clusters emerged from our analysis were merely indicative and served to distinguish each segment readily from the others, clustering provided food for thought and relevant information.

First of all, it was confirmed that consumers still consider the performance of the product as the primary criterion for the final choice of purchase, to the detriment of the green component (Cluster 3). Respondents want products that perform their functions quickly and efficiently. Despite this, however, the weight and relevance given to eco-sustainable attributes is growing, especially in view of the worsening environmental situation and the steady increase in energy costs. This trend can be seen in Clusters 2 and 4, where consumers are increasingly attentive to new features in terms of eco-sustainability, efficiency, and minimization of waste. It is interesting to focus on segment 10, in which consumers begin to conceive of the purchase of a household appliance as an investment that will, despite a significant initial outlay, minimize costs significantly in the medium to long term thanks to the green attributes of the product.

As mentioned above, price still has a major impact on demand decisions, still registering as the most influential factor when the alternatives available on the market are assessed (Cluster 6, 8, 10, 11).

A final relevant consideration is that the number of people who fully and completely embrace the green cause is still very small (9.5%, Cluster 6 and Cluster 9), even if the trend is growing, and that there is a sharp reduction in those individuals who are completely indifferent to such issues (Cluster 13 represents only 1.44% of the total sample).

Finally, when developing new eco-products rather than revising existing ones, quantifying the customer value associated to different virtual product profiles could give important insights and drive the new eco-product development. This gives useful suggestions, first of all, about what the preferred product profile is in case of new eco-product development and, secondary, about the willingness to pay for that profile.

In this application, the utility gap that consumers perceive assumes the value of 0.5836 in favour of "a" eco-product profile. Furthermore, this application might support pricing strategies for eco-products, leading to fix the price as proportional to utility gaps. Indeed, as the gap between the two options is 0.5836, this means that–considering that the monetary value of a utility unit is equal to 0.980–consumers assign to "a" product profile an additional value of 0.5836*336.70 = 196.47 € compared to the one assigned to "b". This means that consumers are willing to pay if anything 196.47 € more moving from product "b" to product "a".

CONCLUSION AND FUTURE RESEARCH DIRECTIONS

This work aims to contribute to the literature dedicated to ecodesign strategies by adopting a customer-based perspective in the context of the Fourth Industrial Revolution. Despite the fact that the existing literature on ecodesign identifies the market and consumers as a significant barrier, few studies have sought to provide operational guidance in the development of eco-strategies from a customer-driven point of view. This is also consistent with the general aim of the book–claiming to a higher customer orientation in innovation as a consequence of the increasing customer attention to the environment and to the ethical issues in the era of the Fourth Industrial Revolution.

Therefore, with regard to the theoretical contribution, this chapter reviews the literature dedicated to the theme of ecodesign, focusing in particular on contributions that highlight the impact that such strategies can have in terms of value for the customer. Through the application of conjoint analysis to the case of "eco" washing machines, the chapter then proposes a useful methodology for quantifying the value to the customer of ecodesign solutions, which could be a starting point for the development of strategies in this area that are increasingly customer-driven.

Specifically, the study gives useful insights for the managers involved in the development of ecodesign strategies to: *i) identify the relative importance of different eco-attributes* included in the product offering; *ii) segment the market according to the different utility* assigned by the customers to the various levels of eco-attributes; *iii) measure the customer value of alternative eco-product profiles.*

The study suffers from certain limitations, however, mainly due to the fact that it proposes only the technique of conjoint analysis as being useful to the development of customer-driven ecodesign strategies. Although we highlight the merits of this technique for quantifying the value for the customer, it is clear that it does not exhaust the range of possible techniques applicable to this purpose. It should also be noted that, in the proposed analysis, only some of the countless possible applications of conjoint analysis have been emphasized, at the expense of others that may also be interesting in relation to ecodesign strategies and worthy of attention (think, for example, on the application of conjoint analysis for the estimation of preference shares).

It should be stressed that the limited representativeness of the sample and the limitation of the analysis to the case of eco-washing machines do not in themselves constitute limitations of this study, since, as already emphasized, the objective of the empirical survey reported here is not to investigate the value of "eco" components in the washing machine sector as such, but rather to provide a methodological proposal to support ecodesign strategies.

REFERENCES

Achabou, M. A., & Dekhili, S. (2013). Luxury and sustainable development: Is there a match? *Journal of Business Research*, *66*(10), 1896–1903. doi:10.1016/j.jbusres.2013.02.011

Adams, R., Jeanrenaud, S., Bessant, J., Overy, P., & Denyer, D. (2012). *Innovating for sustainability: a systematic review of the body of knowledge*. Retrieved from http://nbs.net/wp-content/uploads/NBS-Systematic-Review-Innovation.pdf

Aoe, T. (2007). Eco-efficiency and ecodesign in electrical and electronic products. *Journal of Cleaner Production*, *15*(15), 1406–1414. doi:10.1016/j.jclepro.2006.06.004

Auger, P., Burke, P., Devinney, T. M., & Louviere, J. J. (2003). What will consumers pay for social product features? *Journal of Business Ethics*, *42*(3), 281–304. doi:10.1023/A:1022212816261

Auger, P., Devinney, T. M., Louviere, J. J., & Burke, P. F. (2008). Do social product features have value to consumers? *International Journal of Research in Marketing*, *25*(3), 183–191. doi:10.1016/j.ijresmar.2008.03.005

Bak, A., & Bartlomowicz, T. (2013). *Conjoint analysis method and its implementation in conjoint R package. Department of Econometrics and Computer Science*. Wroclav University of Economics.

Baumann, H., Boons, F., & Bragd, A. (2002). Mapping the green product development field: Engineering, policy and business perspectives. *Journal of Cleaner Production*, *10*(5), 409–425. doi:10.1016/S0959-6526(02)00015-X

Bey, N., Hauschild, M. Z., & McAloone, T. C. (2013). Drivers and barriers for implementation of environmental strategies in manufacturing companies. *CIRP Annals-Manufacturing Technology*, *62*(1), 43–46. doi:10.1016/j.cirp.2013.03.001

Bird, K., & Hughes, D. R. (1997). Ethical consumerism: The case of "Fairly–Traded" coffee. *Business Ethics (Oxford, England)*, *6*(3), 159–167. doi:10.1111/1467-8608.00063

Boks, C. (2006). The soft side of ecodesign. *Journal of Cleaner Production*, *14*(15-16), 1346–1356. doi:10.1016/j.jclepro.2005.11.015

Busacca, B., Bertoli, G., & Chizzoli, C. (2019). *Customer-based View*. Milano, Italy: Egea.

Carrol, J. D., & Green, P. E. (1995). Psychometric methods in marketing research: Part 1, conjoint analysis. *Journal of Marketing*, *32*, 385–391.

Chen, Y. S. (2008). The driver of green innovation and green image – green core competence. *Journal of Business Ethics*, *81*(3), 531–543. doi:10.100710551-007-9522-1

Chen, Y. S., Chang, C. H., & Wu, F. S. (2012). Origins of green innovations: The differences between proactive and reactive green innovations. *Management Decision*, *50*(3), 368–398. doi:10.1108/00251741211216197

Chun, Y. Y., Lee, K. M., Lee, J. S., Lee, J. Y., Lee, M. H., Mishima, N., & Tahara, K. (2018). Identifying key components of products based on consumer- and producer-oriented ecodesign indices considering environmental impacts, costs, and utility value. *Journal of Cleaner Production*, *198*, 1031–1043. doi:10.1016/j.jclepro.2018.07.035

Codini, A., Saccani, N., & Sicco, A. (2012). The relationship between customer value and pricing strategies: An empirical test. *Journal of Product and Brand Management*, *21*(7), 538–546. doi:10.1108/10610421211276321

Conway, S., & Steward, F. (1998). Networks and interfaces in environmental innovation: A comparative study in the UK and Germany. *The Journal of High Technology Management Research*, *9*(2), 239–253. doi:10.1016/S1047-8310(98)90006-2

Dangelico, R. M. (2016). Green product innovation: Where we are and where we are going. *Business Strategy and the Environment*, *25*(8), 560–576. doi:10.1002/bse.1886

Dangelico, R. M., Pontrandolfo, P., & Pujari, D. (2013). Developing sustainable new products in the textile and upholstered furniture industries: Role of external integrative capabilities. *Journal of Product Innovation Management*, *30*(4), 642–658. doi:10.1111/jpim.12013

Dangelico, R. M., & Pujari, D. (2010). Mainstreaming green product innovation: Why and how companies integrate environmental sustainability. *Journal of Business Ethics*, *95*(3), 471–486. doi:10.100710551-010-0434-0

De Medeiros, J. F., Ribeiro, J. L. D., & Cortimiglia, M. N. (2014). Success factors for environmentally sustainable product innovation: A systematic literature review. *Journal of Cleaner Production*, *65*, 76–86. doi:10.1016/j.jclepro.2013.08.035

Dekoninck, E. A., Domingo, L., O'Hare, J. A., Pigosso, D. C., Reyes, T., & Troussier, N. (2016). Defining the challenges for ecodesign implementation in companies: Development and consolidation of a framework. *Journal of Cleaner Production*, *135*, 410–425. doi:10.1016/j.jclepro.2016.06.045

Driessen, P., Hillebrand, B., Kok, R., & Verhallen, T. (2013). Green new product development: The pivotal role of product greenness. *IEEE Transactions on Engineering Management*, *60*(2), 315–326. doi:10.1109/TEM.2013.2246792

Fishbein, M. (1963). An investigation of the relationships between beliefs about an object and the attitude toward that object. *Human Relations*, *16*(3), 233–239. doi:10.1177/001872676301600302

Fishbein, M. (1967). *Readings in attitude theory and measurement.*

Flash Eurobarometer 367. (2013). Attitudes of Europeans towards building the single market for green products. European Commission, Directorate-General for Environment.

Foster, C., & Green, K. (2000). Greening the innovation process. *Business Strategy and the Environment, 9*(5), 287–303. doi:10.1002/1099-0836(200009/10)9:5<287::AID-BSE256>3.0.CO;2-7

Freestone, O. M., & McGoldrick, P. J. (2007). Ethical positioning and political marketing: The ethical awareness and concerns of UK voters. *Journal of Marketing Management, 23*(7-8), 651–673. doi:10.1362/026725707X229984

Galbreth, M. R., & Ghosh, B. (2013). Competition and sustainability: The impact of consumer awareness. *Decision Sciences, 44*(1), 127–159. doi:10.1111/j.1540-5915.2012.00395.x

Gielissen, R., & Graafland, J. (2009). Concepts of price fairness: Empirical research into the Dutch coffee market. *Business Ethics (Oxford, England), 18*(2), 165–178. doi:10.1111/j.1467-8608.2009.01555.x

Gielissen, R. B. (2011). Why do consumers buy socially responsible products? *International Journal of Business and Social Science, 2*(3).

Global Web Index. (2018). Sustainable Packaging Unwrapped.

Green, L., Fristoe, N., & Myerson, J. (1994). Temporal discounting and preference reversals in choice between delayed outcomes. *Psychonomic Bulletin & Review, 1*(3), 383–389. doi:10.3758/BF03213979 PMID:24203522

Green, P. E., & Krieger, A. M. (1991). Segmenting markets with conjoint analysis. *Journal of Marketing, 55*(4), 20–31. doi:10.1177/002224299105500402

Green, P. E., & Krieger, A. M. (2002). What's right with conjoint analysis? *Marketing Research, 14*(1), 24.

Green, P. E., Krieger, A. M., & Wind, Y. J. (2001). Thirty years of conjoint analysis: Reflections and prospects. *Interfaces, 31*(3_supplement), S56–S73. doi:10.1287/inte.31.3s.56.9676

Green, P. E., & Srinivasan, V. (1978). Conjoint analysis in consumer research: Issues and outlook. *The Journal of Consumer Research, 5*(2), 103–123. doi:10.1086/208721

Green, P. E., & Srinivasan, V. (1990). Conjoint analysis in marketing: New developments with implications for research and practice. *Journal of Marketing, 54*(4), 3–19. doi:10.1177/002224299005400402

Guagnano, G. A. (2001). Altruism and market-like behavior: An analysis of willingness to pay for recycled paper products. *Population and Environment, 22*(4), 425–438. doi:10.1023/A:1006753823611

Guoyou, Q., Saixing, Z., Chiming, T., Haitao, Y., & Hailiang, Z. (2013). Stakeholders' influences on corporate green innovation strategy: A case study of manufacturing firms in China. *Corporate Social Responsibility and Environmental Management, 20*(1), 1–14. doi:10.1002/csr.283

Gustaffson, A., Herrmann, A., & Huber, F. (2007). Conjoint analysis as an instrument of market research practice. In A. Gustaffson, A. Hermann, & F. Huber (Eds.), *Conjoint Measurement* (pp. 3–30). London, UK: Springer. doi:10.1007/978-3-540-71404-0_1

Handfield, R. B., Melnyk, S. A., Calantone, R. J., & Curkovic, S. (2001). Integrating environmental concerns into the design process: The gap between theory and practice. *IEEE Transactions on Engineering Management, 48*(2), 189–208. doi:10.1109/17.922478

Hopkins, M. (2010). How sustainability fuels design innovation. Interview with Steven Eppinger. *MIT Sloan Management Review*, *52*(1), 75–81.

Horbach, J., Rammer, C., & Rennings, K. (2012). Determinants of eco-innovations by type of environmental impact—The role of regulatory push/pull, technology push and market pull. *Ecological Economics*, *78*, 112–122. doi:10.1016/j.ecolecon.2012.04.005

Huang, Y. C., Ding, H. B., & Kao, M. R. (2009). Salient stakeholder voices: Family business and green innovation adoption. *Journal of Management & Organization*, *15*(3), 309–326. doi:10.1017/S1833367200002649

Immaculate, P. S. (2013). Consumer awareness of recycled packaging. *International Journal of Retailing and Rural Business Perspectives*, *2*(1), 277–281.

Johansson, G. (2002). Success factors for integration of ecodesign in product development: A review of state of the art. *Environmental Management and Health*, *13*(1), 98–107. doi:10.1108/09566160210417868

Johansson, G. (2006). Incorporating environmental concern in product development: A study of project characteristics. *Management of Environmental Quality Analysis International Journal*, *17*, 421–436.

Kammerer, D. (2009). The effects of customer benefit and regulation on environmental product innovation: Empirical evidence from appliance manufacturers in Germany. *Ecological Economics*, *68*(8-9), 2285–2295. doi:10.1016/j.ecolecon.2009.02.016

Keskin, D., Diehl, J. C., & Molenaar, N. (2013). Innovation process of new ventures driven by sustainability. *Journal of Cleaner Production*, *45*, 50–60. doi:10.1016/j.jclepro.2012.05.012

Kivimaa, P. (2007). The determinants of environmental innovation: The impacts of environmental policies on the Nordic pulp, paper and packaging industries. *European Environment*, *17*(2), 92–105. doi:10.1002/eet.442

Kumar, P. K., & Anand, B. (2014). A new consumer behavior model towards green products: Scale development and validation. *Asian Journal of Research in Social Science and Humanities*, *4*(5), 177–193.

Langerak, F., Peelen, E., & van der Veen, M. (1998). Exploratory results on the antecedents and consequences of green marketing. *Market Research Society*, *40*(4), 1–12. doi:10.1177/147078539804000404

Leenders, M. A., & Chandra, Y. (2013). Antecedents and consequences of green innovation in the wine industry: The role of channel structure. *Technology Analysis and Strategic Management*, *25*(2), 203–218. doi:10.1080/09537325.2012.759203

Leonidou, C. N., Katsikeas, C. S., & Morgan, N. A. (2013). "Greening" the marketing mix: Do firms do it and does it pay off? *Journal of the Academy of Marketing Science*, *41*(2), 151–170. doi:10.100711747-012-0317-2

Lieder, M., Asif, F. M., Rashid, A., Mihelič, A., & Kotnik, S. (2018). A conjoint analysis of circular economy value propositions for consumers: Using 'washing machines in Stockholm' as a case study. *Journal of Cleaner Production*, *172*, 264–273. doi:10.1016/j.jclepro.2017.10.147

Lin, R. J., Tan, K. H., & Geng, Y. (2013). Market demand, green product innovation, and firm performance: Evidence from Vietnam motorcycle industry. *Journal of Cleaner Production*, *40*, 101–107. doi:10.1016/j.jclepro.2012.01.001

Liu, X., Dai, H., & Cheng, P. (2011). Drivers of integrated environmental innovation and impact on company competitiveness: Evidence from 18 Chinese firms. *International Journal of Technology and Globalisation*, *5*(3/4), 255–280. doi:10.1504/IJTG.2011.039767

Mills, B., & Schleich, J. (2010). What's driving energy efficient appliance label awareness and purchase propensity? *Energy Policy*, *38*(2), 814–825. doi:10.1016/j.enpol.2009.10.028

Molteni, L., & Manoforte, R. (1998). *La conjoint analysis e il problema delle interazioni fra gli attributi: un'evidenza empirica*. Roma, Italy: Libero Istituto Universitario Carlo Cattaneo.

Nidumolu, R., Prahalad, C. K., & Rangaswami, M. R. (2009). Why sustainability is now the key driver of innovation. *Harvard Business Review*, *87*(9), 56–64.

O'Hare, J.A. (2010). *Eco-innovation tools for the early stages: an industry-based investigation of tool customisation and introduction.*

Orsato, R. J. (2006). Competitive environmental strategies: When does it pay to be green? *California Management Review*, *48*(2), 127–143. doi:10.2307/41166341

Osburg, V. S., Appelhanz, S., Toporowski, W., & Schumann, M. (2016). An empirical investigation of wood product information valued by young consumers. *Journal of Cleaner Production*, *110*, 170–179. doi:10.1016/j.jclepro.2015.01.068

Pelsmacker, P. D., Janssens, W., Sterckx, E., & Mielants, C. (2006). Fair-trade beliefs, attitudes and buying behaviour of Belgian consumers. *International Journal of Nonprofit and Voluntary Sector Marketing*, *11*(2), 125–138. doi:10.1002/nvsm.47

Pereira, Á. & Vence, X. (2012). *Key business factors for eco-innovation: an overview of recent firm-level empirical studies.*

Petricevic, T. & Bell, R. (2010). *An exploratory study into influence of corporate social responsibility on consumer price sensitivity.*

Plouffe, S., Lanoie, P., Berneman, C., & Vernier, M. F. (2011). Economic benefits tied to ecodesign. *Journal of Cleaner Production*, *19*(6-7), 573–579. doi:10.1016/j.jclepro.2010.12.003

Pujari, D. & Wright, G. H. (1999). *Management of environmental new product development.*

Rao, V. R. (2014). *Applied conjoint analysis*. New York, NY: Springer. doi:10.1007/978-3-540-87753-0

Reinhardt, F. L. (1998). Environmental product differentiation: Implications for corporate strategy. *California Management Review*, *40*(4), 43–73. doi:10.2307/41165964

Rennings, K., Ziegler, A., Ankele, K., & Hoffmann, E. (2006). The influence of different characteristics of the EU environmental management and auditing scheme on technical environmental innovations and economic performance. *Ecological Economics*, *57*(1), 45–59. doi:10.1016/j.ecolecon.2005.03.013

Rokka, J., & Uusitalo, L. (2008). Preference for green packaging in consumer product choices–do consumers care? *International Journal of Consumer Studies*, *32*(5), 516–525. doi:10.1111/j.1470-6431.2008.00710.x

Rossi, M., Germani, M., & Zamagni, A. (2016). Review of ecodesign methods and tools. Barriers and strategies for an effective implementation in industrial companies. *Journal of Cleaner Production*, *129*, 361–373. doi:10.1016/j.jclepro.2016.04.051

Sammer, K., & Wüstenhagen, R. (2005). The influence of eco-labeling on consumer behavior–results of a discrete choice analysis. *Business Strategy and the Environment*, 1–28.

Triebswetter, U., & Wackerbauer, J. (2008a). Integrated environmental product innovation and impacts on company competitiveness: A case study of the automotive industry in the region of Munich. *European Environment*, *18*(1), 30–44. doi:10.1002/eet.475

Triebswetter, U., & Wackerbauer, J. (2008b). Integrated environmental product innovation in the region of Munich and its impact on company competitiveness. *Journal of Cleaner Production*, *16*(14), 1484–1493. doi:10.1016/j.jclepro.2007.09.003

Tsai, M. T., Chuang, L. M., Chao, S. T., & Chang, H. P. (2012). The effects assessment of firm environmental strategy and customer environmental conscious on green product development. *Environmental Monitoring and Assessment*, *184*(7), 4435–4447. doi:10.100710661-011-2275-4 PMID:21818538

Tsen, C. H., Phang, G., Hasan, H., & Buncha, M. R. (2006). Going green: A study of consumers' willingness to pay for green products in Kota Kinabalu. *International Journal of Business and Society*, *7*, 40–54.

Ülkü, M. A., & Hsuan, J. (2017). Towards sustainable consumption and production: Competitive pricing of modular products for green consumers. *Journal of Cleaner Production*, *142*, 4230–4242. doi:10.1016/j.jclepro.2016.11.050

Van Heek, J., Arning, K., & Ziefle, M. (2017). Reduce, reuse, recycle: Acceptance of CO2-utilization for plastic products. *Energy Policy*, *105*, 53–66. doi:10.1016/j.enpol.2017.02.016

Van Hemel, C., & Cramer, J. (2002). Barriers and stimuli for ecodesign in SMEs. *Journal of Cleaner Production*, *10*(5), 439–453. doi:10.1016/S0959-6526(02)00013-6

Venables, W. N. & Smith, D. M. (2002). *An introduction to R.* Retrieved from http://cran.rproject.org/doc/manuals/R-intro. pdf

Vermeir, I., & Verbeke, W. (2006). Sustainable food consumption: Exploring the consumer "attitude–behavioral intention" gap. *Journal of Agricultural & Environmental Ethics*, *19*(2), 169–194. doi:10.100710806-005-5485-3

Visser, W. (2008). Corporate social responsibility in developing countries. In The Oxford handbook of corporate social responsibility.

Ward, D. O., Clark, C. D., Jensen, K. L., Yen, S. T., & Russell, C. S. (2011). Factors influencing willingness-to-pay for the ENERGY STAR® label. *Energy Policy*, *39*(3), 1450–1458. doi:10.1016/j.enpol.2010.12.017

ENDNOTES

1 The attributes and levels taken into account result in the total number of profiles. For example, considering six attributes–two of which are articulated in three discrete levels, three in two levels, and one in four levels–the number of all possible combinations is 288 (3x3×2×2×2×4). Naturally, in order to collect the evaluations of the consumers, it is necessary to identify a subset of offering profiles (usually composed of a minimum of eight, and a maximum of 18, combinations). This is the reason why in this step methods of fractional factorial design are typically used. The main software applications that can be used for this purpose allow a drastic selection of the number of profiles which are acceptable, however, only after verifying the substantial independence of the attributes. The operational advantage connected to the significant containment of the profiles to be submitted to the judgment of the interviewees, can be contrasted with a significant loss of information, consisting in the impossibility of estimating the effects of interaction between the attributes considered. This can significantly distort the results of the survey, as–in the presence of significant interaction effects–the preferences expressed for the levels of one attribute depend on the levels of other attributes. For further information about this step, please refer to Molteni and Manoforte (1998).

2 Many computer programs were carried out since 1970th, for example IBM SPSS Conjoint, Sawtooth Software, SYSTAT Conjoint Analysis, SAS/STAT and online research platforms for various models of conjoint analysis. For the elaboration reported in this chapter we used "R-project" software as it is an integrated suite of software facilities for data manipulation, calculation and graphical display. Among other things it has: *i)* an effective data handling and storage facility; *ii)* a suite of operators for calculations on arrays, in particular matrices; *iii)* a large, coherent, integrated collection of intermediate tools for data analysis; *iv)* graphical facilities for data analysis and display either directly at the computer or on hardcopy; *v)* a well developed, simple and effective programming language which includes conditionals, loops, user defined recursive functions and input and output facilities (Venables and Smith, 2002). The term "environment" is intended to characterize it as a fully planned and coherent system, rather than an incremental accretion of very specific and inflexible tools, as is frequently the case with other data analysis software. R is very much a vehicle for newly developing methods of interactive data analysis (Venables and Smith, 2002). The conjoint R package is easy to use for traditional conjoint analysis based on full-profile collection method and multiple linear regression model with dummy variables. The version of the conjoint package used for our analysis (1.33) has twelve following functions: caBTL, caImportance, caLogit, caMaxUtility, caModel, caPartUtilities, caSegmentation, caTotalUtilitie, ca-Utilities, Conjoint, ShowAllSimulations, ShowAllUtilities. For further details on the usage of R conjoint package functions see Bak and Bartlomowicz (2013).

3 This remembering that the more the values from the "variance in" groups decrease, the more their internal cohesion increases; that the more the "variance in" increases, the more the difference between the segments increases; and, finally, that the higher the percentage value that Pearson's index assumes, the better will be the statistical quality of the cluster analysis.

Chapter 11
The Importance of Consumer Perception of Corporate Social Responsibility to Meet the Need for Sustainable Consumption:
Challenges in the Sportswear Sector

Giovanna Pegan
https://orcid.org/0000-0003-1712-4483
University of Trieste, Italy

Gabriella Schoier
https://orcid.org/0000-0002-4222-9802
University of Trieste, Italy

Patrizia de Luca
https://orcid.org/0000-0001-6418-2534
University of Trieste, Italy

ABSTRACT

Industries have to rethink their value creation processes in a sustainable perspective. In order to satisfy their stakeholders and pursue the well-being of society in the long term, manufacturers must operate under corporate social responsibility (CSR). Embodying the identity of multiple stakeholders, consumers are the key to ensuring the success of sustainability efforts. This chapter analyses the relevance of CSR from the perspective of consumer perception, which has been neglected thus far in literature. The chapter also embraces the idea that CSR and sustainable consumption are two sides of the same coin that need to be integrated in order to create sustainable industrial value. After the theoretical background, this work presents and discusses the results of an empirical research focused on an emblematic industry and brand. The findings support the idea that although a company is trying to seize Industry 4.0. opportunities for sustainability, its efforts can be partly hampered by consumers' lack of perception or their misperception.

DOI: 10.4018/978-1-7998-1419-1.ch011

INTRODUCTION

The issue of corporate social responsibility (CSR) can be considered a mega-trend that is widespread among manufacturers that are increasingly becoming aware of how their response to the challenge of sustainability can affect not only their competitiveness but also the very survival of their business. Indeed, each organization has the task of determining the needs of the target market and satisfying these more effectively and efficiently than the competition does, creating value and preserving or increasing the long-term well-being of consumers and society (Kotler et al., 2012). As key players in promoting global sustainable development, organizations nowadays have to create sustainable industrial value (Stock et al., 2018). In recent years, the creation of this value has undergone radical changes caused by the so-called Fourth Industrial Revolution, or Industry 4.0, which poses new challenges to global sustainable development. Indeed, the paradigm of Industry 4.0, first defined by Kagermann (2011), is significantly influencing the structure of the manufacturing industry through the establishment of smart factories, products, and services and their integration into the Internet of things (IoT) and IoT services (Stock & Seliger, 2016). A recent research (Stock et al., 2018) has highlighted that the potential for sustainable value creation in Industry 4.0 is not easy to realize because it offers not only considerable opportunities but also different threats both in a macro perspective (at the level of business models, value creation networks, and product life cycles) and a micro one (assessment of the value potential of the individual factors of industrial value creation, such as the product, process, organization, and equipment). In brief, several authors (Stock & Seliger, 2016; Stock et al., 2018) have pointed out that the potential for sustainable value creation in Industry 4.0 has yet to be investigated through further studies (Bonilla et al., 2018; Kiel et al., 2017; Muller et al., 2018).

Although there are different definitions of sustainability, which are often focused on the environmental dimension, a consensus is spreading among scholars at the international level (Hoffman & Bazerman, 2007; Sheth et al., 2011) to conceive of sustainability in three dimensions: economic, environmental, and social (Jackson, 2009). The definition of the CSR construct, which will also be adopted in this research is as follows: "a firm's commitment to maximize long-term economic, societal and environmental well-being through business practices, policies and resources" (Du et al., 2011, p. 1; Alvarado-Herrera et al., 2017). From this perspective, a manufacturer's objective of sustainability represents a triple responsibility in which the evaluation of the company's results focuses on the fusion of economic performance and environmental and social impact. This awareness seems widespread among many leading international manufacturers in various sectors, such as Nike, Unilever, Ikea, Patagonia, Adidas, Lavazza, and Illycaffè (Berens et al., 2007; Franklin, 2008; McKinsey Global Survey, 2010; WEF, 2010).

However, the emphasis placed on sustainability research from a company perspective has overlooked the perception and engagement of the consumer, which by embodying multiple stakeholder identities—e.g., citizen, employee, parent and community member— is crucial for sustainability efforts to succeed (Sheth et al., 2011).

The pursuit of sustainability increasingly depends on people's consumption choices.

Sustainable consumption—also known as ethical, responsible, and conscious consumption—generally speaking can be considered a particular form of consumption pursued by those who believe they can influence the choices of companies and brands through their purchasing and consumption decisions and, thus, contribute to the improvement of the environment and society (Cowe & Williams, 2000).

No longer the prerogative of a niche market, this transversal phenomenon identifies a new and growing sensitivity toward the ethical dimension of consumption at a geographical, cultural, and sectoral level.

This figure of the consumer-citizen, a belief-driven consumer, is willing to influence business decisions with healthy consumer decisions toward brands that respond to the call to contribute to making the world a better place by supporting relevant social causes (Kotler et al. 2017; Edelman Earned Brand, 2018). Therefore, consumer social responsibility can be understood as a type of behavior the consumer adopts in order to contribute to the achievement of sustainable development (Buerke et al., 2017, p. 961), which also complements the CSR efforts of companies. The companies' efforts to be successful must focus on constant monitoring of the consumer's actual perception of the types of CSR implemented. Only in this way can companies effectively communicate their CSR activities (Du et al., 2010), correctly inform the consumer, and reduce the skepticism among consumers that CSR is only opportunistic "greenwashing" (de Luca et al., 2017; Matthes & Wonneberger, 2014). In this perspective, information and communication technology (ICT) infrastructure and the availability of big data, which are the fundamentals of Industry 4.0, offer companies numerous opportunities to be transparent and to involve consumers—who often assume the role of employees of these industrial organizations—in sustainable industrial value creation (Stock et al., 2018).

On the contrary, an excessive focus on sustainability from a managerial perspective risks underestimating the importance of involving the customer/employee/citizen, which seriously limits both the efficiency and effectiveness of sustainability efforts (Sheth et al., 2011).

Therefore, given the limited number of studies exploring CSR from a consumer perspective and as an essential link for sustainability (Sheth et al., 2011), the main objective of this chapter is to contribute theoretically to the literature on consumer perceptions of CSR and sustainable consumption by investigating the possible relationships between them. This study combines the three-dimensional conception of CSR and the sustainability of consumption (Alvarado-Herrera et al., 2017) as two sides of the same coin; they must integrate and feed off each other in order to pursue a more sustainable industry and society (Connolly & Prothero, 1998).

This chapter is structured into two main parts. The first one illustrates the theoretical background of the importance of investigating perceptions of CSR as a three-dimensional construct (environmental, social, and economic) from the viewpoint of the consumer, and explores the crucial theme of sustainable consumption. The second part presents an empirical research that investigates the relationships between sustainable consumption of sportswear products and perceptions of the three CSR dimensions of a well-known sportswear firm that has attempted to exploit the potential of Industry 4.0 in creating industrial sustainable value. The third part of the chapter describes the findings, discusses the main results by summarizing the theoretical and managerial implications, and presents the conclusions along with suggestions for future research.

THEORETICAL BACKGROUND

Corporate Social Responsibility to Achieve Sustainability

Scholars agree that the profit logic governing the conduct of business and entrepreneurship is primarily responsible for the current unsustainable lifestyle (Porter & Kramer, 2011; Bonilla et al., 2018). Accused of promoting constant imbalances due to the excessive exploitation of both natural and human resources (Beschorner & Mueller, 2007), industrial manufacturers in particular are increasingly called upon to reduce these imbalances through more ethical and transparent behavior (Carroll, 1979; 1991; Lee & Carroll, 2011) in the joint pursuit of sustainable development (Martínez-Ferrero & García-Sánchez, 2015). These pressures have, therefore, fostered a new awareness among an increasing number of companies that has begun to promote strategies aimed at creating sustainable industrial value.

To date, there is no single definition of CSR (Dahlsrud, 2008). This is testified by the various and numerous definitions (Johnson, 1971; Frederick, 1986; Carroll, 1979; 1991) and names that have been used over time to define it—e.g., "corporate responsibility," "corporate accountability," and "corporate ethics" (European Commission, 2011; Arru & Ruggeri, 2016). The process of integrating CSR is complex and depends on several factors, such as the size of the company, its business nature, and its corporate culture. A definition of CSR that will also be useful for measuring customer perceptions of CSR's corporate activities is as follows: "a firm's commitment to maximize long-term economic, societal and environmental well-being through business practices, policies and resources (Du et al., 2011 p. 1; Alvarado-Herrera et al., 2017). In this perspective, the company's objective of sustainability should be translated into a triple responsibility, in which the evaluation of the company's results would depend on the synthesis of economic performance with its environmental and social impact.

The concept of triple responsibility was clearly explained by Elkington (1997), who defined it as a method of business management based on three specific needs: the company and its need to be profitable, which identifies economic sustainability; the environment and its need to be respected, which identifies environmental sustainability; and the society and its need for well-being, which identifies social sustainability. Following this approach, a company can only be defined as responsible if it is active on all three fronts (Fabris, 2008). This vision is rooted in a growing awareness among scholars and managers that business action goes far beyond the production of products and services and tangible and intangible benefits to include the total satisfaction of the needs of all stakeholders, both direct and secondary (Freeman, 1984). This awareness embraces the conception of the enterprise that detaches itself from a pure logic of profit to become an integral part of the social, economic, and political context in which it operates and to which it must more-or-less directly report (Johnson, 1971). Following this vision, the company assumes the social responsibility for its actions; it precisely assesses where its actions could damage social welfare, works consciously to improve itself, and anticipates the needs of the community in which it operates (Frederick, 1986; Carroll, 1991).

CSR should, therefore, be seen as a strategic orientation that is voluntarily and consciously chosen by the company so that it can take concrete action in support of major social issues. In other words, CSR becomes a sort of operational side of business ethics; it involves the implementation of the abstract principles of business ethics (Fabris, 2008). However, the CSR strategy must be developed in close collaboration with all primary and secondary stakeholders (Freeman, 1984) and implemented through ethical policies that integrate human, social, and environmental rights. The company's adoption of socially responsible practices produces benefits in terms of its corporate image and in its relationships with all stakeholder; these practices also increase the value of the company and reduce business risks (Arru & Ruggieri, 2016) by identifying such specific risks and managing them more consciously. It also improves human resource management and helps to create a stimulating working environment, which promotes increased sales. In fact, a socially responsible company improves brand value and consequently sales performance. When companies engage in CSR activities, their behavior is usually associated with better results (Sen & Bhattacharya, 2001). These results, in turn, trigger a virtuous circle by increasing the company's ability to be sustainable in the long term (Bansal & Roth, 2000).

One of the crucial aspects of CSR is that it must be communicable (Fabris, 2008). Communicating means involving both primary and secondary stakeholders in the responsible actions the company undertakes.

How companies communicate their CSR activities is a fundamental ingredient in sustainability (Bansal, 2005; Barone et al., 2000). In contrast, however, as Sobrero (2006, p. 225) stated, "[w]ithout communication, CSR cannot assume the role it should play in the conscience of those who intend to practice it, but not even in the thought of those who should benefit from it." To build lasting relationships with stakeholders, companies can communicate their CSR activities through various channels and tools, such as websites, advertising, sponsorship etc. However, communicating CSR effectively is a sensitive issue (Du et al., 2010), as stakeholders are often skeptical about it. Consumers appreciate when companies engage in CSR (Sen & Bhattacharya, 2001), but they often do not like when companies boast about their good actions (Morsing et al., 2008). The relevance of the transparency of company activities is even more evident because of the evolution toward Industry 4.0. Indeed, innovative technologies offer companies many opportunities to adequately communicate their commitment to sustainable development. At the same time, ICT and the enormous amount of data available present major challenges to companies (Stock & Seliger, 2018), which now need to meet a growing and more insistent demand for the customization of both products and messages (Muller et al., 2018).

Therefore, it is essential for managers to understand what to communicate and to provide effective messages that are perceived by customer as truthful. To communicate CSR, companies can choose to adopt a general or specific message strategy. Whereas managers may prefer a general message, consumers tend to respond more favorably to specific messages (Burton et al., 2000), as they provide more detailed information and are perceived to be more verifiable (Darley & Smith, 1993). On the contrary, general statements tend to be perceived as more ambiguous and subjective, and may negatively affect the credibility of the CSR message by different stakeholders, primarily the consumer. Its correct perception becomes essential in order to graft a virtuous circle of sustainability.

However, as mentioned above, the focus on CSR has always been from the entrepreneurial point of view, which overlooks the relevance of deepening customer perception and engagement. To fill the gap, this chapter analyses CSR from the perspective of consumer perception, by embracing the idea that CSR (Connolly & Prothero, 1998; Oberseder et al., 2014) and sustainable consumption are two sides of the same coin, and one must necessarily integrate with the other.

Sustainable Consumption and Consumer Perceptions of CSR

The adoption of sustainable behaviors—understood here as those actions that satisfy the needs of the present without compromising the ability of future generations to satisfy their own needs—is strongly determined by people's consumption choices (Brundtland, 1987; Minton et al., 2015). Currently, in more developed societies, consumption is recognized as a phenomenon that characterizes individuals' social lives more than many other phenomena (Solomon et al., 2013), so as to be considered "a cultural sphere capable of producing its own vision of the world, a system of values and a structure of peculiar personalities" (Siri, 2001, p. 13).

The sensitivity toward a greater ethical dimension in consumption originated in the niche market and now extends (Kalamas et al., 2014) across major segments of the world's population—overcoming generational, income, age, social and cultural boundaries—and across different economic sectors, including the food, transportation, construction, and fashion industries. In a world governed by confusion, as pointed out by Kotler et al. (2017), consumers are increasingly looking for shopping and consumption solutions that will appease their anxiety about making today's unjust and globalized world a better place.

The attention and interest that these customers have in what they buy today covers the entire supply chain, starting with the raw materials with which products are made and extending to the environmental and social impact of the distribution channels and the disposal of packaging (Fabris, 2008). Opposed to the traditional *consumer-customer*, the figure of the *citizen-consumer* (de Luca, 2006) is spreading—a figure who is no longer satisfied with choices based on the traditional trade-off of quality and price.

A recent international study (Edelman Earned Brand, 2018) showed how the spread of a transversal global segment called "belief-driven consumers" requires that brands, as the protagonists of the economic system, must share their values and work together to solve the planet's socio-economic and environmental problems. In this way, brands fill the gap often left by governments and institutions. Brands must respond to this call by supporting a more sustainable society and adopting and communicating their commitment to CSR. In some cases, consumer may decide to support specific categories of products and/or brands depending on the degree of approval of the company's conduct and social responsibility (Carrigan & Attalla, 2001). In this *rewarding* dimension, it is possible to recognize a predominantly ecological-environmental component and a predominantly socio-cultural component. In the first component, customers are particularly attentive to the effects of production activities, and for this reason, they favor products made from using more natural production processes (i.e., green products) and, therefore, are attentive to the problems of pollution. In the socio-cultural component, consumers can express their solidarity with curbing the loss of a cultural and social equilibrium or the loss of moral values as well as their desire for social participation (in purchasing fair trade products, typical or ethnic products). Consumers in this category can also express their criticism through "non-consumption" — that is, sanctioning those products or brands considered inconsistent with their value system through individual choices or collective ones, such as boycotts (Hogg, 1998).

Consumer social responsibility for sustainable development is, therefore, to be understood as responsible consumer behavior, which must be coordinated with the efforts of CSR to contribute to the attainment of sustainable development (Buerke et al., 2016, p. 961).

In this perspective, the difficulty for companies is to communicate CSR activities in a way that is correctly perceived by consumers.

Several authors (Brown & Dacin, 1997; Douwn van den Brink et al., 2006; Pivato et al., 2008) have shown a positive relationship between CSR activities and the propensity to buy a brand or even reward it with loyalty only if the consumer perceives the corporate commitment as authentic and long term. Consumers are becoming more critical and skeptical about the authenticity of various firm proposals regarding environmental and social causes (Rozensher, 2013), largely because some companies try to alter their image through "whitewashing," or trying to hide information that may be perceived as negative to consumers (de Luca et al., 2017; Lyon & Maxwell, 2011). For example, a company may try to use greenwashing—a specific form of whitewashing—to make themselves and their products look as though they are helping the environment even when they are not. Over time, these practices have increased consumers' suspicion that activities carried out under the umbrella of CSR may, in fact, may only be short-term opportunistic behavior, leading them, in the most extreme cases, to boycott those companies (de Luca, 2006). Indeed, the consumer, as a citizen and as a member of the community, has become skeptical toward the communication of corporate sustainability activities (Matthes & Wonneberger, 2014). Suh skepticism is a crucial aspect that sometimes causes the incoherence found in the sustainable-green consumption literature between attitudes toward sustainable products that are openly favorable and consumers' actual purchasing behaviors (Pegan & de Luca, 2012). In fact, in the face of a growing sensitivity toward sustainability in consumption, several studies have highlighted inconsistencies in purchasing behaviors and have attributed them to a range factors, including measurement problems[1] (Aizen, 2008) and ambiguous information makes it difficult to grasp the fairness of the cost-benefit ratio of sustainable products versus traditional ones (Thapa, 2010; Lorek & Vergragt, 2015). Since skepticism and a poor understanding of the sustainable information provided by companies can affect how to perceive the different components of CSR as well as the sustainable purchasing attitudes and behaviors of consumers, further research is needed to clarify the various effects of these aspects (Royne et al., 2012; Wannes & Wonneberger, 2014). So far, the literature has not explored how the CSR of a company can be measured correctly to capture the real perception of the consumer in its many dimensions (Alvarado-Herrera et al., 2017). It would also be interesting to investigate how CSR relates to sustainable purchasing attitudes and behaviors. The perception of CSR may vary depending on the interest and familiarity of consumers with the consumption of a particular category of sustainable product. Consumers may express general concern about the social impact of manufacturing activities, but they may not have yet developed clear attitudes or consistent purchasing behaviors toward specific product categories and brands. On the contrary, consumers who are more concerned about the sustainability of the consumption of a particular product may have a stricter attitude to the type of actions that a CSR-oriented company should take. The economic component may seem unrelated to the others because it concerns the company itself, whereas the social and environmental component may vary in intensity even on the basis of the sector under consideration (e.g., labour exploitation scandals in the fashion sector).

EMPIRICAL RESEARCH

Aims, Research Questions, and Method[2]

Given the importance of further understanding consumer perceptions of CSR and its relationship with the pursuit of sustainability in terms of consumption, this work integrates management literature with the following objectives. First, the research wants to understand the relationship between general environmental concerns and specific attitudes and behaviors toward a category of sustainable products. Second, it aims to deepen customer perceptions of CSR—using the multidimensional scale of Alvarado-Herrera et al. (2017)—by studying their relationship with the sustainability of consumption, measured respectively for a company and for a product category, including also skepticism, and consumer perceptions of the usefulness of sustainable advertising.

From a managerial point of view, the research aims to give useful implications to firms for the enhancement of corporate CSR activities with a view to promoting a sustainable industrial system. Specifically, the main questions that have guided the theoretical and empirical investigation are the following:

- What are the relationships between general environmental concerns, attitudes, and specific behaviors toward a category of sustainable products?
- In these relationships, does the informative utility and skepticism perceived toward sustainable advertising play a role?
- How is the consumer perception of CSR for the company X in the sportswear sector?

- What are the relationships among perceptions of a company's CSR dimensions, sustainable attitudes, and behaviors toward a particular category of sustainable product?

To answer the research questions, a quantitative analysis was developed using a structured questionnaire, focused on a specific sustainable product category (sustainable sportswear products) and on a leader company/brand of that sector.

The following are the motivations that have driven the choice of the sector and company:

- *Why the sportswear sector*: the sportswear sector was selected because, in recent years, its impact on global production and consumption has prompted both businesses and consumers to pay attention to sustainability. The global market for sportswear is booming because of more and more people participating in fitness and sports activities. The combination of sportswear and fashion is the major trend in the sportswear market. With the growing demand for fashionable and trendy sportswear, firms are investing in innovation to meet consumers' needs. Some widely known sport technologies (such as insulators, microfibers, and nanotechnologies) are no longer limited to athletes; they have also become popular among consumers interested in sports and adventure activities. Increasing consumer awareness of health and fitness in developing economies, rising per capita income, and increasing participation of women in sports and fitness activities are all driving the growth of the market, and these factors are likely to make sportswear an attractive and driving market in the coming years.[3] Environmentalists and social policy makers, however, consider the fashion industry to be ecologically harmful because it wastes natural resources (Clark, 2008; Chen & Burns, 2006). Moreover, for several years now, the sustainability of the sector has been threatened and has been affected by various scandals involving leading companies in sportswear and fashion—e.g., the production of contaminated clothing, the exploitation of workers, including the use of child labour, in factories in Cambodia,[4] and the death of 1000 workers in in Bangladesh due to poor safety standards of a clothing factory (OECOTEXTILES, 2013). To find a marketing strategy that meets consumers' needs, promotes sustainable consumption, and, thus, generates a sustainable industrial ecosystem, researchers began to analyze consumers' purchasing motives (Song & Ko, 2017). Companies in the sector now recognize sustainability as an important issue and are working hard to integrate it into their marketing strategies (Shen et al., 2014). When it comes to sustainable fashion, however, it is not easy to define, as the concept has several different nuances ranging from the term sustainable fashion to that of eco, organic, and green fashion sportwear (Cervellon et al., 2010). Companies in the sector are therefore faced with the following obstacle: many consumers who, though sensitive to the sustainable dimension, still have several doubts about both the concrete meaning of CSR and sustainable fashion sportswear due to a lack of knowledge or ineffective business communication (Kong et al., 2016).
- *Why that specific company*: The company X[5] was chosen because in addition to being one of the main players in the international sportswear market, it stands out for its commitment to all three dimensions of sustainability and for its effort to exploit potential of Industry 4.0 to create industrial sustainable value. Indeed, in recent years, the company has invested heavily in the digitization of the production process, signing among others an important agreement with a high-tech company. The agreement has resulted in the creation of fully automated production centers, where innovative technology allows the company X to create customized products that satisfy the specific needs of each customer (Randstad, 2017). Further, its reputation has been formally substantiated

through documents (such as the Sustainability Report) as well as through receiving recognition from various external organizations[6]. As mentioned above, one of the most sensitive issues for a sportwear company involved in CSR is to measure its consumers' perceptions to be able to effectively *communicable* its sustainable activities and to guide its customers toward more sustainable consumption choices.

After testing the first draft of the questionnaire on some Italian consumers, we revised it, including two theoretical definitions of sustainable consumption and sustainable sportswear products (Strong, 1996), to overcome the ambiguity of these concepts.

The questionnaire was created using Google Drive modules and had the following structure:

- **Part 1:** A short description of the meaning of sustainable consumption (Strong, 1996, p.5); generic environmental concern (adapted from Schuhwerk & Lefkoff-Hagius, 1995, pp. 47-49; Matthes & Wonneberger, 2014, p.118); skepticism toward sustainable advertising and perceptions of sustainable information usefulness (adapted from Martin & Bateman, 2014; Matthes & Wonneberger, 2014).
- **Part 2:** A short description of the meaning of sustainable sportswear products (adapted from Strong, 1996, p.5); attitudes toward sustainable sportswear products (adapted from Chang 2011; Matthes & Wonneberger, 2014, p. 118); sustainable sportswear purchasing behaviors and sportswear purchasing habits (adapted from Bruner, 2017, pp. 222–224). In this research, the aim was to measure sustainable attitudes and behaviors at the same level of abstraction[7] (sportswear products) in order to guarantee a conceptual correspondence (Ajzen, 2008; Pegan & de Luca, 2012).
- **Part 3:** Knowledge of company X; the multidimensional scale of CSR to measure consumer perception of CSR activities implemented by sportswear company X (adapted from Alvarado-Herrera et al., 2017); the frequency of purchase of sportswear products in general and of the specific brand X; the frequency of purchase of sustainable sportswear products in general and of the specific brand X; and the degree of knowledge of the most recent CSR initiative[8] communicated by the company X.
- **Part 4:** Personal data, including gender, age, nationality, educational qualifications, profession, marital status, family members, perceptions of economic status compared to peers' average, and annual income.

The final questionnaire was mailed to families and friends of Italian students of our courses in economics and management of University of Trieste (Italy), trying to ensure that the main social and demographic characteristics of the respondents were diverse. In addition, we skimmed the respondents only considering those who stated to know the sustainable company chosen to measure CSR. The sample was obtained by non-probabilistic sampling. Between August and November 2018, we collected 207 questionnaires.

Data Analysis and Results

The data collected were analyzed using SPSS Statistics, Version 24.0, and Gretl for Windows. In order to verify the reliability of the constructs, Cronbach's coefficients have been calculated. According to Hair et al. (1998), the minimum requirement for this coefficient is 0.7. In our analysis, the Cronbach's coefficients are greater than 0.7 for all the constructs. Hence, we can conclude that the measurement of this study is acceptable in terms of reliability. The main measures adopted for the research are summarized in Table 1. We used

The characteristics of the sample are briefly described. Regarding gender, the sample is 51.2% female and 48.8% male. Ages ranged from 17 to 85. The highest educational qualifications of the participants are as follows: junior high school (5%); high school (53%); bachelor's degree and master's degree (36%); and PhD (6%). The jobs carried out by the sample are many and include: teachers, entrepreneurs, students, university professors, nurses, doctors, and managers. In addition, the sample (77%) considers its economic situation, compared to its age peers, generally in the average: 17% consider itself above the average and 6% below the average. Regarding the level of family income, most people made between 29,000 and 55,000 euros per year.

Table 1. Measures

Construct/Items	Cronbach Alpha
Environmental concern (EC) (adapted from Schuhwerk & Lefkoff-Hagius 1995, pp. 47-49; Matthes & Wonneberger, 2014, p. 118) Likert 7-point scale - Please evaluate the following statements on a scale of 1 (strongly disagree) to 7 (strongly agree). • I am concerned about the environment (EC1). • The condition of the environment affects the quality of my life (EC2). • I am willing to make sacrifices to protect the environment (EC3).	0.794
Skepticism (toward) sustainable advertising (SSA) (adapted from Matthes e Wonneberger 2014, p.118) - Likert 7-point scale - Most sustainable claims in advertising are intended to mislead rather than to inform consumers (SSA1). • I do not believe most sustainable claims made in advertising (SSA2). • Because sustainable claims are exaggerated, consumers would be better off if such claims in advertising were eliminated (SSA3).	0.791
Informational utility – (IU) (adapted from Matthes & Wonneberger 2014, p.118) - Likert 7-point scale - I find most of the information in sustainable ads useful (IU1). • Sustainable ads help inform my buying decisions. (IU2). • Sustainable ads deliver the information I need for my buying decisions (IU3).	0.826
Sustainable attitudes (ASSP) (adapted for sustainable sportswear products from Chang, 2011; Matthes & Wonneberger, 2014; p. 118) - Likert 7-point scale - - I like sustainable sportswear products (ASSP1). • I feel positive toward sustainable sportswear products (ASSP2). • Sustainable sportswear products are good for the environment (ASSP3). • I feel proud when I buy and use sustainable sportswear products (ASSP4).	0.891
Sustainable behaviors sportswear products (SBSP) (adapted from Bruner, 2017, pp. 222-224) - Likert 7-point scale - • I prefer to buy sportswear products with recycled materials (SBSP1). • I prefer to buy sustainable sportswear products (SBSP2). • I have switched products for sustainable reasons (SBSP3). • When I have a choice between two equal sportswear products, I purchase the one less harmful to the environment (SBSP4).	0.874
Corporate social responsibility (Alvarado-Herrera et al., 2017, p.260) - Likert 7-point scale - In my opinion, regarding the (social impact, environment, economy) company X is really… • Social dimension (CSRsoc) • Environmental dimension (CSRenv) • Economical dimension (CSReco)	0.945 0.905 0.905

Source: Table compiled by authors

In order to answer the research questions, a number of descriptive statistical analyses were first done to provide an overview of the sample's responses in relation to the different parts of the questionnaire (Table 2). The sample in general states a high level of EC with a total average and median value of 6. Respondents are neutral about sustainable advertising, with an average of SAS of 4.3. In terms of sustainability toward sportswear products, the sample reports a moderately positive SASP with an average of 5.3, whereas SBSP achieves an even lower total average score of 4.6.

Focusing on the consumer's perception of the three components of company X's CSR (Alvarado-Herrera et al. 2017), the sample seems not to consider company X as socially responsible. In fact, CSRsoc achieved an overall average score of almost 3.9, similar to CSRenv's score of 3.9, whereas CSReco achieved a higher average score of 5.24. Regarding purchasing habits, the sample participants seem to be buyers of both sportswear products in general and sportswear products of brand X, with an average frequency score of just over 5. Compared with the frequency of purchase of the category of sustainable products of company X, the respondents are more neutral with a frequency score close to 4 (Table 2). It is also interesting to note that 95% of the respondents indicate that they are not aware of the specific CSR initiative of company X mentioned in the questionnaire (see footnote 8).

Some correlation analyses allowed to investigate the relationships between the measured constructs. For this purpose, both Spearman's and Pearson's correlation coefficient[9] were used. Since we observed that both coefficients have a similar tendency, we present only the results for the Pearson's one. First, as illustrated in Figure 1[10] the correlation analysis shows that the two groups of questions relating to SASP and SBSP are strongly and positively correlated with each other, whereas the correlation between SBSP and EC is weaker, though significant and relevant.

It is interesting to highlight the relationship between these measures and the perception of IU and SSA. As illustrated in Figure 1, the SSA is not correlated with any of the examined constructs, whereas IU has significant and medium intensity correlations with EC, SASP, and SBSP.

Table 2. Main descriptive statistics

Constructs	Average	Median
EC	6.029	6
SASP	5.321	5.5
SBSP	4.576	5
SSA	4.288	4
IU	4.327	4
CSRsoc	3.885	4
CSRenv	3.927	4
CSReco	5.250	5.5
Frequency of sportswear products' purchase	5.030	6
Frequency of sustainable products' purchase	3.47	4
Frequency of sportswear products' purchase of brand X	4.34	5
Frequency of sustainable products' purchase of brand X	3.17	3

Source: compiled by authors

Figure 1. Correlations Pearson indices
Source: authors' own figure

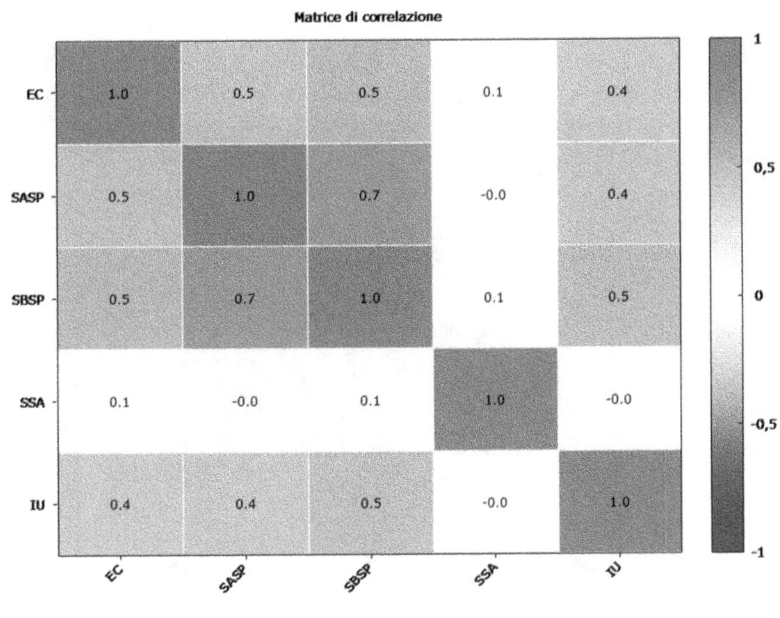

Correlation analyses were then conducted to understand how the three responsibilities underlying the CSR components of the scale (Alvarado-Herrera et al. 2017) relate to one another, with the SASP and SBSP (Figure 2) and then with the perception of IU and SSA (Figure 3). Figure 2 shows that CSRsoc is strongly correlated with CSRenv, whereas both are weakly correlated with CSReco.

The EC is not related to any of the three responsibilities of company X, whereas there are significant but weak correlations between the first two dimensions of CSR with SASP. However, there is no correlation between CSRsoc, CSRenv, and CSReco.

The correlations that emerge with SBSP are similar; there is a significantly higher intensity correlation, but not with CSReco (Figure 2).

It is interesting to note that a general interest in protecting the environment among the respondents is not linked to the perception of specific activities that must be implemented by the company to pursue CSR.

It is also important to underline the difference in the strength of the correlation between the two dimensions of CSRsoc and CSRenv, and between these and the CSReco dimension, where it is very weak. The three components of company X's CSR are not correlated with the SSA, whereas there is a significant but weak correlation between these and the perception of IU by the respondents (Figure 3).

Further correlations were made to deepen the link between the 3 components of CSR and the purchases of both the brand in general and the sustainable product category of brand X. As can be seen from Figure 4, there is a significant correlation of medium strength between CSRsoc and CSRenv of company X and the frequency of purchase of the sample sustainable sportswear product of brand X. Yet the correlations between the components and the frequency of purchase of brand X are significant but very weak. The CSReco is again not related at all to the purchase of the sustainable products of brand X, whereas there is a significant but very weak correlation with the general purchase of brand X.

A factor analysis was then carried out to investigate the actual perception of CSR by the consumers concerning how company X operates in the sportswear sector (Table 3 and 4). As can be seen, the analysis

Figure 2. Correlations Pearson indices
Source: authors' own figure

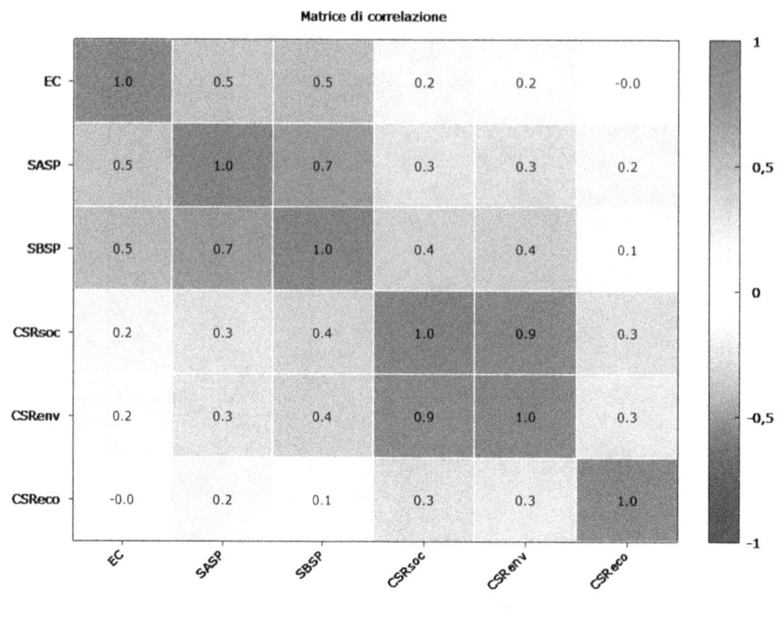

has returned two factors—the environmental-social components and the economic component—instead of three, which explains almost 75% of the variance (Table 4).

In particular, in the perception of respondents, the first factor of CSR, which explains 51.6 of the variance, merges the two original environmental-social dimensions of the scale (Herrera et al., 2017).

Figure 3. Correlations Pearson indices
Source: authors' own figure

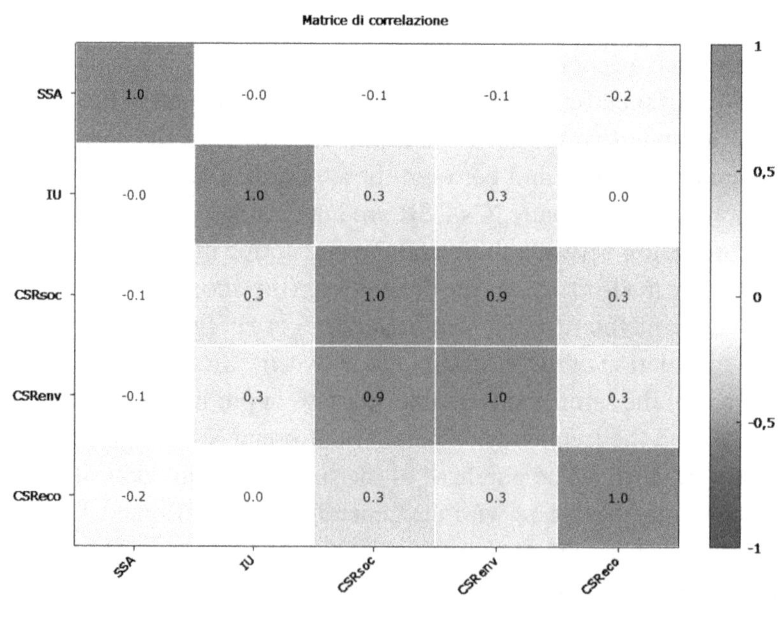

Figure 4. Correlations Pearson indices
Source: authors' own figure

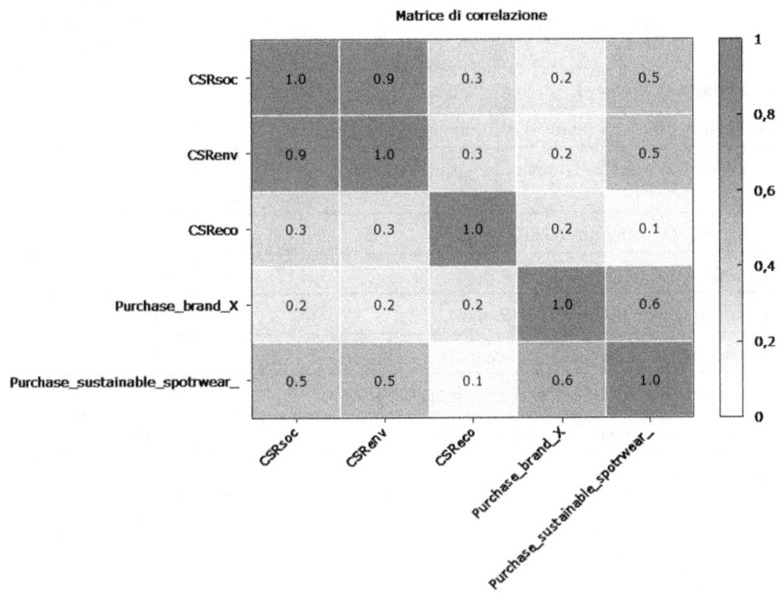

Here, the main share of variability correlates with protection and services aimed at protecting the environment with activities that promote the well-being of the local community in which the company operates (Table 4).

Other aspects that are strongly correlated to the first factor concern programs aimed at safeguarding the environment, reducing waste of resources, reducing pollution, and implementing business conducts that are attentive to ethical principles. The second factor of CSR in the perception of the sample concerns economic sustainability, which explains the 23.4 of the variance. This second factor is mainly linked to aspects of financial and productive performance of the company and to the solid long-term relationships with customers to ensure long-term economic success. It is interesting to note that the factorial analysis carried out has returned a different perception of CSR with only two components, not the three of the original scale by Alvarado-Herrera et al. (2017), which offers interesting insights for discussion.

Table 3. Factor analysis about customers' perception of CSR about company X

	Number of items	Number of factors	Percentage of explained variance	Cumulative percentage of explained variance
CSR	18	1	51,579	51,579
		2	23,374	74,953

Table 4. Factor loadings about customers' perception of CSR about company X

Items of CSR	Factor 1 Env/Social sustainability	Factor 2 Economical sustainability
… trying to protect the environment (CSRenv4).	0,915	
… trying to help to improve quality of life in the local community (SCSsoc6).	0,907	
… trying to allocate resources to offer services compatible with the environment (CSRenv2).	0,904	
…trying to sponsor pro-environmental programs (CSRenv1).	0,902	
…trying to recycle its waste materials properly (CSRenv5).	0,896	
… trying to carry out programs to reduce pollution (CSRenv3).	0,882	
…trying to use only the necessary natural resources (CSRenv6).	0,873	
…trying to be highly committed to well-defined ethical principles (CSRsoc3).	0,871	
…trying to make financial donations to social causes (CSRsoc5).	0,832	
…trying to sponsor educational programs (CSRsoc1).	0,830	
…trying to sponsor cultural programs (CSRsoc4).	0,812	
…trying to sponsor public health programs (CSRsoc2).	0,811	
… trying to always improve its financial performance (CSReco5).		0,883
… trying to do its best to be more productive (CSReco6).		0,865
… trying to build solid relations with its customers to assure its long-term economic success (CSReco2).		0,828
…trying to maximize profits in order to guarantee its continuity (CSReco1).		0,800
… trying to continuously improve the quality of the services they offer (CSReco3)		0,783
… trying to have a competitive pricing policy (CSReco4).		0,715

DISCUSSION OF THE RESULTS

These results, though not generalizable, provide several interesting insights for discussion from both a theoretical and a managerial point of view.

From a theoretical point of view, the results support the importance of studying CSR from a consumer perspective and its relationship with sustainable consumption in order to coordinate them together (Sheth et al., 2011; Alvarado-Herrera et al., 2017), adopting a product-industry specific perspective. Indeed, the results suggest that to get deeper understanding of the multi-faceted phenomenon of sustainable consumption, it is better to study the relationships between consumer attitudes and behavior and adapt them to a specific context, as in the case of sportswear.

In this regard, first of all, the fairly high value of the EC construct agrees with the trend outlined by scholars (Fabris, 2008; Minton et al., 2015; Martin & Bateman, 2014; Kotler et al., 2017) who argue that there is some sensitivity among consumers to environmental issues and consumption. At the same time, however, other data indicate that this sensitivity diminishes when one moves toward measurements of specific sustainable purchasing attitudes and behaviors. The respondents, in fact, show SASP that is only slightly positive and that is lower than the general EC; as well, the SBSP is only slightly positive. A certain neutrality of scores—or uncertainty in perceiving the level of usefulness of sustainable ads (UI) and in judging the truthfulness and credibility of sustainable information within advertising (SSA)—suggests a certain level of uncertainty. Similarly, the low frequency of purchases of sustainable sportswear products may also be due to the lack of clarity about the meaning of these produces. These results may also express a difficulty for the consumer to translate the concept of sustainability in a concrete and industry-specific context. As pointed out by Robert, what is important for marketers is "the ability to separate those who merely express concern for the environment and social issues from those who act on their concerns in the consumer marketplace" (1996, p. 97). In addition, the results seem to support what scholars of attitudes (Aizen, 2008) have expressed about the importance of measuring sustainable attitudes and behaviors at the same level of abstraction. In fact, the correlations that emerged (Figure 1) emphasize, on the one hand, a general consistency between the various constructs of sustainable consumption (EC, SASP, and SBSP), which reflect the greater attention to ethics in consumption (Fabris, 2008). But, on the other hand, it also indicates that this consistency is much more evident between SASP and SBSP (Figure 1). As evidenced in previous research in this field, by ensuring a *conceptual correspondence*, attitudes and behaviors tend to be related (Pegan & de Luca, 2012).

Regarding CSR, the results of the analysis of customer perceptions concerning company X's CSR show that even though the company was selected because of its award-winning and documented commitment to CSR, it is actually not perceived as such by the sample. Although they are buyers of the brand, respondents do not know how to assess its responsibility, as they attribute a neutral value to all CSRsoc and CSRenv items (Table 2). This difficulty, as highlighted above, could be an expression of a lack of consumer knowledge and confusion due to too many ambiguous definitions of sustainable fashion-sportswear, which then hinder the effective implementation of CSR activities of sportswear companies (Kong et al., 2016). The analysis of the correlations has highlighted how there is a significant correlation and quite high strength (Figure 4) between CSRsoc and CSRenv and the propensity to buy sustainable products of the specific company X. The CSReco one is as seen unrelated and not related to purchases of the brand. The results also show that while Alvarado-Herrera et al. (2017) scale confirms its reliability, factor analysis has returned a slightly different perception of respondents with respect to CSR, consisting of only two factors: in the first, CSRsoc and CSRenv merge together, whereas the second identifies CSReco. This result suggests the need not only to capture the real conception that consumers can have of the very concept of CSR, but also to educate them about what triple corporate responsibility should mean so that they can reward businesses with their purchasing choices.

Focusing on the managerial implications, the company analyzed, which—thanks to significant investments in digitalization integrated into its production processes—aims to make Industry 4.0 real, shows that a formal and certified CSR commitment does not guarantee that this is actually perceived by consumers. These results emphasize the strategic importance of monitoring how the company's CRS activities are perceived by the consumers so that company's efforts are effective for the purposes of sustainability. Only in this way will manufacturers be able to exploit the potential of innovative technologies offered by Industry 4.0, by adapting specifically (Burton et al., 2000) to the sectoral context in which they operate. Otherwise, there is a risk that the CSR commitment of companies, as it seems to be the case for the company analyzed, will be partially offset by an erroneous consumer perception of their CSR.

Consumers in their multiple capacities—as citizens, parents, and local community members—are the main actors to either create or destroy a sustainable industrial system (Sheth et al., 2011; Sobrero 2006). Only by constantly monitoring its perception will companies be able to make the most of their efforts and implement corrective actions where necessary (Fredrick, 1986; Carroll, 1991). In order to promote economic sustainability and, thus, increase the competitiveness of the company, it will also be important to be able to communicate CSReco, which is not yet perceived by the consumer to be clearly linked to the concept of CSR. Managers must, therefore, consider that only if the triple responsibility of CSR is enhanced—with specific and exhaustive messages (Burton et al., 2000) capable of simplifying the sustainable purchasing choices of the main beneficiary of the supply chain—can a virtuous circle of sustainability be set in motion. Indeed, consumer social responsibility for sustainable development is to be understood as responsible consumer behavior, which must be coordinated with the efforts of CSR to contribute to attaining sustainable development (Buerke et al., 2016; Connolly & Prothero, 1998)

CONCLUSION AND FUTURE RESEARCH DIRECTIONS

The evolution of production and industrial processes known as Industry 4.0 and the diffusion of its innovative technologies, such as IoT and big data analytics, not only offer new opportunities for sustainable industrial development but also bring with them new challenges for companies (Bonilla et al., 2018; Muller et al., 2018). To satisfy their stakeholders, industries—today considered the main actors in the pursuit of global sustainable development—must rethink their value creation processes from a sustainable perspective by pursuing the well-being of society in the long term (Kotler et al., 2012; Stock & Seliger, 2016; Stock et al., 2018).

Not only as citizens and members of a community but also as employees and parents, consumers increasingly demand customized and healthy products that respect the social and natural environment, and help them make society—which is perceived as unjust—a better place to live in (Kotler et al., 2017). Therefore, the consumer is the main stakeholder to be monitored and satisfied in order to develop a virtuous circle, optimizing the CSR activities implemented by companies (Sheth et al., 2011). CSR, defined as "a company's commitment to maximize long-term economic, social and environmental well-being through business practices, policies and resources" (Alvarado-Herrera et al., 2017; Du et al., 2011, p. 1), indicates that a company has a triple responsibility and that the evaluation of business results must be based on the fusion of economic performance with environmental and social impact (Elkington, 1997).

However, if CSR studies neglect the tasks of measuring and monitoring the market's perception of sustainability industries' commitment, which is what has happened thus far, such a commitment risks being partly wasted or, worse, not implemented (Sheth et al., 2011). The market increasingly calls into question industries and brands, which are considered definitively responsible for sustainable development. If industries respond to this call, citizen-consumers are willing to reward them, thus creating a virtuous circle in which CSR and sustainable consumption become two sides of the same coin.

Our contribution, focusing on a particular industrial context, the sportswear industry, and on a specific company X, an international leader in the sportswear sector, supports the idea that the challenge of sustainability is demanding. The company analyzed, which—thanks to significant investments in digitalization integrated into its production processes—aims to make Industry 4.0 increasingly real, shows that a formal and certified CSR commitment does not guarantee that this is actually perceived by consumers. The perceptual distortion by the final market can concern the meaning that a sustainable industrial value assumes in a specific industrial context (sportswear industry) for a particular category of products (sustainable sportswear product). The effort of the industrial manufacturer X to create sustainable value, exploiting the technological potential of Industry 4.0 incorporated in its production processes, risks being partially undermined unless it is correctly communicated to the main stakeholder. This distortion can hinder the spread of sustainable purchasing and consumption choices, negatively affecting economic performance and demotivating the factory in its efforts to identify sources of sustainable industrial value creation.

Given the relevance of the topic from both a theoretical and a managerial point of view, it is necessary to continue to make further research efforts to overcome the main limitations of this research. First of all, it would be appropriate to replicate the research and involve a more representative sample of brand X buyers, also to include heavy users of brand X to better understand the relationship between the perception of CSR and brand loyalty. From this point of view, it could also be interesting to compare the same sector and the same company in other geographical markets where the company operates. Furthermore, the issue of trust in CSR information given to companies should be explored using other concepts (other than IU and SSA) that capture the assessments of innovative communication technologies used. The opportunity to measure sustainable consumption and the perception of the company's CSR, while maintaining a *conceptual* correspondence as much as possible (Aizen, 2008), that more studies should be done to study the relationships between these phenomena in other sectors and for other companies and organizations. In this way, relevant and useful suggestions could also emerge for institutions and organizations involved in the promotion of sustainability in order to disseminate sustainable industrial systems in an integrated way.

Moreover, adopting the micro perspective in the assessment of the potential for sustainability offered by Industry 4.0 (Stock & Seliger, 2016; Stock et al., 2018), it would be useful to include a specific indicator that takes into account the real perception consumers have of the sustainable value creation of the specific industry. Such an indicator should be included for all three ecological, social, and economic dimensions of CSR.

REFERENCES

Ajzen, I. (2008). Consumer attitudes and behavior. In C. P. Haugtvedt, P. M. Herr, & F. R. Kardes (Eds.), *Handbook of consumer psychology*. New York, NY: Taylor and Francis Group.

Alvarado-Herrera, A., Bigne, E., Aldas-Manzano, J., & Curras-Perez, R. (2017). A scale for measuring consumer perceptions of corporate social responsibility following the sustainable development paradigm. *Journal of Business Ethics, 140*(2), 243–262. doi:10.100710551-015-2654-9

Arru, B. & Ruggieri, M. (2016). I benefici della Corporate Social Responsibility nella creazione di valore sostenibile: il ruolo delle risorse di competenza e del capitale reputazionale. *Economia aziendale online*, 17-41.

Bansal, P. (2005). Envolving sustainable: A longitudinal study of corporate sustainable development. *Strategic Management Journal, 26*(3), 197–218. doi:10.1002mj.441

Bansal, P., & Roth, K. (2000). Why companies go green: A model of ecological responsiveness. *Academy of Management Journal*, 717–736.

Barone, M. J., Miyazaki, A. D., & Taylor, K. A. (2000). The influence of cause-related marketing on consumer choice: Does one good turn deserve another? *Journal of the Academy of Marketing Science, 28*(2), 248–262. doi:10.1177/0092070300282006

Berens, G., Van Riel, C., & van Rekom, J. (2007). The CSR-quality trade-off: When can corporate social responsibility and corporate ability compensate each other? *Journal of Business Ethics*, *74*(3), 233–252. doi:10.100710551-006-9232-0

Bonilla, S. H., Silva, H. R. O., Terra da Silva, M., Franco Gonçalves, R., & Sacomano, J. (2018). Industry 4.0 and sustainability implications: a scenario-based analysis of the impacts and challenges. *Sustainability*, *10*(10), 3740. doi:10.3390u10103740

Brown, T. J., & Dacin, P. A. (1997). The company and the product: Corporate associations and consumer product responses. *Journal of Marketing*, *61*(1), 68–84. doi:10.1177/002224299706100106

Bruner, G. C. (2017). *Marketing scales handbook: multi-item measures for consumer insight research* (Vol. 9). GCBII Productions.

Buerke, A., Straatmann, T., Lin-Hi, N., & Müller, K. (2017). Consumer awareness and sustainability-focused value orientation as motivating factors of responsible consumer behavior. [October.]. *Review of Managerial Science, Springer*, *11*(4), 959–991. doi:10.100711846-016-0211-2

Burton, S., Andrews, J. C., & Netemeyer, R. G. (2000). Nutrition ad claims and disclosures: Interaction and mediation effects for consumer evaluations of the brand and the ad. *Marketing Letters*, *11*(3), 235–247. doi:10.1023/A:1008187110096

Carroll, A. B. (1979). A three-dimensional conceptual model of corporate social performance. *Academy of Management Review*, *4*(4), 497–505. doi:10.5465/amr.1979.4498296

Carroll, A. B. (1991). The pyramid of corporate social responsibility: Toward the moral management of organizational stakeholders. *Business Horizons*, *34*(4), 39–48. doi:10.1016/0007-6813(91)90005-G

Cervellon, M., Hjerth, H., & Ricard, S. (2010). Green in fashion? An exploratory study of national differences in consumers concern for eco-fashion. *Proceedings of 9th International Marketing Trends Conference*, Venice, Italy, Jan. 20-21.

Chang, C. (2011). Feeling ambivalent about going green. *Journal of Advertising*, *40*(4), 19–32. doi:10.2753/JOA0091-3367400402

Chen, H., & Burns, D. (2006). Environmental analysis of textile products. *Clothing & Textiles Research Journal*, *24*(3), 248–261. doi:10.1177/0887302X06293065

Connolly, J., & Prothero, A. (1998). Sustainable consumption: Consumption, consumers and the commodity discourse. *Consumption Markets & Culture*, *6*(4), 275–291. doi:10.1080/1025386032000168311

Cowe, R., & Williams, S. (2000). *Who are the ethical consumers?* London, UK: The Cooperative Bank.

Dahlsrud, A. (2008). How corporate social responsibility is defined: An analysis of 37 definitions. *Corporate Social Responsibility and Environmental Management*, *15*(1), 1–13. doi:10.1002/csr.132

Darley, W. K., & Smith, R. E. (1993). Advertising claim objectivity: Antecedents and effects. *Journal of Marketing*, *57*(4), 100–113. doi:10.1177/002224299305700408 de Luca, P. (2006). Critical consumption: An exploratory research on the social dimension of consumer behaviour. *Proceedings of the International Congress "Marketing Trends,"* Ca' Foscari University, Venice, Italy.

de Luca, P., Schoier, B., & Vessio, A. (2017). Cause-related marketing and trust: Empirical evidence on pinkwashing. *Markets and Competitiveness*, *2*, 49–71.

Du, S., Bhattacharya, C. B., & Sen, S. (2010). Maximizing business returns to corporate social responsibility (CSR): The role of CSR communication. *International Journal of Management Reviews*, *12*(1), 8–19. doi:10.1111/j.1468-2370.2009.00276.x

Du, S., Bhattacharya, C. B., & Sen, S. (2011). Corporate social responsibility and competitive advantage: Overcoming the trust barrier. *Management Science*, *57*(9), 1528–1545. doi:10.1287/mnsc.1110.1403

Edelman Earned Brand. (2018). Brand take a stand. Retrieved from https://www.edelman.com/sites/g/files/aatuss191/files/2018-10/2018_Edelman_Earned_Brand_Global_Report.pdf

Elkington, J. (1997). *Cannibals with forks - Triple bottom line of 21st century business.* Stoney Creek, CT: New Society Publishers.

European Commission. (2011). Green Paper - Promoting a European framework for corporate social responsibility, Brussels European Commission. Renewed EU strategy for 2011-14 on corporate social responsibility. Brussels, Belgium.

Fabris, G. P. (2008). *Societing*. Milan, Italy: Egea.

Franklin, D. (2008). Just good business: A special report of corporate social responsibility. *The Economist*, Jan. 19.

Frederick, C. W. (1986). Towards CSR: Why ethical analysis is indispensable and unavoidable in Corporate affairs. *California Management Review*, *28*(2), 126–141. doi:10.2307/41165190

Freeman, R. E. (1984). *Strategic management: A stakeholder approach.* Boston, MA: Pitman.

Hair, J. F. H., Black, W. C., Babin, J. B., & Anderson, R. E. (1998). *Multivariate data analysis with readings. Englewood Cliffs, NJ: Prentice-Hall .*

Hoffman, A. J., & Bazerman, M. H. (2007). Changing practice on sustainability: Understanding and overcoming the organizational and psychological barriers to action. In S. Sharma, M. Starik, & B. Husted (Eds.), *Organizations and the sustainability mosaic: Crafting long-term ecological and societal solutions*. Northampton, MA: Edward Elgar. doi:10.4337/9781847205544.00012

Hogg, M. K. (1998). Anti-constellations: Exploring the impact of negation on consumption. *Journal of Marketing Management*, *14*(1-3), 1–3. doi:10.1362/026725798784959354

Jackson, T. (2009). *Prosperity without growth: Economics for a finite planet.* London, UK: Earthscan. doi:10.4324/9781849774338

Johnson, H. L. (1971). *Business in contemporary society: Framework and issues.* Belmont, CA: Wadsworth.

Kagermann, H., & Lukas, W. D. (2011). *Industrie 4.0.* VDI, Nachrichten.

Kalamas, M., Cleveland, M., & Laroche, M. (2014). Pro-environmental behaviors for thee but not for me: Green giants, green Gods, and external environmental locus of control. *Journal of Business Research, 67*(2), 12–22. doi:10.1016/j.jbusres.2013.03.007

Kiel, D., Müller, J. M., Arnold, C., & Voigt, K. I. (2017). Sustainable industrial value creation: Benefits and challenges of industry 4.0. *International Journal of Innovation Management, 21*(08). doi:10.1142/S1363919617400151

Kong, H. M., Ko, E., Chae, H., & Mattila, P. (2016). Understanding fashion consumers' attitude and behavioral intention toward sustainable fashion products: Focus on sustainable knowledge sources and knowledge types. *Journal of Global Fashion Marketing, 7*(2), 103–119. doi:10.1080/20932685.2015.1131435

Kotler, P., Kartajaya, H., & Setiawan, I. (2017). *Marketing 4.0.* Milano, Italy: Hoepli.

Kotler, P., Keller, K. L., Ancarani, F., & Costabile, M. (2012). *Marketing management.* Milan, Italy: Pearson.

Lee, S. Y., & Carroll, C. E. (2011). The emergence, variation, and evolution of corporate social responsibility in the public sphere 1980-2004: The exposure of firms to public debate. *Journal of Business Ethics, 104*(1), 115–131. doi:10.100710551-011-0893-y

Lorek, S. & Vergragt, P. (2015). Sustainable consumption as a systemic challenge: Inter- and transdisciplinary research and research questions. In L. Middlemiss (Ed.), Sustainable Consumption: Key Issues. UK: Routledge.

Lyon, T. P., & Maxwell, J. W. (2011). Greenwash: Corporate environmental disclosure under threat of audit. *Journal of Economics & Management Strategy, 20*(1), 3–41. doi:10.1111/j.1530-9134.2010.00282.x

Martin, W. C., & Bateman, C. R. (2014). Consumer religious commitment's influence on ecocentric attitudes and behavior. *Journal of Business Research, 67*(2), 5–11. doi:10.1016/j.jbusres.2013.03.006

Martínez-Ferrero, J., & García-Sánchez, I. (2015). Is corporate social responsibility an entrenchment strategy? Evidence in stakeholder protection environments. *RMS Rev Manag Sci, 9*(1), 89–114.

Matthes, J., & Wonneberger, A. (2014). The skeptical green consumer revisited: Testing the relationship between green consumerism and skepticism toward advertising. *Journal of Advertising, 43*(2), 115–127. doi:10.1080/00913367.2013.834804

McKinsey Global Survey. (2010). How companies manage sustainability. McKinsey & Co. Retrieved from https://www.mckinseyquarterly.com/

Minton, E., Kim, C. H., & Khale, L. R. (2015). Religion and motives for sustainable behaviors: A cross-cultural comparison and contrast. *Journal of Business Research, 68*(9), 1–8. doi:10.1016/j.jbusres.2015.01.003

Morsing, M., Schultz, M., & Nielsen, K. U. (2008). The 'catch 22' of communicating CSR: Findings from a Danish study. *Journal of Marketing Communications, 14*(2), 97–111. doi:10.1080/13527260701856608

Müller, J. M., Kiel, D., & Voigt, K. I. (2018). What drives the implementation of industry 4.0? The role of opportunities and challenges in the context of sustainability. *Sustainability*, *10*(1), 247. doi:10.3390u10010247

Oberseder, M., Schlegelmilch, B. B., Murphy, P. E., & Gruber, V. (2014). Consumers' perceptions of corporate social responsibility: Scale development and validation. *Journal of Business Ethics*, 1–15.

OECOTEXTILES. (2013). True cost of fast fashion. Retrieved from https:// oecotextiles.wordpress.com/2013/08/29/true-cost-of-fast-fashion/

Pegan, G., & de Luca, P. (2012). Can implicit and explicit attitudes predict green product choice under time pressure? An experimental research. *Journal of Management and World Business Research*, *9*, 21–36.

Pivato, S., Misani, N., & Tencati, A. (2008). The impact of corporate social responsibility on consumer trust: The case of organic food. *Business Ethics (Oxford, England)*, 3–12.

Porter, M. E., & Kramer, M. R. (2011). Creating shared value: How to reinvent capitalism - and unleash a wave of innovation and growth. *Harvard Business Review*, *89*(1/2), 62–77.

Decision Processes, 5, 179–211.

Randstad. (2017). Smart manufacturing: grazie a siemens, adidas realizza l'industry 4.0. May 30, 2017. Retrieved from https://www.randstad.it/knowledge360/news-aziende/smart-manufacturing-grazie-a-siemens-adidas-realizza-lindustry-40/

BReport. (1987). Retrieved from https://www.are.admin.ch/are/it/home/sviluppo-sostenibile/cooperazione-internazionale/l_agenda-2030-per-uno-sviluppo-sostenibile/onu-le-pietre-miliari-dello-sviluppo-sostenibile/1987--rapporto-brundtland.html

Roberts, J. A. (1996). Green consumers in the 1990s: Profile and implications for advertising. *Journal of Business Research*, *36*(3), 217–231. doi:10.1016/0148-2963(95)00150-6

Royne, M. B., Martinez, M., Oakley, J., & Fox, A. K. (2012). The effectiveness of benefit type and price endings in green advertising. *Journal of Advertising*, *41*(4), 85–102. doi:10.1080/00913367.2012.10672459

Rozensher, S. (2013). The growth of cause marketing: past, current, and future trends. [JBER]. *Journal of Business & Economics Research*, *11*(4), 181–186. doi:10.19030/jber.v11i4.7746

Schuhwerk, M. E., & Lefkoff-Hagius, R. (1995). Green or non-green? Does type of appeal matter when advertising a green product? *Journal of Advertising*, *24*(2), 45–54. doi:10.1080/00913367.1995.10673475

Sen, S., & Bhattacharya, C. (2001). Does doing good always lead to doing better? Consumer reactions to corporate social responsibility. *Journal of Marketing Research*, *38*(2), 225–243. doi:10.1509/jmkr.38.2.225.18838

Shen, B., Zheng, J. H., Chow, P. Z., & Chow, K. Y. (2014). Perception of fashion sustainability in online community. *Journal of the Textile Institute*, *105*(9), 971–979. doi:10.1080/00405000.2013.866334

Sheth, J. N., Sethia, N. K., & Srinivas, S. (2011). Mindful consumption: A customer-centric approach to sustainability. *Journal of the Academy of Marketing Science*, *39*(1), 21–39. doi:10.100711747-010-0216-3

Siri, G. (2001). *La psiche del consumo. Consumatori, desiderio e identità*. Milano, Italy: Franco Angeli.

Sobrero, R. (2016). *Comunicazione e sostenibilità*. Milano, Italy: Egea.

Solomon, M. R., Bamossy, G. J., Askegaard, S. T., & Hogg, M. K. (2013). *Consumer behaviour - A European perspective* (5th ed.). Harlow, UK: Pearson Education.

Song, S., & Ko, E. (2017). Perceptions, attitudes, and behaviors toward sustainable fashion: Application of Q and Q-R methodologies. *International Journal of Consumer Studies, 41*(3), 264–273. doi:10.1111/ijcs.12335

Stock, T., Obenaus, M., Kunz, S., & Kohl, H. (2018). Industry 4.0 as enabler for a sustainable development: A qualitative assessment of its ecological and social potential. *Process Safety and Environmental Protection, 118*, 254–267. doi:10.1016/j.psep.2018.06.026

Stock, T., & Seliger, G. (2016). Opportunities of sustainable manufacturing in industry 4.0. *Procedia Cirp, 40*, 536–541. doi:10.1016/j.procir.2016.01.129

Strong, C. (1996). Features contributing to the growth of ethical consumerism – a preliminary investigation. *Marketing Intelligence & Planning, 14*(5), 5–13. doi:10.1108/02634509610127518

Thapa, B. (2010). The mediation effect of outdoor recreation participation on environmental attitude–behavior correspondence. *The Journal of Environmental Education, 41*(3), 133–150. doi:10.1080/00958960903439989

van den Brink, D., Odekerken-Schröder, G., & Pauwels, P. (2006). The effect of strategic and tactical cause-related marketing on consumers' brand loyalty. *Journal of Consumer Marketing, 23*(1), 15–2. doi:10.1108/07363760610641127

WEF. (2010). *Redesigning business value: A road map for sustainable consumption.* Geneva, Switzerland: World Economic Forum.

Zani, S., & Cerioli, A. (2007). *Data analysis and data mining for business decisions.* Milan, Italy: Giuffrè Publisher.

ADDITIONAL READING

Kotler, P., Kartajaya, H., & Setiawan, I. (2010). *Marketing 3.0: From Products to Customers to the Human Spirit.* New Delhi: Times Group Books. doi:10.1002/9781118257883

Oberseder, M., Schlegelmilch, B. B., Murphy, P. E., & Gruber, V. (2014). Consumers' perceptions of corporate social responsibility: Scale development and validation. *Journal of Business Ethics*, 1–15.

Peloza, J., & Shang, J. (2011). How can corporate social responsibility activities create value for stakeholders? A systematic review. *Journal of the Academy of Marketing Science, 39*(1), 117–135. doi:10.100711747-010-0213-6

KEY TERMS AND DEFINITIONS

Corporate Social Responsibility: The triple responsibility that a company must fulfil to meet the economic, environmental and social expectations of its stakeholders.

Sportswear Sector: Set of sportswear products (skirts, hats, Underwear and Upper clothing).

Sustainable Consumption: Is the consumption of products/services (brands) that have a minimal impact on the environment, are socially equitable and economically sustainable.

ENDNOTES

1 See footnote 7.

2 This paragraph was written with the contribution of Alberto Giacometti.

3 Obermeyer, Nike, Montbell, Adidas, Volcom, UNDER ARMOUR, Burton, Puma, THE NORTH FACE, Columbia,
Marmot, ASICS, and Patagonia are the leading players in the sportswear market. February 26, 2019, Source: QY Research, retrieved from https://www.globenewswire.com/news-release/2019/02/27/1743035/0/en/Sportswear-Industry-Global-Market-to-reach-US-108-7-Bn-by-the-end-of-2025-QY-Research-Inc.html

4 Retrieved from https://www.corriere.it/esteri/17_June_25/cambodia-selvents-mass-factories-nike-dell-asics-12b7d082-5982-11e7-8109-77a9e9fc44b1.shtml; https://www.theguardian.com/business/2017/jun/25/female-cambodian-garment-workers-mass-fainting; https://www.greenme.it/vivere/lavoro-e-ufficio/7552-6-multinazionali-coinvolte-nello-schiavismo-e-nello-sfruttamento-del-lavoro-minorile

5 The name of the firm is omitted for privacy reasons.

6 For example, in 2015, company X was awarded for being one of top three most sustainable companies on the planet, according to Corporate Knight's Global 100 Index research, and in 2016 it was ranked sixth.

7 The low attitude-behavior consistency found in sustainable consumer behavior studies could be because general environmental concern has been used to predict specific purchase decisions of sustainable products instead of using attitudes toward specific products (Aizen, 2008).

8 In the questionnaire, a specific question was asked to measure if the respondent knew the name of specific company initiative related to the production of sportswear products using plastic collected from the ocean.

9 According to statistical literature, variables measured using Likert scale have to be considered as measured in an "ordinal scale". Therefore, Spearman's correlation coefficients are more appropriate. However, as used in market research (Zani & Cerioli, 2007, p.55), we assume the equidistance criterion among the categories of answers and we consider the means of the answers.

Chapter 12
The Effect of Packaging Material on Consumer Evaluation and Choice:
A Comparison Between Glass and Tetra-Pak in the Olive Oil Sector

Beatrice Luceri
University of Parma, Italy

Donata Tania Vergura
University of Parma, Italy

Cristina Zerbini
University of Parma, Italy

ABSTRACT

Packaging is the last marketing communication tool a company can use before the purchase decision is made. It creates positive or negative brand associations and informs consumers about the product category, personality, and quality. This chapter explains the role of packaging material in influencing the product evaluation process. Specifically, a between-subjects experimental design was conducted to investigate if the product quality judgment and the purchase intention towards extra virgin olive oil differ between tetra-pak and glass bottle. Results showed attitude towards the product, pack and product evaluation, and perceived quality and risk was better in the case of the glass package compared to the tetra-pak. Similarly, the willingness to buy and pay was higher in the case of the glass package compared to the tetra-pak one.

DOI: 10.4018/978-1-7998-1419-1.ch012

INTRODUCTION

In today's increasingly competitive marketplace, packaging represents one of the most important factors in the buying decision process. From the consumers' perspective, it is an important source of information at the point of sale. Its overall features can underline the quality and the uniqueness of the product and, then, influence the purchasing decisions (Silayoi and Speece, 2007; Stewart, 2004). As a consequence, from the manufacturers' standpoint packaging becomes an essential part of the selling strategy, providing the last opportunity to persuade possible buyers before brand selection (e.g., McDaniel and Baker, 1977; Prendergast and Pitt, 1996; Rettie and Brewer, 2000; Silayoi and Speece, 2004).

Starting from these evidences, some authors have defined the packaging as an intrinsic property of the product and the brand, which influences brand recognition, creates positive or negative brand associations and informs consumers about the product category, personality and quality (e.g., Evans and Berman, 1992; Keller, 2009; Orth and Malkewitz, 2008; Silayoi and Speece, 2007). In this perspective, packaging assumes a role similar to other marketing tools, becoming a vehicle for communication and branding (Rettie and Brewer, 2000). This makes choices on the communication elements of the package strategic marketing and positioning decisions. With this premise in mind, a clear understanding of the impact of the package elements is crucial to enhance point of purchase communication and support the selling strategy (Vergura and Luceri, 2018).

A central stream within the marketing research concerns the impact of visual and verbal elements of packaging in the product selection process. Visual elements include colour, shape, material, size and graphics, while verbal elements include information like ingredients, nutritional value, and country of origin. Several authors found that both visual and verbal elements could have a powerful effect on consumers' responses to a product and can influence the purchasing decision (e.g., Andrews et al., 2013; Aschemann-Witzel and Hamm, 2010; Faulkner et al., 2014; Garretson & Burton, 2000; Gorton et al., 2010; Hoegg and Alba, 2011; Hogg et al., 2010; Liaukonyte et al., 2013; Raghubir and Greenleaf, 2006; Saba et al., 2010; Schoormans and Robben, 1997; Silayoi and Speece, 2004; Tan and Tan, 2007; Underwood et al., 2001; Underwood and Klein, 2002; Wansink and Chandon, 2006).

Most of the evidence regarding the cognitive processes induced by different packaging cues focuses principally on elements like colour, shape, graphics (e.g., product imagery) and nutritional claims. A limited marketing research has been conducted about the crucial role of packaging material in consumer evaluation process (Holliwood et al., 2013; Adam and Ali, 2014; Kariyawasam et al., 2006) and most of the existing knowledge focused on the sustainability of materials (e.g., Barber, 2010; Magnier and Schoormans, 2015; Magnier et al., 2016; Marthino et al., 2015). This study aims to fill this gap investigating the impact of two different packaging materials on consumers' perception (measured in terms of product evaluation, perceived quality and perceived risk) and buying intention. To this end, tetra-pak and glass were chosen given their widely use in the food storage. As glass has long been used in the food industry mainly for its impermeability to external contaminants and non-interactivity with foods and drinks, the widespread diffusion of tetra-pak is due to two principal reasons: its environmental sustainability and its characteristics of efficiency, safety and lightness. Only two studies, focused on the milk category, investigated the consumer reaction towards the tetra-pak (Adam and Ali, 2014; Kariyawasam et al., 2006). Shifting the focus on olive oil, the present research aims to enrich the literature on the effect of package material on the consumers' product evaluation. The country under investigation is Italy where olive oil is an essential component of the daily diet. However, its importance is not limited to this country as its use as ingredient for cooking is becoming increasingly widespread in many parts of the world. The market success of olive oil makes it very interesting to explore the consumers' perceptions and evaluation towards different packaging materials. Nevertheless, this product category and the comparison of packaging materials have been neglected by in previous literature. That being stated, a quantitative research (structured questionnaire) with olive oil Italian consumers was conducted in order to investigate if and how tetra-pak and glass differ in terms of consumer perception and behavioural (purchase) intentions towards the product.

The chapter is structured as follows. The next section introduces the research context. Then, the theoretical background is reviewed and the research question formulated. The next two sections present the methodology used for the study and the results. Finally, conclusion and managerial implications are discussed and suggestion for future research are highlighted.

Research Context: Olive Oil Industry in Italy

In the last 25 years, the global olive oil consumption has grown by 49%. This is due to the spread of the Mediterranean Diet, which was declared a World Heritage Site by UNESCO. In 2017, the global consumption of olive oil amounted to 2.95 billion kilos and about 50% was consumed in European Union countries. Among these, Italy stands out with 557 million kilos, followed by Spain (Coldiretti, 2018). In Italy, 9 families out of 10 consume olive oil (especially extra virgin olive oil) every day. This makes it is an essential component of the shopping basket of Italian consumers.

In the country under investigation, olive oil is traditionally sold to the final consumer in glass bottles (60%) or in tin containers (30%). Only recently some manufacturers started to use tetra-pak bottles. This choice is driven not only by environmental reasons but also by the evidence that this material helps to preserve the organoleptic properties of the oil. Not being transparent, it slows down the oxidative degradation of the oil, which instead is accelerated by the light penetration. Oxidation caused by light leads to a loss of some substances of which the olive oil, especially extra virgin oil, is rich, namely polyphenols and vitamins. Furthermore, some studies have shown the good performance of tetra-pak in preserving the sensory properties of the product. Nevertheless, since consumers are not used to buy olive oil packaged in tetra-pak, it is interesting to investigate their perception towards this material, compared to the more traditional glass. In so doing, the present research contributes to the understanding of the ability of this visual element of packaging in influencing the product quality judgment and the purchase intention.

Theoretical Background and Research Question

Traditionally, the main role of the packaging is to protect the product and transport it to the end consumer safely preserving its quality and integrity (against potential damage from climatic, bacteriological and transit hazards). However, in today's crowded marketplace, the packaging also covers more strategic functions (Rundh, 2005). Packaging helps create an overall product perception and promise, and is an important factor in brand recognition and in forming positive brand associations (George, 2005; Keller, 2009; Underwood, 1998). Moreover, it is able to get consumer attention at the point of purchase and to persuade them to buy the product (Rundh, 2005). Pilditch (1957) first defined the packaging as the "silent salesman" and Lewis (1991) added that "good packaging is far more than a salesman, it is a flag of recognition and a symbol of values". In the consumer's minds, the product and package are one and the same: the packaging coincides with the product until the product is consumed and the package is disposed of, reused, or recycled (George, 2005). That's why companies often try to differentiate their products from other offerings in the category leveraging on the packaging features (e.g., structures, shapes, openings, descriptors and colours).

Since packaging has become an important marketing tool for many consumer products, several studies have been conducted on its communicative role. Some authors have suggested that packaging attributes can be classified as verbal and visual cues. Visual cues include colour, design, material, shape, size and graphics. Verbal cues include nutritional information, product information and country of origin. Both visual and verbal elements, communicating favourable or unfavourable implied meaning about the product, are found to be able to attract consumers' attention, set expectations for the product content and influence the decision making process (e.g., Andrews et al., 2013; Aschemann-Witzel and Hamm, 2010; Faulkner et al., 2014; Garretson and Burton, 2000; Gorton et al., 2010; Hoegg and Alba, 2011; Hogg et al., 2010; Liaukonyte et al., 2013; Raghubir and Greenleaf, 2006; Saba et al., 2010; Schoormans and Robben, 1997; Silayoi and Speece, 2004; 2007; Tan and Tan, 2007; Underwood et al., 2001; Underwood and Klein, 2002; Wansink and Chandon, 2006).

Despite the great interest on the effect of various visual and verbal elements of packaging on the consumer response to the product, the many evidence concerns packaging cues like colour, shape, size, graphics, and nutritional information. On the contrary, research into the consumer's perception and evaluation of packaging material is still limited (Holliwood et al., 2013; Adam and Ali, 2014; Kariyawasam et al., 2006).

Technological development has contributed to the enlargement of new materials and to the combination of materials with better properties (Rundh, 2009). This has brought new opportunities for the development of many new packaging products that can ensure greater convenience, functionality, and food safety. Beyond the type of material, one such trend is the ability to introduce transparency into a wide range of product packaging. In order to investigate the impact of seeing the food/drink within the package, various authors provide some insights into the effect of transparency on consumers' product perception and purchase intention (e.g., Billeter et al., 2012; Chandran et al., 2019; Simmons et al., 2018; Vilnai-Yavetz and Koren, 2013). Technological development in the context of package materials was also driven by the growing interest in environmental sustainability. In recent years, individuals and companies are becoming more aware of the damage caused to the environment. Among the actions aimed at reducing the ecological footprint of the products, several programs and initiatives have been instigated to improve the sustainability of packaging. In light of this market interest in environmentally friendly packages, the attention of literature towards consumer perception of sustainable packaging in comparison with regular packaging has also grown (Marthino et al., 2015). Most of the existing knowledge on packaging materials, in fact, is focused on their sustainability. Some scholars investigated the relationship between the sustainable packaging and the consumer (a) evaluation and (b) behaviour during the purchase and near-end-of-life (recycling/disposal) stage (e.g., Barber, 2010; Magnier and Schoormans, 2015; Magnier et al., 2016; Marthino et al., 2015). Among these, Magnier et al. (2016) showed that the perceived quality of a food product is more positive when it is packed in a sustainable packaging compared to a conventional one. Other scholars found a positive relationship between the level of individuals' environmental concern and their attitude and purchase intention towards green product packaging (Barber, 2010; Magnier and Schoormans, 2015). Setting aside the sustainability perspective, to the author knowledge, only three studies emerge which focused the attention on consumers' perception towards different packaging material in the milk sector (Holliwood et al., 2013; Adam and Ali, 2014; Kariyawasam et al., 2006). In the qualitative research by Hollywood et al. (2013) three packaging materials were discussed which includes glass, plastic, and cardboard. Findings revealed different perceptions towards different packaging materials. Despite a general preference for glass packaging, some consumers also highlighted some disadvantages as it is heavier than the plastic containers and have to be washed out after its use. Contextually, cardboard was viewed negatively by the majority of participants as they could not see the product through the packaging and also perceived it did not keep the product as fresh as other forms of packaging. The study of Kariyawasam et al. (2006) measured consumers' perceptions towards fresh milk stored in tetra-pak. They found that consumers who purchase fresh milk in tetra-pak consider it is as safe as other substitutes and are motivated to buy by its "value" and "package" attributes such as the ability to secure purity of the content, the attractiveness of the package and the convenience to handle (small size). Finally, Adam and Ali (2014) found that tetra-pak and glass bottles are positively related with buying intention while plastic bottles are negatively related. Starting from such evidences, the present research intends to enrich the literature on the marketing effect of packaging material, with a specific focus on glass and tetra-pak. The product under investigation is the olive oil. Although some companies have experimented with the use of tetra-pak to package oil (olive or seeds), in most of countries the olive oil is traditionally sold to the final consumer in glass or tin bottles. Therefore, consumers are not used to buy it in tetra-pak. In light of this reasoning, it appears interesting to investigate if the product quality judgment and the purchase intention towards olive oil differ between tetra-pak and glass bottle. More formally, the following research question is formulated:

RQ: How do tetra-pak and glass bottles differ in influencing consumer perception and buying intentions towards extra virgin olive oil?

In order to answer the research question, several important dimensions of consumer's perception were considered and measured including attitude towards the product, perceived quality and perceived risk, besides pack and product evaluation. The selection was made according to their proven relevance in the processes of product evaluation and buying decision. Attitude towards an object (a subject, an event, or a behaviour) refers to the degree to which a person has a favourable or unfavourable evaluation or appraisal of that object (Ajzen and Fishbein, 2005). Consumer attitudes are formed by learning and influenced by personal experience and marketing stimuli (Wang and Heitmeyer, 2006). Acting as marketing stimuli, packaging cues, in general, and packaging material, in particular, are able to influence the creation of the consumer's feeling of favourability towards the product. Perceived product quality is the consumer judgment of the overall excellence or superiority of a product (Anselmsson et al., 2007). In the marketing literature it is well documented that the quality expectation of the various product alternatives is an important factor in the consumer choice behaviour (e.g., Narasimhan and Sen, 1992; Steenkamp, 1989; Steenkamp and Van Trijp, 1996). When product quality information is difficult to pre-obtain, packaging attributes are used as surrogate indicators of product quality (Ampuero and Vila, 2006; Insch and Florek, 2009; Honea and Horsky, 2012; Venter et al., 2011). Among these attributes, sustainable materials emerged as element capable of influencing the quality judgment. The perceived risk construct has received greater attention in the marketing literature for its theoretical and managerial importance. Perceived risk is defined as the degree to which individuals feel the uncertainty and consequences associated with their actions (Bauer, 1960). This construct plays a crucial role in the decision-making process (e.g., Hunter-Jones et al., 2008; Kwun and Oh, 2004; Liao et al., 2010; Pavlou, 2003; Stone and Grønhaug, 1993) because it negatively influences the willingness to engage in a risky behaviour (e.g., Keil et al., 2000; Nicolaou and McKnight, 2006). As a consequence, understanding which elements of the product – and, more specifically, which elements of the packaging – influence the risk associated with the product purchase or consumption is paramount to support marketing decisions. Finally, behavioural intention in terms of willingness to buy and willingness to pay was also assessed.

MATERIALS AND METHOD

A between-subjects experimental design was conducted with a sample of Italian consumers. Two images of the packaging of a known-brand extra virgin olive oil were used as stimuli for the study: a 1 liter tetra-pak bottle and a 1 liter glass bottle. The company is the first one in Italy to adopt a tetra-pak package to protect the extra virgin olive oil from oxygen and light, which are the main causes of oxidation. Contextually, it also continues to market its olive oil in glass bottles. Therefore, Italian consumers can find on the store shelves the same olive oil packaged in two different materials.

Two online questionnaires were prepared for each types of packaging (tetra-pak and glass). Respondents were recruited thanks to the publication of an informative post on social network pages and they were equally and randomly distributed among the two conditions (tetra-pak and glass). After removing people who never buy olive oil from the sample, the number of valid questionnaires was 124 for tetra-pak and 113 for glass.

After the image of the pack, the questionnaire included scales that have been well validated in the literature, in addition to general demographics. The three semantic differential scale of Schoormans and Robben (1997) was used to assess participants' evaluation of the package as a whole. Product evaluation was assessed through the six-items of Meyers-Levy and Tybout (1989) scale. Product perceived quality was measured with an adaptation of the five items developed by Myung-Soo (2007). The four-items scale by Keh and Pang (2010) was used to measure perceived risk. A set of three bipolar adjective was used as measure of attitude towards the product (Muehling et al., 1991). Questions measuring purchase intention were adaptations of the 3-item scale proposed by Putrevu (2008). Finally, willingness to pay (WTP) was collected asking participants the price that they considered suitable for the product. All statements, except for the willingness to pay, were on a seven-point semantic differential/anchored (from "completely disagree" to "completely agree") scale (Table 1). As the scale have been developed in English, to ensure the validity of the translation, a back-to-back translation procedure was conducted (Brislin, 1970). First, all original items were translated from English into Italian by the authors. Then, an expert translator whose native language was English and who was fluent in Italian independently translated the items back to English. Both versions of the scales (the original and the back-translated ones) were then compared for accuracy. Based on this feedback, the Italian version of the questionnaire was modified in order to assess the clarity and the appropriateness of the questions.

Reliability of the scales was assessed as internal consistency using Cronbach's alpha coefficient (Cronbach, 1951) and item-total correlation. The internal consistency reliability was very high for each construct, all items had a high item-total correlation, and the alpha value did not increase when each item was removed (Cronbach's alpha coefficients are shown in Table 1).

Table 1. Measurement scales and reliability indices

Scale	Items	Cronbach's Alpha
Pack evaluation *(Schoormans and Robben, 1997)*	Ugly – Beautiful	0.75
	Badly finished – Very well finished	
	Does not confer quality – Confers quality	
Product evaluation *(Meyers-Levy and Tybout, 1989)*	Appeal – Not appeal	0.96
	Satisfying – Not satisfying	
	Desirable – Undesirable	
	Fresh – Not Fresh	
	Good quality – Bad quality	
	Good taste – Bad taste	
Product perceived quality *(Myung-Soo, 2007)*	This oil has an excellent quality	0.98
	This oil looks to be reliable	
	This oil is safe	
	This oil has excellent quality features	
	This oil will give me excellent consumption experience	
Perceived risk *(Keh and Pang, 2010)*	The thought of using this olive oil made me feel psychologically uncomfortable	0.95
	The thought of using this olive oil gave me a feeling of unwanted anxiety	
	The thought of using this olive oil caused me to experience unnecessary tension	
	I would worry a lot when buying this olive oil	
Attitude towards the product *(Muehling et al., 1991)*	Good-Bad	0.93
	Favourable-Unfavourable	
	Negative-Positive	
Purchase intention *(Putrevu, 2008)*	The next time I buy an olive oil, I will consider this product	0.91
	The next time I consider buying olive oil, I will collect information on this product	
	The next time I buy olive oil, I will buy this product	

RESULTS

To answer the research question, a series of parametric t-tests were performed.

Respondents seem to prefer the olive oil in the glass pack compared to the olive oil in tetra-pak. Specifically, results showed that both pack evaluation (t = -8,595, $p < .01$) and product evaluation (t = -7,909, $p < .01$) were significantly better for the glass package. Moreover, product perceived quality significantly differed between the two stimuli, being better in the case of the glass package compared to the tetra-pak (t = -3,054, $p < .01$). The package material also influenced the risk perception and the attitude towards the product. Consumers exposed to the glass bottle showed a better attitude (t = -5,515, $p < .01$) and a lower risk perception (t = 4,021, $p < .01$) towards the product compared to those exposed to the tetra-pak bottle. Finally, the intention to buy and the price that respondents considered suitable for the observed product were higher in the case of the glass package compared to the tetra-pak one (purchase intention: t = -3,613, p < .01; willingness to pay: t = -5,594, p < .01). In Table 2 means and standard deviations of the measured dimensions for each group are shown.

DISCUSSION

Over the past decades, a growing body of empirical research has highlighted how packaging not only protects the product, but also informs the consumer, both at the point of sale as well as during consumption, influences brand recognition, and contributes to the creation of quality expectations. Packaging is the last marketing communication tool a company can use before the purchase decision is made, and this makes it a fundamental element of the communication mix (Rundh, 2009). In light of these evidences, understanding how consumers perceive visual and verbal elements of the packaging and use them to evaluate products and brands is of strategic importance for marketers, designers and managers.

Prior literature has focused on the effects of several packaging cues on consumers' perception and purchase intention including colour, shape, size, sustainability of materials, nutritional information, and country of origin. Little research has focused on how packaging material, regardless of sustainability, interacts with and influences the product evaluation process. The present study aimed to address this gap by empirically testing how tetra-pak and glass differ in terms of attitude towards the product, product evaluation (taste, appeal, desirability, freshness), perceived quality, perceived risk, purchase intention and willingness to pay. Results revealed that consumers' evaluations significantly differed between the two stimuli, being better in the case of the glass package compared to the tetra-pak one. Similarly, the willingness to buy and pay was higher for glass compared to the tetra-pak.

This chapter contributes to the literature on the role of packaging as a communication vehicle, focusing on one of its visual elements. Specifically, it increases the understanding of the effects of material on consumers' evaluations and behavioural intention in the olive oil sector. This visual element has been overlooked in previous studies, although it is an important marketing element for companies since consumers can assign different values to different materials and, consequently, to identical products packaged in different materials. Comparing consumers' perception towards extra virgin olive oil tetra-pak and glass bottles, the findings of this study suggest that, in the food marketplace, consumers' perceived

Table 2. Cell means and standard deviations

	Glass		*Tetra-pak*	
	Mean	*SD*	*Mean*	*SD*
Pack evaluation	4.50	1.142	3.13	1.292
Product evaluation	4.62	1.314	3.22	1.404
Product perceived quality	3.15	1.653	2.53	1.497
Perceived risk	2.05	1.400	2.87	1.693
Attitude towards the product	4.65	1.549	3.58	1.449
Purchase intention	3.19	1.745	2.44	1.425
Willingness to pay (euros)	4.83	2.415	3.28	1.817

product quality and preference are formed not only through packaging cues like colour, texts, shape, etc., but also through packaging material.

This evidence has practical significance as well. Shedding light on how consumers respond to different packaging materials, the study provides some guidance to manufacturers and product managers for educate consumers and influence their decision making process. In the current competitive market, firms should consider packaging material as one of the core elements for their product development. The values that the consumer associates with the pack material affect the perception of the product quality and values and, consequently, the purchase intention. Although, for some product categories, some materials are equivalent in terms of protection of the organoleptic characteristics of the product, they are perceived – and evaluated – differently by consumers. For example, previous research highlighted that consumers tend to prefer packages with a transparent window. The ability to see a food product inside the pack makes it more salient in the mind of the consumer (compared to just a printed graphic of the product) and increases the willingness to pay (Simmonds et al., 2018). This seems also true in the case of olive oil. Italian consumers, for example, are used to buying olive oil packaged in glass. One of the reasons for this habit is that consumers want to see the oil at the time of purchase: since the main indicator used to understand if it is really olive oil is the green colour, the glass had to be transparent. However, adding a bit of chlorophyll should be enough to make green any type of oil. Therefore, the possibility of seeing the colour thorough a transparent bottle actually gives only a false safety to the consumer. Nevertheless, when consumers consider only certain types of materials to be "standard" for a specific product category, they will naturally attribute them more values than other materials. In this case, the challenge for companies is to help consumers to overcome their resistance to change. The information and the education appear as the most appropriate means for pursue this goal and influence the buying choices.

FUTURE RESEARCH DIRECTIONS

The results of this study are a stepping stone towards future research. First, the research design focuses on only one product (extra virgin olive oil). Since the perception of the material should be closely related to the product category, the authors are cautious about generalizing these findings to the all food categories. Second, only two types of material were considered. Therefore, it is interesting to extend the research to other frequently used materials. Furthermore, replicating the results over non-food product categories, such as durables, could represent an interesting approach in the future. Third, the objective of this research is strictly focused on the comparison of the consumers' perception towards extra virgin olive oil packaged with different materials. A further research project could be devoted to the analysis of the variables that impact on the behavioural intentions (willingness to pay and purchase intention). To this end, a causal relationship model in which the material acts as moderation variable could be developed. Fourth, since the material has to do with environmental protection, it could be interesting to test the influence of individual variables, such as environmental concern, on the evaluation process. Finally, the study has been run online with pictorial stimuli and the respondents were not able to interact physically with the products. Further research may seek to replicate these results with real products in order to consider the effect of haptics and handling on consumer responses.

REFERENCES

Adam, M., & Ali, K. (2014). Impact of packaging elements of packaged milk on consumer buying behaviour. *IBAICM, International Conference on Marketing.*

Ajzen, I., & Fishbein, M. (2005). The influence of attitudes on behaviour. In D. Albarracín, B. T. Johnson, & M. P. Zanna (Eds.), *The handbook of attitudes* (pp. 173–221). Mahwah, NJ: Lawrence Erlbaum Associates Publishers.

Ampuero, O., & Vila, N. (2006). Consumer perceptions of product packaging. *Journal of Consumer Marketing, 23*(2), 102–114. doi:10.1108/07363760610655032

Andrews, J. C., Burton, S., & Netemeyer, R. C. (2013). Are some comparative nutrition claims misleading? The role of nutrition knowledge, ad claim type and disclosure conditions. *Journal of Advertising, 29*(3), 29–42. doi:10.1080/00913367.2000.10673615

Anselmsson, J., Johansson, U., & Persson, N. (2007). Understanding price premium for grocery products: A conceptual model of customer-based brand equity. *Journal of Product and Brand Management, 16*(6), 401–414. doi:10.1108/10610420710823762

Aschemann-Witzel, J., & Hamm, U. (2010). Do consumers prefer foods with nutrition and health claims? Results of a purchase simulation. *Journal of Marketing Communications, 16*(2), 47–58. doi:10.1080/13527260903342746

Barber, N. (2010). Green wine packaging: Targeting environmental consumers. *International Journal of Wine Business Research, 22*(4), 423–444. doi:10.1108/17511061011092447

Bauer, R. A. (1960). Consumer behavior as risk taking. In R. S. Hancock (Ed.), *Proceedings of the 43rd Conference of the American Marketing Association.* (pp. 389–398). Chicago, IL: American Marketing Association.

Billeter, D., Zhu, M., & Inman, J. J. (2012). Transparent packaging and consumer purchase decisions. In J. Sevilla (Ed.), *When it's what's outside that matters: Recent findings on product and packaging design.* PA: University of Pittsburgh.

Chandran, S., Batra, R., & Lawrence, B. (2009). Is seeing believing? Consumer responses to opacity of product packaging. In A. L. McGill & S. Shavitt (Eds.), *Advances in consumer research* (Vol. 36, pp. 970–971). Duluth, MN: Association for Consumer Research.

Coldiretti. (2018, May 6). *Coldiretti: olio d'oliva conquista il mondo, +49% in 25 anni.* Retrieved from http://www.askanews.it/economia/2018/05/06/coldiretti-olio-doliva-conquista-il-mondo-49-in-25-anni-pn_20180506_00020/

Cronbach, L. J. (1951). Coefficient alpha and the internal structure of tests. *Psychometrika, 16*(3), 297–334. doi:10.1007/BF02310555

Faulkner, G. P., Pourshahidi, L. K., Wallace, J. M. W., Kerr, M. A., McCaffrey, T. A., & Livingstone, M. B. E. (2014). Perceived healthiness of foods can influence consumers' estimations of energy density and appropriate portion size. *International Journal of Obesity, 38*(1), 106–112. doi:10.1038/ijo.2013.69 PMID:23732657

Garretson, J. A., & Burton, S. (2000). Effects of nutrition facts panel values, nutrition claims, and health claims on consumer attitudes, perceptions of disease-related risks, and trust. *Journal of Public Policy & Marketing, 19*(2), 213–227. doi:10.1509/jppm.19.2.213.17133

George, J. (2005). On paper, a world of opportunities. Packaging World Magazine, April, p. 36.

Gorton, D., Ni Mhurchu, C., Bramley, D., & Dixon, R. (2010). Interpretation of two nutrition content claims: A New Zealand survey. *Australian and New Zealand Journal of Public Health, 34*(1), 57–62. doi:10.1111/j.1753-6405.2010.00474.x PMID:20920106

Hoegg, J., & Alba, J. W. (2011). Seeing is believing (too much): The influence of product form on perceptions of functional performance. *Journal of Product Innovation Management, 28*(3), 346–359. doi:10.1111/j.1540-5885.2011.00802.x

Hoegg, J., Alba, J. W., & Dahl, D. W. (2010). The good, the bad and the ugly: Influence of aesthetics on product feature judgments. *Journal of Consumer Psychology, 20*(4), 419–430. doi:10.1016/j.jcps.2010.07.002

Hollywood, L., Wells, L., Armstrong, G., & Farley, H. (2013). Thinking outside the carton: Attitudes towards milk packaging. *British Food Journal, 115*(6), 899–912. doi:10.1108/BFJ-Jul-2010-0127

Honea, H., & Horsky, S. (2012). The power of plain: Intensifying product experience with neutral aesthetic context. *Marketing Letters, 1*(23), 223–235. doi:10.100711002-011-9149-y

Hunter-Jones, P., Jeffs, A., & Smith, D. (2008). Backpacking your way into crisis: An exploratory study into perceived risk and tourist behaviour amongst young people. *Journal of Travel & Tourism Marketing, 23*(2-4), 237–247. doi:10.1300/J073v23n02_18

Insch, A., & Florek, M. (2009). Prevalence of country of origin associations on the supermarket shelf. *International Journal of Retail & Distribution Management, 37*(5), 453–471. doi:10.1108/09590550910954937

Jo, M.-S. (2007). Should a quality sub-brand be located before or after the parent brand? an application of composite concept theory. *Journal of the Academy of Marketing Science, 35*(2), 184–196. doi:10.100711747-007-0039-z

Kariyawasam, S., Jayasinghe-Mudalige, U., & Weerahewa, J. (2006, May). Assessing consumer attitudes and perceptions towards food quality: The case of consumption of tetra-packed fresh milk in Sri Lanka. *Selected paper presented at the Canadian Agricultural Economics Society Annual Meeting, Montreal, Canada.*

Keh, H. T., & Pang, J. (2010). Customer Reactions to Service Separation. *Journal of Marketing, 74*(2), 55–70. doi:10.1509/jm.74.2.55

Keil, M., Tan, B. C., Wei, K. K., Saarinen, T., Tuunainen, V., & Wassenaar, A. (2000). A cross-cultural study on escalation of commitment behavior in software projects. *Management Information Systems Quarterly*, *24*(2), 299–325. doi:10.2307/3250940

Keller, K. L. (2009). Choosing brand elements to build brand equity. In *Strategic Brand Management* (3rd ed., pp. 187–196). Delhi, India: Dorling Kindersley.

Kwun, J. W., & Oh, H. (2004). Effects of brand, price, and risk on customers' value perceptions and behavioral intentions in the restaurant industry. *Journal of Hospitality & Leisure Marketing*, *11*(1), 31–49. doi:10.1300/J150v11n01_03

Lewis, M. (1991). *Understanding Brands*. London, UK: Kogan Page.

Liao, C., Lin, H. N., & Liu, Y. P. (2010). Predicting the use of pirated software: A contingency model integrating perceived risk with the theory of planned behaviour. *Journal of Business Ethics*, *91*(2), 237–252. doi:10.100710551-009-0081-5

Liaukonyte, J., Streletskaya, N. A., Kaiser, H. M., & Bradley, J. R. (2013). Consumer response to 'contains' and 'free of' labeling: evidence from lab experiments. *Applied Economic Perspectives and Policy*, *35*(3), 476–507. doi:10.1093/aepp/ppt015

Magnier, L., & Schoormans, J. (2015). Consumer reactions to sustainable packaging: The interplay of visual appearance, verbal claim and environmental concern. *Journal of Environmental Psychology*, *44*, 53–62. doi:10.1016/j.jenvp.2015.09.005

Magnier, L., Schoormans, J., & Mugge, R. (2016). Judging a product by its cover: Packaging sustainability and perceptions of quality in food products. *Food Quality and Preference*, *53*, 132–142. doi:10.1016/j.foodqual.2016.06.006

Martinho, G., Pires, A., Portela, G., & Fonseca, M. (2015). Factors affecting consumers' choices concerning sustainable packaging during product purchase and recycling. *Resources, Conservation and Recycling*, *103*, 58–68. doi:10.1016/j.resconrec.2015.07.012

McDaniel, C., & Baker, R. C. (1977). Convenience food packaging and the perception of product quality. *Journal of Marketing*, *41*(4), 57–58. doi:10.1177/002224297704100406

Meyers-Levy, J., & Tybout, A. M. (1989). Schema congruity as a basis for product evaluation. *The Journal of Consumer Research*, *16*(1), 39–54. doi:10.1086/209192

Muehling, D. D., Laczniak, R. N., & Stoltman, J. J. (1991). The moderating effects of ad message involvement: A reassessment. *Journal of Advertising*, *20*(2), 29–38. doi:10.1080/00913367.1991.10673211

Narasimhan, C., & Sen, S. (1992). Measuring quality perceptions. *Marketing Letters*, *3*(2), 147–156. doi:10.1007/BF00993994

Nicolaou, A. I., & McKnight, D. H. (2006). Perceived information quality in data exchanges: Effects on risk, trust, and intention to use. *Information Systems Research*, *17*(4), 332–351. doi:10.1287/isre.1060.0103

Orth, U. R., & Malkewitz, K. (2008). Holistic package design and consumer brand impressions. *Journal of Marketing*, *72*(3), 64–81. doi:10.1509/jmkg.72.3.64

Pavlou, P. A. (2003). Consumer acceptance of electronic commerce: Integrating trust and risk with the technology acceptance model. *International Journal of Electronic Commerce*, *7*(3), 101–134. doi:10.1080/10864415.2003.11044275

Pilditch, J. (1957). *The silent salesman*. London, UK: Harper and Row.

Prendergast, P. G. and Pitt, L. (1996). Packaging, marketing, logistics and the environment: are there trade-offs? *International Journal of Physical Distribution & Logistics Management, 26*(6), pp. 60-72.

Putrevu, S. (2008). Consumer responses toward sexual and nonsexual appeals: The influence of involvement, need for cognition (NFC), and gender. *Journal of Advertising*, *37*(2), 57–70. doi:10.2753/JOA0091-3367370205

Raghubir, P., & Greenleaf, E. A. (2006). Ratios in proportion: What should the shape of the package be? *Journal of Marketing*, *70*(2), 95–107. doi:10.1509/jmkg.70.2.095

Rettie, R., & Brewer, C. (2000). The verbal and visual components of package design. *Journal of Product and Brand Management*, *9*(1), 56–70. doi:10.1108/10610420010316339

Rundh, B. (2005). The multi-faceted dimension of packaging: Marketing logistic or marketing tool? *British Food Journal*, *107*(9), 670–684. doi:10.1108/00070700510615053

Rundh, B. (2009). Packaging design: Creating competitive advantage with product packaging. *British Food Journal*, *111*(9), 988–1002. doi:10.1108/00070700910992880

Saba, A., Vassallo, M., Shepherd, R., Lampila, P., Arvola, A., Dean, M., ... Lähteenmäki, L. (2010). Country-wise differences in perception of health-related messages in cereal based food products. *Food Quality and Preference*, *21*(4), 385–393. doi:10.1016/j.foodqual.2009.09.007

Schoormans, J., & Robben, H. (1997). The effect of new package design on product attention, categorization and evaluation. *Journal of Economic Psychology*, *8*(2/3), 271–287. doi:10.1016/S0167-4870(97)00008-1

Silayoi, P., & Speece, M. (2004). Packaging and purchase decisions: A focus group study on the impact of involvement level and time pressure. *British Food Journal*, *106*(8), 607–628. doi:10.1108/00070700410553602

Silayoi, P., & Speece, M. (2007). The importance of packaging attributes: A conjoint analysis approach. *European Journal of Marketing*, *41*(11/12), 1495–1517. doi:10.1108/03090560710821279

Simmonds, G., Woods, A. T., & Spence, C. (2018). 'Show me the goods': Assessing the effectiveness of transparent packaging vs. product imagery on product evaluation. *Food Quality and Preference*, *63*, 18–27. doi:10.1016/j.foodqual.2017.07.015

Steenkamp, J. B. E. (1989). *Product quality: An investigation into the concept and how it is perceived by consumers*. Wageningen, The Netherlands: Wageningen Academic Publisher.

Steenkamp, J. B. E., & Van Trijp, H. C. (1996). Quality guidance: A consumer-based approach to food quality improvement using partial least squares. *European Review of Agriculture Economics*, *23*(2), 195–215. doi:10.1093/erae/23.2.195

Stewart, B. (2004). *Packaging design strategies* (2nd ed.). The UK: Pira International Ltd.

Stone, R. N., & Grønhaug, K. (1993). Perceived risk: Further considerations for the marketing discipline. *European Journal of Marketing, 27*(3), 39–50. doi:10.1108/03090569310026637

Tan, S. J., & Tan, K. L. (2007). Antecedents and consequences of skepticism toward health claims: An empirical investigation of Singaporean consumers. *Journal of Marketing Communications, 13*(1), 59–82. doi:10.1080/13527260600963711

Underwood, R. L., & Klein, N. M. (2002). Packaging as brand communication: Effects of product pictures on consumer responses to the package and Brand. *Journal of Marketing Theory and Practice, 10*(4), 58–68. doi:10.1080/10696679.2002.11501926

Underwood, R. L., Klein, N. M., & Burke, R. R. (2001). Packaging communication: Attentional effects of product imagery. *Journal of Product and Brand Management, 10*(7), 403–422. doi:10.1108/10610420110410531

Venter, K., van der Merwe, D., de Beer, H., Kempen, E., & Bosman, M. (2011). Consumers perceptions of food packaging: An exploratory investigation in Potchefstroom, South Africa. *International Journal of Consumer Studies, 35*(3), 273–281. doi:10.1111/j.1470-6431.2010.00936.x

Vergura, D. T., & Luceri, B. (2018). Product packaging and consumers' emotional response. Does spatial representation influence product evaluation and choice? *Journal of Consumer Marketing, 35*(2), 218–227. doi:10.1108/JCM-12-2016-2021

Vilnai-Yavetz, I., & Koren, R. (2013). Cutting through the clutter: Purchase intentions as a function of packaging instrumentality, aesthetics, and symbolism. *International Review of Retail, Distribution and Consumer Research, 23*(4), 394–417. doi:10.1080/09593969.2013.792743

Wang, S. T. E. (2013). The influence of visual packaging design on perceived food product quality, value, and brand preference. *International Journal of Retail & Distribution Management, 41*(10), 805–816. doi:10.1108/IJRDM-12-2012-0113

Wang, Y., & Heitmeyer, J. (2006). Consumer attitude toward US versus domestic apparel in Taiwan. *International Journal of Consumer Studies, 30*(1), 64–74. doi:10.1111/j.1470-6431.2005.00450.x

ADDITIONAL READING

Ahmadi, G., Bahrami, H. R., & Ahani, M. (2013). An investigation of visual components of packaging on food consumer behavior. *Business and Economic Review, 3*(2), 1.

Caponio, F., Bilancia, M. T., Pasqualone, A., Sikorska, E., & Gomes, T. (2005). Influence of the exposure to light on extra virgin olive oil quality during storage. *European Food Research and Technology, 221*(1-2), 92–98. doi:10.100700217-004-1126-8

Garber, L. L. (1995). The package appearance in choice. *Advances in Consumer Research. Association for Consumer Research (U. S.), 22*, 653–660.

Hine, T. (1995). *The total package: The secret history and hidden meanings of boxes, bottles, cans, and other persuasive containers*. New York, NY: Little Brown.

Kuvykaite, R., Dovaliene, A., & Navickiene, L. (2009). Impact of package elements on consumer's purchase decision. *Economics and management*, (14), 441-447.

Mukherjee, A., & Hoyer, W. D. (2001). The effect of novel attributes on product evaluation. *The Journal of Consumer Research*, *28*(3), 462–472. doi:10.1086/323733

Rundh, B. (2013). Linking Packaging to Marketing: How packaging is influencing the marketing strategy. *British Food Journal*, *115*(11), 1547–1563. doi:10.1108/BFJ-12-2011-0297

Silayoi, P., & Speece, M. (2004). Packaging and purchase decisions: An exploratory study on the impact of involvement level and time pressure. *British Food Journal*, *106*(8), 607–628. doi:10.1108/00070700410553602

Underwood, R. L., & Ozanne, J. L. (1998). Is your package an effective communicator? A normative framework for increasing the communicative competence of packaging. *Journal of Marketing Communications*, *4*(4), 207–220. doi:10.1080/135272698345762

Westerman, S. J., Sutherland, E. J., Gardner, P. H., Baig, N., Critchley, C., Hickey, C., ... Zervos, Z. (2013). The design of consumer packaging: Effects of manipulations of shape, orientation, and alignment of graphical forms on consumers' assessments. *Food Quality and Preference*, *27*(1), 8–17. doi:10.1016/j.foodqual.2012.05.007

KEY TERMS AND DEFINITIONS

Attitude: The favourable or unfavourable evaluation or appraisal a person has of the object under investigation (a behaviour, an object, a situation, etc.).

Consumer Decision Making Process: The psychological process implemented by consumers before, during, and after the purchase of a good or service.

Experimental Design: A research design which allows the researcher to manipulate the independent variables and observe the reactions caused by such changes.

Packaging Cues: Visual (aesthetic) and verbal components of packaging which act as element of communication in the market-place.

Sustainable Packaging: A package that is designed to be effective and safe to human health or ecosystems, made efficiently with renewable energy, and once used, is recycled or reused efficiently to provide valuable resources for subsequent generations.

T-Test: A type of parametric statistical test that is used to compare the means of two groups.

Willingness to Pay: The maximum amounts consumers consider suitable for purchasing the product.

Chapter 13
The Evolution of Fast Food in a Customer-Driven Era:
Innovation and Sustainability for Customer Needs

Alessandro Bonadonna
University of Turin, Italy

Chiara Giachino
University of Turin, Italy

Francesca Pucciarelli
ESCP Europe, Turin Campus, Italy

Bernardo Bertoldi
University of Turin, Italy

ABSTRACT

*Customers are important for every company and their changes in taste, behavior, and way to decide strongly influence companies' strategy. The food sector follows the new trends and tries to adapt its way to do business, leveraging on innovation and sustainability. In the food sector, an innovation can be linked to tradition. There is a limited change in the offer and fast food restaurants' innovating is key to survive. Thus, authors analyzed how both International Hamburger Foodservices (IHF) such as McDonalds and Burger King, and Local Hamburger Foodservice (LHF), such as M**Bun and Burgheria, are changing their strategies to meet customers' needs. Authors focused on the Piedmont area, in particular the Turin area, which has a long culinary tradition, hostings of important food events, and an increasing trend of new fast food restaurants.*

DOI: 10.4018/978-1-7998-1419-1.ch013

INTRODUCTION

The European food sector has changed in the last decades due to different factors, such as: policy makers decisions, globalizations, and last but not least changes in customers decision making and choices. In particular, in the past twenty years the policies focus was about to safeguard the food traditions, the territory and the food origin through the use of certification labelling schemes (Dias and Mendes, 2018; Bonadonna et al., 2017; Grunert and Aachmann, 2016; Hajdukiewicz, 2014) and, this trend influenced the actual scenario. Private companies, in the meantime, had to reinterpret the meaning of the term globalization and adapt their products and processes to the new competition' rules. In fact, changes in the society and in consumers led many food companies to adapt their vision from a global perspective (implying a standardized approach to the different geographical segments) into a local one. A lot of international companies, to remain competitive in the market, redefined their strategies and operational schemes adapting them to local specificities and expectations e.g. in the quick restaurant service, it takes place in terms of local raw materials and short supply chain (Mathur, 2017; Kashif et al., 2015; Rarick et al., 2012).

The place and/or the local can be considered an adjustment tools for the international food operators that must follow the changes of the consumer's behaviour and attitude on the assessment of food stuffs and the new models of consumption (Annunziata et al., 2019; Carzedda et al., 2018; Conti et al., 2018; Bedin et al., 2018; Vanhonacker et al., 2010). However, the place remain a fundamental element to create *Alternative Food Network* (AFN) that is a tool promoting the safeguard of the environment and the biodiversity, improving the quality of foodstuffs and outcomes of local operators, protecting consumers and increasing the confidence in the food sector (Timpanaro et al., 2018; Brinkley, 2018).

The new rules and requests of the market led companies and operators to rethink their strategies taking into account not only products and processes, but also innovation and sustainability.

Innovation usually is associated with the ability to transform a good idea in a material or immaterial thing with social and/or economic convenience and able to reach the target market (Intzell and Hilton, 1999). Innovation can involve production process such as specific operations or new plants and devices, product e.g. novel foods, or service e.g. delivery at home (Antonelli, 2004) and, it could be also associated with the technologic aspect e.g. increasing the shelf life of food with modified atmosphere, or as sociological e.g. back to the tradition. In any case, the strategic role of innovation is widely recognized to meet targets and reach the goals (Finco et al., 2018; Vrontis et al., 2016; Bresciani et al., 2013). In the food sector, a particular kind of innovation is remaining linked to tradition and change just some aspects of the offer (Klaus and Aachmann, 2015; Giacosa et al, 2014; Bertoldi et al., 2011; DeSoucey, 2010; Guerrero et al., 2009) with the objective to increase the value of specific foods and foodstuffs (Marcoz et al., 2016; Bonadonna et al., 2016; Rodrigo et al., 2015; Dogan and Gokovali, 2012; Schamel, 2007; Jordana, 2000). Indeed, innovation could be defined like a promotional tool whereas consumers tend to maintain their food habits (Boccia and Covino, 2016; Arcese et al., 2015; Dadura and Lee, 2011).

Sustainability is an important element that gathered a lot of importance among customers in the last years. Always more people are influenced in their buying decision process by the presence of sustainable process/products/actions in what are looking for. In the food sector, sustainability can be described by the HLPE food system definition (UN, 2014) i.e. "*A sustainable food system is a food system that delivers food security and nutrition for all in such a way that the economic, social and environmental bases to generate food security and nutrition for future generations are not compromised*". In this context, many agro-food companies of all sizes are giving an increasing attention to sustainability and related issues (Bayer, 2017; Basf, 2017), by considering both the agricultural and industrial side of their activities, which includes both innovation and technology. As just cultivating the two aspects food companies will be able to reach their business goals and the ones given by ethical concerns as environmental and biodiversity protection. Therefore, food operators are often involved in sustainable initiatives as water bottles certified or Tuna tins certified that can be conducted to incremental change or even, worse, of 'greenwashing'.

In the explained scenario, the Italian foodservice sector and, more specifically, the hamburger foodservice subsector represent an interesting case to understand this phenomena. Firstly, because the hamburger foodservice seems living in a phase of transition caused by a consumers' demand that is oriented towards sustainability and health. The origin of raw materials, the intrinsic quality of ingredients, the care in the production process and service phase are emerging as main peculiarities to better reply to the market requests (Bonadonna et al., 2019). With the consequence that on the one hand, the well-known international foodservice enterprises has signed commercial agreements with fast service, low cost and, sometimes, offering Italian PDO and PGI protection consortia for the supply of characterizing ingredients, as in the case of meat originating from native Italian breeds. These raw materials are useful to produce special hamburgers, demonstrating the need to link their gastronomic offer to the territory of consumption (Cappella et al., 2015; McDonald's Italia, 2015). On the other hand, some foodservice enterprises suggest hamburgers and related gastronomic offer with particular attention to the supply chain collecting main raw materials and the production process for the food offer. Secondly because the relevance of hamburger foodservice and its characteristics is a relatively new issue in the research area that justifies more attention by scholars.

Consequently, this chapter would serve to fill the hamburger foodservice gap in literature, with the aim to identify the different hamburger foodservices strategic reactions to customers quest for innovativeness and sustainability and define their peculiarities in an Italian model area. In particular, authors provided an in-depth analysis on main characteristics i.e. raw materials and ingredients, production processes and service contributing to customer satisfaction, by comparing international and local chains operating in the hamburger foodservice. Some differences amongst hamburger operators emerged and some specific peculiarities highlighted. The study was carried out in the Greater Torino, an Italian Metropolitan area that it is an ideal contest to analyse the situation in the food sector. Indeed, the Turin area hosts several international events of the food sector –as for example the Salone del Gusto and Terra Madre which are among the most important initiatives of Slow Food-, brought to the light the most important Italian retailer of high quality foodstuffs -Eataly-, and own one of the biggest italian outdoor market –so called Porta Palazzo.

From a methodological point of view direct interviews were organized with fast food operators to collect information on different kinds of hamburger foodservice in Greater Torino. In particular, 4 fast food restaurant chains were involved: two international chains i.e. McDonald's and Burger King, and two local chains i.e. M** Bun and Burgheria. The choice was made in order to compare two different systems of food processing and service offered to customers.

Background

To understand if a company really has a competitive advantage in the foodservice market, it is necessary to take into account the most relevant factors for customers, considering the moment of the choice, the one in which they consider their satisfaction, and the elements linked to their perceptions and feelings.

On the other hand, it is necessary to carefully analyse the markets and the characteristics of the countries in which the operators want to compete; those analysis are essential to implement a correct strategy sales (Ng et al., 2018; Nguyen et al., 2018; Rodríguez-López et al., 2018).

In this regard, the foodservice sector can be separated into different categories depending on the type of foodservice that is offered. For example, in the case of the quick service restaurant the parameters that can be taken into consideration are the price, the quality of the product and the service offered (Harrington et al., 2017; Bojanic et al. 2007).

Taking into consideration the Italian market, and in particular the Turin market, the research analyzes the role of innovation and sustainability in the foodservice, deepening the three important elements - raw materials, processes and services - in a more international and/or local context.

Innovation and Sustainability in the Italian Foodservice: From Customers to the Role of Raw Materials, Processes and Services

In the food sector innovation is considered an important element to achieve strategic objectives and meet the needs of consumers, who tends to change their tastes periodically.

Thus, innovation is a useful tool to imitate (Lee et al., 2019) and to fight imitations (Harrington, 2004), make the service easier (Neubling et al., 2017), satisfy new customer requests (Lee et al., 2019), introduce new foods and increase technology acceptance (Lee et al., 2019; Costa, 2013); on the other hand, innovation is also considered an improvement of the local recipes of different geographical areas (Maltese et al., 2016), a selection of high quality local raw materials to prepare recipes in restaurants and hotels (Gordin et al., 2016; Mkono, 2012) or a way to implement more environmentally friendly production methods (Mikkelsen et al., 2006) introducing also new systems and devices e.g. novel food, and/or the e.g. service home delivery (Antonelli, 2004).

These new trends are influencing the sector both from a technological point of view e.g. increase the shelf life of food with a modified atmosphere, both from a sociological point of view e.g. return to tradition (Bonadonna et al., 2017; Costa, 2013).

Considering the production process, international quick foodservice operators are the most advanced in terms of effectiveness and efficiency in the catering sector (Chase et al., 2008). In the United States during the 1950s, before the creation of fast-food restaurants, burgers were produced at the moment in the restaurants. Traditionally, the customers' order was based on a choice made on a large menu, with the possibility to decide the degree of cooking, the type of gaskets and ingredients to be inserted with different levels of customization. In this case, the ability of the chef was to understand customers' requests and the service was characterized by a long lead time. From an industrial point of view, this process is called Make to Order (MTO) i.e. the production starts when an explicit request is made (Jacobs and Chase, 2008).

Subsequently, with the revolution brought by the McDonald's brothers and the introduction of fast-food restaurants, the burger production process embraced an approach aimed at achieving large volumes of production reducing both the costs per unit of product and the lead time in satisfying customer requests through a Make To Stock system (MTS). This type of system allowed to have food ready for delivery at the same time of the customer's request. Obviously, in order to pursue this type of industrial system, products had to be limited in numbers and standardized, limiting the menu's choices for customers (Jacobs and Chase, 2008).

In recent times, the need to customize the food products has led to the adoption of hybrid process systems that allow for short lead times and can respond to particular consumer needs (Rahimnia et al., 2009). In fact, the choice of the process depends on the type of consumers served by restaurants (Chase et al., 2008). Companies have thus reinterpreted the meaning of globalization; many food companies have adapted and moved from a global vision to a more local one. Some multinationals have reinforced their strategies and operational schemes, declining the specificities and expectations in local terms e.g. selection of local raw materials or characterized by particular qualitative peculiarities (Mathur, 2017; Kashif et al., 2015; Rarick et al., 2012). In Italy, for example, McDonalds has proposed menus with DOP and IGP ingredients and/or meat obtained from Italian breeds e.g. *Bovino Piemontese* and *Chianina*. These raw materials are useful for producing special burgers, demonstrating the need to link their offer with the territory (McDonalds, 2019; McDonald's Italia, 2015; Cappella et al., 2015).

Since the 1960s, in Italy the concept of local has been integrated for the selection of food and raw materials in the food service, with the introduction of the protection system of wines by law, then extended to meats and cheeses. In the mid-1980s, this sensitivity grew through the Carlo Petrini Manifesto against fast-food and its relative globalization (Pietrykowski, 2004; Parkins, 2004) and the subsequent design of not losing identity and culture in the agricultural sphere (Tencati and Zsolnai, 2012; Petrini, 2005).

This orientation - combined with the food quality policy of the European Union - has led to reconsider the food production processes and fueled the creation of short supply chains and local products, instead of conventional food products (Gava et al., 2018; Carbone, 2018). Therefore, raw materials and ingredients, food processes, food product management and consumption habits were reconsidered based on social and environmental sustainability as well as economic requirements (Massini, 2010; Peri, 2006). Finally, the service that is provided to customers is a further element involved in the innovation process. In foodservice, the quality of service is an essential element for the definition of marketing strategies (Chang, 2009), the achievement of the success (Saleh and Ryan, 1991), the measurement of customer satisfaction levels (Lee & Lyu, 2019; Nguyen et al., 2018; Castellani & Samoggia, 2018; Wu & Mohi, 2015; Keith & Simmers, 2011; Ryu & Han, 2010).

In the latter case, customer surveys allow us to gather useful information to improve the product/service provided for the target consumers and, to this end, the concept of quality should be interpreted in a multidimensional version (Peri, 2006; Wu & Mohi, 2015). At the same time, the point of view of those who provide the service is essential to better define the elements of the service and bring the demands of customers closer together with the peculiarities of the offer (Lee et al., 2019).

With reference to the demand in the fast foodservice sector, several authors have developed and deepened the issues related to the Quick Service Restaurant (QSR) exploring what are the different reasons that lead to choose this type of restaurant (Harrington et al., 2017; Abdelhadi, 2016; Rydell et al., 2008). The main element of the analysis is, by definition, the speed of the service. Consumers, in fact, appreciate and seek a quick and immediate service that can meet the needs of a fast-paced market characterized by reduced pause times during working hours and therefore the need to satisfy a primary need in very limited times (Rydell et al., 2008). This aspect becomes an essential element to guarantee an adequate service in terms of lead time, to the point of being a fundamental element for the application of measurement methods that refer to the lean system used in industrial processes (Abdelhadi, 2016). The places that offer QSR are easily accessible and located in strategic areas and can be considered as centers of socialization, entertainment and leisure time that offer foods characterized by a good taste and with adequate nutritional principles (Rydell et al., 2008).

Furthermore, QSR can be differentiated by three dimensions of the marketing mix such as quality, convenience and price that can differ according to the age of customers (Harrington et al., 2017; Rydell et al., 2008).

Finally, the further element of evaluation of the QSRs is the service that has a strong influence on the consumers' perception. For example, the interaction between personnel and service manager in a QSR can increase or decrease the customers perception of service quality (Mathe and Slevitch, 2013); factors such as responsibility, reliability, competence, courtesy, tangibility and parking can determine a positive or negative perception of the service by the consumer (Chang, 2009); sometimes, even cleaning the environment can be an important factor in customers' perceptions of the quality of the drinks and food offered (Hensel, 2012).

MAIN FOCUS OF THE CHAPTER

Issues, Controversies, Problems

The Italian agro-food sector shows some peculiarities regarding the satisfaction of consumers' demand in the catering service. In this context, innovation is considered a strategic key to achieve success. A particular type of innovation is the return to tradition through the re-elaboration of local recipes and gastronomy or introducing high quality local raw materials. Some operators rewrote the history of fast food introducing local ingredients in their offer and short supply chains.

This study is based on the point of view of managers that operate in fast foods and analyse their strategic choices in terms of production and management of the premises, as well as of customer relations.

In order to make a more detailed analysis, the City of Torino (Greater Torino) and the neighboring area were considered. The Greater Torino was chosen for two main reasons: the centuries-old culinary tradition and its recent success and spread of local burgers. Furthermore, unlike what happened to most sectors, in the last 5 years the foodservice has become one of the most dynamic sectors of the territory, with a significant increase in restaurants' numbers (1.064 units more than in 2012), take-away shops (with 322 more units) and food trucks presence (with an increase of 67 units) (CCIAA, 2018).

The Quick Service Restaurant has a positive trend as well as the burgers' segment. Over the past ten years, in Greater Torino new McDonald's and Burger King restaurants opened as well as many others hamburgers' restaurants, such as M ** Bun, Eataly's Hamburgeria, Fassoneria, Burgheria.

The production and offer of burgers was essential requirement to be involved in the study, in fact traditional chains have been examined, such as McDonald's and Burger King i.e. International Hamburger Foodservice (IHF) and the two of the main local realities that have emerged over the last decade i.e. M** Bun and Burgheria as Local Hamburger Foodservice (LHF) (Bonadonna et al. 2019).

Each restaurant was analysed singularly, firstly, using public and available information on the websites; secondly, interviewing each manager of the identified restaurants. The interviews were focused on processes and outcomes of foodservice. Indeed, a questionnaire was administered to each manager involved, in order to understand the different meanings of the provided foodservice quality. The questionnaire was divided in two parts; in the first part, some questions on particular topics i.e. the corporate philosophy implemented, the production process used and the lead time, the role of human resources within the production process, issues and how they are solved, relationship between product quality and service speed, future strategic choices and changes in the offer system. In the second part, a check-list with a seven-points Likert scale was used to collect information on the interaction's quality of the staff (interaction with customers, problem solving skills and professional skills of employees), the quality of the location (including restaurant cleaning, layout and design of dining rooms and menu design), the quality of the offer (with reference to the experience the customer wants, the quality of the product and the supply chain, as well as the quality of the menu) and the quality-price ratio of the products, raw materials, services offered.

The interviews were conducted during October 2018 and lasted about 45-70 minutes. The interviewer asked questions based on the questionnaire, recorded the answers, filled out the checklist and took note of the main topics. The authors analyzed the results of the different interviews individually, then compared them with the other authors and, finally, the fundamental elements were collectively identified (Atkinson and Shaffir, 1998). Through the analysis of the results it was possible to make a comparison amongst them and highlighting any similarities and differences, both as regards the adopted production process, and in the strategic choices made to increase market share in the Turin area. Below, the summary of the results divided between raw materials, production process and services was reported.

Raw Materials and Ingredients

The selected operators have different strategies to satisfy the consumers' requirements in term of raw materials and ingredients used for their menus. The IHFs have similar proposals i.e. conventional and inexpensive food products, different kind of hamburgers, french fries, international soft drinks. Sometimes, McDonald's introduces local raw materials and ingredients in its meal (e.g. special menu with national ingredients like *Chianina* meat or *Parmigiano Reggiano* PDO).

On the other hand, the LHFs have two different strategies. M** Bun is characterized by the selection of local ingredients and it underlines both the origin of meats, vegetables and ingredients, and the use of a short supply chain. Burgheria is characterized by high quality ingredients and emphasizes the importance of raw material selection i.e. meats, vegetables and ingredients, and handmade products i.e. bread and sauces. Furthermore, the total absence of pre-packaged condiments in M** Bun and Burgheria restaurants is consistent with the similar choice of offering handmade non-frozen and/or local prepared products. Lastly, in addition to the classic burger sandwiches M ** Bun offers dishes similar to those present in local restaurants e.g. knife-beaten raw bovine meat, agnolotti (a particular kind of filled pasta), tomini al verde (fresh cheese with garlic, parsley and oil).

The quality-price ratio is proportional to the raw materials used and the service offered, in line with the relative business model. The IHFs offer menu up to 10 euros with caloric values included between 650 and 1,470 kilocalories. The LHFs menus are more expensive than others mainly due to the local raw materials selected that are more expensive than conventional one (Table 1).

McDonald's and Burger King's pricing policies also include promotions for limited time periods for medium-sized menus with lower prices than the standard ones. However, the conventional offer includes a standard menu that can then be customized by varying ingredients, sizes and/or drinks. M** Bun foresees variations to the conventional proposal only in the choice of the drink while Burgheria does not offer fixed menus but allows different combinations with surcharge for added ingredients. Related to nutritional and caloric intake and in response to consumers' growing attention to these issues McDonald's and Burger King report on their websites detailed information.

Table 1. Prices and caloric value of the menus

	MCDONALD'S	BURGER KING	M** BUN	BURGHERIA
Menu prices*	Min. € 6.60 Max: € 9.90	Min. € 6.30 Max: € 8.50	Min. € 11.50 Max: € 14.00	Min. € 10.00 Max: € 14.50
Caloric Values**	790-1,300 kcal (circa)	650-1,470 kcal (circa)	-	-
* Menu is composed by sandwich, fries and soft drink (special and promotion menus excluded) ** Estimated values based on the indications given on the original websites				

Production Process

To date, the main international chains, such as McDonald's and Burger King, apply a hybrid system between MTS and MTO to their production process. However, on the basis of the interviews carried out in the piedmontese capital, the application of the system in the production phase is different, although there are some analogies between the two chains. Initially, McDonald's was mostly oriented to the first model i.e. MTS, basing its strategy on sales planning and demand estimation through the analysis of historical data. In fact, the lead time target of McDonald's aims at being lower than the one of its competitors i.e. one minute less than the standard set by Burger King, as well as being one of the company's strengths. The speed in the service represent a feature that has always distinguished McDonald's from competitors, nothing appears to be improvised and is everything aimed at satisfying customers' requests as soon as possible. With the recent introduction of the concept of "made-for-you" - whose sole objective is to be able to offer a meal as personalized as much as possible - the combination of the MTS and MTO production processes takes place in the choice of splitting the cooking phase of the meat from the assembly of the final product. Therefore, as far as meat preparation is concerned, they continue to apply a system based on sales forecasts, while the real sandwich is assembled only at the time of ordering. The system adopted is therefore analogous to the Assemble To Order (ATO) (Wortmann, 1983).

As far as Burger King is concerned, the strategy adopted envisages two distinctions. On the one hand, the basic sandwiches are prepared in advance by applying the MTS model, with the aim of being able to regularly guarantee fast service, especially in times of greater turnout. On the other hand, all Burger King restaurants apply a hybrid system, meaning that the meat is cooked to a certain cooking time according to sales forecasts, while the sandwich is then assembled with various ingredients based on customer requests. In this way, the will is to satisfy the consumer's needs, personalizing the offer.

The Local Hamburger Foodservices seem to be based on a MTO model. Indeed, M**Bun e Burgheria use a process where the hamburger cooking phase and subsequent assembly of the other sandwich's components take place at the time of customer's order. This model explains the difference in the lead times achieved to deliver the final product to the customer, requiring significantly longer time intervals than those of the two IHF operators. However, it is necessary to specify that the M** Bun restaurants have the speed of service as an essential requisite in their business model, while Burgheria, even if considers speed of service an important feature, do not list it among the essential ones in its business model.

Table 2. Comparison amongst production systems

	MCDONALD'S	BURGER KING	M** BUN	BURGHERIA
Production process	Hybrid (MTS and MTO)	Hybrid (MTS and MTO)	Make to Order (MTO)	Make to Order (MTO)
Medium Lead time*	1.5 min.	2.5 – 2.75 min	12 – 15 min.	8 - 12 min.
Maximum time MTS	10 min. (meat)	10 min. (MTS products) Fried products (few minutes)		
Meat preparation time	Just in Time	Just in Time	6 min.	6 min.
* Time between the closing of the order and the delivery of the requested product				

Services

The service quality and consequently the customers' satisfaction are the results of numerous aspects i.e. the relationship between the staff and the customers, the restaurant space, communication material and location, and the speed of the service.

The ability of staff to be able to always inform the consumer about their needs and the ability to always behave in a courteous manner are considered very important elements for all operators. specifically, with regards to interaction, problem solving and professional skills, M** Bun assigns the maximum value, while Burgheria and Burger King assign intermediate scores. With reference to the linguistic internationalization of the menus, McDonald's and Burger King are definitely in advantage because their products are sold with the same names all over the world. In this sense, Burgheria tends to have a national approach while M** Bun has chosen a local orientation. In any case, most of the employees working in the different restaurants can speak in English and therefore all the operators are able to serve non-italian customers. The quality of the interaction between employees and customers is considered very important in all the restaurants interviewed and, in general, communication is considered an essential element to guarantee an efficient service.

The internal design of any restaurant is essential and it influences the first impression that the consumer has with the restaurant. All the restaurants belonging to the same chain are homogeneous, presenting the same characteristics, similar furnishings and decorations (city center or suburbs), so that the identification of the restaurant is in line with the expectations of the customer. All the operators interviewed believe that these characteristics are essential for enhancing the quality of the service but they underlined how, in addition to the aesthetic aspects, the arrangement of the tables, the comfort of the chairs and armchairs and the lighting of the rooms are fundamental. Moreover, the cleanliness of tables and all the stuff, as well as the good presence of the operators have an influence on the customers' perception.

The reachability of the restaurants highlights instead the strong discrepancies between the different restaurants i.e. some restaurants are located in the suburbs or in shopping malls where it is possible to access to private parking or buy food directly from the car; other restaurants are located in the city center with more issues related to the access to the restaurant. However, these factors are not perceived as limits or weaknesses because the location satisfies a specific target area identified in the business plan phase.

The waiting time of consumers is proportional to the ordering system adopted by the restaurants. LHFs are characterized by longer preparation times that are partially balanced by waiting for the order to be processed directly at the table. The IHFs are based instead on the speed of order fulfillment with the peculiarity of McDonald's which, recently, offers the delivery service of the tray at the table. In general, the lead times set by each chain are respected by the staff and restaurants tend to fully interpret the type of experience expected by consumers.

CONCLUSION

With reference to the food products and their ingredients the European Union has developed various tools aimed at protecting traditions, safeguarding the territory and enhancing food origin through quality systems (Bentivoglio et al., 2019; Dias and Mendes, 2018; Bonadonna et al., 2017; Finco et al., 2017; Grunert and Aachmann, 2016; Hajdukiewicz, 2014).

Considering the foodservice, the big international chains, such as McDonald's and Burger King, offer an example of the strategic choices made at production level with the aim of delivering a product/service in the shortest possible time i.e. a reduced lead time, at a low price, able to satisfy consumers who, over the years, have changed their perception of quality in the food sector. In addition to this type of strategy, there is sometimes the search for innovative recipes that can also highlight the peculiarities of the territory in which the product is produced. In any case, this type of service offers a relatively reduced proposal of foods and beverages such as to be prepared, cooked and packaged in a more or less modular way, with reasonable prices, lower than those of any other type of catering activity. This type of restaurant can be identified as International Hamburger Foodservice (IHF). At the same time in Italy, this type of foodservice has been flanked by a different one i.e. Local Hamburger Foodservice (LHF). It is characterized by a particular attention to the type of supply chain used for the selection of the main raw materials and to the food preparation process (Bonadonna et al. 2019).

The research results identify two different catering services for hamburgers, international hamburger foodservice (IHF) and local hamburger foodservice (LHF): on the one hand, IHF is characterized by a strong focus on customer service, human resource management and operations management. On the other hand, LHF distinguishes itself for the high quality of the product offered in terms of product requirements and psychological requirements and the selection of local raw materials and ingredients, in support of the local economy and business.

Specifically, it emerges that McDonald's, Burger King and M** Bun restaurants fully fall into the fast food category, as they possess most of the typical characteristics of this type of restaurant: the main product, namely sandwiches with hamburger, and the other dishes offered (although M** Bun also offers products more similar to those of restaurants), as well as the locations and dimensions of the premises, the offer mode, the opening times and the lack of the reservation service. On the other hand, the Burgheria chain acts differently, it is a little less adherent to the parameters of the sector, although there are many elements that associate it to the others, starting from the products offered.

In line with the general data that underlines a growth of the catering sector in Italy, as well as a growth of consumption outside home, the types of restaurants analysed remain faithful to the their basic principle, that is to offer a rapid service, differentiate themselves and personalize the offer.

In all four cases observed, it is present the desire to offer the highest food quality, that is also the characteristic most taken into consideration by customers, with an important research of the right suppliers, above all for what concerns M** Bun and McDonald's.

The accessibility remains a focal point influencing customers' choice and satisfaction. As for reachability through its own means such as cars, Burger King has made it its point of strength.

The other restaurants taken into consideration present a reasonable accessibility in terms of location (near the main streets, city districts, etc., and therefore easily reachable on foot), that is not a casual choice for McDonald's and Burger King, while M** Bun and Burgheria exploited the opportunities presented.

From some studies emerged that 14.5% of those who decide to have breakfast outside declare to go to a fast food restaurant, despite the great part of the population choose bars or pastry shops. From the research carried out, it emerged that only McDonald's offers this type of service in some of its restaurants, thanks also to an extension of the opening hours from the early morning hours. So far, there have been 4 locals in the studied area that provide the McCafé service, a real cafeteria, a comfortable space that in all respects recalls the classic bars.

Burger King, on the other hand, although if McDonalds pursues a specific strategic choices in serving breakfast, has not yet planned to introduce a similar service. In the case of the other two Turin realities the breakfast is not a considered offer.

In general, it emerged that the current and future strategic choices of the two apparently equivalent American fast food giants are someway different.

In addition to what has been said so far, McDonald's underlines a desire to differentiate the customer consumption experience, trying to divert the classical idea of fast food from the mind of the consumer, but to get as close as possible to the concept of restaurant (see the introduction of table service) and of bars (through McCafé). Moreover, given the considerable attention paid in recent years to food and the typical Italian products and their quality, the well-known chain has been moving in this direction for some time now, through the introduction of special sandwiches and the collaborations with important chefs. The opposite strategy is instead the one undertaken by Burger King, which aims at a greater customization of the products as they are considered the company's core business. The focus is therefore on the sandwich and to try to put the customer first, trying to satisfy his requests.

Analogies can be found in terms of digitization, both increasingly focusing on a self-service service, through touch-screen ordering screens (a service already in place in many local McDonald's and recently present also in Burger King, such as in the one recently opened in Corso Novara).

The two realities in Turin examined have similarities in terms of the service offered, as can be seen in the analysis of the questionnaires, but of the differences in the chosen business model. M** Bun, which defines itself an agri-hamburgheria, refers to some features of the largest American chains, with the aim, however, of offering local products, quick to prepare, including them in the fast food world, a fast food at zero and quality. Burgheria was born with the idea of offering a consumer experience equal to that which could be had in a classic American burger, presenting some aspects that recall those of fast food, but others similar to those of restaurants (as well as being a future goal of the chain that of becoming more and more equal to an American dinner).

Finally, in line with the findings regarding the growing demand from home delivery customers, it is noted that the four chains considered are also moving in this direction and are entering the activation of this service within their own plans of investments, either alone (as in the case of Burger King) or through partnerships with the main players in the sector (as in the case of M** Bun with Just Eat etc.

and McDonald's with Glovo). An exception is represented by Burgheria, which at the moment is not able to guarantee this service, but it is in any case part of its future strategies.

FUTURE RESEARCH DIRECTIONS

This chapter deal with the current evolution of food service driven by innovation and sustainability using the case of Hamburger operating in Greater Turin, which translated in fundamental aspects such as: raw materials and ingredients, food processes, the service provided by the foodservice hamburger, a particular type of Quick Service Restaurant. The aspects relating to the selection of raw materials and their processing method for food preparation allow the analysis of the different business models applied in the study area. On the one hand, IHFs are driven by the dual objective of effectiveness and efficiency to reduce costs, offering limited-cost meals, and maximize profits. On the other hand, the LHFs tend to pursue an objective balance of the quality/price ratio that does not affect the first magnitude in favor of the latter, even if the two operators analyzed tend to have a different business model in terms of selected raw materials and related services. The results highlight some theoretical and practical implications in relation to the foodservice literature with particular reference to the chosen production process model and to the need to satisfy different consumer targets, always more careful and demanding, with a product that is basically similar. In particular, the study highlights a market transition in which demand appears to be oriented towards meals with high quality standards in terms of raw materials and ingredients that operators try to satisfy with different strategies. However, the study proves to have several gaps, such as the small number of interviewed operators, which, although representative of the study area, are only a part of the Quick Service Restaurant in the area, and the reduced geographical area, given the fact that the phenomenon of the foodservice hamburger is quite widespread also in other Italian and foreign areas. These gaps could be filled by comparative studies involving other geographical areas of the European Union in order to provide more structured results that allow for an extended understanding of the phenomenon.

ACKNOWLEDGMENT

A special thanks to Giulia Ambrois for the work done during the research project.

REFERENCES

Abdelhadi, A. (2016). Using lean manufacturing as service quality benchmark evaluation measure. *International Journal of Lean Six Sigma*, *7*(1), 25–34. doi:10.1108/IJLSS-02-2015-0003

Annunziata, A., Agovino, M., & Mariani, A. (2019). Sustainability of Italian families' food practices: Mediterranean diet adherence combined with organic and local food consumption. *Journal of Cleaner Production*, *206*, 86–96. doi:10.1016/j.jclepro.2018.09.155

Antonelli, G. (Ed.). (2004). *Marketing agroalimentare. Specificità e temi di analisi* (Vol. 322). FrancoAngeli.

Arcese, G., Flammini, S., Lucchetti, M., & Martucci, O. (2015). Evidence and experience of open sustainability innovation practices in the food sector. *Sustainability*, *7*(7), 8067–8090. doi:10.3390u7078067

Basf (2018). BASF Report 2018. Economic, environmental and social performance. Available at https://www.basf.com/global/en/who-we-are/sustainability.html

Bayer. (2018). Sustainable development reports. Available at https://www.investor.bayer.de/en/reports/sustainability-reports/

Bedin, E., Torricelli, C., Gigliano, S., De Leo, R., & Pulvirenti, A. (2018). Vegan foods: Mimic meat products in the Italian market. *International Journal of Gastronomy and Food Science*, *13*, 1–9. doi:10.1016/j.ijgfs.2018.04.003

Bentivoglio, D., Savini, S., Finco, A., Bucci, G., & Boselli, E. (2019). Quality and origin of mountain food products: The new European label as a strategy for sustainable development. *Journal of Mountain Science*, *16*(2), 428–440. doi:10.100711629-018-4962-x

Bertoldi, B., Giachino, C., & Pucciarelli, F. (2011). The product development process in the family run businesses: an inside vision. In Ifera (pp. 1-18). Edizioni Fotograf.

Boccia, F. & Covino, D. (2016). Innovation and sustainability in agri-food companies: The role of quality. *Rivista di Studi sulla Sostenibilita'*.

Bojanic, D., Warnick, R., & Musante, M. (2007). An extension of burgernomics: using a full-service restaurant product to measure purchasing power parity. *The Journal of Hospitality Financial Management*, *15*(1), 57–69. doi:10.1080/10913211.2007.10653830

Bonadonna, A., Alfiero, S., Cane, M., & Gheribi, E. (2019). Eating hamburgers slowly and sustainably: the fast food market in northwest Italy. *Agriculture*, *9*(4), 77. doi:10.3390/agriculture9040077

Bonadonna, A. & Duglio, S. (2016). A mountain niche production: the case of Bettelmatt cheese in the Antigorio and Formazza valleys (Piedmont–Italy). *Quality-Access to success, 17*(150).

Bonadonna, A., Macar, L., Peira, G., & Giachino, C. (2017). The dark side of the European quality schemes: The ambiguous life of the traditional specialties guaranteed. *Calitatea*, *18*(156), 102.

Bresciani, S., Thrassou, A., & Vrontis, D. (2013). Change through innovation in family businesses: evidence from an Italian sample. *World Review of Entrepreneurship, Management and Sustainable Development 4, 9*(2), 195-215.

Brinkley, C. (2018). The small world of the alternative food network. *Sustainability*, *10*(8), 2921. doi:10.3390u10082921

Cappella, F., Giaccaria, P., & Peira, G. (2015). La filiera della carne piemontese: Scenari possibili. *Politiche Piemonte*, *36*, 6–12.

Carbone, A. (2018). Foods and places: comparing different supply chains. *Agriculture*, *8*(1), 6. doi:10.3390/agriculture8010006

Carzedda, M., Marangon, F., Nassivera, F., & Troiano, S. (2018). Consumer satisfaction in alternative food networks (AFNs): Evidence from northern Italy. *Journal of Rural Studies*, *64*, 73–79. doi:10.1016/j.jrurstud.2018.10.003

Castellini, A., & Samoggia, A. (2018). Customers' perception of fish fast-casual restaurants. *Journal of Food Products Marketing*, *24*(3), 348–371. doi:10.1080/10454446.2017.1266562

Chang, D. Y. (2009). Service quality assessment of a chain steakhouse in Taiwan. *Journal of Quality Assurance in Hospitality & Tourism*, *10*(4), 255–278. doi:10.1080/15280080903183417

Chase, R. B., Jacobs, R. F., Aquilano, N. J., Grando, A., & Sianesi, A. (2008). Operations Management nella produzione e nei servizi (pp. 1-477). McGraw-Hill, Publishing Group Italia.

Conti, C., Costa, A., Balzaretti, C., Russo, V., & Tedesco, D. (2018). Survey on food preferences of university students: from tradition to new food customs? *Agriculture*, *8*(10), 155. doi:10.3390/agriculture8100155

Costa, A. I. A. (2013). Collaborative product innovation in the food service industry. Do too many cooks really spoil the broth? In *Open Innovation in the Food and Beverage Industry* (pp. 154–173). Woodhead Publishing. doi:10.1533/9780857097248.2.154

Dadura, A. M., & Lee, T. R. (2011). Measuring the innovation ability of Taiwan's food industry using DEA. *Innovation (Abingdon)*, *24*(1-2), 151–172. doi:10.1080/13511610.2011.583863

DeSoucey, M. (2010). Gastronationalism: Food traditions and authenticity politics in the European Union. *American Sociological Review*, *75*(3), 432–455. doi:10.1177/0003122410372226

Dias, C., & Mendes, L. (2018). Protected designation of origin (PDO), protected geographical indication (pgi) and traditional speciality guaranteed (TSG): A bibliometric analysis. *Food Research International*, *103*, 492–508. doi:10.1016/j.foodres.2017.09.059 PMID:29389640

Dogan, B., & Gokovali, U. (2012). Geographical indications: The aspects of rural development and marketing through the traditional products. *Procedia: Social and Behavioral Sciences*, *62*, 761–765. doi:10.1016/j.sbspro.2012.09.128

Finco, A., Bentivoglio, D., & Bucci, G. (2017). A label for mountain products? Let's turn it over to producers and retailers. *Quality-Access to Success*, *18*, 198–205.

Finco, A., Bentivoglio, D., & Bucci, G. (2018). Lessons of innovation in the agrifood sector: Drivers of innovativeness performances. *Economia Agro-Alimentare*, (2), 181–192. doi:10.3280/ECAG2018-002004

Gava, O., Galli, F., Bartolini, F., & Brunori, G. (2018). Linking sustainability with geographical proximity in food supply chains. An indicator selection framework. *Agriculture*, *8*(9), 130. doi:10.3390/agriculture8090130

Giacosa, E., Giachino, C., Bertoldi, B., & Stupino, M. (2014). Innovativeness of Ceretto Aziende Vitivinicole: A first investigation into a wine company. *The International Food and Agribusiness Management Review*, *17*(4), 223–236.

Gordin, V., Trabskaya, J., & Zelenskaya, E. (2016). The role of hotel restaurants in gastronomic place branding. *International Journal of Culture, Tourism and Hospitality Research, 10*(1), 81–90. doi:10.1108/IJCTHR-05-2015-0049

Grunert, K. G., & Aachmann, K. (2016). Consumer reactions to the use of EU quality labels on food products: A review of the literature. *Food Control, 59*, 178–187. doi:10.1016/j.foodcont.2015.05.021

Guerrero, L., Guàrdia, M. D., Xicola, J., Verbeke, W., Vanhonacker, F., Zakowska-Biemans, S., ... Hersleth, M. (2009). Consumer-driven definition of traditional food products and innovation in traditional foods. A qualitative cross-cultural study. *Appetite, 52*(2), 345–354. doi:10.1016/j.appet.2008.11.008 PMID:19084040

Hajdukiewicz, A. (2014). European Union agri-food quality schemes for the protection and promotion of geographical indications and traditional specialities: An economic perspective. *Folia Horticulturae, 26*(1), 3–17. doi:10.2478/fhort-2014-0001

Harrington, R. J. (2005). Part I: The culinary innovation process—a barrier to imitation. *Journal of Foodservice Business Research, 7*(3), 35–57. doi:10.1300/J369v07n03_04

Harrington, R. J., Ottenbacher, M. C., & Fauser, S. (2017). QSR brand value: Marketing mix dimensions among McDonald's, KFC, Burger King, Subway and Starbucks. *International Journal of Contemporary Hospitality Management, 29*(1), 551–570. doi:10.1108/IJCHM-06-2015-0300

Hensel, K. (2012). Convenience food. *Food Technology, 66*(1), 34–43.

Inzelt, A., & Hilton, J. (Eds.). (1999). *Technology transfer: from invention to innovation* (Vol. 19). Springer Science & Business Media. doi:10.1007/978-94-015-9145-4

Jacobs, F. R., & Chase, R. B. (2008). *Operations and supply management: The core.* New York, NY: McGraw Hill/Irwin.

Jordana, J. (2000). Traditional foods: Challenges facing the European food industry. *Food Research International, 33*(3-4), 147–152. doi:10.1016/S0963-9969(00)00028-4

Kashif, M., Awang, Z., Walsh, J., & Altaf, U. (2015). I'm loving it but hating US: Understanding consumer emotions and perceived service quality of US fast food brands. *British Food Journal, 117*(9), 2344–2360. doi:10.1108/BFJ-01-2015-0040

Keith, N. K., & Simmers, C. S. (2011). Measuring service quality perceptions of restaurant experiences: The disparity between comment cards and DINESERV. *Journal of Foodservice Business Research, 14*(1), 20–32. doi:10.1080/15378020.2011.548209

Lee, C., Hallak, R., & Sardeshmukh, S. R. (2019). Creativity and innovation in the restaurant sector: Supply-side processes and barriers to implementation. *Tourism Management Perspectives, 31*, 54–62. doi:10.1016/j.tmp.2019.03.011

Lee, K.-A., & Lyu, E.-S. (2019). Importance-performance analysis (IPA) of university foodservice quality by customer group according to the foodservice satisfaction and customer loyalty. *Journal of the Korean Society of Food Science and Nutrition, 48*(1), 109–119.

Maltese, F., Giachino, C., & Bonadonna, A. (2016). The safeguarding of Italian eno-gastronomic tradition and culture around the world: a strategic tool to enhance the restaurant services. *Quality-Access to Success, 17*(154).

Marcoz, E. M., Melewar, T. C., & Dennis, C. (2016). The value of region of origin, producer and protected designation of origin label for visitors and locals: The case of fontina cheese in Italy. *International Journal of Tourism Research, 18*(3), 236–250. doi:10.1002/jtr.2000

Massini, R. (2010). Prospettive di R&S per l'industria alimentare. *Industrie Alimentari, 49*(500), 19–26.

Mathe, K., & Slevitch, L. (2013). An exploratory examination of supervisor undermining, employee involvement climate, and the effects on customer perceptions of service quality in quick-service restaurants. *Journal of Hospitality & Tourism Research (Washington, D.C.), 37*(1), 29–50. doi:10.1177/1096348011413590

Mathur, S. (2017). Glocalization in fast food chains: a case study of McDonald's. In Strategic Marketing Management and Tactics in the Service Industry (pp. 330-347). Hershey, PA: IGI Global. doi:10.4018/978-1-5225-2475-5.ch013

McDonald's Italia. (2015). McDonald's McItaly Piemontese e Chianina. Available at http://www.mcdonalds.it/sites/default/files/mcdonalds_mcitaly_cs_chianina_e_romagnola.pdf

McDonalds. (2019). McDonald's MySelection 2019. Retrieved from https://www.mcdonalds.it/myselection

Mikkelsen, B. E., Kristensen, N. H., & Nielsen, T. (2006). Innovation processes in large-scale public foodservice—case findings from the implementation of organic foods in a Danish County. *Journal of Foodservice Business Research, 8*(2), 87–105. doi:10.1300/J369v08n02_07

Mkono, M. (2012). Slow food versus fast food: A Zimbabwean case study of hotelier perspectives. *Tourism and Hospitality Research, 12*(3), 147–154. doi:10.1177/1467358412470556

Ng, R. Y. X., Wong, Y. S., Yeo, J. Y., Koh, C. L. Z., Wilson, C., & Gan, S. K. E. (2018). The associations between dietary practices and dietary quality, biological health indicators, perceived stress, religiosity, culture, and gender in multicultural Singapore. *Journal of Ethnic Foods, 5*(3), 220–227. doi:10.1016/j.jef.2018.07.003

Nguyen, Q., Nisar, T. M., Knox, D., & Prabhakar, G. P. (2018). Understanding customer satisfaction in the UK quick service restaurant industry: The influence of the tangible attributes of perceived service quality. *British Food Journal, 120*(6), 1207–1222. doi:10.1108/BFJ-08-2017-0449

Nuebling, M., Behnke, C., Hammond, R., Sydnor, S., & Almanza, B. (2017). On tap: Foodservice operators' perceptions of a wine innovation. *Journal of Foodservice Business Research, 20*(3), 251–267. doi:10.1080/15378020.2016.1209722

Parkins, W. (2004). Out of time: Fast subjects and slow living. *Time & Society, 13*(2-3), 363–382. doi:10.1177/0961463X04045662

Peri, C. (2006). The universe of food quality. *Food Quality and Preference, 17*(1-2), 3–8. doi:10.1016/j.foodqual.2005.03.002

Petrini, C. (2005). Buono pulito e giusto. Nuovi principi di neogastronomia.

Pietrykowski, B. (2004). You are what you eat: The social economy of the slow food movement. *Review of Social Economy, 62*(3), 307–321. doi:10.1080/0034676042000253927

Rahimnia, F., Moghadasian, M., & Castka, P. (2009). Benchmarking leagility in mass services: The case of a fast food restaurant chains in Iran. *Benchmarking: An International Journal, 16*(6), 799–816. doi:10.1108/14635770911000123

Rarick, C., Falk, G., & Barczyk, C. (2012). The little bee that could: Jollibee of the Philippines v. Mcdonald's. *Journal of the International Academy for Case Studies, 18*(3), 83.

Rodrigo, I., Cristóvão, A., Tibério, M. L., Baptista, A., Maggione, L., & Pires, M. (2015). The Portuguese agrifood traditional products: Main constraints and challenges. *Revista de Economia e Sociologia Rural, 53*(suppl 1), 23–32. doi:10.1590/1234-56781806-94790053s01002

Rodríguez-López, M. E., Alcántara-Pilar, J. M., & Ahmed-Laroussi, A. (2018). La estrategia de estandarización de Mcdonald´ s.¿ es valorada del mismo modo en todos los países? El caso de los jóvenes en España, Turquía, Italia y Bulgaria. *Globalización, Competitividad y Gobernabilidad de Georgetown/ Universia, 12*(3).

Rydell, S. A., Harnack, L. J., Oakes, J. M., Story, M., Jeffery, R. W., & French, S. A. (2008). Why eat at fast-food restaurants: Reported reasons among frequent consumers. *Journal of the American Dietetic Association, 108*(12), 2066–2070. doi:10.1016/j.jada.2008.09.008 PMID:19027410

Ryu, K., & Han, H. (2010). Influence of the quality of food, service, and physical environment on customer satisfaction and behavioral intention in quick-casual restaurants: Moderating role of perceived price. *Journal of Hospitality & Tourism Research (Washington, D.C.), 34*(3), 310–329. doi:10.1177/1096348009350624

Saleh, F., & Ryan, C. (1991). Analysing service quality in the hospitality industry using the SERVQUAL model. *Service Industries Journal, 11*(3), 324–345. doi:10.1080/02642069100000049

Schamel, G. (2007). Auction markets for specialty food products with geographical indications. *Agricultural Economics, 37*(2-3), 257–264. doi:10.1111/j.1574-0862.2007.00272.x

Tencati, A., & Zsolnai, L. (2012). Collaborative enterprise and sustainability: The case of slow food. *Journal of Business Ethics, 110*(3), 345–354. doi:10.100710551-011-1178-1

Timpanaro, G., Foti, V. T., Scuderi, A., Schippa, G., & Branca, F. (2018). New food supply chain systems based on a proximity model: The case of an alternative food network in the Catania urban area. *Acta Horticulturae*, (1215), 213–217. doi:10.17660/ActaHortic.2018.1215.39

UN. (2014). Food and food waste. Available at https://www.unenvironment.org/explore-topics/resource-efficiency/what-we-do/sustainable-lifestyles/food-and-food-waste

Vanhonacker, F., Verbeke, W., Guerrero, L., Claret, A., Contel, M., Scalvedi, L., ... Hersleth, M. (2010). How European consumers define the concept of traditional food: Evidence from a survey in six countries. *Agribusiness, 26*(4), 453–476. doi:10.1002/agr.20241

Vrontis, D., Bresciani, S., & Giacosa, E. (2016). Tradition and innovation in Italian wine family businesses. *British Food Journal, 118*(8), 1883–1897. doi:10.1108/BFJ-05-2016-0192

Wortmann, J. C. (1983). A classification scheme for master production scheduling. In *Efficiency of manufacturing systems* (pp. 101–109). Boston, MA: Springer. doi:10.1007/978-1-4684-4475-9_10

Wu, H. C., & Mohi, Z. (2015). Assessment of service quality in the fast-food restaurant. *Journal of Foodservice Business Research*, *18*(4), 358–388. doi:10.1080/15378020.2015.1068673

ADDITIONAL READING

DeSoucey, M. (2010). Gastronationalism: Food traditions and authenticity politics in the European Union. *American Sociological Review*, *75*(3), 432–455. doi:10.1177/0003122410372226

Jacobs, F. R., & Chase, R. B. (2008). *Operations and supply management: The core*. New York, NY: McGraw Hill/Irwin.

Kashif, M., Awang, Z., Walsh, J., & Altaf, U. (2015). I'm loving it but hating US: Understanding consumer emotions and perceived service quality of US fast food brands. *British Food Journal*, *117*(9), 2344–2360. doi:10.1108/BFJ-01-2015-0040

Love, J. F., & Miller, A. W. (1986). *McDonald's: Behind the arches* (Vol. 177). New York: Bantam Books.

Mathur, S. (2017). Glocalization in Fast Food Chains Glocalization in Fast Food Chains: A Case Study of McDonald's. In Strategic Marketing Management and Tactics in the Service Industry (pp. 330-347). IGI Global. doi:10.4018/978-1-5225-2475-5.ch013

Sood, T. (Ed.). (2017). *Strategic Marketing Management and Tactics in the Service Industry*. IGI Global. doi:10.4018/978-1-5225-2475-5

Vignali, C. (2001). McDonald's:"think global, act local"–the marketing mix. *British Food Journal*, *103*(2), 97–111. doi:10.1108/00070700110383154

Xin, G. (2015). The Study of Brand Choice Decision of Top 3 Global Brand Quick Serviced Restaurant (KFC, McDonald's, Burger King) in Bangkok.

Yang, N. (2012). Burger king and McDonald's: Where's the spillover? *International Journal of the Economics of Business*, *19*(2), 255–281. doi:10.1080/13571516.2012.684929

KEY TERMS AND DEFINITIONS

Assemble to Order (ATO): It is a manufacturing process in which the basic parts of the product are already manufactured and are assembled after the customers' order. This model allows to a quick reply and a medium level of customization of products.

Fast-Food: A particular kind of quick restaurant service in Italy i.e. initially only the operators as McDonald's, Burger King, currently also with local operators as M** Bun and Burgheria.

Food Innovation: It is considered an important element to achieve strategic objectives and meet the needs of consumers, who tends to change their tastes periodically. In this case, innovation in production system and selection of local ingredients are important elements.

Food Sustainability: It is considered an important element in term of social and environmental targets. In this case, the targets can be reached by local ingredients and short supply chain.

IHF: The production and offer of burgers by conventional chains such as McDonald's and Burger King.

Lead Time: It is the total time required to manufacture an item from customer's order to product delivery. In this case, it is an essential element to compare the selected quick restaurant operators.

LHF: The production and offer of burgers by local realities that have emerged over the last decade i.e. M** Bun and Burgheria.

Make to Order (MTO): It is a manufacturing process in which production starts only after a customer's order is received.

Make to Stock (MTS): It is a manufacturing process in which production is oriented to stock based on forecast demand. This model allows to a very quick reply.

Production Process: The transformation of a range of inputs into those outputs that are required by the market. In this chapter, the comparison of different process is an essential element.

Chapter 14
Consumer Behavior:
Motivational Factors for the Decision to Purchase Organic Products in the Municipality of Guadalajara, Jalisco

José G. Vargas-Hernández
University of Guadalajara, Mexico

Jovanna Nathalie Cervantes Guzmán
University of Guadalajara, Mexico

ABSTRACT

This chapter develops a model of the behavior of the ecological consumer to know what motivates the decision to purchase organic products in citizens 25 to 45 years old in the city of Guadalajara. The methodology used in the research is qualitative and was carried out through the non-experimental design, with respect to the data collection tool. Results of in-depth interviews support the general hypothesis related to the factors that influence the purchase decision. One of the limitations the study faced was a limited literature regarding studies involving Guadalajara.

INTRODUCTION

The society is currently aware and gives greater importance to the care of the environment, therefore the objective of this study is to develop a model of the behavior of the ecological consumer in order to know the motivations that influence the consumption of organic products.

The first part of this study focuses on the problem statement, the objectives, research questions are presented and hypotheses are proposed to continue with the second part of the study where the concepts related to the subject are concentrated. In this way, the concepts of ecological product will be revised so that the term used throughout the investigation is understood. Another concept that is necessary to explain is an ecological consumer that, like the previous one, is mentioned repeatedly throughout the study.

DOI: 10.4018/978-1-7998-1419-1.ch014

In the third part of the research, the motivational factors that influence the decision to purchase organic products are presented, which are concern for health and the environment, social influences, marketing mix (4p's) and consumer knowledge about environmental problems. In the fourth part, the methodology used in the research is presented, followed by the results and analysis of the results obtained from the research. To conclude with the main limitations and guidelines for future research.

THE RESEARCH PROBLEM

Statement of the Problem

In recent years, environmental problems have intensified, especially those related to non-pollution, climate change and ecological awareness in the consumption of products. Currently, at the national and international level, there are four large environmental groups founded in the 60s and 70s that are the current basis of the militant institutional environmental movement. These are basically Greenpeace, WWF-ADENA, Ecologists in Action, and Seo / Birdlife. (Bravo, 2010).

Due to ecological and marketing research that took place at an early stage in the sixties, environmental movements emerged (Hendarwan, 2002). they sought a new lifestyle and global alternatives to the industrial and consumer society, thus seeking to achieve the transformation of ecology. And it is because of this social movement that materializes the new market segment constituted by ecological consumers, individuals more concerned about the environmental consequences of what they consume, and be sensitive to the negative effects that the impact of human activities have on the environment and the health of people (Santesmases, 2004).

According to Fernández, Cea, Santander & Nuñez, (2013) the main reason for purchasing organic products is that consumers consider them to be healthier because their products are subjected to methods that guarantee the care of environment. On the other hand, Tregear, Dent & McGregor, (1994) tells that the environmental factor explains only a small part of organic food purchases, because consumers have a more egocentric behavior, where concern for oneself and, consequently, concern for their health plays a much more important role in the purchase of these products.

Meanwhile the survey conducted by National Geographic; GlobeScan, (2012) showed that consumers with "ecological conscience" are a niche that grows fast in Mexico, creating a trend, but what factors motivates them to buy this type of products? it is just a novelty or the consumers really consider that the consumption of ecological products and / or services help with the care of the environment. Green consumption in Mexico has been a subject little investigated academically, since the few jobs that exist are market studies, such as the Green Study of (TNS Research International, (2010) which mentions that almost 50% of Mexicans prefer consume products that are friendly to the environment

Therefore, it is necessary that more research be done especially in Mexico to decipher the behavior of consumers who prefer organic products. The subject is of interest for various audiences because there is a possible business opportunity for the creation of companies, products and / or services with green features that help differentiate in an increasingly competitive market and of course for associations, movements and people that seek to promote sustainable lifestyles in the population. For these reasons, the object of study is to know the motivations that influence the decision to purchase organic products in citizens from 25 to 45 years of the municipality of Guadalajara.

Justification

To understand the importance of studying the motivational variables of purchase, one must first reflect on the concept, according to Myers, (2005) Quoted in Arana, Meilán, Gordillo, & Carro, J., (2010). Motivation forms together with the emotion the non-cognitive part (practical, irrational, warm) of the human mind. Etymologically, the word motivation comes from the Latin moveo, movere, movi, motum (what moves or has the virtue to move) and is interested in knowing the reason for the behavior. It is the need or desire that directs and energizes the behavior toward a goal.

When explaining ecological behavior, motivational variables can contribute to the understanding of this behavior and explain why it is often found that individuals do not show high stability in their actions and, therefore, it is difficult to make an exact prediction of behavior (Thogersen, 2004). In this research, a review and interpretation is carried out in relation to the behavior of the ecological consumer attending to this research object, the motivational variables that predict an ecological behavior in the consumers between the ages of 25 and 45 years of the municipality of Guadalajara, Jalisco are identified. Being very useful to know the changes that are currently in the buying behavior.

Research Objectives

General Objective

Develop a model of the behavior of the ecological consumer in order to know the motivations that influence the decision to purchase organic products in the 25 to 45-year-old citizens of Guadalajara.

Specific Objectives

1. Determine what is the motivation that influences the decision to purchase organic products in citizens from 25 to 45 years of the municipality of Guadalajara.
2. Identify the degree of knowledge that citizens of 25 to 45 years of the municipality of Guadalajara have about organic products
3. Analyze what actions reflect consumers of organic products from 25 to 45 years of the municipality of Guadalajara in terms of environmental concerns.

General Research Question

Which are the motivations that influence in the decision of purchase of ecological products in the citizens of 25 to 45 years of the municipality of Guadalajara?

Specific Research Questions

1. What is the motivation that influences the decision to purchase organic products among citizens between 25 and 45 years of age in the municipality of Guadalajara?
2. What is the degree of knowledge that citizens of 25 to 45 years of the municipality of Guadalajara have about organic products?

3. What actions do consumers of organic products from 25 to 45 years of age reflect in the municipality of Guadalajara regarding environmental concerns?

Hypothesis

1. General
   a. H: The environmental motivation is not the predominant at the time of preferring organic products.
2. Specific Hypotheses
   a. H1: The concern for health and the environment is a motivational factor that influences the decision to purchase organic products.
   b. H2: Social influences are a motivational factor that influences the decision to purchase organic products.
   c. H3: The Marketing mix (4p's) is a motivational factor that influences the decision to purchase organic products.
   d. H4: The consumer's knowledge about environmental problems is a motivational factor that influences the decision to purchase organic products.

CONCEPTUAL FRAMEWORK

Product

Taking Bonta and Farber (1994) as a reference, they describe the term product as having certain peculiarities to satisfy the needs or desires of the consumer. In the same way, the American Marketing Association (A.M.A., 2017) states that the concept of product from a marketing perspective refers to a set of attributes (characteristics, functions, benefits and uses) that give the ability to be exchanged or used. Usually, it is a combination of tangible and intangible aspects. Thus, a product can be an idea, a physical entity (a good), a service or any combination of the three. The product exists for purposes of exchange and for the satisfaction of individual and organizational objectives.

While Kotler and Armstrong, (2012) offer another more detailed concept: The product concept holds that consumers will favor products that offer the highest quality, the best performance and the most innovative features. Under this concept, the marketing strategy focuses on making continuous improvements to the product. Quality and product improvement are important parts of most marketing strategies. However, concentrating only on the products of the company can also lead to marketing short-sightedness.

Ecological Products

It is important to mention that for the purposes of this work, that it is understood ecological product. According to (Minetti, 2002), in different countries they are called by different names. Foods called organic in the United States and other countries are called "organic" (Singer & Mason, 2009). Also are used interchangeably the terms "biological product" or "organic product" as synonyms (López Eguilaz & Remírez Esparza, 1998). To define the concept of this type of product, Calomarde (2000) says that

Table 1. Matrix of operationalization of variables

Theme	Consumer behavior: Motivational Factors for the decision to purchase organic products in the municipality of Guadalajara, Jalisco
General objective	Develop a model of the behavior of the ecological consumer in order to know the motivations that influence the decision to purchase organic products in the citizens of 25 to 45 years of the municipality of Guadalajara.
Specific objectives	Determine what is the motivation that influences the decision to purchase organic products in citizens from 25 to 45 years of the municipality of Guadalajara. Identify the degree of knowledge that citizens of 25 to 45 years of the municipality of Guadalajara have about organic products. Analyze what actions consumers of organic products from 25 to 45 years of Guadalajara reflect regarding environmental concerns.
General question	Which are the motivations that influence in the decision of purchase of ecological products in the citizens of 25 to 45 years of the municipality of Guadalajara?
Specific questions	What is the motivation that influences the decision to purchase organic products for citizens between 25 and 45 years of age in the municipality of Guadalajara? What is the degree of knowledge that citizens of 25 to 45 years of the municipality of Guadalajara have about organic products? What actions do consumers of organic products from 25 to 45 years of Guadalajara reflect regarding environmental concerns?
General hypothesis	H: The environmental motivation is not the predominant at the time of preferring organic products.
Specific hypothesis	H1: The concern for health and the environment is a motivational factor that influences the decision to purchase organic products H2: Social influences are a motivational factor that influences the decision to purchase organic products. H3: The Marketing mix (4p's) is a motivational factor that influences the decision to purchase organic products H4: The consumer's knowledge about environmental problems is a motivational factor influencing the decision to purchase organic products.
Variables	Dependent: Consumer behavior. Independent: Motivational Factors.
Indicators	Ecological consumer behavior. Concern for health and the environment. Social influence. Marketing Mix (4p's) Consumer knowledge about environmental problems
Methodology	Qualitative

Source: Own elaboration

it is ecological when the product fulfills the same function as a conventional one and causes a lower environmental impact considering its life cycle.

The International Federation of Organic Agriculture Movements (IFOAM, 2009), states that this type of food compared to conventional, show:

1. Lower amount of water, storing a higher density of nutrients.
2. Greater amount of iron, magnesium, vitamin C and antioxidants.
3. Better balance with essential amino acids.

While the animals raised with this system, they present:

1. Better health in general.
2. Reduced risk of contracting or carrying diseases.
3. Less amount of fat.

The Ecological Consumer

Orozco (2003), defines the concept of ecological consumer as one who is willing to change their behavior patterns for others more respectful of the environment. On the other hand, Carrete, et al. (2013) establish five groups of consumers according to their degree of ecological activity:

1. Eco Indifferent are those that focus on reduction activities, with little interest in recycling or buying organic products.
2. Eco-followers of trends buy organic products
3. Eco-savers focus on the reduction and reuse and not so much in the purchase of products.
4. Anti-ecological they are not interested in anything related to reuse, reduction, or recycling or purchase of organic products.
5. Eco-integral, are the most committed to the ecological, reduction, recycling, purchase of organic products and reused.

Profile of Ecological Consumers

Mostafa (2006) determines gender differences in relation to knowledge, pro-environmental concerns and attitudes about green purchases. Their results suggest that men show greater knowledge in environmental issues. The Revista Vinculado, (2005) confirms that in Mexico, as in Latin American and European countries, the people with the greatest willingness to buy are women, who belong to small families, with higher expenses in food and belonging to middle income segments. However, the segment of higher consumption is in the high income and high educational levels as well as coincides with Martínez (2006) which indicates that the the usual consumer of organic products has a high level of education and a high purchasing power.

A study carried out by Fraj Andrés & Martínez Salinas, (2002) define in a general way that the ecological consumer has the following characteristics:

1. They are young people with a medium or higher level of education.
2. In relation to their values and lifestyle they have a high entrepreneurial capacity, they like to be fashionable, lead a healthy life and collaborate in the improvement of the environment
3. Their attitude can be called ecological because they are very concerned about environmental pollution.
4. They show a greater knowledge about environmental issues.

Figure 1. Explains more easily a comparison between social and ecological marketing

Figure 1 Ecological Marketing
Source: Vicente Molina (2001).

THEORETICAL FRAMEWORK

Ecological Marketing

Green marketing consists of all the activities designed to generate and facilitate any exchange the intention of satisfying human needs and desires, in such a way that the satisfaction of these needs and desires occurs, with minimal harmful impact on the natural environment (Rani, Aravind, & Prasad, 2014). From a social point of view, ecological marketing is about educating, informing and changing behaviors that damage the environment (Rivera Camino, 2001).

Eco-marketing has become a means by which environmental issues can be addressed and the company's products can be commercialized (Rani, Aravind, & Prasad, 2014), which is why companies have needed to design and implement environmental programs. Ecological marketing to reach consumer segments sensitive to problems and educate them in their transformation to sustainable consumption patterns (Calomarde, 2000).

The Production and Purchase of Organic Products in Mexico

The Research Institute of Ecological Agriculture (FiBL) and IFOAM (2018) show data from the study "The world of ecological agriculture 2016" where 210,000 of organic producers were registered in Mexico, ranking third in the world. The organic products that are most produced in Mexico are coffee, aromatic and medicinal herbs, vegetables, cocoa and wild grapes. As for the sale of organic foods in self-service stores, they have increased 20 percent annually and in specialty stores, the increase was 10 percent. (SAGARPA, 2013). In Mexico, they can be found in a matter of fresh foods: fruits, vegetables, milk, milk, cheese, egg, chicken, buffalo and processed: juices, sweets, grains, flours, wines, liqueurs, honeys, syrups (Impulso Orgánico Mexicano AC, 2014).

Lifecycle

The lifecycle is used to assess the environmental burden of a product, process or activity throughout its life cycle (Capuz Rizo & Gómez Navarro, 2004). The author Calomarde (2000) says that there is no ecological product by itself, but according to its environmental behavior throughout its life cycle, from the analysis of the raw materials that comprise it, its production processes as a whole, its use, the waste generated by its distribution and transport and, finally, its reuse or disposal.

Therefore, the production of an ecological product is based on obtaining greater human well-being and at the same time reducing environmental risks (United Nations Industrial Development Organization [UNIDO], 2011). The raw materials and materials used in the production processes constitute a flow of materials that includes raw materials of natural origin. (Cervera-Ferri & Ureña, 2017). In the Arroyo, Chamorro and Miranda, (1999) present the stages that a product must go through in its life cycle and this reduces its ecological footprint.

Characteristics of the Ecological Product

The ecological products have certain peculiarities in their elaboration which does not harm the environment and the animals besides that the properties of these products are totally natural (Buenstorf and Cordes, 2008). The ecological attributes can be classified into two types:

1. Specific attributes of the product: duration, its facility to be recycled / reused, the type, the amount of materials used in the product and its packaging.
2. Specific attributes of the process: energy consumption, water or the generation of waste (Hernández & López, 2012).

The Purchase of Organic Products

The purchase of organic products can be defined as a practice of environmental awareness that reduces sources of waste and promotes recycling and reclamation of purchased materials, without adversely affecting the requirements for the execution of such materials (Min & Galle, 2001). A study conducted by Trujillo León & Vera Martínez, (2011) "Green consumption in Mexico: knowledge, attitude and behavior", people are willing to make more responsible purchases, but 41% consider that the prices of green products are higher than traditional products.

Figure 2.

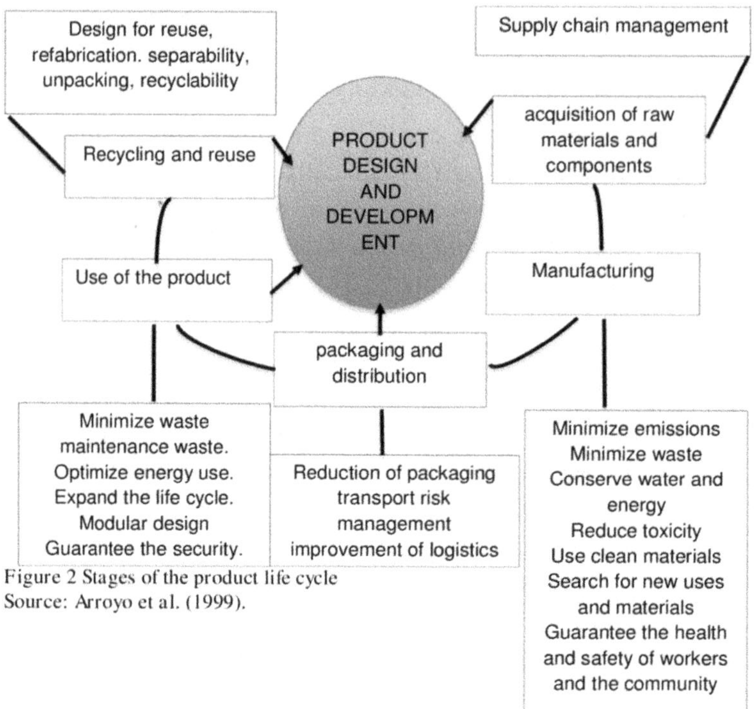

Figure 2 Stages of the product life cycle
Source: Arroyo et al. (1999).

Consumer Behavior

Consumer behavior reflects the decisions of consumers regarding the acquisition, consumption and disposal of goods, services, activities, experiences (Hoyer et al., 2010). There are several theories that try to explain the behavior of the consumer, for this work only the following are briefly explained:

The psychoanalytic theory of Sigmund Freud cited by Kotler and Armstrong (2012), suggests that purchasing decisions are influenced by subconscious motives that even the consumer does not understand. According to Veblen (1899) in his theory of idle class the main reason that guides the behavior of people in their need for integration in their social group. The theory of classical conditioning, demonstrated by the physiologist Ivan Pavlov where Kotler and Armstrong (2012) explain that advertising has to be based on this theory according to which buyers learn to identify a certain product by a symbol repeatedly linked to it. The learning process is through the stimulus-response model.

Ecological Behavior

The ecological consumer has behaviors with different approaches that can range from the purchase of organic products, recycling, voting, activism or others (Izagirre-Olaizola, Fernández-Sainz, & Vicente-Molina, 2013). The ecological consumer is a conscious and sensitive buyer of the repercussions that his consumption habits impose on the sustainable development of the region where he lives. Values the quality of life in terms of respect for the environment, the responsible use of natural resources, the care of their health and the general welfare of their community. Recognizes that this attitude towards life can have additional economic costs and is willing to face them (Martínez Turrubiates & Martín Prieto, 2009).

Consumers have different attitudes that can better explain consumer behavior on organic products (Calomarde, 2000):

1. Ecological conscience. It represents the ecological beliefs and knowledge that are part of the consumer. These can be increased thanks to the information you receive and remember about the benefits of a certain type of consumption.
2. Eco posture. Affective attitude toward organic products. This position is influenced by the culture, education and information that the consumer receives.
3. Eco activity. It is related to personality based on the consumer's tendency to act ecologically.

Purchase Motivation

Motivation forms together with emotion the non-cognitive part of the human mind. Etymologically the word motivation comes from the Latin moveo, moveré, movi, motum (what moves or has the virtue to move) and is interested in knowing the reason for the behavior. It is the need or the desire that directs and energizes the behavior toward a goal (Myers, 2005; Cited in Arana, et al., 2010).

When a consumer is sufficiently motivated to acquire the product, has the ability and the opportunity to do so, he / she will be sure to expose themselves, perceive and pay attention to the information that they consider relevant for their decision (Hoyer, MacInnis, & Pieters, 2010). Another term of motivation suggests that people are driven to act by different types of factors, experiences and highly varied consequences or in other words, people have not only different amounts of motives but also different types of motives (Ryan & Deci, 2000).

Motivational Factors of Ecological Purchase

The factors that intervene in the ecological behavior are internal and external. The first are those sources of information about an ecological product or service that influence the values, ideas, attitudes, intentions, opinions of each person. Externally, they are advertising, information, social groups, family and friends, among others (Shiffman & Kanuk, 2001) (Fraj Andrés & Martínez Salinas, 2002). In this research, four factors studied by several authors are presented:

Concern for Health and the Environment

The ecological consumer manifests his concern for the environment in his buying behavior (Min & Galle, 2001). derived from this concern, another concern appears, the environmental health that is related to all the physical, chemical and biological external factors of a person. That is, it encompasses environmental factors that could affect health. (World Health Organization, [WHO] 2018). According to research on the consumer of organic products, in Mexico, Latin America and Europe, the main reason to buy organic products is related to health (Linked Magazine, 2005).

A study conducted by the Cuidadano Observatory of quality of life: Jalisco as we go, (2017) in the state of Jalisco a percentage of 34% of the population of the lower social strata reported having had a serious health problem the final semester of 2016.

Food

In the state of Jalisco, people's health is affected by several factors (some are congenital); Certain habits such as food can also influence him. (Cuidadano Observatory of quality of life: Jalisco as we go, 2017). The change in the diet of consumers has changed, mainly for health reasons (Del Greco, 2010). Islas García & Sánchez Plascencia, (2013) state that: Healthy consumption has a direct impact not only on the individual sphere, but also on the social sphere and above all on the environment.

Social Influences

To reduce the search and evaluation effort or reduce uncertainty, consumers seek opinions from other people, especially when the perceived risk of the decision increases (Lamb, Hair, & McDaniel 2011). Through coexistence with other people is that consumers form attitudes that influence their lives. (Schiffman, Kanuk, & Wisenblit, 2010). The consumer seeks and issues his opinions based on the information he receives from friends, family, friends, and media that interest him (Rojas, 2012).

Family

For the Mexican it is very important to have family approval and feel accepted. He is very concerned about "what they will say", a situation that is accentuated in more closed societies such as in the province, and manifests itself even more in the lower social classes, since it is not uncommon to find cases in which a family cohabits with its families and close relatives (Galindo, 2010). Lamb, et al. (2011) state that the influencers in the family are the members whose opinions are valued, but who makes the decision to buy or cannot be another member. While Galindo, (2010) states that in Mexican families, the process, from the decision and until the completion of the purchase is the responsibility of the housewife. Although she is the one who makes the decisions, her tastes and needs are always subordinated, in the first place, to family demands and secondly to spending.

In Mexico, each generation of families are transmitters of values and cultural norms, so children learn by observing their parents' consumption patterns, so they will tend to buy in a similar pattern (Lamb, et al., 2011).

Influencer

The use of celebrities in communication increases the credibility of the messages, increases the recall and recognition of the advertised brands, improves the attitude towards the organization that sells the product, and even increases the likelihood of purchase (Agrawal & Kamakura, 1995). Nine of the ten most important influencers come from the digital environment and influence 60% in the decision of the brands that users buy (Expansión, 2017).

Marketing Mix

Kotler & Armstrong, (2012) claim that the marketing mix as the set of controllable tactical marketing tools that the company combines to produce a desired response in the target market. The marketing mix includes everything the company can do to influence the demand for your product. The marketing mix consists of four elements (known as the four p's): product, price, place and promotion (Schiffman, Kanuk, & Wisenblit, 2010).

Price

Kotler & Armstrong, (2012) point out that the consumer can establish a purchase intention based on issues such as their expectations of disposable income, the price to be paid and the benefits to be obtained. However, unexpected events would change their purchase intention. There is a limitation when buying organic products which Caamal Cauich, Pat Fernandez, Ascencio, & Pérez Fernández, (2007) explain that the high price of organic products it is partly due to production costs, which are higher compared to the costs of conventional foods.

A study conducted in 60 countries showed that 66% of the global respondents, being consumers from all types of regions and income levels, acknowledged their willingness to pay more for sustainable products (Nielsen, 2016).

Promotion

The promotion involves activities that communicate the advantages of the product and persuade the target customers to buy it (Kotler & Armstrong, 2012). Lamb, et. al., (2011) states that the promotional strategy uses elements or tools, which may include advertising, public relations, sales promotion and personal sales. Advertising affects the daily life of consumers, informs them about products and services and influences their attitudes, beliefs and, finally, their purchases (Lamb, et al., 2011).

The attitude towards ecological awareness publicity depends on the involvement of the consumer (Zinkhan & Carlson, 1995). It has been shown in various studies that to be credible this publicity consumer must be highly involved while those who feel little involved do not trust in said announcements (D'Souza & Taghian, 2005). Green advertising is about informing customers about the environmental benefits of the products, and its objective is to influence consumers' buying behavior by encouraging them to buy organic products and direct their attention to the positive consequences for them and the environment (Rahbar & Wahid, 2011).

A study conducted by Nielsen, (2016) shows that television ads that highlight a company's commitment to positive social and / or environmental impact influence the purchasing process for 34% of global respondents.

Consumer Awareness of Environmental Problems

The knowledge of the consumer is considered as one of the factors that influence several stages of the decision process (Laroche, Bergeron, & Barbaro-Forleo, 2001).

Several studies found that individuals with greater knowledge of environmental issues were willing to pay more for products considered ecological (Amyx, et al., 1994, cited by Laroche, et al., 2001).

Ecological Awareness

This term is defined as the knowledge and experiences that people actively use in their relationship with the environment (Febles, 2004 cited in Alea, 2006). The degree to which people are aware of environ-

Figure 3.

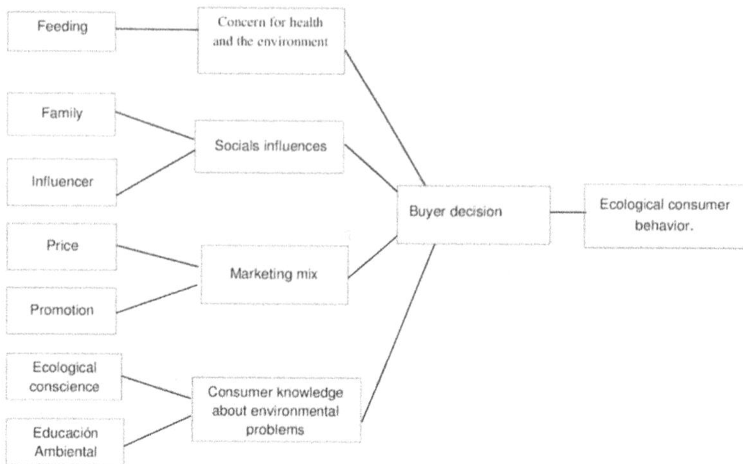

Figure 3 Proposed structural model.
Source: Own elaboration.

mental problems and support efforts to resolve them or manifest a willingness to personally contribute to the solution (Dunlap & Jones, 2002, cited by Romero, s.f.).

Environmental education is a learning process which needs to transform social practices through the habitus which provides human behavior with patterns of perception, thought and action that shape subjectivity (Barbosa Sánchez, 2008). In Mexico, the Secretary of the Environment and Natural Resources (SEMARNAT) is in charge of raising awareness among the population in general about the importance of the global environment and its problems. (Pérez Abuin, 2016)

Environmental education lies in providing a particular knowledge about the interaction of the human being with its biological and social environment (Barbosa Sánchez, 2008)

It is worth mentioning that in Mexico, environmental education is very poor at all levels (Montaño Salas, 2012).

Proposed Structural Model

Based on the theoretical framework, the study seeks to define the relationships between the motivations that influence the decision to purchase organic products, the model presented below was adapted for citizens from 25 to 45 years of the municipality of Guadalajara from a study called "Important Motivators for Buying Green Products" made in Malaysia and which was prepared by Kianpour, Anvari, Jusoh, & Fauzi Othman, (2014).

METHODOLOGY

In this chapter the methodology used for the development of the study is explained. Based on the needs of the study, qualitative research was used, it was carried out through non-experimental design, with respect to the data collection tool they were carried out through in-depth interviews. The methodology of the work is described in more detail below.

Research Focus

The development of this research is of a qualitative nature. It uses data collection without numerical measurement to discover or refine research questions in the interpretation process (Sampieri, Fernández Collado, & Baptista Lucio, 2010). Based on in-depth interviews with consumers who have already shown preference for organic and / or organic products in the municipality of Guadalajara, Jalisco.

Research Design

This research was carried out through the non-experimental design. According to Sampieri, et al., (2010) non-experimental designs are studies that are carried out without the deliberate manipulation of variables and in which only the phenomena are observed in their natural environment and then analyzed. Non-experimental designs can be classified as transactional and longitudinal, for this study we chose the transectional classification that is" collect data in a single moment, in a single time (Sampieri, et al., 2010).

The study being descriptive and exploratory the first one investigates the incidence of the modalities, categories or levels of one or more variables in a population (Sampieri, et al., 2010). The exploratory is ideal for the present investigation. According to Sampieri, et. al., (2010), the exploratory studies serve to familiarize with relatively unknown phenomena, obtain information about the possibility of carrying out a more complete investigation.

Sampling Design

The investigation was carried out by means of a non-probabilistic sampling, so the type of sampling is for convenience. Which is used simply with available cases to which have access (Sampieri, et al., 2010).

Sample Size

The unit of analysis indicates who will be measured, whether the participants or cases to whom in the last instance we will apply the measurement instrument (Sampieri et al., 2010).

Elements: People from 25 to 45 years old from the municipality of Guadalajara Jalisco, who frequent stores, eco-bazaars and organic markets.

Scope: Municipality of Guadalajara, Jalisco.

Time: March 9, 2018 to March 11, 2018.

Data Collection

To carry out the data collection, first a procedure plan was elaborated in which, first, the variables to be measured were established to later build the collection instrument and finally establish the dates to carry it out. The data collection was made on March 9 and 11, 2018, visiting the stores, eco-bazaars and organic markets, to collect the information was done by means of a questionnaire being applied by an interviewer.

Data Collection Instrument

The data collection instrument that was used was through an in-depth interview applied through a questionnaire consisting of questions structured in an open manner. To measure the variables included in the proposed model have been measured individually assigning a series of items for each, obtaining a total of thirteen items.

ANALYSIS OF RESEARCH RESULTS

An analysis of the qualitative data obtained is carried out. As a first step the data has been organized and classified with the most relevant of the interview. Data were analyzed directly from the collection tool as Sampieri et al. (2010) says in the qualitative research data collection and analysis. They usually occur at the same time. Next, representative maps of the results obtained are presented.

Results of the Factors of Concern for Health and the Environment

Next, Figure 4 shows the categories (patterns or responses) most frequently mentioned, health care being the most repetitive concept when it comes to asking the questions assigned to this item and ensuring that while taking care of their health. At the same time, they take care of the planet, in addition to agreeing that conventional products are harmful. So it is concluded that the H1: The concern for health and the environment is a motivational factor that influences the decision to purchase organic products is accepted.

Results of the Social Influences Factors

With respect to social influences, it was obtained that consumers follow a line of recommendations from friends and health professionals, leaving aside the recommendations and opinions of the family. Figure 5 shows the categories (patterns or responses) with the highest frequency of mention. The H2: Social influences are a motivational factor that influences the decision to purchase organic products, it is accepted.

Figure 4.

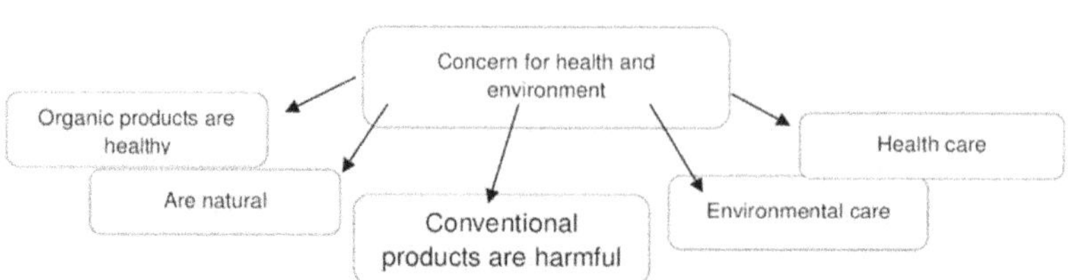

Figure 4. Responses more frequently.
Source: Own elaboration

Figure 5.

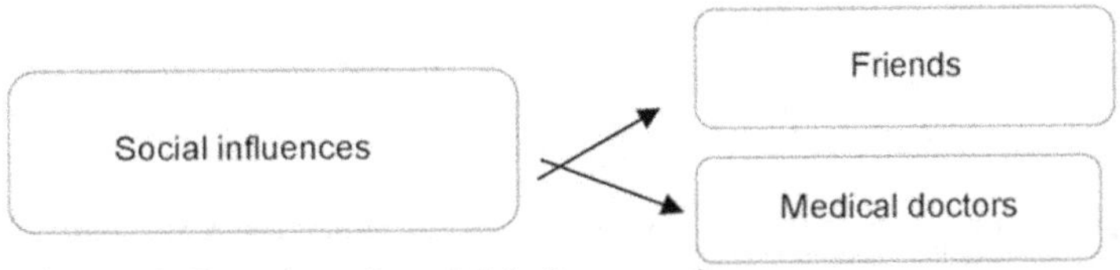

Figure 5. Results of social influence factors
Source: Own elaboration

Results of Marketing Mixing Factors

The categories (patterns or responses) are shown with the highest frequency of mention. For the interviewees, the perception of the price attribute, is valued by consumers as a relevant attribute because they all agreed that they are expensive, so it is considered that it can be a reason to influence when buying the product. On the other hand, they have been exposed to the advertising of these products, they trust in the veracity of the commercial, but most deny having acquired the product only because they have seen the advertising of the product. Based on the results obtained, the H3 is accepted: The Marketing mix (4p's) is a motivational factor that influences the decision to purchase organic products.

Results of the Consumer Knowledge Factors on Environmental Problems

The people interviewed stated that they know the problems that currently exist regarding environmental problems and claim to take action to do something about it and contribute to environmental care, being the recycling and not littering the street the actions most performed by the interviewees.

So the H4: The consumer's knowledge about environmental problems is a motivational factor that influences the decision to purchase organic products is fully accepted. In figure 7, the categories (patterns or responses) are shown with the highest frequency of mention.

Figure 6.

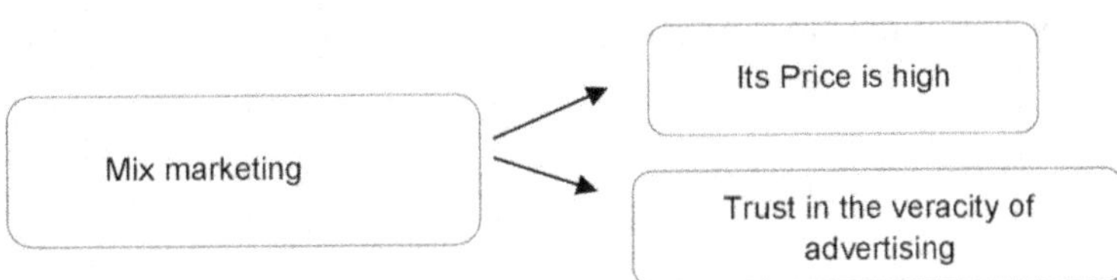

Figure 6: Results of the factors of the marketing mix.
Source: Own elaboration

Figure 7.

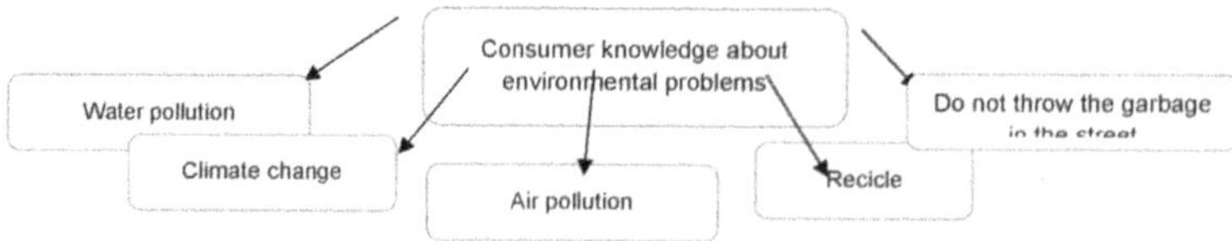

Figure 7: Results of consumer knowledge factors on environmental problems.
Source: Own elaboration

CONCLUSION

There is a great lack of information in terms related to the behavior of the ecological consumer. However, this study allows to know more about the motivations that influence the decision of ecological purchase and the situation in which this market is currently in the municipality of Guadalajara, Jalisco.

At the conclusion of the study, the objectives set for the research are achieved. In relation to the first objective, a structural model is proposed, based on the analyzed theory. Regarding the specific objectives, the first one has been able to conclude that the motivation that most influences the decision to purchase organic products among citizens between 25 and 45 years of age in Guadalajara is the concern for health and the environment. In relation to the second specific objective, it is possible to identify that the citizens of the municipality of Guadalajara are aware of the environmental problems that exist today. In relation to the third specific objective, it has been observed that the citizens of Guadalajara have been forced to modify their habits of life and take action measures such as recycling, care of water and responsible use of resources to contribute to environmental care.

Regarding the general hypothesis raised at the beginning of this study which says that the environmental motivation is not the predominant at the time of preferring organic products, so based on the results obtained it is possible to say that the hypothesis is fully accepted. It should be noted that this research study is one of the first to offer information on ecological behavior in the municipality of Guadalajara. So it is suggested to continue researching in this type of topic since the ecological market is growing and it is important to know about it also that it can be applied in the other municipalities of Jalisco.

Research Limitations

The main limitation in this study is the time that was established for conducting the study. On the other hand, the selection of the sample is another limitation, since it has not been sufficiently representative of the population because the method of data collection used was the in-depth interview, however, allows to obtain information of great interest to design future studies on the subject.

Finally, the study faced a limited literature regarding studies related to it in the case of the city of Guadalajara.

REFERENCES

Agrawal, J., & Kamakura, W. (1995). The economic worth of celebrity endorsers: An event study analysis. *Journal of Marketing*, *59*(3), 56–62. doi:10.1177/002224299505900305

Alea García, A. (2006). Diagnóstico y potenciación de la educación ambiental en jóvenes universitarios. *Odiseo, Revista electrónica de Pedagogía.*, *3*(6).

American Marketing Association. (2017). Ama.org. Retrieved from https://www.ama.org/Pages/default.aspx Sección: Diccionario Términos de Marketing.

Arana, J., Meilán, J., Gordillo, F., & Carro, J. (2010). Estrategias motivacionales y de aprendizaje para fomentar el consumo responsable desde la Escuela. R.E.M.E. *Revista electrónica de Motivación y Emoción, XIII*(35-36), 19-39.

Arroyo, A., Chamorro, A., & Miranda, F. J. (1999). Diseño para el medio ambiente: Hacia una integración entre innovación y medio ambiente. Libro de ponencias del XIII Congreso Nacional de AEDEM

Barbosa Sánchez, A. (2008). Hacia una cultura ambiental con equidad de género. In *U. d. Chiapas, Educación Ambiental para la sustentabilidad en México* (1st ed.). Chiapas, Mexico: UNICACH.

Bonta, P. & Farber, M. (1994). 199 preguntas sobre marketing y publicidad. Bogotá, Colombia: Norma.

Bravo, G. F. (2010). *Partidos verdes y movimientos ecologistas*. Recuperado de www.revistas.unam.mx/index.php/matices/article/download/25725/24217

Buenstorf, G., & Cordes, C. (2008). Can sustainable consumption be learned? A model of cultural evolution. *Ecological Economics*, *67*(4), 646–657. doi:10.1016/j.ecolecon.2008.01.028

Caamal Cauich, I., Pat Fernández, V. G., Ascencio, F. J., & Pérez Fernández, A. (2007). Producción, comercialización y consumo de productos orgánicos en Alemania. *Textual (Chapingo)*, 133–153.

Calomarde, J. (2000). *Marketing Ecológico*. Madrid, Spain: Pirámide ESIC. doi:84-368-1426-6

Capuz Rizo, S., & Gómez Navarro, T. (2004). *Ecodiseño: Ingeniería del ciclo de vida para el desarrollo de productos sostenibles*. México: Alfaomega.

Carrete Lucero, L., González, E. M., Centeno Velázquez, E., Castaño González, R., & Félix, R. (2013). ¿Qué características tienen los consumidores verdes en México? Un enfoque sobre segmentación demográfica fundamentada en las 3R's y la compra de productos ecológicos. Estudios Gerenciales, 30(132), 287-300. Recuperado de http://static1.squarespace.com/static/56228080e4b04bb42a1523da/t/56b39785cf80a1b5f4184f1d/1454610372295/TG2013_Carrete_etal.pdf

Cervera-Ferri, J. L., & Ureña, M. L. (2017). *Indicadores de producción verde: Una guía para avanzar hacia el desarrollo sostenible*. Santiago, Chile: CEPAL.

D'Souza, C., & Taghian, M. (2005). Green advertising effects on attitude and choice of advertising themes. *Asia Pacific Journal of Marketing and Logistics*, *17*(3), 51–66. doi:10.1108/13555850510672386

Del Greco, N. I. (2010). Estudio sobre tendencias de consumo de alimentos. Primera parte-Generalidades y casos. *Datos relevantes para la toma de decisiones en la Agroindustria de Alimentos y Bebidas.*

Diehr, P., & Beresford, S. A. (2003). The relation of dietary patterns to future survival, health, and cardiovascular events in older adults. *Journal of Clinical Epidemiology*, *56*(12), 1224–1235. doi:10.1016/S0895-4356(03)00202-6 PMID:14680674

Expansión. (2017). Influencers 2017. *Expansión*. Obtenido de https://www.pressreader.com/mexico/expansion-m%C3%A9xico/20171115/283128544143988

Fernández, C., Cea Valencia, J., Santander, P., & Nuñez, K. (2013). Consumo verde en Chile: estudio exploratorio sobre consumidor de productos ecológicos. *Global Conference on Business and Finance Proceedings*. Obtenido de https://www.researchgate.net/profile/Cristobal_Fernandez/publication/260364788_Consumo_Verde_en_Chile_Estudio_exploratorio_sobre_consumidor_de_productos_organicos/links/0f317530e614c76869000000/Consumo-Verde-en-Chile-Estudio-exploratorio-sobre-consumidor-

Fraj Andrés, E., & Martínez Salinas, E. (2002). *Comportamiento del consumidor ecológico*. Madrid, Spain: ESIC.

Galindo, A. (2010). Psicología del Consumidor Mexicano. *Revista del Instituto Tecnológico de México*(48), 1-4.

Hendarwan, E. (2002). Seeing green. *Global Cosmetic Industry*, *170*(5), 16–18.

Hernández, Y. & López, D. (2012, Mayo-Agosto). El marketing ecológico y su integración en la planificación estratégica. *Revista de Estudios Interdisciplinarios en Ciencias Sociales, 14*(2), 223-231.

Hopfenbeck, W. (1993). The green management revolution: Lessons in environmental excellence. New York, NY: Prentice Hall.

Hoyer, W., MacInnis, D., & Pieters, R. (2010). Comportamiento del consumidor (5 ed.). (M. E. Ma. del Pilar Carril Villarreal, Trad.) México: Cengage Learning.

IFOAM Federación Internacional de Movimientos de Agricultura Orgánica. (2009). La Agricultura Orgánica y la Salud Humana. Obtenido de http://infohub.ifoam.bio/sites/default/files/page/files/oa_humanhealth_es.pdf

Impulso Orgánico Mexicano, A. C. (2014). *Orgánicos en México*. Obtenido de https://www.impulsoorganicomexicano.com/productos-orgnicos-en-mxico

Islas García, C. & Sánchez Plascencia, M. A. (2013). Consumo saludable: hacia nuevos hábitos de consumo. *Procuraduría Federal del Consumidor*. Obtenido de https://www.profeco.gob.mx/educ_div/educ_y_org_cons/documentos/Consumo%20saludable%20ci.pdf

Izagirre-Olaizola, J., Fernández-Sainz, A., & Vicente-Molina, M.-A. (2013). Antecedentes y barreras a la compra de productos ecológicos. *Universia Business Review*(38), 108-127.

Kianpour, K., Anvari, R., Jusoh, A., & Fauzi Othman, M. (2014). Important motivators for buying green products. *Intangible Capital*, *10*(5), 873–896. doi:10.3926/ic.470

Kotler, P., & Armstrong, G. (2012). *Marketing* (14th ed.). México: Pearson.

Lamb, C., Hair, J., & McDaniel, C. (2011). *Marketing*. México: Cengage Learning.

Laroche, M., Bergeron, J., & Barbaro-Forleo, G. (2001). Targeting consumers who are. *Journal of Consumer Marketing, 18*(6), 503–520. doi:10.1108/EUM0000000006155

López Eguilaz, M. J. & Remírez Esparza, L. (1998). *Marketing ecológico y sector industrial.* Madrid, Spain: UNED.

Martínez Ramón, M. (2006). El mercado de los productos ecológicos en EEUU. *Instituto español del comercio exterior.* Obtenido de http://www.exportapymes.com/documentos/productos/Ie2409_eeuu_ecologicos.pdf

Martínez Turrubiates, A., & Martín Prieto, F. (2009). *Las megatendencias sociales actuales y su impacto en la identificación de oportunidades estratégicas de negocios* (1st ed.). Monterrey, Mexico: Instituto Tecnológico y de Estudios Superiores de Monterrey. Obtenido de http://studylib.es/doc/7253097/las-megatendencias-sociales-actuales-y-su-impacto

Min, H. & Galle, W. (2001). Green purchasing practices of US firms. *Intentions Journal of Operations & Production Management, 21*(9).

Minetti, A. C. (2002). *Marketing de alimentos ecológicos* (1st ed.). Madrid, Spain: Pirámide.

Montaño Salas, F. E. (2012). La educación ambiental en México ante la crisis ambiental. *Revista Vinculando.* Obtenido de http://vinculando.org/ecologia/la-educacion-ambiental-en-mexico-ante-la-crisis-ambiental.html#Educacion_Ambiental_en_Mexico

Mostafa, M. M. (2007). Gender differences in Egyptian consumers' green purchase behaviour: The effects of environmental knowledge, concern and attitude. *International Journal of Consumer Studies, 31*(3), 220–229. doi:10.1111/j.1470-6431.2006.00523.x

National Geographic; GlobeScan. (2012). *Greendex 2012: Consumer Choice and the Environment a worldwide tracking Survey.* Canadá. Obtenido de http://images.nationalgeographic.com/wpf/media-content/file/NGS_2012_Final_Global_report_Jul20-cb1343059672.pdf

Nielsen. (2016). Nuevas percepciones en las expectativas de consumo. *Ganar-Ganar*, 38-43.

Observatorio Cuidadano de calidad de vida: Jalisco como vamos. (2017, July). ¿Como nos vemos los tapatíos? Encuesta de percepción cuidadana sobre la calidad de vida 2016. Obtenido de http://www.jaliscocomovamos.org/encuesta2016

ONUDI (Organización de las Naciones Unidas para el Desarrollo Industrial). (2011). Iniciativa de industria verde para el desarrollo industrial sostenible. Viena. Obtenido de http://www.greenindustryplatform.org/wp-content/uploads/2014/06/green-industry_ES_highres.pdf

Organizacion Mundial de la Salud. (2018). *Organizacion Mundial de la Salud.* Obtenido de http://www.who.int/topics/environmental_health/es/

Orozco Abundis, M. A., Cortes Lamas, A. I., González, M., & Gracia Villar, S. (2003). Mercadotecnia ecológica: actitud del consumidor ante los productos ecológicos. Obtenido de http://www.aeipro.com/files/congresos/2003pamplona/ciip03_1041_1050.2224.pdf

Pérez Abuin, J. A. (2016). *Revista de Educacion y Cultura*. Obtenido de http://www.educacionyculturaaz.com/noticias/educacion-ambiental-en-mexico

Rahbar, E. & Wahid, N. A. (2011). Investigación del efecto de las herramientas de marketing verde 'en el comportamiento de compra de los consumidores. *Serie de estrategia empresarial, 12*(2), 73-83. doi:10.1108/17515631111114877

Rani, A., Aravind, J., & Prasad, T. (2014). Green marketing and its impact. *European Centre for Research Training and Development UK, 2*(8), 45-48. Obtenido de http://www.eajournals.org/wp-content/uploads/Green-Marketing-and-Its-Impact1.pdf

KEY TERMS AND DEFINITIONS

Buying Behavior: Conduct of the consumers relative to the de facto purchase of a product, as well as to the site and the frequency of such purchases.

Consumer Behavior: Consumer behavior is that part of the behavior of people and the decisions that this implies when they are acquiring goods or using services to meet their needs.

Decision Purchase: Important decision process that lies behind the act of buying a product or service, consisting of different stages through which the buyer passes to decide which product or service is best suited to their needs and provides a greater value. If the purchasing decision is satisfactory and provides value to the consumer and, in addition, relational marketing tools are used for the loyalty of the latter, the reiteration of the purchase to the same supplier is highly probable.

Ecological Purchases: The "ecological purchases" suppose the systematic application of compatible criteria with the environment to all the acquisitions and daily operations. In short, it is about meeting the needs of the company with the most appropriate products and favorable to the environment.

Guadalajara: It is the name of the capital of Jalisco, Mexico. Guadalajara is a city and Mexican municipality, capital and most populated city of the state of Jalisco. It is located in western Mexico, in the center of Jalisco.

Motivation Factors: The set of needs that explain the behavior of people are what we call motivating factors or motives: organic motivators and social motivators.

Organic Products: It is called organic food, organic food, or biological food to agricultural or agro-industrial product that is produced under a set of procedures called "ecological." In general, ecological methods avoid the use of synthetic products, such as pesticides, herbicides, and artificial fertilizers.

Psychological Motivators: The motivation is those stimuli that move a person, to perform certain actions, which require an effort to achieve in objective.

APPENDIX

Guide to the interview that was applied

Good day / afternoon. I am a graduate student in Marketing, from the University of Guadalajara. The interview I do is about a survey, to know Motivational Factors that influence the decision to buy organic products. All the data you provide will be treated responsibly for educational purposes.

Name:
Age: ____________ Genre: ____________
Civil status:____________________________
Level of studies: _________________________
Municipality: ______________________________

1. What are organic products for you?
2. What kind of organic products do you buy?

(Organic agricultural products, Hygiene products, keeping the home, Biodegradable materials, Sustainable fashion, Products for physical and emotional well-being)

3. Since when do you consume organic products?
4. Why have you decided to buy organic products?

Consumer knowledge about environmental problems

5. Do you know the main environmental problems that affect the planet?

Mention 3

6. What kind of action do you take to care for the environment?

Concern for health and the environment

7. What are the benefits of buying organic products?
8. What do you think of the phrase? "The purchase of organic products contributes to the improvement of the Environment"
9. Why consume organic products instead of conventional ones?
10. Social influences

11. Has any member of your family, friends or other person influenced your purchase decision to any extent? Specify

Marketing mix

12. What is your opinion about the prices of organic products?
13. Do you trust the veracity of the advertising of organic products?
14. Have you bought an organic product because you saw its advertising? In what medium? what a product?

Chapter 15
Millennial's Involvement in Corporate Social Responsibility

Eleonora Rapiti
https://orcid.org/0000-0003-4394-2965
University of Tuscia, Italy

Cecilia Silvestri
https://orcid.org/0000-0003-2528-601X
University of Tuscia, Italy

ABSTRACT

Corporate Social Responsibility (CSR) has come to be regarded as a great strategic marketing tool and an important part of the business paradigm (Supanti and Butcher, 2019). Several authors (i.e. Choi and La, 2013) studied CSR as a driver of satisfaction and loyalty. This chapter focused on the behavior of Millennials to which CRS is an integral part of their lives. However, studies in the literature on this topic are limited. The chapter fills the gap of existing literature and increases knowledge on this issue by: (1) identifying, through factor analysis, the dimensions of CSR and (2) analyzing, through cluster analysis, the relationships between CSR and Customer Satisfaction (CS) and Customer Loyalty (CL) of different Millennials groups. The results show how the knowledge of the CSR conditions the behavior of millennials by helping to increase their level of satisfaction and loyalty.

INTRODUCTION

In recent years, CSR has come to be regarded as a great strategic marketing tool and an important part of the business paradigm (Supanti and Butcher, 2019). This is because consumers do not ask companies for only a high-quality product, but they are "characterized as being satisfied with products that are developed by socially responsible firms" (Luo and Bhattacharya, 2006, Mohammed and Rashid, 2018 p. 360). Moreover, several authors (e.g. Choi and La, 2013; Kucukusta et al. 2013; Othman e Hemdi, 2015, Paulik et al., 2015) studied CSR as a driver of satisfaction and loyalty. Indeed, Sogari et al. (2017) proved that consumers in their purchase choices focusing on the product/process dimension of envi-

DOI: 10.4018/978-1-7998-1419-1.ch015

ronmental sustainability. Many authors recently (e.g. Formánková et al., 2019; Cavaliere and Ventura, 2018; Bonadonna et al., 2017) concentrated on analyzing the behavior of a precise target of individuals concerning the CSR policies implemented by firms, i.e. Millennials. This generation is composed of individuals born between 1980 and 2000 and they are called Millennials because of their closeness to the new millennium and being raised in a more digital age (Kaifi et al., 2012; Smith and Nichols, 2015). Formánková et al., (2019) claimed that for Millennials, CRS is an integral part of their life and there are more aware of CSR. In fact, in line with the research conducted by Frey (2018) on the topic of Millennials Generation (MG), "one of the long-term trends that continued with millennials [has been] the increase in education attainment" (p. 12) based on an education-oriented to sustainability (Bonadonna et al., 2017). The millennials, therefore, as students, possess extensive knowledge of basic principles of ecology and sustainability and adopt environmentally responsible consumption practices (Earl et al., 2003; Emanuel and Adams, 2011). According to a study led by PricewaterhouseCoopers in 2011, 88% of Millennials prefer companies that emphasize CSR and 86% would consider leaving if their employer's CSR no longer met their expectations. These data are also confirmed by research conducted in the literature. Catano and Morrow Hines, (2016) developed an experimental design in which analyzed how Millennial generation applicants evaluated the firm concerning implementing CSR policies. The results showed as good advertising of such policies increases the initial attractiveness of the organization to job seekers. Instead, Supanti and Butcher (2019) proved that CSR participation has a strong influence over work-related outcomes in the Millennials.

However, in the literature, there are no studies that analyze the topic of CS and CL in the Millennials concerning firms that implement CSR policies. Indeed, based on a literature search conducted on SCOPUS databases (Keywords— TITLE-ABS-KEY "corporate social responsibility" AND TITLE-ABS-KEY "millennial" AND TITLE-ABS-KEY "customer satisfaction" OR TITLE-ABS-KEY "customer loyalty"), no documents were found. While modifying some keywords (TITLE-ABS-KEY "corporate social responsibility" AND TITLE-ABS-KEY "millennial" AND TITLE-ABS-KEY "loyalty" OR TITLE-ABS-KEY "satisfaction"), search provided 3 papers. Eveland et al., (2018) analyzed the CSR topic and study the necessary drivers in order to build a trust-based consumer relationship. The authors proved that Millennial consumers expect organizations/brands to engage in CSR activities and if these policies do not reflect the customer's value system (shared values), the long-term relationship can be impacted negatively. Amoroso and Roman (2019) evaluated the importance of CSR in Millennials and how this can influence their intention to purchase. The results showed that loyalty and trust appear stronger among older-age consumers than among the younger-age consumers. Finally, Lerro et al., (2019) studied the attitude of Millennial consumers towards several CSR activities carried out by food companies. The findings showed that loyalty plays a crucial role in affecting consumers' willingness to support CSR initiatives.

Aim of this study is to fill up the gap of existing literature and increase the knowledge on this topic, through the development of a survey conducted on "Millennial Generation (MG) students" (Cavaliere and Ventura, 2018, p. 641) at the University of Tuscia (Viterbo, Italy). In particular, this study has two objectives: (1) to identify, through factor analysis, the dimensions of CSR and (2) to analyze, through a cluster analysis, the relationships between CSR and CS/CL of different Millennials groups.

The chapter is structured as follows: (1) definition of CRS concept (2) literature review of the relationship between CSR, CS and CL in the last ten years (2009-2019); (3) the relationship between CSR and CS/CL; (3) material and methods; (4) results; (5) discussion and conclusions.

BACKGROUND

Corporate Social Responsibility

Corporate social responsibility (CSR) has been an important and progressing topic since the 1950s "when many people believed that the actions of corporations are closely related to society and the public and should conform to and satisfy social values and expectations" (Bowen, 1953, Lee, 2019, p. 45). McGuire (1963) stated the idea that the corporation has not only economic and legal obligations but also certain responsibilities to society, which extend beyond these obligations contributed to the definition of the concept of socially responsible behavior for firms, a topic widely discussed in the literature in the following years (i.e. Carroll, 1979; Jamali and Mirshak, 2007). Based on "definition of social responsibility that state that companies must make a profit, obey the law and go beyond mere compliance with laws" (Cuesta-Valiño et al. 2018, p. 2), Carroll (1979) developed a model which identifies four dimensions of CRS: economic, legal, ethical, and philanthropic. "Economic responsibility is a baseline requirement that must be met in a competitive business world" (Carroll 2016, p. 3) and include the obligation of satisfying consumers with products of good value, as well as generating enough profits for investors. "Legal responsibilities require firms to obey laws and comply with regulations while fulfilling their economic obligations" (Lee, 2019, p. 46). Ethical responsibilities implicate "that businesses will be responsible for and responsive to the full range of norms, standards, values, principles, and expectations that reflect and honor what consumers, employees, owners and the community regard as consistent with respect to the protection of stakeholders' moral rights" (Carroll, 2016, p. 3). Finally, philanthropic responsibility "includes all forms of business giving. Corporate philanthropy embraces business's voluntary or discretionary activities" (Carroll, 2019, p. 3). This model has been widely accepted and used by several authors, i.e. Lewin et al., 1995; Maignan and Ferrell, 2001; Mohr et al., 2001; del Mar Garcia de los Salmones et al., 2005, which in their study have emphasized these four principle types of responsibilities; economic, legal, ethical and philanthropic (Matten and Crane, 2005; Mandhachitara and Poolthong, 2011).

In the early definitions of CSR, the environmental dimension was not yet considered to be a part of CSR (Carroll, 1999; Dahlsrud, 2008). World Business Council for Sustainable Development (WBCSD) distinguished between 'corporate social responsibility' and 'corporate environmental responsibility' and issue two definitions of CSR, neither of which include the environmental dimension (World Business Council for Sustainable Development, 1999, 2000). However, as claimed by Dahlsrud (2008) "when CSR is explained in more depth, the environmental dimension and the social dimension are equally emphasized"(p. 5). The definition of environmental dimension is developed for the first time by John Brett Elkington who coined a concept of the Triple Bottom Line (TBL) in 1994. As stated by Elkington, companies should be preparing three different bottom lines: (1) corporate profit (and loss) account, (2) company's "people account", (3) the company's "planet" account (Economist, 2009). These three principles represent three pillars of sustainability: economic sustainability (profit), sociopolitical sustainability (people) and environmental sustainability (planet) (Adams, 2006, Tarigan et al., 2012). The TBL concept identified three aspects of CSR (environmental, economic, and social). It has been used by several authors in the following years (e.g., Panwar et al., 2006; Dahlsrud, 2008; Park et al., 2016; Park et al., 2019).

Finally, the third approach regarding CSR is related to the stakeholder's approach which comprises several dimensions of CSR as customers, employees, ethical-legal, and shareholders, environment, and society (Parmar et al., 2010). Based on stakeholder theory, Maignan et al. (1999) defined social responsibility as the degree to which firms assume economic, legal, ethical and discretionary responsibilities towards their stakeholders. Founded on these three scales, authors have used different approaches in order to measure the customer perceptions of CSR and to develop their study in order to analyze the relationship between CSR and customer satisfaction/loyalty (e.g., Öberseder et al., 2014; Pérez and del Bosque, 2013; Lee, 2019; Park, 2019).

CSR, Customer Satisfaction (CS) and Customer Loyalty (CL)

Customer satisfaction (CS) is one of the most debated constructs in customer behavior studies, both in the public and private sectors and represents the only real objective of a business company. It is at the heart of every mission statement and represents the final goal of any strategy (Zairi, 2000). According to Loureiro e Kastenholz, (2011), customer satisfaction, together with customer attitude, plays a crucial mediation role between corporate reputation and CSR. Cuesta-Valiño et al. (2018) suggested that the different dimensions of CSR identified in the research could help improve consumer perception of the firms. Indeed, appropriate social behavior generates the feeling that the company is reliable and honest, which allows consumers to infer a superior quality of service (McWilliams et al., 2005). Also, Luo e Bhattacharya (2006) declared that all other things being equal, customers derive higher satisfaction from a product or service from a socially responsible company. Connelly et al. (2011), proposed a study as a foundation for future marketing research on sustainability through the application of nine prominent organizational theories. Among these, the authors analyzed signaling theory in order to explain organizational activities concerning CSR and they suggested that CSR initiatives could be seen as signals that help to build a reputation and reduce information asymmetry in the market, which in turn can lead to customer satisfaction. In this domain, Pérez and Rodriguez del Bosque (2016), applied the principles of the stakeholder management theory in the bank sector, in order to study the multidimensional perceptions of customers respect to the CSR policies implemented by the bank and how these perceptions affect customer identification and satisfaction with banking companies. Instead, Jean et al., (2016) studied the link between CSR and customer satisfaction in supply chains, in two different institutional contexts: mainland China (a transition economy) and Taiwan (a market economy). The results show that CSR in supply chains do enhance suppliers' reputations, which in turn drives customer satisfaction, in both institutional environments, China and Taiwan. According to Rivera et al., (2016) the customer satisfaction can be considered "as a key metric in evaluating CSR performance" (p.106) and developed two different studies in order to assess under what conditions CSR affects consumer satisfaction. Besides, Loureiro et al., (2012), claimed that Corporate financial performance is impacted by the effect of perceived CSR on consumer satisfaction. The authors developed a study in the automobile industry proving as CSR could contribute to financial performance indirectly by increasing consumer satisfaction. The studies, described above, proved the link between CSR and customer satisfaction. In particular, the authors agree that the implementation of CSR policies helps the consumers have a more favorable and positive attitude toward the firm and purchase of the product and services, as he also stated Wigley (2008). Actually, as believed by several authors (Baker & Crompton, 2000; Mao, 2010; Oliver, 1999; Olsen & Johnson, 2003; Selnes, 1993; Yoon & Uysal, 2005) a satisfied customer is more inclined to buy the product again and to recommend it, starting positive word of mouth with other consumers (Homburg & Giering, 2001; Olsen & Johnson, 2003). The satisfaction is then an antecedent of loyalty as demonstrated in the literature (Oliver, 1999; Bloemer & Kasper, 1995; McDougall & Levesque, 2000; Lewis, 2004; Chang & Tu, 2005; Li & Green, 2011). Choi and La, (2013) proved that CSR is an important component for customer loyalty (CL) and Al-Abdallah and Ahmed (2018), in their research, highlighted the important role CSR represents in directing consumers' behavior, specifically the customer loyalty. Moreover, Liu and Ji, (2010), developed a theoretical framework demonstrating as the perceived CSR indirectly affects customer loyalty through the antecedents of CS. In truth, the CSR and service/goods quality induce consumers to experience greater satisfaction with and trust in the firm, which in turn encouraged customers to be more loyal (Park et al., 2018) and "building a loyal customer base is an important foundation for developing a sustainable competitive advantage" (Mandhachitara, Yaowalak Poolthong, 2011, p. 129).

Relationship Between CSR, CS, and CL in the Literature Review Last Ten Years (2009-2019)

According to Dahlsrud (2008) "the challenge for business is not so much to define CSR, as it is to understand how CSR is socially constructed in a specific context and how to take this into account when business strategies are developed" (p.6). He identified five dimensions of CSR: (1) Environmental dimension, (2) Social dimension, (3) Economic dimension, (4) Stakeholder dimension, (5) Voluntariness dimension. Carroll and Shabana (2010) based on their paper on the study of Dahlsrud (2008) considering the five dimensions of CSR mentioned above. Differently, Yusof et al. (2011) measured CSR by developing four variables, which include six items of philanthropy, four items of legal, four items of ethics and eight items of environment variables. Therefore, they considered the following four CSR dimensions: (1) Philanthropic, (2) Legal, (3) Ethical and (4) Environmental. They examined the effects of a functional store image and CSR in the self-congruity model in influencing store loyalty. The authors developed and tested a structural model in the context of the retailing industry in the self-congruity theory. Findings indicate that self-congruity influence on store loyalty was mediated by both functional store image and social responsibility image. In influencing store loyalty, the findings have shown that social responsibility image has a stronger influence on store loyalty than functional store image. Instead, De Los Salmones et al. (2011), followed guidelines from Carroll (1979, 1991) at the beginning, but they focused, only, on the ethical-legal and social aspects of CSR. They analyzed the influence of CSR on consumer behavior. They started from a literature review about the concept and formulated several hypotheses about the influence of CSR on the traditional antecedents of loyalty, image, and valuation of services. They used methodology support in personal surveys and verified the presence of a direct effect of CSR on service valuation and indirect influence on loyalty and image. Moreover, Stanisavljević (2017), followed the structure of the pyramid of corporate social responsibility of Carroll (1991) to determinate CSR dimensions in order to examine the dependence of customer loyalty on CSR, that is if CSR influences customer loyalty as one possible factor. The author showed that the highest significance is given to the legal followed by the economic dimensions of CSR, then ethical and philanthropic.

On the other hand, Loureiro et al. (2012) designed a conceptual model that links CSR dimensions to consumer satisfaction and perceived value. The CSR dimensions are: (1) Labor practices, (2) Environment, (3) Community development, (4) Consumer price, (5) Consumer quality, (6) Fulfill expectations, (7) Relationship selling (empathy). They studied the contribution of three car manufacturers' perceived CSR regarding labor practices, community development and environmental performance and the relationship between CSR and consumer satisfaction considering a group of 329 Portuguese car buyers and users. They found that these consumers valued environmental performance more than activities related to labor practices and community development. Besides, the overall importance of CSR for consumer satisfaction suggests that in car manufacturing, CSR may not only directly contribute to better corporate financial performance (CFP) by lowering costs and increasing productivity but may also indirectly contribute to better CFP by increasing consumer car purchasing satisfaction. In the same year, Galbreath and Shum (2012) tested a mediated model in understanding the relationship between Corporate Social Responsibility (CSR) and Firm Performance (FP) considering a sample of 280 Australian firms. They thought that reputation and customer satisfaction fully mediate the CSR–FP relationship. Their findings suggested that CSR is linked with FP with an indirect effect: while CSR is linked to both reputation and customer satisfaction, reputation alone mediates the CSR–FP relationship. In the context of the hotel industry, Martìnez and Rodriguez del Bosque (2013) used a survey of Spanish hotel consumers and proposed a model. Their results showed loyalty is indirectly affected by perceived CSR, through the mediation of trust, identification, and satisfaction. Empirical testing confirms most of their hypothesized effects except for the effect of customer trust on customer identification with the company. A year later, He and Lai (2014) provided evidence of an indirect relationship between CSR and brand loyalty through the mediating role of functional and symbolic images. Their findings highlighted two main dimensions of CSR: (1) legal responsibility and (2) ethical responsibility. These dimensions improve brand loyalty by forming positive functional and symbolic images. Furthermore, the fulfillment of legal and ethical responsibilities has different roles in improving brand loyalty. Conversely, Su et al. (2017) investigated the impact of corporate social responsibility (CSR) on consumers' attitudinal and behavioral responses, using data from 451 customers of three hotels in China. The measures of CSR considered are (1) environmental, (2) social, (3) economic and (4) stakeholders' corporate social responsibility. Through Structural equation modeling (SEM), they tested the universality of such impact across various consumer groups. Results show that CSR positively affects perceived corporate reputation and customer satisfaction, which significantly affects customer commitment and behavioral responses (i.e., loyalty intentions and word-of-mouth). They highlighted that the role of CSR is not universal across consumer groups (specifically, the positive effect of CSR on perceived corporate reputation is higher among people with higher income). According to the authors, hospitality managers should allocate their resources to investing in CSR initiatives, in that such practices have proven to cultivate customer loyalty. Otherwise, Mohammed and Rashid (2018) presented a research model based on data relating to the hotel industry, which conceptualized the CSR dimensions-customer satisfaction relationship and proposed the mediating effect of brand image on the stated relationship. The CSR dimensions considered by the authors are (1) economic CSR, (2) legal CSR, (3) ethical CSR and (4) philanthropic CSR. Salmones et al. (2009) considered the ethical and philanthropic responsibility of a financial entity (bank) and analyzed their influence on customer behavior. More specifically, the authors analyzed the relationships between dimensions and different constructs: satisfaction, trust, identification with the company, business performance, relational results, and loyalty. They discover that the relationship of satisfaction, trust and identification is the main determining factor of loyalty, while the ethical and social dimension has an indirect effect. Ethical behavior influences companies increase trust, while corporate philanthropy improves identification with the bank. Instead, as stated by Paulìk et al. (2015) the perception of CSR by bank customers can be divided into four essential elements: (1) bank's involvement in community development (e.g. investing in community projects or supporting of educational activities), (2) following the ethical standards by the bank's employees, (3) need (e.g. supporting of foundations or non-profit organizations as a part of the bank's philanthropic activities) and (4) implementing policies on the environment. Their study focused on CSR and its effects on satisfaction and loyalty of bank customers and employees in the Czech Republic. Based on a conceptual model, they highlighted three types of CSR strategies that the company can adopt: (1) Economic, (2) Social (ethical standards and support of project) and (3) Environmental. Their results showed a positive relationship between customer satisfaction and customer loyalty. However, based on the results, customers' perception of CSR does not have a significant effect on their satisfaction. During the same year, Jo et al. (2015) examined whether corporate environmental responsibility plays a role in enhancing operating performance in the financial services sector considering a unique environmental dataset covering 29 countries. They found that the reducing of environmental costs takes at least 1 or 2 years before enhancing return on assets and that reducing environmental costs has a more immediate and substantial effect on the performance of financial services firms in well-developed financial markets than in less-developed financial markets. Instead, Pèrez and Rodriguez del Bosque (2016) demonstrated that customers' perceptions of CSR and broad legal and ethical issues have significant positive impacts on customer identification and satisfaction with banking companies. Perceptions of shareholder-related CSR also significantly boost customer satisfaction. In contrast, perceptions of employee- and community-related CSR do not have any significant effect on customer identification or satisfaction.

Chung et al. (2015), in their study conducted in China, explored how CSR factors influence customer satisfaction and loyalty considering the presence or not of the moderating effects of corporate image in the relationships between CSR and customer satisfaction and customer loyalty. They used structural equation modeling (SEM) to test the hypotheses and showed that CSR positively affects customer satisfaction and loyalty, and customer satisfaction positively affects customer loyalty. The highlighted some CSR factors with an importance order: (1) Consumer protection, (2) Philanthropic responsibility, (3) Legal responsibility, (4) Ethical responsibility, (5) Economic responsibility, and (6) Environmental contribution. While Rivera et al. (2016), using two different studies, evaluated under what conditions Corporate Social Responsibility (CSR) affects consumer satisfaction. In the first study, based on the American Customer Satisfaction Index, reported positive feedback between CSR and customer satisfaction. The second study, based on an online survey of consumers, points to a positive relationship between CSR and customer satisfaction.

As for the manufacturing sector, Jean et al. (2016) provided some empirical evidence of the influence of three manufacturing sectors (machinery, electronics, and transportation components) on CSR initiatives and their impact on customer satisfaction. They suggested that CSR in supply chains positively impact on customer satisfaction in both mainland China and Taiwan. Yet, the influence on CSR in supply chains of different drivers differs according to the institutional context. In the transition economy of China, CSR initiatives are driven by regulatory and efficiency forces but not by the competitive advantage force. In contrast, in the market economy of Taiwan, CSR initiatives are driven by the competitive advantage force but not by the other two. Xie et al. (2017), also, focused on the manufacturing sector, but they identified three dimensions of CSR: (1) Consumer relations, (2) Community relations, and (3) Environmental issues. Their empirical results present some interesting findings: the relationship between CSR and financial performance is fully mediated by customer satisfaction; good institutional environments positively strengthen the impact of CSR efforts on firms' customer satisfaction. Moreover, there are differences in the moderating effect of institutional environments between the two sampled countries. In the Chinese example, the institutional environment positively moderated the relationship between CSR and customer satisfaction; while in the Vietnamese sample, the institutional environment positively moderated the relationship between CSR and the return on sales (ROS).

Lee (2019) focused his study on Taiwan, but in the insurance sector. He investigated the impact of corporate social responsibility in customer loyalty and examined the role of corporate image and customer satisfaction. He, also, highlighted four dimensions of CSR: (1) Economic responsibility; (2) Legal responsibility; (3) Ethical Responsibility; (4) Discretionary responsibility. He showed the existence of a positive effect of economic and legal corporate social responsibility on customer loyalty, as well as a partial mediating effect of customer satisfaction between corporate social responsibility and customer loyalty. Moreover, he identified the moderating effect of a corporate image between corporate social responsibility and customer loyalty. In the same year, Park (2019) explored activities of corporate social responsibility (CSR) and their effects on corporate reputation, but he focused on the airline service industry (such as Liu and Ji (2010). He considered two factors (customer attitude and satisfaction) as moderators between corporate reputation and CSR. He found that a higher degree of economic responsibility results in improved customer attitude and satisfaction. Moreover, while environmental responsibility has notable effects on customer attitude and satisfaction, corporate reputation is determined by customer attitude and satisfaction. Finally, Cuesta-Valino et al. (2019) revealed that CSR has positive implications for hypermarkets' performance in Spain and illustrated which CSR dimensions are the most important to focus on. They considered three CSR dimensions: (1) Economic, (2) Ethical–legal, (3) Discretionary. They tested the hypothesis applying partial least squares structural equation modeling and found that CSR is positively influencing customer loyalty, and customer satisfaction, image, and quality also intervened in their relationships. More thoroughly, the study highlighted the importance of the mediating role played by image and quality in improving the effect of CSR on satisfaction. They provided useful information to develop a CSR strategy that would enhance customer loyalty.

This study, therefore, wants to contribute increasing the knowledge on this topic, through an empirical study understand how millennials perceive the four dimensions of CSR and to verify the relationship between CSR and CS and CL.

Table 1 shows the studies that analyzed the relationship between CSR and CS and CL described above (2009-2019).

Material and Methods

The research, developed in February-April 2019, was carried out on a sample "Millennial Generation (MG) students" (Cavaliere and Ventura, 2018, p. 641) at the University of Tuscia (Viterbo, Italy). The questionnaire was divided into three different areas of analysis: (1) Customer profile, (2) CSR, (3) CS and CL. The answer to the questions on the customer perception of CSR have been structured based on the Likert-type measurement scale, with a score, assigned by the respondents, between 1 and 7, where 7 expresses the maximum positive evaluation (fully satisfied) and 1 the negative one (very little satisfied) (Likert, 1932). The processing of the collected data was carried also through a multivariate tool analysis and the different elaborations were performed using the statistical program "STATA Statistics/ Data Analysis" (www.stata.com).

RESULTS

Factor Analysis

Data presented in *Table 2* shows that all Corporate Social Responsibility dimensions are strongly important for young people interviewed. All attributes of the Environmental Responsibility dimension are important (the average value is greater than 6), "Reduce the emission of pollutants" (average value of 6.55) and "Use resources efficiently (average value of 6.54). In Economic Responsibility dimension,

Table 1. Relationship between CSR, customer satisfaction, and customer loyalty (2009-2019)

Authors	Environmental responsibility	Social (discretional/ philanthropic/ethical) responsibility	Economic responsibility	Legal responsibility	Customer satisfaction	Customer Loyalty	Sector
Lee (2019)		x	x	x	x	x	Insurance
Lerro et al., (2019)	x	x				x	Food companies
Park (2019)	x	x	x		x		Airline service industry
Cuesta-Valino et al., (2019)		x	x	x	x	x	Hypermarkets
Mohammed and Rashid, (2018)		x	x	x	x		Hotel industry
Stanisavljević (2017)		x	x	x		x	
Su et al. (2017)	x	x	x		x	x	Hospitality industry
Xie et al. (2017)	x				x		Manufacturing
Jean et al. (2016)	x	x		x	x		Manufacturing factories
Pèrez and del Bosque (2016)	x	x	x		x		Banking companies
Rivera et al. (2016)	x	x	x		x		Different industries
Chung et al. (2015)	x	x	x	x	x	x	Business firms
Jo et al. (2015)	x					x	Financial services
Paulík et al. (2015)	x	x	x		x	x	Banking companies
He and Lai, (2014)		x		x		x	Business
Martínez and Rodríguez del Bosque, (2013)	x	x			x	x	Hotel industry
Loureiro et al. (2012)	x				x		Automobile industry
De los Salmones et al. (2011)		x		x		x	Service industry
Yusof et a. (2011)	x	x		x		x	Retailing industry
Liu and Ji (2010)	x				x	x	Airline service industry
Salmones et al. (2009)		x			x	x	Financial companies

Source: our elaborations

"Creating new jobs" is perceived as the most important attribute (average value of 6.37) while in Legal Responsibility and Social Responsibility dimensions, "Meet the minimum legal requirements for goods and services" (average value of 6.10) and "Support the culture, artistic activities and sports activities of the local community" are the attributes most important. The values of the standard deviation show that the data dispersion around the average value is relatively small, thus attesting the homogeneity of the answers given by respondents.

Cronbach α was used to test internal consistency for all items under respective variables (Namukasa, 2013). Following Hair at al. (2006) who stated that the Cronbach α coefficient over 0.6 is adequate for basic research, it is possible to argue that the sample of this study shows good internal consistency. Also performing the Kaiser-Meyer-Olkin (KMO) test whose result must exceed the 0.5 limits (Kaiser, 1974; Hair et al., 2006; Santouridis and Trivellas, 2010), the sample was found appropriate to perform the factor analysis. Finally, the correlation test was used (see Annex A: tables from I to IV) to verify whether the observed variables contain misleading redundancies or make the results insignificant.

Factor analysis is used to synthesize a series of evaluations about the importance of some specific characteristics of the product/service studied, in order to identify the milestone of customer opinions and to perform segmentation. Factor analysis is generally useful to 'condense' and 'reduce' the data, trying to lose the least amount of relevant information (Bracalente et al., 2009).

Table 3 shows the matrix of main components (eigenvectors) of the Environmental Responsibility dimension and the first factor of them has eigenvalues greater than 1 and encompass 85.31% of the information contained in the original data set. For this reason, the first factor was considered to identify the new variable.

Table 4 shows the rotated factor loadings (pattern matrix) and unique variances whit orthogonal Varimax rotation.

Factor interpretation was achieved by considering the so-called saturation matrix (*Table 5*) where the correlation between the original variables and the factors were identified. Each variable is associated according to the highest correlated factor, and then this factor is interpreted according to associated variables. In this case, all the factors are associated with a single variable.

The same analysis of the variables related to the Environmental Responsibility dimension was conducted on the variables related to other dimensions such as Social Responsibility, Economic Responsibility, and Legal Responsibility (see Annex B: tables from I to IX).

Through factor analysis, the number of variables was reduced from 20 to 5. The new variables, as main components, are uncorrelated with each other, then carrying different information content. They are the most relevant to represent the phenomenon observed since they can "explain" most of the variance (or the information content) of the variables themselves (Table 6).

Cluster Analysis

Factor analysis can identify the cornerstones of segmentation, e.g. the macro-benefits which segmentation is built around. This study is preparatory to perform cluster analysis through which individuals are grouped in segments, based on their greater or lesser homogeneity. For research purposes, the hierarchical method of Ward (Fabbris, 1997; Dahl and Næs, 2004; Annunziata and Vecchio, 2013) was used and the number of groups was determined by inspecting the dendrogram. Using the information derived by the Calinski/Harabasz indicator (Table 7) together with the dendrogram analysis, four groups were identified.

Table 8 shows the four groups related to the new variables of Corporate Social Responsibility. Based on the correlation link intensity it is possible to define the characteristics of the four clusters.

Cluster 2 and 4 seem to be indifferent to the issue of Corporate Social Responsibility. Specifically, cluster 4, unlike the other two clusters. Indeed Cluster 1 is characterized by young focused on all Corporate Social Responsibility dimensions, while Environmental (ER), Social Responsibility (SR) and Social Economy (EC2) are fundamental to Cluster 3.

In order to validate the segmentation into 4 clusters, confirmatory analysis (*Table 9*) was developed.

The results of the Analysis of Variance show that the 4-cluster segmentation significantly differentiates the average values of the individual groups (average values calculated on a case-by-factor basis) over the average total value. In this sense, it can be stated that the 4 clusters subdivision has been effective in discriminating statistical units.

Table 10 shows the variables considered for this study in order to characterize the four clusters, and the significance indices used.

Table 2. Descriptive statistics of Corporate Social Responsibility dimensions and reliability analysis

Dimension	Var	Items	Items tot	Mean	Dev. St.	Min	Max	Number of cases	Cronbach's α	KMO
Environmental responsibility	ER1	Recycle the waste	6	6.33	1.20	2	7	241	0.9639	0.9095
	ER2	Reduce waste		6.47	1.09	2	7			
	ER3	Reduce the emission of pollutants		6.55	1.08	2	7			
	ER4	Use resources efficiently		6.54	1.02	2	7			
	ER5	Invest in energy savings		6.47	1.09	2	7			
	ER6	Produce eco-friendly products		6.27	1.19	1	7			
Social responsibility	SR1	Participation in voluntary or charitable activities to improve the quality of life in the local community	6	5.29	1.63	1	7		0.9162	0.8406
	SR2	Support private and public educational institutions		5.05	1.63	1	7			
	SR3	Raise funds for the social cause		5.32	1.66	1	7			
	SR4	Support the culture, artistic activities and sports activities of the local community		5.92	1.43	1	7			
	SR5	Recognizes and abides by new ethical or moral standards		5.90	1.49	1	7			
	SR6	Prevent unethical behavior		5.36	1.54	1	7			
Economic responsibility	EC1	Maximize earnings	5	5.21	1.56	1	7		0.8961	0.8026
	EC2	Search for a profitable business		5.51	1.39	1	7			
	EC3	Acquire a strong competitive position		5.27	1.50	1	7			
	EC4	Contribute to society and the economy		5.87	1.33	1	7			
	EC5	Creating new jobs		6.37	1.14	1	7			
Legal responsibility	LR1	Operate in a manner consistent with the expectations of the government and the law	3	5.58	1.39	1	7		0.9251	0.7693
	LR2	Fulfill legal obligations		6.06	1.31	1	7			
	LR3	Meet the minimum legal requirements for goods and services		6.10	1.27	1	7			

Source: our elaboration from the data set

The statistical significance of "Knowledge of the concept of Corporate Social Responsibility" variables (categorical variables) was validated through the study of test Pearson Chi-square (Adanacioglu and Albayram, 2012) while the statistical significance of numeric variables was validated through the study of Variance (Vermeir and Verbeke, 2008; Yadavalli and Jones, 2014).

Table 3. Matrix of main components (eigenvalues) of the Environmental Responsibility dimension

Factor	Eigenvalue	Difference	Proportion	Cumulative
Factor1	5.1188	4.7848	0.8531	0.8531
Factor2	0.3340	0.0859	0.0557	0.9088
Factor3	0.2481	0.1266	0.0414	0.9502
Factor4	0.1215	0.0181	0.0203	0.9704
Factor5	0.1034	0.0293	0.0172	0.9877
Factor6	0.0741	.	0.0123	1

Source: our elaboration from the data set

Table 4. Rotated factor loadings (pattern matrix) and unique variances of the Environmental Responsibility dimension

Factor	Variance	Difference	Proportion	Cumulative
Factor1	5.1188	.	0.8531	0.8531

Source: our elaboration from the data set

Table 5. Saturation matrix (factor loadings) of the Environmental Responsibility dimension

Variable	Factor1	Uniqueness
ER1	0.8656	0.2507
ER2	0.9357	0.1244
ER3	0.9555	0.0871
ER4	0.9315	0.1323
ER5	0.9472	0.1029
ER6	0.9033	0.1840

Source: our elaboration from the data set

Table 6. New Variables

Dimension	New Variables Code	New Variables
Environmental Responsibility	ER	Environmental Responsibility
Social Responsibility	SR	Social Responsibility
Economic Responsibility	EC1	Firm Economy Responsibility
	EC2	Social Economy Responsibility
Legal Responsibility	LR	Legal Responsibility

Source: our elaboration from the data set

Table 7. Calinski/Harabasz indicator

Number of Clusters	Calinski/Harabasz Pseudo-F
3	113.87
4	*123.71*
5	100.51
6	91.10
7	83.18

Source: our elaboration from the data set

Table 8. Cluster analysis concerning new factors of Corporate Social Responsibility – correlation link intensity

Cluster	ER	SR	EC1	EC2	LR
Cluster1	*0.317873*	*0.234094*	*0.552158*	*0.271402*	*0.438262*
Cluster2	-1.235771	-1.082748	-0.355070	-0.720736	-1.626834
Cluster3	*0.199457*	*0.184727*	-0.758396	*0.001056*	-0.055442
Cluster4	-3.600734	-2.651662	-1.528203	-2.437538	-2.883485
Total	-5.94E-09	3.83E-09	-5.13E-09	6.12E-10	6.04E-09

Source: our elaboration from the data set

Table 11 shows how the largest group is Cluster 1, 58.51% followed by 30.29% of Cluster 3, while Cluster 2 and Cluster 4 are the smallest ones (Cluster 2 represents 6.64% of the sample and Cluster 4 the 11.56%).

Cluster 1 (58.51% of the sample) is mainly composed of young people who know the concept of Corporate Social Responsibility and who attach great importance to the different dimensions of CSR. The results show that the individuals of the cluster 1 have a high predisposition to a positive word of mouth and to the repurchase with respect to a firm that correctly implements the CSR policy (scores assigned on the Likert-scale from 6 to 7), as well as at their level of satisfaction (scores assigned on the Likert-scale from 5 to 7).

Table 9. Analysis of Variance - Confirmatory analysis

Analysis of Variance		
Factor	F	Prob> F
ER	260.81	0.000
SR	62.83	0.000
EC1	108.74	0.000
EC2	101.49	0.000
LR	207.10	0.000

Source: our elaboration from the data set

Table 10. Variables and significance indices

Variables	Items	Pearson Chi-square	F	Pr.>F	Sig.
Knowledge of the concept of Corporate Social Responsibility.	Yes-No	6.0544		0.009	***
Satisfaction with the Corporate Social Responsibility policy implemented by the firms.	Likert scale from 1 (maximum negative evaluation) to (maximum positive evaluation)		43.18	0.000	***
Predisposition to a positive word of mouth of the company that correctly implements the Corporate Social Responsibility policy.	Likert scale from 1 (maximum negative evaluation) to (maximum positive evaluation)		47.6	0.000	***
Make repeat purchases from the firm that correctly implements the Corporate Social Responsibility policy.	Likert scale from 1 (maximum negative evaluation) to (maximum positive evaluation)		36.04	0.000	***

Source: our elaboration from the data set

In cluster 3 (30.29% of the sample) the knowledge of the CSR concept, by the group members, is not discriminating. However, the cluster is composed of young people who attach importance above all to the social aspects of CSR. Their level of satisfaction about a CSR policy implemented by a firm is high (scores assigned on the Likert-scale from 4 to 6), as well as their predisposition to a positive word-of-mouth (scores assigned on the Likert- scale from 5 to 7) and repurchase (scores assigned on the Likert-scale 5 to 7).

Cluster 4 (4.56% of the sample) is composed of young people who do not know the concept of CSR and therefore show a total indifference concerning its dimensions. The results show, in fact, that the individuals of cluster 4 have a low predisposition to word of mouth and repurchase with respect to a firm that correctly implements the CSR policy (scores assigned on the Likert-scale from 1 to 3), as well as at their level of satisfaction (scores assigned on the Likert-scale from 1 to 3).

Table 11. Cluster analysis results

Items	Cluster 1 (n=141; 58.51%)	Cluster 2 (n=16; 6.64%)	Cluster 3 (n=73; 30.29)	Cluster 4 (n=11; 4.56%)
Knowledge of the concept of corporate social responsibility	Yes	No	Non-discriminatory	No
Satisfaction with the Corporate Social Responsibility policy implemented by the firms*	From 5 to 7	From 3 to 4	From 4 to 6	From 1 to 3
Predisposition to a positive word of mouth of the company that correctly implements the Corporate Social Responsibility policy*	From 6 to 7	From 4 to 5	3,5 and 7	From 1 to 3
Make repeat purchases from the firm that correctly implements the Corporate Social Responsibility policy*	From 5 to 7	From 3 to 4	From 4 to 6	From 1 to 3

Notes: * Likert scale from 1 (maximum negative evaluation) to (maximum positive evaluation)
Source: our elaboration from the data set

Finally, cluster 2 (6.64% of the sample) is also composed of young people who do not know the concept of CSR and therefore do not attach importance to the different dimensions of CSR. However, the individuals of the group are on average satisfied with respect to a correct implementation of CSR policy (scores assigned on the Likert-scale from 3 to 4) as their predisposition to word of mouth appears to be (scores assigned on the Likert-scale from 3 to 5) and repurchase (scores assigned on the Likert-scale from 4 to 5).

SOLUTIONS AND RECOMMENDATIONS

Discussion

The first goal of this study has been to identify CSR dimensions through factor analysis. Five factors have been identified. They summarize the variables related to CSR. In particular: (1) Environmental Responsibility; (2) Social Responsibility; (3) Firm Economy Responsibility; (4) Social Economy Responsibility; (5) Legal Responsibility. The results show that all dimensions of the CSR are summarized in a single factor except the Corporate Economic Responsibility dimension. Indeed, the "Maximize earnings", "Search for a profitable business" and "Acquire a strong competitive position" items are summarized in a factor that highlights an economic advantage for the firm. While, the items "Contribute to society and the economy" and "Creating new jobs" are summarized in another factor that highlights the economic advantages for society, generated by the firm. The results are in line with the literature. Carroll (2016) claimed that "as a fundamental condition or requirement of existence, businesses have an economic responsibility to the society that permitted them to be created and sustained" (p. 3) This responsibility consists in guaranteeing profits that will be distributed among the stakeholders, as this is what the company expects and indeed requires: "to be able to sustain themselves and the only way this is possible is by being profitable and able to incentivize owners or shareholders to invest and have enough resources to continue in operation" (p. 3). Another advantage generated by firms, capable of creating profits, is the creation of jobs. In this way, firms contribute to the economic and social development of society (Su et al., 2017; Park, 2019). Moreover, according to Park (2019), in economies that are facing significant job crises, economic responsibility can be more important than social responsibility.

The results of the cluster analysis show the identification of four groups, two of which are sensitive to the CSR theme and two others are indifferent to this issue. The results are in line with the existing literature. Cluster1, which represents 58.51% of the sample, is composed of MG students who know the concept of CSR and who attach great importance to the different dimensions of CSR. According to several authors (i.e. Earl and Lawrence, 2003; Emanuel and Adams 2011; Bonadonna et al., 2017) students have a high level of education and this condition leads them to be more sensitive to the topic of sustainability and CSR. Moreover, individuals in cluster 1 show a high level of satisfaction with companies that adopt CSR policies, which results in loyalty behavior (positive word of mouth and repurchase). Marin, et al., (2009) proved that "CSR initiatives are linked to stronger loyalty both because the consumer develops a more positive company evaluation, and because one identifies more strongly with the company" (p. 65). Indeed, Eveland et al., (2018) highlighted that the sharing of values, between firms and consumers, plays a mediating role between "social performance and behavioral outcomes" (p. 550). Firms must strategically select their CSR activities so that they reflect the values of their customers (Eveland et al., 2018).

The social aspect of CSR is discriminating for Cluster 3 individuals who represent 30.29% of the sample. this cluster has a good level of satisfaction with firms that have adopted CSR policies and that results in loyal behavior a positive word of mouth. The characteristics of the individuals of cluster 3 are in line with the studies conducted by De los Salmones et al. (2011). The authors studied the influence of CSR on consumer behavior focusing only on Social and Ethical-Legal dimensions. The results showed that Social responsibility is regarded as direct determinants of the overall evaluation of the company, and therefore, as having a direct influence on loyalty. Salmones et al. (2009), instead, focuses on the dimension of social responsibility, exploding in ethics and philanthropy, and proved, through the development of a model of structural equations, that ethical and social dimensions have an indirect effect on customer loyalty, through satisfaction and identification.

Finally, the individuals of cluster 2 are not very sensitive to the topic of CSR and those of clusters 4 are indifferent to all the CSR dimensions. However, these are individuals who do not know the concept of CSR and therefore are not able to evaluate, in terms of satisfaction and loyalty, the company that correctly implements good CSR policies as they do not have a perception of what it means. This result indicates how the lack of knowledge about the CRS topic could influence consumer behavior, as demonstrated by McGlone et al., (2011). Indeed, the authors experimented, holding an educational event (Ethics Awareness Week - EAW), on CSR in the College of Business and Technology at a large Western Western University in 2008 and demonstrated how these types of events can have a significant impact on students' attitude towards their social responsibilities. In fact, according to Tucker, 2006, millennials want to get involved in real problems with real situations.

CONCLUSION

Overall, the results of this study provide a more comprehensive theoretical and empirical foundation for understanding the impacts of CSR on the loyalty of young people (specifically, Millennial Generation students). As a final remark, it can be said that factor analysis and cluster analysis allowed to analyze in detail the consumer behavior and his loyalty to some activities of CSR implemented by a firm.

First of all, through factor analysis, it was possible to identify the dimensions of CSR. The factor analysis identified five factors: (1) Environmental Responsibility; (2) Social Responsibility; (3) Firm Economy Responsibility; (4) Social Economy Responsibility; (5) Legal Responsibility. These factors make it possible to understand how the consumer looks at the CSR. It is important to emphasize that all dimensions of the CSR are summed up in a single factor except the Corporate Economic Responsibility dimension. It is outlined in two factors that highlight on the one hand an economic advantage for the firm, on the other hand economic advantage for the company generated by the firm.

After identifying the CSR factors, the second objective of this study was to analyze, through a cluster analysis, the groups of young people relying on their sensitivity to CSR policies implemented by a company in order to examine the nature and the strength of the relationship between CSR and CS and CL. Four groups of young people were identified through cluster analysis: Cluster 1 (58.51% of the sample) composed of who know the concept of CSR; Cluster 3 (30.29%) composed of who gives importance to the social dimension of the CSR; Cluster 4 (4.56% of the sample) and Cluster 2 (6.64% of the sample) composed of who do not know the concept of CSR and does not give importance to the dimensions of CSR. The CSR policies, essentially, implemented by the company affect the satisfaction and loyalty of young people belonging to Cluster 1, who have a greater predisposition to positive word of mouth and repurchase if a firm correctly implements CSR policies. The same result is obtained in Cluster 3, limited to the social dimension of CSR. While in Cluster 4 the same policies do not affect satisfaction and loyalty and in Cluster 2 young people are indifferent to the CSR dimensions.

From the theoretical point of view, this work contributes to further deepen the literature on CSR and CS and CL in Millennial Generation (MG) students, and confirms, through further empirical analysis, what was underlined by other authors. From a managerial point of view, this research provides crucial implications for firms and managers who want to formulate CSR policies in order to increase customer loyalty. Precisely, managers must define CSR activities that are shared by consumers who meet their value system.

The chapter also presents some limitations related to the fact that the research was conducted in a small-sized university, namely that of Tuscia in the city of Viterbo. Furthermore, the sample is accidental. In order to evaluate the results and fill the limits of the research, it would be interesting to develop the research also in other universities of different sizes, thus obtaining a larger sample. Also, some future avenues of research are possible. It would be interesting to learn more about those who have declared that they do not know the CSR topic. It would indeed be appropriate to subject this part of the sample to a further interview, once given a brief explanation of CSR and then to analyze the gap of the perception of CSR before or after.

REFERENCES

Adams, W. M. (2006, January). The future of sustainability: Rethinking environment and development in the twenty-first century. In Report of the IUCN renowned thinkers meeting (Vol. 29, p. 31).

Adanacioglu, H., & Albayram, Z. (2012). A conjoint analysis of consumer preferences for traditional cheeses in Turkey: A case study on tulum cheese. *Han-gug Chugsan Sigpum Hag-hoeji*, *32*(4), 458–466. doi:10.5851/kosfa.2012.32.4.458

Al-abdallah, G. M., & Ahmed, R. S. (2018). The impact of corporate social responsibility on customer loyalty in the Qatari telecommunication sector. *Journal of Business and Retail Management Research*, *13*(1), 253–268. doi:10.24052/JBRMR/V13IS01/ART-25

Annunziata, A., & Vecchio, R. (2013). Consumer perception of functional foods: A conjoint analysis with probiotics. *Food Quality and Preference*, *28*(1), 348–355. doi:10.1016/j.foodqual.2012.10.009

Baker, D. A., & Crompton, J. L. (2000). Quality, satisfaction and behavioral intentions. *Annals of Tourism Research*, *27*(3), 785–804. doi:10.1016/S0160-7383(99)00108-5

Bloemer, J. M., & Kasper, H. D. (1995). The complex relationship between consumer satisfaction and brand loyalty. *Journal of Economic Psychology*, *16*(2), 311–329. doi:10.1016/0167-4870(95)00007-B

Bonadonna, A., Giachino, C., & Truant, E. (2017). Sustainability and mountain tourism: the millennial's perspective. *Sustainability*, *9*(7), 1219. doi:10.3390u9071219

Bowen, H. R. (1953). *Social responsibility of the businessman*. New York, NY: Harper and Row.

Bracalente, B., Cossignani, M., & Mulas, A. (2009). *Statistica aziendale*. Milan, Rome: McGraw-Hill.

Carroll, A. B. (1979). A three-dimensional conceptual model of corporate performance. *Academy of Management Review*, *4*(4), 497–505. doi:10.5465/amr.1979.4498296

Carroll, A. B. (2016). Carroll's pyramid of CSR: taking another look. *International Journal of Corporate Social Responsibility, 1*(1), 3.

Carroll, A. B., & Shabana, K. M. (2010). The business case for corporate social responsibility: A review of concepts, research and practice. *International Journal of Management Reviews*, *12*(1), 85–105. doi:10.1111/j.1468-2370.2009.00275.x

Catano, V. M. & Morrow Hines, H. (2016). The influence of corporate social responsibility, psychologically healthy workplaces, and individual values in attracting millennial job applicants. *Canadian Journal of Behavioural Science/Revue canadienne des sciences du comportement, 48*(2), 142.

Cavaliere, A., & Ventura, V. (2018). Mismatch between food sustainability and consumer acceptance toward innovation technologies among Millennial students: The case of shelf life extension. *Journal of Cleaner Production*, *175*, 641–650. doi:10.1016/j.jclepro.2017.12.087

Chang, C. H., & Tu, C. Y. (2005). Exploring store image, customer satisfaction and customer loyalty relationship: Evidence from Taiwanese hypermarket industry. *The Journal of American Academy of Business, Cambridge*, *7*(2), 197–202.

Choi, B., & La, S. (2013). The impact of corporate social responsibility (CSR) and customer trust on the restoration of loyalty after service failure and recovery. *Journal of Services Marketing*, *27*(3), 223–233. doi:10.1108/08876041311330717

Chung, K. H., Yu, J. E., Choi, M. G., & Shin, J. I. (2015). The effects of CSR on customer satisfaction and loyalty in China: The moderating role of corporate image. *Journal of Economics, Business and Management*, *3*(5), 542–547.

Connelly, B. L., Ketchen, D. J., & Slater, S. F. (2011). Toward a "theoretical toolbox" for sustainability research in marketing. *Journal of the Academy of Marketing Science*, *39*(1), 86–100. doi:10.100711747-010-0199-0

de los Salmones, G., del Mar, M., & Rodriguez del Bosque, I. (2011). Corporate social responsibility and loyalty in services sector. *Esic Market Economic and Business Journal*, *138*, 199–221.

McGlone, T., Spain, J. W., & McGlone, V. (2011). Corporate social responsibility and the millennials. *Journal of Education for Business*, *86*(4), 195–200. doi:10.1080/08832323.2010.502912

Cuesta Valiño, P., Rodríguez, P. G., & Núñez Barriopedro, E. (2019). The impact of corporate social responsibility on customer loyalty in hypermarkets: A new socially responsible strategy. *Corporate Social Responsibility and Environmental Management*, *26*(4), 761–769. doi:10.1002/csr.1718

Dahl, T., & Næs, T. (2004). Outlier and group detection in sensory panels using hierarchical cluster analysis with the Procrustes distance. *Food Quality and Preference*, *15*(3), 195–208. doi:10.1016/S0950-3293(03)00058-2

Dahlsrud, A. (2008). How corporate social responsibility is defined: An analysis of 37 definitions. *Corporate Social Responsibility and Environmental Management*, *15*(1), 1–13. doi:10.1002/csr.132

Earl, C., Lawrence, A., Harris, N., & Stiller, S. (2003). The campus community and the concept of sustainability: An assessment of college of Charleston student perceptions. *Chrestomathy: Annual Review of Undergraduate Research at the College of Charleston*, *2*, 85–102.

Economist. (2009). It consists of three Ps: profit, people and planet. Retrieved from http://goo.gl/BXuE9

Emanuel, R., & Adams, J. N. (2011). College students' perceptions of campus sustainability. *International Journal of Sustainability in Higher Education*, *12*(1), 79–92. doi:10.1108/14676371111098320

Eveland, V. B., Crutchfield, T. N., & Rynarzewska, A. I. (2018). Developing a consumer relationship model of corporate social performance. *Journal of Consumer Marketing*, *35*(5), 543–554. doi:10.1108/JCM-07-2017-2287

Fabbris, L. (1997). *Statistica multivariata: analisi esplorativa dei dati*. McGraw-Hill Libri Italia.

Formánková, S., Trenz, O., Faldík, O., Kolomazník, J., & Sládková, J. (2019). Millennials' awareness and approach to social responsibility and investment—case study of the Czech Republic. *Sustainability*, *11*(2), 504. doi:10.3390u11020504

Frey, W. H. (2018). *The millennial generation: A demographic bridge to America's diverse future*. Brookings Metropolitan Policy Program.

Giese, J. L., & Cote, J. A. (2000). Defining consumer satisfaction. *Academy of Marketing Science Review*, *1*(1), 1–22.

Hair, J., Black, W. C., Babin, B. J., Anderson, R. E., & Tatham, R. (2006). *Multivariate data analysis*. New York, NY: Pearson Education.

Hanks, K., Odom, W., Roedl, D., & Blevis, E. (2008, April). Sustainable millennials: attitudes towards sustainability and the material effects of interactive technologies. In *Proceedings of the SIGCHI Conference on Human Factors in Computing Systems* (pp. 333-342). ACM. 10.1145/1357054.1357111

Hansemark, O. C., & Albinsson, M. (2004). Customer satisfaction and retention: The experiences of individual employees. *Managing Service Quality: An International Journal*, *14*(1), 40–57. doi:10.1108/09604520410513668

Homburg, C., & Giering, A. (2001). Personal characteristics as moderators of the relationship between customer satisfaction and loyalty—An empirical analysis. *Psychology and Marketing*, *18*(1), 43–66. doi:10.1002/1520-6793(200101)18:1<43::AID-MAR3>3.0.CO;2-I

Salmones, M., Crespo, A., & Bosque, I. (2005). Influence of corporate social responsibility on loyalty and valuation of services. *Journal of Business Ethics*, *61*(4), 369–385. doi:10.100710551-005-5841-2

Jamali, D., & Mirshak, R. (2007). Corporate social responsibility (CSR): Theory and practice in a developing country context. *Journal of Business Ethics*, *72*(3), 243–262. doi:10.100710551-006-9168-4

Jean, R. J. B., Wang, Z., Zhao, X., & Sinkovics, R. R. (2016). Drivers and customer satisfaction outcomes of CSR in supply chains in different institutional contexts: A comparison between China and Taiwan. *International Marketing Review*, *33*(4), 514–529. doi:10.1108/IMR-04-2014-0115

Jo, H., Kim, H., & Park, K. (2015). Corporate environmental responsibility and firm performance in the financial services sector. *Journal of Business Ethics*, *131*(2), 257–284. doi:10.100710551-014-2276-7

Kaifi, B. A., Nafei, W. A., Khanfar, N. M., & Kaifi, M. M. (2012). A multi-generational workforce: Managing and understanding millennials. *International Journal of Business and Management*, *7*(24), 88–93. doi:10.5539/ijbm.v7n24p88

Kaiser, H. F. (1974). An index of factorial simplicity. *Psychometrika*, *39*(1), 31–36. doi:10.1007/BF02291575

Kotler, P., & Kevin, L. K. (2007). *Marketing Management*. New York, NY: Pearson.

Kristianto, Y., Ajmal, M. M., & Sandhu, M. (2012). Adopting TQM approach to achieve customer satisfaction: A flour milling company case study. *The TQM Journal*, *24*(1), 29–46. doi:10.1108/17542731211191203

Kucukusta, D., Mak, A., & Chan, X. (2013). Corporate social responsibility practices in four and five-star hotels: Perspectives from Hong Kong visitors. *International Journal of Hospitality Management*, *34*, 19–30. doi:10.1016/j.ijhm.2013.01.010

Lerro, M., Raimondo, M., Stanco, M., Nazzaro, C., & Marotta, G. (2019). Cause related marketing among millennial consumers: the role of trust and loyalty in the food industry. *Sustainability*, *11*(2), 535. doi:10.3390u11020535

Lewin, A. Y., Sakano, T., Stephens, C. U., & Victor, B. (1995). Corporate citizenship in Japan: Survey results from Japanese firms. *Journal of Business Ethics*, *14*(2), 83–101. doi:10.1007/BF00872014

Lewis, M. (2004). The influence of loyalty programs and short-term promotions on customer retention. *JMR, Journal of Marketing Research*, *41*(3), 281–292. doi:10.1509/jmkr.41.3.281.35986

Li, M. L., & Green, R. D. (2011). A mediating influence on customer loyalty: The role of perceived value. *Journal of Management and Marketing Research*, *7*, 1.

Likert, R. (1932). A technique for the measurement of attitudes. *Archives de Psychologie*.

Ling, C. E. & de Run, E. C. (2009). Satisfaction and loyalty: customer perceptions of Malaysian telecommunication service providers. *ICFAI Journal of Services Marketing*, *7*(1).

Liu, Y. & Ji, H. (2010, June). A study on the perceived CSR and customer loyalty based on dairy market in China. In *2010 7th International Conference on Service Systems and Service Management* (pp. 1-6). IEEE. 10.1109/ICSSSM.2010.5530161

Loureiro, S. M., Sardinha, I. M. D., & Reijnders, L. (2012). The effect of corporate social responsibility on consumer satisfaction and perceived value: The case of the automobile industry sector in Portugal. *Journal of Cleaner Production*, *37*, 172–178. doi:10.1016/j.jclepro.2012.07.003

Loureiro, S. M. C., & Kastenholz, E. (2011). Corporate reputation, satisfaction, delight, and loyalty towards rural lodging units in Portugal. *International Journal of Hospitality Management*, *30*(3), 575–583. doi:10.1016/j.ijhm.2010.10.007

Luo, X., & Bhattacharya, C. B. (2006). Corporate social responsibility, customer satisfaction, and market value. *Journal of Marketing*, *70*(4), 1–18. doi:10.1509/jmkg.70.4.001

Maignan, I., & Ferrell, O. C. (2001). Corporate citizenship as a marketing instrument-Concepts, evidence and research directions. *European Journal of Marketing*, *35*(3/4), 457–484. doi:10.1108/03090560110382110

Maignan, I., Ferrell, O. C., & Hult, G. T. M. (1999). Corporate citizenship: Cultural antecedents and business benefits. *Journal of the Academy of Marketing Science*, *27*(4), 455–469. doi:10.1177/0092070399274005

Mandhachitara, R., & Poolthong, Y. (2011). A model of customer loyalty and corporate social responsibility. *Journal of Services Marketing*, *25*(2), 122–133. doi:10.1108/08876041111119840

Mao, J. (2010). Customer brand loyalty. *International Journal of Business and Management*, *5*(7), 213. doi:10.5539/ijbm.v5n7p213

Marin, L., Ruiz, S., & Rubio, A. (2009). The role of identity salience in the effects of corporate social responsibility on consumer behavior. *Journal of Business Ethics*, *84*(1), 65–78. doi:10.100710551-008-9673-8

Matten, D., & Crane, A. (2005). Corporate citizenship: toward an extended theoretical conceptualization. *Academy of Management Review*, *30*(1), 166–179. doi:10.5465/amr.2005.15281448

McDougall, G. H., & Levesque, T. (2000). Customer satisfaction with services: Putting perceived value into the equation. *Journal of Services Marketing*, *14*(5), 392–410. doi:10.1108/08876040010340937

McGuire, J. (1963). *Business and society*. New York, NY: McGraw-Hill.

Mohammed, A., & Rashid, B. (2018). A conceptual model of corporate social responsibility dimensions, brand image, and customer satisfaction in Malaysian hotel industry. *Kasetsart Journal of Social Sciences*, *39*(2), 358–364. doi:10.1016/j.kjss.2018.04.001

Mohr, L. A., Webb, D. J., & Harris, K. E. (2001). Do consumers expect companies to be socially responsible? The impact of corporate social responsibility on buying behavior. *The Journal of Consumer Affairs*, *35*(1), 45–72. doi:10.1111/j.1745-6606.2001.tb00102.x

Namukasa, J. (2013). The influence of airline service quality on passenger satisfaction and loyalty: The case of Uganda airline industry. *The TQM Journal*, *25*(5), 520–532. doi:10.1108/TQM-11-2012-0092

Öberseder, M., Schlegelmilch, B. B., Murphy, P. E., & Gruber, V. (2014). Consumers' perceptions of corporate social responsibility: Scale development and validation. *Journal of Business Ethics*, *124*(1), 101–115. doi:10.100710551-013-1787-y

Oliver, R. L. (1980). A cognitive model of the antecedents and consequences of satisfaction decisions. *JMR, Journal of Marketing Research*, *17*(4), 460–469. doi:10.1177/002224378001700405

Oliver, R. L. (1999). Whence consumer loyalty. *Journal of Marketing*, *63*(4), 33–44. doi:10.1177/00222429990634s105

Oliver, R. L., Rust, R. T., & Varki, S. (1997). Customer delight: Foundations, findings, and managerial insight. *Journal of Retailing*, *73*(3), 311–336. doi:10.1016/S0022-4359(97)90021-X

Olsen, L. L., & Johnson, M. D. (2003). Service equity, satisfaction, and loyalty: From transaction-specific to cumulative evaluations. *Journal of Service Research*, *5*(3), 184–195. doi:10.1177/1094670502238914

Olsen, L. L., & Johnson, M. D. (2003). Service equity, satisfaction, and loyalty: From transaction-specific to cumulative evaluations. *Journal of Service Research*, *5*(3), 184–195. doi:10.1177/1094670502238914

Orel, F. D., & Kara, A. (2014). Supermarket self-checkout service quality, customer satisfaction, and loyalty: Empirical evidence from an emerging market. *Journal of Retailing and Consumer Services*, *21*(2), 118–129. doi:10.1016/j.jretconser.2013.07.002

Othman, N. Z. & Hemdi, M. A. (2015). Predictors of guest retention: Investigating the role of hotel's corporate social responsibility activities and brand image. *Theory and Practice in Hospitality and Tourism Research*, 139-144.

Panwar, R., Rinne, T., Hansen, E., & Juslin, H. (2006). Corporate responsibility. *Forest Products Journal*, *56*(2), 4.

Parasuraman, A., Berry, L. L., & Zeithaml, V. A. (1991). Understanding customer expectations of service. *Sloan Management Review*, *32*(3), 39–48.

Park, E. (2019). Corporate social responsibility as a determinant of corporate reputation in the airline industry. *Journal of Retailing and Consumer Services*, *47*, 215–221. doi:10.1016/j.jretconser.2018.11.013

Park, E., Kwon, S. J., & Kim, K. J. (2016). Assessing the effects of corporate sustainable management on customer satisfaction. *Sustainable Development*, *24*(1), 41–52. doi:10.1002d.1605

Parmar, B. L., Freeman, R. E., Harrison, J. S., Wicks, A. C., Purnell, L., & De Colle, S. (2010). Stakeholder theory: The state of the art. *The Academy of Management Annals*, *4*(1), 403–445. doi:10.1080/19416520.2010.495581

Paulík, J., Kombo, F., & Ključnikov, A. (2015). CSR as a driver of satisfaction and loyalty in commercial banks in the Czech Republic. *Journal of International Studies*.

Pérez, A., & Rodriguez del Bosque, I. (2016). The stakeholder management theory of CSR: A multidimensional approach in understanding customer identification and satisfaction. *International Journal of Bank Marketing*, *34*(5), 731–751. doi:10.1108/IJBM-04-2015-0052

PricewaterhouseCoopers. P. W. C. (2011). Millennials at work. Reshaping the workplace. Retrieved from http://www.pwc.ru/en_RU/ru/hr-consulting/publications/assets/millenials-survey.pdf

Rivera, J. J., Bigne, E., & Curras-Perez, R. (2016). Effects of corporate social responsibility perception on consumer satisfaction with the brand. *Spanish Journal of Marketing-ESIC*, *20*(2), 104–114. doi:10.1016/j.sjme.2016.06.002

Salmones, M. D. M. G. D., Perez, A., & Bosque, I. R. D. (2009). The social role of financial companies as a determinant of consumer behavior. *International Journal of Bank Marketing*, *27*(6), 467–485. doi:10.1108/02652320910988339

Santouridis, I., & Trivellas, P. (2010). Investigating the impact of service quality and customer satisfaction on customer loyalty in mobile telephony in Greece. *The TQM Journal*, *22*(3), 330–343. doi:10.1108/17542731011035550

Selnes, F. (1993). An examination of the effect of product performance on brand reputation, satisfaction and loyalty. *European Journal of Marketing, 27*(9), 19–35. doi:10.1108/03090569310043179

Smith, T. J., & Nichols, T. (2015). Understanding the millennial generation. *Journal of Business Diversity, 15*(1), 39.

Sogari, G., Pucci, T., Aquilani, B., & Zanni, L. (2017). Millennial generation and environmental sustainability: The role of social media in the consumer purchasing behavior for wine. *Sustainability, 9*(10), 1911. doi:10.3390u9101911

Stanisavljević, M. (2017). Does customer loyalty depend on corporate social responsibility?. *Naše gospodarstvo/Our economy, 63*(1), 38-46.

Su, L., Pan, Y., & Chen, X. (2017). Corporate social responsibility: Findings from the Chinese hospitality industry. *Journal of Retailing and Consumer Services, 34*, 240–247. doi:10.1016/j.jretconser.2016.10.013

Supanti, D., & Butcher, K. (2019). Is corporate social responsibility (CSR) participation the pathway to foster meaningful work and helping behavior for millennials? *International Journal of Hospitality Management, 77*, 8–18. doi:10.1016/j.ijhm.2018.06.001

Tarigan, E., Prayogo, D. N., & Mardiono, L. (2012, July). Eco-sustainable campus initiatives: a web content analysis. In *The 3rd International Conference on Technology and Operations Management "Sustaining Competitiveness through Green Technology Management"* (Vol. 3, pp. 59-65). SBM ITB and UUM.

Tucker, P. (2006). Teaching the millennial generation. *The Futurist, 40*(3), 7.

Vermeir, I., & Verbeke, W. (2008). Sustainable food consumption among young adults in Belgium: Theory of planned behavior and the role of confidence and values. *Ecological Economics, 64*(3), 542–553. doi:10.1016/j.ecolecon.2007.03.007

Wigley, S. (2008). Gauging consumers' responses to CSR activities: Does increased awareness make cents? *Public Relations Review, 34*(3), 306–308. doi:10.1016/j.pubrev.2008.03.034

Xie, X., Jia, Y., Meng, X., & Li, C. (2017). Corporate social responsibility, customer satisfaction, and financial performance: The moderating effect of the institutional environment in two transition economies. *Journal of Cleaner Production, 150*, 26–39. doi:10.1016/j.jclepro.2017.02.192

Yadavalli, A., & Jones, K. (2014). Does media influence consumer demand? The case of lean finely textured beef in the United States. *Food Policy, 49*, 219–227. doi:10.1016/j.foodpol.2014.08.002

Yoon, Y., & Uysal, M. (2005). An examination of the effects of motivation and satisfaction on destination loyalty: A structural model. *Tourism Management, 26*(1), 45–56. doi:10.1016/j.tourman.2003.08.016

Yusof, J. M., Musa, R., & Rahman, S. A. (2011). Functional store image and corporate social responsibility image: A congruity analysis on store loyalty. *World Academy of Science, Engineering and Technology, 7*(77), 1233–1240.

Zairi, M. (2000). Managing customer dissatisfaction through effective complaints management systems. *The TQM Magazine, 12*(5), 331–337. doi:10.1108/09544780010341932

KEY TERMS AND DEFINITIONS

Cluster Analysis: It is a set of multivariate data analysis techniques aimed at the selection and grouping of homogeneous elements in a data set.

Customer Loyalty: The set of all those activities aimed at creating a commercial and personal link.

Customer Satisfaction: A measure of how products and services supplied by a company meet or surpass customer expectation.

Factor Analysis: A statistical method used to describe variability between the observed, correlated variables in terms of a potentially lower number of unobserved variables called factors.

Millennials: The people belonging to the new generation.

APPENDIX 1

Table 12. Correlation Matrix of Corporate Social Responsibility Dimension

	SR1	SR2	SR3	SR4	SR5	SR6
SR1	1					
SR2	0,7442	1				
SR3	0,7447	0,7346	1			
SR4	0,5766	0,6047	0,6379	1		
SR5	0,5024	0,5741	0,5811	0,8377	1	
SR6	0,5580	0,7513	0,6270	0,6110	0,6202	1
Number of Obs = 241						

Source: our elaboration

Table 13. Correlation Matrix of Corporate Environmental Responsibility Dimension

	ER1	ER2	ER3	ER4	ER5	ER6
ER1	1					
ER2	0,8284	1				
ER3	0,7535	0,8772	1			
ER4	0,7408	0,8641	0,8998	1		
ER5	0,7597	0,8339	0,9111	0,8662	1	
ER6	0,7314	0,7795	0,8428	0,7825	0,8699	1
Number of Obs = 241						

Source: our elaboration

Table 14. Correlation Matrix of Corporate Economic Responsibility Dimension

	EC1	EC2	EC3	EC4	EC5
EC1	1				
EC2	0,8705	1			
EC3	0,6723	0,7375	1		
EC4	0,5651	0,6049	0,5667	1	
EC5	0,5220	0,5654	0,5265	0,7366	1
Number of Obs = 241					

Source: our elaboration

Table 15. Correlation Matrix of Corporate Legal Responsibility Dimension

	LR1	LR2	LR3
LR1	1		
LR2	0,7917	1	
LR3	0,7323	0,9010	1
Number of Obs = 241			

Source: our elaboration

Table 16. Matrix of main components (eigenvalues) of the Social Responsibility dimension

Factor	Eigenvalue	Difference	Proportion	Cumulative
Factor1	4.23814	3.52272	0.7064	0.7064
Factor2	0.71542	0.25918	0.1192	0.8256
Factor3	0.45624	0.20306	0.0760	0.9016
Factor4	0.25319	0.07067	0.0422	0.9438
Factor5	0.18252	0.02803	0.0304	0.9743
Factor6	0.15449	.	0.0257	1

Source: our elaboration from the data setNote: The first factor of them have eigenvalues greater than 1 and also encompass 70,64% of the information contained in the original data set. For this reason, the first factor was considered to identify the new variable.

APPENDIX 2

Table 17. Rotated factor loadings (pattern matrix) and unique variances of the Social Responsibility dimension

Factor	Variance	Difference	Proportion	Cumulative
Factor1	4.23814	.	0.7064	0.7064

Source: our elaboration from the data set

Table 18. Saturation matrix (factor loadings) of the Social Responsibility dimension

Variable	Factor1	Uniqueness
SR1	0.8185	0.3301
SR2	0.8770	0.2308
SR3	0.8598	0.2607
SR4	0.8454	0.2854
SR5	0.8138	0.3378
SR6	0.8264	0.3171

Source: our elaboration from the data set

Note: Each variable is associated according to the highest correlated factor, and then this factor is interpreted according to associated variables. In this case, all the factors are associated with a single variable.

Table 19. Matrix of main components (eigenvalues) of the Economic Responsibility dimension

Factor	Eigenvalue	Difference	Proportion	Cumulative
Factor1	3.22939	2.87166	0.9750	0.9750
Factor2	0.35774	0.38293	0.1080	1.0830
Factor3	-0.02520	0.07198	-0.0076	1.0753
Factor4	-0.09718	0.05522	-0.0293	1.0460
Factor5	-0.15240	.	-0.0460	1

Source: our elaboration from the data set

Table 20. Rotated factor loadings (pattern matrix) and unique variances of the Economic Responsibility dimension

Factor	Variance	Difference	Proportion	Cumulative
Factor1	2.19146	0.79578	0.6616	0.6616
Factor2	1.39567	.	0.4214	1.0830

Source: our elaboration from the data set

Table 21. Saturation matrix (factor loadings) of the Economic Responsibility dimension

Variable	Factor1	Factor2	Uniqueness
EC1	**0.83970**	0.30410	0.2025
EC2	**0.86100**	0.35200	0.1347
EC3	**0.66400**	0.39910	0.3998
EC4	0.41170	**0.71630**	0.3174
EC5	0.36700	**0.71200**	0.3584

Source: our elaboration from the data set

Note: Each variable is associated according to the highest correlated factor, and then this factor is interpreted according to associated variables. In this case, the variables EC1, EC2 and EC3 are associated with Factor1, while the variables EC4 and EC5 are associated with Factor2.

Table 22. Matrix of main components (eigenvalues) of the Legal Responsibility dimension

Factor	Eigenvalue	Difference	Proportion	Cumulative
Factor1	2.3915	2.40874	1.044	1.044
Factor2	-0.01724	0.06631	-0.0075	1.0365
Factor3	-0.08355	.	-0.0365	1

Source: our elaboration from the data set

Table 23. Rotated factor loadings (pattern matrix) and unique variances of the Legal Responsibility dimension

Factor	Variance	Difference	Proportion	Cumulative
Factor1	2.3915	.	1.044	1.044

Source: our elaboration from the data set

Table 24. Saturation matrix (factor loadings) of the Legal Responsibility dimension

Variable	Factor1	Uniqueness
LR1	0.8069	0.3489
LR2	0.9494	0.0987
LR3	0.9160	0.1609

Source: our elaboration from the data set

Note: Each variable is associated according to the highest correlated factor, and then this factor is interpreted according to associated variables. In this case, all the factors are associated with a single variable.

Compilation of References

Abdelhadi, A. (2016). Using lean manufacturing as service quality benchmark evaluation measure. *International Journal of Lean Six Sigma*, *7*(1), 25–34. doi:10.1108/IJLSS-02-2015-0003

Abhijit, M. & Sanjib, K. S. (2019). Analyzing the barriers of green textile supply chain management in Southeast Asia using interpretive structural modeling. *Sustainable Production and Consumption, 17.*

Achabou, M. A., & Dekhili, S. (2013). Luxury and sustainable development: Is there a match? *Journal of Business Research*, *66*(10), 1896–1903. doi:10.1016/j.jbusres.2013.02.011

Acquaye, A., Ibn-Mohammed, T., Genovese, A., Afrifa, G., Yamoah, F. A., & Oppon, E. (2018). A quantitative model for environmentally sustainable supply chain performance measurement. *European Journal of Operational Research*, *269*(1), 16, 188–205. doi:10.1016/j.ejor.2017.10.057

Adam, M., & Ali, K. (2014). Impact of packaging elements of packaged milk on consumer buying behaviour. *IBAICM, International Conference on Marketing.*

Adams, R., Jeanrenaud, S., Bessant, J., Overy, P., & Denyer, D. (2012). *Innovating for sustainability: a systematic review of the body of knowledge*. Retrieved from http://nbs.net/wp-content/uploads/NBS-Systematic-Review-Innovation.pdf

Adams, W. M. (2006, January). The future of sustainability: Rethinking environment and development in the twenty-first century. In Report of the IUCN renowned thinkers meeting (Vol. 29, p. 31).

Adanacioglu, H., & Albayram, Z. (2012). A conjoint analysis of consumer preferences for traditional cheeses in Turkey: A case study on tulum cheese. *Han-gug Chugsan Sigpum Hag-hoeji*, *32*(4), 458–466. doi:10.5851/kosfa.2012.32.4.458

Afuah, A., & Tucci, C. L. (2001). *Internet business models and strategies*. Boston, MA: McGraw-Hill, Irwin.

Agrawal, J., & Kamakura, W. (1995). The economic worth of celebrity endorsers: An event study analysis. *Journal of Marketing*, *59*(3), 56–62. doi:10.1177/002224299505900305

Ajzen, I. (2008). Consumer attitudes and behavior. In C. P. Haugtvedt, P. M. Herr, & F. R. Kardes (Eds.), *Handbook of consumer psychology*. New York, NY: Taylor and Francis Group.

Ajzen, I., & Fishbein, M. (2005). The influence of attitudes on behaviour. In D. Albarracín, B. T. Johnson, & M. P. Zanna (Eds.), *The handbook of attitudes* (pp. 173–221). Mahwah, NJ: Lawrence Erlbaum Associates Publishers.

Akanbi, L. A., Oyedele, L. O., Omoteso, K., Bilal, M., Akinade, O. O., Ajayi, A. O., ... Owolabi, H. A. (2019). Disassembly and deconstruction analytics system (D-DAS) for construction in a circular economy. *Journal of Cleaner Production*, *223*, 386–396. doi:10.1016/j.jclepro.2019.03.172

Al-abdallah, G. M., & Ahmed, R. S. (2018). The impact of corporate social responsibility on customer loyalty in the Qatari telecommunication sector. *Journal of Business and Retail Management Research, 13*(1), 253–268. doi:10.24052/JBRMR/V13IS01/ART-25

Albertini, E. (2013). Does environmental management improve financial performance? A meta-analytical review. *Organization & Environment, 26*(4), 431–457. doi:10.1177/1086026613510301

Albouy, D., & Adesida, O. (2018). *Sustainable fashion blueprint report.* Cambridge University Judge Business School.

Alea García, A. (2006). Diagnóstico y potenciación de la educación ambiental en jóvenes universitarios. *Odiseo, Revista electrónica de Pedagogía., 3*(6).

Alexy, O., George, G., & Salter, A. J. (2013). Cui bono? The selective revealing of knowledge and its implications for innovative activity. *Academy of Management Review, 38*(2), 270–291. doi:10.5465/amr.2011.0193

Allenby, B. R., & Braden, R. (1999). Industrial ecology: policy framework and implementation. Prentice Hall.

Al-Mulali, U., Fereidouni, H. G., Lee, J. Y., & Sab, C. N. B. C. (2013). Examining the bi-directional long run relationship between renewable energy consumption and GDP growth. *Renewable & Sustainable Energy Reviews, 22*, 209–222. doi:10.1016/j.rser.2013.02.005

Alvarado-Herrera, A., Bigne, E., Aldas-Manzano, J., & Curras-Perez, R. (2017). A scale for measuring consumer perceptions of corporate social responsibility following the sustainable development paradigm. *Journal of Business Ethics, 140*(2), 243–262. doi:10.100710551-015-2654-9

Alvarez, G., Colin Pilbeam, C., & Wilding, R. (2010). Nestlé Nespresso AAA sustainable quality program: An investigation into the governance dynamics in a multi-stakeholder supply chain network. *Supply Chain Management, 15*(2), 165–182. doi:10.1108/13598541011028769

Álvarez-García, J., & del RíoRama, M. (2016). Sustainability and EMAS: Impact of motivations and barriers on the perceived benefits from the adoption of standards. *Sustainability, 8*(10), 1057. doi:10.3390u8101057

American Marketing Association. (2017). Ama.org. Retrieved from https://www.ama.org/Pages/default.aspx Sección: Diccionario Términos de Marketing.

Amit, R., & Zott, C. (2001). Value creation in e-Business. *Strategic Management Journal, 22*(6/7), 493–520. doi:10.1002mj.187

Ampuero, O., & Vila, N. (2006). Consumer perceptions of product packaging. *Journal of Consumer Marketing, 23*(2), 102–114. doi:10.1108/07363760610655032

Anderl, R., Haag, S., Schützer, K., & Zancul, E. (2018). Digital twin technology – An approach for Industrie 4.0 vertical and horizontal lifecycle integration. *Información Tecnológica, 60*(3), 125–132.

Andersen, M., & Skjoett-Larsen, T. (2009). Corporate social responsibility in global supply chains. *Supply Chain Management, 14*(2), 75–86. doi:10.1108/13598540910941948

Anderson, E., & Weitz, B. (1992). The use of pledges to build and sustain commitment in distribution channels. *JMR, Journal of Marketing Research, 29*(1), 18–34. doi:10.1177/002224379202900103

Anderson, L. M., & Bateman, T. S. (2000). Individual environmental initiative: Championing natural environmental issues in US business organizations. *Academy of Management Journal, 43*, 548–570.

Andrews, J. C., Burton, S., & Netemeyer, R. C. (2013). Are some comparative nutrition claims misleading? The role of nutrition knowledge, ad claim type and disclosure conditions. *Journal of Advertising, 29*(3), 29–42. doi:10.1080/00913367.2000.10673615

Annunziata, A., Agovino, M., & Mariani, A. (2019). Sustainability of Italian families' food practices: Mediterranean diet adherence combined with organic and local food consumption. *Journal of Cleaner Production, 206*, 86–96. doi:10.1016/j.jclepro.2018.09.155

Annunziata, A., & Vecchio, R. (2013). Consumer perception of functional foods: A conjoint analysis with probiotics. *Food Quality and Preference, 28*(1), 348–355. doi:10.1016/j.foodqual.2012.10.009

Anselmsson, J., Johansson, U., & Persson, N. (2007). Understanding price premium for grocery products: A conceptual model of customer-based brand equity. *Journal of Product and Brand Management, 16*(6), 401–414. doi:10.1108/10610420710823762

Antikainen, M., Makipaa, M., & Ahonen, M. (2010). Motivating and supporting collaboration in open innovation. *European Journal of Innovation Management, 13*(1), 100–119. doi:10.1108/14601061011013258

Antonelli, G. (Ed.). (2004). *Marketing agroalimentare. Specificità e temi di analisi* (Vol. 322). FrancoAngeli.

Antonioli, D., & Mazzanti, M. (2017). Towards a green economy through innovations: The role of trade union involvement. *Ecological Economics, 131*, 286–299. doi:10.1016/j.ecolecon.2016.09.003

Aoe, T. (2007). Eco-efficiency and ecodesign in electrical and electronic products. *Journal of Cleaner Production, 15*(15), 1406–1414. doi:10.1016/j.jclepro.2006.06.004

Apergis, N., & Payne, J. E. (2010a). Renewable energy consumption and economic growth: Evidence from a panel of OECD countries. *Energy Policy, 38*(1), 656–660. doi:10.1016/j.enpol.2009.09.002

Apergis, N., & Payne, J. E. (2010b). Renewable energy consumption and growth in Eurasia. *Energy Economics, 32*(6), 1392–1397. doi:10.1016/j.eneco.2010.06.001

Apergis, N., & Payne, J. E. (2011). The renewable energy consumption-growth nexus in Central America. *Applied Energy, 88*(1), 343–347. doi:10.1016/j.apenergy.2010.07.013

Apergis, N., & Payne, J. E. (2012). Renewable and non-renewable energy consumption-growth nexus: Evidence from a panel error correction model. *Energy Economics, 34*(3), 733–738. doi:10.1016/j.eneco.2011.04.007

Applegate, L. M. (2001). E-business models: Making sense of the Internet business landscape. In G. W. Dickson & G. DeSanctis (Eds.), Information technology and the future enterprise: New models for managers. Upper Saddle River, NJ: Prentice Hall. 49-94.

Aquilani, B. & Abbate, T. (2016). Co-creation and open innovation: Bridging the two paradigms. In *Proceedings of the R&D Management Conference Titled from Science to Society: Innovation and Value Creation*, Cambridge, UK, July 3–6, 2016.

Aquilani, B., & Abbate, T. (2014). Open Innovation through Customers: Collaborative Web-Based Platforms for Ethically and Socially Responsible New Products Part 1. In Handbook of Research on Consumerism in Business and Marketing: Concepts and Practices (pp. 335-374). IGI Global.

Aquilani, B. (2016). *La co-creazione di valore nei processi di innovazione aperta: verso un modello di analisi.* Padova: Cedam.

Aquilani, B., & Abbate, T. (2013). Le piattaforme di innovazione online: la prospettiva delle imprese. *Proceedings of XXV Convegno annuale di Sinergie*.

Aquilani, B., Abbate, T., & Dominici, G. (2016). Choosing Open Innovation Intermediaries through their web-based platforms. *The International Journal of Digital Accounting Research*, *16*, 35–60. doi:10.4192/1577-8517-v16_2

Aquilani, B., Silvestri, C., Ioppolo, G., & Ruggieri, A. (2018). The challenging transition to bio-economies: Towards a new framework integrating corporate sustainability and value co-creation. *Journal of Cleaner Production*, *172*, 4001–4009. doi:10.1016/j.jclepro.2017.03.153

Arana, J., Meilán, J., Gordillo, F., & Carro, J. (2010). Estrategias motivacionales y de aprendizaje para fomentar el consumo responsable desde la Escuela. R.E.M.E. *Revista electrónica de Motivación y Emoción, XIII*(35-36), 19-39.

Arcese, G., Flammini, S., Lucchetti, M., & Martucci, O. (2015). Evidence and experience of open sustainability innovation practices in the food sector. *Sustainability*, *7*(7), 8067–8090. doi:10.3390u7078067

Armstrong, C. M., Niinimaki, K., Kujala, S., Karell, E., & Lang, C. (2015). Sustainable product-service systems for clothing: Exploring consumer perceptions of consumption alternatives in Finland. *Journal of Cleaner Production*, *97*, 30–39. doi:10.1016/j.jclepro.2014.01.046

Arnold, R. D., & Wade, J. P. (2015). A definition of systems thinking: A systems approach. *Procedia Computer Science*, *44*(C), 669–678. doi:10.1016/j.procs.2015.03.050

Arroyo, A., Chamorro, A., & Miranda, F. J. (1999). Diseño para el medio ambiente: Hacia una integración entre innovación y medio ambiente. Libro de ponencias del XIII Congreso Nacional de AEDEM

Arru, B. & Ruggieri, M. (2016). I benefici della Corporate Social Responsibility nella creazione di valore sostenibile: il ruolo delle risorse di competenza e del capitale reputazionale. *Economia aziendale online*, 17-41.

Aschemann-Witzel, J., & Hamm, U. (2010). Do consumers prefer foods with nutrition and health claims? Results of a purchase simulation. *Journal of Marketing Communications*, *16*(2), 47–58. doi:10.1080/13527260903342746

Atzori, L., Iera, A., & Morabito, G. (2014). From "Smart Objects" to "Social Objects": The Next Evolutionary Step of the Internet of Things. *Communication Magazine, IEEE*, *52*(1), 97–105. doi:10.1109/MCOM.2014.6710070

Auger, P., Burke, P., Devinney, T. M., & Louviere, J. J. (2003). What will consumers pay for social product features? *Journal of Business Ethics*, *42*(3), 281–304. doi:10.1023/A:1022212816261

Auger, P., Devinney, T. M., Louviere, J. J., & Burke, P. F. (2008). Do social product features have value to consumers? *International Journal of Research in Marketing*, *25*(3), 183–191. doi:10.1016/j.ijresmar.2008.03.005

Ayres, R. U. (1989). Industrial Metabolism. In *Technology and Environment*. Washington, DC: National Academy Press.

Ayres, R. U. (1994). Industrial metabolism: Theory and policy. In R. U. Ayres & U. K. Simonis (Eds.), *Industrial Metabolism: Restructuring for Sustainable Development* (pp. 3–20). Tokyo: United Nations University Press.

Badurdeen, F. & Jawahir, I. S. (2017). Strategies for value creation through sustainable manufacturing. *Procedia Manufacturing, 8*(October 2016), 20–27. doi:10.1016/j.promfg.2017.02.002

Bag, S., Telukdarie, A., Pretorius, J. H. C., & Gupta, S. (in press). Industry 4.0 and supply chain sustainability: Framework and future research directions. *Benchmarking: An International Journal.*

Bak, A., & Bartlomowicz, T. (2013). *Conjoint analysis method and its implementation in conjoint R package. Department of Econometrics and Computer Science.* Wroclav University of Economics.

Baker, D. A., & Crompton, J. L. (2000). Quality, satisfaction and behavioral intentions. *Annals of Tourism Research, 27*(3), 785–804. doi:10.1016/S0160-7383(99)00108-5

Baldassarre, B., Schepers, M., Bocken, N., Cuppen, E., Korevaar, G., & Calabretta, G. (2019). Industrial symbiosis: Towards a design process for eco-industrial clusters by integrating circular economy and industrial ecology perspectives. *Journal of Cleaner Production, 216*, 446–460. doi:10.1016/j.jclepro.2019.01.091

Banister, D. (2007). Is paradigm shift too difficult in UK transport? *Journal of Urban Technology, 14*(2), 71–86. doi:10.1080/10630730701531732

Banister, D. (2008). The sustainable mobility paradigm. *Transport Policy, 15*(2), 73–80. doi:10.1016/j.tranpol.2007.10.005

Bansal, P. (2005). Envolving sustainable: A longitudinal study of corporate sustainable development. *Strategic Management Journal, 26*(3), 197–218. doi:10.1002mj.441

Bansal, P., & Roth, K. (2000). Why companies go green: A model of ecological responsiveness. *Academy of Management Journal*, 717–736.

Bányai, T., Tamás, P., Illés, B., Stankevičiūtė, Ž., & Bányai, Á. (2019). Optimization of Municipal Waste Collection Routing: Impact of Industry 4.0 Technologies on Environmental Awareness and Sustainability. *International Journal of Environmental Research and Public Health, 16*(4), 634. doi:10.3390/ijerph16040634

Barber, N. (2010). Green wine packaging: Targeting environmental consumers. *International Journal of Wine Business Research, 22*(4), 423–444. doi:10.1108/17511061011092447

Barbier, E. B. (1987). The concept of sustainable economic development. *Environmental Conservation, 14*(2), 101–110. doi:10.1017/S0376892900011449

Barbosa Sánchez, A. (2008). Hacia una cultura ambiental con equidad de género. In *U. d. Chiapas, Educación Ambiental para la sustentabilidad en México* (1st ed.). Chiapas, Mexico: UNICACH.

Barnett, C., Cloke, P., Clarke, N., & Malpass, A. (2005). Consuming ethics: Articulating the subjects and spaces of ethical consumption. *Antipode, 37*(1), 23–45. doi:10.1111/j.0066-4812.2005.00472.x

Barney, J. (1991). Firm resources and sustained competitive advantage. *Journal of Management, 17*(1), 99–120. doi:10.1177/014920639101700108

Barone, M. J., Miyazaki, A. D., & Taylor, K. A. (2000). The influence of cause-related marketing on consumer choice: Does one good turn deserve another? *Journal of the Academy of Marketing Science, 28*(2), 248–262. doi:10.1177/0092070300282006

Barratt, M. (2004). Understanding the meaning of collaboration in the supply chain. *Supply Chain Management, 9*(1), 30–42. doi:10.1108/13598540410517566

Basf (2018). BASF Report 2018. Economic, environmental and social performance. Available at https://www.basf.com/global/en/who-we-are/sustainability.html

Battaglia, M., Bianchim, L., Frey, M., & Iraldo, F. (2010). An innovative model to promote CSR among SMEs operating in industrial clusters: evidence from an EU project. *Corporate Social Responsibility and Environmental Management, 17*(3), 133–141. doi:10.1002/csr.224

Bauer, R. A. (1960). Consumer behavior as risk taking. In R. S. Hancock (Ed.), *Proceedings of the 43rd Conference of the American Marketing Association.* (pp. 389–398). Chicago, IL: American Marketing Association.

Baumann H. & Tillman A-M. (2004). *The hitchhiker's guide to LCA: an orientation in life cycle*

Baumann, H., Boons, F., & Bragd, A. (2002). Mapping the green product development field: Engineering, policy and business perspectives. *Journal of Cleaner Production, 10*(5), 409–425. doi:10.1016/S0959-6526(02)00015-X

Baumers, M., Dickens, P., Tuck, C., & Hague, R. (2016). The cost of additive manufacturing: Machine productivity, economies of scale and technology-push. *Technological Forecasting and Social Change, 102*, 193–201. doi:10.1016/j.techfore.2015.02.015

Bayer. (2018). Sustainable development reports. Available at https://www.investor.bayer.de/en/reports/sustainability-reports/

B-Corporations. (2017). Why B Corps Matter | B Corporation.

Becker-Olsen, K. L., Cudmore, B. A., & Hill, R. P. (2006). The impact of perceived corporate social responsibility on consumer behavior. *Journal of Business Research, 59*(1), 46–53. doi:10.1016/j.jbusres.2005.01.001

Bedin, E., Torricelli, C., Gigliano, S., De Leo, R., & Pulvirenti, A. (2018). Vegan foods: Mimic meat products in the Italian market. *International Journal of Gastronomy and Food Science, 13*, 1–9. doi:10.1016/j.ijgfs.2018.04.003

Belz, F. M., & Peattie, K. (2010). *Sustainability marketing. A global perspective.* Chichester, UK: John Wiley & Sons.

Bendapudi, N., & Leone, R. P. (2003). Psycologic Implications of Customer Participation in Co-Production. *Journal of Marketing, 67*(1), 14–28. doi:10.1509/jmkg.67.1.14.18592

Bennett, R. (1999). Business associations: Their potential contribution to government policy and the growth of small and medium-sized enterprises. *Environment and Planning. C, Government & Policy, 17*(5), 593–608. doi:10.1068/c170593

Bentivoglio, D., Savini, S., Finco, A., Bucci, G., & Boselli, E. (2019). Quality and origin of mountain food products: The new European label as a strategy for sustainable development. *Journal of Mountain Science, 16*(2), 428–440. doi:10.100711629-018-4962-x

Berens, G., Van Riel, C., & van Rekom, J. (2007). The CSR-quality trade-off: When can corporate social responsibility and corporate ability compensate each other? *Journal of Business Ethics, 74*(3), 233–252. doi:10.100710551-006-9232-0

Bertoldi, B., Giachino, C., & Pucciarelli, F. (2011). The product development process in the family run businesses: an inside vision. In Ifera (pp. 1-18). Edizioni Fotograf.

Bey, N., Hauschild, M. Z., & McAloone, T. C. (2013). Drivers and barriers for implementation of environmental strategies in manufacturing companies. *CIRP Annals-Manufacturing Technology, 62*(1), 43–46. doi:10.1016/j.cirp.2013.03.001

Bhattacharya, C. B., & Sen, S. (2004). Doing better at doing good: When, why, and how consumers respond to corporate social initiatives. *California Management Review, 47*(1), 9–24. doi:10.2307/41166284

Bhat, V. N. (1998). Does environmental compliance pay? *Ecotoxicology (London, England), 7*(4), 221–225. doi:10.1023/A:1008938811813

Bilgili, F., & Ozturk, I. (2015). Biomass energy and economic growth nexus in G7 countries: Evidence from dynamic panel data. *Renewable & Sustainable Energy Reviews, 49*, 132–138. doi:10.1016/j.rser.2015.04.098

Billeter, D., Zhu, M., & Inman, J. J. (2012). Transparent packaging and consumer purchase decisions. In J. Sevilla (Ed.), *When it's what's outside that matters: Recent findings on product and packaging design.* PA: University of Pittsburgh.

Bird, K., & Hughes, D. R. (1997). Ethical consumerism: The case of "Fairly–Traded" coffee. *Business Ethics (Oxford, England), 6*(3), 159–167. doi:10.1111/1467-8608.00063

Birkel, H. S., Veile, J. W., Müller, J. M., Hartmann, E., & Voigt, K. I. (2019). Development of a risk framework for Industry 4.0 in the context of sustainability for established manufacturers. *Sustainability, 11*(2), 384. doi:10.3390u11020384

Birkin, F., & Polesie, T. (2012). *Intrinsic sustainable development epistemes, science, business and sustainability*. Singapore: World Scientific Publishing.

Birtwistle, G., & Moore, C. M. (2007). Fashion clothing–where does it all end up? *International Journal of Retail & Distribution Management, 35*(3), 210–216. doi:10.1108/09590550710735068

Bithas, K. (2011). Sustainability and externalities: Is the internalization of externalities a sufficient condition for sustainability? *Ecological Economics, 70*(10), 1703–1706. doi:10.1016/j.ecolecon.2011.05.014

Bloemer, J. M., & Kasper, H. D. (1995). The complex relationship between consumer satisfaction and brand loyalty. *Journal of Economic Psychology, 16*(2), 311–329. doi:10.1016/0167-4870(95)00007-B

Blome, C., Schoenherr, T., & Kaesser, M. (2013). Ambidextrous governance in supply chains: the impact on innovation and cost performance. *The Journal of Supply Chain Management, 49*(4), 59–80. doi:10.1111/jscm.12033

Blowfield, M., Visser, W., & Livesey, F. (2007). Sustainability innovation - mapping the territory, Cambridge Programme for Sustainability Leadership Paper Series, 2.

Blum, D. W. (2015). Permanent establishments and action 1 on the digital economy of the OECD base erosion and profit shifting initiative – the Nexus criterion redefined? *69 Bulletin of International Taxation*, 6/7, 3.2., *Journals IBFD*. Retrieved from http://www.ibfd.org/sites/ibfd.org/files/

BLUMINE-ACIMIT. (2016). *Le tecnologie green nella filiera tessile: un valore aggiunto nei processi di innovazione sostenibile*. Report presented during the Plenary Meeting of ACIMIT, 21 giugno 2016.

Boccia, F. & Covino, D. (2016). Innovation and sustainability in agri-food companies: The role of quality. *Rivista di Studi sulla Sostenibilita'*.

Bogers, M., Hadar, R., & Bilberg, A. (2016). Additive manufacturing for consumer-centric business models: Implications for supply chains in consumer goods manufacturing. *Technological Forecasting and Social Change, 102*, 225–239. doi:10.1016/j.techfore.2015.07.024

Boiral, O., & Henri, J. F. (2012). Modelling the impact of ISO 14001 on environmental performance: A comparative approach. *Journal of Environmental Management, 99*, 84–97. doi:10.1016/j.jenvman.2012.01.007 PMID:22326757

Bojanic, D., Warnick, R., & Musante, M. (2007). An extension of burgernomics: using a full-service restaurant product to measure purchasing power parity. *The Journal of Hospitality Financial Management, 15*(1), 57–69. doi:10.1080/10913211.2007.10653830

Boks, C. (2006). The soft side of ecodesign. *Journal of Cleaner Production, 14*(15-16), 1346–1356. doi:10.1016/j.jclepro.2005.11.015

Bonadonna, A. & Duglio, S. (2016). A mountain niche production: the case of Bettelmatt cheese in the Antigorio and Formazza valleys (Piedmont–Italy). *Quality-Access to success, 17*(150).

Bonadonna, A., Alfiero, S., Cane, M., & Gheribi, E. (2019). Eating hamburgers slowly and sustainably: the fast food market in northwest Italy. *Agriculture, 9*(4), 77. doi:10.3390/agriculture9040077

Bonadonna, A., Giachino, C., & Truant, E. (2017). Sustainability and mountain tourism: the millennial's perspective. *Sustainability, 9*(7), 1219. doi:10.3390u9071219

Bonadonna, A., Macar, L., Peira, G., & Giachino, C. (2017). The dark side of the European quality schemes: The ambiguous life of the traditional specialties guaranteed. *Calitatea, 18*(156), 102.

Bonan, G. B. & Doney, S. C. (2018). Climate, ecosystems, and planetary futures: The challenge to predict life in Earth system models. *Science*, 359(6375), eaam8328.

Bonilla, S., Silva, H., Terra da Silva, M., Franco Gonçalves, R., & Sacomano, J. (2018). Industry 4.0 and sustainability implications: A scenario-based analysis of the impacts and challenges. *Sustainability*, *10*(10), 3740. doi:10.3390u10103740

Bonta, P. & Farber, M. (1994). 199 preguntas sobre marketing y publicidad. Bogotá, Colombia: Norma.

Boons, F. (2002). Greening products: A framework for product chain management. *Journal of Cleaner Production*, *10*(5), 495–505. doi:10.1016/S0959-6526(02)00017-3

Boons, F., & Lüdeke-Freund, F. (2013). Business models for sustainable innovation: State-of-the-art and steps towards a research agenda. *Journal of Cleaner Production*, *45*, 9–19. doi:10.1016/j.jclepro.2012.07.007

Boons, F., & Wagner, M. (2009). Assessing the relationship between economic and ecological performance: Distinguishing system levels and the role of innovation. *Ecological Economics*, *68*(7), 1908–1914. doi:10.1016/j.ecolecon.2009.02.012

Bos-Brouwers, H. E. J. (2010). Corporate sustainability and innovation in SMEs: Evidence of themes and activities in practice. *Business Strategy and the Environment*, *19*(7), 417–435.

Boudreau, K. J. (2012). Let a Thousand Flowers Bloom? An Early Look at Large Numbers of Software App Developers and Patterns of Innovation. *Organization Science*, *23*(5), 1409–1427. doi:10.1287/orsc.1110.0678

Boureima, F. S., Messagie, M., Matheys, J., Wynen, V., Sergeant, N., Van Mierlo, J., & De Caevel, B. (2009). Comparative LCA of electric, hybrid, LPG and gasoline cars in Belgian context. *World Electric Vehicle Journal*, *3*(3), 469–476. doi:10.3390/wevj3030469

Bouzon, M. & Govindan, K. (2015). Reverse logistics as a sustainable supply chain practice for the fashion industry: an analysis of drivers and the Brazilian Case. In T. C. E. Cheng & T.-M. Choi (Eds.), Sustainable fashion supply chain management (pp. 85-104). Cham, Switzerland: Springer.

Bovea, M. D., & Pérez-Belis, V. (2018). Identifying design guidelines to meet the circular economy principles: A case study on electric and electronic equipment. *Journal of Environmental Management*, *228*(August), 483–494. doi:10.1016/j.jenvman.2018.08.014 PMID:30248643

Bowen, H. R. (1953). *Social responsibility of the businessman*. New York, NY: Harper and Row.

Bowie, N. E. (2000). *Ethical theory and business* (6th ed.). New York, NY: Prentice Hall.

Bracalente, B., Cossignani, M., & Mulas, A. (2009). *Statistica aziendale*. Milan, Rome: McGraw-Hill.

Braccini, A. M., & Margherita, E. G. (2018). Exploring Organizational Sustainability of Industry 4.0 under the Triple Bottom Line: The Case of a Manufacturing Company. *Sustainability*, *11*(1), 1–17. doi:10.3390u11010036

Bradley, J., Loucks, J., Macaulay, J., Noronha, A., & Wade, M. (2015). *Digital vortex how digital disruption is redefining industries. Global Center for Digital Business Transformation*. Retrieved from https://www.cisco.com/c/dam/en/us/solutions/collateral/industry-solutions/digital-vortex-report.pdf

Branger, J., & Pang, Z. (2015). From automated home to sustainable, healthy and manufacturing home: A new story enabled by the Internet-of-Things and Industry 4.0. *Journal of Management Analytics*, *2*(4), 314–332. doi:10.1080/23270012.2015.1115379

Braungart, M., McDonough, W., & Bollinger, A. (2007). Cradle-to-cradle design: Creating healthy emissions - a strategy for eco-effective product and system design. *Journal of Cleaner Production*, *15*(13–14), 1337–1348. doi:10.1016/j.jclepro.2006.08.003

Bravo, G. F. (2010). *Partidos verdes y movimientos ecologistas*. Recuperado de www.revistas.unam.mx/index.php/matices/article/download/25725/24217

BReport. (1987). Retrieved from https://www.are.admin.ch/are/it/home/sviluppo-sostenibile/cooperazione-internazionale/l_agenda-2030-per-uno-sviluppo-sostenibile/onu-le-pietre-miliari-dello-sviluppo-sostenibile/1987--rapporto-brundtland.html

Bresciani, S., Thrassou, A., & Vrontis, D. (2013). Change through innovation in family businesses: evidence from an Italian sample. *World Review of Entrepreneurship, Management and Sustainable Development 4, 9*(2), 195-215.

Bressanelli, G., Adrodegari, F., Perona, M., & Saccani, N. (2018). Exploring how usage-focused business models enable circular economy through digital technologies. *Sustainability*, *10*(3), 639. doi:10.3390u10030639

Brinkley, C. (2018). The small world of the alternative food network. *Sustainability*, *10*(8), 2921. doi:10.3390u10082921

British Petroleum (BP). (2017). Statistical Review of World Energy, June.

British Standards Institution. (2017). *Framework for implementing the principles of the circular economy in organizations : guide*. BSI Standards Limited. Retrieved from https://shop.bsigroup.com/ProductDetail?pid=000000000030334443&_ga=2.150628976.710916583.1559852485-363687714.1559679644

Brousseau, E., & Penard, T. (2007). The economics of digital business models: A framework for analyzing the economics of platforms. *Review of Network Economics*, *6*(2). doi:10.2202/1446-9022.1112

Brown, T. J., & Dacin, P. A. (1997). The company and the product: Corporate associations and consumer product responses. *Journal of Marketing*, *61*(1), 68–84. doi:10.1177/002224299706100106

Bruner, G. C. (2017). *Marketing scales handbook: multi-item measures for consumer insight research* (Vol. 9). GCBII Productions.

Brunori, C., Mancuso, E., Luciano, A., Sbaffoni, S., Barberio, G., La Monica, M., ... Cutaia, L. (2016). L'economia circolare per il contenimento delle emissioni di gas serra. *Energia Ambiente e Innovazione*, *1*, 46–49.

Büchi, Cugno, & Castagnoli. (2018). Economies of Scale and Network Economies in Industry 4.0. *Symphonya*, *2*, 1–11.

Buenstorf, G., & Cordes, C. (2008). Can sustainable consumption be learned? A model of cultural evolution. *Ecological Economics*, *67*(4), 646–657. doi:10.1016/j.ecolecon.2008.01.028

Buerke, A., Straatmann, T., Lin-Hi, N., & Müller, K. (2017). Consumer awareness and sustainability-focused value orientation as motivating factors of responsible consumer behavior. [October.]. *Review of Managerial Science, Springer*, *11*(4), 959–991. doi:10.100711846-016-0211-2

Buguin, J., Dobbs, R., Bisson, P., & Marrs, A. (2013). *Disruptive Technologies: Advances That Will Transform Life, Business, and the Global Economy*. San Francisco, CA: McKinsey Global Institute.

Bullinger, H.-J., Neuhüttler, J., Nägele, R., & Woyke, I. (2017). Collaborative Development of Business Models in Smart Service Ecosystems. PICMET 2017: Technology Management for Interconnected Word, 1-9.

Burgess, K., Singh, P. J., & Koroglu, R. (2006). Supply chain management: A structured literature review and implications for future research. *International Journal of Operations & Production Management*, *26*(7), 703–729. doi:10.1108/01443570610672202

Burritt, R., & Christ, K. (2016). Industry 4.0 and environmental accounting: A new revolution? *Asian Journal of Sustainable Society Responsibility*, *1*(1), 23–38. doi:10.118641180-016-0007-y

Burton, S., Andrews, J. C., & Netemeyer, R. G. (2000). Nutrition ad claims and disclosures: Interaction and mediation effects for consumer evaluations of the brand and the ad. *Marketing Letters, 11*(3), 235–247. doi:10.1023/A:1008187110096

Busacca, B., Bertoli, G., & Chizzoli, C. (2019). *Customer-based View*. Milano, Italy: Egea.

Büyüközkan, G., & Karabulut, Y. (2018). Sustainability performance evaluation: Literature review and future directions. *Journal of Environmental Management, 217*, 253–267. doi:10.1016/j.jenvman.2018.03.064 PMID:29605780

Caamal Cauich, I., Pat Fernández, V. G., Ascencio, F. J., & Pérez Fernández, A. (2007). Producción, comercialización y consumo de productos orgánicos en Alemania. *Textual (Chapingo)*, 133–153.

Calomarde, J. (2000). *Marketing Ecológico*. Madrid, Spain: Pirámide ESIC. doi:84-368-1426-6

Caniato, F., Caridi, M., Crippa, L., & Moretto, A. (2012). Environmental sustainability in fashion supply chains: An exploratory case-based research. *International Journal of Production Economics, 135*(2), 659–670. doi:10.1016/j.ijpe.2011.06.001

Cappella, F., Giaccaria, P., & Peira, G. (2015). La filiera della carne piemontese: Scenari possibili. *Politiche Piemonte, 36*, 6–12.

Capuz Rizo, S., & Gómez Navarro, T. (2004). *Ecodiseño: Ingeniería del ciclo de vida para el desarrollo de productos sostenibles*. México: Alfaomega.

Carayannis, E. G., Sindakis, S., & Walter, C. (2015). Business model innovation as lever of organizational sustainability. *The Journal of Technology Transfer, 40*(1), 85–104. doi:10.100710961-013-9330-y

Carbone, A. (2018). Foods and places: comparing different supply chains. *Agriculture, 8*(1), 6. doi:10.3390/agriculture8010006

Carrete Lucero, L., González, E. M., Centeno Velázquez, E., Castaño González, R., & Félix, R. (2013). ¿Qué características tienen los consumidores verdes en México? Un enfoque sobre segmentación demográfica fundamentada en las 3R's y la compra de productos ecológicos. Estudios Gerenciales, 30(132), 287-300. Recuperado de http://static1.squarespace.com/static/56228080e4b04bb42a1523da/t/56b39785cf80a1b5f4184f1d/1454610372295/TG2013_Carrete_etal.pdf

Carrol, J. D., & Green, P. E. (1995). Psychometric methods in marketing research: Part 1, conjoint analysis. *Journal of Marketing, 32*, 385–391.

Carroll, A. B. (2016). Carroll's pyramid of CSR: taking another look. *International Journal of Corporate Social Responsibility, 1*(1), 3.

Carroll, A. B. (1979). A three-dimensional conceptual model of corporate performance. *Academy of Management Review, 4*(4), 497–505. doi:10.5465/amr.1979.4498296

Carroll, A. B. (1991). The pyramid of corporate social responsibility: Toward the moral management of organizational stakeholders. *Business Horizons, 34*(4), 39–48. doi:10.1016/0007-6813(91)90005-G

Carroll, A. B., & Shabana, K. M. (2010). The business case for corporate social responsibility: A review of concepts, research and practice. *International Journal of Management Reviews, 12*(1), 85–105. doi:10.1111/j.1468-2370.2009.00275.x

Carruthers, K. (2014). How the Internet of Things Changes Everything: the Next Stage of the Digital Revolution. *Australian Journal of Telecommunications and the Digital Economy, 2*(4), 69.1-69.13.

Carsol, R. (1962). *Silent spring*. Boston, MA: Houghton Mifflin Harcourt.

Carter, C. R., & Jennings, M. M. (2002). Logistics social responsibility: An integrative framework. *Journal of Business Logistics*, *23*(1), 145–180. doi:10.1002/j.2158-1592.2002.tb00020.x

Carter, C. R., & Jennings, M. M. (2004). The role of purchasing in the socially responsible management of the supply chain: A structural equation analysis. *Journal of Business Logistics*, *25*(1), 145–186. doi:10.1002/j.2158-1592.2004.tb00173.x

Carvalho, N., Chaim, O., Cazarini, E., & Gerolamo, M. (2018). Manufacturing in the fourth industrial revolution: A positive prospect in sustainable manufacturing. *Procedia Manufacturing*, *21*, 671–678. doi:10.1016/j.promfg.2018.02.170

Carzedda, M., Marangon, F., Nassivera, F., & Troiano, S. (2018). Consumer satisfaction in alternative food networks (AFNs): Evidence from northern Italy. *Journal of Rural Studies*, *64*, 73–79. doi:10.1016/j.jrurstud.2018.10.003

Casadesus-Masanell, R., & Ricart, J. E. (2010). From strategy to business models and onto tactics. *Long Range Planning*, *43*(2–3), 195–215. doi:10.1016/j.lrp.2010.01.004

Castellani, G., De Rossi, D., & Rampa, A. (2016). *L E S OCIETÀ B ENEFIT La nuova prospettiva di una Corporate Social Responsibility con Commitment*. Fondazione Comerciale Dei Comercialisti.

Castellini, A., & Samoggia, A. (2018). Customers' perception of fish fast-casual restaurants. *Journal of Food Products Marketing*, *24*(3), 348–371. doi:10.1080/10454446.2017.1266562

Catano, V. M. & Morrow Hines, H. (2016). The influence of corporate social responsibility, psychologically healthy workplaces, and individual values in attracting millennial job applicants. *Canadian Journal of Behavioural Science/ Revue canadienne des sciences du comportement, 48*(2), 142.

Cavaliere, A., & Ventura, V. (2018). Mismatch between food sustainability and consumer acceptance toward innovation technologies among Millennial students: The case of shelf life extension. *Journal of Cleaner Production*, *175*, 641–650. doi:10.1016/j.jclepro.2017.12.087

Cervellon, M., Hjerth, H., & Ricard, S. (2010). Green in fashion? An exploratory study of national differences in consumers concern for eco-fashion. *Proceedings of 9th International Marketing Trends Conference*, Venice, Italy, Jan. 20-21.

Cervera-Ferri, J. L., & Ureña, M. L. (2017). *Indicadores de producción verde: Una guía para avanzar hacia el desarrollo sostenible*. Santiago, Chile: CEPAL.

Ceschin, F., & Gaziulusoy, I. (2016). Evolution of design for sustainability: From product design to design for system innovations and transitions. *Design Studies*, *47*, 118–163. doi:10.1016/j.destud.2016.09.002

Chaim, O., Muschard, B., Cazarini, E., & Rozenfeld, H. (2018). Insertion of sustainability performance indicators in an industry 4.0 virtual learning environment. *Procedia Manufacturing*, *21*, 446–453. doi:10.1016/j.promfg.2018.02.143

Chalkias, G. (2019). *Industrial Symbiosis: A Circular Manufacturing Strategy for Industry 4.0*. Retrieved from https://www.crit-research.it/wp-content/uploads/2018/04/20180419CRIT_Circular-manufacturing-strategies-for-I40-Chalkias-IRIS.pdf

Chandran, S., Batra, R., & Lawrence, B. (2009). Is seeing believing? Consumer responses to opacity of product packaging. In A. L. McGill & S. Shavitt (Eds.), *Advances in consumer research* (Vol. 36, pp. 970–971). Duluth, MN: Association for Consumer Research.

Chang, C. (2011). Feeling ambivalent about going green. *Journal of Advertising*, *40*(4), 19–32. doi:10.2753/JOA0091-3367400402

Chang, C. H., & Tu, C. Y. (2005). Exploring store image, customer satisfaction and customer loyalty relationship: Evidence from Taiwanese hypermarket industry. *The Journal of American Academy of Business, Cambridge*, *7*(2), 197–202.

Chang, D. Y. (2009). Service quality assessment of a chain steakhouse in Taiwan. *Journal of Quality Assurance in Hospitality & Tourism, 10*(4), 255–278. doi:10.1080/15280080903183417

Chase, R. B., Jacobs, R. F., Aquilano, N. J., Grando, A., & Sianesi, A. (2008). Operations Management nella produzione e nei servizi (pp. 1-477). McGraw-Hill, Publishing Group Italia.

Chellappa, R. K., & Sin, R. G. (2005). Personalization versus privacy: An empirical examination of the online consumer's dilemma. *Information Technology Management, 6*(2-3), 181–202. doi:10.100710799-005-5879-y

Chen, H., & Burns, D. (2006). Environmental analysis of textile products. *Clothing & Textiles Research Journal, 24*(3), 248–261. doi:10.1177/0887302X06293065

Chen, Y. S. (2008). The driver of green innovation and green image – green core competence. *Journal of Business Ethics, 81*(3), 531–543. doi:10.100710551-007-9522-1

Chen, Y. S., Chang, C. H., & Wu, F. S. (2012). Origins of green innovations: The differences between proactive and reactive green innovations. *Management Decision, 50*(3), 369–398. doi:10.1108/00251741211216197

Chertow, M. R. (2000). Industrial Symbiosis: Literature and Taxonomy. *Annual Review of Energy and the Environment, 25*(1), 313–337. doi:10.1146/annurev.energy.25.1.313

Chertow, M. R. (2007). "Uncovering" industrial symbiosis. *Journal of Industrial Ecology, 11*(1), 11–30. doi:10.1162/jiec.2007.1110

Chertow, M. R., Ashton, S. A., & Espinosa, J. C. (2008). Industrial symbiosis in Puerto Rico: Environmentally related agglomeration economies. *Regional Studies, 42*(10), 1299–1312. doi:10.1080/00343400701874123

Chiarello, F., Trivelli, L., Bonaccorsi, A., & Fantoni, G. (2018). Extracting and mapping industry 4.0 technologies using Wikipedia. *Computers in Industry, 100*, 244–257. doi:10.1016/j.compind.2018.04.006

Choi, B., & La, S. (2013). The impact of corporate social responsibility (CSR) and customer trust on the restoration of loyalty after service failure and recovery. *Journal of Services Marketing, 27*(3), 223–233. doi:10.1108/08876041311330717

Cho, S., Heo, E., & Kim, J. (2015). Causal relationship between renewable energy consumption and economic growth: Comparison between developed and less-developed countries. *Geosystem Engineering, 18*(6), 284–291. doi:10.1080/12269328.2015.1053540

Chung, K. H., Yu, J. E., Choi, M. G., & Shin, J. I. (2015). The effects of CSR on customer satisfaction and loyalty in China: The moderating role of corporate image. *Journal of Economics, Business and Management, 3*(5), 542–547.

Chun, Y. Y., Lee, K. M., Lee, J. S., Lee, J. Y., Lee, M. H., Mishima, N., & Tahara, K. (2018). Identifying key components of products based on consumer- and producer-oriented ecodesign indices considering environmental impacts, costs, and utility value. *Journal of Cleaner Production, 198*, 1031–1043. doi:10.1016/j.jclepro.2018.07.035

Clark, H. (2008). SLOW+ FASHION—an oxymoron—or a promise for the future...? *Fashion Theory, 12*(4), 427–446. doi:10.2752/175174108X346922

CNTAC (2015-2017). *Annual report on social responsibility of Chinese textile and apparel industry.*

CNTAC (2016-2017). *Annual report on social responsibility of Chinese textile and apparel industry.*

Codini, A., Saccani, N., & Sicco, A. (2012). The relationship between customer value and pricing strategies: An empirical test. *Journal of Product and Brand Management, 21*(7), 538–546. doi:10.1108/10610421211276321

Coldiretti. (2018, May 6). *Coldiretti: olio d'oliva conquista il mondo, +49% in 25 anni.* Retrieved from http://www.askanews.it/economia/2018/05/06/coldiretti-olio-doliva-conquista-il-mondo-49-in-25-anni-pn_20180506_00020/

Connelly, B. L., Ketchen, D. J., & Slater, S. F. (2011). Toward a "theoretical toolbox" for sustainability research in marketing. *Journal of the Academy of Marketing Science, 39*(1), 86–100. doi:10.100711747-010-0199-0

Connolly, J., & Prothero, A. (1998). Sustainable consumption: Consumption, consumers and the commodity discourse. *Consumption Markets & Culture, 6*(4), 275–291. doi:10.1080/1025386032000168311

Conti, C., Costa, A., Balzaretti, C., Russo, V., & Tedesco, D. (2018). Survey on food preferences of university students: from tradition to new food customs? *Agriculture, 8*(10), 155. doi:10.3390/agriculture8100155

Conway, S., & Steward, F. (1998). Networks and interfaces in environmental innovation: A comparative study in the UK and Germany. *The Journal of High Technology Management Research, 9*(2), 239–253. doi:10.1016/S1047-8310(98)90006-2

Corbetta, P. G. (1999). *Metodologia e tecniche della ricerca sociale (Methodology and methods of the social research).* Bologna, Italy: Il Mulino.

Costa, A. I. A. (2013). Collaborative product innovation in the food service industry. Do too many cooks really spoil the broth? In *Open Innovation in the Food and Beverage Industry* (pp. 154–173). Woodhead Publishing. doi:10.1533/9780857097248.2.154

Cowe, R., & Williams, S. (2000). *Who are the ethical consumers?* London, UK: The Cooperative Bank.

Cronbach, L. J. (1951). Coefficient alpha and the internal structure of tests. *Psychometrika, 16*(3), 297–334. doi:10.1007/BF02310555

Crosby Philip, B. (1997). *Obiettivo qualità.* McGraw-Hil.

Cuesta Valiño, P., Rodríguez, P. G., & Núñez Barriopedro, E. (2019). The impact of corporate social responsibility on customer loyalty in hypermarkets: A new socially responsible strategy. *Corporate Social Responsibility and Environmental Management, 26*(4), 761–769. doi:10.1002/csr.1718

Cullen, J. G. (2017). Educating business students about sustainability: A bibliometric review of current trends and research needs. *Journal of Business Ethics, 145*(2), 424–439. doi:10.100710551-015-2838-3

Cutaia, L., Barberio, G., La Monica, M., Luciano, A., Mancuso, E., Sbaffoni, S., & Scagliarino, C. (2019). *La Prima Piattaforma Italiana per la Simbiosi Industriale.* Retrieved from http://astrolabio.amicidellaterra.it/node/1324

Cutaia, L., La Monica, M., Scagliarino, S., Barberio, G., Sbaffoni, S., Luciano, A., & Mancuso, M. (2015b). Recovery of waste streams from agroindustry through industrial symbiosis in Sicilia. In *LCA for feeding the planet and energy for life, International conference on Life Cycle Assessment as reference methodology for assessing supply chains and supporting global sustainability challenges.* ENEA.

Cutaia, L., Mancuso, E., Barberio, G., Sbaffoni, S., Luciano, A., La Monica, M., & Scagliarino, C. (2015c). The Experience of the First Industrial Symbiosis Platform in Italy. In *Experiences of Industrial Symbiosis in Italy. Proceedings of conferences promoted by ENEA at Ecomondo in 2012, 2013 and 2014.* ENEA.

Cutaia, L., Barberio, B., Luciano, A., Mancuso, E., Sbaffoni, S., La Monica, M., & Scagliarino, C. (2015a). The experience of the first industrial symbiosis platform in Italy. *Environmental Engineering and Management Journal, 14*(7), 1521–1533. doi:10.30638/eemj.2015.164

Cutaia, L., Boncio, E., Barberio, G., Beltrani, T., La Monica, M., Mancuso, E., ... Paoni, S. (2017). Industrial symbiosis network in Umbria, Italy, in methods and tools for the implementation of industrial symbiosis best practices and business cases in Italy. *Proceedings of the first SUN Conference Rome.*

Cutaia, L., Mancuso, E., Sbaffoni, S., Luciano, A., & Barberio, G. (2014c). First results of the implementation of the Industrial Symbiosis Platform in Italy. *Proceedings Symbiosis Conference.*

Cutaia, L., Morabito, R., Barberio, G., Mancuso, E., Brunori, C., Spezzano, P., ... Cappello, F. (2014a). The Project for the Implementation of the Industrial Symbiosis Platform in Sicily: The Progress After the First Year of Operation. In R. Salomone & G. Saija (Eds.), *Pathways to Environmental Sustainability.* Springer International Publishing. doi:10.1007/978-3-319-03826-1_20

Cutaia, L., Sbaffoni, S., Mancuso, E., Barberio, G., Luciano, A., Scagliarino, C., & La Monica, M. (2014b). Un esempio di eco-innovazione di sistema attraverso la valorizzazione territoriale di risorse: Nuovo approccio cooperativo tra mondo industriale, scientifico e istituzionale. *EAI Energia, Ambiente e Innovazione. Energia Ambiente e Innovazione, 60*(5), 76–88.

Cutaia, L., Scagliarino, C., Mencherini, U., & Iacondini, A. (2014d). Industrial symbiosis in Emilia-Romagna region: Results from a first application in the agroindustry sector. *Procedia Environmental Science. Engineering and Management, 2*, 11–36.

Cutaia, L., Scagliarino, C., Mencherini, U., & La Monica, M. (2016). Project green symbiosis 2014 - II phase: Results from an industrial symbiosis pilot project in Emilia Romagna region (Italy). *Environmental Engineering and Management Journal, 15*(9), 1949–1961. doi:10.30638/eemj.2016.210

D'Souza, C., & Taghian, M. (2005). Green advertising effects on attitude and choice of advertising themes. *Asia Pacific Journal of Marketing and Logistics, 17*(3), 51–66. doi:10.1108/13555850510672386

Daddi, T., Gusmerotti, N. M., Iraldo, F., & Frey, M. (2014). EMAS and ISO 14001: The differences in effectively improving environmental performance. *Journal of Cleaner Production, 68*(1), 165–173.

Daddi, T., Magistrelli, M., Frey, M., & Iraldo, F. (2011). Do environmental management systems improve environmental performance? Empirical evidence from Italian companies. *Environment, Development and Sustainability, 13*(5), 845–862. doi:10.100710668-011-9294-8

Daddi, T., Testa, F., Iraldo, F., & Frey, M. (2014). Removing and simplifying administrative costs and burdens for EMAS and ISO 14001 certified organizations: Evidence from Italy. *Environmental Engineering and Management Journal, 13*(3), 689–698. doi:10.30638/eemj.2014.073

Dadura, A. M., & Lee, T. R. (2011). Measuring the innovation ability of Taiwan's food industry using DEA. *Innovation (Abingdon), 24*(1-2), 151–172. doi:10.1080/13511610.2011.583863

Dahlsrud, A. (2008). How corporate social responsibility is defined: An analysis of 37 definitions. *Corporate Social Responsibility and Environmental Management, 15*(1), 1–13. doi:10.1002/csr.132

Dahl, T., & Næs, T. (2004). Outlier and group detection in sensory panels using hierarchical cluster analysis with the Procrustes distance. *Food Quality and Preference, 15*(3), 195–208. doi:10.1016/S0950-3293(03)00058-2

Dallocchio, M., Perrini, F., Russo, A., & Vurro, C. (2010). *Creare valore nella supply chain: Modelli di gestione a confronto.* Milano, Italy: Egea.

Daly, H. E. (1996). *Beyond growth: the economics of sustainable development.* Boston, MA: Beacon Press.

Dangelico, R. M. (2016). Green product innovation: Where we are and where we are going. *Business Strategy and the Environment, 25*(8), 560–576. doi:10.1002/bse.1886

Dangelico, R. M., Pontrandolfo, P., & Pujari, D. (2013). Developing sustainable new products in the textile and upholstered furniture industries: Role of external integrative capabilities. *Journal of Product Innovation Management*, *30*(4), 642–658. doi:10.1111/jpim.12013

Dangelico, R. M., & Pujari, D. (2010). Mainstreaming green product innovation: Why and how companies integrate environmental sustainability. *Journal of Business Ethics*, *95*(3), 471–486. doi:10.100710551-010-0434-0

Darley, W. K., & Smith, R. E. (1993). Advertising claim objectivity: Antecedents and effects. *Journal of Marketing*, *57*(4), 100–113. doi:10.1177/002224299305700408

Dassisti, M., Siragusa, N., & Semeraro, C. (2018). *Exergetic Model as a Guideline for Implementing the Smart-factory Paradigm in Small Medium Enterprises: The Brovedani Case. In Procedia CIRP* (Vol. 67, pp. 534–539). Amsterdam, Netherlands: Elsevier.

Davies, R. (2015). *2015, Industry 4.0 Digitalisation for productivity and growth, EPRS, European Parliamentary.* Research Service.

Davis, J., Edgar, T., Porter, J., Bernaden, J., & Sarli, M. (2012). Smart manufacturing, manufacturing intelligence and demand-dynamic performance. *Computers & Chemical Engineering*, *47*, 145–156. doi:10.1016/j.compchemeng.2012.06.037

De Chiara, A. (2017). *Distretti industriali e sostenibilità. Analisi nei distretti e nei poli industriali della Campania,* University Press, Università degli Studi di Napoli "L'Orientale".

De Chiara, A. (2015). *Stakeholder engagement per strategie di sostenibilità.* Torino, Italy: Giappichelli Editore.

De Chiara, A. (2016). *Implementing sustainability strategies in networks and clusters - principles, tools and new research outcomes, Series: CSR, Sustainability, Ethics & Governance.* Berlin, Germany: Springer.

De Chiara, A. (2018). Strategie sostenibili nei distretti industriali: opportunità per piccole imprese e sistemi locali. In V. Maggioni & P. Stampacchia (Eds.), *L'impresa del XXI secolo. Scritti di economia e gestione delle imprese in onore del prof. Sergio Sciarelli.* Cedam.

de Jesus, A., Antunes, P., Santos, R., & Mendonça, S. (2018). Eco-innovation in the transition to a circular economy: An analytical literature review. *Journal of Cleaner Production*, *172*, 2999–3018. doi:10.1016/j.jclepro.2017.11.111

de los Salmones, G., del Mar, M., & Rodriguez del Bosque, I. (2011). Corporate social responsibility and loyalty in services sector. *Esic Market Economic and Business Journal*, *138*, 199–221.

de Luca, P. (2006). Critical consumption: An exploratory research on the social dimension of consumer behaviour. *Proceedings of the International Congress "Marketing Trends,"* Ca' Foscari University, Venice, Italy.

de Luca, P., Schoier, B., & Vessio, A. (2017). Cause-related marketing and trust: Empirical evidence on pinkwashing. *Markets and Competitiveness*, *2*, 49–71.

de Man, J. C., & Strandhagen, J. O. (2017). *An Industry 4.0 research agenda for sustainable business models. In Procedia CIRP* (Vol. 63, pp. 721–726). Amsterdam, Netherlands: Elsevier.

De Medeiros, J. F., Ribeiro, J. L. D., & Cortimiglia, M. N. (2014). Success factors for environmentally sustainable product innovation: A systematic literature review. *Journal of Cleaner Production*, *65*, 76–86. doi:10.1016/j.jclepro.2013.08.035

de Reuver, M., Bouwman, H., & MacInnes, I. (2007, July). What drives business model dynamics? A case survey. In *Eighth World Congress on the Management of eBusiness* (WCMeB 2007). IEEE.

de Reuver, M., Sørensen, C., & Basole, R. C. (2018). The digital platform: A research agenda. *Journal of Information Technology*, *33*(2), 124–135. doi:10.105741265-016-0033-3 de Sousa Jabbour, A. B. L., Jabbour, C. J. C., Foropon, C., & Godinho Filho, M. (2018). When titans meet–Can industry 4.0 revolutionise the environmentally-sustainable manufacturing wave? The role of critical success factors. *Technological Forecasting and Social Change, 132*, 18–25. doi:10.1016/j.techfore.2018.01.017

de Sousa Jabbour, A. B. L., Jabbour, C. J. C., Godinho Filho, M., & Roubaud, D. (2018). Industry 4.0 and the circular economy: A proposed research agenda and original roadmap for sustainable operations. *Annals of Operations Research, 270*(1-2), 273–286. doi:10.100710479-018-2772-8

Decision Processes, 5, 179–211.

Dekoninck, E. A., Domingo, L., O'Hare, J. A., Pigosso, D. C., Reyes, T., & Troussier, N. (2016). Defining the challenges for ecodesign implementation in companies: Development and consolidation of a framework. *Journal of Cleaner Production, 135*, 410–425. doi:10.1016/j.jclepro.2016.06.045

Del Greco, N. I. (2010). Estudio sobre tendencias de consumo de alimentos. Primera parte-Generalidades y casos. *Datos relevantes para la toma de decisiones en la Agroindustria de Alimentos y Bebidas.*

Deloitte, M. (2017). Car sharing in Europe: Business models. National variations and upcoming disruptions.

Deming, W. E., & De Vio, S. (1991). *L'impresa di qualità*. Petrini.

Denning, S. (2014). Navigating the phase change to the creative economy. *Strategy and Leadership, 42*, 3–11.

DeSoucey, M. (2010). Gastronationalism: Food traditions and authenticity politics in the European Union. *American Sociological Review, 75*(3), 432–455. doi:10.1177/0003122410372226

Desrochers, P., & Leppälä, S. (2010). Industrial symbiosis: Old wine in recycled bottles? Some perspective from the history of economic and geographical thought. *International Regional Science Review, 3*(3), 338–361. doi:10.1177/0160017610375441

Dias, C., & Mendes, L. (2018). Protected designation of origin (PDO), protected geographical indication (pgi) and traditional speciality guaranteed (TSG): A bibliometric analysis. *Food Research International, 103*, 492–508. doi:10.1016/j.foodres.2017.09.059 PMID:29389640

Diehr, P., & Beresford, S. A. (2003). The relation of dietary patterns to future survival, health, and cardiovascular events in older adults. *Journal of Clinical Epidemiology, 56*(12), 1224–1235. doi:10.1016/S0895-4356(03)00202-6 PMID:14680674

Dillman, D. A. (2000). *Mail and internet surveys: the Taylored design method* (2nd ed.). New York, NY: John Wiley & Sons.

Ding, B. (2018). Pharma industry 4.0: Literature review and research opportunities in sustainable pharmaceutical supply chains. *Process Safety and Environmental Protection, 119*, 115–130. doi:10.1016/j.psep.2018.06.031

Dogan, B., & Gokovali, U. (2012). Geographical indications: The aspects of rural development and marketing through the traditional products. *Procedia: Social and Behavioral Sciences, 62*, 761–765. doi:10.1016/j.sbspro.2012.09.128

Dossou, P. E. (2018). *Impact of Sustainability on the supply chain 4.0 performance. In Procedia Manufacturing* (Vol. 17, pp. 452–459). Amsterdam, Netherlands: Elsevier.

Dragomir, V.D. (2013). Environmental performance and responsible corporate governance: An empirical note. *Ekonomika a management*, 16, 33-51.

Driessen, P., Hillebrand, B., Kok, R., & Verhallen, T. (2013). Green new product development: The pivotal role of product greenness. *IEEE Transactions on Engineering Management, 60*(2), 315–326. doi:10.1109/TEM.2013.2246792

Drucker, P. F. (1992). The new society of organizations. *Harvard Business Review*, (September–August), 95–104.

Dubosson-Torbay, M., Osterwalder, A., & Pigneur, Y. (2002). E-business model design, classification, and measurements. *Thunderbird International Business Review*, *44*(1), 5–23. doi:10.1002/tie.1036

Dukić, B., Dugandžić, S., & Dukić, S. (2017). Conceptual CRM Application database Model in the Function of Physical products distribution for Known Customer. *17th International Scientific Conference Business Logistics in Modern Management*, 369-383.

Durakbasa, N. M., Bas, G., & Krauter, L. G. (2013). The Assessment of Industrial Manufacturing Systems Towards Advanced Operations by Means of Integrated Modeling Approach. *Vision 2020: Innovation, Development Sustainability, and Economic Growth, 21st International-Business-Information-Management-Association Conference on Vision 2020: Innovation, Development Sustainability, and Economic Growth*, 1418-1426.

Du, S., Bhattacharya, C. B., & Sen, S. (2010). Maximizing business returns to corporate social responsibility (CSR): The role of CSR communication. *International Journal of Management Reviews*, *12*(1), 8–19. doi:10.1111/j.1468-2370.2009.00276.x

Du, S., Bhattacharya, C. B., & Sen, S. (2011). Corporate social responsibility and competitive advantage: Overcoming the trust barrier. *Management Science*, *57*(9), 1528–1545. doi:10.1287/mnsc.1110.1403

Dyer, J., & Singh, H. (1998). The relational view: Cooperative strategy and sources of interorganizational competitive advantage. *Academy of Management Review*, *23*(4), 660–679. doi:10.5465/amr.1998.1255632

Earl, C., Lawrence, A., Harris, N., & Stiller, S. (2003). The campus community and the concept of sustainability: An assessment of college of Charleston student perceptions. *Chrestomathy: Annual Review of Undergraduate Research at the College of Charleston*, *2*, 85–102.

Economist. (2009). It consists of three Ps: profit, people and planet. Retrieved from http://goo.gl/BXuE9

Edelman Earned Brand. (2018). Brand take a stand. Retrieved from https://www.edelman.com/sites/g/files/aatuss191/files/2018-10/2018_Edelman_Earned_Brand_Global_Report.pdf

Efthymiou, D., Antoniou, C., & Waddell, P. (2013). Factors affecting the adoption of vehicle sharing systems by young drivers. *Transport Policy*, *29*, 64–73. doi:10.1016/j.tranpol.2013.04.009

Egels-Zandén, N., & Wahlqvist, E. (2007). Post-partnership strategies for defining corporate responsibility: The business social compliance initiative. *Journal of Business Ethics*, *70*(2), 75–189. doi:10.100710551-006-9104-7

Ehrenfeld, J., & Gertler, N. (1997). Industrial ecology in practice: The evolution of interdependence at Kalundborg. *Journal of Industrial Ecology*, *1*(1), 67–79. doi:10.1162/jiec.1997.1.1.67

Eisenhardt, K. M. (1989). Building theories from case study research. *Academy of Management Review*, *14*(4), 532–550. doi:10.5465/amr.1989.4308385

Eisenhardt, K. M., & Graebner, M. E. (2007). Theory building from cases: Opportunities and challenges. *Academy of Management Journal*, *50*(1), 25–32. doi:10.5465/amj.2007.24160888

Elkington, J. (2004). Enter the triple bottom line. In *The triple bottom line: Does it all add up, 11*(12), 1-16. Retrieved from http://www. johnelkington.com

Elkington, J. (1987). Towards the Sustainable Corporation. Win-Win-Win Business Strategies for Sustainable Development. *California Management Review*, *36*(2), 90–100. doi:10.2307/41165746

Elkington, J. (1997). *Cannibals with forks - Triple bottom line of 21st century business*. Stoney Creek, CT: New Society Publishers.

Elkington, J. (1997). *Cannibals with Forks: The Triple Bottom Line of 21st Century Business*. Oxford, UK: Capstone Publishing.

Elkington, J. (1998). Partnerships from cannibals with forks: The triple bottom line of 21st-century business. *Environmental Quality Management*, *8*(1), 37–51. doi:10.1002/tqem.3310080106

Elkington, J. (2013). Enter the triple bottom line. In *The triple bottom line* (pp. 23–38). Routledge.

Ellen-MacArthur Foundation. (2013). Toward the circular economy.

Ellis, J. L., McCracken, V. A., & Skuza, N. (2012). Insights into willingness to pay for organic cotton apparel. *Journal of Fashion Marketing and Management*, *16*(3), 290–305. doi:10.1108/13612021211246053

Emanuel, R., & Adams, J. N. (2011). College students' perceptions of campus sustainability. *International Journal of Sustainability in Higher Education*, *12*(1), 79–92. doi:10.1108/14676371111098320

EMAS. (2013). *EMAS implementation in the EU: level of adoption, benefits, barriers and regulatory relief, BRAVE Project – Survey on European EMAS organizations.* Scuola Superiore Sant'Anna, November.

Enkel, E., & Mezger, F. (2013). Imitation Processes and their Application for Business Model Innovation: An Explorative Study. *International Journal of Innovation Management*, *17*(1), 1340005. doi:10.1142/S1363919613400057

Erro-Garcés, A. (2019). Industry 4. 0: Defining the research agenda. *Benchmarking: An International Journal*, (ahead-of-print). doi:10.1108/BIJ-12-2018-0444

Espino-Rodrìguez, T., & Rodrìguez-Diaz, F. M. (2008). A model of strategic evaluation of a tourism destination based on internal and relational capabilities. *Journal of Travel Research*, *45*(4), 368–380. doi:10.1177/0047287507308324

Etzkowitz, H., & Zhou, C. (2006). Triple helix twins: Innovation and sustainability. *Science & Public Policy*, *33*(1), 77–83. doi:10.3152/147154306781779154

EU COM. (2018) *Proposal for a COUNCIL DIRECTIVE laying down rules relating to the corporate taxation of a significant digital presence*. Brussels, Belgium. 21.3.2018, 147 final 2018/0072 (CNS). Retrieved from https://ec.europa.eu/taxation_customs/business/company-tax/fair-taxation-digital-economy_en

Euchner, J. (2018). The Internet of Things. *Research Technology Management*, *61*(5), 10–11. doi:10.1080/08956308.2018.1495971

European Commission. (2011). Communication from the Commission to the European Parliament, the Council, the European Economic and Social Committee and the Committee of the Regions. A renewed EU strategy 2011–14 for Corporate Social Responsibility. COM (2011) 681, Brussels, Belgium.

European Commission. (2011). Green Paper - Promoting a European framework for corporate social responsibility, Brussels European Commission. Renewed EU strategy for 2011-14 on corporate social responsibility. Brussels, Belgium.

European Commission. (2013). *La responsabilità sociale d'impresa per le piccole e medie imprese. Consigli e Strategie per i consulenti.*

Evans, S., Vladimirova, D., Holgado, M., Van Fossen, K., Yang, M., Silva, E., & Barlow, C. (2017). Business model innovation for sustainability: Towards a unified perspective for creation of sustainable business models. *Business Strategy and the Environment*, *26*(5), 597–608. doi:10.1002/bse.1939

Eveland, V. B., Crutchfield, T. N., & Rynarzewska, A. I. (2018). Developing a consumer relationship model of corporate social performance. *Journal of Consumer Marketing*, *35*(5), 543–554. doi:10.1108/JCM-07-2017-2287

Expansión. (2017). Influencers 2017. *Expansión*. Obtenido de https://www.pressreader.com/mexico/expansion-m%C3%A9xico/20171115/283128544143988

Fabbris, L. (1997). *Statistica multivariata: analisi esplorativa dei dati*. McGraw-Hill Libri Italia.

Fabris, G. P. (2008). *Societing*. Milan, Italy: Egea.

Fang, Y. (2011). Economic welfare impacts from renewable energy consumption: The China experience. *Renewable & Sustainable Energy Reviews*, *15*(9), 5120–5128. doi:10.1016/j.rser.2011.07.044

Farrer, J. (2018). Remediation: discussing fashion textiles sustainability. In A. Gwilt & T. Rissanen (Eds.), *Shaping sustainable fashion*. Washington, DC: Earthscan.

Faulkner, G. P., Pourshahidi, L. K., Wallace, J. M. W., Kerr, M. A., McCaffrey, T. A., & Livingstone, M. B. E. (2014). Perceived healthiness of foods can influence consumers' estimations of energy density and appropriate portion size. *International Journal of Obesity*, *38*(1), 106–112. doi:10.1038/ijo.2013.69 PMID:23732657

Ferber, S. (2013). *How the Internet of Things Changes Everything*. HBR Blog Network.

Ferenhof, H. A., Vignochi, L., Selig, P. M., Lezana, A. G. R., & Campos, L. M. S. (2014). Environmental management systems in small and medium-sized enterprises: An analysis and systematic review. *Journal of Cleaner Production*, *74*, 44–53. doi:10.1016/j.jclepro.2014.03.027

Fernández, C., Cea Valencia, J., Santander, P., & Nuñez, K. (2013). Consumo verde en Chile: estudio exploratorio sobre consumidor de productos ecológicos. *Global Conference on Business and Finance Proceedings*. Obtenido de https://www.researchgate.net/profile/Cristobal_Fernandez/publication/260364788_Consumo_Verde_en_Chile_Estudio_exploratorio_sobre_consumidor_de_productos_organicos/links/0f317530e614c76869000000/Consumo-Verde-en-Chile-Estudio-exploratorio-sobre-consumidor-

Ferrera, E., Rossini, R., Baptista, A. J., Evans, S., Hovest, G. G., Holgado, M., & Silva, E. J. (2017). Toward Industry 4.0: efficient and sustainable manufacturing leveraging MAESTRI total efficiency framework. In *International Conference on Sustainable Design and Manufacturing* (pp. 624-633). Springer. 10.1007/978-3-319-57078-5_59

Finco, A., Bentivoglio, D., & Bucci, G. (2017). A label for mountain products? Let's turn it over to producers and retailers. *Quality-Access to Success*, *18*, 198–205.

Finco, A., Bentivoglio, D., & Bucci, G. (2018). Lessons of innovation in the agrifood sector: Drivers of innovativeness performances. *Economia Agro-Alimentare*, (2), 181–192. doi:10.3280/ECAG2018-002004

Finkbeiner, M., Schau, E. M., Lehmann, A., & Traverso, M. (2010). Towards life cycle sustainability assessment. *Sustainability*, *2*(10), 3309–3322. doi:10.3390u2103309

Fishbein, M. (1967). *Readings in attitude theory and measurement.*

Fishbein, M. (1963). An investigation of the relationships between beliefs about an object and the attitude toward that object. *Human Relations*, *16*(3), 233–239. doi:10.1177/001872676301600302

Flash Eurobarometer 367. (2013). Attitudes of Europeans towards building the single market for green products. European Commission, Directorate-General for Environment.

Fletcher, K. (2007). Slow fashion. *The Ecologist*, *37*(5), 61.

Fletcher, K. (2008). *Sustainable fashion & textiles: design journeys*. Oxford, UK: Earthscan.

Florida, R. (2010). *The Great Reset: how new ways of living and working drive post- crash prosperity*. New York, NY: HarperCollins.

Fogliatto, F. S., da Silvera, G. J., & Borestein, D. (2012). The mass customization decade: An updated review of the literature. *International Journal of Production Economics*, *138*(1), 14–25. doi:10.1016/j.ijpe.2012.03.002

Fondazione Symbola. (2015). *Certificare per Competere. Dalle certificazioni ambientali nuova forza al made in Italy*.

Formánková, S., Trenz, O., Faldík, O., Kolomazník, J., & Sládková, J. (2019). Millennials' awareness and approach to social responsibility and investment—case study of the Czech Republic. *Sustainability*, *11*(2), 504. doi:10.3390u11020504

Foss, N. J., & Saebi, T. (2017). Fifteen years of research on business model innovation: How far have we come, and where should we go? *Journal of Management*, *43*(1), 200–227. doi:10.1177/0149206316675927

Foss, N. J., & Saebi, T. (2018). Business models and business model innovation: Between wicked and paradigmatic problems. *Long Range Planning*, *51*(1), 9–21. doi:10.1016/j.lrp.2017.07.006

Foster, C., & Green, K. (2000). Greening the innovation process. *Business Strategy and the Environment*, *9*(5), 287–303. doi:10.1002/1099-0836(200009/10)9:5<287::AID-BSE256>3.0.CO;2-7

Fraj Andrés, E., & Martínez Salinas, E. (2002). *Comportamiento del consumidor ecológico*. Madrid, Spain: ESIC.

Franciosi, C., Iung, B., Miranda, S., & Riemma, S. (2018). Maintenance for Sustainability in the Industry 4.0 context: a Scoping Literature Review. In *IFAC-PapersOnLine* (vol. 51(11), pp. 903-908). Laxenburg, Austria: IFAC (International Federation of Automatic Control).

Frankfurt School of Finance and Management (FS). (2018). *Global trends in renewable energy investment 2018*. Frankfurt School-UNEP Centre/BNEF.

Franklin, D. (2008). Just good business: A special report of corporate social responsibility. *The Economist*, Jan. 19.

Frederick, C. W. (1986). Towards CSR: Why ethical analysis is indispensable and unavoidable in Corporate affairs. *California Management Review*, *28*(2), 126–141. doi:10.2307/41165190

Freeman, R. E. (1984). *Strategic management: A stakeholder approach*. Boston, MA: Pitman.

Freestone, O. M., & McGoldrick, P. J. (2007). Ethical positioning and political marketing: The ethical awareness and concerns of UK voters. *Journal of Marketing Management*, *23*(7-8), 651–673. doi:10.1362/026725707X229984

Frey, W. H. (2018). *The millennial generation: A demographic bridge to America's diverse future*. Brookings Metropolitan Policy Program.

Frolov, V. G., Kaminchenko, D. I., Kovylkin, D. Y., Alex, J., & Alex, A. (2017). The Main Economic Factors of Sustainable Manufacturing within the Industrial Policy Concept of Industry 4.0. *Academy Strategic Management Journal*, *16*, 1–11.

Frosch, R. A. (1992). Industrial ecology: A philosophical introduction. *Proceedings of the National Academy of Sciences of the United States of America*, *89*(3), 800–803. doi:10.1073/pnas.89.3.800

Galaskiewicz, J. (2011). Studying supply chains from a social network perspective. *The Journal of Supply Chain Management*, *47*(1), 4–8. doi:10.1111/j.1745-493X.2010.03209.x

Galbreth, M. R., & Ghosh, B. (2013). Competition and sustainability: The impact of consumer awareness. *Decision Sciences*, *44*(1), 127–159. doi:10.1111/j.1540-5915.2012.00395.x

Galindo, A. (2010). Psicología del Consumidor Mexicano. *Revista del Instituto Tecnológico de México*(48), 1-4.

Gallego-Álvarez, I., García-Sánchez, I. M., & Vieira, C. D. (2014). Climate change and financial performance in times of crisis. *Business Strategy and the Environment*, *23*(6), 361–374. doi:10.1002/bse.1786

Garcés-Ayerbe, C., & Cañón-de-Francia, J. (2017). The relevance of complementarities in the study of the economic consequences of environmental proactivity: Analysis of the moderating effect of innovation efforts. *Ecological Economics*, *142*, 21–30. doi:10.1016/j.ecolecon.2017.06.022

García-Gutiérrez, I., & Martínez-Borreguero, F. J. (2016). The innovation pivot framework. Fostering business model innovation in startups. *Research Technology Management*, (September-October): 48–56.

Garcia-Muiña, F., González-Sánchez, R., Ferrari, A., & Settembre-Blundo, D. (2018). The Paradigms of Industry 4.0 and Circular Economy as Enabling Drivers for the Competitiveness of Businesses and Territories: The Case of an Italian Ceramic Tiles Manufacturing Company. *Social Sciences*, *7*(12), 255. doi:10.3390ocsci7120255

Garg, S. K., & Buyya, R. (2012). Green cloud computing and environmental sustainability. *Harnessing Green IT: Principles and Practices*, 315-340.

Gärling, T., Ettema, D., & Friman, M. (2013). *Handbook of sustainable travel*. Heidelberg, Germany: Springer.

Garretson, J. A., & Burton, S. (2000). Effects of nutrition facts panel values, nutrition claims, and health claims on consumer attitudes, perceptions of disease-related risks, and trust. *Journal of Public Policy & Marketing*, *19*(2), 213–227. doi:10.1509/jppm.19.2.213.17133

Garrido-Hidalgo, C., Hortelano, D., Roda-Sanchez, L., Olivares, T., Ruiz, M. C., & Lopez, V. (2018). IoT Heterogeneous Mesh Network Deployment for Human-in-the-Loop Challenges Towards a Social and Sustainable Industry 4.0. *IEEE Access: Practical Innovations, Open Solutions*, *6*, 28417–28437. doi:10.1109/ACCESS.2018.2836677

Gava, O., Galli, F., Bartolini, F., & Brunori, G. (2018). Linking sustainability with geographical proximity in food supply chains. An indicator selection framework. *Agriculture*, *8*(9), 130. doi:10.3390/agriculture8090130

Gawer, A., & Cusumano, M. A. (2014). Industry platforms and ecosystem innovation. *Journal of Product Innovation Management*, *31*(3), 417–433. doi:10.1111/jpim.12105

Geissdoerfer, M., Morioka, S. N., de Carvalho, M. M., & Evans, S. (2018). Business models and supply chains for the circular economy. *Journal of Cleaner Production*, *190*, 712–721. doi:10.1016/j.jclepro.2018.04.159

Geissdoerfer, M., Vladimirova, D., & Evans, S. (2018). Sustainable business model innovation: A review. *Journal of Cleaner Production*, *198*, 401–416. doi:10.1016/j.jclepro.2018.06.240

Genovese, A., Acquaye, A. A., Figueroa, A., & Koh, S. C. L. (2017). Sustainable supply chain management and the transition towards a circular economy: Evidence and some applications. *Omega (United Kingdom)*, *66*. doi:10.1016/j.omega.2015.05.015

Genovese, A., Morris, J. L., Piccolo, C., & Koh, S. C. L. (2017). Assessing redundancies in environmental performance measures for supply chains. *Journal of Cleaner Production*, *167*, 1290–1302. doi:10.1016/j.jclepro.2017.05.186

George, J. (2005). On paper, a world of opportunities. Packaging World Magazine, April, p. 36.

George, G., & Bock, A. J. (2011). The business model in practice and its implications for entrepreneurship research. *Entrepreneurship Theory and Practice*, *35*(1), 83–111. doi:10.1111/j.1540-6520.2010.00424.x

Gerbert, P., Lorenz, M., Rüßmann, M., Waldner, M., Justus, J., Engel, P., & Harnisch, M. (2015). *Industry 4.0: The future of Productivity and growth in Manufacturing Industries*. BCG Perspectives.

Gershenfeld, N. G., & Euchner, J. (2015). Atoms and bits: Rethinking manufacturing. Conversations. *Research Technology Management, 58*(5), 16–21. doi:10.5437/08956308X5805003

Ghisellini, P., Cialani, C., & Ulgiati, S. (2016). A review on circular economy: The expected transition to a balanced interplay of environmental and economic systems. *Journal of Cleaner Production, 114*, 11–32. doi:10.1016/j.jclepro.2015.09.007

Giacosa, E., Giachino, C., Bertoldi, B., & Stupino, M. (2014). Innovativeness of Ceretto Aziende Vitivinicole: A first investigation into a wine company. *The International Food and Agribusiness Management Review, 17*(4), 223–236.

Giannakis, G., & Papadopoulos, T. (2016). Supply chain sustainability: A risk management approach. *International Journal of Production Economics, 171*(4), 455–470. doi:10.1016/j.ijpe.2015.06.032

Gibbert, M., Ruigrok, W., & Wicki, B. (2008). What passes as a rigorous case study? *Strategic Management Journal, 29*(13), 1465–1474. doi:10.1002mj.722

Gibbs, D. (2008). Industrial Symbiosis and Eco-Industrial Development: An Introduction. *Geography Compass, 2*(4), 1138–1154. doi:10.1111/j.1749-8198.2008.00123.x

Gielissen, R. B. (2011). Why do consumers buy socially responsible products? *International Journal of Business and Social Science, 2*(3).

Gielissen, R., & Graafland, J. (2009). Concepts of price fairness: Empirical research into the Dutch coffee market. *Business Ethics (Oxford, England), 18*(2), 165–178. doi:10.1111/j.1467-8608.2009.01555.x

Giese, J. L., & Cote, J. A. (2000). Defining consumer satisfaction. *Academy of Marketing Science Review, 1*(1), 1–22.

Glaser, B. G., & Strauss, A. (1967). *The discovery of grounded theory*. New York, NY: Aldine.

Glavič, P., & Lukman, R. (2007). Review of sustainability terms and their definitions. *Journal of Cleaner Production, 15*(18), 1875–1885. doi:10.1016/j.jclepro.2006.12.006

Global Web Index. (2018). Sustainable Packaging Unwrapped.

Gordin, V., Trabskaya, J., & Zelenskaya, E. (2016). The role of hotel restaurants in gastronomic place branding. *International Journal of Culture, Tourism and Hospitality Research, 10*(1), 81–90. doi:10.1108/IJCTHR-05-2015-0049

Gorecky, D., Schmitt, M., Loskyll, M., & Zühlke, D. (2014). Human-machine-interaction in the industry 4.0 era. *2014 12th IEEE International Conference on Industrial Informatics (INDIN)*.

Gorton, D., Ni Mhurchu, C., Bramley, D., & Dixon, R. (2010). Interpretation of two nutrition content claims: A New Zealand survey. *Australian and New Zealand Journal of Public Health, 34*(1), 57–62. doi:10.1111/j.1753-6405.2010.00474.x PMID:20920106

Grant, G. B., Seager, T. P., Massard, G., & Nies, L. (2010). Information and communication technology for industrial symbiosis. *Journal of Industrial Ecology, 14*(5), 740–753. doi:10.1111/j.1530-9290.2010.00273.x

Green, L., Fristoe, N., & Myerson, J. (1994). Temporal discounting and preference reversals in choice between delayed outcomes. *Psychonomic Bulletin & Review, 1*(3), 383–389. doi:10.3758/BF03213979 PMID:24203522

Green, P. E., & Krieger, A. M. (1991). Segmenting markets with conjoint analysis. *Journal of Marketing, 55*(4), 20–31. doi:10.1177/002224299105500402

Green, P. E., & Krieger, A. M. (2002). What's right with conjoint analysis? *Marketing Research, 14*(1), 24.

Green, P. E., Krieger, A. M., & Wind, Y. J. (2001). Thirty years of conjoint analysis: Reflections and prospects. *Interfaces, 31*(3_supplement), S56–S73. doi:10.1287/inte.31.3s.56.9676

Green, P. E., & Srinivasan, V. (1978). Conjoint analysis in consumer research: Issues and outlook. *The Journal of Consumer Research*, *5*(2), 103–123. doi:10.1086/208721

Green, P. E., & Srinivasan, V. (1990). Conjoint analysis in marketing: New developments with implications for research and practice. *Journal of Marketing*, *54*(4), 3–19. doi:10.1177/002224299005400402

Greenwood, M. (2007). Stakeholder engagement: Beyond the myth of corporate responsibility. *Journal of Business Ethics*, *34*(4), 315–327. doi:10.100710551-007-9509-y

Gregori, F., Papetti, A., Pandolfi, M., Peruzzini, M., & Germani, M. (2017). *Digital manufacturing systems: a framework to improve social sustainability of a production site. In Procedia CIRP* (Vol. 63, pp. 436–442). Amsterdam, Netherlands: Elsevier.

Gregori, F., Papetti, A., Pandolfi, M., Peruzzini, M., & Germani, M. (2018). *Improving a production site from a social point of view: an IoT infrastructure to monitor workers condition. In Procedia CIRP* (Vol. 72, pp. 886–891). Amsterdam, Netherlands: Elsevier.

Grönroos, C., & Gummerus, J. (2014). The service revolution and its marketing implications: Service logic vs service-dominant logic. *Managing Service Quality*, *24*(3), 206–229. doi:10.1108/MSQ-03-2014-0042

Grönroos, C., & Voima, P. (2013). Critical Service Logic: Making Sense of Value Creation and Co-creation. *Journal of the Academy of Management Science*, *41*(2), 133–150. doi:10.100711747-012-0308-3

Grunert, K. G., & Aachmann, K. (2016). Consumer reactions to the use of EU quality labels on food products: A review of the literature. *Food Control*, *59*, 178–187. doi:10.1016/j.foodcont.2015.05.021

Guagnano, G. A. (2001). Altruism and market-like behavior: An analysis of willingness to pay for recycled paper products. *Population and Environment*, *22*(4), 425–438. doi:10.1023/A:1006753823611

Guerrero, L., Guàrdia, M. D., Xicola, J., Verbeke, W., Vanhonacker, F., Zakowska-Biemans, S., ... Hersleth, M. (2009). Consumer-driven definition of traditional food products and innovation in traditional foods. A qualitative cross-cultural study. *Appetite*, *52*(2), 345–354. doi:10.1016/j.appet.2008.11.008 PMID:19084040

Gu, F., Guo, J., Hall, P., & Gu, X. (2018). An integrated architecture for implementing extended producer responsibility in the context of Industry 4.0. *International Journal of Production Research*, 1–20.

Guglielmetti Mugion, R., Toni, M., Raharjo, H., Di Pietro, L., & Sebathu, S. P. (2018). Does the service quality of urban public transport enhance sustainable mobility? *Journal of Cleaner Production*, *174*, 1566–1587. doi:10.1016/j.jclepro.2017.11.052

Guimarães, J. C. F., Severo, E. A., & Vasconcelos, C. R. M. (2018). The influence of entrepreneurial, market, knowledge management orientations on cleaner production and the sustainable competitive advantage. *Journal of Cleaner Production*, *174*, 1653–1663. doi:10.1016/j.jclepro.2017.11.074

Guoyou, Q., Saixing, Z., Chiming, T., Haitao, Y., & Hailiang, Z. (2013). Stakeholders' influences on corporate green innovation strategy: A case study of manufacturing firms in China. *Corporate Social Responsibility and Environmental Management*, *20*(1), 1–14. doi:10.1002/csr.283

Gupta, S., & Lehmann, D. R. (2006). *Customers as Assets*. Milano: Pearson.

Gustaffson, A., Herrmann, A., & Huber, F. (2007). Conjoint analysis as an instrument of market research practice. In A. Gustaffson, A. Hermann, & F. Huber (Eds.), *Conjoint Measurement* (pp. 3–30). London, UK: Springer. doi:10.1007/978-3-540-71404-0_1

Haghshenas, H., & Vaziri, M. (2012). Urban sustainable transportation indicators for global comparison. *Ecological Indicators*, *15*(1), 115–121. doi:10.1016/j.ecolind.2011.09.010

Hair, J. F. H., Black, W. C., Babin, J. B., & Anderson, R. E. (1998). *Multivariate data analysis with readings. Englewood Cliffs, NJ: Prentice-Hall .*

Hair, J., Black, W. C., Babin, B. J., Anderson, R. E., & Tatham, R. (2006). *Multivariate data analysis*. New York, NY: Pearson Education.

Hajdukiewicz, A. (2014). European Union agri-food quality schemes for the protection and promotion of geographical indications and traditional specialities: An economic perspective. *Folia Horticulturae*, *26*(1), 3–17. doi:10.2478/fhort-2014-0001

Hajer, M., Hoen, A., & Huitzing, H. (2012). Shifting gear: beyond classical mobility policies and urban planning. In B. van Wee (Ed.), Keep Moving. The Hague, The Netherlands: Eleven International Publishing.

Hamel, G. (2000). *Leading the revolution*. Boston, MA: Harvard Business School Press.

Hamel, G. (2002). *Leading the revolution: How to thrive in turbulent times by making innovation a way of life*. Boston, MA: Harvard Business School Press.

Handfield, R. B., Melnyk, S. A., Calantone, R. J., & Curkovic, S. (2001). Integrating environmental concerns into the design process: The gap between theory and practice. *IEEE Transactions on Engineering Management*, *48*(2), 189–208. doi:10.1109/17.922478

Hanks, K., Odom, W., Roedl, D., & Blevis, E. (2008, April). Sustainable millennials: attitudes towards sustainability and the material effects of interactive technologies. In *Proceedings of the SIGCHI Conference on Human Factors in Computing Systems* (pp. 333-342). ACM. 10.1145/1357054.1357111

Hansemark, O. C., & Albinsson, M. (2004). Customer satisfaction and retention: The experiences of individual employees. *Managing Service Quality: An International Journal*, *14*(1), 40–57. doi:10.1108/09604520410513668

Harhoff, D., Henkel, J., & Von Hippel, E. (2003). Profiting from voluntary information spillovers: How users benefit by freely revealing their innovations. *Research Policy*, *32*(10), 1753–1769. doi:10.1016/S0048-7333(03)00061-1

Harrington, R. J. (2005). Part I: The culinary innovation process—a barrier to imitation. *Journal of Foodservice Business Research*, *7*(3), 35–57. doi:10.1300/J369v07n03_04

Harrington, R. J., Ottenbacher, M. C., & Fauser, S. (2017). QSR brand value: Marketing mix dimensions among McDonald's, KFC, Burger King, Subway and Starbucks. *International Journal of Contemporary Hospitality Management*, *29*(1), 551–570. doi:10.1108/IJCHM-06-2015-0300

Hart, S. L. (2007). *Capitalism at the crossroads aligning business, Earth, and humanity*. Upper Saddle River, NJ: Wharton School Publishing.

Harvey, B., Van Luijk, K., & Corbetta, G. (1991). *Market morality and company size*. London, UK: Kluver. doi:10.1007/978-94-011-3556-6

Hawken, P. (1993). *The Ecology of Commerce*. New York: Harper Business.

Hawkins, T. R., Singh, B., Majeau-Bettez, G., & Strømman, A. H. (2013). Comparative environmental life cycle assessment of conventional and electric vehicles. *Journal of Industrial Ecology*, *17*(1), 53–64. doi:10.1111/j.1530-9290.2012.00532.x

Hawley, J. M. (2018). Textile recycling options: Exploring what could be. In A. Gwilt & T. Rissanen (Eds.), *Shaping sustainable fashion*. Washington, DC: Earthscan.

Heiskanen, E. (2002). The institutional logic of life cycle thinking. *Journal of Cleaner Production, 10*(5), 427–437. doi:10.1016/S0959-6526(02)00014-8

Hendarwan, E. (2002). Seeing green. *Global Cosmetic Industry, 170*(5), 16–18.

Henkel, J. (2006). Selective revealing in open innovation processes: The case of embedded Linux. *Research Policy, 35*(7), 953–969. doi:10.1016/j.respol.2006.04.010

Hensel, K. (2012). Convenience food. *Food Technology, 66*(1), 34–43.

Heras-Saizarbitoria, I., Arana, G., & Boiral, O. (2015). Exploring the dissemination of environmental certifications in high and low polluting industries. *Journal of Cleaner Production, 89*, 50–58. doi:10.1016/j.jclepro.2014.10.088

Hermann, M., Pentek, T., & Otto, B. (2015). *Design Principles for Industrie 4.0 Scenarios: A Literature Review*. Dortmund: Technische UniversitäT Dortmund.

Hernández, Y. & López, D. (2012, Mayo-Agosto). El marketing ecológico y su integración en la planificación estratégica. *Revista de Estudios Interdisciplinarios en Ciencias Sociales, 14*(2), 223-231.

Hoegg, J., & Alba, J. W. (2011). Seeing is believing (too much): The influence of product form on perceptions of functional performance. *Journal of Product Innovation Management, 28*(3), 346–359. doi:10.1111/j.1540-5885.2011.00802.x

Hoegg, J., Alba, J. W., & Dahl, D. W. (2010). The good, the bad and the ugly: Influence of aesthetics on product feature judgments. *Journal of Consumer Psychology, 20*(4), 419–430. doi:10.1016/j.jcps.2010.07.002

Hoffman, A. J., & Bazerman, M. H. (2007). Changing practice on sustainability: Understanding and overcoming the organizational and psychological barriers to action. In S. Sharma, M. Starik, & B. Husted (Eds.), *Organizations and the sustainability mosaic: Crafting long-term ecological and societal solutions*. Northampton, MA: Edward Elgar. doi:10.4337/9781847205544.00012

Hogg, M. K. (1998). Anti-constellations: Exploring the impact of negation on consumption. *Journal of Marketing Management, 14*(1-3), 1–3. doi:10.1362/026725798784959354

Højberg, A. L., Troldborg, L., Stisen, S., Christensen, B. B. S., & Henriksen, H. J. (2013). Stakeholder driven update and improvement of a national water resources model. *Environmental Modelling & Software, 40*, 202–213. doi:10.1016/j.envsoft.2012.09.010

Holgado, M., Benedetti, M., Evans, S., Baptista, A. J., & Lourenço, E. J. (2018). Industrial symbiosis implementation by leveraging on process efficiency methodologies. *Procedia CIRP, 69*(May), 872–877. doi:10.1016/j.procir.2017.11.078

Hollywood, L., Wells, L., Armstrong, G., & Farley, H. (2013). Thinking outside the carton: Attitudes towards milk packaging. *British Food Journal, 115*(6), 899–912. doi:10.1108/BFJ-Jul-2010-0127

Homburg, C., & Giering, A. (2001). Personal characteristics as moderators of the relationship between customer satisfaction and loyalty—An empirical analysis. *Psychology and Marketing, 18*(1), 43–66. doi:10.1002/1520-6793(200101)18:1<43::AID-MAR3>3.0.CO;2-I

Honea, H., & Horsky, S. (2012). The power of plain: Intensifying product experience with neutral aesthetic context. *Marketing Letters, 1*(23), 223–235. doi:10.100711002-011-9149-y

Hongle, P. & Pistone, P. (2015). *Blueprints for a new PE Nexus to tax business income in the era of the digital economy*. White Papers IBFD. Retrieved from http://www.ibfd.org/sites/ibfd.org/files/

Hopfenbeck, W. (1993). The green management revolution: Lessons in environmental excellence. New York, NY: Prentice Hall.

Hopkins, M. (2010). How sustainability fuels design innovation. Interview with Steven Eppinger. *MIT Sloan Management Review, 52*(1), 75–81.

Horbach, J., Rammer, C., & Rennings, K. (2012). Determinants of eco-innovations by type of environmental impact—The role of regulatory push/pull, technology push and market pull. *Ecological Economics, 78*, 112–122. doi:10.1016/j.ecolecon.2012.04.005

Horne, R. E. (2009). Limits to labels: The role of eco-labels in the assessment of product sustainability and routes to sustainable consumption. *International Journal of Consumer Studies, 33*(2), 175–182. doi:10.1111/j.1470-6431.2009.00752.x

Horváthová, E. (2010). Does environmental performance affect financial performance? A meta-analysis. *Ecological Economics, 70*(1), 52–59. doi:10.1016/j.ecolecon.2010.04.004

Horváthová, E. (2012). The impact of environmental performance on firm performance: Short-term costs and long-time benefits. *Ecological Indicators, 84*, 91–97.

Hotelling, H. (1931). The economics of exhaustible resources. *Journal of Political Economy, 39*(2), 137–175. doi:10.1086/254195

Hoyer, W., MacInnis, D., & Pieters, R. (2010). Comportamiento del consumidor (5 ed.). (M. E. Ma. del Pilar Carril Villarreal, Trad.) México: Cengage Learning.

Høyer, K. G. (1997). Sustainable development. In D. Brune, D. Chapman, M. Gwynne, & J. Pacyna (Eds.), *The Global Environment. Science, Technology and Management.* Weinheim, Germany: VCH. doi:10.1002/9783527619658.ch74

Huang, M. C., Cheng, H. L., & Tseng, C. Y. (2014). Re-examining the direct and interactive effects of governance mechanisms upon buyer–supplier cooperative performance. *Industrial Marketing Management, 43*(4), 704–716. doi:10.1016/j.indmarman.2014.02.001

Huang, Y. C., Ding, H. B., & Kao, M. R. (2009). Salient stakeholder voices: Family business and green innovation adoption. *Journal of Management & Organization, 15*(3), 309–326. doi:10.1017/S1833367200002649

Hunkeler, D., Saur, K., Rebitzer, G., Schmidt, W., Jensen, A., Stranddorf, H., & Christiansen, K. (2004). *Life cycle management.* Pensacola, FL: SETAC.

Hunter-Jones, P., Jeffs, A., & Smith, D. (2008). Backpacking your way into crisis: An exploratory study into perceived risk and tourist behaviour amongst young people. *Journal of Travel & Tourism Marketing, 23*(2-4), 237–247. doi:10.1300/J073v23n02_18

Husted, B. W., & de Jesus Salazar, J. (2006). Taking Friedman seriously: Maximizing profits and social performance. *Journal of Management Studies, 43*(1), 75–91. doi:10.1111/j.1467-6486.2006.00583.x

Husted, B., & Allen, D. (2007). Corporate social strategy in multinational enterprises: antecedents and value creation. *Journal of Business Ethics, 74*(4), 345–361. doi:10.100710551-007-9511-4

Iacondini, A., Mencherini, U., Morselli, L., Passarini, F., & Vassura, I. (2014). Industrial symbiosis in Italy as a tool for sustainability: Case study analysis and replicability, *Procedia Environmental Science. Engineering and Management, 1*, 19–24.

IEFE Bocconi & Ricardo-AEA (2015). *Evaluation of the Implementation of the EU Ecolabel Regulation.*

IFOAM Federación Internacional de Movimientos de Agricultura Orgánica. (2009). La Agricultura Orgánica y la Salud Humana. Obtenido de http://infohub.ifoam.bio/sites/default/files/page/files/oa_humanhealth_es.pdf

Immaculate, P. S. (2013). Consumer awareness of recycled packaging. *International Journal of Retailing and Rural Business Perspectives*, *2*(1), 277–281.

Impulso Orgánico Mexicano, A. C. (2014). *Orgánicos en México.* Obtenido de https://www.impulsoorganicomexicano.com/productos-orgnicos-en-mxico

Ind, N., Iglesias, O., & Schultz, M. (2013). Building brands together. *California Management Review*, *55*(3), 5–26. doi:10.1525/cmr.2013.55.3.5

Insch, A., & Florek, M. (2009). Prevalence of country of origin associations on the supermarket shelf. *International Journal of Retail & Distribution Management*, *37*(5), 453–471. doi:10.1108/09590550910954937

International Energy Agency (IEA). (2013). Renewable energy: Medium-term market report, OECD/IEA, Paris.

Inzelt, A., & Hilton, J. (Eds.). (1999). *Technology transfer: from invention to innovation* (Vol. 19). Springer Science & Business Media. doi:10.1007/978-94-015-9145-4

Iraldo, F., Lanzini, P., Melis, M., Kahlenborn, W., Freier, I., Rubik, F., ... Petersen, A. (2006). *EVER: Evaluation of EMAS and Eco-Label for their revision.* Research Findings.

Ireland, R. & Bruce, R. (2000). CPFR: only the beginning of collaboration, *Supply Chain Management Review*, September/October, 80-88.

Islas García, C. & Sánchez Plascencia, M. A. (2013). Consumo saludable: hacia nuevos hábitos de consumo. *Procuraduría Federal del Consumidor.* Obtenido de https://www.profeco.gob.mx/educ_div/educ_y_org_cons/documentos/Consumo%20saludable%20ci.pdf

Ismail, M. S., Ramli, A., & Darus, F. (2014). Environmental management accounting practices ad Islamic corporate social responsibility compliance: Evidence from ISO14001 companies. *Procedia: Social and Behavioral Sciences*, *145*, 343–351. doi:10.1016/j.sbspro.2014.06.043

ISO 14040 and ISO 14044, Environmental Management – Life Cycle Assessment – Principles and Framework

ISO. (2015). *ISO 14001:2015 Environmental management systems – Requirements with guidance of use.* Geneva, Switzerland: International Organization for Standardization.

ISO. (2018). *The ISO survey of management system standard certifications – 2017.* International Organization for Standardization. Available at https://isotc.iso.org/livelink/livelink?func=ll&objId=18808772&objAction=browse&viewType=1

Izagirre-Olaizola, J., Fernández-Sainz, A., & Vicente-Molina, M.-A. (2013). Antecedentes y barreras a la compra de productos ecológicos. *Universia Business Review*(38), 108-127.

Jackson, T. (2009). *Prosperity without growth: Economics for a finite planet.* London, UK: Earthscan. doi:10.4324/9781849774338

Jacobs, F. R., & Chase, R. B. (2008). *Operations and supply management: The core.* New York, NY: McGraw Hill/Irwin.

Jacoby, J., Berning, C. K., & Dietvorst, T. F. (1977). What about disposition. *Journal of Marketing*, *41*(2), 22–28. doi:10.1177/002224297704100212

Jamali, D., & Mirshak, R. (2007). Corporate social responsibility (CSR): Theory and practice in a developing country context. *Journal of Business Ethics*, *72*(3), 243–262. doi:10.100710551-006-9168-4

Janssen, Blankers, Moolenburgh, & Posthumus. (2014). *The Impact of 3-D Printing on Supply-Chain Management.* TNO Transport and Mobility.

Jawahir, I. S., & Bradley, R. (2016). Technological elements of circular economy and the principles of 6R-based closed-loop material flow in sustainable manufacturing. *Procedia CIRP*, *40*, 103–108. doi:10.1016/j.procir.2016.01.067

Jean, R. J. B., Wang, Z., Zhao, X., & Sinkovics, R. R. (2016). Drivers and customer satisfaction outcomes of CSR in supply chains in different institutional contexts: A comparison between China and Taiwan. *International Marketing Review*, *33*(4), 514–529. doi:10.1108/IMR-04-2014-0115

Jensen, J. P. & Remmen, A. (2017). Enabling circular economy through product stewardship. *Procedia Manufacturing*, *8*(October 2016), 377–384. doi:10.1016/j.promfg.2017.02.048

Jhonson, M. W., Christensen, C. M., & Kagermann, H. (2008). Reinventing your Business Model. *Harvard Business Review*, *86*(12), 51–59.

Jiang, R., Kleer, R., & Piller, F. T. (2017). Predicting the future of additive manufacturing: A Delphi study on economic and societal implications of 3D printing for 2030. *Technological Forecasting and Social Change*, *117*, 84–97. doi:10.1016/j.techfore.2017.01.006

Jiang, Z., Wang, H., Zhang, H., Mendis, G., & Sutherland, J. W. (2019). Value recovery options portfolio optimization for remanufacturing end of life product. *Journal of Cleaner Production*, *210*, 419–431. doi:10.1016/j.jclepro.2018.10.316

Jin Gam, H., Cao, H., Farr, C., & Heine, L. (2009). C2CAD: A sustainable apparel design and production model. *International Journal of Clothing Science and Technology*, *21*(4), 166–179. doi:10.1108/09556220910959954

Joergens, C. (2006). Ethical fashion: Myth or future trend?, *Journal of Fashion Marketing and Management*: An *International Journal (Toronto, Ont.)*, *10*(3), 360–371.

Jo, H., Kim, H., & Park, K. (2015). Corporate environmental responsibility and firm performance in the financial services sector. *Journal of Business Ethics*, *131*(2), 257–284. doi:10.100710551-014-2276-7

Johansson, G. (2002). Success factors for integration of ecodesign in product development: A review of state of the art. *Environmental Management and Health*, *13*(1), 98–107. doi:10.1108/09566160210417868

Johansson, G. (2006). Incorporating environmental concern in product development: A study of project characteristics. *Management of Environmental Quality Analysis International Journal*, *17*, 421–436.

Johnson, H. L. (1971). *Business in contemporary society: Framework and issues*. Belmont, CA: Wadsworth.

Jo, M.-S. (2007). Should a quality sub-brand be located before or after the parent brand? an application of composite concept theory. *Journal of the Academy of Marketing Science*, *35*(2), 184–196. doi:10.100711747-007-0039-z

Jordana, J. (2000). Traditional foods: Challenges facing the European food industry. *Food Research International*, *33*(3-4), 147–152. doi:10.1016/S0963-9969(00)00028-4

Jørgensen, M. S., & Jensen, C. L. (2012). The shaping of environmental impacts from Danish production and consumption of clothing. *Ecological Economics*, *83*, 164–173. doi:10.1016/j.ecolecon.2012.04.002

Joyce, A., & Paquin, R. L. (2016). The triple layered business model canvas: A tool to design more sustainable business models. *Journal of Cleaner Production*, *135*, 1474–1486. doi:10.1016/j.jclepro.2016.06.067

Kagermann, H., Wahlster, W., & Helbig, J. (2013). *Recommendations for implementing the strategic initiative Industrie 4.0*. Final report of the Industrie 4.0 Working Group. Frankfurt am Main, Germany: acatech.

Kagermann, W. W. H., Helbig, J., & Wahlster, W. (2013). Recommendations for implementing the strategic initiative Industrie 4.0. Final report of the Industrie 4.0 working group.

Kagermann, H., & Lukas, W. D. (2011). *Industrie 4.0*. VDI, Nachrichten.

Kaifi, B. A., Nafei, W. A., Khanfar, N. M., & Kaifi, M. M. (2012). A multi-generational workforce: Managing and understanding millennials. *International Journal of Business and Management*, *7*(24), 88–93. doi:10.5539/ijbm.v7n24p88

Kaiser, H. F. (1974). An index of factorial simplicity. *Psychometrika*, *39*(1), 31–36. doi:10.1007/BF02291575

Kajikawa, Y. (2008). Research core and framework of sustainability science. *Sustainability Science*, *3*(2), 215–239. doi:10.100711625-008-0053-1

Kalamas, M., Cleveland, M., & Laroche, M. (2014). Pro-environmental behaviors for thee but not for me: Green giants, green Gods, and external environmental locus of control. *Journal of Business Research*, *67*(2), 12–22. doi:10.1016/j.jbusres.2013.03.007

Kalmykova, Y., Sadagopan, M., & Rosado, L. (2018). Circular economy – From review of theories and practices to development of implementation tools. *Resources, Conservation and Recycling*, *135*, 190–201. doi:10.1016/j.resconrec.2017.10.034

Kamble, S. S., Gunasekaran, A., & Gawankar, S. A. (2018). Sustainable Industry 4.0 framework: A systematic literature review identifying the current trends and future perspectives. *Process Safety and Environmental Protection*, *117*, 408–425. doi:10.1016/j.psep.2018.05.009

Kammerer, D. (2009). The effects of customer benefit and regulation on environmental product innovation: Empirical evidence from appliance manufacturers in Germany. *Ecological Economics*, *68*(8-9), 2285–2295. doi:10.1016/j.ecolecon.2009.02.016

Kariyawasam, S., Jayasinghe-Mudalige, U., & Weerahewa, J. (2006, May). Assessing consumer attitudes and perceptions towards food quality: The case of consumption of tetra-packed fresh milk in Sri Lanka. *Selected paper presented at the Canadian Agricultural Economics Society Annual Meeting, Montreal, Canada.*

Kashif, M., Awang, Z., Walsh, J., & Altaf, U. (2015). I'm loving it but hating US: Understanding consumer emotions and perceived service quality of US fast food brands. *British Food Journal*, *117*(9), 2344–2360. doi:10.1108/BFJ-01-2015-0040

Katiyar, R., Meena, P. L., Barua, M. K., Tibrewala, R., & Kumar, G. (2018). Impact of sustainability and manufacturing practices on supply chain performance: Findings from an emerging economy. *International Journal of Production Economics*, *197*, 303–316. doi:10.1016/j.ijpe.2017.12.007

Kayikci, Y. (2018). *Sustainability impact of digitization in logistics. In Procedia Manufacturing* (Vol. 21, pp. 782–789). Amsterdam, Netherlands: Elsevier.

Keh, H. T., & Pang, J. (2010). Customer Reactions to Service Separation. *Journal of Marketing*, *74*(2), 55–70. doi:10.1509/jm.74.2.55

Keil, M., Tan, B. C., Wei, K. K., Saarinen, T., Tuunainen, V., & Wassenaar, A. (2000). A cross-cultural study on escalation of commitment behavior in software projects. *Management Information Systems Quarterly*, *24*(2), 299–325. doi:10.2307/3250940

Keith, N. K., & Simmers, C. S. (2011). Measuring service quality perceptions of restaurant experiences: The disparity between comment cards and DINESERV. *Journal of Foodservice Business Research*, *14*(1), 20–32. doi:10.1080/15378020.2011.548209

Keller, K. L. (2009). Choosing brand elements to build brand equity. In *Strategic Brand Management* (3rd ed., pp. 187–196). Delhi, India: Dorling Kindersley.

Kenett, R. S., Zonnenshain, A., & Fortuna, G. (2018). *A road map for applied data sciences supporting sustainability in advanced manufacturing: the information quality dimensions. In Procedia Manufacturing* (Vol. 21, pp. 141–148). Amsterdam, Netherlands: Elsevier.

Keskin, D., Diehl, J. C., & Molenaar, N. (2013). Innovation process of new ventures driven by sustainability. *Journal of Cleaner Production*, *45*, 50–60. doi:10.1016/j.jclepro.2012.05.012

Khmara, Y., & Kronenberg, J. (2018). Degrowth in business: An oxymoron or a viable business model for sustainability? *Journal of Cleaner Production*, *177*, 721–731. doi:10.1016/j.jclepro.2017.12.182

Kianpour, K., Anvari, R., Jusoh, A., & Fauzi Othman, M. (2014). Important motivators for buying green products. *Intangible Capital*, *10*(5), 873–896. doi:10.3926/ic.470

Kiel, Müller, Arnold, & Voigt. (2017). Sustainable Industrial Value Creation: Benefits And Challenges Of Industry 4.0. *International Journal of Innovation Management, 21*(8).

Kiel, D., Müller, J. M., Arnold, C., & Voigt, K. I. (2017). Sustainable industrial value creation: Benefits and challenges of industry 4.0. *International Journal of Innovation Management*, *21*(08), 1740015. doi:10.1142/S1363919617400151

Kinsy, M., Khan, O., Ivan, C., Majstorovic, D., Celanovic, N., & Devadas, S. (2011). Time-predictable computer architecture for cyber-physical systems: digital emulation of power electronics systems. *Proceedings of 2011 IEEE 32nd Real-Time Systems Symposium (RTSS)*, 305-316. 10.1109/RTSS.2011.35

Kirchherr, J., Reike, D., & Hekkert, M. (2017). Conceptualizing the circular economy: An analysis of 114 definitions. *Resources, Conservation and Recycling*, *127*(September), 221–232. doi:10.1016/j.resconrec.2017.09.005

Kivimaa, P. (2007). The determinants of environmental innovation: The impacts of environmental policies on the Nordic pulp, paper and packaging industries. *European Environment*, *17*(2), 92–105. doi:10.1002/eet.442

Kleine, A., & Von Hauff, M. (2009). Sustainability-driven implementation of corporate social responsibility: Application of the integrative sustainability triangle. *Journal of Business Ethics*, *85*(3), 517–533. doi:10.100710551-009-0212-z

Klingenberg, C. O., Viana Borges, M. A., & Valle Antunes Jr, J. A. (2019). Industry 4.0 as a data-driven paradigm: A systematic literature review on technologies. *Journal of Manufacturing Technology Management*, JMTM-09-2018-0325. doi:10.1108/JMTM-09-2018-0325

Kloepffer, W. (2008). Life cycle sustainability assessment of products. *The International Journal of Life Cycle Assessment*, *13*(2), 89–95. doi:10.1065/lca2008.02.376

Knox, S., & Maklan, S. (2004). Corporate social responsibility: Moving beyond investment towards measuring outcome. *European Management Journal*, *22*(5), 508–516. doi:10.1016/j.emj.2004.09.009

Koberg, E., & Longoni, A. (2019). A systematic review of sustainable supply chain management in global supply chains. *Journal of Cleaner Production*, *207*, 1084–1098. doi:10.1016/j.jclepro.2018.10.033

Kogg, B., & Mont, O. (2012). Environmental and social responsibility in supply chains: The practice of choice and inter-organisational management. *Ecological Economics*, *83*, 154–163. doi:10.1016/j.ecolecon.2011.08.023

Kollmann, K., & Prakash, A. (2001). Green by choice? Cross-national variation in firms' responses to EMS-based environmental regimes. *World Politics*, *53*(3), 399–430. doi:10.1353/wp.2001.0010

Kong, H. M., Ko, E., Chae, H., & Mattila, P. (2016). Understanding fashion consumers' attitude and behavioral intention toward sustainable fashion products: Focus on sustainable knowledge sources and knowledge types. *Journal of Global Fashion Marketing*, *7*(2), 103–119. doi:10.1080/20932685.2015.1131435

Kotler, P., & Armstrong, G. (2012). *Marketing* (14th ed.). México: Pearson.

Kotler, P., Kartajaya, H., & Setiawan, I. (2017). *Marketing 4.0.* Milano, Italy: Hoepli.

Kotler, P., Keller, K. L., Ancarani, F., & Costabile, M. (2012). *Marketing management.* Milan, Italy: Pearson.

Kotler, P., & Kevin, L. K. (2007). *Marketing Management.* New York, NY: Pearson.

Kozinets, R. V. (2002). The field behind the screen: Using netnography for marketing research in online communities. *JMR, Journal of Marketing Research, 39*(1), 61–72. doi:10.1509/jmkr.39.1.61.18935

Kristianto, Y., Ajmal, M. M., & Sandhu, M. (2012). Adopting TQM approach to achieve customer satisfaction: A flour milling company case study. *The TQM Journal, 24*(1), 29–46. doi:10.1108/17542731211191203

Kucukusta, D., Mak, A., & Chan, X. (2013). Corporate social responsibility practices in four and five-star hotels: Perspectives from Hong Kong visitors. *International Journal of Hospitality Management, 34*, 19–30. doi:10.1016/j.ijhm.2013.01.010

Kumar, P. K., & Anand, B. (2014). A new consumer behavior model towards green products: Scale development and validation. *Asian Journal of Research in Social Science and Humanities, 4*(5), 177–193.

Kumar, R., Singh, S. P., & Lamba, K. (2018). Sustainable robust layout using Big Data approach: A key towards industry 4.0. *Journal of Cleaner Production, 204*, 643–659. doi:10.1016/j.jclepro.2018.08.327

Kusiak, A. (2019). Fundamentals of smart manufacturing: A multi-thread perspective. *Annual Reviews in Control, 47*, 214–220. doi:10.1016/j.arcontrol.2019.02.001

Kwun, J. W., & Oh, H. (2004). Effects of brand, price, and risk on customers' value perceptions and behavioral intentions in the restaurant industry. *Journal of Hospitality & Leisure Marketing, 11*(1), 31–49. doi:10.1300/J150v11n01_03

La Monica, M., Cutaia, L., & Franco, S. (2014). La simbiosi industriale come modello per lo sviluppo sostenibile dei sistemi economici territoriali. *Proceedings XXVI Convegno annuale di Sinergie —Manifattura: quale futuro?*, 151-164.

Lafferty, W., & Langhelle, O. (1995). *Bærekraftig Utvikling.* Oslo, Norway: Ad Notam.

Lane, C., Zeng, H., Dhingra, C., & Carrigan, A. (2015). Car sharing, A vehicle for sustainable mobility in emerging markets. *World Resources Institute Centre for Sustainable Cities.*

Lane, R., & Watson, M. (2012). Stewardship of things: The radical potential of product stewardship for re-framing responsibilities and relationships to products and materials. *Geoforum, 43*(6), 1254–1265. doi:10.1016/j.geoforum.2012.03.012

Langerak, F., Peelen, E., & van der Veen, M. (1998). Exploratory results on the antecedents and consequences of green marketing. *Market Research Society, 40*(4), 1–12. doi:10.1177/147078539804000404

Laplume, A. O., Petersen, B., & Pearce, J. M. (2016). Global value chains from a 3D printing perspective. *Journal of International Business Studies, 47*(5), 595–609. doi:10.1057/jibs.2015.47

Laroche, M., Bergeron, J., & Barbaro-Forleo, G. (2001). Targeting consumers who are. *Journal of Consumer Marketing, 18*(6), 503–520. doi:10.1108/EUM0000000006155

Lasi, H., Fettke, P., Kemper, H.-G., Feld, T., & Hoffmann, M. (2014). Industry 4.0. *Business & Information Systems Engineering, 6*(8), 239–242. doi:10.100712599-014-0334-4

Latorre-Biel, J. I., Faulín, J., Juan, A. A., & Jiménez-Macías, E. (2018). Petri net model of a smart factory in the frame of Industry 4.0. *IFAC-PapersOnLine, 51*(2), 266–271. doi:10.1016/j.ifacol.2018.03.046

Lawrence, S. R., Collins, E., Pavlovich, K., & Arunachalam, M. (2006). Sustainability practices of SMEs: The case of NZ. *Business Strategy and the Environment*, *15*(4), 242–257. doi:10.1002/bse.533

Lawrence, T., Dyck, B., Maitlis, S., & Mauws, K. M. (2006). The underlying structure of continuous change. *MIT Sloan Management Review*, *47*, 59–66.

Leavy, B. (2014). Venkat Ramaswamy–how value co-creation with stakeholders is transformative for producers, consumers and society. *Strategy and Leadership*, *42*(1), 9–16. doi:10.1108/SL-09-2013-0072

Lee, C., Hallak, R., & Sardeshmukh, S. R. (2019). Creativity and innovation in the restaurant sector: Supply-side processes and barriers to implementation. *Tourism Management Perspectives*, *31*, 54–62. doi:10.1016/j.tmp.2019.03.011

Lee, J., Bagheri, B., & Kao, H. A. (2015). A Cyber-Physical Systems architecture for Industry 4.0-based manufacturing systems. *Manufacturing Letters*, *3*, 18–23. doi:10.1016/j.mfglet.2014.12.001

Lee, K.-A., & Lyu, E.-S. (2019). Importance-performance analysis (IPA) of university foodservice quality by customer group according to the foodservice satisfaction and customer loyalty. *Journal of the Korean Society of Food Science and Nutrition*, *48*(1), 109–119.

Leenders, M. A., & Chandra, Y. (2013). Antecedents and consequences of green innovation in the wine industry: The role of channel structure. *Technology Analysis and Strategic Management*, *25*(2), 203–218. doi:10.1080/09537325.2012.759203

Lee, S. M., Noh, Y., Choi, D., & Rha, J. S. (2017). Environmental policy performances for sustainable development: From the perspective of ISO 14001 certification. *Corporate Social Responsibility and Environmental Management*, *24*(2), 108–120. doi:10.1002/csr.1395

Lee, S. Y., & Carroll, C. E. (2011). The emergence, variation, and evolution of corporate social responsibility in the public sphere 1980-2004: The exposure of firms to public debate. *Journal of Business Ethics*, *104*(1), 115–131. doi:10.100710551-011-0893-y

Leigh, M., & Li, X. (2015). Industrial ecology, industrial symbiosis and supply chain environmental sustainability: A case study of a large UK distributor. *Journal of Cleaner Production*, *106*, 632–643. doi:10.1016/j.jclepro.2014.09.022

Leminen, S., Westerlund, M., Rajahonka, M., & Siuruanien, R. (2012). Towards IOT Ecosystems and Business Models. In S. Andreev, S. Balandin, & Y. Koucheryavy (Eds.), *Internet of Things, Smart Spaces, and Next Generation Networking* (pp. 15–26). Berlin: Springer. doi:10.1007/978-3-642-32686-8_2

Leonidou, C. N., Katsikeas, C. S., & Morgan, N. A. (2013). "Greening" the marketing mix: Do firms do it and does it pay off? *Journal of the Academy of Marketing Science*, *41*(2), 151–170. doi:10.100711747-012-0317-2

Lerro, M., Raimondo, M., Stanco, M., Nazzaro, C., & Marotta, G. (2019). Cause related marketing among millennial consumers: the role of trust and loyalty in the food industry. *Sustainability*, *11*(2), 535. doi:10.3390u11020535

Letaifa, S. B. (2015). How to Strategise Smart Cities: Revealing the SMART model. *Journal of Business Research*, *68*(7), 1414–1419. doi:10.1016/j.jbusres.2015.01.024

Lewin, A. Y., Sakano, T., Stephens, C. U., & Victor, B. (1995). Corporate citizenship in Japan: Survey results from Japanese firms. *Journal of Business Ethics*, *14*(2), 83–101. doi:10.1007/BF00872014

Lewis, H. (2005). Defining product stewardship and sustainability in the Australian packaging industry. *Environmental Science & Policy*, *8*(1), 45–55. doi:10.1016/j.envsci.2004.09.002

Lewis, M. (1991). *Understanding Brands*. London, UK: Kogan Page.

Lewis, M. (2004). The influence of loyalty programs and short-term promotions on customer retention. *JMR, Journal of Marketing Research, 41*(3), 281–292. doi:10.1509/jmkr.41.3.281.35986

Liao, C., Lin, H. N., & Liu, Y. P. (2010). Predicting the use of pirated software: A contingency model integrating perceived risk with the theory of planned behaviour. *Journal of Business Ethics, 91*(2), 237–252. doi:10.100710551-009-0081-5

Liao, Y., Deschamps, F., Loures, E., & Ramos, L. F. P. (2017). Past, present and future of Industry 4.0 - a systematic literature review and research agenda proposal. *International Journal of Production Research, 55*(12), 3609–3629. doi:10.1080/00207543.2017.1308576

Liaukonyte, J., Streletskaya, N. A., Kaiser, H. M., & Bradley, J. R. (2013). Consumer response to 'contains' and 'free of' labeling: evidence from lab experiments. *Applied Economic Perspectives and Policy, 35*(3), 476–507. doi:10.1093/aepp/ppt015

Lieder, M., Asif, F. M., Rashid, A., Mihelič, A., & Kotnik, S. (2018). A conjoint analysis of circular economy value propositions for consumers: Using 'washing machines in Stockholm' as a case study. *Journal of Cleaner Production, 172*, 264–273. doi:10.1016/j.jclepro.2017.10.147

Li, G., Hou, Y., & Wu, A. (2017). Fourth Industrial Revolution: Technological drivers, impacts and coping methods. *Chinese Geographical Science, 27*(4), 626–637. doi:10.100711769-017-0890-x

Lii, Y. S., & Lee, M. (2012). Doing right leads to doing well: When the type of CSR and reputation interact to affect consumer evaluations of the firm. *Journal of Business Ethics, 105*(1), 69–81. doi:10.100710551-011-0948-0

Likert, R. (1932). A technique for the measurement of attitudes. *Archives de Psychologie.*

Lillywhite, S. (2007). Corporate social responsibility home and away. *Age, 14*(June).

Li, M. L., & Green, R. D. (2011). A mediating influence on customer loyalty: The role of perceived value. *Journal of Management and Marketing Research, 7*, 1.

Limba, T., Stankevičius, A., & Andrulevičius, A. (2019). Industry 4.0 and national security: The phenomenon of disruptive technology. *Entrepreneurship and Sustainability Issues, 6*(3), 1528–1535. doi:10.9770/jesi.2019.6.3(33)

Lim, S. J., & Phillips, J. (2008). Embedding CSR values: The global footwear industry's evolving governance, structure. *Journal of Business Ethics, 81*(1), 143–156. doi:10.100710551-007-9485-2

Ling, C. E. & de Run, E. C. (2009). Satisfaction and loyalty: customer perceptions of Malaysian telecommunication service providers. *ICFAI Journal of Services Marketing, 7*(1).

Lin, K. Y. (2018). User experience-based product design for smart production to empower industry 4.0 in the glass recycling circular economy. *Computers & Industrial Engineering, 125*, 729–738. doi:10.1016/j.cie.2018.06.023

Lin, K., Shyu, J., & Ding, K. (2017). A cross-strait comparison of innovation policy under industry 4.0 and sustainability development transition. *Sustainability, 9*(5), 786. doi:10.3390u9050786

Linneman, R. E., & Stanton, J. L. (1995). *Marketing planning in a total quality environment.* Psychology Press.

Lin, R. J., Tan, K. H., & Geng, Y. (2013). Market demand, green product innovation, and firm performance: Evidence from Vietnam motorcycle industry. *Journal of Cleaner Production, 40*, 101–107. doi:10.1016/j.jclepro.2012.01.001

Lintukangas, K., Kähkönen, A. K., & Ritala, P. (2016). Supply risks as drivers of green supply management adoption. *Journal of Cleaner Production, 112*(3), 1901–1909. doi:10.1016/j.jclepro.2014.10.089

Littig, B., & Griessler, E. (2005). Social sustainability. A catchword between political pragmatism and social theory. *International Journal of Sustainable Development*, *8*(1-2), 65–78. doi:10.1504/IJSD.2005.007375

Liu, Y. & Ji, H. (2010, June). A study on the perceived CSR and customer loyalty based on dairy market in China. In *2010 7th International Conference on Service Systems and Service Management* (pp. 1-6). IEEE. 10.1109/ICSSSM.2010.5530161

Liu, X., Dai, H., & Cheng, P. (2011). Drivers of integrated environmental innovation and impact on company competitiveness: Evidence from 18 Chinese firms. *International Journal of Technology and Globalisation*, *5*(3/4), 255–280. doi:10.1504/IJTG.2011.039767

Li, Y., Zhao, X., Shi, D., & Li, X. (2014). Governance of sustainable supply chains in the fast fashion industry. *European Management Journal*, *32*(5), 823–836. doi:10.1016/j.emj.2014.03.001

Llorach-Massana, P., Farreny, R., & Oliver-Sol, J. (2016). Are cradle to cradle certified products environmentally preferable? Analysis from an LCA approach'. *Journal of Cleaner Production*, *113*, 715–716. doi:10.1016/j.jclepro.2015.11.008

Locke, K. (2001). *Grounded theory in management research.* London, UK: Sage.

López Eguilaz, M. J. & Remírez Esparza, L. (1998). *Marketing ecológico y sector industrial.* Madrid, Spain: UNED.

Lorek, S. & Vergragt, P. (2015). Sustainable consumption as a systemic challenge: Inter- and transdisciplinary research and research questions. In L. Middlemiss (Ed.), Sustainable Consumption: Key Issues. UK: Routledge.

Loureiro, S. M. C., & Kastenholz, E. (2011). Corporate reputation, satisfaction, delight, and loyalty towards rural lodging units in Portugal. *International Journal of Hospitality Management*, *30*(3), 575–583. doi:10.1016/j.ijhm.2010.10.007

Loureiro, S. M., Sardinha, I. M. D., & Reijnders, L. (2012). The effect of corporate social responsibility on consumer satisfaction and perceived value: The case of the automobile industry sector in Portugal. *Journal of Cleaner Production*, *37*, 172–178. doi:10.1016/j.jclepro.2012.07.003

Lovelock, C., & Gummesson, E. (2004). Whither services marketing?: In search of a new paradigm and fresh perspectives. *Journal of Service Research*, *7*(1), 20–41. doi:10.1177/1094670504266131

Luederitz, C., Meyer, M., Abson, D. J., Gralla, F., Lang, D. J., Rau, A. L., & von Wehrden, H. (2016). Systematic student-driven literature review in sustainability science—An effective way to merge research and teaching. *Journal of Cleaner Production*, *119*, 229–235. doi:10.1016/j.jclepro.2016.02.005

Lugert, A., Batz, A., & Winkler, H. (2018). Empirical assessment of the future adequacy of value stream mapping in manufacturing industries. *Journal of Manufacturing Technology Management*, *29*(5), 886–906. doi:10.1108/JMTM-11-2017-0236

Luo, X., & Bhattacharya, C. B. (2006). Corporate social responsibility, customer satisfaction, and market value. *Journal of Marketing*, *70*(4), 1–18. doi:10.1509/jmkg.70.4.001

Luthra, S., & Mangla, S. K. (2018). Evaluating challenges to Industry 4.0 initiatives for supply chain sustainability in emerging economies. *Process Safety and Environmental Protection*, *117*, 168–179. doi:10.1016/j.psep.2018.04.018

Lu, Y. (2017). Industry 4.0: A survey on technologies, applications and open research issues. *Journal of Industrial Information Integration*, *6*, 1–10. doi:10.1016/j.jii.2017.04.005

Lu, Y., Papagiannidis, S., & Alamanos, E. (2018). Internet of Things: A systematic review of the business literature from the user and organisational perspectives. *Technological Forecasting and Social Change*, *136*, 285–297. doi:10.1016/j.techfore.2018.01.022

Lyon, T. P., & Maxwell, J. W. (2011). Greenwash: Corporate environmental disclosure under threat of audit. *Journal of Economics & Management Strategy*, *20*(1), 3–41. doi:10.1111/j.1530-9134.2010.00282.x

MacMillan, I., Roberts, E., Livada, V., & Wang, A. (2008). *Corporate venture capital (CVC): Seeking innovation and strategic growth.* National Institute of Standards and Technology-US Department of Commerce 08-916.

Magnier, L., & Schoormans, J. (2015). Consumer reactions to sustainable packaging: The interplay of visual appearance, verbal claim and environmental concern. *Journal of Environmental Psychology*, *44*, 53–62. doi:10.1016/j.jenvp.2015.09.005

Magnier, L., Schoormans, J., & Mugge, R. (2016). Judging a product by its cover: Packaging sustainability and perceptions of quality in food products. *Food Quality and Preference*, *53*, 132–142. doi:10.1016/j.foodqual.2016.06.006

Maignan, I., & Ferrell, O. C. (2001). Corporate citizenship as a marketing instrument-Concepts, evidence and research directions. *European Journal of Marketing*, *35*(3/4), 457–484. doi:10.1108/03090560110382110

Maignan, I., Ferrell, O. C., & Hult, G. T. M. (1999). Corporate citizenship: Cultural antecedents and business benefits. *Journal of the Academy of Marketing Science*, *27*(4), 455–469. doi:10.1177/0092070399274005

Maignan, I., Hillebrand, B., & McAlister, D. (2002). Managing socially-responsible buying. *European Management Journal*, *20*(6), 641–648. doi:10.1016/S0263-2373(02)00115-9

Maksimchuk, O., & Pershina, T. (2017). A new paradigm of industrial system optimization based on the conception "Industry 4.0". *MATEC Web of Conferences*, 1-5.

Maltese, F., Giachino, C., & Bonadonna, A. (2016). The safeguarding of Italian eno-gastronomic tradition and culture around the world: a strategic tool to enhance the restaurant services. *Quality-Access to Success, 17*(154).

Manavalan, E., & Jayakrishna, K. (2019). A review of Internet of Things (IoT) embedded sustainable supply chain for industry 4.0 requirements. *Computers & Industrial Engineering*, *127*, 925–953. doi:10.1016/j.cie.2018.11.030

Mandhachitara, R., & Poolthong, Y. (2011). A model of customer loyalty and corporate social responsibility. *Journal of Services Marketing*, *25*(2), 122–133. doi:10.1108/08876041111119840

Manninen, K., Koskela, S., Antikainen, R., Bocken, N., Dahlbo, H., & Aminoff, A. (2018). Do circular economy business models capture intended environmental value propositions? *Journal of Cleaner Production*, *171*, 413–422. doi:10.1016/j.jclepro.2017.10.003

Mao, J. (2010). Customer brand loyalty. *International Journal of Business and Management*, *5*(7), 213. doi:10.5539/ijbm.v5n7p213

Marcoz, E. M., Melewar, T. C., & Dennis, C. (2016). The value of region of origin, producer and protected designation of origin label for visitors and locals: The case of fontina cheese in Italy. *International Journal of Tourism Research*, *18*(3), 236–250. doi:10.1002/jtr.2000

Maresova, P., Soukal, I., Svobodova, L., Hedvicakova, M., Javanmardi, E., Selamat, A., & Krejcar, O. (2018). Consequences of Industry 4.0 in business and economics. *Economies*, *6*(3), 46. doi:10.3390/economies6030046

Marin, L., Ruiz, S., & Rubio, A. (2009). The role of identity salience in the effects of corporate social responsibility on consumer behavior. *Journal of Business Ethics*, *84*(1), 65–78. doi:10.100710551-008-9673-8

Marshall, S., & Banister, D. (2000). Travel reduction strategies: Intentions and outcomes. *Transportation Research Part A, Policy and Practice*, *34*(5), 321–338. doi:10.1016/S0965-8564(99)00034-8

Martínez Ramón, M. (2006). El mercado de los productos ecológicos en EEUU. *Instituto español del comercio exterior.* Obtenido de http://www.exportapymes.com/documentos/productos/Ie2409_eeuu_ecologicos.pdf

Martínez Turrubiates, A., & Martín Prieto, F. (2009). *Las megatendencias sociales actuales y su impacto en la identificación de oportunidades estratégicas de negocios* (1st ed.). Monterrey, Mexico: Instituto Tecnológico y de Estudios Superiores de Monterrey. Obtenido de http://studylib.es/doc/7253097/las-megatendencias-sociales-actuales-y-su-impacto

Martínez-Ferrero, J., & García-Sánchez, I. (2015). Is corporate social responsibility an entrenchment strategy? Evidence in stakeholder protection environments. *RMS Rev Manag Sci*, *9*(1), 89–114.

Martinho, G., Pires, A., Portela, G., & Fonseca, M. (2015). Factors affecting consumers' choices concerning sustainable packaging during product purchase and recycling. *Resources, Conservation and Recycling*, *103*, 58–68. doi:10.1016/j.resconrec.2015.07.012

Martin, W. C., & Bateman, C. R. (2014). Consumer religious commitment's influence on ecocentric attitudes and behavior. *Journal of Business Research*, *67*(2), 5–11. doi:10.1016/j.jbusres.2013.03.006

Massa, L., Tucci, C., & Afuah, A. (2017). A critical assessment of business model research. *The Academy of Management Annals*, *11*(1), 73–104. doi:10.5465/annals.2014.0072

Massini, R. (2010). Prospettive di R&S per l'industria alimentare. *Industrie Alimentari*, *49*(500), 19–26.

Mathe, K., & Slevitch, L. (2013). An exploratory examination of supervisor undermining, employee involvement climate, and the effects on customer perceptions of service quality in quick-service restaurants. *Journal of Hospitality & Tourism Research (Washington, D.C.)*, *37*(1), 29–50. doi:10.1177/1096348011413590

Mathur, S. (2017). Glocalization in fast food chains: a case study of McDonald's. In Strategic Marketing Management and Tactics in the Service Industry (pp. 330-347). Hershey, PA: IGI Global. doi:10.4018/978-1-5225-2475-5.ch013

Matinaro, V., Liu, Y., Le, T. R. J. S., & Poesche, J. (2019). Extracting key factors for sustainable development of enterprises: Case study of SMEs in Taiwan. *Journal of Cleaner Production*, *209*, 1152–1169. doi:10.1016/j.jclepro.2018.10.280

Matten, D., & Crane, A. (2005). Corporate citizenship: toward an extended theoretical conceptualization. *Academy of Management Review*, *30*(1), 166–179. doi:10.5465/amr.2005.15281448

Matthes, J., & Wonneberger, A. (2014). The skeptical green consumer revisited: Testing the relationship between green consumerism and skepticism toward advertising. *Journal of Advertising*, *43*(2), 115–127. doi:10.1080/00913367.2013.834804

Mattia, G., Mugion, R. G., & Principato, L. (2019). Shared mobility as a driver for sustainable consumptions: The intention to re-use free-floating car sharing. *Journal of Cleaner Production*, 237.

Mattioda, R. A., Mazzi, A., Canciglieri, O., & Scipioni, A. (2015). Determining the principal references of the social life cycle assessment of products. *The International Journal of Life Cycle Assessment*, *8*(8), 1155–1165. doi:10.100711367-015-0873-z

Mattsson, S., Fast-Berglund, Å., Li, D., & Thorvald, P. (in press). Forming a cognitive automation strategy for Operator 4.0 in complex assembly. *Computers & Industrial Engineering*.

Maynard, A. D. (2015). Navigating the fourth industrial revolution. *Nature Nanotechnology*, *10*(1), 1005–1006. doi:10.1038/nnano.2015.286

Mazzi, A., Toniolo, S., Manzardo, A., Ren, J., & Scipioni, A. (2016, Nov. 19). (2016/a). Exploring the direction on the environmental and business performance relationship at the firm level. Lessons from a literature review. *Sustainability*, *8*(11), 1200. doi:10.3390u8111200

Mazzi, A., Toniolo, S., Mason, M., Aguiari, F., & Scipioni, A. (2016, December). (2016/b). What are the benefits and difficulties in adopting an environmental management system? The opinion of Italian organizations. *Journal of Cleaner Production, 139*, 873–885. doi:10.1016/j.jclepro.2016.08.053

McAfee, A., & Brynjolfsson, E. (2012a). Big data: The management revolution. *Harvard Business Review, 90*(10), 61–67.

McAffee, A., & Brynjolfsson, E. (2012b). Big Data: The Management Revolution Exploiting vast new flows of information can radically improve your company's performance. But first you'll have to change your decision-making culture. *Harvard Business Review*, 3–9.

McCarthy, S., & Golocic, S. (2002). Implementing collaborative planning to improve supply chain performance. *International Journal of Physical Distribution & Logistics Management, 32*(6), 431–454. doi:10.1108/09600030210437960

McDaniel, C., & Baker, R. C. (1977). Convenience food packaging and the perception of product quality. *Journal of Marketing, 41*(4), 57–58. doi:10.1177/002224297704100406

McDonald's Italia. (2015). McDonald's McItaly Piemontese e Chianina. Available at http://www.mcdonalds.it/sites/default/files/mcdonalds_mcitaly_cs_chianina_e_romagnola.pdf

McDonalds. (2019). McDonald's MySelection 2019. Retrieved from https://www.mcdonalds.it/myselection

McDougall, G. H., & Levesque, T. (2000). Customer satisfaction with services: Putting perceived value into the equation. *Journal of Services Marketing, 14*(5), 392–410. doi:10.1108/08876040010340937

McEvily, B., Perrone, V., & Zaheer, A. (2003). Trust as an organizing principle. *Organization Science, 14*(1), 91–103. doi:10.1287/orsc.14.1.91.12814

McGlone, T., Spain, J. W., & McGlone, V. (2011). Corporate social responsibility and the millennials. *Journal of Education for Business, 86*(4), 195–200. doi:10.1080/08832323.2010.502912

McGuire, J. (1963). *Business and society*. New York, NY: McGraw-Hill.

McKinsey Global Survey. (2010). How companies manage sustainability. McKinsey & Co. Retrieved from https://www.mckinseyquarterly.com/

McWilliams, A., Parhankangas, A., Coupet, J., Welch, E., & Barnum, D. T. (2016). Strategic Decision Making for the Triple Bottom Line. *Business Strategy and the Environment, 25*(3), 193–204. doi:10.1002/bse.1867

Meadows, D. H., Meadows, D. L., Randers, J., & Behrens, W. W. (1972). The limits to growth. New York, NY: Potomac Associates - Universe Books.

Mebratu, D. (1998). Sustainability and sustainable development: Historical and conceptual review. *Environmental Impact Assessment Review, 18*(6), 493–520. doi:10.1016/S0195-9255(98)00019-5

Mehta, P. (2019). E-Waste, Chemical Toxicity, and Legislation in India. In Advanced Methodologies and Technologies in Engineering and Environmental Science. IGI Global.

Mejtoft, T. (2011). Internet of Things and Co-Creation of Value. *2011 International Conference on Internet of things & 4th International Conference on Cyber, Physical and Social Computing*, 672-677.

Menegaki, A. N. (2011). Growth and renewable energy in Europe: A random effect model with evidence for neutrality hypothesis. *Energy Economics, 33*(2), 257–263. doi:10.1016/j.eneco.2010.10.004

Merli, R., & Preziosi, M. (2018). The EMAS impasse : Factors influencing Italian organizations to withdraw or renew the registration. *Journal of Cleaner Production, 172*, 4532–4543. doi:10.1016/j.jclepro.2017.11.031

Merli, R., Preziosi, M., & Ippolito, C. (2016). Promoting sustainability through EMS application: A survey examining the critical factors about EMAS registration in Italian organizations. *Sustainability*, *8*(3), 197. doi:10.3390u8030197

Meyers-Levy, J., & Tybout, A. M. (1989). Schema congruity as a basis for product evaluation. *The Journal of Consumer Research*, *16*(1), 39–54. doi:10.1086/209192

Michelini, G., Moraes, R. N., Cunha, R. N., Costa, J. M. H., & Ometto, A. R. (2017). From linear to circular economy: PSS conducting the transition. *Procedia CIRP*, *64*, 2–6. doi:10.1016/j.procir.2017.03.012

Miemczyk, J., Johnsen, T. E., & Macquet, M. (2012). Sustainable purchasing and supply management: A structured literature review of definitions and measures at the dyad, chain and network levels. *Supply Chain Management*, *17*(5), 478–496. doi:10.1108/13598541211258564

Mikkelsen, B. E., Kristensen, N. H., & Nielsen, T. (2006). Innovation processes in large-scale public foodservice—case findings from the implementation of organic foods in a Danish County. *Journal of Foodservice Business Research*, *8*(2), 87–105. doi:10.1300/J369v08n02_07

Mildenberger, U., & Khare, A. (2000). Planning for an environment-friendly car. *Technovation*, *20*(4), 205–214. doi:10.1016/S0166-4972(99)00111-X

Miles, M. B., & Huberman, A. M. (1994). *Qualitative data analysis: An expanded sourcebook.* Thousand Oaks, CA: Sage.

Millard-Ball, A., Murray G., ter Schure J., Fox, C., & Burkhardt, J., (2005). Car sharing: *Where and how it succeeds.* Transit Cooperative Research Program (TCRP) Report, 108.

Mills, B., & Schleich, J. (2010). What's driving energy efficient appliance label awareness and purchase propensity? *Energy Policy*, *38*(2), 814–825. doi:10.1016/j.enpol.2009.10.028

Min, H. & Galle, W. (2001). Green purchasing practices of US firms. *Intentions Journal of Operations & Production Management, 21*(9).

Minetti, A. C. (2002). *Marketing de alimentos ecológicos* (1st ed.). Madrid, Spain: Pirámide.

Minton, E., Kim, C. H., & Khale, L. R. (2015). Religion and motives for sustainable behaviors: A cross-cultural comparison and contrast. *Journal of Business Research*, *68*(9), 1–8. doi:10.1016/j.jbusres.2015.01.003

Mirata, M., & Emtairah, T. (2005). Industrial symbiosis networks and the contribution to environmental innovation: The case of the Landskrona industrial symbiosis programme. *Journal of Cleaner Production*, *13*(10-11), 993–1002. doi:10.1016/j.jclepro.2004.12.010

Mitcham, C. (1995). The concept of sustainable development: Its origins and ambivalence. *Technology in Society*, *17*(3), 311–326. doi:10.1016/0160-791X(95)00008-F

Mitchell, D. W., & Coles, C. B. (2004). Business Model Innovation breakthrough moves. *The Journal of Business Strategy*, *25*(1), 16–26. doi:10.1108/02756660410515976

Mitra, A., O'Regan, N., & Sarpong, D. (2018). Cloud resource adaptation: A resource based perspective on value creation for corporate growth. *Technological Forecasting and Social Change*, *130*, 28–38. doi:10.1016/j.techfore.2017.08.012

Mkono, M. (2012). Slow food versus fast food: A Zimbabwean case study of hotelier perspectives. *Tourism and Hospitality Research*, *12*(3), 147–154. doi:10.1177/1467358412470556

Mohammed, A., & Rashid, B. (2018). A conceptual model of corporate social responsibility dimensions, brand image, and customer satisfaction in Malaysian hotel industry. *Kasetsart Journal of Social Sciences*, *39*(2), 358–364. doi:10.1016/j.kjss.2018.04.001

Mohr, L. A., Webb, D. J., & Harris, K. E. (2001). Do consumers expect companies to be socially responsible? The impact of corporate social responsibility on buying behavior. *The Journal of Consumer Affairs, 35*(1), 45–72. doi:10.1111/j.1745-6606.2001.tb00102.x

Mol, A. P. J. (2015). Transparency and value chain sustainability. *Journal of Cleaner Production, 107*, 154–161. doi:10.1016/j.jclepro.2013.11.012

Molteni, M. & Todisco, A. (2008). *Piccole e medie imprese e CSR. La CSR come leva di differenziazione*. Retrieved from http://www.isvi.org

Molteni, L., & Manoforte, R. (1998). *La conjoint analysis e il problema delle interazioni fra gli attributi: un'evidenza empirica*. Roma, Italy: Libero Istituto Universitario Carlo Cattaneo.

Molteni, M. (2004). *Responsabilità sociale e performance d'impresa*. Milano, Italy.

Molteni, M., Antoldi, F., & Todisco, A. (2016). SMEs and CSR: An empirical survey in Italian industrial district. In *EABIS/CBS International Conference on The Social Responsibility of Small and Medium Sized Enterprises. Integration of CSR into SMEs Business Practice*, Copenhagen, Vol. 26.

Molteni, M., Pedrini, M., & Bertolini, S. (Eds.). (2006). *La responsabilità sociale d'impresa nelle aziende familiari italiane*. Milano, Italy: Franco Angeli.

Montaño Salas, F. E. (2012). La educación ambiental en México ante la crisis ambiental. *Revista Vinculando*. Obtenido de http://vinculando.org/ecologia/la-educacion-ambiental-en-mexico-ante-la-crisis-ambiental.html#Educacion_Ambiental_en_Mexico

Moore, J. F. (2006). Business ecosystems and the view from the firm. *The Antitrust Bulletin, 51*(1), 31-75.

Moore, J. F. (1993). Predators and prey: A new ecology of competition. *Harvard Business Review, 71*(3), 75–86. PMID:10126156

Moraga, G., Huysveld, S., Mathieux, F., Blengini, G. A., Alaerts, L., Van Acker, K., & ... Dewulf, J. (2019). Circular economy indicators: What do they measure? *Resources, Conservation and Recycling, 146*, 452–461. doi:10.1016/j.resconrec.2019.03.045

Morioka, S. N., Bolis, I., Evans, S., & Carvalho, M. M. (2017). Transforming sustainability challenges into competitive advantage: Multiple case studies kaleidoscope converging into sustainable business models. *Journal of Cleaner Production, 167*, 723–738. doi:10.1016/j.jclepro.2017.08.118

Morsing, M., Schultz, M., & Nielsen, K. U. (2008). The 'catch 22' of communicating CSR: Findings from a Danish study. *Journal of Marketing Communications, 14*(2), 97–111. doi:10.1080/13527260701856608

Mosconi, M. (2015). *The New European Industrial Policy*. London, UK: Routledge. doi:10.4324/9781315761756

Mostafa, M. M. (2007). Gender differences in Egyptian consumers' green purchase behaviour: The effects of environmental knowledge, concern and attitude. *International Journal of Consumer Studies, 31*(3), 220–229. doi:10.1111/j.1470-6431.2006.00523.x

Muehling, D. D., Laczniak, R. N., & Stoltman, J. J. (1991). The moderating effects of ad message involvement: A reassessment. *Journal of Advertising, 20*(2), 29–38. doi:10.1080/00913367.1991.10673211

Müller, J., Dotzauer, V., & Voigt, K. I. (2017). Industry 4.0 and its impact on reshoring decisions of German manufacturing enterprises. In Supply Management Research (pp. 165-179). Springer Gabler.

Müller, J. M. (2019a). Business model innovation in small-and medium-sized enterprises: Strategies for industry 4.0 providers and users. *Journal of Manufacturing Technology Management*. doi:10.1108/JMTM-01-2018-0008

Müller, J. M. (2019b). Antecedents to Digital Platform Usage in Industry 4.0 by Established Manufacturers. *Sustainability, 11*(4), 1121. doi:10.3390u11041121

Müller, J. M., Buliga, O., & Voigt, K.-I. (2018b). Fortune favors the prepared. How SMEs approach business model innovation in Industry 4.0. *Technological Forecasting and Social Change, 132*, 2–17. doi:10.1016/j.techfore.2017.12.019

Müller, J. M., & Däschle, S. (2018). Business Model Innovation of Industry 4.0 Solution Providers Towards Customer Process Innovation. *Processes, 6*(12), 260. doi:10.3390/pr6120260

Müller, J. M., Kiel, D., & Voigt, K. I. (2018a). What drives the implementation of industry 4.0? The role of opportunities and challenges in the context of sustainability. *Sustainability, 10*(1), 247. doi:10.3390u10010247

Müller, J. M., & Voigt, K. I. (2018). Sustainable industrial value creation in SMEs: A comparison between industry 4.0 and Made in China 2025. *International Journal of Precision Engineering and Manufacturing-Green Technology, 5*(5), 659–670. doi:10.100740684-018-0056-z

Müller, J., & Voigt, K. I. (2016). Industrie 4.0 für kleine und mittlere Unternehmen. *Productivity Management, 3*, 28–30.

Murmura, F., & Bravi, L. (2018). Additive manufacturing in the wood-furniture sector: Sustainability of the technology, benefits and limitations of adoption. *Journal of Manufacturing Technology Management, 29*(2), 350–371.

Nadvi, K. (2008). Global standards, global governance and the organization of global value chains. *Journal of Economic Geography, 8*(3), 323–343. doi:10.1093/jeg/lbn003

Nagy, J., Oláh, J., Erdei, E., Máté, D., & Popp, J. (2018). The Role and Impact of Industry 4.0 and the Internet of Things on the Business Strategy of the Value Chain—The Case of Hungary. *Sustainability, 10*(10), 3491. doi:10.3390u10103491

Namukasa, J. (2013). The influence of airline service quality on passenger satisfaction and loyalty: The case of Uganda airline industry. *The TQM Journal, 25*(5), 520–532. doi:10.1108/TQM-11-2012-0092

Narasimhan, C., & Sen, S. (1992). Measuring quality perceptions. *Marketing Letters, 3*(2), 147–156. doi:10.1007/BF00993994

Nascimento, D. L. M., Alencastro, V., Quelhas, O. L. G., Caiado, R. G. G., Garza-Reyes, J. A., Lona, L. R., & Tortorella, G. (2018). Exploring Industry 4.0 technologies to enable circular economy practices in a manufacturing context: A business model proposal. *Journal of Manufacturing Technology Management, 30*(3), 607–627. doi:10.1108/JMTM-03-2018-0071

National Geographic; GlobeScan. (2012). *Greendex 2012: Consumer Choice and the Environment a worldwide tracking Survey*. Canadá. Obtenido de http://images.nationalgeographic.com/wpf/media-content/file/NGS_2012_Final_Global_report_Jul20-cb1343059672.pdf

Neuteleers, S., & Engelen, B. (2015). Talking money: How market-based valuation can determine environmental protection. *Ecological Economics, 117*, 253–260. doi:10.1016/j.ecolecon.2014.06.022

New, S. (2010). The transparent supply chain. *Harvard Business Review, 88*(10), 1–11.

Ngan, S. L., How, B. S., Teng, S. Y., Promentilla, M. A. B., Yatim, P., Er, A. C., & Lam, H. L. (2019). Prioritization of sustainability indicators for promoting the circular economy: The case of developing countries. *Renewable & Sustainable Energy Reviews, 111*(May), 314–331. doi:10.1016/j.rser.2019.05.001

Ng, R. Y. X., Wong, Y. S., Yeo, J. Y., Koh, C. L. Z., Wilson, C., & Gan, S. K. E. (2018). The associations between dietary practices and dietary quality, biological health indicators, perceived stress, religiosity, culture, and gender in multicultural Singapore. *Journal of Ethnic Foods*, *5*(3), 220–227. doi:10.1016/j.jef.2018.07.003

Nguyen, Q., Nisar, T. M., Knox, D., & Prabhakar, G. P. (2018). Understanding customer satisfaction in the UK quick service restaurant industry: The influence of the tangible attributes of perceived service quality. *British Food Journal*, *120*(6), 1207–1222. doi:10.1108/BFJ-08-2017-0449

Ni, B. (2018). Productivity, capital intensity, and ISO 14001 adoption: Theory and evidence. *Review of Development Economics*, *23*(1), 395–414. doi:10.1111/rode.12547

Nicolaou, A. I., & McKnight, D. H. (2006). Perceived information quality in data exchanges: Effects on risk, trust, and intention to use. *Information Systems Research*, *17*(4), 332–351. doi:10.1287/isre.1060.0103

Nidumolu, R., Prahalad, C. K., & Rangaswami, M. R. (2009). Why sustainability is now the key driver of innovation. *Harvard Business Review*, *87*(9), 56–64.

Nielsen. (2016). Nuevas percepciones en las expectativas de consumo. *Ganar-Ganar*, 38-43.

Niero, M., & Rivera, X. C. S. (2018). The role of life cycle sustainability assessment in the implementation of circular economy principles in organizations. *Procedia CIRP*, *69*(May), 793–798. doi:10.1016/j.procir.2017.11.022

Nieuwenhuis, L. J. M., Ehrenhard, M. L., & Prause, L. (2018). The shift to Cloud Computing: The impact of disruptive technology on the enterprise software business ecosystem. *Technological Forecasting and Social Change*, *129*, 308–313. doi:10.1016/j.techfore.2017.09.037

Niinimaki, K. (2010). Eco-clothing, consumer identity and ideology. *Sustainable Development*, *18*(3), 150–162. doi:10.1002d.455

Niinimaki, K. (2015). Ethical foundations in sustainable fashion. *Textiles and Clothing Sustainability*, *1*(1), 3. doi:10.118640689-015-0002-1

Niinimaki, K., & Hassi, L. (2011). Emerging design strategies in sustainable production and consumption of textiles and clothing. *Journal of Cleaner Production*, *19*(16), 1876–1883.

Nijland, H., & van Meerkerk, J. (2017). Mobility and environmental impacts of car sharing in the Netherlands. *Environmental Innovation and Societal Transitions*, *23*, 84–91. doi:10.1016/j.eist.2017.02.001

Niray, R., Gupta, M., & Narasimhan, C. (2001). Customer profitability in a Supply Chain. *Journal of Marketing*, *65*(3), 1–16. doi:10.1509/jmkg.65.3.1.18332

Nishitani, K., Kaneko, S., Fujii, H., & Komatsu, S. (2012). Are firms' voluntary environmental management activities beneficial for the environment and business? An empirical study focusing on Japanese manufacturing firms. *Journal of Environmental Management*, *105*, 121–130. doi:10.1016/j.jenvman.2012.03.054

Nižetić, S., Djilali, N., Papadopoulos, A., & Rodrigues, J. J. P. C. (2019). Smart technologies for promotion of energy efficiency, utilization of sustainable resources and waste management. *Journal of Cleaner Production*, *231*, 565–591. doi:10.1016/j.jclepro.2019.04.397

Normann, R., & Ramirez, R. (1993). From value chain to value constellation: Designing interactive strategy. *Harvard Business Review*, *71*(4), 65–77. PMID:10127040

Norman, W., MacDonald, C., & Arnold, D. G. (2004). Getting to the Bottom of "Triple Bottom Line". *Business Ethics Quarterly*, *14*(2), 243–262. doi:10.5840/beq200414211

Norris, G. A. (2001). Integrating life cycle cost analysis and LCA. *The International Journal of Life Cycle Assessment, 6*(2), 118–120.

Nosratabadi, S., Mosavi, A., Shamshirband, S., Kazimieras Zavadskas, E., Rakotonirainy, A., & Chau, K. W. (2019). Sustainable business models: A review. *Sustainability, 11*(6), 1663. doi:10.3390u11061663

Nuebling, M., Behnke, C., Hammond, R., Sydnor, S., & Almanza, B. (2017). On tap: Foodservice operators' perceptions of a wine innovation. *Journal of Foodservice Business Research, 20*(3), 251–267. doi:10.1080/15378020.2016.1209722

O'Hare, J.A. (2010). *Eco-innovation tools for the early stages: an industry-based investigation of tool customisation and introduction.*

O'Rourke, D. (2014). The science of sustainable supply chains. *Science, 344*(6188), 1124–1127. doi:10.1126cience.1248526 PMID:24904157

Oberseder, M., Schlegelmilch, B. B., Murphy, P. E., & Gruber, V. (2014). Consumers' perceptions of corporate social responsibility: Scale development and validation. *Journal of Business Ethics*, 1–15.

Observatorio Cuidadano de calidad de vida: Jalisco como vamos. (2017, July). ¿Como nos vemos los tapatíos? Encuesta de percepción cuidadana sobre la calidad de vida 2016. Obtenido de http://www.jaliscocomovamos.org/encuesta2016

OECD. (2015). *Addressing the tax challenges of the digital economy, action 1 - 2015 Final Report, OECD/G20 base erosion and profit shifting project.* Paris, France: OECD Publishing. doi:10.1787/9789264241046-

OECOTEXTILES. (2013). True cost of fast fashion. Retrieved from https:// oecotextiles.wordpress.com/2013/08/29/true-cost-of-fast-fashion/

Oehmen, J., De Nardo, M., Schonsleben, P., & Boutellier, R. (2010). Supplier code of conduct - state of the art and customisation in the electronics industry. *Production Planning and Control, 21*(7), 664–679. doi:10.1080/09537280903547785

Okorie, O., Salonitis, K., Charnley, F., Moreno, M., Turner, C., & Tiwari, A. (2018). Digitisation and the circular economy: A review of current research and future trends. *Energies, 11*(11), 3009. doi:10.3390/en11113009

Oliver, R. L. (1980). A cognitive model of the antecedents and consequences of satisfaction decisions. *JMR, Journal of Marketing Research, 17*(4), 460–469. doi:10.1177/002224378001700405

Oliver, R. L. (1999). Whence consumer loyalty. *Journal of Marketing, 63*(4), 33–44. doi:10.1177/00222429990634s105

Oliver, R. L., Rust, R. T., & Varki, S. (1997). Customer delight: Foundations, findings, and managerial insight. *Journal of Retailing, 73*(3), 311–336. doi:10.1016/S0022-4359(97)90021-X

Olsen, L. L., & Johnson, M. D. (2003). Service equity, satisfaction, and loyalty: From transaction-specific to cumulative evaluations. *Journal of Service Research, 5*(3), 184–195. doi:10.1177/1094670502238914

ONUDI (Organización de las Naciones Unidas para el Desarrollo Industrial). (2011). Iniciativa de industria verde para el desarrollo industrial sostenible. Viena. Obtenido de http://www.greenindustryplatform.org/wp-content/uploads/2014/06/green-industry_ES_highres.pdf

Orel, F. D., & Kara, A. (2014). Supermarket self-checkout service quality, customer satisfaction, and loyalty: Empirical evidence from an emerging market. *Journal of Retailing and Consumer Services, 21*(2), 118–129. doi:10.1016/j.jretconser.2013.07.002

Organizacion Mundial de la Salud. (2018). *Organizacion Mundial de la Salud.* Obtenido de http://www.who.int/topics/environmental_health/es/

Orozco Abundis, M. A., Cortes Lamas, A. I., González, M., & Gracia Villar, S. (2003). Mercadotecnia ecológica: actitud del consumidor ante los productos ecológicos. Obtenido de http://www.aeipro.com/files/congresos/2003pamplona/ciip03_1041_1050.2224.pdf

Orsato, R. J. (2006). Competitive environmental strategies: When does it pay to be green? *California Management Review*, *48*(2), 127–143. doi:10.2307/41166341

Orth, U. R., & Malkewitz, K. (2008). Holistic package design and consumer brand impressions. *Journal of Marketing*, *72*(3), 64–81. doi:10.1509/jmkg.72.3.64

Osburg, V. S., Appelhanz, S., Toporowski, W., & Schumann, M. (2016). An empirical investigation of wood product information valued by young consumers. *Journal of Cleaner Production*, *110*, 170–179. doi:10.1016/j.jclepro.2015.01.068

Osterwalder, A., & Pigneur, Y. (2003). Modeling value propositions in e-Business. In *Proceedings of the 5th International Conference on Electronic Commerce*, 429-436.

Osterwalder, A., Pigneur, Y., & Tucci, C. L. (2005). Clarifying business models: origins, present, and future of the concept. *Communications of the Association for Information Systems*, *16*(1), 1–25.

Othman, N. Z. & Hemdi, M. A. (2015). Predictors of guest retention: Investigating the role of hotel's corporate social responsibility activities and brand image. *Theory and Practice in Hospitality and Tourism Research*, 139-144.

Ozturk, I., & Bilgili, F. (2015). Economic growth and biomass consumption nexus: Dynamic panel analysis for Sub-Sahara African countries. *Applied Energy*, *137*, 110–116. doi:10.1016/j.apenergy.2014.10.017

Paillé, P., Chen, Y., Boirla, O., & Jin, J. (2014). The impact of human resource management on environmental performance: An employee-level study. *Journal of Business Ethics*, *121*(3), 451–466. doi:10.100710551-013-1732-0

Pan, M., Sikorski, J., Kastner, C. A., Akroyd, J., Mosbach, S., Lau, R., & Kraft, M. (2015). Applying Industry 4.0 to the Jurong Island Eco-Industrial Park. *Energy Procedia*, *75*, 1536–1541. doi:10.1016/j.egypro.2015.07.313

Pan, S. Y., Du, M. A., Te Huang, I., Liu, I. H., Chang, E. E., & Chiang, P. C. (2014). Strategies on implementation of waste-to-energy (WTE) supply chain for circular economy system: A review. *Journal of Cleaner Production*, *108*, 409–421. doi:10.1016/j.jclepro.2015.06.124

Panwar, R., Rinne, T., Hansen, E., & Juslin, H. (2006). Corporate responsibility. *Forest Products Journal*, *56*(2), 4.

Parasuraman, A., Berry, L. L., & Zeithaml, V. A. (1991). Understanding customer expectations of service. *Sloan Management Review*, *32*(3), 39–48.

Paravizo, E., Chaim, O. C., Braatz, D., Muschard, B., & Rozenfeld, H. (2018). *Exploring gamification to support manufacturing education on industry 4.0 as an enabler for innovation and sustainability. In Procedia Manufacturing* (Vol. 21, pp. 438–445). Amsterdam, Netherlands: Elsevier.

Parboteeah, K., Addae, H., & Cullen, J. B. (2012). Propensity to support sustainability initiatives: A cross- national model. *Journal of Business Ethics*, *105*(3), 403–413. doi:10.100710551-011-0979-6

Park, E. (2019). Corporate social responsibility as a determinant of corporate reputation in the airline industry. *Journal of Retailing and Consumer Services*, *47*, 215–221. doi:10.1016/j.jretconser.2018.11.013

Park, E., Kwon, S. J., & Kim, K. J. (2016). Assessing the effects of corporate sustainable management on customer satisfaction. *Sustainable Development*, *24*(1), 41–52. doi:10.1002d.1605

Parkins, W. (2004). Out of time: Fast subjects and slow living. *Time & Society*, *13*(2-3), 363–382. doi:10.1177/0961463X04045662

Parmar, B. L., Freeman, R. E., Harrison, J. S., Wicks, A. C., Purnell, L., & De Colle, S. (2010). Stakeholder theory: The state of the art. *The Academy of Management Annals*, *4*(1), 403–445. doi:10.1080/19416520.2010.495581

Patton, M. Q. (2001). *Qualitative evaluation and research methods*. Thousand Oaks, CA: Sage.

Paulík, J., Kombo, F., & Ključnikov, A. (2015). CSR as a driver of satisfaction and loyalty in commercial banks in the Czech Republic. *Journal of International Studies*.

Pauliuk, S. (2018). Critical appraisal of the circular economy standard BS 8001:2017 and a dashboard of quantitative system indicators for its implementation in organizations. *Resources, Conservation and Recycling*, *129*, 81–92. doi:10.1016/j.resconrec.2017.10.019

Pavlou, P. A. (2003). Consumer acceptance of electronic commerce: Integrating trust and risk with the technology acceptance model. *International Journal of Electronic Commerce*, *7*(3), 101–134. doi:10.1080/10864415.2003.11044275

Pegan, G., & de Luca, P. (2012). Can implicit and explicit attitudes predict green product choice under time pressure? An experimental research. *Journal of Management and World Business Research*, *9*, 21–36.

Pelsmacker, P. D., Janssens, W., Sterckx, E., & Mielants, C. (2006). Fair-trade beliefs, attitudes and buying behaviour of Belgian consumers. *International Journal of Nonprofit and Voluntary Sector Marketing*, *11*(2), 125–138. doi:10.1002/nvsm.47

Pereira, Á. & Vence, X. (2012). *Key business factors for eco-innovation: an overview of recent firm-level empirical studies*.

Pérez Abuin, J. A. (2016). *Revista de Educacion y Cultura*. Obtenido de http://www.educacionyculturaaz.com/noticias/educacion-ambiental-en-mexico

Pérez, A., & Rodriguez del Bosque, I. (2016). The stakeholder management theory of CSR: A multidimensional approach in understanding customer identification and satisfaction. *International Journal of Bank Marketing*, *34*(5), 731–751. doi:10.1108/IJBM-04-2015-0052

Pérez-Calderón, E., Milanés-Montero, P., & Ortega-Rossel, F. J. (2012). Environmental performance and firm value: Evidence from Dow Jones Sustainability Index Europe. *International Journal of Environmental of Research*, *6*, 1007–1014.

Peri, C. (2006). The universe of food quality. *Food Quality and Preference*, *17*(1-2), 3–8. doi:10.1016/j.foodqual.2005.03.002

Perrini, F. & Pivato, S. (2007). Responsabilità sociale e competitività delle piccole-medie imprese. In R. Benini (Ed.), L'impresa responsabile e la comunità intraprendente (73–94). Halley Editrice, MC.

Perrini, F., & Tencati, A. (2008). *Corporate social responsibility*. Milano, Italy: Egea.

Pesce, M., Shi, C., Critto, A., Wang, X., & Marcomini, A. (2018). SWOT analysis of the application of International Standard ISO 14001 in the Chinese context. A case study of Guangdong Province. *Sustainability*, *10*(9), 3196. doi:10.3390u10093196

Petersen, A. (2006). *EVER: Evaluation of EMAS and Eco-Label for their Revision*. Research Findings.

Petricevic, T. & Bell, R. (2010). *An exploratory study into influence of corporate social responsibility on consumer price sensitivity*.

Petrini, C. (2005). Buono pulito e giusto. Nuovi principi di neogastronomia.

Petrovic, O., Kittl, C., & Teksten, R. D. (2001). Developing business models for eBusiness. *International Conference on Electronic Commerce* 2001, Vienna, Austria.

Pfahl, S. (2005). Institutional sustainability. *International Journal of Sustainable Development*, *8*(1/2), 80–96. doi:10.1504/IJSD.2005.007376

Phu-Hop, M. (2017). The corporate social responsibility in Vietnam today. *Journal of Business and Economic Development*, *2*(3), 170–175.

Piccarozzi, M., Silvestri, C., & Aquilani, B. (forthcoming). Achieving environmental sustainability: the role of Industry 4.0 in industrial symbiosis processes (work-in-progress). *Conference Proceedings Sinergie-Sima 2019.*

Piccarozzi, M. (2017). Does Social Innovation Contribute to Sustainability? The Case of Italian Innovative Start-Ups. *Sustainability*, *9*(12), 2376. doi:10.3390u9122376

Piccarozzi, M., Aquilani, B., & Gatti, C. (2018). Industry 4.0 in management studies: A systematic literature review. *Sustainability*, *10*(10), 3821. doi:10.3390u10103821

Pieroni, M. P. P., McAloone, T. C., & Pigosso, D. C. A. (2019). Business model innovation for circular economy and sustainability: A review of approaches. *Journal of Cleaner Production*, *215*, 198–216. doi:10.1016/j.jclepro.2019.01.036

Pietrykowski, B. (2004). You are what you eat: The social economy of the slow food movement. *Review of Social Economy*, *62*(3), 307–321. doi:10.1080/0034676042000253927

Pilditch, J. (1957). *The silent salesman*. London, UK: Harper and Row.

Pivato, S., Misani, N., & Tencati, A. (2008). The impact of corporate social responsibility on consumer trust: The case of organic food. *Business Ethics (Oxford, England)*, 3–12.

Plambeck, E. L., Lee, H. L., & Yatsko, P. (2012). Improving environmental performance in your Chinese supply chain. *MIT Sloan Management Review*, *53*(2), 43–52.

Plouffe, S., Lanoie, P., Berneman, C., & Vernier, M. F. (2011). Economic benefits tied to ecodesign. *Journal of Cleaner Production*, *19*(6-7), 573–579. doi:10.1016/j.jclepro.2010.12.003

Pomponi, F., & Moncaster, A. (2017). Circular economy for the built environment: A research framework. *Journal of Cleaner Production*, *143*, 710–718. doi:10.1016/j.jclepro.2016.12.055

Pookulangara, S., & Shephard, A. (2013). Slow fashion movement: Understanding consumer perceptions— An exploratory study. *Journal of Retailing and Consumer Services*, *20*(2), 200–206. doi:10.1016/j.jretconser.2012.12.002

Pookulangara, S., Shephard, A., & Mestres, J. (2011). University community's perception of sweatshops: A mixed method data collection. *International Journal of Consumer Studies*, *35*(4), 476–483. doi:10.1111/j.1470-6431.2010.00950.x

Poponi, S., Colantoni, A., Cividino, S., & Mosconi, E. (2019). The stakeholders' perspective within the B corp certification for a circular approach. *Sustainability*, *11*(6), 1584. doi:10.3390u11061584

Porter, M. & Kramer, M. (2011). Creating shared value, *Harvard Business Review*, Jan-Feb, 1-17.

Porter, M. E. (1991). America's green strategy. *Scientific American*, *264*(4), 168. doi:10.1038cientificamerican0491-168

Porter, M. E., & Heppelmann, J. E. (2014). How smart, connected products are transforming competition. *Harvard Business Review*, *92*(11), 64–88.

Porter, M. E., & Kramer, M. (2011). Creating shared value. How to reinvent capitalism and unleash the wave of innovation and growth. *Harvard Business Review*, *89*, 62–77.

Porter, M. E., & Kramer, M. R. (2002). The competitive advantage of corporate philanthropy. *Harvard Business Review*, *80*(12), 56–68.

Porter, M. E., & Kramer, M. R. (2011). Creating shared value: How to reinvent capitalism - and unleash a wave of innovation and growth. *Harvard Business Review*, *89*(1/2), 62–77.

Porter, M., & Kramer, M. (2006). Strategy and society: the link between competitive advantage and corporate social responsibility. *Harvard Business Review*, (December): 78–93.

Powell, W. W. (1990). Neither market nor hierarchy. *Research in Organizational Behavior*, *12*, 295–336.

Prahalad & Ramaswamy. (2003). Experience Innovation. *MIT Sloan Business Review*, *44*(4), 12-18.

Prahalad, C. K. (2005). *The fortune at the bottom of the pyramid, Pearson Education, Inc*. Upper Saddle River, NJ: Publishing as Warthon School Publishing.

Prahalad, C. K., & Ramaswamy, V. (2000). Co-Opting Customer Competence. *Harvard Business Review*, 79–87.

Prahalad, C. K., & Ramaswamy, V. (2003). The new frontier of experience innovation. *MIT Sloan Management Review*, *44*, 4, 12–18.

Prahalad, C. K., & Ramaswamy, V. (2004). *The future of competition: Co-creating unique value with customers*. Boston, MA: Harvard Business School Publishing.

Prahalad, C. K., & Ramaswamy, V.The Experience Economy. (2004). *Work is Theatre & Every Business a Stage*. Boston: Harvard Business School Press.

Prause, G. (2015). Sustainable Business Models and Structures for Industry 4.0. *Journal of Secure Sustainability*, *5*(2), 159–169. doi:10.9770/jssi.2015.5.2(3)

Prause, G., & Atari, S. (2017). On sustainable production networks for Industry 4.0. *Entrepreneurship and Sustainability Issues*, *4*(4), 421–431. doi:10.9770/jesi.2017.4.4(2)

Prendergast, P. G. and Pitt, L. (1996). Packaging, marketing, logistics and the environment: are there trade-offs? *International Journal of Physical Distribution & Logistics Management, 26*(6), pp. 60-72.

Presenza, A., Messeni Petruzzelli, A., & Natalicchio, A. (2019). Business model innovation for sustainability. Highlights from the tourism and hospitality industry. *Sustainability*, *11*(1), 212–216. doi:10.3390u11010212

PricewaterhouseCoopers. P. W. C. (2011). Millennials at work. Reshaping the workplace. Retrieved from http://www.pwc.ru/en_RU/ru/hr-consulting/publications/assets/millenials-survey.pdf

Prieto-Sandoval, V., Jaca, C., & Ormazabal, M. (2018). Towards a consensus on the circular economy. *Journal of Cleaner Production*, *179*, 605–615. doi:10.1016/j.jclepro.2017.12.224

Pui-Yan Ho, H., & Choi, T.-M. (2012). A five-R analysis for sustainable fashion supply chain management in Hong Kong: A case analysis. *Journal of Fashion Marketing and Management: An International Journal*, *16*(2), 161–175. doi:10.1108/13612021211222815

Pujari, D. & Wright, G. H. (1999). *Management of environmental new product development.*

Putrevu, S. (2008). Consumer responses toward sexual and nonsexual appeals: The influence of involvement, need for cognition (NFC), and gender. *Journal of Advertising*, *37*(2), 57–70. doi:10.2753/JOA0091-3367370205

Qorri, A., Mujkić, A., & Kraslawski, A. (2018). A conceptual framework for measuring sustainability performance of supply chains. *Journal of Cleaner Production*, *189*, 570–584. doi:10.1016/j.jclepro.2018.04.073

Raabe, B., Low, J. S. C., Juraschek, M., Herrmann, C., Tjandra, T. B., Ng, Y. T., & Tan, Y. S. (2017). Collaboration platform for enabling industrial symbiosis: Application of the by-product exchange network model. *Procedia CIRP*, *61*, 263–268. doi:10.1016/j.procir.2016.11.225

Raghubir, P., & Greenleaf, E. A. (2006). Ratios in proportion: What should the shape of the package be? *Journal of Marketing*, *70*(2), 95–107. doi:10.1509/jmkg.70.2.095

Rahbar, E. & Wahid, N. A. (2011). Investigación del efecto de las herramientas de marketing verde 'en el comportamiento de compra de los consumidores. *Serie de estrategia empresarial, 12*(2), 73-83. doi:10.1108/17515631111114877

Rahimnia, F., Moghadasian, M., & Castka, P. (2009). Benchmarking leagility in mass services: The case of a fast food restaurant chains in Iran. *Benchmarking: An International Journal*, *16*(6), 799–816. doi:10.1108/14635770911000123

Rajput, S., & Singh, S. P. (2019). Connecting circular economy and industry 4.0. *International Journal of Information Management*, *49*, 98–113. doi:10.1016/j.ijinfomgt.2019.03.002

Ramaswamy, V., & Gouillart, F. (2010). Building the co-creative enterprise. *Harvard Business Review*, (October): 100–109.

Ramaswamy, V., & Ozcan, K. (2014). *The co-creation paradigm*. Stanford University Press.

Ramaswamy, V., & Ozcan, K. (2014). *The Co-creation Paradigm*. Stanford, CA: Stanford University Press.

Randstad. (2017). Smart manufacturing: grazie a siemens, adidas realizza l'industry 4.0. May 30, 2017. Retrieved from https://www.randstad.it/knowledge360/news-aziende/smart-manufacturing-grazie-a-siemens-adidas-realizza-lindustry-40/

Rani, A., Aravind, J., & Prasad, T. (2014). Green marketing and its impact. *European Centre for Research Training and Development UK, 2*(8), 45-48. Obtenido de http://www.eajournals.org/wp-content/uploads/Green-Marketing-and-Its-Impact1.pdf

Ranta, V., Aarikka-Stenroos, L., & Mäkinen, S. J. (2018). Creating value in the circular economy: A structured multiple-case analysis of business models. *Journal of Cleaner Production*, *201*, 988–1000. doi:10.1016/j.jclepro.2018.08.072

Rao, V. R. (2014). *Applied conjoint analysis*. New York, NY: Springer. doi:10.1007/978-3-540-87753-0

Rarick, C., Falk, G., & Barczyk, C. (2012). The little bee that could: Jollibee of the Philippines v. Mcdonald's. *Journal of the International Academy for Case Studies*, *18*(3), 83.

Rauch, E., Dallasega, P., & Matt, D. T. (2017). Distributed manufacturing network models of smart and agile mini-factories. *International Journal of Agile Systems and Management*, *10*(3-4), 185–205. doi:10.1504/IJASM.2017.088534

Raut, R. D., Mangla, S. K., Narwane, V. S., Gardas, B. B., Priyadarshinee, P., & Narkhede, B. E. (2019). Linking big data analytics and operational sustainability practices for sustainable business management. *Journal of Cleaner Production*, *224*, 10–24. doi:10.1016/j.jclepro.2019.03.181

Rayport, J. F., & Jaworski, B. J. (2001). *Cases in e-Commerce*. Boston, MA: McGraw-Hill/Irwin.

Rebitzer, G., Ekvall, T., Frischknecht, R., Hunkeler, D., Norris, G., Rydberg, T., & Pennington, D. W. (2004). Life cycle assessment: Part 1: Framework, goal and scope definition, inventory analysis, and applications. *Environment International*, *30*(5), 701–720. doi:10.1016/j.envint.2003.11.005 PMID:15051246

Reike, D., Vermeulen, W. J. V., & Witjes, S. (2018). The circular economy: New or Refurbished as CE 3.0? — Exploring controversies in the conceptualization of the circular economy through a focus on history and resource value retention options. *Resources, Conservation and Recycling*, *135*(August 2017), 246–264. doi:10.1016/j.resconrec.2017.08.027

Reinhardt, F. L. (1998). Environmental product differentiation: Implications for corporate strategy. *California Management Review*, *40*(4), 43–73. doi:10.2307/41165964

Reischauer, G. (2018). Industry 4.0 as policy-driven discourse to institutionalize innovation systems in manufacturing. *Technological Forecasting and Social Change*, *132*, 26–33. doi:10.1016/j.techfore.2018.02.012

Remmen, A., Jensen, A. A., & Frydendal, J. (2007). *Life cycle management. A business guide to sustainability*. UNEP DTIE.

Ren, S., He, D., Zhang, T., & Chen, X. (2019). Symbolic reactions or substantive pro-environmental behavior? An empirical study of corporate environmental performance under the government's environmental subsidy scheme. *Business Strategy and the Environment*, in press. doi:10.1002/bse.2308

Renewable Energy Policy Network for the 21st Century (REN21). (2019). Renewables 2019 Global Status Report. Paris, REN21 Secretariat.

Rennings, K., Ziegler, A., Ankeleb, K., & Hoffmann, E. (2006). The influence of different characteristics of the EU environmental management and auditing scheme on technical environmental innovations and economic performance. *Ecological Economics*, *57*(1), 45–59. doi:10.1016/j.ecolecon.2005.03.013

Rennung, F., Luminosu, C. T., & Draghici, A. (2016). Service Provision in the framework of Industry 4.0. *Procedia: Social and Behavioral Sciences*, *221*, 372–377. doi:10.1016/j.sbspro.2016.05.127

Repubblica, D. (2019). Moda sostenibile: da trend a realtà. La richiesta di abiti etici cresce in tutto il mondo, 9 aprile. Retrieved from https://d.repubblica.it/moda/2019/04/09

Rettie, R., & Brewer, C. (2000). The verbal and visual components of package design. *Journal of Product and Brand Management*, *9*(1), 56–70. doi:10.1108/10610420010316339

Rio, M., Riel, A., & Brissaud, D. (2017). Design to environment: information model characteristics. *Procedia CIRP*, *60*, 494–499. doi:10.1016/j.procir.2017.02.006

Rivas-Asanza, W., Celleri-Pacheco, J., Andrade-Garda, J., García-Vázquez, R., Mato-Abad, V., Rodríguez-Yáñez, S., & Suárez-Garaboa, S. (2018). Environmental sustainability in information technologies governance. *Sustainability*, *10*(12), 4792. doi:10.3390u10124792

Rivera, J. J., Bigne, E., & Curras-Perez, R. (2016). Effects of corporate social responsibility perception on consumer satisfaction with the brand. *Spanish Journal of Marketing-ESIC*, *20*(2), 104–114. doi:10.1016/j.sjme.2016.06.002

Roberts, J. A. (1996). Green consumers in the 1990s: Profile and implications for advertising. *Journal of Business Research*, *36*(3), 217–231. doi:10.1016/0148-2963(95)00150-6

Robinson, C. J., & Malhotra, M. K. (2005). Defining the concept of supply chain quality management and its relevance to academic and industrial practice. *International Journal of Production Economics*, *96*(3), 315–337. doi:10.1016/j.ijpe.2004.06.055

Rockström, J., Steffen, W., Noone, K., Persson, Å., Chapin, F. S., Lambin, E., ... Foley, J. (2009). Planetary boundaries: exploring the safe operating space for humanity. *Ecology and Society*, *14*(2), 32. doi:10.5751/ES-03180-140232

Rodič, B. (2017). Industry 4.0 and the New Simulation Modelling Paradigm. *Organizacija*, *50*(3), 193–207. doi:10.1515/orga-2017-0017

Rodrigo, I., Cristóvão, A., Tibério, M. L., Baptista, A., Maggione, L., & Pires, M. (2015). The Portuguese agrifood traditional products: Main constraints and challenges. *Revista de Economia e Sociologia Rural*, *53*(suppl 1), 23–32. doi:10.1590/1234-56781806-94790053s01002

Rodríguez-López, M. E., Alcántara-Pilar, J. M., & Ahmed-Laroussi, A. (2018). La estrategia de estandarización de Mcdonald´ s.¿ es valorada del mismo modo en todos los países? El caso de los jóvenes en España, Turquía, Italia y Bulgaria. *Globalización, Competitividad y Gobernabilidad de Georgetown/Universia, 12*(3).

Rodriguez-Melo, A., & Mansouri, S. A. (2011). Stakeholder engagement: Defining strategic advantage for sustainable construction. *Business Strategy and the Environment, 20*(8), 539–552. doi:10.1002/bse.715

Rokka, J., & Uusitalo, L. (2008). Preference for green packaging in consumer product choices–do consumers care? *International Journal of Consumer Studies, 32*(5), 516–525. doi:10.1111/j.1470-6431.2008.00710.x

Rong, K., Hu, G., Lin, Y., Shi, Y., & Guo, L. (2015). Understanding business ecosystem using a 6C framework in Internet-of-Things-based sectors. *International Journal of Production Economics, 159*, 41–55. doi:10.1016/j.ijpe.2014.09.003

Rosa, P., Sassanelli, C., & Terzi, S. (2019). Towards circular business models: A systematic literature review on classification frameworks and archetypes. *Journal of Cleaner Production, 236*, 117696. doi:10.1016/j.jclepro.2019.117696

Rossi, M., Germani, M., & Zamagni, A. (2016). Review of ecodesign methods and tools. Barriers and strategies for an effective implementation in industrial companies. *Journal of Cleaner Production, 129*, 361–373. doi:10.1016/j.jclepro.2016.04.051

Roulet, T., & Touboul, S. (2015). The intentions with which the road is paved: Attitudes to liberalism as determinants of greenwashing. *Journal of Business Ethics, 128*(2), 305–320. doi:10.100710551-014-2097-8

Royne, M. B., Martinez, M., Oakley, J., & Fox, A. K. (2012). The effectiveness of benefit type and price endings in green advertising. *Journal of Advertising, 41*(4), 85–102. doi:10.1080/00913367.2012.10672459

Rozensher, S. (2013). The growth of cause marketing: past, current, and future trends. [JBER]. *Journal of Business & Economics Research, 11*(4), 181–186. doi:10.19030/jber.v11i4.7746

Ruggieri, A., Mosconi, E. M., & Poponi, S. (2018). Can the B corp certification activate the circular economy pathway in a multiple stakeholder perspective? In *ISDRS - The 24th Annual Conference, Actions for a Sustainable World: from theory to practice.*

Ruggieri, A., Mosconi, E. M., & Poponi, S. (2018). The B corp certification as a standard of the entrepreneurial pathway towards the circular economy perspective. In *XXVIII National Congress of Commodity Sciences, Firenze, Italy, Feb. 21-23, 2018.*

Ruggieri, A., Braccini, A. M., Poponi, S., & Mosconi, E. M. (2016). A meta-model of inter-organisational cooperation for the transition to a circular economy. *Sustainability (Switzerland), 8*(11). doi:10.3390u8111153

Rundh, B. (2005). The multi-faceted dimension of packaging: Marketing logistic or marketing tool? *British Food Journal, 107*(9), 670–684. doi:10.1108/00070700510615053

Rundh, B. (2009). Packaging design: Creating competitive advantage with product packaging. *British Food Journal, 111*(9), 988–1002. doi:10.1108/00070700910992880

Rupo, D., Perano, M. & Vargas-Sanchez, A. (2018). A framework based on sustainability, open innovation, and value cocreation paradigms—a case in an Italian maritime cluster. *Sustainability, 10*(3), 729. 1-28. doi:10.3390u10030729

Russo Spena, T., & De Chiara, A. (2012). CSR, innovation strategy and supply chain management: Toward an integrated perspective. *International Journal of Technology Management, 58*(1/2), 83–108. doi:10.1504/IJTM.2012.045790

Rydell, S. A., Harnack, L. J., Oakes, J. M., Story, M., Jeffery, R. W., & French, S. A. (2008). Why eat at fast-food restaurants: Reported reasons among frequent consumers. *Journal of the American Dietetic Association, 108*(12), 2066–2070. doi:10.1016/j.jada.2008.09.008 PMID:19027410

Ryu, K., & Han, H. (2010). Influence of the quality of food, service, and physical environment on customer satisfaction and behavioral intention in quick-casual restaurants: Moderating role of perceived price. *Journal of Hospitality & Tourism Research (Washington, D.C.), 34*(3), 310–329. doi:10.1177/1096348009350624

Saarijärvi, H., Kannan, P. K., & Kuusela, H. (2013). Value co-creation: Theoretical approaches and practical implications. *European Business Review, 25*(1), 1, 6–19. doi:10.1108/09555341311287718

Saba, A., Vassallo, M., Shepherd, R., Lampila, P., Arvola, A., Dean, M., ... Lähteenmäki, L. (2010). Country-wise differences in perception of health-related messages in cereal based food products. *Food Quality and Preference, 21*(4), 385–393. doi:10.1016/j.foodqual.2009.09.007

Sabath, R., & Fontanella, J. (2002). The unfulfilled promise of supply chain collaboration. *Supply Chain Management Review, 6*(4), 24–29.

Sadorsky, P. (2009). Renewable energy consumption and income in emerging economies. *Energy Policy, 37*(10), 4021–4028. doi:10.1016/j.enpol.2009.05.003

Salah, B., Abidi, M. H., Mian, S. H., Krid, M., Alkhalefah, H., & Abdo, A. (2019). Virtual Reality-Based Engineering Education to Enhance Manufacturing Sustainability in Industry 4.0. *Sustainability, 11*(5), 1477. doi:10.3390u11051477

Saleh, F., & Ryan, C. (1991). Analysing service quality in the hospitality industry using the SERVQUAL model. *Service Industries Journal, 11*(3), 324–345. doi:10.1080/02642069100000049

Salim, R. A., & Rafiq, S. (2012). Why do some emerging economies proactively accelerate the adoption of renewable energy? *Energy Economics, 34*(4), 1051–1057. doi:10.1016/j.eneco.2011.08.015

Salmones, M., Crespo, A., & Bosque, I. (2005). Influence of corporate social responsibility on loyalty and valuation of services. *Journal of Business Ethics, 61*(4), 369–385. doi:10.100710551-005-5841-2

Salmones, M. D. M. G. D., Perez, A., & Bosque, I. R. D. (2009). The social role of financial companies as a determinant of consumer behavior. *International Journal of Bank Marketing, 27*(6), 467–485. doi:10.1108/02652320910988339

Sammer, K., & Wüstenhagen, R. (2005). The influence of eco-labeling on consumer behavior–results of a discrete choice analysis. *Business Strategy and the Environment*, 1–28.

Santouridis, I., & Trivellas, P. (2010). Investigating the impact of service quality and customer satisfaction on customer loyalty in mobile telephony in Greece. *The TQM Journal, 22*(3), 330–343. doi:10.1108/17542731011035550

Sarkis, J., Zhu, Q., & Lai, K. H. (2011). An organizational theoretic review of green supply chain management literature. *International Journal of Production Economics, 130*(1), 1–15. doi:10.1016/j.ijpe.2010.11.010

Sasson, A., & Johnson, J. C. (2016). The 3D printing order: Variability, supercenters and supply chain configurations. *International Journal of Physical Distribution & Logistics Management, 46*(1), 82–94. doi:10.1108/IJPDLM-10-2015-0257

Savastano, M., Amendola, C., Bellini, F., & D'Ascenzo, F. (2019). Contextual Impacts on Industrial Processes Brought by the Digital Transformation of Manufacturing: A Systematic Review. *Sustainability, 11*(3), 891. doi:10.3390u11030891

Schaltegger, S., Lüdeke-Freund, F., & Hansen, E. G. (2012). Business cases for sustainability: the role of business model innovation for corporate sustainability. *International Journal of Innovation and Sustainable Development, 6*(2), 95-119.

Schaltegger, S., Hansen, E. G., & Lüdeke-Freund, F. (2016). Business models for sustainability: Origins, present research, and future avenues. *Organization & Environment, 29*(1), 3–10. doi:10.1177/1086026615599806

Schamel, G. (2007). Auction markets for specialty food products with geographical indications. *Agricultural Economics, 37*(2-3), 257–264. doi:10.1111/j.1574-0862.2007.00272.x

Scharl, S., & Praktiknjo, A. (2019). The Role of a Digital Industry 4.0 in a Renewable Energy System. *International Journal of Energy Research, 43*(8), 3891–3904. doi:10.1002/er.4462

Schlechtendahl, J., Keinert, M., Kretschmer, F., Lechler, A., & Verl, A. (2015). Making Existing Production Systems Indutry 4.0-ready, production. *Engineering, 9*(1), 143–148.

Schmidt, M.-C., Veile, J. W., Müller, J. M., & Voigt, K.-I. (2019). *Kick-start for connectivity – How to implement digital platforms successfully.* Paper presented at the International Society for Professional Innovation Management (ISPIM) Innovation Conference, Florence, Italy.

Schmidt, R., Möhring, M., Härting, R. C., Reichstein, C., Neumaier, P., & Jozinović, P. (2015). Industry 4.0 - Potentials for Creating Smart Products: Empirical Research Results. In W. Abramowicz (Ed.), *Business Information Systems, 18th International Conference, BIS.* Poznan, Poland: Springer International Publishing.

Schneider, A., & Meins, E. (2013). Two dimensions of corporate sustainability assessment: Towards a comprehensive framework. *Business Strategy and the Environment, 21*(4), 211–222. doi:10.1002/bse.726

Schoolman, E. D., Bush, J. S., & Bell, K. F. (2012). How interdisciplinary is sustainability research? Analyzing the structure of an emerging scientific field. *Sustainability Science, 7*(1), 67–80. doi:10.100711625-011-0139-z

Schoormans, J., & Robben, H. (1997). The effect of new package design on product attention, categorization and evaluation. *Journal of Economic Psychology, 8*(2/3), 271–287. doi:10.1016/S0167-4870(97)00008-1

Schuhwerk, M. E., & Lefkoff-Hagius, R. (1995). Green or non-green? Does type of appeal matter when advertising a green product? *Journal of Advertising, 24*(2), 45–54. doi:10.1080/00913367.1995.10673475

Sciarelli, S. (1999). Responsabilità sociale ed etica d'impresa: una relazione finalizzata allo sviluppo aziendale, *Finanza, Marketing e Produzione, 17(1).*

Sciarelli, S. (2007). *Etica e responsabilità sociale nell'impresa.* Milano, Italy: Giuffrè Editore.

Selnes, F. (1993). An examination of the effect of product performance on brand reputation, satisfaction and loyalty. *European Journal of Marketing, 27*(9), 19–35. doi:10.1108/03090569310043179

Sénéchal, O. (2018). Performance indicators nomenclatures for decision making in sustainable conditions based maintenance. *IFAC-PapersOnLine, 51*(11), 1137–1142. doi:10.1016/j.ifacol.2018.08.438

Sen, S., & Bhattacharya, C. (2001). Does doing good always lead to doing better? Consumer reactions to corporate social responsibility. *Journal of Marketing Research, 38*(2), 225–243. doi:10.1509/jmkr.38.2.225.18838

Shafer, S. M., Smitha, H. J., & Linder, J. C. (2005). The power of business models. *Business Horizons, 48*(3), 199–207. doi:10.1016/j.bushor.2004.10.014

Shaheen, S. (2015). Mobility + sharing economy: past, present and future. (2015). *International Sharing Economy Symposium. Utrecht,* The Netherlands.

Shaheen, S., Meyn, M., & Wipyewski, K. (2003). US shared-use vehicle survey findings on carsharing and station car growth: Obstacles and opportunities. *Transportation Research Record: Journal of the Transportation Research Board,* (1841), 90-98.

Shaheen, S. A., & Cohen, A. P. (2007). Growth in worldwide carsharing: An international comparison. *Transportation Research Record: Journal of the Transportation Research Board, 1992*(1), 81–89. doi:10.3141/1992-10

Shaheen, S. A., & Cohen, A. P. (2013). Carsharing and personal vehicle services: Worldwide market developments and emerging trends. *International Journal of Sustainable Transportation, 7*(1), 5–34. doi:10.1080/15568318.2012.660103

Shankar, V., Smith, A. K., & Rangaswamy, A. (2003). Customer satisfaction and loyalty in online and offline environments. *International Journal of Research in Marketing, 20*(2), 153–175. doi:10.1016/S0167-8116(03)00016-8

Shapiro, C., & Varian, H. R. (1999). *Information rules: A strategic guide to the network economy*. Boston, MA: Harvard Business School Press.

Shaw, D. S., & Connolly, J. (2006). Identifying fair trade in consumption choice. *Journal of Strategic Marketing, 14*(4), 353–368. doi:10.1080/09652540600960675

She, B. (2014). Sustainable fashion supply chain: Lessons from H&M. *Sustainability, 6*(9), 6236–6249. doi:10.3390u6096236

Shen, B., Wang, Y., Lo, C., & Shum, M. (2012). The impact of ethical fashion on consumer purchase behaviour. *Journal of Fashion Marketing and Management, 16*(2), 234–245. doi:10.1108/13612021211222842

Shen, B., Zheng, J. H., Chow, P. S., & Chow, K. Y. (2014). Perception of fashion sustainability in online community. *Journal of the Textile Institute, 105*(9), 971–979. doi:10.1080/00405000.2013.866334

Sheth, J. N., Sethia, N. K., & Srinivas, S. (2011). Mindful consumption: A customer-centric approach to sustainability. *Journal of the Academy of Marketing Science, 39*(1), 21–39. doi:10.100711747-010-0216-3

Siggelkow, N. (2007). Persuasion with case studies. *Academy of Management Journal, 50*(1), 20–24. doi:10.5465/amj.2007.24160882

Silayoi, P., & Speece, M. (2004). Packaging and purchase decisions: A focus group study on the impact of involvement level and time pressure. *British Food Journal, 106*(8), 607–628. doi:10.1108/00070700410553602

Silayoi, P., & Speece, M. (2007). The importance of packaging attributes: A conjoint analysis approach. *European Journal of Marketing, 41*(11/12), 1495–1517. doi:10.1108/03090560710821279

Silverman, D. (2008). *Qualitative Research: Theory, Method and Practice*. Sage.

Silverman, D. (2011). *Qualitative Research*. London, UK: Sage.

Simmonds, G., Woods, A. T., & Spence, C. (2018). 'Show me the goods': Assessing the effectiveness of transparent packaging vs. product imagery on product evaluation. *Food Quality and Preference, 63*, 18–27. doi:10.1016/j.foodqual.2017.07.015

Singh, N., Jain, S., & Sharma, P. (2015). Motivations for implementing environmental management practices in Indian industries. *Ecological Economics, 109*, 1–8. doi:10.1016/j.ecolecon.2014.11.003

Siri, G. (2001). *La psiche del consumo. Consumatori, desiderio e identità*. Milano, Italy: Franco Angeli.

Sjödin, D. R., Parida, V., Leksell, M., & Petrovic, A. (2018). Smart Factory Implementation and Process Innovation: A Preliminary Maturity Model for Leveraging Digitalization in Manufacturing Moving to smart factories presents specific challenges that can be addressed through a structured approach focused on people, processes, and technologies. *Research Technology Management, 61*(5), 22–31. doi:10.1080/08956308.2018.1471277

Smith, T. J., & Nichols, T. (2015). Understanding the millennial generation. *Journal of Business Diversity, 15*(1), 39.

Sobrero, R. (2016). *Comunicazione e sostenibilità*. Milano, Italy: Egea.

Sogari, G., Pucci, T., Aquilani, B., & Zanni, L. (2017). Millennial generation and environmental sustainability: The role of social media in the consumer purchasing behavior for wine. *Sustainability, 9*(10), 1911. doi:10.3390u9101911

Solomon, M. R., Bamossy, G. J., Askegaard, S. T., & Hogg, M. K. (2013). *Consumer behaviour - A European perspective* (5th ed.). Harlow, UK: Pearson Education.

Sommer, L. (2015). Industrial revolution-industry 4.0: Are German manufacturing SMEs the first victims of this revolution? *Journal of Industrial Engineering and Management, 8*(5), 1512–1532. doi:10.3926/jiem.1470

Song, S., & Ko, E. (2017). Perceptions, attitudes, and behaviors toward sustainable fashion: Application of Q and Q-R methodologies. *International Journal of Consumer Studies, 41*(3), 264–273. doi:10.1111/ijcs.12335

Sonnemann, G., & Margni, M. (Eds.). (n.d.). *Life cycle management, LCA compendium.* The Complete World of Life Cycle Assessment.

Sousa-Zomer, T. T., Magalhães, L., Zancul, E., Campos, L. M. S., & Cauchick-Miguel, P. A. (2018). Cleaner production as an antecedent for circular economy paradigm shift at the micro-level: Evidence from a home appliance manufacturer. *Journal of Cleaner Production, 185*, 740–748. doi:10.1016/j.jclepro.2018.03.006

Stachová, K., Papula, J., Stacho, Z., & Kohnová, L. (2019). External partnerships in employee education and development as the key to facing industry 4.0 challengesn. *Sustainability, 11*(2), 345. doi:10.3390u11020345

Stanisavljević, M. (2017). Does customer loyalty depend on corporate social responsibility?. *Naše gospodarstvo/Our economy, 63*(1), 38-46.

Stark, R., Grosser, H., Beckmann-Dobrev, B., & Kind, S. (2014). Advanced technologies in life cycle engineering. *Procedia CIRP, 22*, 3–14. doi:10.1016/j.procir.2014.07.118

Steenkamp, J. B. E. (1989). *Product quality: An investigation into the concept and how it is perceived by consumers.* Wageningen, The Netherlands: Wageningen Academic Publisher.

Steenkamp, J. B. E., & Van Trijp, H. C. (1996). Quality guidance: A consumer-based approach to food quality improvement using partial least squares. *European Review of Agriculture Economics, 23*(2), 195–215. doi:10.1093/erae/23.2.195

Steffen, W., Richardson, K., Rockström, J., Cornell, S. E., Fetzer, I., Bennett, E. M., ... Sörlin, S. (2015). Planetary boundaries: Guiding human development on a changing planet. *Science, 347*(6223). doi:10.1126cience.1259855 PMID:25592418

Stewart, B. (2004). *Packaging design strategies* (2nd ed.). The UK: Pira International Ltd.

Stock, T., Obenaus, M., Kunz, S., & Kohl, H. (2018). Industry 4.0 as enabler for a sustainable development: A qualitative assessment of its ecological and social potential. *Process Safety and Environmental Protection, 118*, 254–267. doi:10.1016/j.psep.2018.06.026

Stock, T., & Seliger, G. (2016). *Opportunities of sustainable manufacturing in industry 4.0. In Procedia CIRP* (Vol. 40, pp. 536–541). Amsterdam, Netherlands: Elsevier.

Stock, T., & Seliger, G. (2016). Opportunities of sustainable manufacturing in Industry 4.0. *Procedia Cirp, 40*, 536–541. doi:10.1016/j.procir.2016.01.129

Stone, R. N., & Grønhaug, K. (1993). Perceived risk: Further considerations for the marketing discipline. *European Journal of Marketing, 27*(3), 39–50. doi:10.1108/03090569310026637

Strandhagen, J. O., Vallandingham, L. R., Fragapane, G., Strandhagen, J. W., Stangeland, A. B. H., & Sharma, N. (2017). Logistics 4.0 and emerging sustainable business models. *Advances in Manufacturing, 5*(4), 359–369. doi:10.100740436-017-0198-1

Strauss, A., & Corbin, J. (1998). *Basics of qualitative research techniques.* Thousand Oaks, CA: Sage.

Strong, C. (1996). Features contributing to the growth of ethical consumerism – a preliminary investigation. *Marketing Intelligence & Planning, 14*(5), 5–13. doi:10.1108/02634509610127518

Stubbs, W. (2017). Characterising B corps as a sustainable business model: An exploratory study of B corps in Australia. *Journal of Cleaner Production, 144*, 299–312. doi:10.1016/j.jclepro.2016.12.093

Su, L., Pan, Y., & Chen, X. (2017). Corporate social responsibility: Findings from the Chinese hospitality industry. *Journal of Retailing and Consumer Services, 34*, 240–247. doi:10.1016/j.jretconser.2016.10.013

Supanti, D., & Butcher, K. (2019). Is corporate social responsibility (CSR) participation the pathway to foster meaningful work and helping behavior for millennials? *International Journal of Hospitality Management, 77*, 8–18. doi:10.1016/j.ijhm.2018.06.001

Swaen, V., & Vanhamme, J. (2005). The use of corporate social responsibility arguments in communication campaigns: does source credibility matter. *Advances in Consumer Research. Association for Consumer Research (U. S.), 32*, 590–591.

Szalavetz. (2018). Industry 4.0 and capability development in manufacturing subsidiaries. *Technological Forecasting and Social Change.*

Tachizawa, E. M., & Wong Chee, Y. (2015). Towards a theory of multi-tier sustainable supply chains: A systematic literature review. *Supply Chain Management, 19*(5/6), 643–663. doi:10.1108/SCM-02-2014-0070

Taddeo, R., Simboli, A., Ioppolo, G., & Morgante, A. (2017). Industrial symbiosis, networking and innovation: The potential role of innovation poles. *Sustainability, 9*(2), 169. doi:10.3390u9020169

Taghikhah, F., Voinov, A., & Shukla, N. (2019). Extending the supply chain to address sustainability. *Journal of Cleaner Production, 229*, 652–666. doi:10.1016/j.jclepro.2019.05.051

Tanner, C., & Wölfing Kast, S. (2003). Promoting sustainable consumption: Determinants of green purchases by Swiss consumers. *Psychology and Marketing, 20*(10), 883–902. doi:10.1002/mar.10101

Tan, S. J., & Tan, K. L. (2007). Antecedents and consequences of skepticism toward health claims: An empirical investigation of Singaporean consumers. *Journal of Marketing Communications, 13*(1), 59–82. doi:10.1080/13527260600963711

Tarigan, E., Prayogo, D. N., & Mardiono, L. (2012, July). Eco-sustainable campus initiatives: a web content analysis. In *The 3rd International Conference on Technology and Operations Management "Sustaining Competitiveness through Green Technology Management"* (Vol. 3, pp. 59-65). SBM ITB and UUM.

Teece, D. J. (2010). Business models, business strategy and innovation. *Long Range Planning, 43*(2–3), 172–194. doi:10.1016/j.lrp.2009.07.003

Tencati, A., & Zsolnai, L. (2008). The collaborative enterprise. *Journal of Business Ethics, 85*(3), 367–376. doi:10.100710551-008-9775-3

Tencati, A., & Zsolnai, L. (2012). Collaborative enterprise and sustainability: The case of slow food. *Journal of Business Ethics, 110*(3), 345–354. doi:10.100710551-011-1178-1

Testa, F., Battaglia, M., & Bianchi, L. (2012). The diffusion of CSR initiatives among SMEs in industrial clusters: Some findings from Italian experiences. *International Journal of Technology Management, 58*(1-2), 152–170. doi:10.1504/IJTM.2012.045793

Teuscher, P., Grüninger, B., & Ferdinand, N. (2006). Risk management in sustainable supply chain management (SSCM) lessons learnt from the case of GMO-free soybeans. *Corporate Social Responsibility and Environmental Management, 13*(1), 1–10. doi:10.1002/csr.81

Thapa, B. (2010). The mediation effect of outdoor recreation participation on environmental attitude–behavior correspondence. *The Journal of Environmental Education, 41*(3), 133–150. doi:10.1080/00958960903439989

The Natural Step. (2018). *Strategic Life Cycle Assessment (SLCA).* Available at https://thenaturalstep.org/wp-content/uploads/2018/01/SLCA-matrix-structure.pdf

Thoben, K. D., Wiesner, S., & Wuest, T. (2017). "Industrie 4.0" and smart manufacturing-a review of research issues and application examples. *International Journal of Automotive Technology, 11*(1), 4–16.

Tilson, D., Sørensen, C., & Lyytinen, K. (2012). Change and Control Paradoxes in Mobile Infrastructure Innovation: The Android and iOS Mobile Operating Systems Cases. *45th Hawaii International Conference on System Science (HICSS 45).* 10.1109/HICSS.2012.149

Timpanaro, G., Foti, V. T., Scuderi, A., Schippa, G., & Branca, F. (2018). New food supply chain systems based on a proximity model: The case of an alternative food network in the Catania urban area. *Acta Horticulturae*, (1215), 213–217. doi:10.17660/ActaHortic.2018.1215.39

Tischner, U., Schmincke, E., Rubik, F., & Prosler, M. (2000). *How to do ecodesign? - A guide for environmentally and economically sound design.* Berlin, Germany: German Federal Environmental Agency.

Tiwana, A., Konsynsky, B., & Bush, A. A. (2010). Platform Evolution: Coevolution of Platform Architecture, Governance, and Environmental Dynamics. *Information Systems Research, 21*(4), 675–687. doi:10.1287/isre.1100.0323

Tiwari, A. K. (2011). A structural VAR analysis of renewable energy consumption, real GDP and CO2 emissions: Evidence from India. *Economic Bulletin, 31*(2), 1793–1806.

Toniolo, S., Mazzi, A., Mazzarotto, G., & Scipioni A. (2019/a). International standards with a life cycle perspective: which dimension of sustainability is addressed? *International Journal of Life Cycle Assessment*, (in press). doi:10.100711367-019-01606-w

Toniolo, S., Mazzi, A., Simonetto, M., Zuliani, F., & Scipioni, A. (2019/b). Mapping diffusion of environmental product declarations released by European program operators. *Sustainable Production and Consumption*, 17, 85-94.

Triebswetter, U., & Wackerbauer, J. (2008a). Integrated environmental product innovation and impacts on company competitiveness: A case study of the automotive industry in the region of Munich. *European Environment, 18*(1), 30–44. doi:10.1002/eet.475

Triebswetter, U., & Wackerbauer, J. (2008b). Integrated environmental product innovation in the region of Munich and its impact on company competitiveness. *Journal of Cleaner Production, 16*(14), 1484–1493. doi:10.1016/j.jclepro.2007.09.003

Trimi, S., & Berbegal-Mirabent, J. (2012). Business model innovation in entrepreneurship. *The International Entrepreneurship and Management Journal, 8*(4), 449–465. doi:10.100711365-012-0234-3

Tsai, M. T., Chuang, L. M., Chao, S. T., & Chang, H. P. (2012). The effects assessment of firm environmental strategy and customer environmental conscious on green product development. *Environmental Monitoring and Assessment, 184*(7), 4435–4447. doi:10.100710661-011-2275-4 PMID:21818538

Tsai, W. H., & Lu, Y. H. (2018). A framework of production planning and control with carbon tax under industry 4.0. *Sustainability, 10*(9), 3221. doi:10.3390u10093221

Tsen, C. H., Phang, G., Hasan, H., & Buncha, M. R. (2006). Going green: A study of consumers' willingness to pay for green products in Kota Kinabalu. *International Journal of Business and Society*, *7*, 40–54.

Tseng, Jiao, & Wang. (2010). Design for mass personalization. *CIRP Annals Manufacturing Technology, 59*(1), 175-178.

Tseng, M. L., Chiu, A. S., Chien, C. F., & Tan, R. R. (2019). Pathways and barriers to circularity in food systems. *Resources, Conservation and Recycling*, *143*, 236–237. doi:10.1016/j.resconrec.2019.01.015

Tseng, M. L., Tan, R. R., Chiu, A. S., Chien, C. F., & Kuo, T. C. (2018). Circular economy meets industry 4.0: Can big data drive industrial symbiosis? *Resources, Conservation and Recycling*, *131*, 146–147. doi:10.1016/j.resconrec.2017.12.028

Tucker, P. (2006). Teaching the millennial generation. *The Futurist*, *40*(3), 7.

Tugcu, C. T., Ozturk, I., & Aslan, A. (2012). Renewable and non-renewable energy consumption and economic growth relationship revisited: Evidence from G7 countries. *Energy Economics*, *34*(6), 1942–1950. doi:10.1016/j.eneco.2012.08.021

Tukker, A. (2015). Product services for a resource-efficient and circular economy - A review. *Journal of Cleaner Production*, *97*, 76–91. doi:10.1016/j.jclepro.2013.11.049

Tuptuk, N., & Hailes, S. (2018). Security of smart manufacturing systems. *Journal of Manufacturing Systems*, *47*, 93–106. doi:10.1016/j.jmsy.2018.04.007

Turcu, C. (2013). Re-thinking sustainability indicators: Local perspectives of urban sustainability. *Journal of Environmental Planning and Management*, *56*(5), 1–25. doi:10.1080/09640568.2012.698984

Ülkü, M. A., & Hsuan, J. (2017). Towards sustainable consumption and production: Competitive pricing of modular products for green consumers. *Journal of Cleaner Production*, *142*, 4230–4242. doi:10.1016/j.jclepro.2016.11.050

Ullmann, A. (1985). Data in search of a theory: A critical examination of the relationship among social performance, social disclosure and economic performance of U.S. firms. *Academy of Management Review*, *10*, 540–557.

UN. (1992). *Report of the United Nations Conference on Environment and Development. Annex I - Rio Declaration on Environment and Development*. United Nations, Rio de Janeiro. Retrieved from https://www.un.org/documents/ga/conf151/aconf15126-1annex1.htm

UN. (2002). *Plan of implementation of the world summit on sustainable development. United Nations, UN Documents*, A/CONF.199/20. United Nations, Johannesburg. Retrieved from http://www.un-documents.net/jburgpln.htm

UN. (2014). Food and food waste. Available at https://www.unenvironment.org/explore-topics/resource-efficiency/what-we-do/sustainable-lifestyles/food-and-food-waste

Ünal, E., & Shao, J. (2019). A taxonomy of circular economy implementation strategies for manufacturing firms: Analysis of 391 cradle-to-cradle products. *Journal of Cleaner Production*, *212*, 754–765. doi:10.1016/j.jclepro.2018.11.291

Underwood, R. L., & Klein, N. M. (2002). Packaging as brand communication: Effects of product pictures on consumer responses to the package and Brand. *Journal of Marketing Theory and Practice*, *10*(4), 58–68. doi:10.1080/10696679.2002.11501926

Underwood, R. L., Klein, N. M., & Burke, R. R. (2001). Packaging communication: Attentional effects of product imagery. *Journal of Product and Brand Management*, *10*(7), 403–422. doi:10.1108/10610420110410531

UNEP. (2009). *SETAC. Guidelines for social life cycle assessment of products. United Nations Environment Programme (UNEP) and Society of Environmental Toxicology and Chemistry*. Belgium: SETAC.

UNIDO. (2007). *The UN global compact operational guide for medium-scale enterprise*. July.

United Nations Global Compact. (2010). *Supply chain sustainability. A practical guide for continuous improvement.*

United Nations Global Compact. (2015). Supply chain sustainability. A practical guide for continuous improvement, Second Edition.

Urbinati, A., Chiaroni, D., & Chiesa, V. (2017). Towards a new taxonomy of circular economy business models. *Journal of Cleaner Production, 168*, 487–498. doi:10.1016/j.jclepro.2017.09.047

Valdivia, S., Ugaya, C. M. L., Hildenbrand, J., Traverso, M., Mazijn, B., & Sonnemann, G. (2013). A UNEP/SETAC approach towards a life cycle sustainability assessment—Our contribution to Rio+20. *The International Journal of Life Cycle Assessment, 18*(9), 1673–1685. doi:10.100711367-012-0529-1

van den Brink, D., Odekerken-Schröder, G., & Pauwels, P. (2006). The effect of strategic and tactical cause-related marketing on consumers' brand loyalty. *Journal of Consumer Marketing, 23*(1), 15–2. doi:10.1108/07363760610641127

Van Heek, J., Arning, K., & Ziefle, M. (2017). Reduce, reuse, recycle: Acceptance of CO2-utilization for plastic products. *Energy Policy, 105*, 53–66. doi:10.1016/j.enpol.2017.02.016

Van Hemel, C., & Cramer, J. (2002). Barriers and stimuli for ecodesign in SMEs. *Journal of Cleaner Production, 10*(5), 439–453. doi:10.1016/S0959-6526(02)00013-6

Vanhaverbeke, W. & Cloodt, M. (2006). Open innovation in value networks. *Open innovation: Researching a new paradigm*, 258-281.

Vanhonacker, F., Verbeke, W., Guerrero, L., Claret, A., Contel, M., Scalvedi, L., ... Hersleth, M. (2010). How European consumers define the concept of traditional food: Evidence from a survey in six countries. *Agribusiness, 26*(4), 453–476. doi:10.1002/agr.20241

Varela, L., Araújo, A., Ávila, P., Castro, H., & Putnik, G. (2019). Evaluation of the Relation between Lean Manufacturing, Industry 4.0, and Sustainability. *Sustainability, 11*(5), 1439. doi:10.3390u11051439

Vargo, S. L., & Lush, R. F. (2008). Service-dominant logic: Continuing the evolution. *Journal of the Academy of Marketing Science, 36*(1), 1–10. doi:10.100711747-007-0069-6

Veile, J. W., Kiel, D., Müller, J. M., & Voigt, K.-I. (2019). *Ecosystem 4.0: A Supply Chain Perspective on Business Model Innovation.* Paper presented at the International Society for Professional Innovation Management (ISPIM) Innovation Conference, Florence, Italy.

Veleva, V., & Bodkin, G. (2018). Corporate-entrepreneur collaborations to advance a circular economy. *Journal of Cleaner Production, 188*, 20–37. doi:10.1016/j.jclepro.2018.03.196

Venables, W. N. & Smith, D. M. (2002). *An introduction to R.* Retrieved from http://cran.rproject.org/doc/manuals/R-intro. pdf

Venkatraman, N. V., El Sawy, O. A., Pavlou, P. A., & Bharadwaj, A. (2014). Theorizing digital business innovation: platforms and capabilities in ecosystems. *Fox School of Business Research Paper,* (15-080).

Venter, K., van der Merwe, D., de Beer, H., Kempen, E., & Bosman, M. (2011). Consumers perceptions of food packaging: An exploratory investigation in Potchefstroom, South Africa. *International Journal of Consumer Studies, 35*(3), 273–281. doi:10.1111/j.1470-6431.2010.00936.x

Vergura, D. T., & Luceri, B. (2018). Product packaging and consumers' emotional response. Does spatial representation influence product evaluation and choice? *Journal of Consumer Marketing, 35*(2), 218–227. doi:10.1108/JCM-12-2016-2021

Vermeir, I., & Verbeke, W. (2006). Sustainable food consumption: Exploring the consumer "attitude–behavioral intention" gap. *Journal of Agricultural & Environmental Ethics*, *19*(2), 169–194. doi:10.100710806-005-5485-3

Vermeir, I., & Verbeke, W. (2008). Sustainable food consumption among young adults in Belgium: Theory of planned behavior and the role of confidence and values. *Ecological Economics*, *64*(3), 542–553. doi:10.1016/j.ecolecon.2007.03.007

Vezzoli, C. (2007). *System design for sustainability. Theory, methods and tools for a sustainable "satisfaction-system" design*. Milan, Italy: Maggioli Editore.

Vildåsen, S. S., Keitsch, M., & Fet, A. M. (2017). Clarifying the epistemology of corporate sustainability. *Ecological Economics*, *138*, 40–46. doi:10.1016/j.ecolecon.2017.03.029

Vilnai-Yavetz, I., & Koren, R. (2013). Cutting through the clutter: Purchase intentions as a function of packaging instrumentality, aesthetics, and symbolism. *International Review of Retail, Distribution and Consumer Research*, *23*(4), 394–417. doi:10.1080/09593969.2013.792743

Visser, W. (2008). Corporate social responsibility in developing countries. In The Oxford handbook of corporate social responsibility.

Vrontis, D., Bresciani, S., & Giacosa, E. (2016). Tradition and innovation in Italian wine family businesses. *British Food Journal*, *118*(8), 1883–1897. doi:10.1108/BFJ-05-2016-0192

Vurro, C., Russo, A., & Perrini, F. (2009). Shaping sustainable value chains: Network determinants of supply chain governance models. *Journal of Business Ethics*, *90*(4), 607–621. doi:10.100710551-010-0595-x

Waibel, M. W., Oosthuizen, G. A., & du Toit, D. W. (2018). *Investigating current smart production innovations in the machine building industry on sustainability aspects. In Procedia Manufacturing* (Vol. 21, pp. 774–781). Amsterdam, Netherlands: Elsevier.

Waibel, M. W., Steenkamp, L. P., Moloko, N., & Oosthuizen, G. A. (2017). *Investigating the effects of smart production systems on sustainability elements. In Procedia Manufacturing* (Vol. 8, pp. 731–737). Amsterdam, Netherlands: Elsevier.

Wamba, S. F., Akter, S., Edwards, A., Chopin, G., & Gnanzou, D. (2015). How 'big data' can make big impact: Findings from a systematic review and a longitudinal case study. *International Journal of Production Economics*, *165*, 234–246. doi:10.1016/j.ijpe.2014.12.031

Wang, Y. & Fesenmaie, D. R. (2007). Collaborative destination marketing: A case study of Elkhart County, Indiana, *Tourism Management, 28*, 863-875.

Wang, S. T. E. (2013). The influence of visual packaging design on perceived food product quality, value, and brand preference. *International Journal of Retail & Distribution Management*, *41*(10), 805–816. doi:10.1108/IJRDM-12-2012-0113

Wang, S., Wan, J., Li, D., & Zhang, C. (2016). Implementing smart factory of industrie 4.0: An outlook. *International Journal of Distributed Sensor Networks*, *12*(1), 3159805. doi:10.1155/2016/3159805

Wang, Y., & Heitmeyer, J. (2006). Consumer attitude toward US versus domestic apparel in Taiwan. *International Journal of Consumer Studies*, *30*(1), 64–74. doi:10.1111/j.1470-6431.2005.00450.x

Wan, J., Cai, H., & Zhou, K. (2015). Industrie 4.0: Enabling Technologies. *International Conference on Intelligent Computing and Internet of Things (ICIST)*, 135-140.

Ward, D. O., Clark, C. D., Jensen, K. L., Yen, S. T., & Russell, C. S. (2011). Factors influencing willingness-to-pay for the ENERGY STAR® label. *Energy Policy*, *39*(3), 1450–1458. doi:10.1016/j.enpol.2010.12.017

WCED. (1987, December). Report of the World Commission on Environment and Development. *General Assembly Resolution, 42/187*, 11.

WEF. (2010). *Redesigning business value: A road map for sustainable consumption.* Geneva, Switzerland: World Economic Forum.

Weill, P., & Vitale, M. R. (2001). *Place to space. Migrating to eBusiness models.* Boston, MA: Harvard Business School Press.

Wei, Z., Song, W., & Wang, D. (2017). Manufacturing flexibility, business model design, and firm performance. *International Journal of Production Economics, 193*, 87–97. doi:10.1016/j.ijpe.2017.07.004

Weller, C., Kleer, R., & Piller, F. T. (2015). Economic implications of 3D printing: Market structure models in light of additive manufacturing revisited. *International Journal of Production Economics, 164*, 43–56. doi:10.1016/j.ijpe.2015.02.020

Werbach, A. (2009). *Strategy for sustainability: A business manifesto.* London, UK: McGraw-Hill.

Wiemer, J. & Plugge, L. (2007). Transparency in the supply chain GRI, *Briefing Paper*, July 23, 2007.

Wigley, S. (2008). Gauging consumers' responses to CSR activities: Does increased awareness make cents? *Public Relations Review, 34*(3), 306–308. doi:10.1016/j.pubrev.2008.03.034

Wijethilake, C. (2017). Proactive sustainability strategy and corporate sustainability performance: The mediating effect of sustainability control systems. *Journal of Environmental Management, 196*, 569–582. doi:10.1016/j.jenvman.2017.03.057 PMID:28351823

Wilburn, K., & Wilburn, R. (2014). The double bottom line: Profit and social benefit. *Business Horizons, 57*(1), 11–20. doi:10.1016/j.bushor.2013.10.001

Williamson, O. E. (1981). The economics of organization: The transaction cost approach. *American Journal of Sociology, 87*(3), 548–577. doi:10.1086/227496

Witjes, S., & Lozano, R. (2016). Towards a more circular economy: Proposing a framework linking sustainable public procurement and sustainable business models. *Resources, Conservation and Recycling, 112*, 37–44. doi:10.1016/j.resconrec.2016.04.015

Wognum, P. M., Bremmers, H., Trienekens, J. H., van der Vorst, J. G. A. L., & Bloemhof, J. M. (2011). Systems for sustainability and transparency of food supply chains-current status and challenges. *Advanced Engineering Informatics, 25*, 65–76. doi:10.1016/j.aei.2010.06.001

Woodall. (2003). Conceptualizing Value for the Customer. An Attributional Structural and Dispositional Analysis. *Academy of Marketing Science Review, 12*, 1-44.

World Commission on Environment and Development. (1987). *Our Common Future.* Oxford University Press.

Wortmann, J. C. (1983). A classification scheme for master production scheduling. In *Efficiency of manufacturing systems* (pp. 101–109). Boston, MA: Springer. doi:10.1007/978-1-4684-4475-9_10

Wrana, J., & Revilla Diez, J. (2018). Multinational enterprises or the quality of regional institutions – What drives the diffusion of global CSR certificates in a transition economy? Evidence from Vietnam. *Journal of Cleaner Production, 186*, 168–179. doi:10.1016/j.jclepro.2018.03.113

Wu, H. C., & Mohi, Z. (2015). Assessment of service quality in the fast-food restaurant. *Journal of Foodservice Business Research, 18*(4), 358–388. doi:10.1080/15378020.2015.1068673

Xie, X., Jia, Y., Meng, X., & Li, C. (2017). Corporate social responsibility, customer satisfaction, and financial performance: The moderating effect of the institutional environment in two transition economies. *Journal of Cleaner Production, 150*, 26–39. doi:10.1016/j.jclepro.2017.02.192

Xu, L. D., He, W., & Li, S. (2014). Internet of Things in industries: A survey. *IEEE Transactions on Industrial Informatics, 10*(4), 2233–2243. doi:10.1109/TII.2014.2300753

Xu, X., Zeng, S., & Chen, H. (2018). Signaling good by doing good: How does environmental corporate social responsibility affect international expansion? *Business Strategy and the Environment, 27*(7), 946–959. doi:10.1002/bse.2044

Yadavalli, A., & Jones, K. (2014). Does media influence consumer demand? The case of lean finely textured beef in the United States. *Food Policy, 49*, 219–227. doi:10.1016/j.foodpol.2014.08.002

Yang, S., MR, A., Kaminski, J., & Pepin, H. (2018). Opportunities for industry 4.0 to support remanufacturing. *Applied Sciences, 8*(7), 1177. doi:10.3390/app8071177

Yazdi, G. P., Azizi, A., & Hashemipour, M. (2018). An empirical investigation of the relationship between overall equipment efficiency (OEE) and manufacturing sustainability in Industry 4.0 with time study approach. *Sustainability, 10*(9), 3031. doi:10.3390u10093031

Yin, R. K. (1984). *Case study research: design and methods*. Beverly Hills, CA: Sage.

Yin, R. K. (1994). *Case study research, design and methods*. Londres, UK: Sage.

Yin, R. K. (2002). *Case study research: Design and methods*. Thousand Oaks, CA: SAGE Publications.

Yin, Y., Stecke, K. E., & Li, D. (2017). The evolution of production systems from Industry 2.0 through Industry 4.0. *International Journal of Production Research, 7543*, 1–14.

Yoon, Y., & Uysal, M. (2005). An examination of the effects of motivation and satisfaction on destination loyalty: A structural model. *Tourism Management, 26*(1), 45–56. doi:10.1016/j.tourman.2003.08.016

Yunus, M., Moingeon, B., & Lehmann-Ortega, L. (2010). Building Social Business Models: Lessons from the Grameen Experience. *Long Range Planning, 43*(2), 308–325. doi:10.1016/j.lrp.2009.12.005

Yusof, J. M., Musa, R., & Rahman, S. A. (2011). Functional store image and corporate social responsibility image: A congruity analysis on store loyalty. *World Academy of Science, Engineering and Technology, 7*(77), 1233–1240.

Zairi, M. (2000). Managing customer dissatisfaction through effective complaints management systems. *The TQM Magazine, 12*(5), 331–337. doi:10.1108/09544780010341932

Zani, S., & Cerioli, A. (2007). *Data analysis and data mining for business decisions*. Milan, Italy: Giuffrè Publisher.

Zeller, V., Towa, E., Degrez, M., & Achten, W. M. J. (2018). Integration of waste supply and use data into regional footprints: case study on the generation and use of waste from consumption and production activities in Brussels. *Procedia CIRP, 69*(May), 100–105. doi:10.1016/j.procir.2017.11.116

Zott, C., Amit, R., & Massa, L. (2011). The business model: Recent developments and future research. *Journal of Management, 37*(4), 1019–1042. doi:10.1177/0149206311406265

About the Contributors

Cecilia Silvestri is Assistant Professor of Commodity Science at the Department of Economics, Engineering, Society and Business Organization (DEIM) of the University of Tuscia, Viterbo (Italy) where she held the course Quality and Customer Relationships. She had her PhD in 2011 in "Economics and local development" at the University of Tuscia. Consistent with carried out studies, her research has developed along the following guidelines: (1) Quality of goods, products and services. Studies and research on the quality according to the approaches of "Total Quality Management" and standards "ISO 9000", (2) The relationship between quality and consumers, with particular reference to satisfaction and loyalty, (3) Quality and innovation in the agro -food, (4) Innovation and technology transfer, with particular attention to the role of technological innovation for territorial development.

Michela Piccarozzi is an Assistant Professor at the Department of Economics, Engineering, Society and Business Organization (DEIM) of the University of Tuscia, Italy, where she teaches courses in Economics and Business Management and International Marketing. In 2010 he obtained a Ph.D. in "Planning and Control" at the University of Florence discussing a thesis entitled "Creating value at the University: financial and management problems in academic spin-offs". The research topics concern university spin-offs and innovative start-ups from the point of view of the difficulties of start-up and management.

Barbara Aquilani is Full Professor of Management at the Department of Economics, Engineering, Society and Business Organization (DEIM) of University of Tuscia (Italy) where she held the courses of Management and International Marketing. She worked as Assistant Professor at the Siena University from 2005 to 2009 - Communication Department, Faculty of Letter and Philosophy where she held the courses of Marketing and Marketing Communication. She has been involved, as presenter, in several national and international conferences and in several national/international research projects, as member or scientific coordinator. Her research interests refer to: (1) firm management and especially on firm growth (on which she published a book) and corporate governance; (2) marketing (among others she published papers on university marketing and online marketing); (3) innovation and open innovation.

* * *

Tindara Abbate, PhD in Business Administration, is Assistant Professor of Business Economics and Management at the University of Messina (Italy). She teaches Territorial Marketing and Tourism Marketing. She has been involved, as presenter o chairman, in several national and international conferences and workshops. Also, she has been involved in different national and international research projects focused on tourism themes, as member and scientific coordinator. Her research interests refer to territorial marketing and territorial certification; market orientation; open innovation declined in PMI context; creativity and gastronomy.

Patrizia Accordino, after a Master's Degree in Law Level II and a Ph.D. in Company Income Tax in The Eu, won a postdoctoral fellowship in Company Income Tax in The Eu and in 2007 she became Assistant Professor of Tax Law at the University of Messina. In 2019, she obtained twice the National academic qualification as Associate Professor and of the scientific committee of the Ph.D. Course in Law at the University of Messina and of several Editorial Boards. Principal investigator of several projects of research on Tax law, she took part at several national and international conferences as a speaker. She is the author of several articles about Tax law - printed on specialized magazines - and of three monographs published in book series.

Michelangelo Arezzo di Trifileti is academically disciplined in Political Economy at "Sapienza" University of Rome, having presented his final thesis on the economical assessment of a large-scale photovoltaic plant in Rovigo, Italy. He is currently employed at the U.S. Embassy in Rome, Italy. Mr. Arezzo assumed employment with the U.S. embassy in 1998. Prior to that, Mr. Arezzo was employed in the United States as a Sales and Service Associate for BankBoston in Hartford, Connecticut.

Bernardo Bertoldi teaches Family Business Strategy and Marketing at the Department of Management (University of Turin). His main research interests are linked to family business and entrepreneurship. He is vice president of the Investors Club of Turin, the first Italian business angel club.

Giuseppe Bertoli is Full Professor of Corporate Economics and Management and chairman of the board of courses of study in Economics and Management at the University of Brescia, where he teaches Marketing Management. He is also a general secretary of Italian Marketing Society. His research interests refer to Brand Management and International Business.

Alessandro Bonadonna, PhD in Culture and Enterprise at the University of Torino. He is Assistant Professor at the Department of Management - Commodity Science Area - of the University of Torino. His research interests concern Commodity science, food quality, the enhancement of typical products and agriculture production. He has published several contributions, among which "Street food and innovation: the food truck phenomenon" (in British Food Journal – 2016), "The Management of Unsold Food in Outdoor Market Areas: Food Operators' Behaviour and Attitudes" (in Sustainability – 2018), "Eating Hamburgers Slowly and Sustainably: The Fast Food Market in North-West Italy" (in agriculture – 2019). He is a Member of AISME - Italian Academy of Commodity Science, as from 2004. He is also a Member of NATRISK - Research Centre on Natural Risks in Mountain and Hilly Environments, as from 2014.

Giacomo Büchi, M. Sc. (Oxford) Ph.D. (Padova). Full Professor of Business Economics and Management at the Department of Management, School of Management and Economics, University of Torino.

Rebecca Castagnoli, Ph.D. student in Business and Management, Department of Management, School of Management and Economics, University of Torino.

Anna Paola Codini is Associate Professor of Corporate Economics and Management at the University of Brescia, where she teaches Operations Management and International Business. Her research interests refer to Innovation Management and Green Consumption.

Raffaella Coppolino, Assistant Professor of Organization and Human Resource Management, University of Messina, Department of Economics. She teaches Organization Theory and Human Resource Management in several undergraduate and postgraduate courses. Her main research interests concern knowledge management and organizational behaviour.

Monica Cugno, Ph.D. in Statistics applied to the economic and social sciences – University of Padova. Assistant Professor of Business Economics and Management at the Department of Management, School of Management and Economics, University of Torino.

Alessandra de Chiara is a Full professor of Management. She teaches International Management at the I level degree and Corporate Social Responsibility at the II level degree of the University of Naples "L'Orientale".

Patrizia de Luca is Associate Professor of Marketing and Management at the University of Trieste (Italy), where she teaches marketing and marketing research. She is the author or co-author of books, chapters and articles in national and international publications. Her research interests concern marketing channels and innovation, with particular attention to the experiential and sustainable perspective.

Simona Fortunati, PhD student in Economics,management and quantitative methods at the University of Tuscia, Italy.

Giuseppe Garofalo is Full Professor of Economics at Tuscia University in Viterbo (Italy) after a long activity at Sapienza University in Rome. He trained as a researcher under the supervision of Prof. Giorgio Fuà, at the University of Ancona (Italy). His main fields of interest include finance (see, among others, the paper in Physica A_2007 and the one in Journal of Economic Behavior & Organization_2019), economic interaction (Economics Letters_2013), territorial and individual educational inequality (Economic Modelling_2017).

Corrado Gatti, Full Professor of Business Management at Sapienza University of Rome. Research interests include strategic decision making, corporate restructuring, negotiations, the systems approach to management, corporate finance, performance measurement. Author, co-author, or co-editor of over 50 publications on management theory and practice, including research articles in Italian and international academic journals, book chapters, conference papers, book reviews, and books. Serves as board member in listed companies, both in the financial and industrial sectors.

Chiara Giachino teaches Marketing and Industrial Marketing at the Department of Management (University of Turin). Her main research interests are linked to marketing, tourism and family business.

Floriana Iannone is Research Fellow at the University of Naples "L'Orientale". PHD in 'Entrepreneurship and Innovation' she's teaches Management of Cultural Organizations at the International University of Rome - UNINT.

Elvira Tiziana La Rocca is Assistant Professor in Management at the University of Messina (Italy), where she teaches "International Marketing" and "Corporate Governance". Her research interests concern international management, corporate governance and firm value. She is author and co-author of many contributions published in International and Italian journals.

Beatrice Luceri is Full Professor at the Department of Economics and Management of the University of Parma, Italy. She teaches International Marketing and Consumer Behavior Analysis. Her research interests include topics related to consumer behavior, retail marketing and logistics.

Anna Mazzi, from 2017: Assistant Professor at University of Padova, Department of Industrial Engineering. From 2004 to 2017: Research grant holder at University of Padova, Department of Industrial Engineering, in the fields of Sustainability management and Environmental Life Cycle Assessment. From 1999 to 2004: Research scolarship holder at University of Padova, Department of Engineering Chemical Processes, in the fields of Sustainability assessment and Management systems. Author and coauthor of more than 90 publications. Senior expert in European projects, in the following founds: LIFE Environment, Intelligent Energy Europe (IEE), EQUAL, INTERREG IVC, CIP Innovation. Senior expert in more than 30 local and national projects.

Patrizio Morganti is a research fellow at the Department of Economics, Engineering, Society and Business Organization of the University of Tuscia (Italy). His area of expertise is macroeconomics and finance. He joined the Department in September 2016 after receiving his PhD from Sapienza University in Rome in May, with a dissertation titled "The economics of shadow banking: a theoretical approach to the securitized credit intermediation process". He has been a visiting graduate student at the Department of Economics at Johns Hopkins University, where he conducted research on shadow banking and financial regulation. His current research focuses on i) shadow banking, ii) the impact of finance and indebtedness on economic growth, iii) the role of renewables and energy efficiency in sustainable development goals.

Enrico Mosconi, Full Professor of Technology and Management of Production, Operation Management and Quality Assurance at the Department of Engineering, Economics and Management at the "Università degli Studi della Tuscia". Chairman of the Master's degree in Circular Economy. President at Consortium Università per Civitavecchia Consortium (Italy). Author of international publications on Technology and Environmental Management, Commodity Science and Circular Economy issues.

Julian Marius Müller is professor for logistics and operations Management at Salzburg University of Applied Sciences. He holds a PhD from Friedrich-Alexander University Erlangen-Nürnberg. His research areas include Industry 4.0 with special regard to supply chain management, the integration of small and medium-sized enterprises, as well as business model innovation and sustainability.

Giovanna Pegan is Associate Professor of Marketing and Management at the University of Trieste (Italy), where she teaches consumer behavior, business communication and consumer psychology. She is the author or co-author of numerous national and international publications, and her research focuses on sustainable consumption, marketing innovation and the country of origin effect on international distribution channels. From May 2016 to July 2019 she was delegated by the Rector for the specific area "Communication strategies of the University of Trieste".

Stefano Poponi, Researcher of Commodity Sciences at the Niccolò Cusano University. His research interests are focused on quality, spin-off enterprises, management of innovation and circular economy. His past experience relates to patents, technology placement systems, technological support and innovation of SMEs. He participated in European and national projects. He is co-founder and President of Gentox-chem srl, a spin-off enterprises of University of Tuscia. He worked also as expert for the technological park PST Alto Lazio in project to support the innovation development of SME.

Francesca Pucciarelli is Assistant Professor in Marketing at ESCP Europe and Academic Director of MBA in IM for the Turin Campus.

Eleonora Rapiti is enrolled in the second year of the PhD in Economics Management and Quantitative Methods at the University of Tuscia, Viterbo (Italy). Among the subjects of my interest: circular economy, quality, consumer behavior, political economy. She received a bachelor's degree in "Business Economics-Curriculum Banca e Finanza" with the mark of 110 cum laude in the Academic Year 2013-2014 with a thesis titled " Stochastic approach to the determination of the capital requirement to cover Premium Risk from a Solvency II perspective. She received a specialist degree in "Administration, Finance and Control-Curriculum Finance" with a grade of 110 and honors in the 2015-2016 Academic Year with a thesis titled "The impact of terrorism on financial markets". Among the subjects of her interest: circular economy, quality, consumer behavior, political economy.

Frassine Riccardo is an Area Commercial Manager at Poste Italiane S.p.a.. He graduated in Marketing Management and Comunication at the Economy University of Brescia and passed the Financial Advisor National Exam.

Daniela Rupo, PhD, is Associate Professor of Business Administration at the Department of Economics, University of Messina, Italy. Her teaching assignments range from financial accounting in private and public sector to business valuation. She has participated and currently is working on various national and international research projects about: Human capital, Intangible assets and Business Valuation, Sustainability, Corporate Social Responsibility and Environmental Reporting, Integrated reporting, Accounting and governance in the public sector. She is author of a number of journal papers and books. He is Certified Public Accountant and Certified Auditor.

Gabriella Schoier is Associate Professor of Statistics at the University of Trieste. She is and has been member in different academic commitees. She is involved in the ERASMUS + project. She has been professeur visiteur at the Groupe de Statistique, at the Institut de l'Entreprise and at the Institut de Statistique of the University of Neuchâtel. In 2012 she has been visiting professor at the University of Plymouth. She has been a member of the Scientific Committee in different Congresses. She has participated in several funded projects. She is currently a member of different Italian and International Statistical Society. She is a reviewer for MIUR. She has been a reviewer for several International Journals.

Research interests: Big Data, Data Mining, Spatial Data Mining Web Mining and Text Mining, Social Network analysis applied to the Web, Customer Satisfaction and Consumer Perception, Pink washing, Time Series Analysis, Operational and Credit Risk, Statistical Matching.

Luca Silvestri has a degree in Mechanical Engineering and PhD at the University of Rome "Torvergata" and Southern Lazio. Currently, she is a Researcher at University Niccolo Cusano (Department of Engineering)where she conducts research activities on multi-criteria decision analysis(MCDA), industrial plant, logistic and safety.

José Vargas-Hernández, Research Professor Professor José G. Vargas-Hernández, M.B.A.; Ph.D. Member of the National System of Researchers of Mexico and a research professor at University Center for Economic and Managerial Sciences, University of Guadalajara. Professor Vargas-Hernández has a Ph. D. in Public Administration and a Ph.D. in Organizational Economics. He has undertaken studies in Organisational Behaviour and has a Master of Business Administration, published four books and more than 200 papers in international journals and reviews (some translated to English, French, German, Portuguese, Farsi, Chinese, etc.) and more than 300 essays in national journals and reviews. He has obtained several international Awards and recognition.

Donata Tania Vergura is a Researcher at the Department of Economics and Management of the University of Parma, Italy. She teaches "E-business and E-commerce" and "Digital Marketing" and her main areas of research interest include consumer behavior, e-commerce and neuromarketing.

Cristina Zerbini is Ph.D. in Economics and Business. She teaches Neuromarketing at the Department of Economics and Management of the University of Parma, Italy. Her research interests include topics related to consumer behavior, social marketing and neuromarketing.

Index

www.ingramcontent.com/pod-product-compliance
Lightning Source LLC
LaVergne TN
LVHW062116300926
849161LV00010B/2474
* 9 7 8 1 7 9 9 8 1 4 1 9 1 *